Slang Across Societies

Slang Across Societies is an introductory reference work and textbook which aims to acquaint readers with key themes in the study of youth, criminal and colloquial language practices.

Focusing on key questions such as speaker identity and motivations, perceptions of use and users, language variation, and attendant linguistic manipulations, the book identifies and discusses more than 20 in-group and colloquial varieties from no fewer than 16 different societies worldwide.

Suitable for advanced undergraduate and postgraduate students working in areas of slang, lexicology, lexicography, sociolinguistics and youth studies, *Slang Across Societies* brings together extensive research on youth, criminal and colloquial language from different parts of the world.

Jim Davie pursued an academic career as a researcher and lecturer in Russian at the University of Portsmouth (1993–98) before moving on to work in the civil service. He has written *Slang Across Societies* as an independent researcher.

Slang Across Societies
Motivations and Construction

Jim Davie

LONDON AND NEW YORK

First published 2019
by Routledge
2 Park Square, Milton Park, Abingdon, Oxon OX14 4RN

and by Routledge
711 Third Avenue, New York, NY 10017

Routledge is an imprint of the Taylor & Francis Group, an informa business

© 2019 Jim Davie

The right of Jim Davie to be identified as author of this work has been asserted by him in accordance with sections 77 and 78 of the Copyright, Designs and Patents Act 1988.

All rights reserved. No part of this book may be reprinted or reproduced or utilised in any form or by any electronic, mechanical, or other means, now known or hereafter invented, including photocopying and recording, or in any information storage or retrieval system, without permission in writing from the publishers.

Trademark notice: Product or corporate names may be trademarks or registered trademarks, and are used only for identification and explanation without intent to infringe.

British Library Cataloguing-in-Publication Data
A catalogue record for this book is available from the British Library

Library of Congress Cataloging-in-Publication Data
A catalog record has been requested for this book

ISBN: 978-1-138-55882-3 (hbk)
ISBN: 978-1-138-55883-0 (pbk)
ISBN: 978-1-315-15140-3 (ebk)

Typeset in Sabon
by Deanta Global Publishing Services, Chennai, India

Visit the eResources: www.routledge.com/9781138558830

For Dad

Contents

Acknowledgements — xii
List of figures — xiii
List of tables — xiv
Reference boxes — xv
Transliteration, transcription systems and note on translation — xvi
Guide to abbreviations — xvii

Introduction — 1

Slang – what kind of language? 1
A key role for youth 3
Why another book looking at youth? 5
Studying youth and criminal language together 7
Comparing colloquial, criminal and youth language 9
Stylistic headaches, stereotypes and indexicality 20
The structure of the book 23
What this book doesn't investigate 26
Notes 28
References 29

PART I — 41

1 Linguistic data – varieties, sources and methodologies — 43

Introduction 43
Varieties and sources 43
    Youth, criminal and colloquial language in France 44
    German youth language 45
    The Caló of Spanish Roma and Pachuco Caló 46
    Lunfardo – underworld and colloquial language in
      Argentina 47

viii   Contents

      Youth, criminal and colloquial language in
         peninsular Spain   47
      US college practice   48
      Russian youth language, colloquial usage, criminal and
         traders' practices   48
      The language of criminals in 1960s West Bengal   49
      Indonesian youth language, Bahasa Prokem and
         Bahasa Gay   50
      The language practices of Japan's Kogals   51
      Prisoner language practices in Israel   52
      Sheng – youth-associated language in Kenya   52
      Randuk – youth-associated language in Sudan   53
      Camfranglais – youth-associated language in Cameroon   54
      Nouchi – youth-associated language in Côte d'Ivoire   54
      Youth language in Zimbabwe   55
      Lusaka's Town Nyanja   55
Data collection: an overview of methods used by researchers   56
Summary   58
Notes   58
References   60

2   Non-standard language – concepts and perspectives   68

Introduction   68
Antilanguage   68
Resistance and resistance identities   74
Style (stylistic practice) as an explanation of linguistic variation   78
Repertoires   82
Identity and identification   88
Summary   96
Notes   99
References   99

3   Youth and criminal language practices – attitudes and motivations   108

Introduction   108
Criminal language practices and how we understand them – threads
   through time   108
Why cryptolect is used: beyond the criminal   113
Youth language practices: how they're perceived   116
Youth language practices: an impenetrable threat?   122
Identity for the self and others   128

*What kind of difference? Many actors, many contexts,
   many Others   129*
Youth language practices: not just about men and boys   134
Youth language practices and class: not just the lower rungs   138
Youth, age and language practices: one age group or many?   141
Difference within groups   143
Verbal contests and ritual insults   146
*The global and the local: youth language practice
   in a connected world   148*
Moving beyond fixed positions   149
Crossing boundaries: youth language, race and ethnicity   153
The diffusion of youth and criminal language into broader usage   157
The media: enabling diffusion, and movement on the stylistic radar   161
What does the Internet mean for youth and colloquial language?   163
Internet Russian: is it contagious?   166
Taking other options   173
Summary   175
Notes   178
References   181

PART II   207

4   Invention and borrowing   209

Introduction   209
Coining and currency   210
Lexical borrowing across languages: why?   211
Semantic change in the borrowing process   214
Functional shift   216
Adapting borrowed words to a new system   217
Mimicry, and altering how a borrowed word sounds   219
Hybrids and mixed text   220
Calques and literal translation   226
Borrowing within a language   226
Difficulties in defining word origin   230
Summary   232
Notes   233
References   235

5   Semantic change   240

Introduction   240
Popular thematic areas and richness of options   244

x   Contents

    Metaphor: comparison to create new meaning   248
    Metonymy: associations and connections   254
    Synecdoche   257
    Over- and understatement   258
    Euphemism and dysphemism   260
    Expansion and contraction of meaning   261
    Polysemy   262
    Antiphrasis   263
    Context and culture   265
    Summary   267
    Notes   267
    References   269

6   The role of affixation   274

    Introduction: a focus on suffixes   274
    Prefixing   280
    Infixing   281
    Circumfixes: before and after   283
    Dummy affixes   284
    Back formation   285
    Summary   285
    Notes   286
    References   288

7   Compounding and reduplication   292

    Introduction   292
    Composition, and extending expressive and
        descriptive boundaries   293
    Blends   295
    Satire about officialdom: stump compounds   296
    Hybrid forms   296
    Reduplication   298
    Summary   299
    Note   300
    References   300

8   Phonetics and phonology   302

    Introduction   302
    Changing how a word sounds (or looks)   303
    Substitution strategies: some examples   306

Contents xi

Reduction: making it short and sweet 308
Sounds like ... 309
Insertion 312
Rhyming and alliteration 313
Backslang and reordering 314
The case of Verlan 316
Inversion and reordering in other languages 318
Double metathesis (reverlanisation) 321
Largonji and Largonji des Louchébems 321
Onomatopoeia and ideophones 322
Summary 323
Notes 325
References 327

9 **Clipping and the use of acronyms and other abbreviations** 332

Introduction 332
Apocope 333
Aphaeresis 336
*Truncation in phrases, change in meaning,
   and shortening names* 336
Truncation and affixation 337
Abbreviations 338
Acronyms 339
Abbreviations and vocalisation 341
Borrowed and named abbreviations 343
Summary 343
Notes 344
References 344

10 **Final comments** 347

Some general points for reflection 348
Looking forward 351
Note 354
References 354

Index 357

Acknowledgements

It takes many people to write a book, and this one is no exception. First and foremost, I would like to express my heartfelt thanks to all those colleagues who commented on the various manuscripts. Each and every person shared insights that made the project all the more interesting and instructive for me as a linguist and, more importantly, made the book both richer and rounder. Their names are too numerous to mention, but my very sincere gratitude goes to all those who shared their knowledge and helped in so many ways.

I am also grateful to Camille Burns, Claire Margerison, Geraldine Martin and Andrea Hartill at Routledge and Lisa Keating at Deanta for their friendly advice and supportive guidance and to the anonymous reviewer for their hugely helpful comments and feedback. I would also like to thank the staff at Bar Kvartira 148/2 in Almaty for permission to reproduce posters; Duncker & Humblot GmbH for permission to cite material from Stein-Kanjora's article in 'Sociologus'; and Cambridge University Press for permission to cite work by Ana Deumert from Cutler and Røyneland's *Multilingual Youth Practices in Computer Mediated Communication* (in press). While every effort has been made to trace copyright holders, this has not been possible in all cases. Any omissions brought to the publisher's attention will be remedied in further editions.

I'd also like to express my appreciation of those friends and family who encouraged me as I travelled along what seemed at times a hugely challenging road. Their support and encouragement were indeed very sustaining and helped me enormously to get from A to Z. The same goes for those who provided insights through discussing how some of the questions raised in the book mattered or related to them: special shout-outs in this respect go to Louise B and Rachel C ('Indi! Δ').

Finally, I'd like to pay two special tributes. Firstly, to the lovely Louise Crompton, whose insight and encouragement were hugely instrumental in getting the book project off the ground; and secondly to my wonderful wife Ruth who – on too many occasions to count – so supportively provided me with the context within which to write a book I've always wanted to write.

Figures

A new saint, Florence, 2012	195
'All cops are bastards', Bordeaux, 2015	196
'Blank walls = silent people', Paris, 2013	197
'ILY' ('JtM'), near Rambouillet, 2013	198
'Illuminati' or '*Kill*uminati'?, Florence, 2012	199
Rabzette and friends, Strasbourg, 2013	200
Electricity 'for nowt', Saintes, 2015	201
'New Year shindig …', Almaty, 2016	202
'Treize (13) NRV': 'Très énervé' ('very irritated') or 'Trop déter(miné') ('Too determined')?, Paris, 2013	203
'Keuj', Metz, 2011	204
'À ma mifa' ('To my family'), Geneva, 2013	205
'The Little Diner', Strasbourg, 2013	205
'Shut Your Trap!' ('Ta gueule'), Rouen, 2013	206

Tables

0.1	Youth language and age ranges in research	15
0.2	Comparative stylistic attribution of non-standard Russian items	20
2.1	Overlexicalisation in selected varieties	70
3.1	Mallik: motives for using the language of the underworld of West Bengal	113
3.2	Stein-Kanjora: adults' views on the use of Camfranglais	123
3.3	Bardsley: motives of students at Victoria University of Wellington, New Zealand, for using slang	125
3.4	Nad'iarova: motives of students in Simferopol', Crimea, for using in-group youth language	125
3.5	Stein-Kanjora: youth explanations for learning Camfranglais	143
4.1	Examples of inter-group borrowing among Russian criminals and sailors	227

Reference boxes

Overt and covert prestige	73
Social dialects, speech communities and Communities of Practice	84
In-groups and out-groups	90
Multilingualism	111
Language ideology	127
Contemporary Urban Vernaculars	156
Youth Internet use: statistics and significance	173
Communication Accommodation Theory (CAT)	222
Youth language and links to criminal communities	229
Appropriation	243
Counterlanguage	264
Enregisterment	280
Conscious choice in language practice	297
Devices used to create new words and phrases in literature	311
Opposite in name	315
Evaluation and stance	334
The Rebus Principle, and abbreviation in text- and computer-speak	342

Transliteration, transcription systems and note on translation

Where required, pronunciation is noted using the International Phonetic Alphabet. The transliteration system used for Cyrillic is a modified version of the Library of Congress system. Items from languages such as Hebrew, Arabic and others are given as found in sources. In most cases, translations are as provided in the original source material. However, on some occasions, additional or updated meanings are given.

Guide to abbreviations

The following abbreviations are used to qualify examples. In many cases, the descriptions are those provided by source authors.

coll. *colloquial*
crim. *criminal*
dr. *drugs*
joc. *jocular*
mil. *military*
neg. *negative*
prost. *prostorechie (stigmatised colloquial Russian)*
sch. *school*
yth. *youth*

Introduction

Slang – what kind of language?

This book has been written to serve as an introductory reference and supporting textbook that identifies and considers the drivers behind and manipulations typically associated with the use of youth, criminal and colloquial language. The book is entitled *Slang Across Societies*, and thus from the outset draws the reader's attention to a social and linguistic phenomenon of considerable interest to many people. Some researchers investigate the use of youth slang associated with adolescent and young adult social actors – for example, Androutsopoulos (2000) considers German youth slang, Miller (2004) reflects on the use of youth and Kogal slang by rebellious young women in Japan, and Shlyakhov and Adler include vocabulary from youth slang in their 2006 *Dictionary of Russian Slang and Colloquial Expressions*, as does Mahler in his 2008 Spanish equivalent. At the same time, researchers such as Mallik (1972), Cooper (1989) and Szabó (2006) note the slang of criminals and prisoners in West Bengal, Russia and Hungary, commentators such as Åke-Nilsson (1960) and Eble (2014) analyse Soviet (Russian) and US student slang, Dalzell (2014) explores English hip hop slang, Shlyakhov and Adler (2006) consider Russian army slang, Coleman (2012) discusses the slang of US film-makers, journalists and musicians, Victor (2014) addresses the question of 'gestural slang' and journalists in South Africa talk about largely negative "HIV/AIDS slang" (*IRIN/News* 2008). We can also discern interests in slang in the works of commentators such as Kripke (2014), who investigates New York inner-city slang, Bardsley (2014: 98), who talks of "the national slang in New Zealand", and Thorne who, in his *Dictionary of Contemporary Slang* (2005), incorporates in-group usage (e.g. youth and criminal language), expletives and more general colloquial language.

Slang certainly has great appeal to many researchers. However, as those well acquainted with its study will no doubt know, and as the previous instances suggest, 'slang' can often be understood by different commentators in different ways. For instance, while all described as examples of 'slang', the previous illustrations capture the communicative behaviours of what may be in some respects very different speech communities: in some cases what is described is the language of discrete groups, some of which are socially valued and legitimised and have an overt role in society (e.g. students, journalists, the army), some less so or not at all (e.g. criminals). In others, what is described is the language of a wide and heterogeneous social cohort (youth) or a subgroup of it (Kogals); a collective defined entirely or in no small part geographically (e.g. New York youth, New Zealand slang); a variety based on topic (hip hop, HIV/AIDS); or colloquial language, which encompasses the relaxed usage of social collectives that stretch beyond youth as a social configuration.

Given that some of these speaker communities can be so very different and that their reasons for and methods of using in-group language in particular can potentially vary, this book focuses not on the language of all those who are described as exponents of slang but on the language practices associated with discrete groups and particular situations. More specifically, it looks at the language practices of youth and criminals and the language that is indicative of relaxed or casual usage (colloquial language) in different societies and seeks to shed light on key principles for understanding these phenomena, including commonalities and differences.

At the same time, the book places analytical emphasis on the way in which speakers may actively use language to negotiate social meaning as dynamic social personae in different contexts and as members of potentially different Communities of Practice (for more on which, see pages 84–5); that is to say, as agentive interactants who employ language practices situationally with (social) outcomes in mind. Focusing on language as practice in this way is important, particularly insofar as the volume considers the language practices of social actors across societies (for more see also **Comparing colloquial, criminal and youth language** later in this chapter). Such comparison requires us to identify criteria that are more granular than the sometimes generic use of 'slang' allows as a broad-ranging and differently understood umbrella term or concept that may be equally generalising about the motivations and acts of speakers. Greater specificity is needed to compare the dynamics that underpin and emerge from usage across groups and societies, to comprehend the practices that comparable actors undertake and how those practices are perceived, and to explore the social meanings they negotiate.

The book therefore focuses on youth, criminal and colloquial language practices and discusses why they occur. It also identifies the corresponding linguistic mechanisms used to enable speakers to meet their social and communicative aims. Although it looks for common strands in particular, this is not to say that the varieties are regarded as identical. As readers will see in Chapter Three, the language practices of the criminal underworld (often known as 'criminal slang', 'cant' or 'argot') and those occupying the social margins are and have often been viewed as serving to hide meaning from others, in many cases for criminal ends. The language of beggars, traders and criminals is thus often painted as a form of largely nefarious, deceptive or underhand *cryptolect* (see, for instance, discussions in Zhirmunskii 1936 on Russia and Europe; Chambert-Loir 1984 on Indonesia; Robert L'Argenton 1991 on France; Mazrui 1995 on Kenya; Kouassi Ayewa 2005 on Côte d'Ivoire). Youth language practices (often known as 'youth slang'), on the other hand, while also enabling speakers to conceal meaning and concurrently underscore social distance or sharedness, are often represented with a different emphasis, with greater attention paid to alternative primary motivations such as expressing evaluation, identity, social affiliation or distance, establishing social credentials as and/or in a peer group, and so on (e.g. Danesi 1994; de Klerk 2005; González and Stenström 2011; although see, for example, Kerswill 2010 on African youth languages). This does not mean that there are no commonalities between the two sets of practices, either. While Part Two of the book highlights shared linguistic manipulations, Chapter Three will show that there can be other common ground. For example, the use of criminal language in prison prompts us to consider its social and psychological implications, including for identity construction and individual status. Some of these aspects may also apply to the language practices of youth.

Equally, the book also considers colloquial language, particularly insofar as the manipulations used to create colloquial varieties are also often those employed to form youth and criminal language. While the latter are associated with discrete groups in society (that is, where such distinctions as youth exist), colloquial language is seen to typify the casual, informal language that we all use in relaxed situations. In this respect it does not necessarily share the same *raisons d'être* as youth and criminal language – while it can enable solidarity, its user community is generally much bigger for a start, and it is not so group-defined in the same ways. However, insofar as it also departs from stylistically neutral language and enables speakers to express some form of attitude or evaluation in those more informal contexts (for more on **Evaluation and stance**, see page 334), and insofar as it shares some common lexical and word-formation features with youth and criminal language, it deserves to be studied. Indeed, as Chapter Three indicates, some words and expressions can originate in small, tight-knit groups as youth or criminal practice, but gain sufficient currency within larger social bodies as to become part of everyday colloquial usage, or even standard in the formal, stylistically neutral sense.

A key role for youth

A key focus of the book falls on the study of youth language practices, in part due to the significant role that youth play as heterogeneous, core social actors in a number of societies and in view of their concordant reach into a variety of communities (e.g. street vendors and other traders, social and political movements, the criminal world, both *petty* and serious, music scenes and transnational movements such as hip hop, etc.). Interest in the language practices of youth is not an altogether new area, and there have been many individual studies across the world going back several decades – for example, Magner's (1957) and Åke-Nilsson's (1960) records of youth language in the USSR, Labov's (1973) early 1970s study of *the dozens* (also known as *sounding*) in the US, Mallik's (1972) discussion of youth practice within his investigation of the language practices of criminals in 1960s West Bengal, Chambert-Loir's (1984) overview of Bahasa Prokem in Indonesia, Lefkowitz's (1989) analysis of Verlan in France in the 1980s and Salmons' (1991) exploration of youth language in the German Democratic Republic, to name but a few. Furthermore, academic interest in urban youth language practices is growing and attracting the attention of anthropologists,

4   *Introduction*

linguistic anthropologists, sociolinguists, social psychologists and sociologists worldwide (e.g. Miller 2003, 2004 on Kogals in Japan; Bucholtz 2004 on Laotian American youth in the US; Wyn 2005 on youth in the UK, US, New Zealand and Australia; Smith-Hefner 2007 on Bahasa Gaul in Indonesia; Hurst 2007, 2015 on youth practices in South Africa; Wolfer 2011 on Arabic varieties; Nassenstein and Hollington's 2015 edited volume on African youth language). In this regard, the study of youth language in multiethnic urban environments has been particularly noteworthy for those charting the use of language in social contexts (e.g. Dorleijn and Nortier 2013; Cheshire, Nortier and Adger 2015; Nortier and Svendsen's 2015 edited volume).

This growing interest should not surprise us. Given that youth play an active, if not central, role in pushing sociocultural and linguistic boundaries (Miles 2000; Eckert 2005: 94, citing Chambers 1995; de Klerk 2005; Stenström 2014; Lebedeva and Astakhova 2016: 126, citing Khimik 2004), the study of youth language practice is certainly important if we want to better understand key issues surrounding language and society. This, it could be argued, is especially the case in times of diversity or super-diversity, where migration and the unfolding rapid advancements of the digital age have further fostered the adoption of linguistic resources across groups and the creation of new forms, requiring a reconceptualisation of who is typically held to use what language for identity or other purposes, especially in urban areas in Europe, Africa and the US (see, for example, Blommaert and Backus 2011; Blommaert and Rampton 2011; Beyer 2015). What is more, if we reasonably assume that the language practices of youth are relatively widespread among many populations of the world, particularly as some varieties proceed to the status of more widely used vernaculars, then we should pay close attention to youths' communicative practices. This is all the more evident if we consider the substantial cohort that youth represent as a demographic constituency in various parts of the world. For example:

- In sub-Saharan Africa, extending from northern Senegal and Sudan to South Africa, in 2012 more than 70% of the region's population was aged below 30 (Boumphrey 2012) – the population that year was estimated to be 923 million people (World Bank). In 2015, in Africa as a whole, 60% of the population was under 25 years of age, while 19% was between 15 and 24 years alone (UN 2015c: 7). That same year, African youth aged 15–24 accounted for 19% of the world's youth; the number of youth in Africa is expected to more than double by 2055 (UN 2015b: 1).
- In India in 2000, 300 million people between the ages of 10 and 24 accounted for roughly 30% of the population (Verma and Saraswathi 2002: 106). In early 2012, there were 704 million people aged below 30 in the country (Boumphrey 2012) in a population exceeding 1.2 billion (Population Reference Bureau 2012: 2).
- In eight Southeast Asian states such as Malaysia, Thailand and the Philippines in 2001, youth aged 12–23 accounted for roughly 23% of the population (Santa Maria 2002: 172). While the youth population in Thailand, for

example, is expected to fall by more than 20% over the period 2015–2030 (UN 2015a: 13), it will still remain substantial with an anticipated populace of circa 68 million (UN 2015c: 22).
- At the beginning of the current century in Latin America, individuals between 10 and 24 years old comprised circa 30% of the population (Welti 2002: 281). In 2015, 17% of the population was aged between 15–24, while 43% of the population was under 25 years of age (UN 2015c: 7).

This is not to argue, of course, that such statistics enable entirely like-for-like comparison: definitions of youth can vary across organisations and societies, and surveying does not always allow for comparison in finer terms regarding, for example, educational opportunities, peer group importance and so on (for instance, sometimes the statistics are not in place). Nonetheless, although young people can and do often belong to different speech communities, the statistics do point to young people representing substantial proportions of populations of interest to those studying youth practice and language development.

Why another book looking at youth?

In view of the key role that youth play in many societies and the growing interest in the group as a wider social category, those researching youth language in particular may ask: "So, why add another book to literature examining youth and language?" The reasons are manifold. First of all, although many works have been dedicated to youth cultural practices over the last few years, and interest is increasing in comparing youth practice in Europe (e.g. Aarsæther, Marzo, Nistov and Ceuleers 2015), across Europe and North America (e.g. Boyd, Hoffman and Walker 2015; Cutler and Røyneland 2015) and across individual European and African urban speech styles (e.g. Dorleijn, Mous and Nortier 2015), this does not mean that the analytical picture is complete. There is still room to explore questions surrounding language practices and identity and the impact of diversity within countries and within and across continents, for example. And, of course, more work will be needed on an ongoing basis as factors such as migration continue to bring social and linguistic impacts.

At the same time, several scholars have called for more far-reaching comparative studies to be conducted of (youth) in-group language practices. In their excellent collection of studies of youth language practices in Africa, Hollington and Nassenstein (2015b: 355) conclude that a broader comparative scope would be welcomed to "expand the view from the African focus and also take into account youths' identity constructions and practices that have emerged worldwide". Additionally, in their interesting study of emerging multiethnolects in Europe, Cheshire, Nortier and Adger call attention to the importance of comparative study of linguistic manipulations:

> The mechanisms by which the relevant linguistic forms [in multiethnolects] are generated may be the same, perhaps worldwide, but the actual linguistic

forms are changing continuously, with not only words but also other elements becoming outdated years – or sometimes only months – later. *What is important in these cases, therefore, is to attempt to understand the mechanisms that are involved rather than document the specific forms that are used.*

(Cheshire, Nortier and Adger 2015: 21; my italics)

Finally, Coleman (2014b), in the conclusions to her engaging compilation of articles on global English 'slang', identifies four key constituent elements: informal terms used by English speakers across the globe; items limited to social subgroups spanning national boundaries; English items used by speakers of other languages; and the extra-lexical impact of English on informal usage in other languages. This leads her to underline the value of broader comparative analysis, couched in terms of Englishes vis-à-vis these further-reaching systemic questions, when she states:

The question that remains is whether any of these phenomena is truly global. A book of this size cannot cover the whole world in adequate detail and there have been some significant omissions. Africa, the Middle East, South America and East Asia are among the regions that offer fertile ground for future research into the use of English slang and the influence of English on the slang of other languages.

(Coleman 2014b: 212–13)

That is to say, if we extend the core questions that Coleman identifies to other languages, we can ascertain whether any or all of them are "truly global" or at least very widespread.

These researchers are inviting, then, a broader focus, including hypotheses and/or conclusions as to whether the language practices of in-groups, primarily young people as important social actors, in the settings they consider resemble or coincide with those in other parts of the globe.

Work to meet these invitations requires, of course, a measure of comparability to be effective – this subject is treated in more detail later in the chapter. However, the first steps have already been taken on a cross-continental basis, with a notable study that of Dorleijn, Mous and Nortier (2015), who studied Kenyan and Dutch Urban Youth Speech Styles (UYSS) and found that they were comparable insofar as they represented the creative efforts of multilingual urban youth and in that they emerged as a stylistic option instead of through communicative need (as opposed to pidgins, for instance). The very publication of this study – and others like it – is significant for a number of reasons, not least because it opens up comparative analysis of identity, the use of linguistic form and the negotiation of social meaning in ostensibly different settings (here: in Northern Europe and Africa), and uses the resultant analysis as a basis for initial hypotheses. This is an important cross-continental step involving considerably different environments, and further efforts in the same vein will also no doubt provide valuable insights. In light of such comparative work and the calls by Hollington and Nassenstein,

Cheshire, Nortier and Adger, and Coleman, it is reasonable to state that the kind of discussion this book brings, of manipulations and motivations across language settings and groups, is an endeavour that academics working in this field consider important for further understanding youth language practices.

An additional consideration relates not only to the potential value to be gained from comparative analysis, but more specifically to academic understanding of the varieties being sufficiently evolved for comparison to be undertaken – a notion implicit in Dorleijn, Mous and Nortier's study. In his overview of the challenges of studying youth language practices in Africa, Beyer (2015: 44) suggests that the time is now ripe for comparisons to be made regarding youth language practices in African settings and beyond so that "interesting generalizations" might be made. Dorleijn, Mous and Nortier's study aside, research has been conducted that supports this proposition across various spaces – for instance, across Belgium and Norway (Aarsæther, Marzo, Nistov and Ceuleers 2015) and across Norway and the US (Cutler and Røyneland 2015). And we have seen some cross-cultural strands figure in other discussions – for instance, Eckert (2005) considers the behaviours of some Western youth but also those of France and Indonesia, while Dorleijn and Nortier (2013) briefly profile a number of varieties, including Verlan in France, Citétaal in Belgium, Kanaksprak in Germany, Straattaal in the Netherlands, and Prokem and Bahasa Gaul in Indonesia, as well as a small selection of African varieties. In most of these cases, there are fairly solid ideas or hypotheses about the nature of the youth language variety and its use over time. The question is: what patterns emerge? This is an important consideration that underpins questions about, for example, whether the creative means mobilised by present-day youth actors are truly new or unique; for establishing whether comparison between varieties is really feasible; and for studying the process of diffusion of forms from tight-knit youth groups to the broader populace. This does not mean that the same mechanisms are always used for the same communicative purposes – of course, context and setting are always important. However, investigation of the manipulations typically found in youth language practices as witnessed across time and space, when contextualised by examination of potential motivations behind local usage, certainly holds value for ongoing discussions in this area.

Studying youth and criminal language together

In addition to investigating the language practices of youth, we also explore the practices of social marginals such as criminals. At first glance, some may question why analysis of the language practices of two such groups should be included, if not in some places intertwined, in the same work. However, such dual exploration – which also presupposes sufficient contrast or commonality to make for meaningful investigation – can be justified for a number of reasons:

- The two groups are often associated with non-standard language varieties (for example, see variously Chambert-Loir 1984; Stenström, Andersen and Hasund 2002; Mutonya 2007; Nassenstein 2015b).

8   *Introduction*

- Their language practices evidence a strong co-occurrence of linguistic manipulations, often for similar purposes (e.g. metathesis or semantic mechanisms to hide meaning, whether by youth actors or criminals).
- The practices of both groups serve as good starting points for exploring questions such as the role of and motivations behind cryptolect.
- Both are often contrasted with social mainstreams, thus inviting consideration and comparison of the motivations behind their respective in-group membership and activities. In this regard, both are also often painted as countercultural or antisocieties and as users of antilanguage (e.g. Halliday 1978 and Mayr 2004 on criminal groups; Kiessling and Mous 2004; Veit-Wild 2009; González and Stenström 2011 on youth groups; for more details see **Antilanguage** in Chapter One).
- Statistics indicate that between two-thirds and three-quarters of all crimes that young people commit are carried out by gangs or group members, and that tens of millions of children and youth (between 15 and 24) live or work on the street, where they are often involved in illegal activities such as begging or petty crime – mostly in large cities in India, Latin America and sub-Saharan Africa (UN *Fact Sheet on Juvenile Justice*, undated: 1, 3). The participation in or exposure of youth to criminal groups or activities (e.g. Mallik 1972; Chambert-Loir 1984; Lafage 1991; Boellstorff 2004; Roth-Gordon 2009) provides promising ground for exploring questions of shared practice, but also linguistic diffusion.
- Youth in conflict (whether social, military or other) figure strongly as gang members (Hagedorn 2005). In this connection it is also noteworthy that some gangs become permanent, institutionalised social agents in locations such as cities or nations, in some cases competing with or even replacing political groups (Hagedorn 2005: 154).

This is not to say, of course, that youth are by necessity synonymous with criminality or that all criminal gang members are youths – clearly neither is the case, nor does this volume wish to feed any stigma in those directions. However, in view of the considerations listed, we can reasonably claim sufficient grounds for studying youth and criminal language practices together.

At the same time, it should also be noted that although the book draws on research on and data from diverse language varieties and social collectives, it is not seeking to establish sociological, linguistic or other universals, or to draw conclusions about the development of language and society or societies writ large.[1] Nor does it claim to be definitive either in terms of charting the various speech aims that social agents might pursue in the multitude of situations in which they may find themselves or in terms of covering the entirety of manipulations that could be brought to bear (indeed, even items associated with standard varieties can be used in an unconventional or *non-standard* way). Instead, as stated previously, its aim is to give the reader sufficient grounding to identify key questions that should be borne in mind when attending to what some might paint as non-standard usage in colloquial, youth and criminal sociocultural practice.

Indeed, if I as the author must confess to any particular perspective, then it is rather to shed light on the ways in which items thought to typify colloquial usage and youth and criminal in-group practices are created as a means of *understanding the drivers behind and synergy between creativity, expression and effect in the practices studied*. In this regard, I echo the thoughts of Carter (2004), where he points to the ubiquity and artfulness of linguistic creativity in everyday language; to how, often spontaneously through language, speakers dynamically co-create and co-define relationships as they interact within developing contexts; and where he suggests:

> Creative language is not a capacity of special people but a special capacity of all people. It shows speakers as language makers and not simply as language users.
>
> (Carter 2004: 215)

Comparing colloquial, criminal and youth language

To draw together data pointing to speaker motivations, as well as to lexical, semantic, morphological and phonological manipulations in a number of languages is no small undertaking, and rests on the notion that data must be comparable in some way, shape or form. The question arises as to how this can be done when some of the languages are structured very differently, and when popular concepts such as colloquial language, slang and argot, not to mention jargon (which I am treating here as in-group language practices linked most commonly to socially approved professions) might be viewed differently both within and across languages: commentators on French colloquial and in-group usage, for example, have had difficulty arriving at universal definitions of these phenomena, variously using terms such as 'français populaire', 'français familier', 'français branché' and 'argot' (Lodge 1993: 3–9, 17, 230–60; see also Abecassis 2002 and Chapter One). Furthermore, whereas in Russian criminal language practice is often known as 'argo', and in French as 'argot', in England the language of thieves, vagabonds and ne'erdowells was traditionally known as 'cant', while in Spain the language of the underworld was known as 'Germanía' and also 'Caló', and in West Bengal 'Ulṭi' or 'Ulṭibātolā'. At first glance, as with the term 'slang', this looks like a difficult terminological circle to square, so to speak. Moreover, and perhaps more importantly, how can we be sure that understandings of these varieties are comparable, let alone the terms used? How might it be possible to find common strands in youth and criminal practices in particular across many societies?

To establish some measure of comparability across these different language varieties, I propose looking at commonalities in five areas: speaker motivation; youth as a life stage; diffusion; mainstream perceptions vis-à-vis the standard; and trends in lexical supplementation and word-formation.

Speaker motivation: there is merit in comparing the motives behind in-group usage as attested in the literature and recognising that there can be similarities across groups with similar profiles in this regard. The criminals of 1960s

West Bengal (Mallik 1972) to a great extent wished to hide meaning for the same reasons as criminals in sixteenth- and seventeenth-century England (e.g. Beier 1995), nineteenth-century Spain (e.g. Salillas 1896), nineteenth-century Buenos Aires (e.g. Grayson 1964), 1980s Cameroon (e.g. Kouega 2003), and late twentieth-century Russia (e.g. Grachëv 1994) – for example, to evade capture and punishment. Similarly, young Kenyan speakers of Sheng wished to communicate beyond the ken of their parents and grandparents or others in much the same way as speakers of Cameroon's Camfranglais (Kießling 2004; Ogechi 2005) or children in Indonesia (Beazley 2003); 1970s–1990s US college students undoubtedly wished to engage in language play (known as the *ludic function,* hence the term *ludling* to mean *play language*) to identify and represent their world, express evaluation and mark their differences from other groups, broadly speaking, in much the same way as French youth did over the same period, and still do (e.g. Eble 1996, 2014; Goudailler 2002); and French and Russian traders no doubt sought to gain the same advantages over unsuspecting customers and/or rival sellers as they sold their wares at various points throughout the nineteenth and twentieth centuries (e.g. Mandelbaum-Reiner 1991; Davie 1998). This is not to say, of course, that the sociolinguistic environments, driving principles and *raisons d'être* of the groups, and communicative aims enabled by the practices reflected in this book were or are uniform, or that context has no role to play in determining how and why linguistic forms associated with a particular variety may be used for different ends (indeed, context is important). And it is not to say that all language varieties are typologically identical – speakers of Caló, for instance, might be more properly regarded as speakers of a *mixed language* where Romani lexis is used with Spanish syntax and morphology. Nonetheless, there is sufficient commonality in the ascribed and assessed motivations behind the language varieties studied in this book to enable comparison.

Youth as a life stage: the United Nations Educational, Scientific and Cultural Organisation (UNESCO) see youth as best understood as "a period of transition from the dependence of childhood to adulthood's independence and awareness of our interdependence as members of a community" (UNESCO 2016). In doing so, it outlines youth as "a more fluid category than a fixed age-group" (UNESCO 2016), employing different definitions of youth depending on the context.

At the same time, however, the UN acknowledges that an acceptable way of defining youth lies in terms of age, especially when aligned with education and employment. For this reason, the notion of youth often applies to those falling between the ages when they may leave compulsory education and gain their first employment. Furthermore, to ensure a measure of statistical consistency across the globe, the UN identifies as youth those people aged between 15 and 24, while acknowledging that national-level or multilateral conceptualisations may differ. For example, the African Youth Charter defines youth as everyone between 15 and 35 years of age (UNESCO 2016).

When comparing youth in terms of life stage (age-defined or not), significant analytical value can be attained through assessment in two distinct respects – across societies and within. Both have real merit. Looking at intra-societal views of youth, Wilson (2015), in her study of urban youth language in Kisangani, Democratic Republic of Congo, points to the heterogeneity of youth as a social group where youth cannot be defined in terms of a single age range, and where people with different occupations and statuses are to be found. And in his mainly UK-focused discussion, Miles (2000: 123–4) notes moves away from definitions of youth based on age range, stating: "In effect, taste rather than age became the defining feature of youth culture … 'youth' came to mean more than simply a particular age group, but a lifestyle in its own right".

Assessing the potential for comparing youth *across* societies, Hollington and Nassenstein discern some respects in which cross-societal comparison is possible:

> Adolescents, after all, regardless of their set of linguistic or social practices, their larger communities or sociocultural background, still have to struggle with generational conflicts, societal expectations, debatable values and norms as well as with the process of growing up itself (in terms of their agency and responsibility).
>
> (Hollington and Nassenstein 2015b: 355)

Also with a broad set of collectives in mind, Danesi (1994: xi) draws distinctions in cross-societal comparison where he posits that in the general Western societal model, teenagerhood and the requirement to attend school at that time of life exist to meet the requirements of adult institutions such as the market. At the same time, however, he observes that the concept of teenagerhood might not be found in other social configurations at all, notably those societies where the onset of puberty coincides with marriage (Danesi 1994: xi, 5). Bucholtz (2002: 527) similarly observes that "[y]outh or adolescence is not a highly salient life stage in all cultures, although this is changing in many societies".

With these comparative tenets in mind, it is important to consider whether we can indeed compare concepts such as youth cross-societally with a view to comparing youth language practices. In their significant book *The World's Youth* (2002), Brown, Larson and Saraswathi suggest that a measure of sociological comparison can be realised across societies by comparing a number of factors. These include, for example, the roles of peer groups, media influence, the family, health matters, education and employment. Brown and Larson observe:

> Across nations, families and educational systems – and to an increasing extent, experiences with peers – play a central role in shaping an individual's experiences during this phase of life. There is even some evidence of convergence across the world in the experiences an adolescent has within each of these contexts.
>
> (Brown and Larson 2002: 18)

However, as they also acknowledge, the extent to which these discrete factors influence youth as a consolidated social cohort across or within societies can also be societally contingent. Brown and Larson (2002: 2) indicate, for example, that there are "markedly different 'adolescences'" in non-Western parts of the world and that the principles that characterise the period between childhood and adulthood are not universal. Such variability is also underlined by the UN where they note that a progression to autonomy is not necessarily present, articulated or pursued in some societies as in the West (UNESCO and UNICEF 2013; UNESCO 2014). Saraswathi and Larson (2002: 348) describe "a world of disturbing contrasts and glaring inequalities, both between and within nations", while Jensen Arnett (2002) posits that, in the West alone, youth by and large constitute a very diverse social category. Indeed, youth are not homogeneous in terms of their cultural values and social norms (e.g. Labov 1992; Verma and Saraswathi 2002; Thurlow 2003, 2005; Wilson 2015), or their material circumstance and access to social support.

The very concept of whether there is such a thing as a youth or adolescence to experience (terms that are often seen as largely synonymous, though note also references to young adulthood as a further distinction) is a fundamental underlying question. Western ideas of youth are, in many respects, the product of adolescence being seen as institutionally segregated from the adult world, a "time of experimental leisure and playful violation of norms before the standards of adult society are accepted and adult roles are entered" (Jensen Arnett 2002: 308). This is an understanding that seems to have been taking root at least partially in other parts of the globe. Booth (2002), for example, noted that at the turn of this century the Arab world, a diverse one that does not tend to embrace Western sociocultural practices wholesale (see also Schade-Poulsen 1995; Kraidy and Khalil 2008; Moussalli 2016 [2003]), witnessed an emergent adolescent phase where some youth met in malls and in and through cyber cafés, spent longer periods in education, enjoyed greater access to the media and possessed their own means of personal communication. This meant a separation of this phase from early adulthood, mostly among youth in urban areas with the requisite economic resources. Bucholtz (2002: 527, citing Condon 1990) similarly points to the emergence of adolescence as a social phenomenon among Canadian Inuits in a fast-moving economic and cultural milieu.

However, even if some social strata or cohorts outside the West as we understand it are moving in something akin to a Western direction, as Brown and Larson intimate the Western model of youth experience is patently not a global one. In some regions, young people more routinely head households at puberty or marry at a very young age, thereby moving straight into adulthood from childhood and bypassing youth as we know it in the West (Welti 2002; UNESCO 2014).

Indeed, drilling down into some of the factors identified by Brown, Larson, Saraswathi and others is highly instructive in bringing out some of the real differences in adolescent experience and determining whether youth is pervasive as a life stage across the globe. Economic circumstances, for example, can play a determining role in whether young people experience adolescence. Bucholtz (2002: 527) suggests that for some individuals even in late industrial societies, adolescence may be absent as a result of economic or other constraints, while Saraswathi and Larson point to such limitations more broadly:

poor youth in many parts of the world do not have an 'adolescence,' they do not have a period of moratorium from labor to develop the capabilities that are necessary for adequate employment in the new economy.
(Saraswathi and Larson 2002: 350)

The notion of whether there is a "moratorium from labor" is certainly an important one, and differences in economic circumstances both within and across societies can result in major impacts on life paths, life stages and life chances. In Africa, for example, contributing to income through street trading is, among other things, one of the roles required of many youth; street life for family- and self-support is a "continent-wide, urban phenomenon" (Nsamenang 2002: 76). While not unknown in Western societies as we typically conceive them, the issue is almost certainly more acute on the African continent. At the same time, in some countries the converse may be seen: a lack of employment can prevent young people from entering the mainstream adult space (Miles 2000).

Nor is access to education equal. While the progression to adult roles is comparatively delayed in industrialised countries in East Asia, North America and Europe in favour of education (Fussell and Greene 2002), not all societies have the same level of access to education across, for instance, social class, location or gender (UNESCO and UNICEF 2013; UNESCO 2014). Or the same levels of enrolment, attendance or completion. For example, only 20% of countries with low incomes have gender parity in primary education, 10% at lower secondary level and 8% at upper secondary (UNESCO 2014: 77). Indeed, some cultures put greater obstacles in the way of girls pursuing certain careers, engaging in leisure activities or attaining dominant roles among family and friends, with traditional roles often marked out for them as wives and mothers (Brown and Larson 2002; Fussell and Greene 2002; UNESCO and UNICEF 2013; UNESCO 2014) or as family members charged with household chores and greater sibling care (Nsamenang 2002). In 2010, for instance, 42% of girls and young women between 14 and 19 in South Asia and 26% in sub-Saharan Africa were neither in paid work nor studying (United Nations 2011, citing the World Bank 2010).

In point of fact, educational opportunities can be negated by a variety of factors, such as the need to work at home, the need to contribute to familial income, family mobility, parental attitude to education, overcrowding and inadequate facilities, poor health, disability, poverty, class and location, not to mention endemic disease, hunger and starvation, wars and armed conflicts, and low life expectancy (Nsamenang 2002; UNESCO and UNICEF 2013).

One area where there does seem to be a relatively strong degree of similarity across many societies concerns peer groups. Brown and Larson (2002) saw the peer group as increasingly important across societies in the early years of this century. Such groups are commonplace in a variety of environments, ranging from sub-Saharan Africa to Europe and North America, and – while local circumstances naturally vary – the peer group as a phenomenon appears to be enjoying great or assuming increasing importance more broadly (see, for instance, Miles 2000 on peer groups in the UK, and Stenström 2014: 12 on their "vital importance for

14 *Introduction*

the formation of teenage identity"). However, we must again note variability and difference in respect of the nature of peer group support, and the discrete groups in question. Collectives and forms of support are indeed varied, ranging from the importance of groups for survival on the streets in parts of Africa (e.g. Mutonya 2007) to their roles as ensembles within which to spend significant chunks of available free time, as Welti observed in 2002 with regard to some groups in Latin America. A different picture from that painted by Welti has been seen in India, where outside peer groups have been regarded as less socially important depending on the location, gender, socio-economic circumstances and social class of the youth in question (Verma and Saraswathi 2002).

So far, we have addressed comparative questions regarding youth as a life stage in terms of access to education and work, as well as the significance of peer groups. However, for those who accommodate youth as a life stage, when exactly within a lifetime are we talking about? And do they see this life stage in the same terms?

To be sure, the answer to this question is mostly addressed earlier – this depends on socio-economic, sociocultural and other factors such as access to education, class, community, location, gender and familial attitudes. However, as UNESCO suggest for their own comparative purposes, if we are to establish comparability of the language practices of youth groups across societies, it is also germane to consider the age ranges that scholars identify *where they see youth as a viable social category*, assuming that comparability in other social terms can also be established.

If we look at sociological and communication studies literature, we can see that in many cases the concept of youth starts in the early years of puberty and extends in some instances to upwards of 30 or even 35 years, depending in part on when full maturity or respect may be earned or when there is an appreciably full onset of adult responsibilities:

- In a volume devoted most of all to youth in Western contexts, Thurlow (2005: 4) suggests that adolescence refers to 11–21/22 years, while Garret and Williams (2005: 37) see adolescence as usually spanning 12–17 years and young adulthood 18–26.
- In India, according to the Draft National Youth Policy, the concept of youth stretches from 10 to 35 (Verma and Saraswathi 2002: 107). In their own study, Verma and Saraswathi included some older youth aged 20–25+ (Verma and Saraswathi 2002: 106).
- In South Africa, youth typically falls between 14 and 35 years (Nsamenang 2002: 91, citing Mokwena 1999).
- In Thailand, youth are described as between 15 and 25 years (Santa Maria 2002: 172, citing UN 1997).
- In Malaysia, according to the state Youth Council, the age range stretches from 15 to 40 years (Santa Maria 2002: 172, citing UN 1997).

These ranges are instructive. The evidence cited by Brown, Larson, Saraswathi and others is indeed compelling in respect of the diversity of circumstances in which young people find themselves and how life stages are conceptualised and demarcated across societies. However, just as the age ranges listed have been identified in sociological and communication studies, so at the same time it is also worth acknowledging that certain language practices can and have become enregistered (for a definition of **Enregisterment**, see page 280) so as to be typically associated with particular social groups, youth included, and that these groups are often associated with particular age ranges. I therefore employ the term *youth* to cover a broad temporal waterfront, including those who are emerging from childhood and those who are young or emerging adults. At the same time, I include those youth or *youth scene* actors in their early to mid-30s. It is, of course, noteworthy that this definition departs from the UN age range and does not accord with the move to taste-based definition that Miles discussed regarding the UK. And, of course, due recognition is given to the fact that not all youth actors engage in language practices thought to be typical of youth groups. However, considerable comparative gain can be accrued by working from the principle that in many studies of youth language practices an understanding of *prototypical* speakers/ social actors is provided to help make sense of usage, and that those social agents are often described among other things in what emerge (for the most part) as broadly comparable age ranges (see Table 0.1).

We will explore how people view youth language and its users in more detail in Chapter Three. For the time being, however, it is worth noting that these age ranges make for interesting reading. Firstly, their rather wide chronological scope generally appears to match those long spans outlined in the more sociologically focused discussion (i.e. Santa Maria 2002 on Malaysia; Verma and Saraswathi 2002 on India). Secondly, from what we might know of the societies and collectives involved, the figures also invite the inference that users of (mainly urban)

Table 0.1 Youth language and age ranges in research

Commentator	Variety	Min. age	Max. age	Year
Riordan/Davie	Russian youth language	14	32	1988/1998
Méla	Verlan (French)	10	30	1991
Berjaoui	Moroccan Ġawṣ*	19	25	1997
Androutsopoulos	German fanzines	18	30	2000
Kießling	Camfranglais	10	30	2004
Miller	Kogal language (Japan)	14	22	2004
Kouadio N'guessan	Nouchi (Côte d'Ivoire)	10	30	2006
Stein-Kanjora	Camfranglais	12/30	20–24/40	2008
Roth-Gordon	Brazilian youth language	Early teens	Early 20s	2009
Namyalo	Luyaaye (Uganda)	15	45	2015

*Ġawṣ is not one of the main language varieties explored in this book. It was documented as spoken by youth in many parts of El Jadida in 1997, when it was largely used by friends with a common bond, such as going to the same school (Berjaoui 1997). Interestingly, Berjaoui (1997: 150–3, 155) also describes another secret language variety known as Ṣawġ which was used by adults aged 23–30 years in the same town. Ṣawġ relied greatly on reordering, for example, 'lawu' for 'walu' ('nothing'). Indeed, the word 'Ṣawġ' itself is a transposed form of 'Ġawṣ'. A third variety is known as a "secret youth language", which Berjaoui describes as being spoken by the "young generation (17–25 years old)".

youth language are heterogeneous and operate as actors in different social circumstances (of course, this depends on what we know of the societies). By this we mean that those held to typically use youth language are not simply those who go to school or university, or are of an age to do so, but are people who are to be found in different circumstances or social situations, and with different responsibilities or obligations – however these are formed and whatever shape they take. They may be marginalised (e.g. Krohn and Suazo 1995; Beazley 1998, 2002, 2003; Mugaddam 2012b); they may have everyday preoccupations and responsibilities that have little to do with education, and thus may be people who continue to use elements of youth language in other domains – such as street vendors – as they construct different identities (Githinji 2006; Mutunda 2007; Mugaddam 2012b); they may belong to or socialise with diverse social groups or Communities of Practice (Eckert and McConnell-Ginet 1992; Eckert 2006); and they may be older-than-teenage speakers who have carried elements of youth practice and language with them into later life, including into the workplace and recreational spaces (see, for example, Stein-Kanjora 2008; Rampton 2015). But they are neither all the same age nor modelled from a single, strictly defined social identikit. A good example of this principle can be seen in Stein-Kanjora's (2008: 137) analysis of Camfranglais, where she noted that speakers claimed to use it as a means of everyday communication up to the age of 20–24, at which point they might assume certain responsibilities such as getting a job and getting married. However, some adults aged between 30 and 40 also used certain Camfranglais words and phrases when talking with friends.

Diffusion: very much following on from the last point is the principle of diffusion. Discussion of many youth and criminal language practices indicates that there can be an enriching of what are held to be standard and colloquial vocabularies through diffusion from the lexicons of smaller in-groups. This can happen for a number of reasons: as a result of social policy or enforcement, e.g. through forced or compulsory population movement, as happened in parts of Paris in the nineteenth century (Lodge 1993; Ellis 2002) and in South Africa (Molamu 1995); language contact through increasing urbanisation, as can be seen, for example, in Côte d'Ivoire and Sudan (e.g. Kouadio N'guessan 2006 and Aboa 2011 on Côte d'Ivoire; Manfredi 2008 and Mugaddam 2015 on Sudan); social change, as happened with the stylistic democratisation of Russian after the fall of the Soviet Union (e.g. Davie 1998); the popularising of in-group terms in literature and by the media (e.g. Samper 2004; Ferrari 2006; Smith-Hefner 2007; Veit-Wild 2009; Coleman 2012; Mugaddam 2012a, 2015; Widawski 2012, 2015), be this as a result of the development and growth of new media vehicles, the depiction of crime in entertainment, the expansion of practices such as hip hop, or the creation of mainstream TV programmes for youth groups; the expansion of the Internet (e.g. Hendry and Kloep 2005; McKay, Thurlow and Toomey Zimmerman 2005; Cutler and Røyneland 2015; Hollington and Nassenstein 2015b; Nassenstein 2015b); people mixing in the same social systems, such as in prison or in military service (e.g. Mallik 1972; Einat and Einat 2000; Higgs 2014; Green 2016); major or large-scale sociocultural or socio-political events such as war and reintegration into civilian life (e.g. Beregovskaia 1996; Coleman 2012; Widawski 2012, 2013). And so on. This is a common phenomenon and one seen happening with many of the language varieties cited in the book. For example, suffixes once associated with criminal or youth speak have been adopted into colloquial French (for example, '-oche' in 'téloche' ('telly'), 'cantoche' ('diner' – see page 205)), as have some terms created through *backslang* (Verlan), while elements of GDR youth language penetrated "into general usage in the Spoken Standard" in the former East Germany (Salmons 1991: 7). So, it is possible to say in fairly broad-brush terms that informal colloquial language can often adopt words and expressions from smaller in-groups as these terms gain currency among the wider (often national) speech community, and that this diffusion occurs in many of the societies we study (see Chapter One and pages 84–5 for discussion of the **Speech community**).

Mainstream perceptions vis-à-vis the standard: in our general understanding, a standard language is a – often *the* – language variety which is believed to most clearly embody a language's fundamental and authoritative rules in terms of appropriate use in different contexts (e.g. Montgomery 2008; Eckert 2012). In other words, it sets the parameters for what is inside and outside the language, and for what is correct or permitted in different situations, and what is not.

The standard is often based on a privileged dialect that comes to be promoted as normative – most often by those with greater social status and power (e.g. Bucholtz and Hall 2003; Morgan 2004; de Klerk and Antrobus 2004; Eckert 2012). In many cases, this norm is highly idealised (Agha 2003). Nonetheless, the standard variety becomes seen as appropriate for promoting a form of linguistic commonality and shared identity across subgroups within society (i.e. among groups who may use other dialects) and for official and/or national-level communication (e.g. Bucholtz and Hall 2003; Montgomery 2008). It may also be regarded as appropriate for teaching second language learners. Given that a standard language is often thus a social or institutional construct where a particular dialect is especially valued, both it and those who speak it, or are typified by it, are often accorded higher social status (Lodge 1993; Agha 2003; Eckert 2012; Lytra 2015) – although the use of standard language need not necessarily highlight in and of itself alignment with, or belonging to, the mainstream or establishment (Coupland 2007).[2] Usage that is considered to deviate from these rules and norms, both in linguistic and social terms, is often regarded as non-standard, although the use of such variables can in fact cover a variety of pragmatic purposes (Coupland 2007).

In some language communities, ideas about standard (idealised) usage have developed from a strong association not only between a privileged dialect and those who speak it (e.g. academics, professionals, *good* people), but also the written mode – partly because of the use of that mode by those with social power and of the supposed expressive and cultural superiority of written exposition (e.g. Lodge 1993 on French;[3] Carter 2004 on English;[4] Andrews 2012 on Russian[5]). Indeed, in some languages, such as Russian, the standard language can be known as the 'literary language' ('literaturnyi iazyk'; Levikova 2004; Biblieva 2007; Artemova, Katyshev, Olenev *et al.* 2014; Oganian and Ishkhanova 2015; Ozhegov 2016), while older forms of written exposition may be viewed as superior to newer ones (see, for example, Thurlow 2014 on digital discourse in English).

While the structure, shape and rules of standard varieties can vary across different languages, some consistency can be discerned in how youth, criminal and some colloquial language are characterised by representatives of out-groups and/or the dominant mainstream. In many cases, youth and criminal practices in particular can be viewed as either non-standard or *substandard* (a qualification with different connotations) and therefore become liable to draw disapproval. If standard language is thought to bring linguistic and social uniformity, for example, youth and criminal language can be seen to do the opposite in marking subgroups from others as they, seemingly or in reality, reject mainstream values. If the standard is felt to enable order, accuracy and clarity of thought and expression, colloquial, youth and criminal language might be held to variously bring vagueness, lack of structure and inaccuracy in their spontaneity and unpredictability. Associated with a spoken form that is often traditionally less valued than the written, and in some cases tied to accusations of a lack of social or intellectual completeness or suitability, youth and criminal language especially thus become painted as lesser forms of language (e.g. Halliday 1978; Bucholtz and Hall 2003; Beck 2015; Cornips, Jaspers and de Rooij 2015; Milani, Jonsson and Mhlambi 2015). Lodge's (1993) summary of top-down beliefs and attitudes towards standardisation in French, which draws on Milroy and Milroy's *ideology of the standard*, is noteworthy in this regard:

> The ideal state of a language is one of *uniformity* – everyone should (ideally) speak (and write) in the same way. Non-standard usage is always to some degree improper, and language change is to be deplored.
>
> The most valid form of the language is to be found in *writing* ... Although prestige norms for speech do exist, speaking is generally considered to be 'less grammatical' than writing. The purest form of the language is to be found in the work of the community's 'best' authors ...
>
> This form is *inherently better* than other varieties (i.e. more elegant, clearer, more logical, etc.) – it also happens to be the variety used by persons of the highest status with the greatest potential for exercising power. Other social dialects are *debased* corruptions of the standard, i.e. sloppy, slovenly, uncultivated, failed attempts to express oneself properly – these tend to be used by people of lower status and who exercise little power.
>
> (Lodge 1993: 156–7; Lodge's emphasis)

Lodge's description focuses on French as it is, and has traditionally been, viewed by certain parts of French society (for more on the *ideology of the standard* in France, see Doran 2004, 2007). However, as questionable as the views are, they resonate in a number of societies. As some of the complaints made about the use of Sheng (Mazrui 1995; Beck 2015), Bahasa Gaul (Smith-Hefner 2007), Kogal language practices (Miller 2004) and Camfranglais (Stein-Kanjora 2008) are explored in Chapter Three, social, cultural and linguistic antagonisms are identified regarding many languages and societies that put the user of the stigmatised form in a similar social and even intellectual space, even though standard varieties represent an abstracted and idealised form of language (see also **Language ideology** on page 127).

Trends in lexical borrowing and semantic, morphological and phonological manipulations: in their studies of colloquial, youth and criminal language practices, many linguists cite the lengths to which speakers will go to create group-specific lexis through the creation of new items (e.g. Sornig 1981; Robert L'Argenton 1991; Berjaoui 1997; Sourdot 1997; Slone 2003; Miller 2004; García 2005; Vázquez Ríos 2009; Wolfer 2011; Coleman 2014a; Hasund and Drange 2014; Hollington and Makwabarara 2015; Nassenstein 2015a, 2015b). Over and above this, some suggest that discourse identified as colloquial, youth and/or criminal across a range of languages bears the same lexical, semantic and word-formation hallmarks. Writing in 1936 about the development of argotic language and slang in a number of the languages of Western Europe (including English, French and German), the Russian linguist Zhirmunskii noted that, as a secret, special or professional language variety, argot had three main methods of restricting access to meaning: through word distortion (such as metathesis, syllable addition and insertion); borrowing from other languages; and semantic transfer (which might occur in tandem with other means of word-creation). This description chimed quite closely with a qualification of word-creation in Spanish criminal language practices produced in the late nineteenth century that indicated that concealment took three main forms: "phonetic" alteration (inversion, metathesis, truncation, compounding); lexical substitution (the use of loanwords); and semantic change (Salillas 1896: 34–43).[6] Indeed, comparison of word-formation mechanisms identified across very different languages sheds light on some interesting parallels:

- Khomiakov (1992) identified word-formation similarities in non-standard Russian, English and French, such as compounding, metathesis and reduplication.
- Goudaillier (2002) saw street French as typically comprising words created by semantic means (with emphasis on metaphor and metonymy), borrowing from other languages and older argots, Verlan, reduplication, and truncation with or without resuffixation.[7]
- Smith-Hefner's (2007: 191–2) examination of Indonesia's Bahasa Gaul focused on "backwards language", borrowing from other languages and informal usage, and abbreviation (blends, clipping and acronyms).
- Bosire's (2009) profile of Sheng identified the use of coining, borrowing, ideophones, semantic change, calques, metathesis, truncation, and truncation and affixation.
- Hollington and Nassenstein's (2015a) overview of mainly African youth practices identified phonological (metathesis, truncation, acronyms, Bantuisation of loanwords), morphological (hybridisation, dummy affixation) and semantic manipulations (metaphor, metonymy, euphemism, dysphemism and coinage), as well as borrowing and code-switching as highly productive.

Introduction

Again, a measure of consistency, this time in terms of methods of linguistic manipulation, can be discerned.

Stylistic headaches, stereotypes and indexicality

So far it has been suggested that there is sufficient commonality across the practices and motivations reflected in the book to justify comparison. However, inevitably there is one major challenge to this comparison, and that is that the stylistic categorisation and perception of many words within a language can often find itself up for debate. Given the propensity for speakers to associate linguistic forms with certain styles or personae (e.g. Agha 2003), and as we noted previously regarding 'français familier', 'français branché' and other designations in French, can we ever be certain that a word will be uniformly viewed as characteristic of colloquial, criminal or youth practice in any given language, let alone when comparing with analogues in other languages? With Russian, for example, some commentators disagree variously on the meanings, typical users, stylistic categorisation and connotations of some items. In Table 0.2, we can see the use of various qualifications such as 'zhargon',[8] 'razgovornaia rech'' (colloquial), 'sleng' ('slang')[9] and 'prostorechie' (a stigmatised form of colloquial, mainly urban speech, often viewed as less educated[10]) for the words 'babakhnutyi' ('loopy', 'not right in the head'), 'bashka' ('nut', 'noggin'), 'obaldet'' ('to get out of it') and 'alkash' ('alkie').

Although we allow for the possibility that meanings can change over time and between groups, this brief comparison shows that views can differ as to the stylistic categorisation and semantic reference of any given item. With 'babakhnutyi', for instance, Kveselevich (2005: 18) sees it as 'prostorechie', while Shlyakhov and Adler (2006: 9) consider it to be indicative of 'youth slang'. With 'obaldet'', Kveselevich (2005: 511) notes that it is regarded as 'prostorechie' where it means 'to become mad', but 'zhargon' – which could be either a general 'slang' or something more group-specific – where it means either 'to be on cloud nine' or 'to get high'. Nikitina (2009: 525), on the other hand, sees it as 'youth slang', meaning both 'to be ecstatic' and 'to be astonished'. Then there are different attitudinal markers: Shlyakhov and Adler (2006: 3) view 'alkash', for example, as "rude", while Nikitina (2009: 20) considers her example – cited in a dictionary of youth language and serving as an epithet for a well-known individual – to be "jocular–ironic". In fact, both these hues are possible, depending on factors such as context,

Table 0.2 Comparative stylistic attribution of non-standard Russian items

Commentator	Babakhnutyi	Bashka	Obaldet'	Alkash	Year
Marder	Slang	Colloq.	Slang	Colloq.	1994
Elistratov	–	Prost.	–	Colloq./Argot	1994
Kveselevich	Prost.	Prost.	Prost./Zhar.	Zhar.	2005
Shlyakhov and Adler	Youth	–	Negative	Rude	2006
Nikitina	–	–	Youth	Joc.-iron.	2009

the relationships between speakers and delivery (e.g. tone, facial expression). Although a brief treatment, we can see from Table 0.2 that questions of meaning, connotation and stylistic categorisation might not be quite so clear-cut as some reference works might make out, perhaps due to the life experiences, positionality and linguistic ideologies of researchers.[11] And this isn't just a problem for Russian – similar challenges have been recorded for other languages such as English (e.g. B. Moore 2014) and French (e.g. Wise 1997).

Then there is a second problem: if the experts diverge in their interpretation and definitions, how can we have any confidence in our own analysis?

There is no doubt that the interpretation and definition of linguistic practices conceptualised as colloquial, youth and criminal language can be problematic. In some cases we see competing definitions of what are believed to be clearly demarcated stylistic categories ('argot' versus 'slang') or of which lexis or word-formation elements any given category is said to definitively *contain* (e.g. 'obaldet'', 'alkash', certain suffixes). Somewhat tied to this thinking is the suggestion that whether a word is 'slang' or 'argot' may also depend on perceived unique users at any given time: a word is a 'criminal argot' item if perceived to be non-standard and used by criminals; it may then be borrowed by youth and become part of the 'youth slang' lexicon, by which time it ceases being viewed as 'criminal argot' – a linear transfer between categories is thus effected. Finally, we may also see definition through perceived motivation, for example, the use of words to conceal meaning being representative of criminal in-group language.

However, there is another way of understanding youth, criminal and colloquial language practices that offers some help – to consider how some forms of language are commonly regarded as emblematic of certain socially recognisable personas, identities, stances and situations of use and are then deployed by speakers on the basis of that understanding in specific situations. This is the notion of indexicality (for engaging discussions, see Ochs 1992; Podesva, Roberts and Campbell-Kibler 2001; Reyes 2005; Eckert 2008, 2012). With this approach, the focus is on a connection that is formed and popularly maintained by speakers between certain linguistic variables and the kinds of people *who are widely thought to use them*, between the variables *and perceived personal or social characteristics*. For example, and to move for a moment beyond youth and criminal language practices in particular, people may draw certain conclusions about another's level of education, intelligence or socio-economic status – aspects of their personal and social identity – judging by popular understandings of the latter's accent, or of the person's accent and clothing (multiple indices). Another example may be where certain language forms index a regional identity – again, based on the association of certain linguistic forms with particular social types.

So, indexicality means that certain language forms point to certain types of people, whose social value, identities, activities, status and characteristics are also judged (Agha 1998). And when the resulting associations between language form and user take hold and acquire greater currency within society, they become essentialised as popular stereotypes: the language a person is held to use thus becomes a marker of their positive or negative social identity, value and status, the kind of person they are thought to be. At the same time, the use of certain *variant* words or expressions by certain individuals becomes converted into *perceived difference* in terms of identity and character (Agha 1998; see also Kiesling 2009; Lacoste, Leimgruber and Breyer 2014).

With indexicality we therefore focus on the question of what identity, stance, characteristics or situation is/are being indexed by a speaker through use of a given language variable or variables within a given context and cotext (the surrounding text) – taking care to note that combinations of these stances, characteristics and so on can be indexed simultaneously, and that *A, B* or *C* linguistic forms may be used to index more than one identity, activity, situation, characteristic or stance (e.g. Agha 1998; Reyes 2005; Aarsæther, Marzo, Nistov and Ceuleers 2015). For example, is a speaker using a particular non-standard linguistic form or forms because it/they index(es) sophistication (e.g. in language play), coolness, in-groupness, lack of education, opposition to social mainstream rules and structures, particular social status, or another particular social persona held to have these attributes? Is more than one characteristic, for example, ethnicity, stance and in-groupness, being indexed?

In the examples we consider in this book, we see that words typically associated with youth practice primarily index sociocultural conceptions of what is it to be a youth, to have a youth style and a youth identity, of what young people are believed to be typically concerned with, of the situations of language use in which they act as agents, and of how they linguistically negotiate their social universe. So, when considering youth language practice, we may wish to consider whether its use indexes social rebellion or coolness, for example, and/or whether it indexes a particular youth identity in any given situation or instance. We may wish to consider other indices that may be involved (e.g. non-verbal cues, discourse topics, clothing, posture) and how this multiple indexing might manifest itself in interaction as it unfolds (e.g. Verma and Saraswathi 2002; Reyes 2005). Indeed, the expression and interpretation of identity and stance as emergent processes is of no little importance, as Bucholtz (2009) observes:

> The social meaning of linguistic forms is most fundamentally a matter not of social categories such as gender, ethnicity, age, or region but rather of subtler and more fleeting interactional moves through which speakers take stances, create alignments, and construct personas.
>
> (Bucholtz 2009: 146)

The same principle can be extended to criminal language practices, of course.

In these cases, then, what is indexed by the linguistic variables is a stereotypical *social image* of an individual or group (and/or situation of use), and of what they are believed to represent as social actors. The individual or group is believed to have recognisable social attributes – a particular identity or values that others may oppose or alternatively with which they may seek to establish some form of commonality. One way or another, with an indexical approach we are stepping back from focusing on whether a discrete (even widely agreed) group of words falls into a single stylistic category such as 'slang', 'argot' or 'prostorechie' – to continue the Russian example – or whether a person employs a particular language practice *because* they fall within a particular social bracket (youth, criminal) or need a cryptolect (motivation), and are concentrating instead on what people believe to be typical users, stances, identities, activities, characteristics and use. We are thus looking at linguistic resources that can be employed by a variety of speakers who mobilise prototypical understandings of users and use within a given context and for a given reason: with language practices associated with criminals, for instance, forms need not be used exclusively by criminals in order to index *images* of criminality.

Of course, this need not mean that language practices typically conceptualised as youth or criminal language no longer exist. Indeed, they do. However, they exist as collections of linguistic forms that speakers or authors believe to typify users, their identities and situations of usage, and not as strictly demarcated or absolute either/or stylistic categories. So, in a given context, a Russian word such as 'obaldet'' may well index lack of sophistication, social grace or even education where it means 'to become mad' ('prostorechie'), while in other situations it may index drug use or inebriation and the social meaning this brings when used to mean 'to get high' (youth- or drugs-related usage), or relaxed situations where someone is 'on cloud nine' (as colloquial usage) (see also **Enregisterment** on page 280).

The structure of the book

The book has been designed using a structure commonly found in analyses of youth, criminal and colloquial language. A great many of the chapters in Nassenstein and Hollington's (2015) recent volume mainly centring on African practice, and in Coleman's (2014c) *Global English Slang*, for example, initially characterise the sociolinguistic environment, discussing factors such as increasing urbanisation and questions of ethnicity before moving on to analyse aspects such as speaker motivation, how linguistic variation is defined and typical linguistic manipulations. This is an approach that has also been used in a number of prior studies of youth and criminal practices (e.g. Einat and Einat 2000; Bosire 2009). It works well for exploring complementarity between background, motives and manipulations and is thus employed in this book for the same reason.

This book also builds on previous approaches in terms of the individual subtopics covered. Most fundamentally, it incorporates the themes addressed by Androutsopoulos (2005) in his helpful outline of sociolinguistic research into youth language. In its thematic scope, Androutsopoulos' overview identifies key questions and premises, including relevant age range, youth control and agentivity, and linguistic innovation and variation; and outlines perspectives on colloquial usage by youth; vocabulary creation and non-standard word-formation processes; speech aims (e.g. expressive and interactive goals); the wider diffusion of terms; research using macrosociological variables such as gender, age and class; the influence of peer groups and status within them; questions of language contact; issues of language attitudes and stereotypes; social–psychological dimensions such as the negotiation of identity, resistance and social differentiation; cross-linguistic and -societal comparison; and media influence (e.g. on local and global levels).

Of course, although Androutsopoulos' excellent summary provides an assessment of the status of research at that time across the various subthemes relating to youth language, research has moved on since 2005. Therefore, a number of matters that have attracted attention in more recent times are also discussed in the book. These include: multiethnolects and super-diversity; questions of stylistic practice and repertoires as explanatory constructs for language variation; and evaluation/verdictiveness, to name but a few. It is hoped that, between the 2005 overview topics and discussion of subsequent developments, the primary questions relevant to youth and criminal practice over the last 15–20 years or so in particular are thus identified and explored.

In terms of content, the book is effectively split into two parts. Part One consists of:

- Chapter One, which outlines the main sources used for language examples cited in the book and briefly profiles how associated varieties have been understood in the literature. It also provides a brief overview of methods used by scholars in the collection of source material.
- Chapter Two, which attends to theories and perspectives that have been most prominent in literature on youth and criminal linguistic practices in the past few years. In specific terms, we consider antilanguage, resistance identity, style as a means of explaining linguistic variation, the concept of repertoires, and questions of identity and identification.
- Chapter Three, which considers why youth and criminal practices are undertaken and perceptions of them: here we move beyond theoretical frameworks and discuss many of the more specific questions that obtain in discussion of these practices. This chapter explores, for example, why in-groups may choose to employ certain linguistic practices and what those in out-groups think of such usage; what types of Other are identified through usage; how practices may be used for status within a group; conceptualisation of youth language practices relative to class, age and gender; and what the implications are for language practices online, using Russian as an initial basis for discussion. We also acquaint readers with questions regarding the diffusion of items from in-groups to broader social configurations.

Part Two focuses on the various lexical, semantic and other manipulations that are commonly reflected in the literature on those varieties outlined in Chapter One:

- Chapter Four (lexical borrowing between and within languages and the invention of new words): this primarily familiarises readers with the various motivations for borrowing items, not just between languages but between varieties, as social agents look to meet various social–communicative needs or goals. Additionally, it acquaints readers with the different changes that may obtain when a word is borrowed from a donor lexicon (semantic change, change in grammatical number, etc.). A key section of this chapter concerns the forms that hybridity may take, such as through merging orthographic systems.

- Chapter Five (semantic manipulations): attends to how meaning is changed as a vehicle for supplementing a group's lexical repertoire across a number of languages. Key areas covered in this chapter are the many ways in which new items can be created through metaphor and metonymy, as well as discussion of hyperbole, *litotes*, euphemism and dysphemism.
- Chapter Six (morphological manipulations): in this chapter we chiefly focus on affixation, paying particular attention to *stylistically marked* suffixes as used in languages such as Spanish, French and Russian. We discuss the connotations attached to the use of new items created through suffixation and address dummy affixation as a means of hiding meaning or socially marking an item. Prefixation, circumfixation and back-formation are also outlined.
- Chapter Seven (compounding and reduplication): here we discuss the many ways in which items can be concatenated to create new vocabulary, again across many different languages. We discuss different types of concatenation (ranging from noun and numeral to the fusion of items with different orthographic representations) and shed light on ways in which different types of reduplication (full and partial) may be employed for particular effect.
- Chapter Eight (phonetic and phonological considerations): here we look at the ways in which changes in sound or structure may be used to create new items. We explore the use of consonant addition and replacement and onomatopoeia as options on the expressive palettes of a number of speakers. Particular attention is paid to phonotactic manipulations such as syllable reordering (metathesis) to invent new items, and to how such methods as inversion and transposition are employed in language practices by several in-groups across the globe.
- Chapter Nine: other manipulations such as truncation are addressed as means to create new in-group and colloquial vocabulary. Similarly outlined in this section are the use of acronyms and abbreviations, again across languages.
- Chapter Ten: in this chapter we consider some of the key points to emerge in the book and outline some questions that require further investigation.

In each chapter in Part Two, the manipulations are principally explored vis-à-vis the main language varieties outlined in Chapter One. These include criminal language in Indonesia, West Bengal and Israel; youth language varieties in Cameroon, Kenya, the US, Germany and Japan; and colloquial French, Russian and Spanish (see Chapter One for a full list). Where examples of practices involving these key varieties are provided in explanatory text and illustrations, specific source details are not given (although they are indicated in Chapter One where the core varieties and sources are introduced). However, in select instances observations relating to

26 *Introduction*

Estonian, Hungarian, Finnish, Italian, Turkish, Arabic, Brazilian and a number of other languages are also provided for comparative, contextual or other illustrative purposes. In these cases sources are identified.

Finally, to support readers new to the subject, a number of reference boxes briefly outlining theories, concepts and questions pertinent to the use of the language varieties studied in the book have also been included (for example, **Overt and covert prestige**, **Appropriation**). Study questions and images illustrating usage have additionally been provided online on the book's accompanying *eResource* at www.routledge.com/9781138558830.

What this book doesn't investigate

Naturally, it is also germane to highlight what this book does not cover: non-standard grammar; expletives/swearing; and code-switching.

Grammar in colloquial language and in-group varieties: researchers note that there are grammatical and syntactic considerations that are relevant to colloquial usage and in-group practices in many languages. Lodge (1993: 247), for example, observes with respect to French that "[t]here exist a large number of non-standard grammatical forms which are heavily stigmatised and attributed to the less-educated social groups". Molamu, in his paper on Tsotsitaal in South Africa (i.e. urban youth practice often associated with young males to demonstrate modernity and street smarts, among other things), notes how it "often defies the formal constraints of grammar" (Molamu 1995: 148–9) and documents how "[g]rammatical creativity and spontaneity were sometimes accompanied by peculiar violations of structured syntax" (Molamu 1995: 149). In his study of English, Carter (2004) draws attention to various mechanisms by which a sense of solidarity, informality and shared viewpoint can be dynamically co-established and co-consolidated in exchanges (e.g. through the use of affective vocatives), while Ochs and Schieffelin (1989) demonstrate how pronouns, voice, particles, case-marking and change in grammatical gender, animacy and number, among others, can be variously employed to reflect attitudes, moods and dispositions in a number of languages, including Japanese, Samoan, Spanish, Italian and Russian.

More recently, a number of works have variously investigated grammatical innovation in German Kiezdeutsch ('hood German', 'street German'; Wiese 2009); pragmatic and grammatical function words in Kiezdeutsch, Swedish and Norwegian youth practices (Ekberg, Opsahl and Wiese 2015); instances of non-standard grammar in the language practices of youth in London and Madrid (Stenström 2014); and syntactic developments in a range of European multiethnolects (Cheshire, Nortier and Adger 2015). Multiethnolects are globally found, mainly urban youth peer-group language varieties typically of speakers from multiple ethnic backgrounds, often including the host community, that incorporate elements from migrant languages as a means of indexing social identity (Dorleijn and Nortier 2013).

While I note the importance of the elements that Lodge, Carter, Stenström and others discuss and draw attention to them in a few places, the focus in this book essentially rests on ways in which lexis is borrowed or created to meet communicative aims. It is for this same reason that intonation, gestures and facial expression are also acknowledged but not pursued to any real degree.

Expletives: here I have in mind the use of what we might call *curse words*, *vulgarisms* or *swearwords or expressions* (which are often linked to notions of taboo). They *can* be used to meet the same ends as words popularly categorised as youth or criminal language, although this is often context-dependent. For example, Mayr (2004) notes the use of swearing by prisoners for evaluation, amplification, assertiveness, group cohesion and resistance (compare, for example, the section on **Verbal contests** in Chapter Three); Widawski (2015) discusses the use of swearwords to demonstrate toughness; while Danesi (1994: 100) calls attention to swearing serving a need for constant emotional and forceful expression, to shock outsiders and to foster group solidarity among teenagers – although persistent use may ultimately lessen emotiveness and render relevant items "mere conversational gambits or verbal protocols" (Danesi 1994: 115). And, of course, there is the jocular use of cursing among and about friends to foster solidarity (e.g. Stenström, Andersen and Hasund 2002; Widawski 2015; Nassenstein 2016).

Notably, while some commentators combine the use of in-group youth language practices and swearwords within the same study (e.g. Beazley 2003; de Klerk and Antrobus 2004; de Klerk 2005; Jørgensen 2013; Stenström 2014; see also Green 2016 for discussion of obscenities as part of English 'slang'), there are grounds to suggest that they are *not* the same linguistic phenomenon. In his analysis of this question with regard to English, Moore (2012, 2014) suggests, for example, that while both can entail the expression of emotion (affect) and can co-occur, in some societies expletives may carry greater shock value. De Klerk (2005) additionally posits that swearwords tend to constitute a relatively limited group of words and expressions, do not change with any great regularity (in both regards much unlike youth practices),[12] and can effect considerably more emotive and offensive impact (in this regard see also Molamu 1995 on swearing and Tsotsitaal).

The view of this work is that there is sufficient difference between youth and criminal in-group language practices and swearing to justify seeing them as different entities. Correspondingly, expletives do not form a focus of study in the book. That being said, where colloquial usage involves euphemism, such as in abbreviation, then this is mentioned, and there are some limited examples involving expletives in various chapters to exemplify certain salient points, especially around linguistic manipulations.

Code-switching: this is where speakers move between languages or dialects as they interact. This is undoubtedly an important part of the linguistic reality for some groups, such as those in urban spaces in Africa (e.g. Hollington and Nassenstein 2015a). However, while I acknowledge this reality, the focus in this book is more on the borrowing of discrete lexical items and what happens to them when adopted from one lexicon into another.

It is very much hoped that the book considerably helps readers as they seek to learn more about colloquial, youth and criminal language practices. However, it is acknowledged that, although many examples and mechanisms are included as indicative or typical of relevant language varieties, there will inevitably be limitations in the book's coverage as an introductory guide: both in terms of encompassing the full breadth and depth of manipulations and inventiveness associated with any given variety, group or speaker, and in terms of covering every potential means of creating new items more widely. Readers are therefore invited to seek out the key texts from which examples and other insights are drawn (outlined in Chapter One) and to consult references for further information.

This introduction draws to a close with three final points. Firstly, readers are requested to note that the book contains examples of what some may see as offensive language. It is hoped that readers will view the inclusion of any such material as important to the book's integrity. Secondly, where timescales are indicated in examples of usage, these relate to dates of source publication and not of usage *per se*: items may continue to be used. And thirdly, any errors in this work are, of course, the responsibility of the author.

Jim Davie, December 2017

Notes

1 Kis (2006: 138) provides some thought-provoking reflections on whether 'slang' can be claimed to be universal. He concludes by stating: "I believe that, as a conclusion to the arguments considered, I can say yes: the use of slang must be a characteristic of the *Homo sapiens* since the formation of language. Slang is an absolute universal, its existence is and has always been legitimate in every human language. Furthermore, as the reasons creating slang (and thus language) derived from the most basic human characteristics, the social features of the *Homo sapiens*, we can also state that it was created not primarily for linguistic reasons but for biological–ethological–social reasons, thus slang is not only a linguistic but a 'human' universal".
2 An engaging discussion of the value and rise of standard varieties can be found in Joseph's *Language and Identity*. Joseph (2004: 208) indicates that during and after the Renaissance there was fierce debate in a number of nations as to which dialect would serve as the basis of the national language, adding that "[t]heir ferocity would defy belief were it not that the location of the common soul was at stake". His list, which he admits is by no means exclusive, includes such discussions in France, the Iberian Peninsula, Germany, Scandinavia, the British Isles, and subsequently in the Balkans, Poland, Turkey and India.
3 Also referring to French, Abecassis (2003: 117) has stated: "Standard French is given prestige and is an advantage in a social and educational sense, whereas non-standard varieties of French, such as local vernaculars are highly stigmatised ... Institutional hostility towards the vernacular adopts two lines of attack: the first favours written, planned discourse over spoken, spontaneous discourse and the second favours upper-class over lower-class usages".
4 Carter (2004: 54–5) opines with regard to English: "There is a corresponding tendency to value written language highly, especially in comparison with spoken language ... For many centuries dictionaries and grammars of the English language have taken the written language as a benchmark for what is proper and standard in the language and have incorporated written and often 'literary' examples to illustrate the best usage. What is written and what is literate are accorded high cultural status and what is spoken is accordingly not privileged".
5 According to some scholars, the superior status of the standard and the written word is also echoed in Russian. Andrews (2012: 26; his italics) notes: "As is well known, many

commentators in Russia are greatly alarmed by the erosion of language standards there over the past two decades. These complaints include the large influx of English borrowings ... but extend far beyond that, from previously impermissible usages in verbal government ... and word stress ... to the proliferation of vulgarities (*mat*) and other non-standard lexicon ... It is unsurprising that these developments are so disturbing to the intelligentsia, for whom the Russian language has traditionally held enormous symbolic power. Indeed, for many it has been a virtual object of veneration, along with Russian literature. If literature is regarded as the crowning achievement of Russian culture, then these perceived assaults on the standard language are a threat to the very culture itself". Utekhin (2012: 250) also offers the following comment with regard to online Russian and the status of the written word: "It is characteristic that the audience of *ZhZh* [Russian LiveJournal blogging site] ... is more 'literate' than that of other blogging services that appeared later. For Russian culture, its orientation towards the written language and texts is so important that blogging logically became an affordable way of virtual self-expression and socializing".
6 Zhirmunskii (1936: 124) points to an older heritage, indicating that the first work citing Germanía was in 1609, for example.
7 Lodge (1993) also notes that the non-standard character of much adolescent speech in French is reflected in syntax and phonology but is most evident in lexis. He observes that the mechanisms involved in lexical innovation are semantic shift, a change in word class, derivation (such as the use of new suffixes), abbreviation and borrowing from English.
8 Kveselevich (2005: 3) sees 'zhargon' as consisting of general slang, youth slang, military slang, criminal argot, drug users' slang and the slang of sexual minorities.
9 Marder (1994: vi) suggests that 'slang' is ephemeral and geographically specific, with some exceptions.
10 Ozhegov and Shvedova (1995: 611) define 'prostorechie' as: "The speech of poorly educated native speakers (mainly town-dwellers); pronunciation features, words and expressions, grammatical forms and constructions characteristic of non-literary colloquial usage". A later edition of Ozhegov's dictionary (2016: 503) defines it as "Words and grammatical forms of mass urban colloquial speech used in the literary language as a stylistic means for giving speech a humorous, contemptuous, ironic, somewhat crude and other shade". It is noteworthy that the use of such language was explicitly linked with a poor level of education in the first definition but not, or perhaps not so directly, in the second. In both definitions, "(non-)literary" can be read as a reference to the (non-)standard variety.
11 It is also worth noting that Offord (1996: 19–20) leaves room for alternative interpretations of register in Russian, where he points out that theoretical demarcation may not easily fit with actual practice, and that there is a lack of complete agreement as to where stylistic boundaries are to be found.
12 In her discussion of the learning of American English taboo words by second language learners, Register (1996: 48) appears to echo de Klerk regarding the longevity and lesser turnover of swearwords by comparison with some other varieties: "The majority of present day unmentionables identifiably date back to the Middle Ages, while slang words, catch phrases, and other colloquial types continually come in and out of vogue and further vary with social class, geographic region, and age group". The limited number of obscene lexical items in English is also reported by Green (2016: 21) to be a "micro-lexis".

References

Aarsæther, F., Marzo, S., Nistov, I. and Ceuleers, E. (2015) 'Indexing locality: contemporary urban vernaculars in Belgium and Norway', in J. Nortier and B.A. Svendsen (eds.) *Language, Youth and Identity in the 21st Century*, Cambridge: Cambridge University Press. 249–70.

Abecassis, M. (2002) 'The origins of the collocation "le français populaire" and of stylistic labels in dictionaries and in linguistic studies', *Calliope: Journal de Littérature et de Linguistique*, 5(1, Janvier–Février). www.mediom.qc.ca/~extrudex/home1.html, accessed July 2012.

Abeccasis, M. (2003) 'Le français populaire: a valid concept?', *Marges Linguistiques*, 6(Novembre), 116–32.

Aboa, A.L.A. (2011) 'Le Nouchi – a-t-il un avenir?', *Revue Electronique Internationale de Sciences du Langage*, 16(Décembre), 44–54.

Agha, A. (1998) 'Stereotypes and registers of honorific language', *Language in Society*, 27, 151–193.

Agha, A. (2003) 'The social life of cultural value', *Language and Communication*, 23, 231–73.

Åke-Nilsson, N. (1960) 'Soviet Student Slang', *Scando-Slavica*, 6, 113–23.

Andrews, D.R. (2012) 'Attitudes toward the Russian and English languages in Russia and the United States: perceptions of self and the other', in R. Alapuro, A. Mustajoki and P. Pesonen (eds.) *Understanding Russianness*, London: Routledge. 19–31.

Androutsopoulos, J. (2000) 'Non-standard spellings in media texts: The case of German fanzines', *Journal of Sociolinguistics*, 4(4), 514–33.

Androutsopoulos, J. (2005) 'Research on youth language', in U. Ammon, D. Norbert, K.J. Mattheier and P. Trudgill (eds.) *Sociolinguistics/Soziolinguistik: An International Handbook of the Science of Language and Society (Ein internationales Handbuch zur Wissenschaft von Sprache und Gesellschaft), Vol. 2*, Berlin: de Gruyter. 1496–1505.

Artemova, T.V., Katyshev, P.A., Olenev, S.V., Pauli, Iu.S. and Sokolova, S.K. (2014) 'Funktsii zhargona narkomanov i slovoobrazovatel′nye sredstva ikh osushchestvleniia', *Vestnik Kemerovskogo Gosudarstvennogo Universiteta*, 3(59), T. 3, 166–9.

Bardsley, D. (2014) 'Slang in Godzone (Aotearoa – New Zealand)', in J. Coleman (ed.), *Global English Slang*, London: Routledge. 96–106.

Beazley, H. (1998) 'Homeless street children in Yogyakarta, Indonesia', *Development Bulletin*, Australian Development Studies Network, 44, 40–2.

Beazley, H. (2002) '"Vagrants wearing make-up": negotiating spaces on the streets of Yogyakarta, Indonesia', *Urban Studies*, 39(9), 1665–83.

Beazley, H. (2003) 'The construction and protection of individual and collective identities by street children and youth in Indonesia', *Children, Youth and Environments*, 13(1). www.colorado.edu/journals/cye/13_1/Vol13_1Articles/CYE_CurrentIssue_Article_ChildrenYouthIndonesia_Beazley.htm, accessed July 2015.

Beck, R.M. (2015) 'Sheng: an urban variety of Swahili in Kenya', in N. Nassenstein and A. Hollington (eds.) *Youth Language Practices in Africa and Beyond*, Berlin/Boston: Walter de Gruyter, Inc. 51–79.

Beier, L. (1995) 'Anti-language or jargon? canting in the English underworld in the 16th and 17th centuries', in P. Burke and R. Porter (eds.) *Languages and Jargons: Contributions to a Social History of Language*, Cambridge: Polity Press. 64–101.

Beregovskaia, E.M. (1996) 'Molodëzhnyi sleng: formirovanie i funktsionirovanie', *Voprosy iazykoznaniia*, 3, 32–41.

Berjaoui, N. (1997) 'Parlers secrets d'El-Jadida: notes préliminaires', *Estudios de dialectología norteafricana y andalusí*, 2, 147–58.

Beyer, K. (2015) 'Youth language practices in Africa: achievements and challenges', in N. Nassenstein and A. Hollington (eds.) *Youth Language Practices in Africa and Beyond*, Berlin/Boston: Walter de Gruyter, Inc. 23–50.

Biblieva, O.V. (2007) 'Molodëzhnyi sleng kak forma reprezentatsii molodëzhnoi kul'tury v sredstvakh massovoi informatsii', *Vestnik Tomskogo Gosudarstvennogo Universiteta*, *304*(Noiabr'), 62–5.
Blommaert, J. and Backus, A. (2011) 'Repertoires revisited: "knowing language" in superdiversity', in *Working Papers in Urban Language and Literacies*, 67.
Blommaert, J. and Rampton, B. (2011) 'Language and superdiversity', *Diversities*, *13*(2), 1–21.
Boellstorff, T. (2004) '*Gay* language and Indonesia: registering belonging', *Journal of Linguistic Anthropology*, *14*(2), 248–68.
Booth, M. (2002) 'Arab adolescents facing the future: enduring ideals and pressures to change', in B.B. Brown, R.W. Larson and T.S. Saraswathi (eds.) *The World's Youth*, Cambridge: CUP. 207–42.
Bosire, M. (2009) 'What makes a Sheng word unique? Lexical manipulation in mixed languages', in A. Ojo and L. Moshi (eds.) *Selected Proceedings of the 39th Annual Conference on African Linguistics*, Somerville, MA. 77–85.
Boumphrey, S. (2012) *Special Report: The World's Populations*, 13 February. blog.euromonitor.com/2012/02/special-report-the-worlds-youngest-populations.html, accessed July 2016.
Boyd, S., Hoffman, M.F. and Walker, J.A. (2015) 'Sociolinguistic variation among multicultural youth: comparing Swedish cities and Toronto', in J. Nortier and B.A. Svendsen (eds.) *Language, Youth and Identity in the 21st Century*, Cambridge: Cambridge University Press. 290–306.
Brown, B.B. and Larson, R.W. (2002) 'The kaleidoscope of adolescence: experiences of the world's youth at the beginning of the 21st century', in B.B. Brown, R.W. Larson and T.S. Saraswathi (eds.) *The World's Youth*, Cambridge: Cambridge University Press. 1–20.
Brown, B.B., Larson, R.W. and Saraswathi, T.S. (eds.) (2002) *The World's Youth*, Cambridge: Cambridge University Press.
Bucholtz, M. (2002) 'Youth and cultural practice', *Annual Review of Anthropology*, *31*, 525–52.
Bucholtz, M. (2004) 'Styles and stereotypes: the linguistic negotiation of identity among Laotian American youth', *Pragmatics*, *14*(2/3), 127–47.
Bucholtz, M. (2009) 'From stance to style: gender, interaction, and indexicality in Mexican immigrant youth slang', in A. Jaffe (ed.) *Stance: Sociolinguistic Perspectives*, Oxford: Oxford University Press. 146–70.
Bucholtz, M. and Hall, K. (2003) 'Language and identity', in A. Duranti (ed.) *A Companion to Linguistic Anthropology*, Oxford: Blackwell. 369–94.
Carter, R.A. (2004) *Language and Creativity*, London: Routledge.
Chambers, J.K. (1995) *Sociolinguistic Theory*, Oxford: Blackwell.
Chambert-Loir, H. (1984) 'Those who speak Prokem', *Indonesia*, *37*, 105–17.
Cheshire, J., Nortier, J. and Adger, D. (2015) 'Emerging multiethnolects in Europe', in *Queen Mary's Occasional Papers Advancing Linguistics*, 33.
Coleman, J. (2012) *The Life of Slang*, Oxford: Oxford University Press.
Coleman, J. (2014a) 'Slang used by students at the University of Leicester', in J. Coleman (ed.) *Global English Slang*, London: Routledge. 49–61.
Coleman, J. (2014b) 'Global English slang in the era of big data', in J. Coleman (ed.) *Global English Slang*, London: Routledge. 205–13.
Coleman, J. (ed.) (2014c) *Global English Slang*, London: Routledge.

32 Introduction

Condon, R.G. (1990) 'The rise of adolescence: social change and life stage dilemmas in the central Canadian Arctic', *Human Organ*, *49*(3), 266–79.

Cooper, B. (1989) 'Russian underworld slang and its diffusion into the standard language', *Australian Slavonic and East European Journal*, *3*(2), 61–89.

Cornips, L, Jaspers, J. and de Rooij, V. (2015) 'The politics of labelling youth vernaculars in the Netherlands and Belgium', in J. Nortier and B.A. Svendsen (eds.) *Language, Youth and Identity in the 21st Century*, Cambridge: Cambridge University Press. 45–69.

Coupland, N. (2007) *Style: Language Variation and Identity*, Cambridge: Cambridge University Press.

Cutler, C. and Røyneland, U. (2015) 'Where the fuck am I from? Hip-hop youth and the (re)negotiation of language and identity in Norway and the US', in J. Nortier and B.A. Svendsen (eds.) *Language, Youth and Identity in the 21st Century*, Cambridge: Cambridge University Press. 139–63.

Dalzell, T. (2014) 'Hip-hop slang', in J. Coleman (ed.) *Global English Slang*, London: Routledge. 15–24.

Danesi, M. (1994) *Cool: The Signs and Meanings of Adolescence*, Toronto: University of Toronto Press.

Davie, J.D. (1998) *Making sense of the nonstandard: a study of borrowing and word-formation in 1990s Russian youth slang, with particular reference to the language of the fanzine* (Doctoral dissertation, 2 volumes). University of Portsmouth.

de Klerk, V. (2005) 'Slang and swearing as markers of inclusion and exclusion in adolescence', in A. Williams and C. Thurlow (eds.) *Talking Adolescence: Perspectives on Communication in the Teenage Years*, New York: Peter Lang Publishing, Inc. 111–27.

de Klerk, V. and Antrobus, R. (2004) 'Swamp-donkeys and rippers: The use of slang and pejorative terms to name 'the other'', *Alternation*, *11*(2), 264–82.

Doran, M. (2004) 'Negotiating between bourge and racaille: Verlan as youth identity practice in suburban Paris', in A. Pavlenko and A. Blackledge (eds.) *Identities in Multilingual Contexts*, Clevedon, UK: Multilingual Matters Ltd. 93–124.

Doran, M. (2007) 'Alternative French, alternative identities: situating language in la banlieue', *Contemporary French and Francophone Studies*, *11*(4), 497–508.

Dorleijn, M., Mous, M. and Nortier, J. (2015) 'Urban youth speech styles in Kenya and the Netherlands', in J. Nortier and B.A. Svendsen (eds.) *Language, Youth and Identity in the 21st Century*, Cambridge: Cambridge University Press. 271–89.

Dorleijn, M. and Nortier, J. (2013) 'Multi-ethnolects: Kebabnorsk, Perkerdansk, Verlan, Kanakensprache, Straattaal, etc.', in P. Bakker and Y. Matras (eds.) *Contact Languages: A Comprehensive Guide*, Berlin: de Gruyter. 229–72.

Eble, C. (1996) *Slang and Sociability*, Chapel Hill, NC: University of North Carolina Press.

Eble, C. (2014) 'American college student slang: University of North Carolina (2005–12)', in J. Coleman (ed.) *Global English Slang*, London: Routledge. 36–48.

Eckert, P. (2005) 'Stylistic practice and the adolescent social order', in A. Williams and C. Thurlow (eds.) *Talking Adolescence: Perspectives on Communication in the Teenage Years*, New York: Peter Lang Publishing, Inc. 93–110.

Eckert, P. (2006) 'Communities of Practice', *Encyclopedia of Language and Linguistics*, Elsevier. Pre-publication copy. pdfs.semanticscholar.org/a4c6/ade3f09be4a074655b543 d02055029099059.pdf, accessed February 2013.

Eckert, P. (2008) 'Variation and the indexical field', *Journal of Sociolinguistics*, *12*(4), 453–76.

Eckert, P. (2012) 'Three waves of variation study: the emergence of meaning in the study of sociolinguistic variation', *Annual Review of Anthropology*, *41*, 87–100.
Eckert, P. and McConnell-Ginet, S. (1992) 'Communities of Practice: where language, gender, and power all live', in K. Hall, M. Bucholtz and B. Moonwomon (eds.) *Locating Power, Proceedings of the 1992 Berkeley Women and Language Conference*, Berkeley: Berkeley Women and Language Group. 89–99.
Einat, T. and Einat, H. (2000) 'Inmate argot as an expression of prison subculture: the Israeli case', *The Prison Journal*, *80*(3), 309–25.
Ekberg, L. Opsahl, T. and Wiese, H. (2015) 'Functional gains: a cross-linguistic case study of three particles in Swedish, Norwegian and German', in J. Nortier and B.A. Svendsen (eds.) *Language, Youth and Identity in the 21st Century*, Cambridge: Cambridge University Press. 93–115.
Elistratov, V.S. (1994) *Slovar' moskovskogo argo*, Moscow: Russkie slovari.
Ellis, Y. (2002) 'Argot and Verlan', *Contemporary France Online*, www.well.ac.uk/cfol/argot.asp, accessed May 2011.
Ferrari, A. (2006) 'Vecteurs de la propagation du lexique sheng et invention perpétuelle de mots', *Le Français en Afrique*, 21, 227–37.
Fussell, E. and Greene, M. (2002) 'Demographic trends affecting youth around the world', in B.B. Brown, R.W. Larson and T.S. Saraswathi (eds.) *The World's Youth*, Cambridge: Cambridge University Press. 21–60.
García, M. (2005) 'Influences of gypsy *Caló* on contemporary Spanish slang', *Hispania*, *88*(4), 800–12.
Garrett, P. and Williams, A. (2005) 'Adults' perceptions of communication with young people', in A. Williams and C. Thurlow (eds.) *Talking Adolescence: Perspectives on Communication in the Teenage Years*, New York: Peter Lang Publishing, Inc. 35–52.
Githinji, P. (2006) 'Bazes and their shibboleths: lexical variation and Sheng speakers' identity in Nairobi', *Nordic Journal of African Studies*, *15*(4), 443–72.
González, F.R. and Stenström, A. (2011) 'Expressive devices in the language of English- and Spanish-speaking youth', *Revista Alicantina de Estudios Ingleses*, *24*, 235–56.
Goudaillier, J.-P. (2002) 'De l'argot traditionnel au français contemporain des cités', *La Linguistique*, *1*(38), 5–24.
Grachëv, M.A. (1994) 'Ob etimologii v russkom argo', *Russkaia rech'*, *4*, 67–70.
Grayson, J. (1964) 'Lunfardo, Argentina's unknown tongue', *Hispania*, *47*(1), 66–8.
Green, J. (2016) *Slang: A Very Short Introduction*, Oxford: Oxford University Press.
Hagedorn, J.M. (2005) 'The global impact of gangs', *Journal of Contemporary Criminal Justice*, *21*(2), 153–69.
Halliday, M.A.K. (1978) *Language as Social Semiotic*, London: Edward Arnold.
Hasund, I.K. and Drange, E. (2014) 'English influence on Norwegian teenage slang', in J. Coleman (ed.) *Global English Slang*, London: Routledge. 139–49.
Hendry, L. and Kloep, M. (2005) 'Talkin', doin' and bein' with friends': leisure and communication in adolescence', in A. Williams and C. Thurlow (eds.) *Talking Adolescence: Perspectives on Communication in the Teenage Years*, New York: Peter Lang Publishing, Inc. 163–84.
Higgs, E. (2014) 'Inmate subcultures', in J.S. Albanese (ed.) *The Encyclopedia of Criminology and Criminal Justice*, Chichester: John Wiley and Sons, Ltd. shareslide.org/inmate-subcultures-higgs, accessed June 2015.
Hollington, A. and Makwabarara, T. (2015) 'Youth language practices in Zimbabwe', in N. Nassenstein and A. Hollington (eds.) *Youth Language Practices in Africa and Beyond*, Berlin/Boston: Walter de Gruyter, Inc. 257–70.

Hollington, A. and Nassenstein, N. (2015a) 'Youth language practices in Africa as creative manifestations of fluid repertoires and markers of speakers' social identity', in N. Nassenstein and A. Hollington (eds.) *Youth Language Practices in Africa and Beyond*, Berlin/Boston: Walter de Gruyter, Inc. 1–22.

Hollington, A. and Nassenstein, N. (2015b) 'Conclusion and outlook: taking new directions in the study of youth language practices', in N. Nassenstein and A. Hollington (eds.) *Youth Language Practices in Africa and Beyond*, Berlin/Boston: Walter de Gruyter, Inc. 345–56.

Hurst, E. (2007) 'Urban discourses and identity in a South African township: an analysis of youth culture in Cape Town', paper presented at the African Studies Association 50th Annual Meeting, New York, 18–21 October.

Hurst, E. (2015) 'Overview of the tsotsitaals of South Africa; their different base languages and common core lexical items', in N. Nassenstein and A. Hollington (eds.) *Youth Language Practices in Africa and Beyond*, Berlin/Boston: Walter de Gruyter, Inc. 169–84.

IRIN/Plus News (2008) 'AFRICA: Mind your language – a short guide to HIV/AIDS slang', *IRIN*, 18 June. www.irinnews.org/news/2008/06/18/mind-your-language-short-guide-hivaids-slang, accessed June 2014.

Jensen Arnett, J. (2002) 'Adolescents in Western countries in the 21st century: vast opportunities – for all?', in B.B. Brown, R.W. Larson and T.S. Saraswathi (eds.) *The World's Youth*, Cambridge: Cambridge University Press. 307–43.

Jørgensen, A.M. (2013) 'Spanish teenage language and the COLAm-corpus', *Bergen Language and Linguistic Studies*, 3(1), 151–66 (shared through https://creativecommons.org/licenses/by/3.0/legalcode).

Joseph, J. (2004) *Language and Identity*, Basingstoke, UK: Palgrave MacMillan.

Kerswill, P. (2010) 'Youth languages in Africa and Europe: linguistic subversion or emerging vernaculars?', *Language in Africa: An Inter-University Research Seminar Exploring Language Usage and Values in a Range of Contexts*, Edge Hill University, 24 November.

Khimik, V.V. (2004) 'Iazyk sovremennoi molodëzhi', *Sovremennaia russkaia rech': sostoianie i funktsionirovanie*. Sankt-Peterburg. 7–66.

Khomiakov, V.A. (1992) 'Nekotorye tipologicheskie osobennosti nestandartnoi leksiki angliiskogo, frantsuzskogo i russkogo iazykov', *Voprosy iazykoznaniia*, 3, 94–105.

Kiesling, S.F. (2009) 'Style as stance', in A. Jaffe (ed.) *Stance: Sociolinguistic Perspectives*, Oxford: Oxford University Press. 171–94. www.academia.edu/983606/Style_as_ Stance, accessed June 2014.

Kiessling, R. and Mous, M. (2004) 'Urban youth languages in Africa', *Anthropological Linguistics*, 46(3), 1–39.

Kießling, R. (2004) 'bàk mwà mè dó – Camfranglais in Cameroon', *Lingua Posnaniensis*, 47. www.aai.uni-hamburg.de/afrika/personen/kiessling/medien/kiessling-2004-camfranglais.pdf, accessed September 2012.

Kis, T. (2006) 'Is slang a linguistic universal?', *Revue d'Etudes Françaises*, 11, 125–41.

Kouadio N'guessan, J. (2006) 'Le Nouchi et les rapports Dioula-Français', *Le Français en Afrique*, 21, 177–91.

Kouega, J.-P. (2003) 'Word formative processes in Camfranglais', *World Englishes*, 22(4), 511–38.

Kraidy, M.M. and Khalil, J.F. (2008) 'Youth, media and culture in the Arab world', in K. Drotner and S. Livingstone (eds.) *International Handbook of Children, Media and Culture*, London: Sage. 330–44.

Kripke, M. (2014) 'Inner-city slang of New York', in J. Coleman (ed.) *Global English Slang*, London: Routledge. 25–35.
Krohn, F.B. and Suazo, F.L. (1995) 'Contemporary urban music: controversial messages in hip-hop and rap lyrics', *Et cetera: A Review of General Semantics*, *52*(2), 139–54.
Kveselevich, D.I. (2005) *Tolkovyi slovar' nenormativnoi leksiki russkogo iazyka*, Moscow: Astrel' AST.
Labov, T. (1992) 'Social and language boundaries among adolescents', *American Speech*, *67*(4), 339–66.
Labov, W. (1973) *Language in the Inner City*, University of Pennsylvania Press.
Lacoste, V., Leimgruber, J. and Breyer, T. (2014) 'Authenticity: a view from inside and outside sociolinguistics', in V. Lacoste, J. Leimgruber and T. Breyer (eds.) *Indexing Authenticity: Perspectives from Linguistics and Anthropology*, Berlin: de Gruyter. 1–13. www.researchgate.net/publication/287699206_Authenticity_A_view_from_inside_and_outside_sociolinguistics, accessed August 2015.
Lafage, S. (1991) 'L'argot des jeunes Ivoiriens, marque d'appropriation du français?', *Langue française*, *90*, 95–105.
Lebedeva, S.V. and Astakhova, N.V. (2016) 'Main features of youth jargon: synchronic analysis', *Russian Linguistic Bulletin*, *3*(7), 125–6.
Lefkowitz, N.J. (1989) 'Verlan: talking backwards in French', *The French Review*, *63*(2), 312–22.
Levikova, S.I. (2004) 'Molodëzhnyi sleng kak svoeobraznyi sposob verbalizatsii bytiya', *Bytie i iazyk*, 167–73.
Lodge, R.A. (1993) *French: From Dialect to Standard*, London: Routledge.
Lytra, V. (2015) 'Language and language ideologies among Turkish-speaking young people in Athens and London', in J. Nortier and B.A. Svendsen (eds.) *Language, Youth and Identity in the 21st Century*, Cambridge: Cambridge University Press. 183–204.
Magner, T. (1957) 'The Stiljaga and his language', *Slavic and East European Journal*, *15*(1), 192–5.
Mahler, M. (2008) *Dictionary of Spanish Slang and Colloquial Expressions*, New York: Barron's.
Mallik, B. (1972) *Language of the Underworld of West Bengal*, Calcutta: Sanskrit College Research Series No. LXXVII.
Mandelbaum-Reiner, F. (1991) 'Secrets de bouchers et Largonji actuel des Louchébèm', *Langage et société*, *56*, 21–49.
Manfredi, S. (2008) 'Rendók: a youth secret language in Sudan', *Estudios de dialectología norteafricana y andalusí*, *12*, 113–29.
Marder, S. (1994) *A Supplementary Russian–English Dictionary*, Columbus Ohio: Slavica Publishers Inc.
Mayr, A. (2004) *Prison Discourse: Language as a Means of Control and Resistance*, Basingstoke, UK: Palgrave MacMillan.
Mazrui, A.M. (1995) 'Slang and code-switching: the case of Sheng in Kenya', *Afrikanistische Arbietspapier*, *42*, 168–79.
McKay, S., Thurlow, C. and Toomey Zimmerman, H. (2005) 'Wired whizzes or techno-slaves? Young people and their emergent communication technologies', in A. Williams and C. Thurlow (eds.) *Talking Adolescence: Perspectives on Communication in the Teenage Years*, New York: Peter Lang Publishing, Inc. 185–203.
Méla, V. (1991) 'Le verlan ou le langage du miroir', *Langages*, 101, 73–94.
Milani, T.M., Jonsson, R. and Mhlambi, I.J. (2015) 'Shooting the subversive: when non-normative linguistic practices go mainstream in the media', in J. Nortier and

B.A. Svendsen (eds.) *Language, Youth and Identity in the 21st Century*, Cambridge: Cambridge University Press. 119–38.

Miles, S. (2000) *Youth Lifestyles in a Changing World*, Buckingham: Open University Press.

Miller, L. (2003) 'Graffiti photos: expressive art in Japanese girls' culture', *Harvard Asia Quarterly*, 7(3), 31–42.

Miller, L. (2004) 'Those naughty teenage girls: Japanese Kogals, slang, and media assessments', *Journal of Linguistic Anthropology*, 14(2), 225–47.

Mokwena, S. (1999) 'A perspective on youth and social justice in South Africa', *New Designs for Youth Development*, 15(3), 1–5.

Molamu, L. (1995) 'Wietie: the emergence and development of Tsotsitaal in South Africa', *Alternation*, 2(2), 139–58.

Montgomery, M. (2008) *An Introduction to Language and Society* (3rd ed.), London: Routledge.

Moore, B. (2014) 'Australian slang', in J. Coleman (ed.) *Global English Slang*, London: Routledge. 87–95.

Moore, R. (2012) 'On swearwords and slang', *American Speech*, 87(2), 170–89.

Moore, R. (2014) 'Affect-marked lexemes and their relational model correlates', *Faculty Publications*, Rollins College, Paper 107. scholarship.rollins.edu/cgi/viewcontent.cgi?article=1212&context=as_facpub, accessed January 2015.

Morgan, M. (2004) 'Speech community', in A. Duranti (ed.) *A Companion to Linguistic Anthropology*, Oxford: Blackwell. 3–22.

Moussalli, M. (2016) 'Impact of globalization', *Global Policy Forum*, www.globalpolicy.org/component/content/article/162/27627.html, blog entry, originally published on 25 August 2003 in *Lebanon Daily Star*, accessed November 2016.

Mugaddam, A.H. (2012b) 'Identity construction and linguistic manipulation in Randuk', paper presented at the *Youth Languages and Urban Languages in Africa Workshop*, Institut für Afrikanistik, Cologne University, Germany.

Mugaddam, A.H. (2015) 'Identity construction and linguistic manipulation in Randuk', in N. Nassenstein and A. Hollington (eds.) *Youth Language Practices in Africa and Beyond*, Berlin/Boston: Walter de Gruyter, Inc. 99–118.

Mugaddam, A.R.H. (2012a) 'Aspects of youth language in Khartoum', in M. Brenzinger and A-M. Fehn (eds.) *Proceedings of 6th World Congress of African Linguistics*, Cologne: Rüdiger Köppe Verlag. 87–98.

Mutonya, M. (2007) 'Redefining Nairobi's streets: a study of slang, marginalization, and identity', *Journal of Global Initiatives*, 2(2), 169–85.

Mutunda, S. (2007) 'Language behavior in Lusaka: the use of Nyanja slang', *The International Journal of Language, Society and Culture*, 21. www.edu.utas.au/users/tle/JOURNAL/

Namyalo, S. (2015) 'Linguistic strategies in Luyaaye: word play and conscious language manipulation', in N. Nassenstein and A. Hollington (eds.) *Youth Language Practices in Africa and Beyond*, Berlin/Boston: Walter de Gruyter, Inc. 313–44.

Nassenstein, N. (2015a) 'Imvugo y'Umuhanda: youth language practices in Kigali (Rwanda)', in N. Nassenstein and A. Hollington (eds.) *Youth Language Practices in Africa and Beyond*, Berlin/Boston: Walter de Gruyter, Inc. 185–204.

Nassenstein, N. (2015b) 'The emergence of Langila in Kinshasa (DR Congo)', in N. Nassenstein and A. Hollington (eds.) *Youth Language Practices in Africa and Beyond*, Berlin/Boston: Walter de Gruyter, Inc. 81–98.

Nassenstein, N. (2016) 'The new urban youth language Yabacrâne in Goma (DR Congo)', *Sociolinguistic Studies*, *10*(1–2), 235–59.
Nassenstein N. and Hollington, A. (eds.) (2015) *Youth Language Practices in Africa and Beyond*, Berlin/Boston: Walter de Gruyter, Inc.
Nikitina, T.G. (2009) *Molodëzhnyi sleng: tolkovyi slovar'*, Moscow: AST: Astrel'.
Nortier, J. and Svendsen, B.A (eds.) (2015) *Language, Youth and Identity in the 21st Century*, Cambridge: Cambridge University Press.
Nsamenang, A.B. (2002) 'Adolescence in sub-Saharan Africa: an image constructed from Africa's triple inheritance', in B.B. Brown, R.W. Larson and T.S. Saraswathi (eds.) *The World's Youth*, Cambridge: Cambridge University Press. 61–104.
Ochs, E. (1992) 'Indexing gender', in A. Duranti and C. Goodwin (eds.), *Rethinking Context: Language as an Interactive Phenomenon*, Cambridge: Cambridge University Press. 335–58.
Ochs, E. and Schieffelin, B. (1989) 'Language has a heart', *Text*, *9*(1), 7–25.
Offord, D. (1996) *Using Russian*, Cambridge: Cambridge University Press.
Oganian, A.A. and Ishkhanova, D.I. (2015) 'Osobennosti iazyka molodëzhnykh subkul'tur: khippi, baykerov i gotov', *Unikal'nye issledovaniia XXI veka*, *5*(5), 151–3.
Ogechi, N.O. (2005) 'On lexicalization in Sheng', *Nordic Journal of African Studies*, *14*(3), 334–55.
Ozhegov, S.I. (2016) *Tolkovyi slovar' russkogo iazyka*, Moscow: Izdatel'stvo AST: Mir i Obrazovanie.
Ozhegov, S.I. and Shvedova, N.Iu. (1995) *Tolkovyi slovar' russkogo iazyka*, Moscow: Az'.
Podesva, R.J., Roberts, S.J. and Campbell-Kibler, K. (2001) 'Sharing resources and indexing meanings in the production of gay styles', in K. Campbell-Kibler, R.J. Podesva, S.J. Roberts and A. Wong (eds.) *Language and Sexuality: Contesting Meaning in Theory and Practice*, CSLI Publications. 175–89.
Population Reference Bureau (2012) *2012 World Population Data Sheet*, www.prb.org/pdf12/2012-population-data-sheet_eng.pdf, accessed May 2017.
Rampton, B. (2015) 'Contemporary urban vernaculars', in J. Nortier and B.A. Svendsen (eds.) *Language, Youth and Identity in the 21st Century*, Cambridge: Cambridge University Press. 24–44.
Register, N.A. (1996) 'Second-language learners and taboo words in American English', *English Today*, *12*(3), 44–9.
Reyes, A. (2005) 'Appropriation of African American slang by Asian American youth', *Journal of Sociolinguistics*, *9*(4), 509–32.
Riordan, J. (1988) 'Soviet youth: pioneers of change', *Soviet Studies*, *XL*(4), 556–72.
Robert L'Argenton, F. (1991) 'Larlépeem largomuche du louchébem. Parler l'argot du boucher', *Langue française*, *90*, 113–25.
Roth-Gordon, J. (2009) 'The language that came down the hill', *American Anthropologist*, *111*(1), 57–68.
Salillas, R. (1896) *El Delincuente español – El Lenguaje (studio filológico, psicológico y sociológico) con dos vocabularios jergales*, Read Books. 2011 reprint.
Salmons, J. (1991) 'Youth language in the German Democratic Republic: its diversity and distinctiveness', *American Journal of German Linguistics and Literature*, *3*, 1–30.
Samper, D.A. (2004) '"Africa is still our mama": Kenyan rappers, youth identity, and the revitalization of traditional values', *African Identities*, *2*(1), 37–51.
Santa Maria, M. (2002) 'Youth in Southeast Asia: living within the continuity of tradition and the turbulence of change', in B.B. Brown, R.W. Larson and T.S. Saraswathi (eds.) *The World's Youth*, Cambridge: Cambridge University Press. 171–206.

Saraswathi, T.S. and Larson, R.W. (2002) 'Adolescence in global perspective: an agenda for social policy', in B.B. Brown, R.W. Larson and T.S. Saraswathi (eds.) *The World's Youth*, Cambridge: Cambridge University Press. 344–62.
Schade-Poulsen, M. (1995) 'The power of love: raï music and youth in Algeria', in V. Amit-Talai and H. Wulff (eds.) *Youth Cultures: A Cross-Cultural Perspective*, London: Routledge. 81–113.
Shlyakhov V. and Adler, E. (2006) *Dictionary of Russian Slang and Colloquial Expressions*, New York: Barron's.
Slone, T.H. (2003) *Prokem. An Analysis of a Jakartan Slang*, Oakland: Masalai Press.
Smith-Hefner, N.J. (2007) 'Youth language, *Gaul* sociability, and the new Indonesian middle class', *Journal of Linguistic Anthropology*, *17*(2), 184–203.
Sornig, K. (1981) *Lexical Innovation: A Study of Slang, Colloquialisms and Casual Speech*, Amsterdam: John Benjamins.
Sourdot, M. (1997) 'La dynamique du français des jeunes: sept ans de mouvement à travers deux enquêtes (1987–1994)', *Langue française*, *114*, 56–81.
Stein-Kanjora, G. (2008) "'Parler comme ça, c'est vachement cool!'", *Sociologus*, *58*(2), 117–41.
Stenström, A. (2014) *Teenage Talk: From General Characteristics to the Use of Pragmatic Markers in a Contrastive Perspective*, Basingstoke, UK: Palgrave MacMillan.
Stenström, A., Andersen, G. and Hasund, I.K. (2002) *Trends in Teenage Talk: Corpus Compilation, Analysis and Findings*, Amsterdam/Philadelphia: John Benjamins Publishing Company.
Szabó, E. (2006) 'Hungarian prison slang today', *Revue d'Études Françaises*, *11*, 219–29.
Thorne, T. (2005) *Dictionary of Contemporary Slang*, (3rd ed.), London: A & C Black.
Thurlow, C. (2003) 'Generation txt? The sociolinguistics of young people's text-messaging', *Discourse Analysis Online*, *1*(1), 1–27. www.researchgate.net/publication/259258527_Generation_Txt_The_sociolinguistics_of_young_people%27s_text-messaging, accessed August 2016.
Thurlow, C. (2005) 'Deconstructing adolescent communication', in A. Williams and C. Thurlow (eds.) *Talking Adolescence: Perspectives on Communication in the Teenage Years*, New York: Peter Lang Publishing, Inc. 1–20.
Thurlow, C. (2014) 'Disciplining youth: language ideologies and new technologies', in A. Jaworski and N. Coupland (eds.) *The Discourse Reader*, (3rd ed.), London: Routledge. 481–96.
UNESCO (2014) *Teaching and Learning: Achieving Quality for All*, EFA Global Monitoring Report 2013/14. unesdoc.unesco.org/images/0022/002256/225660e.pdf, accessed October 2016.
UNESCO (2016) *Learning to Live Together*. www.unesco.org/new/en/social-and-human-sciences/themes/youth/youth-definition/, accessed July 2016.
UNESCO and UNICEF (2013) *Asia–Pacific End of Decade Notes on Education for All: Universal Primary Education*. unesdoc.unesco.org/images/0022/002212/221200E.pdf, accessed October 2016.
United Nations (undated), *Fact Sheet on Juvenile Justice*, New York: United Nations. www.un.org/esa/socdev/unyin/documents/wyr11/FactSheetonYouthandJuvenileJustice.pdf, accessed September 2016.
United Nations (2011) *United Nations World Youth Report*. unworldyouthreport.org/index.php?option=com_k2&view=item&id=10:conclusions&Itemid=131, accessed October 2016.

United Nations (2015a) *Integrating Population Issues into Sustainable Development, Including the Post-2015 Development Agenda*, New York: United Nations Department of Economic and Social Affairs. www.un.org/en/development/desa/population/commission/pdf/48/CPD48ConciseReport.pdf, accessed September 2016.

United Nations (2015b) *Population Facts*, New York: United Nations Department of Economic and Social Affairs, May. www.un.org/en/development/desa/population/publications/pdf/popfacts/PopFacts_2015-1.pdf, accessed July 2016.

United Nations (2015c) *World Population Prospects. The 2015 Revision*, New York: United Nations. esa.un.org/unpd/wpp/publications/files/key_findings_wpp_2015.pdf, accessed July 2016.

Utekhin, I. (2012) 'Social networking on the internet: is the Russian way special?', in R. Alapuro, A. Mustajoki and P. Pesonen (eds.) *Understanding Russianness*, Abingdon: Routledge. 245–56.

Vakunta, P. (undated) 'Nouchi – the making of a new Ivorian language: an interview with Mema Bamba', blog entry. vakunta.blogspot.co.uk/p/interviews_02.html, accessed July 2016.

Vázquez Ríos, J. (2009) 'Linguistique et sociolinguistique du verlan à travers le monde', *AnMal Electronica*, 26, 197–214.

Veit-Wild, F. (2009) '"Zimbolicious" – the creative potential of linguistic innovation: the case of Shona-English in Zimbabwe', *Journal of Southern African Studies*, 35(3, September), 683–97.

Verma, S. and Saraswathi, T.S. (2002) 'Adolescence in India: street urchins or Silicon Valley millionaires?', in B.B. Brown, R.W. Larson and T.S. Saraswathi (eds.) *The World's Youth*, Cambridge: Cambridge University Press. 105–40.

Victor, T. (2014) 'Gestural slang', in J. Coleman (ed.) *Global English Slang*, London: Routledge. 194–204.

Welti, C. (2002) 'Adolescents in Latin America: facing the future with skepticism', in B.B. Brown, R.W. Larson and T.S. Saraswathi (eds.) *The World's Youth*, Cambridge: Cambridge University Press. 276–306.

Widawski, M. (2012) 'Twentieth century American slang and its sociocultural context: part one', *Kwartalnik Neofilologiczny*, LIX(3), 381–91.

Widawski, M. (2013) 'Twentieth century American slang and its sociocultural context: part two', *Kwartalnik Neofilologiczny*, LX(1), 115–25.

Widawski, M. (2015) *African American Slang*, Cambridge: Cambridge University Press.

Wiese, H. (2009) 'Grammatical innovation in multi-ethnic urban Europe: New linguistic practices among adolescents', *Lingua*, 119, 782–806.

Wilson, C. (2015) 'Kindoubil: urban youth languages in Kisangani', in N. Nassenstein and A. Hollington (eds.) *Youth Language Practices in Africa and Beyond*, Berlin/Boston: Walter de Gruyter, Inc. 293–311.

Wise, H. (1997) *The Vocabulary of Modern French*, London: Routledge.

Wolfer, C. (2011) 'Arabic secret languages', *Folia Orientalia*, 47, part II.

World Bank, *Sub-Saharan Africa*. data.worldbank.org/region/sub-saharan-africa, accessed September 2016.

Zhirmunskii, V. (1936) *Natsional'nyi iazyk i sotsial'nye dialekty*, Leningrad: Khudozhestvennaia literatura.

Part I

1 Linguistic data – varieties, sources and methodologies

Introduction

In this chapter, we identify the main sources providing language examples cited in the book and briefly explore how related varieties have been understood in the literature. We then briefly profile some of the methods that have been used by researchers to gather these data vis-à-vis methods generally employed by scholars working in the field.

Varieties and sources

As noted in the Introduction, this book essentially consists of two parts: (a) an exploration of certain theoretical perspectives on youth and criminal language practices, followed by investigation into the reasons for use and related attitudes of members of corresponding in- and out-groups; and (b) identification of the main linguistic manipulations found across a cross-section of varieties in a number of languages and societies.

In order to explore themes relevant to both parts, a number of varieties – all briefly profiled in this chapter – have been selected after a wide literature review. These varieties span criminal and youth language practice in a number of societies across the globe, separated both temporally and spatially, and they have been selected to support and illuminate discussion of key questions on which scholars have generally focused their attention, whether in studies of individual varieties (e.g. Grayson 1964; Chambert-Loir 1984; Grachëv 1994; García 2005; Ferrari 2006; Stein-Kanjora 2008; Einat and Livnat 2012; Eble 2014), limited comparative analyses (e.g. Chamberlain 1981; Khomiakov 1992; Vázquez Ríos 2009; Dorleijn and Nortier 2013), or broader overviews (e.g. Zhirmunskii 1936; Sornig 1981; Androutsopoulos 2005; Beck 2010; Hollington and Nassenstein 2015a, 2015b; see also the discussion of comparability in the Introduction). They have been selected not to exemplify all youth or criminal practice in any one society but to provide sufficient information to support broad discussion and, where relevant, comparison.

As readers will appreciate, amassing and analysing such a far-reaching data set in the form of primary sources in the various languages, and supporting valuable discussion (and, where appropriate, comparison), is a far from inconsiderable task.

Therefore, the accent in the book falls mainly on the use of secondary literature supplemented by primary data from the author's own research into Russian youth language practices in the 1990s, and by altogether more recent examples from online sources such as French graffiti artists' (taggers') fora, to bring together and explore common analytical strands. Of course, the status of investigation of different varieties will differ: in some cases, there is a rather rich history of research into the language practices in the literature (e.g. North American and French youth language practices), and comparison and debate are readily available from within those literature sets to support broader exploration here; in others (e.g. Israeli prison language, youth language practices in Zimbabwe), the debate is less broad. However, there is value in including select examples of the latter category of (often breakthrough) studies to illuminate manipulations and motivations for use that relevant scholars have highlighted and discussed in their exploratory (and sometimes follow-up or complementary) studies, accepting that a less established literature does not mean less authoritative findings *per se*. In other words, where examples of language practices are effectively captured and established as representative data in less broad or developed discussion they can still be instructive, particularly to support analysis of manipulations. Of course, in this respect the use of such material is of particular relevance to the second part of the book, where similarities in the use of certain linguistic mechanisms are highlighted.

The book utilises the following sources to provide core data for discussion and analysis:

Youth, criminal and colloquial language in France

Several works have been devoted to colloquial French and to in-group youth and criminal language. In some cases, researchers (e.g. Bullock 1996) have suggested that the term 'argot' – often used to designate both in-group varieties – particularly refers to the secret languages of criminal gangs. However, the term has also been associated more widely with technical terminology, and also with colloquial or 'street French', which is also known as 'français branché' (e.g. Verdelhan-Bourgade 1991).

The concept and translation of the term 'colloquial French' have also been addressed by commentators who have pointed to many attempts to find appropriate French designations. Abecassis (2003), for example, points to how terms such as 'français populaire' and 'français familier' have sometimes been used interchangeably, as have 'populaire', 'familier' and 'argot'. Furthermore, Verdelhan-Bourgade (1991) has suggested that 'français branché' is not necessarily the language of the socially marginalised and need not be youth-specific; that it is seen in both verbal and written forms, including in the media; and that it has syntactic features.[1]

The idea of youth language practices expressing or symbolising social marginalisation and/or opposition to dominant mainstream ideas has been explored by a number of researchers (e.g. Bachmann and Basier 1984; Méla 1988, 1991; Goudailler 2002). One example of this practice is where lexis is created through Verlan (French urban backslang), which was initially created by socially and economically marginalised suburban youths, often with immigrant backgrounds, but has spread more widely.

When citing examples, this book draws distinctions between language practices that many French speakers perceive to index criminals and youth (not to mention their identities, values and practices) and colloquial usage, which indexes situations of use. Items cited derive from a number of sources, but in particular from the works of Méla (1988, 1991, 1997) and Lefkowitz (1989) on Verlan; Verdelhan-Bourgade (1991) on 'street French', borrowing and word-formation; Mandelbaum-Reiner (1991) on Largonji and Largonji des Louchébems; Bullock (1996) on Javanais and Verlan; Sourdot (1997) on Parisian student usage across 1987–1994; Červenková (2001) and Goudaillier (2002) on Verlan and other forms of word-formation; Doran (2004, 2007) on suburban youth practices and identity; and Strutz (2009). Examples of graffiti containing forms popularly considered to represent colloquial French and French youth language have also been added from the author's own collection (some of these can be seen on the book's *eResource*), as have illustrations of youth language online.

German youth language

Information on the use of language practices to index German youth spans two countries and two eras. Firstly, from analysis of the youth language of the former East Germany (GDR). This comes exclusively from Joe Salmons' (1991) article 'Youth language in the German Democratic Republic: its diversity and distinctiveness'. Drawing largely on data derived from work with students and young teachers from about 21 to 30 years of age, Salmons analyses the social aspects of this language use, cites instances of borrowing and semantic transfer (among other processes), and points to expressivity in practice. Although he invited further study to enable broader conclusions to be reached, Salmons (1991: 23) noted that East German youth language "closely paralleled" its West German counterpart and that GDR youth speak involved complex interaction with regional language varieties and the spoken standard.

The second set of information comes from the work of Androutsopoulos, who looks at West German youth culture in the late 1990s and the first decade of the twenty-first century.[2] His work is wide-ranging and includes: analysis of the motivations behind youth language practices; the role of globalisation vis-à-vis hip hop (2009; see also Androutsopoulos and Scholz 2002); investigation of the online language practices of German hip hop practitioners (2007); description of fanzine style (e.g. punk fanzines) (2000a); and lexical creation in youth language (2000b). Androutsopoulos' work on hip hop is also complemented by Cheeseman's (1998) account of the German hip hop scene in the mid- to late 1990s.

Finally, supporting information on German youth language practices, particularly with regard to the Kiezdeutsch ('hood German', 'street German') multiethnolect – an urban youth peer variety that incorporates elements of immigrant languages to mark identity and demarcate youth from others such as adults, teachers, parents and siblings (Paul, Freywald and Wittenberg 2009) – is provided by Wiese (2009) and by Paul, Freywald and Wittenberg (2009).

The Caló of Spanish Roma[3] and Pachuco Caló

The term 'Caló' refers to a language variety consisting largely of Romani vocabulary and phraseology used within Spanish morphological, syntactic and grammatical structures. In this sense, it may be regarded as a mixed language.

The Roma first settled in Spain in the early to mid-fifteenth century, bringing their Romani language with them. However, their integration into Spanish society was to prove problematic. For their part, the 'gitanos' – as they were called by non-Roma – maintained a clearly defined sense of cultural independence and socialised primarily within their own circles and in Roma quarters ('gitanerías'). However, they were also variously marginalised, oppressed and forcibly integrated into non-Roma communities (Geipel 1995; García 2005; Council of Europe 2012).

In time, their Romani language mixed with Spanish – the result was Caló. This too was undoubtedly used by Roma to shape and maintain a distinct culture and identity. However, it was also used as a cryptolect to communicate beyond the understanding of others and to aid stealing and deception (Geipel 1995; García 2005). By the end of the nineteenth century, Caló had contributed many items to Spanish criminal language, together with what remained of the traditional lexicon of the criminal underworld, Germanía. Indeed, the term 'Caló' became synonymous with criminal practice (García 2005; Buzek 2012). Furthermore, whether through the filter of criminal language practices or otherwise, some Caló vocabulary had also become more widely used in Spanish society, circulating to the extent that some items are now used in colloquial Spanish (Geipel 1995). As before, nowadays peninsular Spanish speakers of Caló largely use Spanish syntax and morphology with Romani vocabulary and expressions interposed. However, Geipel (1995) suggests that Caló terms can still be used by Spanish Roma to obscure meaning, emphasise Roma affiliation and/or exclude outsiders.[4]

Caló terms were also adopted outside Spain. By the first half of the twentieth century, some items appear to have spread to the in-group language of Mexican American Pachucos in the US Southwest. The precise origins of Pachuco Caló (or Pachuco) are much debated, although a strong link is thought to exist particularly with El Paso (Daniels 1997; De Katzew 2004; García 2005; Ramírez 2006). Often linked to the 1930s–1960s in particular, the lexicon of Pachuco Caló contained items from indigenous American languages such as Nahuatl, as well as Spanish, English and Spanish Caló.

The Pachucos are reputed to have used their Caló for a number of reasons: to underscore a sophisticated peer group identity where they perceived a lack of identification with either their heritage or adopted cultures (i.e. Hispanic Mexican and Anglophone US; Daniels 1997; De Katzew 2004; García 2005); as a sign of style, street smarts and hipness (Daniels 1997; Ramírez 2006); to demonstrate social resistance and counterculture (De Katzew 2004; Ramírez 2006); and, in some cases, to conceal criminal activity (García 2005). In socio-economic terms, they were often marginalised, with some unemployed and/or working as seasonal labourers – along with the popularity of Pachuco songs on the radio, the latter are possibly responsible for Pachuco Caló's circulation after World War Two, although other vectors for diffusion are also likely (Daniels 1997). Many Pachuco Caló terms yet exist and may be recognised as such by some in the Mexican American population, while some original Caló terms are still found in broader colloquial Mexican Spanish and are also associated with Mexican criminal language practices – also called Caló – and the criminal underworld (Buzek 2012).

The main sources of information on Caló are Geipel's (1995) 'Caló: the "secret" language of the gypsies of Spain' and García's (2005) 'Influences of gypsy Caló on contemporary Spanish slang' – both focus on the known history of Caló and borrowings from it into other Spanish varieties. Lexis from these studies is also compared with vocabulary found in Salillas' 1896 *El Delincuente español – El Lenguaje (studio filológico, psicológico y sociológico) con dos vocabularios jergale* and Veraldi-Pasquale's (2011 reprint) *Vocabulario de caló-español*, while Buzek (2012) provides additional background on individual items and their transmission and retention. Insights into the development and use of Pachuco Caló comes primarily from Daniels' (1997) study of Pachuco culture and the zoot-suit rioting of 1943; De Katzew's (2004) analysis of Chicano language; García's (2005) account of the influence of Caló on modern-day Spanish language practices; and Ramírez's (2006) study of Pachuca identity and resistance.

Lunfardo – underworld and colloquial language in Argentina

With its name believed to be derived from the non-standard Italian 'lombardo' ('criminal') (Blake 2010: 235),[5] Lunfardo was originally associated with the Buenos Aires underworld and lower classes. It contained items from the indigenous language of the gauchos, as well as from such foreign sources as Italian, English and French. However, after its development in the nineteenth century, Lunfardo became more widespread within Argentinian society, partly due to its association with the tango (Grayson 1964; Chamberlain 1981). As a result, many terms previously attributed to Lunfardo are still documented and indeed used as part of colloquial Argentinian Spanish today. Examples of broader Argentinian Spanish usage are thus provided for illustration of more recently used colloquial forms. The main sources of information on Lunfardo are Grayson (1964), Chamberlain (1981) and Vázquez Ríos (2009).

Youth, criminal and colloquial language in peninsular Spain

To supplement information regarding Caló and Lunfardo, items viewed as representative of *peninsular* colloquial Spanish and Spanish youth and criminal language practices and their respective practitioners have been analysed. These primarily derive from Mahler's 2008 *Dictionary of Spanish Slang and Colloquial Expressions*, which contains items popularly viewed as indicative of colloquial, youth and criminal language as found in mainland Spain, but also in other countries where Spanish is spoken. Items cited from Mahler, as well as García (2005) and Geipel's (1995) studies of Caló, have been further cross-referenced with and supplemented by lexis found in online dictionary websites, and further contextualised by González and Stenström's (2011) discussion of English- and Spanish-speaking youth and Jørgensen's (2013) analysis of Spanish teenage usage. In the case of Caló and Lunfardo, cross-referencing has been carried out to determine ongoing use and meaning.

US college practice

Data on US college student language are taken primarily from Eble's (1996, 2014) analyses of the language practices of students of the University of North Carolina at Chapel Hill. In her engaging 1996 study, *Slang and Sociability*, Eble studied more than 4,500 words and expressions submitted to her by students from 1972 to 1993 as examples of "good, current campus slang" (Eble 1996: 1). Most of Eble's contributors were undergraduate student residents of North Carolina, aged between 19 and 23, white, female, and working towards certification as teachers. In this study, Eble (1996: 2) underlined that "slang is ordinary language, not a peripheral embellishment either for good or for ill", and viewed it as "part of the common core of language rather than an anomaly".

Eble's 2014 discussion is no less informative. Here she examined the use of some 5,000 words and expressions gathered over 14 semesters from 2005 to 2012. Her source profile was almost identical to that of her previous study – predominantly white students, resident in North Carolina, aged between 18 and 22, and majoring in English or Education. In all some 600 students supplied material. In this study, Eble not only provided examples of more recent usage, but also addressed questions of social networking and the role of the Internet in the use and proliferation of vocabulary.

Supplementary information on US student language is provided by Breva Claramonte and García Alonso's (1993) article on the use of slang in graffiti at the University of Colorado in Boulder. Although graffiti differs from more conventional forms of written communication in that it is often anonymous and is not generally designed for interaction in the same way, it does allow for the expression of individual and group attitudes in an often emphatic and innovative manner.[6]

Russian youth language, colloquial usage, criminal and traders' practices

The study of Russian youth language has been somewhat patchy over the last 100–150 years. Although there were some studies of Russian criminal language practices in the 1920s and early 1930s (in which the language viewed as typical of – often delinquent – youth was partially captured, e.g. Tonkov 1930), it was not until the 1950s and 1960s (e.g. Magner 1957) that attention gradually turned to the language forms commonly associated with Soviet youth, with much work emerging in the 1990s after the collapse of the USSR. The main sources on Russian youth language are von Timroth (1986), Zaikovskaia (1993), Elistratov (1994), Kovalev (1995), Beregovskaia (1996), Davie (1998), Levikova (2004), Shlyakhov and Adler (2006), Gromov (2009), Nikitina (2009), Nad'iarova

(2014), Oganian and Ishkhanova (2015) and Lebedeva and Astakhova (2016). Russian youth language practice is understood in this work to be largely indexical of perceived identities, activities and stance.

The term 'argo' ('argot') is commonly used in Russian with regard to the language practices of criminals and traders with devious or nefarious intent. To this end, its cryptolectal function is emphasised. In some cases, like the language of the Coquillards and other past French groups, it was taught by instructors (Zhirmunskii 1936). Investigation of Russian criminal and trader language practices gained momentum in the mid- to late nineteenth century, while by the 1930s, a number of studies had been produced of criminal language in particular (e.g. Tonkov 1930). These accumulated discussions highlighted, among other things, borrowing from other languages (e.g. from German, Greek, Yiddish) and criminal and trader lexicons, as well as the use of dialectal forms (Davie 1998). As with Russian youth language, comparatively little was produced on this subject during the Soviet era. However, many researchers have sought to understand the development of criminal language since the break-up of the Soviet Union and have written on the subject. The main sources providing information on Russian language forms as a way of indexing criminal and traders' identity and activity are Tikhanov (1895), Smirnov (1902), Grachëv (1992, 1994, 2003), Elistratov (1994) and Davie (1997/98, 1998). Information on the use of language in the drugs sphere is provided by Davie (1998), Nikitina (2009) and Artemova, Katyshev, Olenev et al. (2014).

There have been a number of discussions of colloquial Russian, known in places also as 'demotic' Russian, published over the years (see, for example, Offord 1996; Ryazanova-Clarke and Wade 1999). Furthermore, some usage cited as colloquial has also been characterised by some linguists as 'prostorechie' (which indexes individuals through uneducated, socially stigmatised usage). The main sources for examples of colloquial Russian over the period 1990s–2006 are Davie (1998), Kveselevich (2005) and Shlyakhov and Adler (2006). Prokutina (2009) additionally provides information on language play and foreign loans.

Finally, the use of Russian online has attracted no small measure of attention over the last 20 years or so. Questions surrounding the role that new technological affordances such as the Internet have played in the development of modern Russian and how their influence has been perceived have been an important part of the debate. Contributions by Gorny (2004), Dunn (2006), Schmidt and Teubener (2006), Lysenko (2008), Lapina-Kratasiuk (2009), Berdicevskis (2011, 2012), Doludenko (2012) and Zvereva (undated) have been used in particular to explore this discussion. These are complemented by works by Biblieva (2007) and Garza (2008) on youth language and the media, online included.

The language of criminals in 1960s West Bengal

Known as Ulṭi or Ulṭibātolā, this is the language variety thought to be typically used by a number of criminal, near-criminal and anti-social groups, from kidnappers and pimps to burglars and dacoits (armed robbers), operating in West Bengal in the 1960s to early 1970s. Mallik's seminal 1972 book, *Language of* the *Underworld of West Bengal*, was a breakthrough account of the underworld language of West Bengal and was based mainly on material collected in the 1960s from over 2,000 interviews. The majority of the language Mallik studied was Bengali and Hindi. Hindi speakers mainly originated in Bihar and Uttar Pradesh; those from Western Uttar Pradesh also brought Urdu and Perso-Arabic terms, while those from Bihar imported Bhojpuri and Magahi forms. Not only does Mallik's study provide numerous examples of the language practices of various criminals, but it also includes a comprehensive list of linguistic mechanisms that were held to be representative of the language and criminals of the time. It therefore serves as the key text for information on this language variety.

Indonesian youth language, Bahasa Prokem and Bahasa Gay

The main sources for examples of these language varieties are Chambert-Loir (translated by Collins in 1984), Slone (2003), Boellstorff (2004) and Smith-Hefner (2007).

In 1983, Chambert-Loir published an article in which he described the emergence over the previous five years of a language variety amounting to a few hundred words. The variety, Bahasa Prokem, had probably been created before the 1960s and was commonly associated with criminals, street kids and some students in Jakarta, who were reported to use it as a form of cryptolect and creative means of expression (Chambert-Loir 1984). Its grammar and much of its lexis were Indonesian, and it borrowed new words which were sometimes of unclear origin. Speakers also created items through meaning transfer, metathesis and affixation (almost always using an Indonesian or Jakartan affix) (Chambert-Loir 1984).

Prokem was also studied by Slone (2003), who analysed circa 4,400 words and phrases drawn from three written sources, including work by Rahardja and Chambert-Loir in 1988 and 1990. According to Slone (2003: 45), Prokem's vocabulary is 95% derived from Indonesian and may possibly derive from Cakap Balik (lit. 'reverse words'), a variety based mainly on inversion, from Negri Sembilan State in Malaysia. Slone similarly qualified Prokem as a slang, mainly of youth (school and university students, and street gang members, who were instrumental in transferring Prokem from criminals to students) who spoke the Jakartan dialect of Indonesian, and posited that it was most likely created as a secret criminal language variety. However, he also suggested that a growth in the use of Prokem may have been the result of the repressive regime of General Suharto, who replaced Sukarno as president, ruling from 1968 until 1998.

Both Chambert-Loir (1984) and Slone (2003) note that Prokem is not the only non-standard variety used in Indonesia. For example, both additionally point to the Béncong variety, which is associated with Jakartan transvestites and transsexuals.[7]

Another study of language practices in Indonesia is Boellstorff's (2004) account of Bahasa Gay, language practices associated with gay men. While it can serve as a cryptolect to enable Indonesian men to communicate securely about their homosexuality, Boellstorff reports that Bahasa Gay functions largely to support notions of association and community. Mechanisms used to create new items include suffixation, and substitution involving words that share syllables.

A key source of information on language practices associated with Indonesian youth, a variety known as Bahasa Gaul, is that of Smith-Hefner (2007). Borrowing considerably from the Jakartan dialect of Indonesian, Bahasa Gaul is believed to be used by Indonesian university students and youth, including those of the middle class. Through its use, speakers are believed to index shared social affiliation, belonging, coolness and modernity, as well as a rejection of traditional social expectations and the official standard language (Smith-Hefner 2007).[8] Gaul is also held to borrow terms from Prokem. Smith-Hefner's study examines both the reasons underpinning its use and the lexical and word-formation methods found in the several hundred items she examined.

Finally, these studies are complemented by the work of Beazley (1998, 2002, 2003) on street children and youth in Indonesia. Beazley has produced social analyses of the subcultural worlds of street boys and girls in Yogyakarta, Central Java. Studying the lives of boys typically aged between 7 and 18 and girls between 12 and 20, she has explored questions of, *inter alia*, social marginality, gender, agency, resistance to the state and social mainstream, identities and group values, as well as – to a lesser extent – the use of in-group language. Although Beazley did not provide a substantial corpus of linguistic material, some of the manipulations employed by the children and youth to communicate merit inclusion insofar as group composition and/or linguistic mechanisms are comparable to those of other collectives, both within Indonesia and beyond.

The language practices of Japan's Kogals

This is language that is typically associated with the Kogal subculture that emerged in the early 1990s involving assertive and bold young Japanese girls between 14 and 22 (Miller 2003). These girls and young women seek to construct and project identities and lifestyles different from those expected of them by broader society, particularly those of their parents' generation and/or of the middle class. Where girls and young women are expected to value restraint and modesty, Kogals ('kogyaru') are commonly painted as self-assertive and expressive. The communicative style for which they are popularly known includes emphatic prefixes, varied orthographic characters and symbols, and truncation, all of which are held to index their opposition and resistance to the expected model of a docile, innocent and deferential young woman (Miller 2004). Correspondingly, Kogals are often depicted in the media as indecent, egocentric, brash and loud. The origin of the subculture's name is subject to debate; however, Miller (2003: 41, endnote 1) suggests that it is likely to be a clipped form of 'high school girls' – 'kôkôsei gyaru'.

Information on Kogal culture, identity and language use comes from Laura Miller's (2003, 2004) engaging work on Kogals, their language practices and their portrayal in the media, and from her work on "cool Japan" (2011). It is supported by insights from Okamoto's (1995) work on women's language in Japan and Stanlaw's (2014) description of the use of English loanwords and Roman script in contemporary Japanese youth practices.

Prisoner language practices in Israel

The main sources of information on Israeli prisoner language are Einat and Einat's (2000) study of the language used by, and associated with, those incarcerated in Israeli prisons, and subsequent analyses by Einat and Wall (2006) and Einat and Livnat (2012). The 2000 study in particular, the first of its kind in Israel and described as "one of the most extensive linguistic studies of prison argot" (Higgs 2014: 8), examined prisoner language practices as a reflection of the norms and values of Israeli inmate subculture – subjects also explored in the 2006 and 2012 examinations. It established the existence of an 'argot' and discussed the thematic domains covered by a lexicon of some 482 items collected from 30 Hebrew-speaking male prisoners who had served at least six years as part of long-term sentences.[9] Examples, almost none of which were to be found in regular Hebrew dictionaries, were provided to illustrate usage. Among the reported *raisons d'être* of the variety were its use in establishing and communicating prisoners' own rules and values and prisoner need to define status (see, for example, Einat and Wall 2006; Einat and Livnat 2012).

Sheng – youth-associated language in Kenya

The term 'Sheng' is thought by some to be an abbreviated form of 'Swahili–English Slang' (Githinji 2006), although this explanation is not universally embraced (Beck 2015). Viewed mainly as an urban language with many group varieties, Sheng, also known in some instances as 'Mtaa' ('neighbourhood', 'streets', 'suburbs'; Mazrui 1995), largely consists of vocabulary drawn from English and Swahili – Kenya's two official languages – and from other traditional languages such as Kikuyu and Luo. Descriptions of Sheng indicate that it is generally used within a framework of Swahili grammar and syntax (e.g. Githinji 2006; Ferrari 2006; Mutonya 2007), although other languages can be prominent when they serve as the local base (e.g. Githinji 2006; Kioko 2015).

Sheng is principally associated with marginalised urban Kenyan youth – mainly, but not exclusively, of the lower class and the slums. However, its rise had been so prolific that it has become the first language of many young people born in the shanty towns and beyond, and the most used informal language variety in everyday life (Ferrari 2006; Vierke 2015). It is also used in the Kenyan diaspora (e.g. Ferrari 2014).

Its genesis is subject to some debate: some commentators suggest that it arose as a youth variety in the poor areas of Nairobi's Eastlands in the 1960s or 1970s (Githinji 2006; Ferrari 2006; Ferrari 2014; Vierke 2015 suggests criminal origins in the same period); others posit that it emerged as an urban youth variety from a criminal variety associated with a multiethnic underworld at least as far back as the colonial 1930s (Mazrui 1995; see also Mutonya 2007; Beck 2015); a third view focuses on its rise and diffusion – that it was used in the early 1950s but became more widely used in the 1970s (as discussed in Ogechi 2005).

Sheng is believed to serve many purposes and to have a number of varieties by virtue of different forms used in distinct estates or 'bazes' within Nairobi, and by dint of items being exported to rural areas and integrated into different mother tongues (Kioko 2015). It is generally reported to foreground an urban youth identity that expresses and emphasises in-group solidarity as well as distance from older, rural and more traditional groups (e.g. Dorleijn, Mous and Nortier 2015, although note Kioko 2015 on rural practices). Another explanation is that it is used as a form of youth cryptolect to hide secrets from parents (see Ogechi 2005). Importantly, as Bosire (2009: 85, citing Samper 2002) observes, Sheng "gives the youth a unique 'hybrid' identity – the transcending of the ethnic and official languages 'status quo' into a fused, *Sheng sub-culture*, constructed at their own terms" (Bosire's emphasis), where Sheng's "structural and semantic malleability allows speakers to be creators" (Bosire 2009: 84). It has also been associated with the expression of verbal art known as 'ki-noki' – 'the language of the rebels or transgressors' – although ki-noki (also seen as 'Kinoki') has also been recorded as indexing street smarts and membership of the ranks of the homeless, while Sheng indexes urban sophistication and an association with the lower class (Bosire 2009, citing Mutonya 2006; for more on Kinoki, see Mutonya 2007).[10] Sheng can be found in everyday speech, rap, literature, advertising, the media and graffiti (e.g. Kioko 2015; Vierke 2015). The main sources on Sheng and associated practices are Mazrui (1995), Samper (2004), Ogechi (2005), Ferrari (2006, 2007, 2014), Githinji (2006), Mutonya (2007), Mwihaki (2007), Bosire (2009), Beck (2015), Dorleijn, Mous and Nortier (2015), Kioko (2015), Mukhwana (2015) and Vierke (2015).[11]

Randuk – youth-associated language in Sudan

Also known as Rendók, this variety is Arabic-based and indexes the identity of urban youth, primarily in Northern and Central Sudan. It developed in the 1970s after war, desertification and resultant massive urbanisation in Khartoum, which brought large numbers of rural migrants to the city and its environs. When more urbanisation and population flow occurred in the late 1980s and 1990s, it spread to all the urban centres of Arabic-speaking Sudan (Manfredi 2008; Mugaddam 2015).[12]

Randuk was originally invented by street boys known as 'Shamasha' as a cryptolect to protect them from oppressing groups such as the police, but also to foster a shared identity that set them apart from others (Manfredi 2008; Mugaddam 2012b, 2015). While this enabled and enables speakers to make their communication incomprehensible to the dominant linguistic community, Randuk terms have nonetheless spread among broader society, for example among school pupils and university students (Mugaddam 2015).

One of the prototypical methods in Randuk for creating new items is metathesis; however, speakers also draw on others such as borrowing and semantic transfer.[13] Data cited in this work derive primarily from Manfredi's (2008) study of Randuk as spoken in Khartoum and Kadugli in the Southern Kordofan State, but also from information on Khartoum youth practice provided by Dimmendaal

(2009) and from studies published by Mugaddam (2008, 2012a, 2012b, 2015), where he compares the Randuk used by different groups.

Camfranglais – youth-associated language in Cameroon

Also known as Francamglais, Camfranglais is a blend of the terms 'Cameroun', 'Français' and 'Anglais' (Kießling 2004). It is an urban hybrid language variety associated principally with youth in the cities of Yaoundé and Douala and has been spreading more widely within society to literary and other sociocultural domains. It is thought to have emerged in the 1960s–1970s, possibly from a criminal language known as 'français makro' ('yob' or 'hooligan French') (de Féral 2004; Ngo Ngok-Graux 2007), although Fonkoua (2015) suggests a precursor in a youth criminal variety known as 'Mboko'. The main purposes behind its use have traditionally concerned the desire by youth to signal their identity as in-group members (e.g. Vakunta 2008), especially of a modern and mainly urban social collective (Stein-Kanjora 2008). As such, they stand in contrast to older generations and rural populations. However, they also stand apart from the Cameroonian élites who define themselves as Francophone or Anglophone – especially as mastery of French in particular is needed for advancement but remains uncommon among the majority of the population (Kießling 2004; see also Vakunta 2008 on its use for opposing authority). The motivations for creating Camfranglais do not end there, however: it can also reportedly be used to support secret, in-group communication (Kouega 2003; Stein-Kanjora 2008; Vakunta 2008); for amusement (Stein-Kanjora 2008); to be *in* (Stein-Kanjora 2008); to cross ethnic bridges (Kießling 2004); and to demonstrate linguistic dexterity or virtuosity for status or sociocultural cachet (Stein-Kanjora 2008). Its popularity is such that it is used widely in informal situations but also in the workplace and school playground.

In addition to the creation of new vocabulary through mechanisms such as semantic transfer, its lexicon contains vocabulary borrowed from languages such as English, Pidgin English, French and Cameroonian languages such as Duala. Used within a French morphosyntactic structure, these items are often deliberately distorted. The main sources of information on Camfranglais are Kouega (2003), de Féral (2004), Kießling (2004), Ngo Ngok-Graux (2007), Stein-Kanjora (2008), Vakunta (2008), Ngefac (2010) and Fonkoua (2015).

Nouchi – youth-associated language in Côte d'Ivoire

Also known as Abidjanese French, and arising against a backdrop of considerable immigration (Kiessling and Mous 2004), Nouchi is a language variety that mainly indexes urban youth in Côte d'Ivoire. It is thought to have been created in the 1970s–1980s by young people who had dropped out of or had been left without education, and who needed a form of secret communication as a means of identity and survival. These youngsters created their own language variety which would be inaccessible to adults and would reportedly help them to pick pockets, among other things (e.g. Lafage 1991, 1998; Kouassi Ayewa 2005; Aboa 2011).

Nouchi has been associated with youths aged between 10 and 30, including pupils and students, for whom it has become the main means of communication (Kouadio N'guessan 2006). However, it has spread through increasing use in the media and music, as well as through urbanisation, so that it is no longer the preserve of the young.

Nouchi, thought to be a Susu or Dioula term,[14] borrows words from a variety of sources, including languages native to Côte d'Ivoire such as Dioula, Susu, Baoulé and Bété, as well as French, English, Spanish and German. Its core syntactic structure relies greatly on popular French ('français populaire') as it is spoken in Côte d'Ivoire, although Vakunta (2011) notes that Nouchi has some syntactic "peculiarities". The main sources of information on Nouchi are Lafage (1991, 1998), Kouassi Ayewa (2005), Ahua (2006, 2008), Kouadio N'guessan (2006), Aboa (2011) and Vakunta (2011).

Youth language in Zimbabwe

Zimbabwe is a country with three main languages – English, Shona and Ndebele. Each of these languages serves as a base for different youth language varieties which, depending on the speaker, can also figure within the same repertoire. At the same time, the corresponding gamut of youth actors also varies, ranging from youth of lower class status to those who are more educated (Hollington and Makwabarara 2015).

Core information on youth practices in Zimbabwe comes from Hollington and Makwabarara's (2015) engaging initial study. Although their outline is a preliminary one, it reflects many motivations behind such practices: to build group identity, express solidarity and social sharedness with peers, to underline social distance from others, such as older generations and those in rural areas, and to conceal meaning from the uninitiated. In addition, it also importantly highlights the linguistic manipulations that figure most in their sample, including morphological hybridisation, semantic transfer and metathesis; and complements discussion of language practices in the country as provided by authors such as Veit-Wild (2009).

Further insights regarding lexis associated with youth actors and the more general Harare population derive mainly from Mawadza's (2000) study of 'Harare Shona slang'. Shona is a Bantu language spoken by Shona people mainly in Zimbabwe, Mozambique, Zambia and Botswana. Mawadza considers that the variety largely works to Standard Shona's grammatical patterns and mainly relies on phonological processes, meaning transfer and borrowing to create new items with connotations of informality.

Lusaka's Town Nyanja

With English and Bemba, Nyanja is one of Zambia's three major *lingua francas* and is one of the 15–20 most widely spoken 'language groupings' in the country. As such it is used in education, the media and government. However, in Zambia's capital city Lusaka and elsewhere, a variety known as Town Nyanja consisting of borrowed lexis from languages such as English, Bemba, and Nsenga and Chewa mixes is widely used.[15] Mutunda (2007) notes that Town Nyanja (which he calls "Nyanja slang") generally consists of lexis that lends a sense of informality, and that it is typically associated with youth, educated and uneducated alike. Users include children of school age, attendants at bus stations, and hawkers, both young and adult.[16]

Data collection: an overview of methods used by researchers

There are a number of ways in which researchers can acquire linguistic data for analysis. In some cases, the methodology may be influenced by particularities in the object of study which will have a bearing on materials used to support analysis – for example, analysis of computer-mediated communication in specific online fora (e.g. Berdicevskis 2011); examination of usage in fanzines (e.g. Androutsopoulos 2000a); or investigation of graffiti content (e.g. Breva Claramonte and García Alonso 1993). In others, the researcher might select an alternative single method for data collection, such as participant questionnaires on language use and attitudes (e.g. Ngefac 2010).

Other methods may also be applied where subjects are requested to bring the researcher examples of current youth or other language with the result that an index or corpus builds up over time (e.g. Eble 1996, 2014), or where corpora may be constructed for subsequent linguistic investigation through the (often self-) recording of speech. Two examples of corpora based on recorded speech that have been later transcribed for analysis are the German *Kiezdeutschkorpus* (or *KiDKo*), which consists of informal peer-group conversations, mainly in German, among speakers aged 14–17 from 2008 to 2015, and the Norwegian UPUS–Oslo spoken language corpus comprising data collected over 2006–2010 in Oslo among 13–23-year-olds (for examples of analysis using both sources, see Ekberg, Opsahl and Wiese 2015; Aarsæther, Marzo, Nistov and Ceuleers 2015. Harchaoui 2015 has also made use of the UPUS data).[17]

A number of researchers apply multi-stranded approaches. In her study of Verlan, Lefkowitz (1989) drew on recorded spontaneous speech, informant interviews, a survey capturing speakers and usage, and language found in graffiti, advertising, articles, books and translations. Stein-Kanjora (2008) adopted a similarly varied approach in her study of Camfranglais, in which she collated information from 500 questionnaires and interviews and studied usage in newspapers, advertisements, magazines and photographs. Some projects may adopt an ethnographic approach where there is close observation of social actors as they deploy their linguistic resources in interaction. Reyes (2005), for example, carried out a four-year ethnographic and discourse analytic study of an Asian American video-making project at a community arts organisation in Philadelphia. Here teenage subjects, supported by volunteers and adult artists, discussed matters of particular importance to them, developed a script on the basis of their discussions, and then put together a short video. As a volunteer in the video project and member of staff of the initiative in question, Reyes was able to take part in the video creation process. She was ultimately able to collect data through audio and video recordings, participant observation, interviews and field notes.

As we can see with Reyes (and others such as Mayr 2004 and Miller 2004), sometimes the researcher is present to witness the use of language in exchanges; however, this is not always the case. Aarsæther, Marzo, Nistov and Ceuleers (2015), for instance, used data collected through questionnaires and video-recorded interviews by a researcher, as well as peer conversations where the researcher was not in attendance. Moreover, Stenström, Andersen and Hasund (2002) and Stenström (2014) used the self-recording approach to real effect where youth speakers were asked to record conversations in which they took part. This approach provided data from interactions in a number of settings, such as in the classroom, at home with family, in informal peer-group situations, and so on, and enabled the researchers to provide statistical analysis of usage as well as examination of pragmatic meaning.

Clearly, not all in-groups are going to be approached and engaged in the same way. Not only are prisoners, for example, representative of a broader age range of speakers, but access to them often has to occur within certain constraints that may not – for reasons of safety – be encountered elsewhere. Einat and Livnat (2012), for example, describe the collection method that brought them over 500 items: 158 prisoners aged between 22 and 65 and located in a number of correctional facilities voluntarily took part in in-depth, semi-structured interviews. These interviews took place in the prisons' education wings during the prisoners' spare time and, although no prison officers were present during the interviews, they nonetheless accompanied the prisoners to these sessions.

This volume uses data collected in a number of different ways, ranging from prisoner interviews (e.g. Einat and Einat 2000; Einat and Livnat 2012), the requested provision of lexical items by subjects (e.g. Eble 1996, 2014), the use of questionnaires (Ngefac 2010) and recorded speech (e.g. Beck 2015), to analysis of graffiti (e.g. Breva Claramonte and García Alonso 1993) and various combined approaches (e.g. Lefkowitz 1989; Méla 1997; Davie 1998; Ngo Ngok-Graux 2007; Smith-Hefner 2007; Stein-Kanjora 2008; Mugaddam 2015). In addition to the methods outlined, it also makes use of dictionaries as a source of linguistic data, principally for comparative study of manipulations. The use of dictionaries and glossaries is not without complications. Some may have more of an autobiographical slant where they reflect the life experiences of the compiler to a greater degree than might ordinarily be the case (e.g. Nikol'ski 1993); others cater for specific varieties (e.g. Stavsky, Mozeson and Mozeson's 1995 dictionary of US hip hop and rap slang) or contain a broad range of non-standard forms, reflecting the usage of a number of groups or subgroups as well as broader colloquial usage (e.g. Mahler 2008; Nikitina 2009; Strutz 2009); while others still may include usage from fiction (which is a representation of persona language more than a recording of social agents, although usage can sometimes be cross-referenced with other sources). Nonetheless, notwithstanding differences in compiler experience and perspective, and although dictionaries do not typically disclose the frequency of an item's use, with circulation of an item inferred through its inclusion in the publication, dictionaries can represent solid sources of linguistic material to variously explore questions of group association, etymology, manipulations and reasons for use (see, for example García's 2005 use of dictionaries in her study of Pachuco Caló).

Summary

In this chapter, we have briefly considered a variety of data collection methodologies that are used to gather information on the use of youth, criminal and colloquial language. These methodologies have been used in studies serving as key sources for the book and in broader research. In each case, researchers have identified data that they consider to be generally representative of the practices they are studying.

The data and sources outlined in this chapter are cited in discussions of attitudes and motivations believed to underpin the use of colloquial, youth and criminal language (Part One), as well as in exploration of the main associated linguistic manipulations (Part Two). Most of the varieties cited are well documented (e.g. North American youth usage, colloquial French), but some are not. This means that, in some cases, breakthrough studies, or discussion which may be less broad or evolved than that of the well-documented varieties, are cited. Where there is a less expansive literature or debate (e.g. youth practice in Zimbabwe), the total number of publications is not necessarily a reflection of the quality of the studies or representativeness of the data.

In all cases, source material has been selected on the basis of extensive literature review of the motivations behind and reactions to usage, as well as of particularly prominent and productive mechanisms. This has enabled a broad view of questions on which to alight. As noted in the Introduction, supporting information is also cited where required from a number of other languages such as Estonian, Italian, Turkish and Brazilian. The data relating to colloquial, youth and criminal language in these languages have been selected using the same criteria as for data from the key texts (for example, certain linguistic manipulations are seen as typical of colloquial usage or youth practice).

Notes

1 Wise (1997) provides an interesting example of the verb 'flinguer' ('to shoot') being regarded as *populaire*, *familier* and *argotique* in different reference works, and notes that "Such discrepancies are legion" (Wise 1997: 182). She also suggests the following difference between *familier* and *populaire*: "If the relationship between the speakers is closer, and the situation more informal, then they may move into a register termed ***familier***: not strictly adhering to the grammatical norm, and using lexical items that would be incongruous in a more formal setting, but which in no way mark the speakers as uneducated. The label ***populaire***, however, is often used with pejorative overtones, and implies the word is characteristic of the social dialect of the relatively uneducated lower working class; the label may be considered a tacit warning to the reader to avoid such items as being *déclassants*!" (Wise 1997: 181; her emphasis).
2 It should be noted that Germany is thought to have a far-reaching history of criminal and other in-group usage. Beier (1995: 66) reports that a German criminal language variety known as Rotwelsch apparently originated in the thirteenth century, and that

usage was documented in municipal records in 1342–3. Zhirmunskii (1936) suggests that the word Rotwelsch was first noted referring to secret language in 1250, and that a series of materials was produced in Germany from the beginning of the fifteenth century about the déclassé (beggars, vagabonds, brigands) and their secret language. He further indicates that an eighteenth-century criminal group had its own king, had members in a number of areas (such as Bavaria, Hannover and Saxony) and that their criminal language was taught and changed, where necessary.

3 The term 'Roma' is employed in this volume in line with the Council of Europe's (2012: 4) recommended usage: "The term 'Roma' used at the Council of Europe refers to Roma, Sinti, Kale and related groups in Europe, including Travellers and the Eastern groups (Dom and Lom), and covers the wide diversity of the groups concerned, including persons who identify themselves as Gypsies". In this book, the main focus is on the language practices of Spanish Roma, known as "Calé" or "Kale", although some reference is also made to the use of Romani in other language varieties in other parts of Europe.

4 In the mid-1990s Geipel reported that there were some 400,000 Spanish citizens who were identified as 'gitanos', and that the Romani language had a core vocabulary of basic terms that were found in all or most Romani dialects; indeed, this core vocabulary mainly derived from the languages of India (Geipel 1995: 102–3). Furthermore, the terms used by Spanish gitanos to refer to themselves – 'Calé', the plural of 'Caló' – and to their ancestral language, derive from the Hindi 'kālā' ('black').

5 Chamberlain's (1981: 422) glossary of Lunfardo terms gives 'lunfardo' the meaning of 'thief'. He also notes that many terms common to Lunfardo and Brazil's Gíria have been recorded as coming from Italian or Italian dialects, particularly Genoese and Piedmontese (Chamberlain 1981: 418).

6 Crystal (1998: 117) provides food for thought in his description of graffiti: "By its nature, graffiti inhabits a rule-breaking, anarchic world, and we would expect to find in it many kinds of language play, alongside the political, lavatorial, absurdist and other forms of situational comment which the genre invites".

7 Indeed, Slone (2003) lists a number of ludlings from Indonesia, Malaysia and Brunei, such as Seselan, a Javanese student language variety used possibly circa 1958 in Kediri, East Java Province, and the Malay Bahasa Rahsia, a children's variety used in Johor State in 1995.

8 Smith-Hefner (2007) points out that formal Standard Indonesian, a form of Malay, is learned almost uniquely in schools and is associated with printed publications, government announcements and official media; however, it is not used in everyday informal contexts. By contrast, informal Indonesian is learned outside the education system and is often influenced by the regional language background of its speakers. It expresses familiarity and solidarity.

9 Topics identified as part of Einat and Einat's (2000) study included: prisoner status; drugs (over a quarter of all terms were narcotics-related); sexual relations; violence; prisoner behaviours; nicknames for police officers and prison staff; and 'other' (general) items.

10 Used by street people (including children) to survive in hostile streets and to create a sense of social sharedness, Kinoki hides the illegal activities of its speakers from outgroupers.

It is noteworthy that Mutonya (2007: 178) points to a "symbiotic relationship" between Sheng and Kinoki (especially concerning lexical exchange), but proposes that Kinoki differs from Sheng, which he regards as the "dominant urban slang": "while Sheng is widely perceived to index urban sophistication and an association with the lower class, Kinoki indexes street sophistication and membership of a different group of the lower class: those with a shared knowledge of the experiences and harsh realities of homelessness" (Mutonya 2007: 170). He further notes that: "Sheng facilitates the transmission of the culture and reality of Nairobi's lower class, but Kinoki provides the homeless community with a tool to help form its own

images and perspectives of the world, and to distinguish friend from foe" (Mutonya 2007: 172).
11 Ogechi (2005) and Kioko (2015) also note the use of 'Engsh' that is spoken in the more affluent Westlands area of Nairobi. 'Engsh' appears to be based on English grammatical–syntactic structure, with a greater preponderance of English lexis.
12 Although not a focus of this book, Arabic has a rich tradition of criminal language. The first Arabic criminal variety is believed to have been that of the Banu Sāsān. Recorded from the tenth until the fourteenth century, it was spoken by beggars and crooks, and is thought to have provided a large amount of lexical material for a later variety, known as Sīm, which was noted as being used by travelling people and entertainers in Egypt since the nineteenth century (Wolfer 2011).
13 In a presentation at the University of Cologne Institute for African Studies, Abdel Rahim Mugaddam (2008) observed that "[t]he only salient phonological manipulation that occurs in youth language in Khartoum is the process of metathesis". He also pointed to the use of other methods, such as semantic transfer and borrowing, for instance, as methods for supplementing the youth lexicon.
   The spread of Randuk has also been reported by Justice Africa (2002: 9; their italics), who recorded with regard to Sudan's displaced population that "The displaced camps have witnessed the development of a new version of colloquial Arabic, '*randuk*', which is replacing customary tribal languages".
14 One theory is that it is derived from Dioula 'nou' ('nostril') and 'chi' ('hairs') (Kouadio N'guessan 2006: 182). Kiessling and Mous (2004: 3) suggest that the term may also have arisen through metathesis of the French 'chez nous' or (citing Lafage 1998) from Dioula 'nún síí' ('nose-skin').
15 Chewa is the language of inhabitants of Malawi, Eastern Zambia and Northern Zimbabwe. Nsenga is a Bantu language spoken in Mozambique and Zambia.
16 Much of the structure of Mutunda's article appears to echo that of Mawadza (2000) on Harare Shona slang. That said, it has sufficiently new material in its own right to add to the book's overall exploration of motivations and manipulations.
17 UPUS-Oslo is a corpus of Norwegian as spoken by youth aged between 13 and 23 years old (according to information as of September 2016). It aims to capture the language of urban multiethnic youth and consists of video-recorded interviews and conversations in schools, in family settings, and among friends. The *KiDKo* corpus comprises spontaneous speech data derived from informal peer groups in both mono- and multiethnic environments. The data were acquired through self-recordings of young people aged between 14 and 17 at two schools. The language was mostly German as used in informal conversations between friends.

References

Aarsæther, F., Marzo, S., Nistov, I. and Ceuleers, E. (2015) 'Indexing locality: contemporary urban vernaculars in Belgium and Norway', in J. Nortier and B.A. Svendsen (eds.) *Language, Youth and Identity in the 21st Century*, Cambridge: Cambridge University Press. 249–270.
Abeccasis, M. (2003) 'Le français populaire: a valid concept?', *Marges Linguistiques*, 6 116–132.
Aboa, A.L.A. (2011) 'Le Nouchi – a-t-il un avenir?', *Revue Electronique Internationale de Sciences du Langage*, *16*, 44–54.
Ahua, B.M. (2006) 'La Motivation dans les créations lexicales en Nouchi', *Le Français en Afrique*, *21*, 143–157.
Ahua, B.M. (2008) 'Mots, phrases et syntaxe du Nouchi', *Le Français en Afrique*, *23*, 135–150.
Androutsopoulos, J. (2000a) 'Non-standard spellings in media texts: The case of German fanzines', *Journal of Sociolinguistics*, *4*(4), 514–533.

Androutsopoulos, J.K. (2000b) 'Extending the concept of the (socio)linguistic variable to slang', in T. Kis (ed.) *Mia szleng*, Debrecen: Kossuth Lajos University Press. 1–21. jannisandroutsopoulos.files.wordpress.com/2009/09/slangvar.pdf, accessed April 2014.

Androutsopoulos, J. (2005) 'Research on youth language', in U. Ammon, D. Norbert, K.J. Mattheier and P. Trudgill (eds.) *Sociolinguistics/Soziolinguistik: An International Handbook of the Science of Language and Society (Ein internationales Handbuch zur Wissenschaft von Sprache und Gesellschaft), Vol. 2*, Berlin: de Gruyter. 1496–1505.

Androutsopoulos, J. (2007) 'Style online: doing hip-hop on the German-speaking web', in P. Auer (ed.) *Style and Social Identities: Alternative Approaches to Linguistic Heterogeneity*, Berlin/New York: de Gruyter. 279–317.

Androutsopoulos, J. (2009) 'Language and the three spheres of hip-hop', in A. Ibrahim, H.S. Alim and A. Pennycook (eds.) *Global Linguistic Flows: Hip Hop Cultures, Identities, and the Politics of Language*, New Jersey: Lawrence Erlbaum. 43–62.

Androutsopoulos, J. and Scholz, A. (2002) 'On the recontextualization of hip-hop in European communities: a contrastive analysis of rap lyrics'. www.fu_berlin.de/phon/phin19/p19t1.htm, accessed April 2012.

Artemova, T.V., Katyshev, P.A., Olenev, S.V., Pauli, Iu.S. and Sokolova, S.K. (2014) 'Funktsii zhargona narkomanov i slovoobrazovatel'nye sredstva ikh osushchestvleniia', *Vestnik Kemerovskogo Gosudarstvennogo Universiteta*, 3(59), T. 3, 166–169.

Bachmann, C. and Basier, L. (1984) 'Le verlan: argot d'école ou langue des Keums?', *Mots*, 8, 169–187.

Beazley, H. (1998) 'Homeless street children in Yogyakarta, Indonesia', *Development Bulletin*, Australian Development Studies Network, 44, 40–2.

Beazley, H. (2002) '"Vagrants wearing make-up": negotiating spaces on the streets of Yogyakarta, Indonesia', *Urban Studies*, 39(9), 1665–83.

Beazley, H. (2003) 'The construction and protection of individual and collective identities by street children and youth in Indonesia', *Children, Youth and Environments*, 13(1). www.colorado.edu/journals/cye/13_1/Vol13_1Articles/CYE_CurrentIssue_Article_ChildrenYouthIndonesia_Beazley.htm, accessed July 2015.

Beck, R.M. (2010) 'Urban languages in Africa', *Africa Spectrum*, 45(3), 11–41.

Beck, R.M. (2015) 'Sheng: an urban variety of Swahili in Kenya', in N. Nassenstein and A. Hollington (eds.) *Youth Language Practices in Africa and Beyond*, Berlin/Boston: Walter de Gruyter, Inc. 51–79.

Beier, L. (1995) 'Anti-language or jargon? Canting in the English underworld in the 16th and 17th centuries', in P. Burke and R. Porter (eds.) *Languages and Jargons: Contributions to a Social History of Language*, Cambridge: Polity Press. 64–101.

Berdicevskis, A. (2011) 'Elektronnaia pochta vs. Chat: vliianie kanala kommunikatsii na iazyk', in *Computational Linguistics and Intellectual Technologies. Papers from the Annual International Conference "Dialogue"*, Moscow: RGGU. 84–93.

Berdicevskis, A. (Berdichevskiy, A.) (2012) '"Orfograficheskii" srednii rod: grammaticheskaia innovatsiia v iazyke russkogo interneta', in L.L. Fedorova (ed.) *Variativnost' v iazyke i kommunikatsii*, Moscow: RGGU. www.uib.no/filearchive/berdichevskij_neuter.pdf, accessed June 2014.

Beregovskaia, E.M. (1996) 'Molodëzhnyi sleng: formirovanie i funktsionirovanie', *Voprosy iazykoznaniia*, 3, 32–41.

Biblieva, O.V. (2007) 'Molodëzhnyi sleng kak forma reprezentatsii molodëzhnoi kul'tury v sredstvakh massovoi informatsii', *Vestnik Tomskogo Gosudarstvennogo Universiteta*, 304, 62–5.

Blake, B. (2010) *Secret Language*, Oxford: Oxford University Press.

Boellstorff, T. (2004) '*Gay* language and Indonesia: registering belonging', *Journal of Linguistic Anthropology*, *14*(2), 248–68.
Bosire, M. (2009) 'What makes a Sheng word unique? Lexical manipulation in mixed languages', in A. Ojo and L. Moshi (eds.) *Selected Proceedings of the 39th Annual Conference on African Linguistics*, Somerville, MA. 77–85.
Breva Claramonte, M. and García Alonso, J.I. (1993) 'Categories, morphological features, and slang in the graffiti of a United States Western university', *Revista Alicantina de Estudios Ingleses*, *6*, 19–31.
Bullock, B. (1996) 'Popular derivation and linguistic inquiry: Les Javanais', *The French Review*, *70*(2), 180–191.
Buzek, I. (2012) 'Presence of gypsy origin vocabulary in Latin American Spanish varieties: the case of Mexican Spanish and its *Caló*', paper presented at the *Tenth International Conference on Romani Linguistics*, Barcelona, 5–7 September.
Červenková, M. (2001) 'L'influence de l'argot sur la langue commune et les procédés de sa formation en français contemporain', *Studia Minora Facultatis Philosophicae Universitatis Brunensis*, *L*(22), 77–86.
Chamberlain, B.J. (1981) 'Lexical similarities of Lunfardo and Gíria', *Hispania*, *64*(3), 417–425.
Chambert-Loir H. (1984) 'Those who speak Prokem', *Indonesia*, *37*, 105–117.
Cheeseman, T. (1998) 'Hip hop in Germany', *Debatte*, *6*(2), 191–214.
Council of Europe (2012) *Council of Europe Descriptive Glossary of Terms Relating to Roma Issues*, 18 May.
Crystal, D. (1998) *Language Play*, London: Penguin Books.
Daniels, D.H. (1997) 'Los Angeles zoot: race "riot", the Pachuco, and black music culture', *The Journal of Negro History*, *82*(2), 201–220.
Davie, J.D. (1997/98) 'Missing presumed dead? The *baikovyi iazyk* of the St. Petersburg *mazuriki* and other pre-Soviet argots', *Slavonica*, *4*(1), 28–45.
Davie, J.D. (1998) *Making sense of the* nonstandard*: a study of borrowing and word-formation in 1990s Russian youth slang, with particular reference to the language of the fanzine* (Doctoral dissertation, 2 volumes). University of Portsmouth.
De Féral, C. (2004) 'Français et langues en contact chez les jeunes en milieu urbain: vers de nouvelles identités', in *Penser la francophonie: concepts, actions et outils linguistiques, Actes des premières Journées scientifiques communes des réseaux de chercheurs concernant la langue*, Ouagadougou (Burkina Faso), 31 mai–1er juin.
De Katzew, L. (2004) 'Interlingualism: the language of Chicanos/as', in A. Muñoz (ed.) *Chican@ Critical Perspectives and Praxis at the Turn of the 21st Century*, National Association for Chicana and Chicano Studies. 61–76.
Dimmendaal, G.J. (2009) 'Randuk: Arabisch in Khartoum/Sudan', 2 November.
Doludenko, E. (2012) 'Morphological analysis of the lexicon used in the Russian social network "Vkontakte"', *Studies in the Linguistic Sciences: Illinois Working Papers*, 17–31.
Doran, M. (2004) 'Negotiating between bourge and racaille: Verlan as youth identity practice in suburban Paris', in A. Pavlenko and A. Blackledge (eds.) *Identities in Multilingual Contexts*, Clevedon, UK: Multilingual Matters Ltd. 93–124.
Doran, M. (2007) 'Alternative French, alternative identities: situating language in la banlieue', *Contemporary French and Francophone Studies*, *11*(4), 497–508.
Dorleijn, M., Mous, M. and Nortier, J. (2015) 'Urban youth speech styles in Kenya and the Netherlands', in J. Nortier and B.A. Svendsen (eds.) *Language, Youth and Identity in the 21st Century*, Cambridge: Cambridge University Press. 271–89.

Dorleijn, M. and Nortier, J. (2013) 'Multi-ethnolects: Kebabnorsk, Perkerdansk, Verlan, Kanakensprache, Straattaal, etc.', in P. Bakker and Y. Matras (eds.) *Contact Languages: A Comprehensive Guide*, Berlin: de Gruyter. 229–72.

Dunn, J.A. (2006) 'It's Russian – but not as we know it', *Rusistika*, *31*, 3–6.

Eble, C. (1996) *Slang and Sociability*, Chapel Hill, NC: University of North Carolina Press.

Eble, C. (2014) 'American college student slang: University of North Carolina (2005–12)', in J. Coleman (ed.) *Global English Slang*, London: Routledge. 36–48.

Einat, T. and Einat, H. (2000) 'Inmate argot as an expression of prison subculture: the Israeli case', *The Prison Journal*, *80*(3), 309–25.

Einat T. and Livnat, Z. (2012) 'Words, values and identities: the Israeli argot (jargon) of prisoners', *International Journal of Political Science, Law and International Relations*, *2*(2), 97–118.

Einat, T. and Wall, A. (2006) 'Language, culture, and behavior in prison: The Israeli case', *Asian Criminology*, *1*, 173–89.

Ekberg, L. Opsahl, T. and Wiese, H. (2015) 'Functional gains: a cross-linguistic case study of three particles in Swedish, Norwegian and German', in J. Nortier and B.A. Svendsen (eds.) *Language, Youth and Identity in the 21st Century*, Cambridge: Cambridge University Press. 93–115.

Elistratov, V.S. (1994) *Slovar' moskovskogo argo*, Moscow: Russkie slovari.

Ferrari, A. (2006) 'Vecteurs de la propagation du lexique sheng et invention perpétuelle de mots', *Le Français en Afrique*, *21*, 227–37.

Ferrari, A. (2007) 'Hip-hop in Nairobi: recognition of an international movement and the main means of expression for the urban youth in poor residential areas', in K. Njogu and H. Maupeu (eds.) *Songs and Politics in Eastern Africa*, Dar es Salaam/Nairobi: IFRA and Mkuki na Nyoka Publishers. 107–128.

Ferrari, A. (2014) 'Evolution of Sheng during the last decade', *Les Cahiers de l'Afrique de l'Est*, *47*, 29–54. rekebisho.wixsite.com/aureliaferrari/publications, accessed March 2015.

Fonkoua, H.K. (2015) *A Dictionary of Camfranglais*, Frankfurt am Main: Peter Lang AG, Volume 107.

García, M. (2005) 'Influences of gypsy *Caló* on contemporary Spanish slang', *Hispania*, *88*(4), 800–12.

Garza, T.J. (2008) '«Ne trozh' molodëzh'!» A portrait of urban youthspeak and the Russian language in the 21st century', *Russian Language Journal*, *58*. www.academia.edu/1974996/Не_трожь_молодджь_A_Portrait_of_Urban_Youthspeak_and_the_Russian_Language_in_the_21st_Century, accessed December 2016.

Geipel, J. (1995) 'Caló: the 'secret' language of the gypsies of Spain', in P. Burke and R. Porter (eds.) *Languages and Jargons: Contributions to a Social History of Language*, Cambridge: Polity Press. 102–32.

Githinji, P. (2006) 'Bazes and their shibboleths: lexical variation and Sheng speakers' identity in Nairobi', *Nordic Journal of African Studies*, *15*(4), 443–72.

González, F.R. and Stenström, A. (2011) 'Expressive devices in the language of English- and Spanish-speaking youth', *Revista Alicantina de Estudios Ingleses*, *24*, 235–56.

Gorny, E. (2004) 'Russian LiveJournal: national specifics in the development of a virtual community', Version 1.0, 13 May. www.ruhr-uni-bochum.de/russ-cyb/library/texts/en/gorny_rlj.pdf, accessed June 2012.

Goudaillier, J.-P. (2002) 'De l'argot traditionnel au français contemporain des cités', *La Linguistique*, *1*(38), 5–24.

Grachëv, M.A. (1992) 'Tret'ia volna', *Russkaia rech'*, *4*, 61–4.

Grachëv, M.A. (1994) 'Ob etimologii v russkom argo', *Russkaia rech'*, *4*, 67–70.
Grachëv, M.A. (2003) *Slovar' tysiacheletnego russkogo argo*, Moscow: RIPOL KLASIK.
Grayson, J. (1964) 'Lunfardo, Argentina's unknown tongue', *Hispania*, *47*(1), 66–8.
Gromov, D.V. (2009), 'Sleng molodëzhnykh subkul'tur: leksicheskaia struktura i osobennosti formirovaniia', extended version of article in *Russkii iazyk v nauchnom osveshchenii*, *1*(17), 228–40.
Harchaoui, S. (2015) 'Lexical innovations in the speech of adolescents in Oslo, Norway', *Proceedings of ConSOLE XXIII*, 220–47.
Higgs, E. (2014) 'Inmate subcultures', in J.S. Albanese (ed.) *The Encyclopedia of Criminology and Criminal Justice*, Chichester: John Wiley and Sons, Ltd. shareslide.org/inmate-subcultures-higgs, accessed June 2015.
Hollington, A. and Makwabarara, T. (2015) 'Youth language practices in Zimbabwe', in N. Nassenstein and A. Hollington (eds.) *Youth Language Practices in Africa and Beyond*, Berlin/Boston: Walter de Gruyter, Inc. 257–70.
Hollington, A. and Nassenstein, N. (2015a) 'Youth language practices in Africa as creative manifestations of fluid repertoires and markers of speakers' social identity', in N. Nassenstein and A. Hollington (eds.) *Youth Language Practices in Africa and Beyond*, Berlin/Boston: Walter de Gruyter, Inc. 1–22.
Hollington, A. and Nassenstein, N. (2015b) 'Conclusion and outlook: taking new directions in the study of youth language practices', in N. Nassenstein and A. Hollington (eds.) *Youth Language Practices in Africa and Beyond*, Berlin/Boston: Walter de Gruyter, Inc. 345–56.
Jørgensen, A.M. (2013) 'Spanish teenage language and the COLAm-corpus', *Bergen Language and Linguistic Studies*, *3*(1), 151–66 (shared through https://creativecommons.org/licenses/by/3.0/legalcode).
Khomiakov, V.A. (1992) 'Nekotorye tipologicheskie osobennosti nestandartnoi leksiki angliiskogo, frantsuzskogo i russkogo iazykov', *Voprosy iazykoznaniia*, *3*, 94–105.
Kießling, R. (2004) 'bàk mwà mè dó – Camfranglais in Cameroon', *Lingua Posnaniensis*, *47*. www.aai.uni-hamburg.de/afrika/personen/kiessling/medien/kiessling-2004-camfranglais.pdf, accessed September 2012.
Kiessling, R. and Mous, M. (2004) 'Urban youth languages in Africa', *Anthropological Linguistics*, *46*(3), 1–39.
Kioko, E.M. (2015) 'Regional varieties and "ethnic" registers of Sheng', in N. Nassenstein and A. Hollington (eds.) *Youth Language Practices in Africa and Beyond*, Berlin/Boston: Walter de Gruyter, Inc. 119–47.
Kouadio N'guessan, J. (2006) 'Le Nouchi et les rapports Dioula-Français', *Le Français en Afrique*, *21*, 177–91.
Kouassi Ayewa, N. (2005) 'Mots et contexts en FPI et en Nouchi', *JS LTT/AUF, AUF*, Bruxelles. 1–11.
Kouega, J-P. (2003) 'Word formative processes in Camfranglais', *World Englishes*, *22*(4), 511–38.
Kovalev, A. (1995) 'Molodye o molodëzhnom zhargone', *Russkii iazyk za rubezhom*, *1*, 90–9.
Kveselevich, D.I. (2005) *Tolkovyi slovar' nenormativnoi leksiki russkogo iazyka*, Moscow: Astrel' AST.
Lafage, S. (1991) 'L'argot des jeunes Ivoiriens, marque d'appropriation du français?', *Langue française*, *90*, 95–105.
Lafage, S. (1998) '"Le français des rues", une variété avancée du français Abidjanais', *Faits de langues*, *11–12*, 135–44.

Lapina-Kratasiuk, E. (2009) 'News in the Russian internet: the growing indifference of a closing society', *Russian Analytical Digest*, *69*(9), 12–14.
Lebedeva, S.V. and Astakhova, N.V. (2016) 'Main features of youth jargon: synchronic analysis', *Russian Linguistic Bulletin*, *3*(7), 125–26.
Lefkowitz, N.J. (1989) 'Verlan: talking backwards in French', *The French Review*, *63*(2), 312–22.
Levikova, S.I. (2004) 'Molodëzhnyi sleng kak svoeobraznyi sposob verbalizatsii bytiya', *Bytie i iazyk*, 167–73.
Lysenko, S.A. (2008) 'Oralizatsiia kak tendentsiia razvitiia Internet-kommunikatsii', *Vestnik VGU, Seriia: Filologiia. Zhurnalistika*, *2*, 69–71.
Magner, T. (1957) 'The Stiljaga and his language', *Slavic and East European Journal*, *15*(1), 192–5.
Mahler, M. (2008) *Dictionary of Spanish Slang and Colloquial Expressions*, New York: Barron's.
Mallik, B. (1972) *Language of the Underworld of West Bengal*, Calcutta: Sanskrit College Research Series No. LXXVII.
Mandelbaum-Reiner, F. (1991) 'Secrets de bouchers et Largonji actuel des Louchébèm', *Langage et société*, *56*, 21–49.
Manfredi, S. (2008) 'Rendók: a youth secret language in Sudan', *Estudios de dialectología norteafricana y andalusí*, *12*, 113–29.
Mawadza, A. (2000) 'Harare Shona slang: a linguistic study', *Zambezia*, *XXVII*(i), 93–101.
Mayr, A. (2004) *Prison Discourse: Language as a Means of Control and Resistance*, Basingstoke, UK: Palgrave MacMillan.
Mazrui, A.M. (1995) 'Slang and code-switching: the case of Sheng in Kenya', *Afrikanistische Arbietspapier*, *42*, 168–79.
Méla, V. (1988) 'Parler verlan: règles et usages', *Langage et société*, *45*, 47–72.
Méla, V. (1991) 'Le verlan ou le langage du miroir', *Langages*, *101*, 73–94.
Méla, V. (1997) 'Verlan 2000', *Langue française*, *114*, 16–34.
Miller, L. (2003) 'Graffiti photos: expressive art in Japanese girls' culture', *Harvard Asia Quarterly*, *7*(3), 31–42.
Miller, L. (2004) 'Those naughty teenage girls: Japanese Kogals, slang, and media assessments', *Journal of Linguistic Anthropology*, *14*(2), 225–47.
Miller, L. (2011) 'Taking girls seriously in "cool Japan" ideology', *Japan Studies Review*, *15*, 97–106.
Mugaddam, A.R. (2008) 'Youth language in Khartoum', paper presented at the University of Cologne Institute for African Studies, 28 May.
Mugaddam, A.R.H. (2012a) 'Aspects of youth language in Khartoum', in M. Brenzinger and A-M. Fehn (eds.) *Proceedings of 6th World Congress of African Linguistics*, Cologne: Rüdiger Köppe Verlag. 87–98.
Mugaddam, A.H. (2012b) 'Identity construction and linguistic manipulation in Randuk', paper presented at the *Youth Languages and Urban Languages in Africa Workshop*, Institut für Afrikanistik, Cologne University, Germany.
Mugaddam, A.H. (2015) 'Identity construction and linguistic manipulation in Randuk', in N. Nassenstein and A. Hollington (eds.) *Youth Language Practices in Africa and Beyond*, Berlin/Boston: Walter de Gruyter, Inc. 99–118.
Mukhwana, A. (2015) 'Sheng and Engsh: what they are and what they are not', *International Journal of Scientific Research and Innovative Technology*, *2*(1), 94–102.
Mutonya, M. (2007) 'Redefining Nairobi's streets: a study of slang, marginalization, and identity', *Journal of Global Initiatives*, *2*(2), 169–85.

Mutunda, S. (2007) 'Language behavior in Lusaka: the use of Nyanja slang', *The International Journal of Language, Society and Culture*, 21. www.edu.utas.au/users/ tle/JOURNAL/

Mwihaki, A. (2007) 'Viewing Sheng as a social dialect: a linguistic approach', *ChemChemi*, Kenyatta University, 4(2), 57–75.

Nad'iarova, E.Sh. (2014) 'Rasprostranenie slengovykh vyrazhenii v molodëzhnoi polilingvokul'turnoi srede', *Uchënye zapiski Tavricheskogo natsional'nogo universiteta im. V.I. Vernadskogo. Seriia "Filologiia. Sotsial'nye kommunikatsii"*, 27(66), No. 2, 64–74.

Ngefac, A. (2010) 'Linguistic choices in postcolonial multilingual Cameroon', *Nordic Journal of African Studies*, 19(3), 149–64.

Ngo Ngok-Graux, E.N. (2007) 'Les Représentations du Camfranglais chez les Locuteurs de Douala et Yaoundé', *Le Français en Afrique*, 21, 219–25.

Nikitina, T.G. (2009) *Molodëzhnyi sleng: tolkovyi slovar'*, Moscow: AST: Astrel'.

Nikol'ski, V. (1993) *Dictionary of Contemporary Russian Slang*, Moscow: Panorama.

Offord, D. (1996) *Using Russian*, Cambridge: Cambridge University Press.

Oganian, A.A. and Ishkhanova, D.I. (2015) 'Osobennosti iazyka molodëzhnykh subkul'tur: khippi, baykerov i gotov', *Unikal'nye issledovaniia XXI veka*, 5(5), 151–53.

Ogechi, N.O. (2005) 'On lexicalization in Sheng', *Nordic Journal of African Studies*, 14(3), 334–55.

Okamoto, S. (1995) '"Tasteless" Japanese: less "feminine" speech among young Japanese women', in K. Hall and M. Bucholtz (eds.) *Gender Articulated: Language and the Socially Constructed Self*, New York: Routledge. 297–325.

Paul, K. Freywald, U. and Wittenberg, E. (2009) '"*Kiezdeutsch* goes school" – a multiethnic variety of German from an educational perspective', *JoLIE*, 2(1), 91–113.

Prokutina, E.V. (2009) 'Iazykovaia igra kak sposob obrazovaniia nestandartnoi leksiki russkogo iazyka na baze angliiskikh zaimstvovanii', *Vestnik Cheliabinskogo gosudarstvennogo universiteta*, 7(188), Vyp. 41, 123–7.

Ramírez, C.S. (2006) 'Saying "nothin": pachucas and the languages of resistance', *Frontiers: A Journal of Women Studies*. muse.jhu.edu/journals/frontiers/v027/27.3ramirez.html, accessed August 2012.

Reyes, A. (2005) 'Appropriation of African American slang by Asian American youth', *Journal of Sociolinguistics*, 9(4), 509–32.

Ryazanova-Clarke L. and Wade, T. (1999) *The Russian Language Today*, London: Routledge.

Salillas, R. (1896) *El Delincuente español – El Lenguaje (studio filológico, psicológico y sociológico) con dos vocabularios jergales*, Read Books. 2011 reprint.

Salmons, J. (1991) 'Youth language in the German Democratic Republic: its diversity and distinctiveness', *American Journal of German Linguistics and Literature*, 3, 1–30.

Samper, D. A. (2002) *Talking Sheng: the role of a hybrid language in the construction of identity and youth culture in Nairobi, Kenya* (Dissertation). University of Pennsylvania.

Samper, D.A. (2004) '"Africa is still our mama": Kenyan rappers, youth identity, and the revitalization of traditional values', *African Identities*, 2(1), 37–51.

Schmidt, H. and Teubener, K. (2006) '"Our Runet"? Cultural identity and media usage', in H. Schmidt, K. Teubener and N. Konradova (eds.) *Control + Shift. Public and Private Usages of the Russian Internet*, Norderstedt, Germany: Books on Demand. 14–20.

Shlyakhov V. and Adler, E. (2006) *Dictionary of Russian Slang and Colloquial Expressions*, New York: Barron's.

Slone, T.H. (2003) *Prokem. An analysis of a Jakartan slang*, Oakland: Masalai Press.

Smirnov, I.T. (1902) 'Melkie torgovtsy g. Kashina Tverskoi gub. i ikh uslovnyi iazyk', *Izvestiia otdeleniia ruskogo iazyka i slovesnosti*, III(VII), 89–114.

Smith-Hefner, N.J. (2007) 'Youth language, *Gaul* sociability, and the new Indonesian middle class', *Journal of Linguistic Anthropology*, *17*(2), 184–203.
Sornig, K. (1981) *Lexical Innovation: A Study of Slang, Colloquialisms and Casual Speech*, Amsterdam: John Benjamins.
Sourdot, M. (1997) 'La dynamique du français des jeunes: sept ans de mouvement à travers deux enquêtes (1987–1994)', *Langue française*, *114*, 56–81.
Stanlaw, J. (2014) 'Some trends in Japanese slang', in J. Coleman (ed.) *Global English Slang*, London: Routledge. 160–170.
Stavsky, L., Mozeson, I.E. and Mozeson, D.R. (1995) *A2Z: The Book of Rap and Hip-Hop Slang*, New York: Boulevard.
Stein-Kanjora, G. (2008) '"Parler comme ça, c'est vachement cool!"', *Sociologus*, *58*(2), 117–41.
Stenström, A. (2014) *Teenage Talk: From General Characteristics to the Use of Pragmatic Markers in a Contrastive Perspective*, Basingstoke, UK: Palgrave MacMillan.
Stenström, A., Andersen, G. and Hasund, I.K. (2002) *Trends in Teenage Talk: Corpus Compilation, Analysis and Findings*, Amsterdam/Philadelphia: John Benjamins Publishing Company.
Strutz, H. (2009) *Dictionary of French Slang and Colloquial Expressions*, New York: Barron's.
Tikhanov, P.N. (1895) *Brianskie startsy: tainyi iazyk nishchikh. Etnologicheskii ocherk*, Briansk.
Tonkov, V. (1930) *Opyt issledovaniia vorovskogo iazyka*, Kazan': TATPOLIGRAF.
Vakunta, P.W. (2008) 'On translating Camfranglais and other Camerounismes', *Meta Translators' Journal*, *53*(4), 942–47.
Vakunta, P.W. (2011) 'Ivorian Nouchi, cousin to Cameroonian Camfranglais'. www.postnewslive.com/2011, accessed September 2012.
Vázquez Ríos, J. (2009) 'Linguistique et sociolinguistique du verlan à travers le monde', *AnMal Electronica*, *26*, 197–214.
Veit-Wild, F. (2009) '"Zimbolicious" – the creative potential of linguistic innovation: the case of Shona-English in Zimbabwe', *Journal of Southern African Studies*, *35*(3), 683–97.
Veraldi-Pasquale, G. (2011) *Vocabulario de caló-español*, Madrid: Bubok Publishing S.L.
Verdelhan-Bourgade, M. (1991) 'Procédés sémantiques et lexicaux en francais branché', *Langue française*, *90*(1), 65–79.
Vierke, C. (2015) 'Some remarks on poetic aspects of Sheng', in N. Nassenstein and A. Hollington (eds.) *Youth Language Practices in Africa and Beyond*, Berlin/Boston: Walter de Gruyter, Inc. 227–56.
von Timroth, W. (1986) *Russian and Soviet Sociolinguistics and Taboo Varieties of the Russian Language*, Munich: Verlag Otto Sagner.
Wiese, H. (2009) 'Grammatical innovation in multi-ethnic urban Europe: New linguistic practices among adolescents', *Lingua*, *119*, 782–806.
Wise, H. (1997) *The Vocabulary of Modern French*, London: Routledge.
Wolfer, C. (2011) 'Arabic secret languages', *Folia Orientalia*, *47*, Part II.
Zaikovskaia, T.V. (1993) 'Mozhno mozzhechoknut'sia? Sabo samoi!', *Russkaia rech'*, *6*, 40–3.
Zhirmunskii, V. (1936) *Natsional'nyi iazyk i sotsial'nye dialekty*, Leningrad: Khudozhestvennaia literatura.
Zvereva, V. (undated) 'Comments on Ru.net news: speech formulas and cultural meanings'. www.uib.no/filearchive/zvereva2.pdf, accessed July 2012.

2 Non-standard language – concepts and perspectives

Introduction

Before exploring some of the reasons why speakers choose to undertake linguistic practices as part of youth or criminal activity and how such usage is often perceived by others, in this chapter we provide an introduction to some of the theoretical perspectives that are advanced as explanatory constructs. We focus on those perspectives to which particular attention has been paid in studies over recent years. These are:

- antilanguage;
- resistance and resistance identities;
- style (stylistic practice) as an explanation of linguistic variation;
- repertoires.

Additionally, given the pervasive references in current and past literature to the use of such language practices in terms of the negotiation and expression of identity, we additionally consider some perspectives on identity and identification.

Antilanguage

Introduced as a concept by M.A.K. Halliday in 1976, the antilanguage is a language variety used by antisocieties – collectives set up within another society as a "conscious alternative" and "mode of resistance" to the social mainstream (Halliday 1978: 164). Antisocieties create antilanguage to reflect the social, ideological or other phenomena that are problematic or especially salient to them. Antilanguage not only serves as a way of expressing an alternative subjective reality, but of "actively creating and maintaining it" (Halliday 1978: 172), where "the process is one not of construction, but of reconstruction" (Halliday 1978: 170). In this sense, Halliday (1978: 168) sees an antilanguage as "no different from a language 'proper': both are reality-generating systems".

The antilanguage is built on the basis of "same grammar, different vocabulary" (Halliday 1978: 165), on the principle of new words for old – although not all words in the standard lexicon need have antilanguage equivalents. A variety of mechanisms may be used to create new vocabulary – including metaphor, metathesis, lexical borrowing, compounding and suffixation. Not unsurprisingly, the vocabulary of an antilanguage tends to focus on particular subject areas: typically, those that are especially important or pertinent to the antisociety and most reflect and relate to its distance from, and tension with, the established social mainstream. For this reason, vocabularies may contain a multitude of words and expressions for particular concepts or phenomena (such as the police, weapons, etc.). Indeed, in this connection Halliday notes that an antilanguage "is not merely *re*lexicalized in these areas; it is *over*lexicalized" (Halliday 1978: 165; his italics); and it is partly through this overlexicalisation that the antilanguage can become opaque to outsiders while helping to consolidate social solidarity among users. As examples of this overlexicalisation, Halliday points to the proliferation of synonyms (or near-synonyms) in two of the three varieties he cites in advancing his theory, noting that the language of the underworld of West Bengal had 41 words referring to the police and 21 for bomb, while the cant of criminals – also described as vagabonds – in Elizabethan England contained approximately 20 terms for different types of vagabond (Halliday 1978: 165). The third variety cited by Halliday was the Grypserka of those incarcerated in Polish prisons and reform schools.

The concept of the antilanguage has been frequently cited since its introduction and – either in its entirety or in considerable part – still holds appeal as a theoretical construct for contemporary researchers exploring language practices associated with youth and criminal sub-/countercultures (e.g. Veit-Wild 2009; González and Stenström 2011; Mugaddam 2012a, 2012b, 2015; Dalzell 2014; Hollington 2015). Key points often cited by researchers are the construction of an identity and means of expressing ideology to oppose those of the mainstream. For instance:

- Dalzell (2014: 18–9) regards hip hop culture as indicative of an antisociety whose lexicon, in containing items such as 'sick' and 'bad', suggests an altered, inverted or "upside down" view of the world. For Dalzell, the word that represents hip hop as an antisociety more than any other is 'gangsta' (as in 'gangsta rap') – with its roots in illegal inner-city troubles and conflict, it connotes admiration of violence and crime.
- Mayr (2004: 22), analysing the language of Scottish prisoners, points to resistance taking the shape of "oppositional discourse people set up and use as a conscious alternative to the dominant or established discourse type in the form of an antilanguage".
- Kießling (2004: 16–8) views Camfranglais as a clear example of an antilanguage in that its speakers use a variety of linguistic strategies to mark a distinct identity and opposition to the dominant collective. One way in which this is done is through deliberate distortion of the languages of the mainstream (French and English). Its use also underscores distance between the subgroup and older generations and traditional ways of life.
- In their study of expressive devices in London and Madrid youth language, González and Stenström (2011: 236) observe that "[t]he humour and irony

in youth slang often reflect a kind of rebellion, giving rise to a subversive language, an 'anti-language', as it implies values set against the established society".
- Hollington (2015: 161) sees an association between the use of Yarada K'wank'wa by some youth in Ethiopia and an antisociety identity: the language practices she considers facilitate group identity as well as difference from the dominant group.

Further to this, a number of researchers have set considerable store by overlexicalisation in the practices they encounter. While some agree with Halliday that overlexicalisation is an important feature of the varieties they study, which they explicitly hold to be antilanguages (e.g. Mayr 2004; Vierke 2015; Mugaddam 2015), others either allude or more explicitly point to the relevance of overlexicalisation in the language practices they observe while not necessarily drawing on antilanguage as a theoretical basis (e.g. Einat and Einat 2000, Einat and Wall 2006 on 'intensity'; Githinji 2006 on variant generation; Kouadio N'guessan 2006 on synonyms; Brook 2010 on overlexicalisation in tsotsitaals).[1] Indeed, observations about the productivity of lexis reflecting certain semantic domains preceded Halliday's publication in 1976 – for example, Mallik's study, which was published in 1972. Table 2.1 outlines some of those studies where antilanguage is not posited as an explanatory theoretical framework but where overlexicalisation is nonetheless evident.

From this discussion, it is apparent that some scholars see antilanguage as a viable concept for explaining the social and linguistic behaviours and trends they observe. And it is clear why it has appeal, not least insofar as the tenets proposed regarding resistance, identity and characteristic linguistic features have been seen as resonant in multiple studies (e.g. Einat and Einat 2000; Sherzer 2002; Zarzycki 2015), not to mention the crosscurrents that exist with other perspectives such as resistance identity (discussed later in the chapter). However, it is equally correct to say that the concept of the antilanguage is not universally espoused or, where it is cited, accepted wholly or without caveats.

Some scholars question the degree to which the concept *completely* explains the varieties they study. Although the US college language she analysed shares certain manipulations held to be typical of antilanguages, and although it shows a clear tendency towards overlexicalisation, Eble (1996: 125–7, 137–8) posits that

Table 2.1 Overlexicalisation in selected varieties

Language variety	Standard meaning	Number of items	Source/Year
US college language	drunk	31	Eble (1996)
Colloquial Russian	face	>50	Nikitina (2005)
Israeli prison language	informer	>20	Einat and Wall (2006)
Sheng	fool	52	Githinji (2006)
Tsotsitaals	girlfriend, woman	15	Brook (2010)
UK student language	good, great	>65	Coleman (2014)

the semantic areas reflected in the lexicon do not represent those domains which set students off most distinctly from the mainstream. Instead, they reflect taboos held by the society at large or centre on inter-student relationships. Moreover, although it has a high lexical turnover that might prevent others from knowing what is being communicated, and although it irreverently conveys opposition to social and academic authority, she holds that college student language is "only mildly and occasionally adversarial" (Eble 1996: 129) and not "cautiously secret" in the way that a "full-fledged antilanguage" is normally understood to be (Eble 1996: 127).

A second respect in which the application or full relevance of the antilanguage is questioned concerns resistance and opposition; more specifically, whether this is always a driver behind youth language practice. Examining the use of elements of African American Vernacular English (AAVE) by young Asian Americans, Reyes (2015) points out that such practices do not always serve to index resistance. This point is also made by Kerswill (2010) who, citing language practice involving the Indoubil variety in the Democratic Republic of Congo, indicates its use for discussing everyday topics where confrontation is not an issue – although this may be the result of the variety possibly having moved in the direction of a widely used vernacular and its being replaced by another youth variety in Lingala ya Bayankee.

Another question extends to the polarisation within which understandings of resistance can often be framed. Here too Reyes raises an important question about how antilanguage is typically understood and the degree to which this understanding applies to the practice she observes. She points in particular to the danger of interpreting resistance and opposition in binary society versus antisociety terms – a light in which the concept of antilanguage is often read. As an example, she cites work by Bucholtz in which the latter observes that "despite the dominant view of slang as a form of youthful rebellion against the older generation, the divisions between different groups of teenagers are often far more relevant in teenagers' daily lives than the division between adolescents and adults" (Reyes 2005, citing Bucholtz 2006: 5). This is certainly an important consideration and one that is shared in other analyses: in her study of US youth language practices, Labov (1992: 358–9) observes that "[e]ach subset of youth culture has its own bases for differentiating itself, for being less readily penetrated by other people, including other youth". More recent research on youth language and hip hop in Norway and the US, for example, has also noted that speakers sought to project difference from others, *including non-hip hop youth,* as well as to signal resistance to standard language ideologies and traditional ethnic categories (Cutler and Røyneland 2015; see also Stenström, Andersen and Hasund 2002, and Vierke's 2015 discussion of hip hop and Sheng for more discussion in the same vein).

Of course, this is not to say that youth language practices never involve directed differentiation such as distancing from members of older generations. Indeed, the antisociety and antilanguage presuppose distinction from and opposition to a perceived Other. However, as we will see in the next chapter, there can be many Others from whom youth may wish to establish clear blue water in social and/or ideological terms (see, for example, Hollington and Makwabarara 2015 on youth language in Zimbabwe; and Hollington 2015 on Yarada K'wank'wa in Addis Ababa), and many antagonisms can be in evidence simultaneously. As we see in Cutler and Røyneland's (2015) analysis, motivations for use can be both multiple and varied.

This evidence suggests that care should be taken to avoid seeing resistance or certain types of resistance as givens, not to mention the kinds of binary social distinctions to which some may feel Halliday's theory points. It is possible that there could be a number of antisocieties that demonstrate resistance to the dominant mainstream as well as resistance to or distinctiveness from one another (Drury 2005; Bucholtz 2006) and who may do so in different ways. Youth are not a single homogeneous social cohort (e.g. Labov 1992; Thurlow 2003a, 2003b, 2005), but instead comprise a variety of different Communities of Practice with distinct identities (for a definition of **Communities of Practice**, see pages 84–5). Mugaddam's 2015 study of the use of Randuk by three distinct communities in Khartoum – university students, mechanics and street boys – serves as a good example of this principle.

A further respect in which the notion of the antilanguage is challenged concerns not necessarily the question of whether the language practice of a given Community of Practice constitutes an antilanguage, either partially or entirely, but whether it corresponds to the concept of antilanguage as Halliday envisaged it. Boellstorff, for example, considers that Bahasa Gay, a variety associated with gay men in Indonesia which can serve as a cryptolect but also acts largely to support ideas of association and community, does not function as an antilanguage in the sense that Halliday proposed it. For Boellstorff (2004: 254–5), the "fundamental logic" of Bahasa Gay is not one of "alterity but of creative transformation of a dominant discourse". Here the dominant discourse – that of the Indonesian state – is recast and reshaped from "within its horizon" (Boellstorff 2004: 255) rather than opposed from another space, while the reality in question is also not an alternative one, but a "queer take on a dominant reality" (Boellstorff 2004: 255). This is an eminently interesting perspective on how antilanguage and those who speak it might be differently understood. The implication is that other understandings of the stances of social actors often seen as atypical of or opposing the mainstream, and how these stances are articulated and interpreted, need to be considered, if Halliday's concept as it was originally expounded is not felt to cover the theoretical bases. And, in parallel, it poses questions about how the social and ideological spaces within and from which such stances are taken and articulated are interpreted, about how we understand difference relative to mainstream discourses and identities.

Finally, and as we will see later in this chapter, it is also noteworthy that youth language practices may involve grammatical innovation, thereby potentially posing a challenge to the traditional concept of the antilanguage as constructed on the basis of "same grammar, different vocabulary". An important point here is captured in the qualification *potentially*. Grammatical innovation has certainly been recorded in a number of studies of youth language practice – for example, developments in the use of grammatical function words in German Kiezdeutsch

(Wiese 2009), as well as comparison of German, Swedish and Norwegian youth practices (Ekberg, Opsahl and Wiese 2015). However, for the most part the rules of the base language in youth and criminal language varieties are generally observed. As further analysis is provided of the grammatical dimensions of varieties such as Kiezdeutsch and others, it will be interesting to chart the degree to which Halliday's tenet remains supported.

Overt and covert prestige

Overt prestige relates to social standing from linguistic behaviour that is widely viewed as indicative of prestigious/socially esteemed groups. Sometimes individuals may be drawn to it by institutional pressures. The linguistic behavioural norms are often set by high-status groups associated with the creation and maintenance of a standard variety (e.g. Trudgill 1983; Lodge 1993 on French).

Covert prestige refers to the positive value that members of a social subgroup attach to the non-standard linguistic norms and behaviours of their community. In this way, the members use or favour linguistic forms that are regarded more widely in society or by social institutions as less prestigious, often to establish solidarity. For example, in his discussion of French, Lodge (1993) indicates that some men might be considered more manly by workmates the less their speech accords with the social norms of the standard variety. Where 'slang' is concerned, Kis (2006: 134) posits that "[o]vert prestige is never attributed to slang because of its stigmatisation but covert prestige is a typical characteristic of slang".

An example of covert prestige from among the varieties we look at in this book is provided by García (2005: 801), who suggests that, in the 1940s and 1950s, Pachuco Caló may have given some young people a way of being part of a socially defiant in-group as well as gaining esteem by appearing to be in tune with the times. As that group then aged, so more Pachuco Caló words and phrases diffused into the broader speech community and became more widely recognised. A second is provided by Thorne (2006), who reported the results of a limited survey conducted in three West London secondary schools to identify a common core youth lexicon. This survey showed that over 80% of the items collated had originated in the speech of the black community, and that "transgressive language" was viewed as "prestigious" (Thorne 2006: 2).

Notably, in some instances questions of prestige may not always be universal or clear-cut: what might be regarded as prestigious in one area may potentially be viewed less favourably, or even seen as stigmatised, in another.

Resistance and resistance identities

In our exploration of Halliday's antilanguage, we saw how ideas of opposition and resistance are often regarded as key drivers for the creation of the antisociety. We noted that antisocieties are created as a "mode of resistance" to the dominant society (Halliday 1978: 164).

A number of scholars link youth language practices with notions of resistance. Discussing poetic aspects of Sheng, Vierke (2015: 231) reports that it is used in hip hop by virtue of its popular association with an identity that is tied to concepts of resistance and opposition where "counter-identity necessitates counter-form". Hurst (2007), in an account of South African tsotsitaals, records the way in which speaker subcultures were initially created in part due to the need for a resistance identity as a response to apartheid. Ferrell (1995) observes how youth in Europe and the US use graffiti to resist authority in legal, political and religious regards, and that hip hop graffiti in particular disrupts this authority and serves to resist the constraints imposed upon youth in social and spatial respects; Mensah (2016: 5) similarly underlines the use of graffiti in urban areas in Africa as "a means of resistant identity, where young people initiate a platform to talk back to the establishment". A similar tension is addressed in terms of "geographies of resistance" by Indonesian street children who use railways to avoid state control (Beazley 1998), and who – in the case of girls – visit numerous places to contest limitations on single female mobility and frame a distinctive culture through their attachment to a particular urban location. This fosters a positive identity for them as street girls, provides a sense of security and belonging, enables them to survive the rigours of street life and facilitates a freedom to act as they wish in their own space (Beazley 2002). Finally, Miller (2003, 2004) charts how Japanese girls and young women, through highly unconventional communicative styles, emphatically construct and project identities that convey their opposition and resistance to the expected model of a conservative, docile and compliant young woman. Resistance can thus be found in a number of different youth practices.

Antilanguage aside, the theoretical construct that is perhaps most applied to explain resistance in accounts of youth language practices, as well as those of other social subgroups and countercultures, is that of Castells (2010 [2007]). Castells sees the construction of social identity as occurring within frameworks of power and subdivides the notion of identity into three types:

- Legitimising identity: this is introduced by dominant institutions in a society to both enhance and rationalise their dominance.
- Resistance identity: this type of identity is created by those who occupy social positions with low social value or are stigmatised. Those who create a resistance identity therefore construct "trenches of resistance and survival on the basis of principles different from, or opposed to, those permeating the institutions of society" (Castells 2010: 8).
- Project identity: this is where social agents construct a new identity that redefines the position they occupy within the social fabric and, by dint of these actions, look to alter the social structure overall (Castells 2010: 8).

In considering the different kinds of identity construction, Castells proposes that resistance identity in particular may be the most socially important insofar as it generates collective resistance to "otherwise unbearable oppression" (Castells 2010: 9).

As we might imagine, and indeed as we can see in Hurst's thoughts earlier in the chapter, we need not go far to see youth, criminal and other countercultural practices described in terms of resistance identity. Hagedorn (2005), for example, suggests that the failings of modern state institutions and uncertainty over a better future have, in some cases, served to consolidate resistance identity in gangs that have formed in opposition to dominant cultures. Furthermore, he proposes that the considerable cultural capital enjoyed by hip hop can also be used to foster a resistance identity that draws on concepts of African American rebellion to white authority among youth, an identity that can be complex given the various scenarios of adoption and social actors involved (Hagedorn 2005). In his discussion of Camfranglais, Vakunta (2008: 942) indicates that it too serves urban youth speakers as "an icon of 'resistance identity'", one which is used in "an effort to mark off their identity as a new social group – the modern Cameroonian urban youth – in opposition to other groups such as the older generation, the rural population and the elite". Indeed, Vakunta not only theoretically explains the use of Camfranglais in terms of resistance identity, but also posits that the various linguistic manipulations used to create Camfranglais vocabulary "reflect the provocative attitude of its speakers and their jocular disrespect of linguistic norms and purity, clearly revealing its function as an *anti-language*" (Vakunta 2008: 943; my italics). Finally, Beyer (2015: 32–3) notes that "the beginnings of specific youth ways of speaking are usually traced back to marginalized groups, often situated in juvenile male-dominated low income and low-education class milieus where specific ways of speaking become a marker of 'resistance identities'".

Clearly, then, many commentators – although not all (e.g. Coleman 2014) – address questions of identity construction and projection and the language that is correspondingly utilised with particular regard to resistance identity. However, what of the other two types, in particular project identity? These tend not to be cited so widely in the literature, and there may be a number of potential reasons why this is the case. It is possible, for example, that researchers may focus on identities where sociocultural agents have not been able to operate sufficiently, if at all, in mainstream spaces and thus share linguistic and other practices more widely and/or with the requisite degree of broader transformational impact. Equally, given the currency enjoyed by concepts of resistance and opposition as witnessed in part by the continuing application of Halliday's antilanguage, not to mention academic discourse centring on constraint in institutional, life stage (e.g. Amit-Talai 1995; Eckert 2005) or socio-economic terms (e.g. Jensen Arnett 2002), or language ideology and powerlessness (e.g. Sherzer 2002), commentators may feel it more appropriate to explain language practices through a prism of social antagonism. In relative terms, they may find little or no evidence of project identity in their fieldwork, but more indications of the resistance identity practices of marginalised and/or stigmatised communities (see, for example, Beazley 1998, 2002, 2003).

That said, although the focus tends to fall on resistance identity, some scholars have sought to illuminate cases where youth and countercultural language practices have been used for project identities – that is to say, where speakers alter their social position and, in doing so, effect change in the broader social edifice. Kerswill (2010: 12), for example, has proposed that speakers of African youth languages have all progressed to project identities from "symbolising resistance identities". In more specific terms, youth have carved out identities associated with the mainstream through a number of vehicles – notably music, print media and online – and have correspondingly further legitimised their identity and associated practices as the number of speakers has grown (Kerswill 2010: 15). In a similar vein, Kiessling and Mous (2004: 11, citing Castells 1997) also suggest that, where African youth languages are concerned, what begins as a resistance identity can develop into a project identity when youth "use the emblematic nature of their new code to 'build a new identity that redefines their position in society and, by doing so, seek the transformation of overall social structure'". Indeed, the expansion in their use can be such that they grow

> more and more into emblems of a newly emerging project identity. By being adopted by larger portions of the urban population, these sociolects cease to be antilanguages; instead they become established as norms themselves, and might be on their way to becoming new national languages.
> (Kiessling and Mous 2004: 32)

Finally, Beyer (2015) also addresses shifts from resistance to project identities on a broader scale, suggesting that, as markers of resistance identities associated with socially marginal (youth) groups are used more widely, acquire social prestige and become seen as indexical of an urban way of life, so they become indicative of project identities.

These observations reflect and indeed invite key questions regarding the expansion of youth language practices to the point where they become commonly used or vernacularised within society more broadly (as we see with Sheng, Nouchi and Camfranglais, for example) and what impact this has on identity. In particular, what happens once the project identity stage has been reached and the stigma generally lost? Do those with the project identity seek to create new resistance identities, as Kerswill (2010) asks in his discussion of African varieties? With many youth language varieties being viewed as emerging or *de facto* vernaculars in Africa and elsewhere, and in view of the rising use of global means of communication, increasing urbanisation and the significant numbers of youth constituting major percentages of (particularly) urban populations, the scene may be set to appreciate further the conditions under which language practices mark out a maintained project identity, or alternatively, project identities are replaced with resistance identities by particular groups.

From the discussion of both antilanguage and resistance identities, we can see that many researchers frame their explanations of youth and countercultural language practices in terms of resistance and opposition. And, indeed, in many cases the connections may be clear or difficult to dispute. We can readily appreciate why Mayr's prisoners may use language to underscore their resistance to mainstream norms of communication and the people, institutions and values associated with them, or how they might interrupt, express counterpoints and refuse to answer to actively resist positions adopted by *the man* and/or to signal non-acceptance of his authority (Mayr 2004). Moreover, it is not difficult to envision the ways in which hip hop taggers might resist constraints imposed upon them by authorities through their graffiti (Ferrell 1995), or the ways in which language practices linked with US and Norwegian hip hop enable the expression of resistance to standard language ideologies as well as social pressure to adopt standard practices (Cutler and Røyneland 2015). Such kinds of alternative practices may well be in evidence, and Castells' concepts of resistance and project identity may provide entirely satisfactory explanation for understanding these practices. However, whether we apply the perspective of Castells or others, the extent to and ways in which concepts of resistance satisfactorily explain *all* youth and sub- or countercultural practices may be more nuanced than appears at first glance.

There are, for instance, considerations that concern resistance and social class. In certain societies, notions of resistance may enjoy particular associations with certain cultural styles linked to specific social classes, and many youth may well create their identities against this social backdrop (Bucholtz 2006). However, it is by no means certain that youth identities will remain tied to those class-based styles; indeed – for whatever reason – they may become further distanced from them. Thus, it is possible that the notion of resistance may become less relevant as a means of explaining youth identity (Bucholtz 2006). This consideration is broadly consistent with that of Drury (2005), who points to elucidation of adolescent subculture in terms of "powerful forces of resistance and counterhegemony" having become less firmly espoused in psychology and sociology in the last 15 or 20 years of the twentieth century, perhaps as a result of the "relative weakness of working class resistance more generally" (Drury 2005: 235) – although Drury's observations were not intended to reflect the working class and resistance on a global scale.

A second consideration concerns the framing of resistance, where care must be taken not to see resistance in political terms alone. In point of fact, resistance can have cultural and aesthetic as well as political drivers (although the act itself may be political). Hagedorn (2005), for instance, reports that gangs proliferate in what is mainly an urban world by virtue of a combination of economic and political marginalisation. However, he also draws attention to the importance of their cultural resistance. Furthermore, while some earlier subcultures may have been openly and directly linked to economic or political stances, it may now be the case that certain cultural practices are dominated more by aesthetics – especially where those cultural styles are linked to the middle class (Bucholtz 2006). Opposition need not therefore be predicated on traditional ideas of social, political or economic powerlessness but instead on "a rejection of an undiscerning mainstream culture" (Bucholtz 2006: 541). Of course, that is not to say that youth have left behind the idea of political resistance.

To be sure, where they are evident, resistance identities can be complex, and we cannot assume that social, ideological or other drivers and modes of expression of opposition and resistance will be the same across contexts. Instead, "analysts would do well to be attentive to local meanings of such practices" (Bucholtz 2006: 541). Moreover, and more fundamentally, as intimated previously, analysts may face questions regarding the relevance of resistance as a sole or even relevant driver for youth cultural practice *tout court*. The implication from Drury's observation that sociology and psychology had found less value in explaining youth practice in terms of resistance is that room is left for other explanations. Drury intimates, for example, that peer groups can also be a "source of solidarity and liberating constructions for young people – important issues when considering their interaction with powerful adults" (Drury 2005: 235). Indeed, as we will see in Chapter Three, the proposition that there may be alternative, potentially multiple complex motivations driving language use is important.

Style (stylistic practice) as an explanation of linguistic variation

One perspective that has gained much attention in recent years concerns style and stylistic practice. As Bucholtz and Hall note (2005: 596–7, citing Labov 1972), traditionally in sociolinguistics the term 'style' has related to intraspeaker variation, and it has been seen as "different ways of saying the same thing" (Eckert 2008: 456). Eckert (2003b, 2012), however, has suggested a different conceptualisation of style and linguistic variation where, to understand the meaning of linguistic variation, and thus the construction of social categories and social meaning, we should focus rather on the style and stylistic practices of personae – the ways a person or people contextually mobilise and combine resources such as dress, dance, demeanour or language, for instance. In this sense, and where language is concerned, style constitutes a "repertoire of linguistic forms associated with personas or identities" (Bucholtz and Hall 2005: 596–7) and variables are viewed as "components of styles" (Eckert 2008: 456).

To understand the significance of this reinterpretation of style as an explanatory vehicle for youth and countercultural language practice and variation, it is important to situate it within broader sociolinguistic thinking. Eckert (2012) achieves this by suggesting that sociolinguistic variation studies have proceeded in three waves:

- The first wave began with Labov's ground-breaking work on variation in the 1960s. It involved the use of quantitative methods to identify broad correlations between linguistic variables and demographic brackets such as ethnicity, age, class and gender. Analyses looked at patterns of linguistic variation relative to large urban populations, with variables considered to directly mark membership of, or association with, those demographic categories (Eckert 2003b, 2012).
- The second wave consisted of ethnographic studies of variation where it was understood and defined at a more local level. Particular groups were studied

and linguistic variation assessed in terms of social factors such as class and local identity. This wave brought a focus on social networks as a means of tracing how people within a network interact with one another relative to those outside the community (Eckert 2012). What is more, while identity assumed a more central focus in the second wave than in the first, it was still seen as fixed and stable (Drummond and Schleef 2016).

- The third wave is the one in which Eckert situates her thinking. Here researchers become less occupied with the study of static, macro-level social categories as the key drivers and explications of linguistic variation and instead centre on the moment-by-moment stylistic practices of agentive speakers as they construct social identities and social meaning and contextually situate themselves in the social terrain. The emphasis is thus on the ways in which variables are brought together to construct the kinds of people that constitute social categories, rather than on the way in which variables directly correlate with demographic brackets (Eckert 2012). Whereas the first two waves correlated variables with broad social categories, the third wave is predicated on the principles that:

  o variation can be regarded as a semiotic system that conveys the entire scope of a community's social preoccupations;
  o variation serves not only to reflect social meaning but also to create it; and
  o the meanings of variables become more concrete when used within styles (Eckert 2012).

Instead of reflecting belonging to a set social bracket, variation in language can thus be considered part of a speaker's active contextual construction of social differentiation (Eckert 2012). Individual variables gain more specific meanings through the construction of speech styles; the use of language, as well as its interpretation, is not fixed, but dynamic and locally negotiated by speakers who act

> not as passive and stable carriers of dialect, but as stylistic agents, tailoring linguistic styles in ongoing and lifelong projects of self-construction and differentiation. It has become clear that patterns of variation do not simply unfold from the speaker's structural position in a system of production, but are part of the active – stylistic – production of social differentiation.
> (Eckert 2012: 97–8)

In advancing her case for looking at linguistic practice and social meaning through the prism of the third wave, Eckert acknowledges that it represents a notable departure from previous approaches to the study of language variation (Eckert 2003b). However, she suggests that, if anything, the third wave is an extension and not a replacement of those previous approaches (Eckert 2003b). She recognises, for instance, that larger survey-based approaches have merit for studying variables in the greater static social terrain (even though macrosociological patterns are "only a distant reflection of what is happening moment to moment on the ground" (Eckert 2008: 472)), and that second wave studies brought a more local dimension to the analysis of variation than during the first. However, these still leave a need for enquiry where speakers and their identities are not seen in static terms, and where "speakers make socio-semiotic moves, reinterpreting variables and combining and recombining them in a continual process of bricolage" (Eckert 2012: 94). Complementarity between approaches is also possible: to understand the broad demographic patterns, researchers need to investigate how everyday local meaning relates to what is observed at the macro level (Eckert 2003b).

Analysing language variation in light of Eckert's third wave has a number of merits. For one thing, style is viewed as a *practice*, the dynamic "activity in which people create social meaning" (Eckert 2003b: 43). This brings a focus on how resources such as linguistic variables, but also other semiotic markers such as clothing, hair style, music, tattoos, substance use, etc. that jointly contribute to the building and expression of new social meanings, are actively combined by social actors as a form of *bricolage* (Eckert 2003b; Eckert 2008; Drummond and Schleef 2016). Linguistic variables are not seen in isolation from other types but rather form part of a complex semiotic collage composed by social agents who, through their practices, are correspondingly understood as people who are typical of or who comprise social categories within an interpreted social universe (Eckert 2003b, 2012).

A further merit concerns the way in which the third wave accommodates the interpretation of variables, insofar as they are incorporated into a style, as not having a fixed or static meaning. Rather, they take on meaning as the style is being constructed. Indeed, the components that make up styles acquire meanings as they are used across styles – both in terms of the new combinations in which they come to feature, and in terms of the ways in which they may be modified (Eckert 2012). A good example of this lack of fixedness to create social meaning can be seen in the appropriation or re-appropriation of language practices for youth identity construction, where language forms may be fluidly adopted and adapted across social groups and woven into personal or group styles and their stylistic practice (Bucholtz 2004). Bucholtz (1999, cited in Eckert 2012: 94), for example, points to ways in which speakers may draw on others' social dialects as important sources to feed stylistic performance, such as the use of elements of AAVE by white American youth to align with the positively evaluated status that can come with African American and hip hop identity.

A no less important benefit of the third wave involves the way in which it enables a more fine-grained examination of variation and social meaning in ways that direct quantitative approaches cannot. Eckert (2008: 455) holds that insofar as variables may "stratify regularly" with more than one macrosociological category such as ethnicity and class, their meanings cannot be directly related to each of these brackets but to something that has a relation to all of them. Given that this is the case, a new approach is required that provides understandings beyond those provided by quantitative survey-based approaches (Eckert 2008). Eckert sees a solution to this challenge in the shape of indirect indexicality, which was previously applied to language and gender (Ochs 1992). Here, linguistic forms index social categories *indirectly* through pointing to social stances, values or qualities that are in turn associated with the social categories in question. This principle of indirect indexicality rests on the creation and understanding of stereotypes. For example, members of one social group can use the linguistic variables understood to be typical of another group – not to be seen as members of the other group, but to identify with the social values or qualities which the second group is said to possess (Eckert 2003b). This type of analytical approach has important implications for the way in which style and variation are understood. In taking us away from the quantitative approach and in taking us more toward questions of direct and indirect indexicality, the third wave provides greater scope for understanding how linguistic variables may be used in more discrete ways to create social meaning in context.

One qualification is, however, worth noting: far from suggesting otherwise, Eckert notes there was a recognition during the first wave that linguistic variables could in effect be used to index particular types of identity and explore social meaning, but in general terms researchers opted not to pursue this line of enquiry at the time (Eckert 2012; see also Drummond and Schleef 2016 on identity and the three waves).

A final merit of the third wave approach relates to the various forms that stylistic activity can take. Stylistic activity can be manifested in a number of ways, ranging from automatic accommodation to the styles and practices of others to engineered or concocted performances (for a definition of **Communication Accommodation Theory [CAT]**, see pages 222–3). The third wave approach to stylistic activity provides latitude for understanding the many ways in which linguistic variables may be used, catering for practices such as the unconscious expression of social solidarity between interlocutors on the one hand and conscious performance, e.g. mimicking the characteristics (accent, etc.) of another person, on the other.

The third wave approach suggested by Eckert has recently been embraced by a number of scholars exploring youth language practices. In her analysis of tsotsitaals, Hurst (2015) observes that style and linguistic repertoire (see **Repertoires** later in the chapter) are the main theoretical premises that hold value for understanding youth language practice, while drawing attention to other means such as gesture at the same time. Mugaddam (2015) similarly underlines the merit of the third wave approach insofar as the speakers of the Randuk he investigates use language that reflects their speech style. In his study of Imvugo y'Umuhanda, a youth language variety in Kigali (Rwanda), Nassenstein (2015) additionally points to the way in which Imvugo y'Umuhanda's stylistic variables serve to convey all the social preoccupations of its speakers, for instance, ideas of identity construction, social distinction, resistance, expressing non-conformity and the recasting of social hierarchy, and to how relevant variables acquire social meaning through stylistic practice. Finally, Namyalo's (2015) study of Luyaaye, a youth language practice chiefly encountered in Kampala, Uganda, is also situated within the third wave approach, emphasising the agency of speakers as they negotiate constant processes of identity construction and differentiation.

That such studies cite the third wave practice approach as a means of conceptualising youth language is not surprising; indeed, Rampton (2015: 24–5) notes that it is currently superseding the variety-based approach used in studies which examine usage relative to a standard or regional variety, an approach which "by formal description of speech argued that certain contact-induced linguistic traits are characteristic of historically more recent 'varieties' or 'lects', be it a 'dialect' or a 'sociolect' ..., a 'multiethnolect' ... or an 'ethnolect'" (Svendsen 2015: 6–7). However, as Rampton (2015) equally importantly observes, there is no absolute division between the variety and practice approaches insofar as important variety-based analyses have incorporated practice thinking into assessment of quantitative patterns. As more studies are conducted into youth language, it remains to be seen how the practice-based approach might be further integrated with quantitative data on the use of linguistic forms by social actors, as well as how well it can be applied to thus far under- or unstudied language practices.

Repertoires

In recent years an approach to analysing language practices has emerged that focuses on usage as indicative of the differing repertoires of individual social agents, rather than as reflective of forms associated with set speech communities (see pages 84–5 for a definition of **Speech community**). In past sociolinguistic thinking, repertoires were seen as collections of communicative resources that were shared among, linked with, and characteristic of particular speech communities, which in turn were often treated as stable sociolinguistic entities with relatively fixed and similar memberships (for overviews, see Blommaert and Backus 2011; Blommaert and Rampton 2011; Busch 2012; Bristowe, Oostendorp and Anthonissen 2014). However, the utility of seeing repertoires in this way has been challenged by the onset of greater sociolinguistic and sociocultural diversity, fluidity and complexity.

The importance of looking at language in terms of individual repertoires has arisen in great part as a result of a sociolinguistic diversity that has become so pronounced as to be latterly regarded as *super-diversity*. This term was introduced by Vertovec (2007) to reflect the tremendous variability, in quantitative and qualitative terms, that has come with two particular social developments: the marked rise of migration from the early 1990s onwards, when ever-greater numbers of migrants with increasingly diverse socio-economic, cultural, linguistic, legal and other profiles flowed from many more countries and through more migration channels than previously; and the advent of the Internet and mobile communications (Vertovec 2007; Blommaert and Backus 2011; Arnaut and Spotti 2014; although notably some highly multilingual parts of Africa, for example, were super-diverse before the early 1990s). Both factors have significantly affected how we might identify, relate to and/or socialise with others, and how we conceptualise the self and Other (Blommaert and Backus 2011; Parkin and Arnaut 2012). They have also influenced the ability of people to occupy social roles transnationally – some émigrés, for example, have been able to act as agents in their new places of settlement while reaching back to and remotely participating in the affairs of their society of origin and/or diasporas (Vertovec 2007; Blommaert and Rampton 2011).

Factors such as globalisation, migration and the digital age have had very real impacts on how youth use language – although it is noteworthy that globalisation and the benefits of the computer age are not evenly distributed. In Europe, for example, great numbers of people have migrated to large urban areas and have participated in multiple social networks. In so doing they have altered the ethnic, sociocultural and sociolinguistic environment. In countries such as Sweden, Norway and Germany, large numbers of speakers of contemporary urban vernaculars have now grown up with two or more languages, notionally bringing greater scope for linguistic flexibility among local groups. With rising migration and mobility have come opportunities for youth from different ethnic backgrounds to seek out, embrace or become exposed to sociocultural knowledge and multiple practices beyond those traditionally associated with their own heritage (Boyd, Hoffman and Walker 2015). In the Netherlands, for instance, urban youth speech styles have emerged where lexis from languages such as Sranan (a creole based on English and widely spoken in Suriname) becomes utilised while Dutch serves as the base language. At the same time, great store is particularly set by use of elements of languages such as Moroccan: a Moroccan accent and lexis are prized by speakers of other languages who want to identify or associate with those of Moroccan provenance (Dorleijn, Mous and Nortier 2015). Indeed, both Moroccans and their language are held to have "very strong covert prestige" in the Netherlands (Dorleijn, Mous and Nortier 2015: 275; for more on **Overt and covert prestige**, see page 73).

The impact of migration and convergence on the sociolinguistic environment is evident in other parts of the world also: population movement has led to convergence and the creation of new youth language varieties and forms in spaces such as Khartoum (Manfredi 2008; Mugaddam 2012b), Abidjan (Lafage 1998; Kouadio N'guessan 2006), Nairobi (Bosire 2009; Karanja 2010) in Africa, and Jakarta in Indonesia (Smith-Hefner 2007), to name just a few.

In such diverse urban, multilingual settings, the circumstances thus exist for speakers with different backgrounds and languages to come into contact, borrow and/or share linguistic practices, and to define and/or (re)cast new identities. What is more, given the multiple linguistic and sociolinguistic results that can notionally ensue, this diversity can unfold and contribute to social meaning-making in different ways. In some cases, as we saw with Moroccan in the Netherlands, particular aspects of a specific language may enjoy particular prestige (Dorleijn, Mous and Nortier 2015), and speakers may try to assume qualities they believe to be associated with a particular group. Speakers may also come into contact and share communicative practices that accentuate ties to a location or some other commonality (e.g. Cutler and Røyneland 2015 and Harchaoui 2015 on Eastern Oslo; see also Gidley 2007, for example, on attachment to locales). New patterns of linguistic variation and identity construction can thus emerge, not only among migrants or those from migrant families, but also among those from the host community, including monolingual speakers of the dominant language (e.g. Wiese 2009; Cheshire, Nortier and Adger 2015; Freywald, Cornips, Ganuza et al. 2015).

Social dialects, speech communities and Communities of Practice

Social dialects (sociolects) have been defined as language varieties that are distinguished or "used by groups defined according to class, education, occupation, age, sex, and a number of other social parameters" (Yule 1985: 190), and as "differences in speech associated with various social groups or classes" (Wardhaugh 1998: 45–6). They reflect linguistic variation vis-à-vis different social configurations.

Manfredi (2008: 114) describes Randuk as a "cryptic sociolect" as its use masks communication while marking an urban youth identity; Vakunta (2011, online) views Nouchi as a sociolect "created by Ivorian youths to talk about the things that are of interest to them to the exclusion of non-initiates – drugs, sex, scams and so on", where "a sociolect is the language spoken by a social group, social class or subculture"; while Mwihaki (2007: 69, 72), noting claims about Sheng's use by "youth of different backgrounds for their everyday social interaction", considers it a social dialect of Swahili because its speakers "are prominent social categories that differentiate themselves through language use".

A **speech community** is often defined as a group sharing a common language, ways of using language, attitudes to language and social bonds (Montgomery 2008). However, it can be difficult to find cases where all these criteria are met, especially where the focus is on communities in terms of location and/or population: e.g. national-level communities often contain great linguistic diversity, if not division, within them, and rely upon imagined, perhaps even idealised, social and linguistic commonality (Montgomery 2008).[2] In the present book, the term is mostly used with reference to larger collectives (e.g. 'speakers of British English'), but it is recognised that such groups are not monolithic or homogeneous, and that smaller subgroups can also be speech communities.

The feasibility of the speech community as an analytical tool for understanding varieties associated with communities has been questioned. For one thing, speech communities have often been understood in terms of broad categories such as class, race, ethnicity, age and sex; however, these categories might not be stable, and people create identities from membership of many groups at the same time. Further, although the use of linguistic variables can index social groups directly, it mostly does so *indirectly* by *contextually* indexing stances and practices that are *in turn* associated with a group (Podesva, Roberts and Campbell-Kibler 2001; Eckert 2003). Eckert (2002: 4), while also stating that linguistic variation "does not simply reflect, but also constructs, social categories and social meaning", observes that "[t]he meaning of variables is located not in the categories of people who employ them, but in the performance of identities that populate categories. This performance is a stylistic enterprise that employs linguistic variables as resources for constructing styles that come to be associated with individual or group personae".

A concept more recently applied in sociolinguistics is the **Community of Practice** (COP). This is a group of people who, through joint engagement, develop ways of doing things, shared norms, values, beliefs, identities and ways of speaking (practices) (Eckert 2006, after Lave and Wenger's 1991 work on learning theories). People can take part in several COPs at the same time and base their identity on what they draw experientially from those various memberships. Each time members identify themselves "as a group with respect to the world around them" (Eckert 2006: 1), and both interpret their own local practice and other COPs and situate themselves as a group within the wider social universe. They also develop and deploy a style (including linguistic) that encompasses how they see the world and as a means of articulating their identity. Because people develop identities in this way on a fluid, ongoing basis, identity is not seen as fixed (Eckert 2006). At the same time, the concept avoids identifying groups through abstract categories such as age, class or race, or collocation, but accentuates COPs as sites of social engagement (Eckert 2006).

A number of scholars view the language practices of youth through the repertoire lens. Hollington and Nassenstein (2015), for instance, believe that the repertoire approach aids analysis of African youth language practices that stem from a variety of linguistic and non-linguistic sources and are constantly prone to alteration, in view of both flux among Communities of Practice and an ongoing need for secrecy. The multiplicity of linguistic resources that Hollington and Nassenstein outline is reflected, for example, by Kioko (2015), who describes a large variety of new codes which bring mobility and fluidity to the creation and use of Sheng in urban, peri-urban and rural settings. Kioko contends, for instance, that rural Sheng has a number of registers and that rural varieties can include Swahili or English loans, while a different (mother) tongue can serve as the base language. At the same time, urban speakers in Nairobi might also use elements of regional varieties, loans from English and other European languages, hip hop terminology, and different neologisms, among other things. All of these linguistic elements correspondingly feed the repertoires of several discrete Communities of Practice. Additionally, in their treatment of language and youth identity in a multilingual context in Johannesburg, Bristowe, Oostendorp and Anthonissen (2014: 229) are clear that, despite what they see as its relatively rare use as an analytical instrument in South African research, "the notion of 'repertoire', rather than that of 'language', is a useful tool for analysing how a group of adolescents use their linguistic resources to construct multiple identities in diverse environments". Indeed, they posit that repertoire is a "more productive" method for understanding the manner in which questions of identity are entwined with issues such as multilingualism (Bristowe, Oostendorp and Anthonissen: 229, 242).

When examining the repertoire approach in analyses of youth or criminal usage, a number of considerations are particularly noteworthy.

The first concerns the way in which the concept of repertoire affects how we understand linguistic knowledge, or *competence*. Given exposure to more diverse opportunities for language contact and social agency through conditions of super-diversity, researchers such as Blommaert and Backus (2011) argue that there needs to be a new way of accounting for people's linguistic knowledge. They posit that we can learn or acquire linguistic knowledge in many ways, and to greater or lesser degrees, and we can unlearn what we learn. We can acquire linguistic knowledge deeply as native speakers, often through significant socialisation; we can learn it less extensively but still to a high level through formal instruction; equally, we can learn elements of a language to a much lesser or even minimal extent such as with phrases for holidays; we can learn to recognise foreign language terminology used in pastimes and interests, and so on. Equally, we may use language at particular life stages, as is often thought to happen with youth language practices (Blommaert and Backus 2011, but see also Stein-Kanjora 2008; Rampton 2015). Whether learned formally or informally, and in whatever measure, the picture of our linguistic competence as a dynamically changing "set of resources" (Blommaert and Backus 2011: 8) challenges more conventional representations of language as a unitary, discretely bounded entity harnessed by speakers (Blommaert and Backus 2011; Busch 2012; Arnaut and Spotti 2014). Rather, a more representative approach is required that focuses on real-life usage through emergent practice – in effect, through the repertoires that speakers develop through ongoing multifaceted/multi-layered life experience.

With the repertoire approach, analytical emphasis therefore falls on how a person uses this combined linguistic repertoire, one which is reflective of fluid and dynamic real-life learning experiences as the product of an individual's own life path or biography. Given that super-diversity brings together a multitude of social actors as well as considerable movement "of people, language resources, social arenas, technologies of learning and learning environments" (Blommaert and Backus 2011: 22), a focus on repertoires provides a conceptual scaffold for analysing language in conditions where mobility, fluidity and complexity are very much in evidence among different social configurations – for example the urban multiethnolectal repertoires of immigrant youth and those of non-migrant descent in Europe (for further discussion of multiethnolects, see, for example, Wiese 2009; Dorleijn and Nortier 2013; Cheshire, Nortier and Adger 2015; Cutler and Røyneland 2015).

A focus on repertoires as the products of complex linguistic life stories also invites discussion of how we understand the use of linguistic resources vis-à-vis notions of performance and identity, and social currency. We have previously noted a challenge to the notion of repertoires as characteristic of set speech communities, and that scholars studying youth language practices have shed light on the ways in which youth actors draw from a variety of sociocultural and linguistic wells to develop their repertoires, often in complex multilingual settings (see also Hollington 2015 on Yarada K'wank'wa in Ethiopia, and Hurst 2015 on different tsotsitaals and repertoires in South Africa). In Chapter Four, we will see many examples where a speaker or group's lexicon is supplemented through borrowing a word or phrase from another language, or through the creation of hybrid forms where affixes and lexical items from different languages are conjoined (which might also involve items with different orthographies); or expressed through non-transliteration or the articulation of set expressions with particular subcultural salience or value (e.g. 'X is in the house'). The push to reconsider what constitutes linguistic competence as outlined previously reminds us that mastery of a foreign or another language is not a pre-requisite for effectively, even artfully, employing items of foreign provenance (Blommaert 2013; see also Cheshire, Nortier and Adger 2015). Further, if we assume that there will be more individual difference in communities with more pronounced diversity than in homogeneous collectives (Blommaert and Backus 2011); that in super-diverse contexts there will be many ways in which people from different backgrounds create and share new forms of social practice and identities; and that speakers dynamically change social memberships as they progress down their life paths (e.g. Blommaert and Backus 2011; Hollington and Nassenstein 2015), then questions centring on borrowing, code-switching and language crossing – where speech forms typically associated with one group are adopted by others, e.g. across ethnicities (Rampton 2015 [1995]) – may become more important to understanding how we view questions such as how contextually performed youth identities are (re)negotiated or shifting; to how we consider and assess the agency of sociocultural personae; and, more fundamentally and by extension, to what it means to be a credible youth actor.

Following from that is the question of how we account for the repertoires of youth actors as they age, and what studies across life stages might show us. If we accept Bowie's (2010: 65; my italics) observation that "just as adolescents have a wide repertoire of linguistic behaviours from which they can choose depending on their social needs, adults – *including those well beyond adolescence* – also have a range of behaviours to choose from", then it behoves us to consider how we understand those who take elements of language practice normally associated with youth with them on their life journey and what they do with them. In other words, what happens to the repertoires of young social agents who move on to another life stage? Rampton (2015) has already begun to address this question in his study of how such practices extend into middle age, and further questions are sure to arise about how dynamic repertoires in a polycentric environment are understood across different life stages, given moves away from treating linguistic forms as belonging to bounded varieties used in the construction of "stable identities" (Parkin and Arnaut 2012: 4).

Finally, there is the matter of multimodality. Blommaert (2013: 4; his italics) favours a wider view of the repertoire insofar as "[t]he collective resources available to anyone at any point in time are a *repertoire* ... Repertoires include *every* resources [sic] used in communication – linguistic ones, semiotic ones, sociocultural ones". This view accords with the observations of Eckert (2003a), Parkin and Arnaut (2012) and Victor (2014), who underline the preponderance of resources social actors can deploy in meaning-making. In this sense, the concept of resource encompasses not just verbal or written communication, but also other means of social signalling. There is a challenge thus to remain conscious of the different modes of expression and meaning-making that dynamic – in this case youth – actors may employ, such as graffiti in its various forms (e.g. images, messages or slogans), the sharing of musical practice (e.g. choice of instruments, genre, sampling), dance, clothing, the sharing of online gaming experience, blog design, and so on. And there is a challenge to remain conscious of potentially different degrees and methods of mobilisation in the use of such resources within different contexts as identities become altered, emphasised and de-emphasised. Here too there is real potential to study repertoires, communities and identities in a very full way, paying due attention to a number of semiotic dimensions, as well as to how agents themselves understand how and why those repertoires are contextually employed.

Identity and identification

As we saw in our discussion of antilanguage, resistance identity and style, questions of identity are often highlighted by scholars in their analyses of the language practices of youth as well as criminals and other social marginals. In a certain sense, this is to be expected: Tajfel and Turner's seminal exposition of Social Identity Theory (SIT) attests to research into in- and out-group identities before their initial publication in 1979 and update in 1986.

The SIT theoretical model, one developed within social psychological enquiry, is an important one. It sees the self as an accumulation of social identities and focuses both on how an individual's self-perception relates to their group membership(s), and on how such membership provides a sense of social identity and belonging (Tajfel and Turner 1986). It suggests that when we belong to an in-group we may look to enhance its status to improve our own self-esteem – in this way, our sense of self is tied to the fate of the group.

We may also negatively assess relevant out-groups for the same reason. The process on which this identification and evaluation rests has three phases. In general terms, we initially categorise ourselves and others in terms of definable groups; we then assume the identity of the groups to which we consider we belong and act according to the perceived norms of that ensemble. We also invest in this identity emotionally. Finally, we compare our group favourably with out-groups to enhance and keep our self-esteem, which suggests an aspiration "to maintain or achieve superiority over an out-group on some dimensions" (Tajfel and Turner 1986: 17). SIT has since become a theoretical pillar of Communication Accommodation Theory.

Sociological studies have provided conceptualisations of youth where the question of identity has been of considerable importance. Adolescence has, for example, been variously depicted as a time when social identity is constructed and modified through "successive interpersonal encounters and experiences that make up ... ontogenetic history" (Nsamenang 2002: 69, regarding youth identity in Africa); when self-identity may be enhanced through reliance on peer groups (Booth 2002: 221, citing Melikian 1981); or when youth might seek to create an identity through selecting prominent media figures with whom to identify and whom they might emulate (Jensen Arnett 2002: 325, citing Steele and Brown 1995). Furthermore, in their study of adults' perceptions of communication with youth, Garrett and Williams (2005: 40) also affirm that identity development is a "major issue" for adolescents. At the same time, other scholars (not all sociologists) suggest that negotiating identity is not the sole preserve of youth, but instead occurs across different life stages (e.g. Thurlow 2005; Bowie 2010. Androutsopoulos 2007 makes a similar point concerning style).

Equally, researchers have also explored questions of identity among criminal groups. Analyses of prison inmates, for instance, acknowledge the significance of identity to those incarcerated within the prison system, not to mention how important language is in that regard. For example, in an exploration of Israeli prisoners' everyday experiences, norms, values and in-group language, Einat and Wall (2006) suggest that prisoners consolidate a sense of common identity through the use of shared secret language practices; Hensley, Wright, Tewksbury and Castle (2003) address not only how male sexual identities relate to prisoner hierarchies in US corrective facilities, but also to how prisoner designations reinforce those identities (see also Higgs 2014 on hypermasculinity in prisons). Higgs (2014: 8) posits that "[m]astery of prison argot indicates the criminal's status in prison and his commitment to the convict identity". Finally, in his discussion of Polish and American prisoner language practices, Zarzycki (2015) agrees with Einat and Einat (2000) that prisoner language practices enable social identification and group belonging. Given the relative lack of liberty that prisoners experience, not to mention the social and psychological stresses of resocialisation to survive prison (Einat and Einat 2000) – including operating within both official *and* unofficial networks – it is perhaps not surprising that many scholars alight on the question of identity for such cohorts.

In-groups and out-groups

In-groups are collectives with which social actors strongly identify. The opposite of the in-group is the out-group, where the process is correspondingly one of non-identification.

In-groups express identification through a variety of semiotic means, including dress, dance, language and other practices. Language practices in particular play a significant role in the expression of in- and out-group membership, both consciously and unconsciously, by the speaker.

Questions of in- and out-group membership and identity are highly pertinent in the study of youth and criminal language practices. Hollington and Nassenstein (2015: 1; my emphases), for instance, suggest that "[e]ncoding and marking in-group identity of the respective community of practice has been recognized as *the key function* of youth language practices (in Africa); it is a function which plays a role *in all* of the linguistic varieties created by African youths that have been described so far". In parallel, Einat and Livnat (2012: 97) observe that, akin to other subcultures, prisoners employ a particular "linguistic repertoire" to frame and express in-group membership and social status, among other things.

For more on the nexus between language and identification, see **Identity and identification** (this chapter) and **Communication Accommodation Theory (CAT)** on pages 222–3.

Progress within linguistics, and particularly the development of sociolinguistics as a discipline, has also added considerably to the study of identity. Over the last few decades this new field (relatively speaking) has brought studies of language attitudes and variation that have not just recorded linguistic and demographic correlations but, as we saw in our discussion of style earlier, have also asked why and/or how different linguistic forms become associated with certain social cohorts and stances (see, for instance, Agha 1998, 2003). Sociolinguistic and, increasingly, associated linguistic–anthropological studies have also assessed how the language practices of social groups might be perceived by others and indeed used as part of ongoing identity work (e.g. Bucholtz 2004; Reyes 2005), as well as what the social meaning of such practices might be (e.g. Aarsæther, Marzo, Nistov and Ceuleers 2015; Cutler and Røyneland 2015). To be sure, research into language and identity has gained increasing prominence more broadly within linguistics over the last 20–30 years, with scholars such as Joseph (2004: 224) stating unequivocally that:

> identity is itself at the very heart of what language is about, how it operates, why and how it came into existence and evolved as it did, how it is learned and how it is used, every day, by every user, every time it is used.

Such emphasis on the significance of the language and identity nexus is also shared by scholars such as Llamas and Watt. Together with contributors to their 2010 volume *Language and Identities*, these researchers demonstrate the many ways in which language folds into questions of identity (for example, changes in identity over time, variation in African American English, accent imitation), pointing to the paramount importance of this same nexus where they state that "[t]he connection between language and identity is a fundamental element of our experience of being human" (Llamas and Watt 2010: 1). Not all scholars necessarily subscribe to the pervasiveness of identity construction, however. While not underestimating the importance of this combination in stating that "there is much identity work going on in the intersection between linguistic form, language use and the ideologies of language associable by a society at large", Svendsen (2015: 14) arguably take a less committed approach to the ubiquity of identity work in language where she notes that "not every language choice is an identity act".

As actors in local, transnational, inter-generational, multiethnic and other social spaces, youth are often painted as agents negotiating matters of identity through linguistic practices. In their review of identity in variationist sociolinguistics, Drummond and Schleef (2016: 58), for instance, observe that "[a]dolescence is a crucial time in the construction of identity", a concern variously reflected by a number of researchers looking at why youth engage in the language practices they undertake. For example:

- Méla (1997) suggests that while it still allowed speakers to communicate without being understood, Verlan more enabled youth to express their difference and attachment to a French identity at the same time.[3]
- de Klerk (2005) links 'slang' with the articulation of social or linguistic identity by groups at odds with a dominant culture through underscoring the subculture's values and attitudes.
- In their study of youth language practices in Zimbabwe, Hollington and Makwabarara (2015) examine the ways in which the practices are part of identity formation where signalling group identity is a major function.
- Dorleijn, Mous and Nortier (2015) posit that certain urban youth speech styles in the Netherlands entail, *inter alia*, the use of language to indicate group belonging and an urban and hip hop identity.
- Cutler and Røyneland (2015) document how language linked to hip hop is used by young people of immigrant descent in the US and Norway to convey their frustration at non-acceptance by the host society. It gives them a means of expression in a new language while enabling them to maintain a connection with their own identity.

In view of the importance that identity seems to enjoy in questions of youth and countercultural language practice, in this section we investigate some of the perspectives surrounding identity that have not been assessed so far in this chapter. Explorations of identity span a number of disciplines, including psychology, linguistics and anthropology. Correspondingly, we consider some of the individual and multi-disciplinary approaches to identity and discuss their relevance to the language practice of youth and communities such as criminals. Our point of departure lies within questions of social psychology. We then proceed to cross-currents between this discipline and questions of language variation and discuss how they may influence our understanding of youth and countercultural language practices.

Literature in the field of social psychology talks of two types of identity: personal and social. The former is the "individuated self – those characteristics that differentiate one individual from others within a given social context" (Brewer 1991: 476). It refers to individual as opposed to group identity. Social identity, on the other hand, relates to how individuals define themselves based on membership of groups and feelings towards that membership (e.g. Deaux 2001; Feitosa, Salas and Salazar 2012). The categorisation of identity in terms of the personal and the social has attracted great attention in the literature (e.g. Brewer 1991; Deaux 2001). However, this need not mean that the two are separable in terms of identity construction (e.g. Deaux 1993; Joseph 2004).

Social identity does not necessarily equate to membership of a group or social category, which may be voluntary or imposed; instead, social identities are selected (Brewer 1991). As a concept it is regarded as widespread, with some academics pointing to certain conceptualisations of social identity spanning many studies of diverse populations, from geographical and Internet communities to the exploration of gender and race identification (see Obst and White 2005 for an engaging overview).

There are many reasons why social identity is believed to exist. It is thought, for example, that individuals are more attracted to similar others and will seek encounters with them because this provides a certain level of comfort where they can seek positive social outcomes such as self-enhancement, as well as lesser uncertainty about others' feelings and behaviours. Furthermore, similar others may be perceived as more predictable (Feitosa, Salas and Salazar 2012) – although it is important to note that individuals have multiple social identities available to them (e.g. Burke and Stets 2000; Feitosa, Salas and Salazar 2012).

What social identity covers conceptually is not easy or straightforward to define. There is no one universally accepted model for it, although some have gained popularity. In one conception, Deaux (2001) considers cognitive processes, emotional association, and motivational–functional drivers to be important aspects of social identification. Cameron (2004) has also proposed a model for social identification which consists of three dimensions:

- centrality: the prominence of the group in self-conception and thought;
- in-group ties: the perceived connection and belonging that people feel with other members of the group;
- in-group affect: the positivity of feelings that emerge from being a member of the group.

(Cameron 2004, cited in Cameron, Duck, Terry and Lalonde 2005: 77)

A third, and by no means final, definition of social identification is provided by Feitosa, Salas and Salazar (2012), who – while also underscoring the importance of cultural orientation – pinpoint three core dimensions emerging from an extensive body of research:

- categorisation (cognitive): knowledge about one's membership; "the comparisons individuals make cognitively between themselves and either the group as a whole or the ingroup members" (Feitosa, Salas and Salazar 2012: 532);
- sense of belonging (affective): commitment to the in-group and feeling part of it;
- positive attitude (affective): an individual's feelings about being a member of the collective. Belonging is therefore a level of connection between the person and, for example, an organisation (Feitosa, Salas and Salazar 2012: 531–3).

As we can see, the question of identity has attracted much attention within academia. However, the notion of identity is not without its challenges. Two particular loci for discussion concern ideas of fixedness and singularity.

The perceived fixedness of identity as a concept has been questioned on a number of fronts, with greater benefit being perceived through focusing on identification as a constant negotiation and renegotiation of self-view, group membership and interpersonal positioning. In his analysis of language and emotion, Wilce (2009: 198; his emphases), for instance, notes that "[i]n contrast with the fixity implied in the noun **identity**, the choice to write about **identification** indicates a commitment to look at dynamic processes that may never settle into fixed form". Focusing on language and identity in a slightly different vein, Bucholtz and Hall (2010) also hold that identity is not static and does not precede but rather emerges in interaction, observing that "[t]he semiotics of language concerns not identity as a set of fixed categories but identification as an ongoing social and political process" (Bucholtz and Hall 2003: 376). Identity, then, is not a unitary, static property – sensitive to situation, it may change in reaction to circumstances as interlocutors engage one another (Bucholtz and Hall 2003). Insofar as levels of engagement between interactants are not constant but subject to ongoing adjustment, this perspective on the negotiation of identity also aligns with Tannen's (2007) position on conversational engagement (involvement), which she posits is not a given but must be achieved by interlocutors within discourse as it unfolds. This notion of the continual positioning of interlocutors as they converge and diverge with others, moves that undoubtedly involve the negotiation of identity in the moment, also echoes some of the key principles of Communication Accommodation Theory.

The second challenge to the notion of identity concerns the multiplicity of identities that are believed to be presented or negotiated by the individual. Here, people are seen as identifying with separate groups simultaneously (see, for example, Deaux 2001; Feitosa, Salas and Salazar 2012). Writing from a social psychological perspective, Deaux (1993: 102) posits that

> people can claim membership in a variety of groups in describing themselves. Ascribed categories such as gender, race, and ethnicity are forms of identity

that provide a basis for self-definition. So, too, are groups that evolve to provide support or political clout to those who identify with them such as Gray Panthers or associations of family members of people with Alzheimer's disease.

The proposition that individuals have a number of identities is also supported in the linguistic literature. Joseph (2004) has pointed to the various roles we have with regard to those around us as child, friend, parent, colleague, manager, and so on; to how identities can co-exist within us; and to how our identity changes depending on who we are with. Bucholtz and Hall (2003: 375) underscore the complexity of the links between language and identity where they indicate that they are influenced by context and suggest that we can have multiple identities – or at least multiple aspects of our identity – that co-occur on three levels: in terms of macro-level demographic categories; in local, ethnographically specific cultural positions; and in temporary and interactionally specific stances and participant roles (Bucholtz and Hall 2010).

Where youth identity is concerned, a number of scholars researching the expression of identity in youth groups also discuss its complexity and fluidity. Eble (2014) posits that the identities of US college learners as students are deliberately temporary insofar as they will graduate and move on to other social domains; Beazley (2003) indicates that street boys in Yogyakarta, Indonesia, alter or refocus their identities in line with changing environments and circumstances; Drury (2005) draws attention to (young) people having multiple social identities more generically; while Thurlow (2005) underlines the need to consider young people in terms beyond their youth – for example, youth is also intertwined with gender, class, nationality, ethnicity, etc. The substance of Thurlow's call has not gone unnoticed: Rampton (2010), for example, has explored language crossing and class; Cornips and de Rooij (2013) look at how young men in Rotterdam who self-identify as Surinamese negotiate multi-layered identities as they interlink ideas of language, place and race; and Eckert (2005) has pointed to how some middle-class youth adopt the language practices of marginalised and/or disaffected youth from lower classes, but nonetheless maintain their middle-class associations and identity.

In their study of hip hop language in Norway and the US, Cutler and Røyneland (2015: 143) similarly postulate that identity is neither static nor monolithic but "potentially multiple, dynamic, multilayered and negotiable". They cite the example of a Norwegian–Chilean–Peruvian rapper who puts the manifold memberships and affiliations of youth with immigrant backgrounds under the spotlight and counters the proposition that belonging is either "simple or singular" (Cutler and Røyneland 2015: 158). In point of fact, the complexity and variability of identity is becoming an increasingly important question in studies of youth language practice, especially in conditions of super-diversity. The multi-stranded nature of migration into urban areas in Europe, for example, and the various linguistic behaviours to emerge as a result, have brought further to the fore questions of how complex identities are negotiated and conveyed linguistically (see, for example, Cornips and de Rooij 2013; Beyer 2015; Nortier and Svendsen 2015).

From these cursory examples, it is clear, then, that discussion of youth identity, whether defined by social psychologists or the result of sociological or linguistic research, or all three, is far from a simple cut-and-dried, either–or matter. Instead, it requires close attention in a number of respects.

The first relates to the need to understand the use of language for identity work on a local level. The rise of global sociocultural practices such as hip hop, where an American model has given rise to, and been fused with, many local variants, ineluctably brings questions of degrees of identification with the global, and how this identification may be fused with and/or amended by local practices and values. A number of researchers point to the ways in which US models of hip hop, even the idea of a transnational hip hop nation, have not been simply mimicked or imported by various groups in foreign locations, but have been merged with local sociocultural practices in a number of countries to create new variants that enable the expression of local concerns (e.g. Androutsopoulos and Scholz 2002; Samper 2004; Roth-Gordon 2007; Gidley 2007; see also Svendsen 2015). Fox's observation when applied in this case to hip hop – that "the intricate weave of interdependent factors underlying [issues of identity] must be unravelled for each unique community and possibly for each of its individual members" (Fox 2010: 156) – gains particular resonance when considered in this respect.

A second consideration concerns where language practices associated with certain youth groups transcend ethnic boundaries and what this means in social terms. Adopting certain practices enables youth to cross ethnic and linguistic boundaries to share and/or (re)create identity. A good example of this phenomenon can be found in Multiethnic London English (MLE), where the language of some members of the black community is prominent in the usage of non-black youth, thus helping to overcome class, ethnic and/or racial barriers (Green 2014; see also Thorne 2006; Rampton 2010). Another notable example of ethnic boundaries being crossed is Sheng, which has traditionally been depicted as a variety that brings speakers of different ethnicities speaking national and indigenous languages together – it began as a (supra-ethnic) marker of urban as opposed to ethnic identity (Dorleijn, Mous and Nortier 2015). Indeed, the creation of supra-ethnic identities is pronounced in certain African urban settings, aided in some cases by the global appeal and spread of hip hop. In this connection, the fact that certain language practices can form part of contemporary urban usage, where the linguistic practice of speakers in areas with linguistic and/or ethnic diversity might underscore ties to specific locations as opposed to individual ethnicities, represents a highly interesting and relevant strand of research, and not just in Africa – Ekberg, Opsahl and Wiese (2015), for example, profile similar research in Sweden, Norway and Germany.

A third dimension to the exploration of identity and youth language practices concerns affiliation with several groups at the same time – i.e. the second of the challenges we recognised earlier with regard to the notion of identity in a broader sense. The concept of Community of Practice, where people come together to engage in joint endeavours and develop common outlooks, forms of expression and identity, views language as practice in line with Eckert's thoughts on style and also allows for individuals to be members of a number of ensembles at the same time. Through taking part in a number of Communities of Practice and constructing shared social identities, individuals build up their overall sense of identity (Eckert and McConnell-Ginet 1992; see also Burke and Stets 2000 on the composite nature of the self-concept). This plurality makes identity not just multifaceted but implies a moving and complex picture where degrees of identification are consistently revisited and recalibrated (Bucholtz and Hall 2010). Indeed, it invites us to consider the possibility that identification with one group can be activated, emphasised or de-emphasised depending on the situation and – presumably – network (Brewer 1991; Jones and McEwen 2000; Deaux 2001). We certainly see complex and concurrent identification in the youth sphere: Eble (2014) implies that US college students in her sample had a multifaceted identity in that they belonged to many different networks simultaneously, while Coleman (2014) suggests that the UK university students in her study might have amended their speech as they moved from one network to another. The question arises as to what extent identification across groups is maintained at similar levels, and to what degree and how it is re- or de-emphasised as it is negotiated within a given context.

A final point relates again to perspective – not in the sense of whether the accent should fall on multiple ongoing instances of identification with different collectives as opposed to unitary concepts of fixed identities – but in terms of the centring of analytical questions about youth and identification. By this we mean that inasmuch as members of many societies consider youth to be a discrete life stage, there can still be a tendency to relate to it not in terms of what it is in and of itself, or in terms of the commonality of social practices and motivations that youth share with non-youth, but in terms of what youth is not – i.e. not adult in different senses of the term (e.g. Brown and Larson 2002; Jensen Arnett 2002; Nsamenang 2002; Santa Maria 2002; Eckert 2004, 2005). Caputo (1995) and Eckert (2005) cite the example of Western concepts of adolescence where youth tends to be compared with adulthood rather than with childhood; consequently, comparisons can be negative. As we also note in Chapter Three, there is a danger that we address questions of identification and associated activities undertaken by youth from a similarly skewed perspective, relegating their identity work to a lesser form of social practice.

Summary

In this chapter, we profiled some of the theoretical perspectives that have been cited and applied in literature on youth and criminal language practices over the last few years. We addressed them individually; however, we can also discern overlap and common themes.

One such cross-current concerns resistance. This is a central principle in the antilanguage insofar as antisocieties are established within a larger social collective as a "mode of resistance" (Halliday 1978: 164). The antilanguage is created chiefly through overlexicalisation in semantic domains deemed to be a source of tension for the antisociety, and on the basis of "same grammar, different vocabulary" (Halliday 1978: 165). A number of manipulations might be used to create this vocabulary, including metaphor and metathesis. The exemplar groups cited by Halliday were criminals, prisoners and vagabonds as found in India, Poland and Elizabethan England. As a construct, the antilanguage is frequently cited. However, its application in studies of youth language practice is neither wholesale, nor universal, and questions have been posed as to whether it applies wholly, in part or at all to the social groups and language practices scholars observe (e.g. Eble 1996; Boellstorff 2004; Reyes 2005).

Resistance identity also foregrounds the need to create identity and to oppose among those in low or stigmatised social positions – that is to say, among people who set up "trenches of resistance and survival on the basis of principles different from, or opposed to, those permeating the institutions of society" (Castells 2010: 8). While Halliday suggested linguistic features for the antilanguage, resistance identity is not framed in such linguistic terms. Nonetheless, while some scholars observe that the language practices of youth (or, it could be suggested, criminals) cannot always be characterised in terms of resistance (e.g. Mensah 2016), resistance identity is a theoretical anchor which – in its generality – is fairly frequently referenced with regard to marginal social actors in studies of their language practices (e.g. Ferrell 1995; Hurst 2007).

We have also seen that Castells' notion of identity has been applied to certain groups, such as youth groups in Africa (see Kerswill 2010), who move from the resistance identity to the project identity stage, and that it holds some conceptual appeal insofar as some in-group youth language varieties can become so widespread as to become popular vernaculars (e.g. Nouchi, Sheng). In such cases, youth social actors "construct a new identity that redefines the position they occupy within the social fabric and, by dint of these actions, look to alter the social structure overall" (Castells 2010: 8). As certain youth language practices grow within substantially broad communities, so Castells' construct may become more attractive as a means for testing an in-group's perceived identity, not to mention potentially its social, political or other resonance – although, as with antilanguage, attention should be given to the multiplicity and fluidity of social actor identification.

Indeed, a second key theme that emerges from this chapter is that of identity. In the great majority of literature on youth and language practice reviewed for and utilised in this book, questions of identity are cited as an important concern underpinning creation and use (e.g. Danesi 1994; de Klerk 2005; Stenström 2014; Cutler and Røyneland 2015; Hollington and Nassenstein 2015; Mugaddam 2015, to cite but a few). A number of studies of criminal language practices also pay great attention to it as a crucial factor (e.g. Hensley, Wright, Tewksbury and Castle 2003; Einat and Wall 2006; Einat and Livnat 2012; Zarzycki 2015). In many instances the precise definition of identity is taken as something of a given and it is implied that the creation and negotiation of shared identity by speakers as social actors will be commonly understood by writer and reader alike – references to specific models accounting for social identity are rather infrequent, although the work of Tajfel and Turner, for example, is occasionally cited (e.g. Mukhwana 2015). However, although a generic understanding of identity represents a reasonable assumption on the part of researchers, there is merit nonetheless in understanding commonalities and differences regarding the definition of identity both within disciplines (e.g. Cameron's model as compared with the thoughts of Feitosa, Salas and Salazar) and across (e.g. principles of sociolinguistics and social psychology combine in Communication Accommodation Theory). Indeed, investigation of whether the youth or criminal language practices of any given group correspond to any given model of social identity in social psychological research represents a promising area of study.

In the same vein, we have also considered the potential complementarity of multidisciplinary or methodological approaches to the study of youth and criminal language practices. Eckert, for example, suggests a certain complementarity in approaches where she discusses the utility of both large-scale quantitative and more local ethnographic study of language practices. Her concept of style, where the on-the-ground negotiation of social meaning through the stylistic agency of *bricoleurs* who utilise linguistic and non-linguistic means (e.g. hair styles, posture, clothing, etc.) forms a central focus, is one which is frequently cited in current research, and shares some commonality with the concept of repertoires where exploration of linguistic and social identities and practice on the micro level is also important. As Eckert intimates, such locally based research does not preclude the use of larger-scale sociolinguistic enquiry. However, it does provide for a more fine-grained analysis of the local and dynamic use of language as style. Furthermore, it facilitates important work in terms of speaker/actor perspective and (self-)perception – both regarding their use of stylistic variables (e.g. why, how, what) within a given sociolinguistic context, and with respect to their personal and social identities.

Another thread in this chapter – and one explored further in Chapter Three – concerns dichotomisation and polarity. It will be remembered that the antilanguage was predicated on the existence of an antisociety that was created in opposition to a mainstream social structure. Although the concept of resistance against a dominant social configuration may be validated by some practices, we noted that there can be a number of tensions which involve differentiation or antagonism, not just between society and antisociety, but also between what might be understood as different antisocieties. In this respect (and others), binary notions of youth or criminal language practices may be limiting.

Questioning the value of such binary thinking also appears to be valid in other respects. In their example of the Norwegian–Chilean–Peruvian rapper, Cutler and Røyneland (2015: 158) show that identity, for example, is not monolithic but "potentially multiple, dynamic, multilayered and negotiable"; in doing so, they are pointing to a complexity that is becoming increasingly evident and studied in youth language practice, particularly with the advent of super-diversity. This multiplicity is a reality that is captured well in the Communities of Practice model (Eckert and McConnell-Ginet 1992; Eckert 2006), where speakers enjoy a number of affiliations simultaneously and fluidly engage in multiple practices. Speakers may be members of several in-groups at the same time, some of which may even be in a state of tension. As they continue to negotiate their identities as *bricoleurs* and active social agents who construct meaning situationally through stylistic practice, they may draw on complex practices that they encounter in a range of contexts.

Similarly, we have seen in this chapter that questions have been raised about linguistic competence stemming from knowledge of language as discretely demarcated entities. The concept of the repertoire poses questions about bounded perceptions of language. It postulates that we can acquire linguistic knowledge in a number of ways, and to greater or lesser degrees, and that we can unlearn what we learn. As a result, we emerge as speakers with a dynamically evolving "set of resources" (Blommaert and Backus 2011: 8) that challenge more established understandings of language as unitary and delimited (Blommaert and Backus 2011; Busch 2012; Arnaut and Spotti 2014). We thus develop mixed, multifaceted repertoires through emergent practice in our life paths, and apply these in a fluid, dynamic way.

As we have considered the merits and demerits of each of these perspectives, one way or another we have continually raised questions of complexity, and of whether any given perspective adequately allows for the multifacetedness that underpins and sits alongside youth and criminal language practices. The question thus arises as to how best capture, conceptualise and analyse this complexity from a theoretical and a methodological point of view.

Notes

1 Hurst (2015: 169–70) indicates that many languages in South Africa, both official and non-official, have their own tsotsitaal. Furthermore, a tsotsitaal can have different designations, for example Iscamtho. Hurst states that the term can thus be used as a noun rather than the name of a single variety. In this book, the use of upper and lower cases reflects references to Tsotsitaal as a single variety and tsotsitaals as nouns.
2 Interesting discussions of the speech community can also be found in Hudson (1980), Wardhaugh (1998) and Morgan (2004).
3 "C'est beaucoup plus un moyen pour les jeunes d'exprimer à la fois leur différence et leur attachement à une identité française" (my translation).

References

Aarsæther, F., Marzo, S., Nistov, I. and Ceuleers, E. (2015) 'Indexing locality: contemporary urban vernaculars in Belgium and Norway', in J. Nortier and B.A. Svendsen (eds.) *Language, Youth and Identity in the 21st Century*, Cambridge: Cambridge University Press. 249–70.

Agha, A. (1998) 'Stereotypes and registers of honorific language', *Language in Society*, 27, 151–93.

Agha, A. (2003) 'The social life of cultural value', *Language and Communication*, 23, 231–73.

Amit-Talai, V. (1995) 'The waltz of sociability: intimacy, dislocation and friendship in a Quebec high school', in V. Amit-Talai and H. Wulff (eds.) *Youth Cultures: A Cross-Cultural Perspective*, London: Routledge. 144–65.

Androutsopoulos, J. (2007) 'Style online: Doing hip-hop on the German-speaking web', in P. Auer (ed.) *Style and Social Identities: Alternative Approaches to Linguistic Heterogeneity*, Berlin/New York: de Gruyter. 279–317.

Androutsopoulos, J. and Scholz, A. (2002) 'On the recontextualization of hip-hop in European communities: a contrastive analysis of rap lyrics'. www.fu_berlin.de/phon/phin19/p19t1.htm, accessed April 2012.

Arnaut, K. and Spotti, M. (2014) 'Superdiversity discourse', *Working Papers in Urban Language and Literacies*, 122.

Beazley, H. (1998) 'Homeless street children in Yogyakarta, Indonesia', *Development Bulletin*, Australian Development Studies Network, 44, 40–2.

Beazley, H. (2002) '"Vagrants wearing make-up": negotiating spaces on the streets of Yogyakarta, Indonesia', *Urban Studies*, 39(9), 1665–83.

Beazley, H. (2003) 'The construction and protection of individual and collective identities by street children and youth in Indonesia', *Children, Youth and Environments*, 13(1). www.colorado.edu/journals/cye/13_1/Vol13_1Articles/CYE_CurrentIssue_Article_ChildrenYouthIndonesia_Beazley.htm, accessed July 2015.

Beyer, K. (2015) 'Youth language practices in Africa: achievements and challenges', in N. Nassenstein and A. Hollington (eds.) *Youth Language Practices in Africa and Beyond*, Berlin/Boston: Walter de Gruyter, Inc. 23–50.

Blommaert, J. (2013) 'Language and the study of diversity', in *Working Papers in Urban Language and Literacies*, 113.

Blommaert, J. and Backus, A. (2011) 'Repertoires revisited: "knowing language" in superdiversity', in *Working Papers in Urban Language and Literacies*, 67.

Blommaert, J. and Rampton, B. (2011) 'Language and superdiversity', *Diversities*, 13(2), 1–21.

Boellstorff, T. (2004) '*Gay* language and Indonesia: registering belonging', *Journal of Linguistic Anthropology*, 14(2), 248–68.

Booth, M. (2002) 'Arab adolescents facing the future: enduring ideals and pressures to change', in B.B. Brown, R.W. Larson and T.S. Saraswathi (eds.) *The World's Youth*, Cambridge: CUP. 207–42.

Bosire, M. (2009) 'What makes a Sheng word unique? Lexical manipulation in mixed languages', in A. Ojo and L. Moshi (eds.) *Selected Proceedings of the 39th Annual Conference on African Linguistics*, Somerville, MA. 77–85.

Bowie, D. (2010) 'The ageing voice: changing identity over time', in C. Llamas and D. Watt (eds.) *Language and Identities*, Edinburgh: Edinburgh University Press. 55–66.

Boyd, S., Hoffman, M.F. and Walker, J.A. (2015) 'Sociolinguistic variation among multicultural youth: comparing Swedish cities and Toronto', in J. Nortier and B.A. Svendsen (eds.) *Language, Youth and Identity in the 21st Century*, Cambridge: Cambridge University Press. 290–306.

Brown, B.B. and Larson, R.W. (2002) 'The kaleidoscope of adolescence: experiences of the world's youth at the beginning of the 21st century,' in B.B. Brown, R.W. Larson and T.S. Saraswathi (eds.) *The World's Youth*, Cambridge: Cambridge University Press. 1–20.

Brewer, M.B. (1991) 'The social self: on being the same and different at the same time', *Personality and Social Psychology Bulletin*, 17(5), 475–82.

Bristowe, A., Oostendorp, M. and Anthonissen, C. (2014) 'Language and youth identity in a multilingual setting: a multimodal repertoire approach', *South African Linguistics and Applied Language Studies*, 37(2), 229–45.

Brook, K. (2010) 'Interactions of South African languages: case study of Tsotsitaal', paper presented at the *GlobalWordnet Conference*, Mumbai, India. www.cfilt.iitb. ac.in/gwc2010/pdfs/13_challenges_Tsotsitaal_wordnet__Brook.pdf, accessed 20 May 2016.

Bucholtz, M. (1999) 'You da man: narrating the racial other in the production of white masculinity', *Journal of Sociolinguistics*, *3*, 443–60.

Bucholtz, M. (2004) 'Styles and stereotypes: the linguistic negotiation of identity among Laotian American youth', *Pragmatics*, *14*(2/3), 127–47.

Bucholtz, M. (2006) 'Word up: social meanings of slang in Californian youth culture', in J. Goodman and L. Monaghan (eds.) *A Cultural Approach to Interpersonal Communication: Essential Readings*, Malden, MA: Blackwell. cloudfront.escholarship.org/dist/prd/content/qt0c7141bs/qt0c7141bs.pdf;v=lg, accessed November 2016.

Bucholtz, M. and Hall, K. (2003) 'Language and identity', in A. Duranti (ed.) *A Companion to Linguistic Anthropology*, Oxford: Blackwell. 369–94.

Bucholtz, M. and Hall, K. (2005) 'Identity and interaction: a sociocultural linguistic approach', *Discourse Studies*, *7*(4–5), 585–614.

Bucholtz, M. and Hall, K. (2010) 'Locating identity in language', in C. Llamas and D. Watt (eds.) *Language and Identities*, Edinburgh: Edinburgh University Press. 18–28.

Burke, P.J. and Stets, J.E. (2000) 'Identity theory and social identity theory', *Social Psychology Quarterly*, *63*(3), 224–37.

Busch, B. (2012) 'The linguistic repertoire revisited', *Applied Linguistics*, *33*(5), 503–23.

Cameron, J.E. (2004) 'A three-factor model of social identity', *Self and Identity*, *35*(3), 239–62.

Cameron, J.E., Duck, J.M., Terry, D.J. and Lalonde, R.N. (2005) 'Perceptions of self and group in the context of a threatened national identity: a field study', *Group Processes and Intergroup Relations*, *8*(1), 73–88.

Caputo, V. (1995) 'Anthropology's silent "others": a consideration of some conceptual and methodological issues for the study of youth and children's cultures', in V. Amit-Talai and H. Wulff (eds.) *Youth Cultures: A Cross-Cultural Perspective*, London: Routledge. 19–42.

Castells, M. (2010) *The Power of Identity* (2nd ed.), Oxford: Wiley-Blackwell.

Cheshire, J., Nortier, J. and Adger, D. (2015) 'Emerging multiethnolects in Europe', in *Queen Mary's Occasional Papers Advancing Linguistics*, *33*.

Coleman, J. (2014) 'Slang used by students at the University of Leicester', in J. Coleman (ed.) *Global English Slang*, London: Routledge. 49–61.

Cornips, L. and de Rooij, V.A. (2013) 'Selfing and othering through categories of race, place, and language among minority youths in Rotterdam, The Netherlands', in P. Siemund, I. Gogolin, M.E. Schulz and J. Davydova (eds.) *Multilingualism and Language Diversity in Urban Areas: Acquisition, Identities, Space, Education*, Amsterdam/Philadelphia: John Benjamins Publishing Company. 129–64.

Cutler, C. and Røyneland, U. (2015) 'Where the fuck am I from? Hip-hop youth and the (re)negotiation of language and identity in Norway and the US', in J. Nortier and B.A. Svendsen (eds.) *Language, Youth and Identity in the 21st Century*, Cambridge: Cambridge University Press. 139–63.

Dalzell, T. (2014) 'Hip-hop slang', in J. Coleman (ed.) *Global English Slang*, London: Routledge. 15–24.

Danesi, M. (1994) *Cool: The Signs and Meanings of Adolescence*, Toronto: University of Toronto Press.

Deaux, K. (1993) 'Reconstructing social identity', *Personality and Social Psychology Bulletin*, *19*, 102–11.

Deaux, K. (2001) 'Social identity', in J. Worrell (ed.) *Encyclopedia of Women and Gender, Volume Two*, San Diego: Academic Press. pdfs.semanticscholar.org/97b3/929263667b f754777da7a94260ecbad9f625.pdf, accessed May 2016.

de Klerk, V. (2005) 'Slang and swearing as markers of inclusion and exclusion in adolescence', in A. Williams and C. Thurlow (eds.) *Talking Adolescence: Perspectives on Communication in the Teenage Years*, New York: Peter Lang Publishing, Inc. 111–27.

Dorleijn, M., Mous, M. and Nortier, J. (2015) 'Urban youth speech styles in Kenya and the Netherlands', in J. Nortier and B.A. Svendsen (eds.) *Language, Youth and Identity in the 21st Century*, Cambridge: Cambridge University Press. 271–89.

Dorleijn, M. and Nortier, J. (2013) 'Multi-ethnolects: Kebabnorsk, Perkerdansk, Verlan, Kanakensprache, Straattaal, etc.', in P. Bakker and Y. Matras (eds.) *Contact Languages: A Comprehensive Guide*, Berlin: de Gruyter. 229–72.

Drummond, R. and Schleef, E. (2016) 'Identity in variationist sociolinguistics', in S. Preece (ed.) *The Routledge Handbook of Language and Identity*, London: Routledge. 50–65.

Drury, J. (2005) 'Young people's communication with adults in the institutional order', in A. Williams and C. Thurlow (eds.) *Talking Adolescence: Perspectives on Communication in the Teenage Years*, New York: Peter Lang Publishing, Inc. 229–40.

Eble, C. (1996) *Slang and Sociability*, Chapel Hill, NC: University of North Carolina Press.

Eble, C. (2014) 'American college student slang: University of North Carolina (2005–12)', in J. Coleman (ed.) *Global English Slang*, London: Routledge. 36–48.

Eckert, P. (2002) 'Constructing meaning in sociolinguistic variation', paper presented at the Annual Meeting of the American Anthropological Association, New Orleans, November.

Eckert, P. (2003a) 'Language and adolescent peer groups', *Journal of Language and Social Psychology*, 22(1), 112–18.

Eckert, P. (2003b) 'The meaning of style', *Texas Linguistic Forum 47, Proceedings of the Eleventh Annual Symposium about Language and Society*, Austin, April, 41–53.

Eckert, P. (2004) 'Adolescent language', in E. Finegan and J. Rickford (eds.) *Language in the USA*, Cambridge and New York: Cambridge University Press. Pre-publication copy. web.stanford.edu/~eckert/PDF/adolescentlanguage.pdf, accessed February 2013.

Eckert, P. (2005) 'Stylistic practice and the adolescent social order', in A. Williams and C. Thurlow (eds.) *Talking Adolescence: Perspectives on Communication in the Teenage Years*, New York: Peter Lang Publishing, Inc. 93–110.

Eckert, P. (2006) 'Communities of Practice', *Encyclopedia of Language and Linguistics*, Elsevier. Pre-publication copy. pdfs.semanticscholar.org/a4c6/ade3f09be4a074655b543 d02055029099059.pdf, accessed February 2013.

Eckert, P. (2008) 'Variation and the indexical field', *Journal of Sociolinguistics*, 12(4), 453–76.

Eckert, P. (2012) 'Three waves of variation study: the emergence of meaning in the study of sociolinguistic variation', *Annual Review of Anthropology*, 41, 87–100.

Eckert, P. and McConnell-Ginet, S. (1992) 'Communities of Practice: where language, gender, and power all live', in K. Hall, M. Bucholtz, M. and B. Moonwomon (eds.) *Locating Power, Proceedings of the 1992 Berkeley Women and Language Conference*, Berkeley: Berkeley Women and Language Group. 89–99.

Einat, T. and Einat, H. (2000) 'Inmate argot as an expression of prison subculture: the Israeli case', *The Prison Journal*, 80(3), 309–25.

Einat T. and Livnat, Z. (2012) 'Words, values and identities: the Israeli argot (jargon) of prisoners', *International Journal of Political Science, Law and International Relations*, 2(2), 97–118.

Einat, T. and Wall, A. (2006) 'Language, culture, and behavior in prison: the Israeli case', *Asian Criminology*, *1*, 173–89.
Ekberg, L. Opsahl, T. and Wiese, H. (2015) 'Functional gains: a cross-linguistic case study of three particles in Swedish, Norwegian and German', in J. Nortier and B.A. Svendsen (eds.) *Language, Youth and Identity in the 21st Century*, Cambridge: Cambridge University Press. 93–115.
Feitosa, J., Salas, E. and Salazar, M.R. (2012) 'Social identity: clarifying its dimensions across cultures', *Psychological Topics*, *21*(3), 527–48.
Ferrell, J. (1995) 'Urban graffiti: crime, control, and resistance', *Youth and Society*, *27*, 73–92.
Fox, S. (2010) 'Ethnicity, religion and practices: adolescents in the East End of London', in C. Llamas and D. Watt (eds.) *Language and Identities*, Edinburgh: Edinburgh University Press. 144–56.
Freywald, U., Cornips, L., Ganuza, N., Nistov, I. and Opsahl, T. (2015) 'Beyond verb second – a matter of novel information-structural effects? Evidence from Norwegian, Swedish, German and Dutch', in J. Nortier and B.A. Svendsen (eds.) *Language, Youth and Identity in the 21st Century*, Cambridge: Cambridge University Press. 73–92.
García, M. (2005) 'Influences of gypsy *Caló* on contemporary Spanish Slang', *Hispania*, *88*(4), 800–12.
Garrett, P. and Williams, A. (2005) 'Adults' perceptions of communication with young people', in A. Williams and C. Thurlow (eds.) *Talking Adolescence: Perspectives on Communication in the Teenage Years*, New York: Peter Lang Publishing, Inc. 35–52.
Gidley, B. (2007) 'Youth culture and ethnicity: emerging youth interculture in South London', in P. Hodkinson and W. Deicke (eds.) *Youth Cultures: Scenes, Subcultures and Tribes*, New York: Routledge. 145–60.
Githinji, P. (2006) 'Bazes and Their Shibboleths: Lexical Variation and Sheng Speakers' Identity in Nairobi', *Nordic Journal of African Studies*, *15*(4), 443–72.
González, F.R. and Stenström, A. (2011) 'Expressive devices in the language of English- and Spanish-speaking youth', *Revista Alicantina de Estudios Ingleses*, *24*, 235–56.
Green, J. (2014) 'Multicultural London English: the new "youthspeak"', in J. Coleman (ed.) *Global English Slang*, London: Routledge. 62–71.
Hagedorn, J.M. (2005) 'The global impact of gangs', *Journal of Contemporary Criminal Justice*, *21*(2), 153–69.
Halliday, M.A.K. (1978) *Language as Social Semiotic*, London: Edward Arnold.
Harchaoui, S. (2015) 'Lexical innovations in the speech of adolescents in Oslo, Norway', *Proceedings of ConSOLE XXIII*. 220–47.
Hensley, C., Wright, J., Tewksbury, R. and Castle, T. (2003) 'The evolving nature of prison argot and sexual hierarchies', *The Prison Journal*, *83*, 289–300.
Higgs, E. (2014) 'Inmate subcultures', in J.S. Albanese (ed.) *The Encyclopedia of Criminology and Criminal Justice*, Chichester: John Wiley and Sons, Ltd. shareslide.org/inmate-subcultures-higgs, accessed June 2015.
Hollington, A. (2015) 'Yarada K'wank'wa and urban youth identity in Addis Ababa', in N. Nassenstein and A. Hollington (eds.) *Youth Language Practices in Africa and Beyond*, Berlin/Boston: Walter de Gruyter, Inc. 149–68.
Hollington, A. and Makwabarara, T. (2015) 'Youth language practices in Zimbabwe', in N. Nassenstein and A. Hollington (eds.) *Youth Language Practices in Africa and Beyond*, Berlin/Boston: Walter de Gruyter, Inc. 257–70.
Hollington, A. and Nassenstein, N. (2015) 'Youth language practices in Africa as creative manifestations of fluid repertoires and markers of speakers' social identity', in

N. Nassenstein and A. Hollington (eds.) *Youth Language Practices in Africa and Beyond*, Berlin/Boston: Walter de Gruyter, Inc. 1–22.
Hudson, R.A. (1980) *Sociolinguistics*, Cambridge: Cambridge University Press.
Hurst, E. (2007) 'Urban discourses and identity in a South African township: an analysis of youth culture in Cape Town', paper presented at the African Studies Association 50th Annual Meeting, New York, 18–21 October.
Hurst, E. (2015) 'Overview of the tsotsitaals of South Africa; their different base languages and common core lexical items', in N. Nassenstein and A. Hollington (eds.) *Youth Language Practices in Africa and Beyond*, Berlin/Boston: Walter de Gruyter, Inc. 169–84.
Jensen Arnett, J. (2002) 'Adolescents in Western countries in the 21st century: vast opportunities – for all?', in B.B. Brown, R.W. Larson and T.S. Saraswathi (eds.) *The World's Youth*, Cambridge: Cambridge University Press. 307–43.
Jones, S.R. and McEwen, M.K. (2000) 'A conceptual model of multiple dimensions of identity', *Journal of College Student Development*, *41*(4), 405–14.
Joseph, J. (2004) *Language and Identity*, Basingstoke, UK: Palgrave MacMillan.
Karanja, L. (2010) '"Homeless" at home: linguistic, cultural and identity hybridity and third space positioning of Kenyan urban youth', *Education canadienne et internationale*, *39*(2, juin), 1–11.
Kerswill, P. (2010) 'Youth languages in Africa and Europe: linguistic subversion or emerging vernaculars?', *Language in Africa: An Inter-University Research Seminar Exploring Language Usage and Values in a Range of Contexts*, Edge Hill University, 24 November.
Kießling, R. (2004) 'bàk mwà mè dó – Camfranglais in Cameroon', *Lingua Posnaniensis*, *47*. www.aai.uni-hamburg.de/afrika/personen/kiessling/medien/kiessling-2004-camfranglais.pdf, accessed September 2012.
Kiessling, R. and Mous, M. (2004) 'Urban youth languages in Africa', *Anthropological Linguistics*, *46*(3), 1–39.
Kioko, E.M. (2015) 'Regional varieties and 'ethnic' registers of Sheng', in N. Nassenstein and A. Hollington (eds.) *Youth Language Practices in Africa and Beyond*, Berlin/Boston: Walter de Gruyter, Inc. 119–47.
Kis, T. (2006) 'Is slang a linguistic universal?', *Revue d'Etudes Françaises*, *11*, 125–41.
Kouadio N'guessan (2006) 'Le Nouchi et les rapports Dioula-Français', *Le Français en Afrique*, *21*, 177–91.
Labov, T. (1992) 'Social and language boundaries among adolescents', *American Speech*, *67*(4), 339–66.
Lafage, S. (1998) '"Le français des rues", une variété avancée du français Abidjanais', *Faits de langues*, *11–12*(Octobre), 135–44.
Lave, J. and Wenger, E. (1991) *Situated Learning: Legitimate Peripheral Participation*, Cambridge: Cambridge University Press.
Llamas, C. and Watt, D. (2010) *Language and Identities*, Edinburgh: Edinburgh University Press.
Lodge, R.A. (1993) *French: From Dialect to Standard*, London: Routledge.
Mallik, B. (1972) *Language of the Underworld of West Bengal*, Calcutta: Sanskrit College Research Series No. LXXVII.
Manfredi, S. (2008) 'Rendók: a youth secret language in Sudan', *Estudios de dialectología norteafricana y andalusí*, *12*, 113–29.
Mayr, A. (2004) *Prison Discourse: Language as a Means of Control and Resistance*, Basingstoke, UK: Palgrave MacMillan.

Méla, V. (1997) 'Verlan 2000', *Langue française*, *114*, 16–34.
Mensah, E. (2016) 'The dynamics of youth language in Africa: an introduction', *Sociolinguistic Studies*, *10*(1–2), 1–14.
Miller, L. (2003) 'Graffiti photos: expressive art in Japanese girls' culture', *Harvard Asia Quarterly*, *7*(3), 31–42.
Miller, L. (2004) 'Those naughty teenage girls: Japanese Kogals, slang, and media assessments', *Journal of Linguistic Anthropology*, *14*(2), 225–47.
Montgomery, M. (2008) *An Introduction to Language and Society*, third edition, London: Routledge.
Morgan, M. (2004) 'Speech community', in A. Duranti (ed.) *A Companion to Linguistic Anthropology*, Oxford: Blackwell. 3–22.
Mugaddam, A.H. (2012b) 'Identity construction and linguistic manipulation in Randuk', paper presented at the *Youth Languages and Urban Languages in Africa Workshop*, Institut für Afrikanistik, Cologne University, Germany.
Mugaddam, A.H. (2015) 'Identity construction and linguistic manipulation in Randuk', in N. Nassenstein and A. Hollington (eds.) *Youth Language Practices in Africa and Beyond*, Berlin/Boston: Walter de Gruyter, Inc. 99–118.
Mugaddam, A.R.H. (2012a) 'Aspects of youth language in Khartoum', in M. Brenzinger and A-M. Fehn (eds.) *Proceedings of 6th World Congress of African Linguistics*, Cologne: Rüdiger Köppe Verlag. 87–98.
Mukhwana, A. (2015) 'Sheng and Engsh: what they are and what they are not', *International Journal of Scientific Research and Innovative Technology*, *2*(1), 94–102.
Mwihaki, A. (2007) 'Viewing Sheng as a social dialect: a linguistic approach', *ChemChemi*, Kenyatta University, *4*(2), 57–75.
Namyalo, S. (2015) 'Linguistic strategies in Luyaaye: word play and conscious language manipulation', in N. Nassenstein and A. Hollington (eds.) *Youth Language Practices in Africa and Beyond*, Berlin/Boston: Walter de Gruyter, Inc. 313–44.
Nassenstein, N. (2015) 'Imvugo y'Umuhanda: youth language practices in Kigali (Rwanda)', in N. Nassenstein and A. Hollington (eds.) *Youth Language Practices in Africa and Beyond*, Berlin/Boston: Walter de Gruyter, Inc. 185–204.
Nikitina, T.G. (2009) *Molodëzhnyi sleng: tolkovyi slovar'*, Moscow: AST: Astrel'.
Nortier, J. and Svendsen, B.A. (eds.) (2015) *Language, Youth and Identity in the 21st Century*, Cambridge: Cambridge University Press.
Nsamenang, A.B. (2002) 'Adolescence in sub-Saharan Africa: an image constructed from Africa's triple inheritance', in B.B. Brown, R.W. Larson and T.S. Saraswathi (eds.) *The World's Youth*, Cambridge: Cambridge University Press. 61–104.
Obst, P.L. and White, K.M. (2005) 'Three-dimensional strength of identification across group memberships: a confirmatory factor analysis', *Self and Identity*, 4. www.researchgate. net/publication/27466106_Three-Dimensional_Strength_of_Identification_Across_ Group_Memberships_A_Confirmatory_Factor_Analysis, accessed May 2016.
Ochs, E. (1992) 'Indexing gender', in A. Duranti and C. Goodwin (eds.), *Rethinking Context: Language as an Interactive Phenomenon*, Cambridge: Cambridge University Press. 335–58.
Parkin, D. and Arnaut, K. (2012) 'Super-diversity – a digest', Göttingen: Max Planck Institute for the Study of Religious and Ethnic Diversity.
Podesva, R.J., Roberts, S.J. and Campbell-Kibler, K. (2001) 'Sharing resources and indexing meanings in the production of gay styles', in K. Campbell-Kibler, R.J. Podesva, S.J. Roberts and A. Wong (eds.) *Language and Sexuality: Contesting Meaning in Theory and Practice*, Stanford, CA: CSLI Publications. 175–89.

Rampton, B. (2010) 'Crossing into class: language, ethnicities and class sensibility in England', in C. Llamas and D. Watt (eds.) *Language and Identities*, Edinburgh: Edinburgh University Press. 134–43.

Rampton, B. (2015) 'Contemporary urban vernaculars', in J. Nortier and B.A. Svendsen (eds.) *Language, Youth and Identity in the 21st Century*, Cambridge: Cambridge University Press. 24–44.

Reyes, A. (2005) 'Appropriation of African American slang by Asian American youth', *Journal of Sociolinguistics*, 9(4), 509–32.

Roth-Gordon, J. (2007) 'Racing and erasing the playboy: slang, transnational youth subculture, and racial discourse in Brazil', *Journal of Linguistic Anthropology*, 17(2), 246–65.

Samper, D.A. (2004) '"Africa is still our mama": Kenyan rappers, youth identity, and the revitalization of traditional values', *African Identities*, 2(1), 37–51.

Santa Maria, M. (2002) 'Youth in Southeast Asia: living within the continuity of tradition and the turbulence of change', in B.B. Brown, R.W. Larson and T.S. Saraswathi (eds.) *The World's Youth*, Cambridge: Cambridge University Press. 171–206.

Sherzer, J. (2002) *Speech Play and Verbal Art*, Austin, TX: University of Texas Press.

Smith-Hefner, N.J. (2007) 'Youth language, *Gaul* sociability, and the new Indonesian middle class', *Journal of Linguistic Anthropology*, 17(2), 184–203.

Stein-Kanjora, G. (2008) '"Parler comme ça, c'est vachement cool!"', *Sociologus*, 58(2), 117–41.

Stenström, A. (2014) *Teenage Talk: From General Characteristics to the Use of Pragmatic Markers in a Contrastive Perspective*, Basingstoke, UK: Palgrave MacMillan.

Stenström, A., Andersen, G. and Hasund, I.K. (2002) *Trends in Teenage Talk: Corpus Compilation, Analysis and Findings*, Amsterdam/Philadelphia: John Benjamins Publishing Company.

Svendsen, B.A. (2015) 'Language, youth and identity in the 21st century: content and continuations' in J. Nortier and B.A. Svendsen (eds.) *Language, Youth and Identity in the 21st Century*, Cambridge: Cambridge University Press. 3–23.

Tajfel, H. and Turner, J.C. (1986) 'The social identity theory of intergroup behavior', in S. Worchel and L.W. Austin (eds.) *Psychology of Intergroup Relations*, Chicago: Nelson-Hall. 7–24.

Tannen, D. (2007) *Talking Voices*, Cambridge: Cambridge University Press.

Thorne, T. (2006) 'Slanguistics or just lemon meringue?', *Proceedings from the Crossing Frontiers: Languages and the International Dimension Conference*, Cardiff University, 6–7 July. www.llas.ac.uk/cardiff2006, accessed June 2012.

Thurlow, C. (2003a) 'Generation txt? The sociolinguistics of young people's text-messaging', *Discourse Analysis Online*, 1(1), 1–27. www.researchgate.net/publication/259258527_ Generation_Txt_The_sociolinguistics_of_young_people%27s_text-messaging, accessed August 2016.

Thurlow, C. (2003b) 'Teenagers *in* communication, teenagers *on* communication', *Journal of Language and Social Psychology*, 22(1), 50–7.

Thurlow, C. (2005) 'Deconstructing adolescent communication', in A. Williams and C. Thurlow (eds.) *Talking Adolescence: Perspectives on Communication in the Teenage Years*, New York: Peter Lang Publishing, Inc. 1–20.

Trudgill, P. (1983) *Sociolinguistics: An Introduction to Language and Society*, Harmondsworth, UK: Penguin Books.

Vakunta, P.W. (2008) 'On translating Camfranglais and other Camerounismes', *Meta Translators' Journal*, 53(4), 942–7.

Vakunta, P.W. (2011) 'Ivorian Nouchi, cousin to Cameroonian Camfranglais'. www.postnewslive.com/2011, accessed September 2012.

Veit-Wild, F. (2009) '"Zimbolicious" – the creative potential of linguistic innovation: the case of Shona-English in Zimbabwe', *Journal of Southern African Studies*, *35*(3), 683–97.

Vertovec, S. (2007) *New Complexities of Cohesion in Britain: Super-Diversity, Transnationalism and Civil-Integration*, UK Commission on Integration and Cohesion.

Victor, T. (2014) 'Gestural slang', in J. Coleman (ed.) *Global English Slang*, London: Routledge. 194–204.

Vierke, C. (2015) 'Some remarks on poetic aspects of Sheng', in N. Nassenstein and A. Hollington (eds.) *Youth Language Practices in Africa and Beyond*, Berlin/Boston: Walter de Gruyter, Inc. 227–56.

Wardhaugh, R. (1998) *An Introduction to Sociolinguistics* (3rd ed.), Malden: Blackwell.

Wiese, H. (2009) 'Grammatical innovation in multi-ethnic urban Europe: new linguistic practices among adolescents', *Lingua*, *119*, 782–806.

Wilce, J.M. (2009) *Language and Emotion*, Cambridge: Cambridge University Press.

Yule, G. (1985) *The Study of Language*, Cambridge: Cambridge University Press.

Zarzycki, Ł. (2015) 'Socio-lingual phenomenon of the anti-language of Polish and American prison inmates', *Crossroads: A Journal of English Studies*, Wydział Filologiczny Uniwersytetu w Białymstoku, *8*, 11–23.

3 Youth and criminal language practices – attitudes and motivations

Introduction

Before exploring the ways in which in-group–associated lexis is created, we should dig deeper into why it is used in the first place – considering those often described as typical users, the social and cultural contexts for its appearance, and the assessed or stated motivations for its use. As we saw in the Introduction and in Chapters One and Two, there are different types of in-group language and social meaning attached to usage. Furthermore, the motivations behind usage can often vary. In this chapter, we consider some of the stances, identities and activities that have been popularly viewed as indexed by the use of criminal and youth language practices, and attitudes towards both the language used and speakers. We begin with criminal language practices in France.

Criminal language practices and how we understand them – threads through time

The association of certain language forms and varieties with criminals and other in-groups is nothing new for the people living in what is now modern-day France. For example, if we look back even just over the last millennium, a reference to beggars' and thieves' talk ('gergons') can be found in the twelfth-century Old Occitan (also known as Old Provençal) work *Donats proensals* (Lodge 2004; Heller-Roazen 2013).

The most complete account of early criminal language practices in France concerns the language of the Coquillard criminal beggars and brigands of the thirteenth to fifteenth centuries. A glossary of their secret terminology – known as Jobelin or Jargon – was produced as part of their trial in Dijon in 1455. The Coquillards had members in many French provinces, and they replaced in-group terms if they became well known. They reportedly had their own king and were not the only criminal collective using in-group terms in France at the time: another beggar group, the Caymands, was documented as operating in the Paris area in 1448 (Zhirmunskii 1936).

The use of criminal language varieties in France did not end with the Coquillards' trial. In the eighteenth century, for instance, a criminal band known as the Chauffeurs d'Orgères roamed the French countryside, torturing farmers to reveal where they had hidden their savings and using a variety drawing on Romani and local French forms for in-group communication (Green 2008).[1] A century later, Parisian butchers used in-group terms when referring to cuts of meat and pricing in front of unwitting customers (Robert L'Argenton 1991). This variety – the Largonji des Louchébems – employed a mechanism for creating lexis that is believed to have a precedent in Hanoi butchers' language (Robert L'Argenton 1991; Strutz 2009 also notes possible derivation from former French Indochina) and in a French criminal variety known as Largonji ('argot', 'criminal jargon') (Robert L'Argenton 1991; Roffé 1993). In the case of Largonji, the first letter of a word was substituted by *l*; the original first letter and a suffix, which also served to mask meaning, were then added to the end of the new base. So, 'jargon' ('jargon') would become 'largonji', and 'boucher' ('butcher') – 'louchébem', sometimes also seen as 'loucherbem' or 'louchébèm'. Although there was undoubtedly an element of enjoyment in and social use of Largonji des Louchébems by butchers, the need for a form of communication limited to initiates was important, and knowledge of Largonji des Louchébems terms and how to create them was passed on between people in that trade even in the late twentieth century (Robert L'Argenton 1991).[2] Indeed, both those butchers who spoke Largonji des Louchébems and the Chauffeurs, who broke up in 1800, had among their ranks instructors with a specific responsibility to teach in-group terms to those who joined the group (Zhirmunskii 1936; Robert L'Argenton 1991). This is a practice that appears to live on in some places. Higgs (2014: 6, citing Kaminski 2003) reports that Polish prison inmates have to undergo instruction and examinations covering behavioural codes, language games and "secret argot" before being initiated into prison culture.

Although the use of in-group language forms by criminals has continued since the days of the Coquillards, how we understand the concept of in-group French and its users has broadened and evolved. Accounts documenting the use of Jobelin, Jargon and, later, Argot tell us about popular associations between restricted language varieties and beggars and criminals, as well as their activity, roughly across the thirteenth to nineteenth centuries (e.g. Roffé 1993; Lodge 2004). However, by the sixteenth century the term 'jargon', for example, was not only associated with criminals and social marginals but also came to index student talk (Lodge 1993), while by the 1860s some commentators began to talk about 'argot' more broadly – not only as language typical of vagabonds, beggars and thieves, but also of people involved in a common activity or profession (Roffé 1993).[3] The term later became associated with technical language and even colloquial or street French, while some trade-related language varieties (for example, rural and itinerant trades) gradually waned during the nineteenth and twentieth centuries with the rise of urbanisation, industrialisation and centralising social and political institutions. By 2001, one commentator, Červenková (2001: 77), qualified modern argot as:

> no longer really a secret language but rather one of the elements on the palette of choice at the disposal of the speaker ... To follow fashion, some people use

argotic words that they discover thanks to the media. Others, who have created these words, will create others to maintain distance between their group and those who imitate it.[4]

So far, we have looked at France. However, a long thread of in-group usage has been woven in other countries, too. The sixteenth century, for example, saw a real interest in those occupying the margins of society (including the criminal underworld) and the language they used, or were held to use, across Europe (Nedelec 1986; Beier 1995; Burke 1995; Green 2016). A good example of the language of socially marginal groups in that continent can be seen in Caló, the language variety of Roma in Spain, which developed from Romani and Spanish.

By the early to mid-fifteenth century, Roma had settled in Spain and had brought their language, Romani, with them. Their integration into local societies was a far from easy road. The Roma had a strong sense of cultural independence, which was no doubt consolidated by their socialising mainly within their own circles and living in specific Roma quarters ('gitanerías'). However, they were also variously subjected to travel restrictions, marginalisation, oppression and forced integration with non-Roma communities (Geipel 1995; García 2005; Council of Europe 2012). In time their language mixed with Spanish to produce Caló. This largely consisted of Romani lexis used within Spanish syntax and morphology. Undoubtedly used to craft, convey and maintain a distinct culture and identity, Caló was also used by some Roma as a cryptolect to act beyond the wit of others and to aid stealing and deception. This was no doubt one reason why it was viewed by out-group members with suspicion (Geipel 1995; García 2005).

By the end of the nineteenth century, Caló had lent a great many terms to criminal language, along with remnants of the traditional language of the criminal underworld, Germanía, which had been principally in use during the fifteenth to seventeenth centuries. Indeed, the term 'Caló' had become synonymous with criminal language and criminality (Geipel 1995; García 2005; Buzek 2012). At this time, Caló was a largely hispanicised criminal lexicon that, through diffusion, also contributed words and phrases to colloquial Spanish; it would eventually be used to extend in-group lexicons in the wider Spanish-speaking world, including Pachuco Caló in the US (García 2005; Buzek 2012). As before, nowadays peninsular Spanish speakers of Caló largely use Spanish syntax and morphology with Romani vocabulary and expressions interposed (Geipel 1995).[5]

The Roma were far from being the only people linked to or even known by in-group language in Spain. As with France, in-group varieties were often associated with beggars, traders and itinerant workers, particularly over the fifteenth to seventeenth centuries, as they reportedly sought to mask their intentions and/or carry out their work (Roffé 1993). One example of a trader variety is Gacería, the language of travelling salesmen from Cantalejo in Segovia. These salesmen sold livestock and harrows and possessed a vocabulary that sourced words from popular and standard Castilian, Germanía, Caló, Arabic, Basque, Catalan and other regional varieties. Many of the occupations on which traders depended survived until the end of the nineteenth century, when again changes in economic conditions prompted a reduction in or the disappearance of itinerant and/or seasonal traders and thus a decline in the use of substantial elements of their language (Roffé Gómez 1994).

In both the French and Spanish cases, flux in the socio-economic situations of some speakers, as well as the need to respond to changing social and/or socio-political realities, played some part in how those language varieties were used and developed, particularly in the nineteenth century. However, it would be incorrect to think that in-group practices declined, either in those countries or more generally, once the New Year bells of 1 January 1900 began to toll. Indeed, the twentieth century also saw prolific use of criminal in-group language as underworld circles operated and as people on the street found ways to get by. In the US, for example, the introduction of the Harrison Act in 1914 made many narcotics illegal; those involved in procuring, selling and using drugs therefore created their own in-group terms to communicate beyond the wit of the law (Slone 2003; indeed, Green (2016: 64) suggests that the Act multiplied the number of terms referring to narcotics "by a factor of 10"). In the Soviet Union of the 1920s and 1930s, individuals from various walks of life mixed in labour camps and other corrective institutions, thereby facilitating the transmission of prisoner lexis among hitherto unconnected groups as a means of identity construction and survival (e.g. Davie 1997/1998). And in such diverse parts of the world as Indonesia and Africa criminals are reported to have used in-group language varieties, among other things, to operate beyond the ken of the authorities, from at least the middle of the twentieth century onwards (Boellstorff 2004; Ogechi 2005).

Multilingualism

Many social actors have access to a number of languages, with greater or lesser degrees of ability, within their repertoires (e.g. working knowledge of French as a language of the workplace, native-level Arabic as the main language at home or of religion, more limited holiday Spanish, etc.). Some countries have more than one official language, for example, Swahili and English in Kenya, while other languages may also be spoken or understood by parts of the populace (e.g. Luo and Kikuyu).

Many youth operate within complex multilingual environments, which can be reflected in their language practices. A good example is provided by Harchaoui (2015). In a study of lexical innovation among adolescents in Oslo, she analysed 663 lexical forms. Of these, 245 examples could be classed as Norwegian 'slang', 353 as borrowings from English, and 65 from other languages which included non-(Indo-)European languages (such as Berber and Arabic) and

Indo-European languages apart from Norwegian and English. Of the 65 latter examples, youth from parts of the poorer multiethnic and multilingual Eastern Oslo, where there is greater language contact involving several languages, employed 58. Conversely, those from the better-off west of the city, where there are fewer immigrant groups mainly originating in other Nordic countries, the EU and the US, only used seven forms. Harchaoui (2015: 221) suggests that "real innovative features (such as non-European loan words) seem to result from multilingual urban environments where speakers grow up", and that speakers thus use language to convey their belonging to specific areas of the city.

The study of multilingualism is a large field and encompasses many different situations (e.g. the use of imposed foreign official languages at a state level alongside indigenous languages or vernaculars, multiple language use in local neighbourhoods, etc.). Moreover, multilingual environments have gained prominence as sites of study in terms of linguistic and social practice over recent years. Freywald, Cornips, Ganuza et al. (2015: 73) consider that "[m]ultilingual settings support new linguistic variation and the emergence of new linguistic patterns", a view echoed by Ekberg, Opsahl and Wiese (2015: 93), who posit that multilingual urban settings (in Europe) "lead to rich sources of language contact involving the majority languages and a range of typologically diverse minority languages" and are "particularly open to linguistic variation and innovation, and might also support a faster pace of language change" when compared to informal varieties and styles found in more monolingual settings and to national standard varieties. Many speakers may thus be multilingual, adept in or draw on more than one language, although knowledge across them may be quite uneven and/or limited.

A key question therefore concerns how and why social agents harness any given linguistic resource at any given time and what patterns emerge among groups and localities. There may be reasons why speakers engage in code-switching (e.g. topic, self-identification, to show affiliation, cryptolect, etc.), for example, or borrow individual items from other languages (e.g. social cachet, language play). How individual and group resources are mobilised in multilingual environments and to what ends are sure to continue to represent important fields of enquiry as we witness ongoing linguistic super-diversity, particularly within many urban and peri-urban spaces, as well as the progress of computer-mediated communication.

Why cryptolect is used: beyond the criminal

As the Largonji des Louchébems and Caló examples suggest, there can be more to the language practices of criminals and traders than masking intention for the purpose of crime or deception. Červenková's qualification that (French) argot is but one of a number of tools to be used to meet a speaker's social or other requirements is important in this respect – although admittedly this depends on how we understand and define the practice at hand.

If we stay with criminal groups for the moment, as clear as the relationship between illegal activity and the need to communicate securely no doubt is, the question arises as to whether criminal groups use specific forms for other reasons, including some that might not necessarily relate to criminal activity at all. After all, criminals also eat and drink and socialise while negotiating questions of identity and articulating their world view and values. Might these factors also be conveyed in their language? For a brief discussion of these questions, we consider the language used by criminals in 1960s West Bengal.

In his seminal study *Language of the Underworld of West Bengal*, Bhaktiprasad Mallik (1972: 19, 21) suggested that the motives underpinning the formation of what he termed "slang" vocabulary could be manifold, including fear or resistance; dispute, quarrel or distrust; wit and humour; and the romance of innovation. Indeed, as can be seen in Table 3.1, he ranked in more detailed fashion the motivations behind the use of in-group language practices by the criminals and "anti-social elements" he studied (in order of frequency).

The figures in Table 3.1 are significant. Importantly, they highlight the danger of attributing a single motivation to the language use of any given group and, crucially, underline the deliberate use of alternative vocabulary or linguistic forms for a given purpose or purposes that are not necessarily criminal or crime-related. We see motivations that relate to social play, clarity, and achieving an expressive, emotive or other effect that sit alongside the need to operate beyond the law. This variety in motivations is important; it stretches beyond the criminal–cryptic and into the social–interactive, suggesting that criminals are more than law-breakers and people who need secrecy to survive. They are people who

Table 3.1 Mallik: motives for using the language of the underworld of West Bengal

To disguise the utterance	85
For fear of arrest	73
Slang is more terse, has different effect	72
It creates fun	60
Speech is not clear without its use	51
Didn't know why	26
Acquired by association	18

(Adapted from Mallik 1972: 58)*

*Mallik (1972: 3–5, 24–5, 58) notes that criminal language forms can be learned through association. However, he also proposes in his discussion of the language of the underworld of West Bengal that "[c]riminality may be either professional or anti-social. Slangs as codes are widely current only among the professional criminals. Non-professional criminals do not come within the purvue of this discussion".

socialise with others within (and most probably beyond) socio-'professional' networks, and people who express attitudes and interpret and operate within social contexts. In these senses, Mallik's data draw our attention to subtler arguments that are closer to the nuanced palette of choice alluded to by Červenková: to what a speaker is seeking to achieve individually and socially through their (here: linguistic) practices.

Although these social dimensions of criminal language practices seem like a reasonable proposition to us when we consider those practices as group usage, they don't always attract attention in studies of such practices and those considered to be *typical* speakers. Yet, some of the drivers behind usage by the West Bengal criminals and near-criminals and the speakers of Largonji des Louchébems considered previously seem to have a distinctly social dimension. Indeed, if we turn our attention to other varieties associated with the criminal world we see that they too have many in-group words for items that might not be *expressly* crime-related, and may well simply refer to everyday realia: although Beier's (1995: 76, 89) study of the cant of the English underworld in the sixteenth and seventeenth centuries suggests that it was principally used to talk about types of criminal or victim, thieves' tools and deception in gaming, for instance, there were also terms for the Church, and for animals, food, drink, clothing and household goods and furnishings (although, of course, some of these could have figured in criminal acts in some way, e.g. as objects for theft). Tonkov's (1930) study of Russian criminal language also points to a wide range of everyday phenomena referenced by those considered to be typical speakers, including items that were arguably not central to the acts of thieving or deception (e.g. insects, birds and so on). And in more recent times, some 30 years after Mallik, Einat and Einat (2000) and later Einat and Livnat (2012) indicate that while prison inmates may use in-group forms for criminal purposes, they may also employ them defensively to cope with the strenuous demands of prison life.[6] This is certainly one conclusion that emerges in a number of studies of prisoner language varieties, with other explanations focusing on the use of criminal language to convey and reinforce organisation and status within the prison subculture (Hensley, Wright, Tewksbury and Castle 2003; Zarzycki 2015); the underscoring of positive gender identity and associated attributes (Einat and Livnat 2012); the mitigation of pains that come with imprisonment (Einat and Wall 2006); the facilitation of social cohesiveness and shared identity among the prisoner group (Einat and Wall 2006); demonstrating adherence to values (particularly to prisoner codes of conduct); and conveying hierarchy, standing and behaviours, etc. (Einat and Einat 2000; Einat and Livnat 2012; Higgs 2014). In functional terms, therefore, although such in-group language may thrive among collectives that conflict with the mainstream structure (de Klerk 2005), criminal language practices have not necessarily served solely to safely and accurately designate criminals or their acts as a form of cryptolect – comparisons with the motivations behind New Zealand student language (Bardsley 2014) and Camfranglais (Stein-Kanjora 2008; Ngefac 2010) also throw up some interesting social parallels (see pages 125 and 143) – although secrecy has clearly been a key facet of its use.[7]

Youth and criminal language practices 115

Indeed, as we strive to understand the motives behind the use of criminal language, and how criminals and their language are painted, we are also drawn to the conclusion that cryptic language is not just the preserve of criminal groups. That people not involved in criminal activity might also use language so that other individuals or groups, such as members of the opposite sex, different generations or even guests, don't understand what they are saying points to other reasons or tensions which might explain why cryptolect is used in some instances. Manfredi (2008a, 2008b) sees the main purpose of Randuk, a language variety developed by *urban youth* in Sudan, as making communication incomprehensible to the dominant linguistic community, but also as *underscoring group identity*. Wolfer (2011: 25), in her study of Arabic secret language, indicates that the

> most typical situation for the use of ludlings in Damascus is the communication between *family members in front of guests, or women in front of men*, thus reflecting the traditional Muslim life with its *rituals of hospitality and politeness* and with its strict rules of *segregation* between the two sexes.

Kawase (2005), describing the use of a secret language by Ethiopian *musicians*, the Azmari, considers its central function to be communicating information the Azmari don't want outsiders to know (it is taboo to share the language variety with outsiders), but also to share a sense of *exclusivity and community*. In her analysis of the language of the Fulɓe, an ethnic group found in many parts of West Africa, Storch (2011: 57–61, 72, 84) reports that the "secret language used specifically by *young people* among the Fulɓe [in this case in Nigeria and Cameroon] is designed to become practically incomprehensible to adults, especially after they have not used it for a period of time", while some men in the same part of the world use secret language to *maintain an exclusive command of spirits and shrines*. In his discussion of Indonesia's Bahasa Gay, Boellstorff (2004) notes that, while it can serve as a cryptolect to enable *gay Indonesian men* to communicate securely about their homosexuality, Bahasa Gay functions more to support ideas of *association and community* (my emphases throughout). Furthermore, we can also posit that language that is used to avoid, evade, exclude or conceal need not always be conceived in the criminal language terms in which we generally understand it (i.e. mostly distinct secret words and phrases): in a fascinating article, Fortier (2002) describes the use of proverbs and evasive replies by a nomadic Tibeto–Burman-speaking hunting and gathering society, the Rāute, to conceal their cultural practices from enquiring Nepalese villagers.

Finally, no less careful consideration should be given to instances where the very acts of communication are hidden, such as concealed SMS exchanges when interactants are in close physical proximity – for example, students texting one another discreetly during a lecture – which do not constitute cryptolect *per se* but centre on the confidential nature of the act (Thurlow 2003a).

So, whereas it has been viewed in some societies as the language of the déclassé, of the social depths and criminal groups – people who have been seen to typically require secret or in-group language to commit crime or deceive, and also as socially remote from and/or hostile to social and linguistic rule-makers (e.g. Halliday 1978; Lodge 1993; Green 2016) – cryptolect can be used to meet other needs, such as survival, the maintenance of social harmony or networks or the expression of beliefs and group identity. Indeed, it is highly likely that social views of criminals and the déclassé and their language over time have led to stereotypical descriptions in some societies of cryptolect as the language of crime and/or social subversion and little else.[8]

Youth language practices: how they're perceived

Although in Europe and North America young people are often held to be at the vanguard of social and linguistic innovation, experimentation and change (e.g. Miles 2000; Stenström, Andersen and Hasund 2002; Eckert 2005; Stenström 2014) – which in some cases may be influenced by a multilingual environment (Cheshire, Nortier and Adger 2015; Harchaoui 2015) – youth language has often been portrayed in ways that have arguably failed to capture its true social and linguistic significance (Thurlow 2006). And yet, however the category is defined, youth often constitute an important cross-section of society – one that is sensitive to and instrumental in creating and implementing change, be it social, cultural or political; one that represents a significant bridge between today's and tomorrow's society; and often one that captures and interprets what is happening in the broader world and translates it for, integrates it into, and merges it with the local.

Indeed, in a number of societies, young people and their associated practices can often be viewed with suspicion, concern or even derision. There are many reasons for this. As a number of commentators variously intimate, in some societies adolescents are often depicted by adults as sloppy, inept, rebellious, risk-taking, subversive or irresponsible, and both they and their language can become viewed in the same light (e.g. Stenström, Andersen and Hasund 2002; Eckert 2003, 2004, 2005; Jørgensen 2013; see also Miles 2000 and Bucholtz 2002 for a broader view of this depiction). They are not regarded as children, but not quite as adults, either; instead, they may be seen as negotiating a transition to adulthood (e.g. James 1995) and in a "state of becoming" (Smaill 2008: 3). In some cases, they may be compared to adults rather than to children, often to negative effect (Caputo 1995; Eckert 2005), and assessed as unable to adopt roles in adult life or enter the adult world (e.g. Levikova 2004). They may therefore be regarded as less-than-adult (Bucholtz 2002; Eckert 2004, 2005), serving as an Other that, *inter alia,* supports adult self-definition (Thurlow 2006, 2007).

Furthermore, as they work to define both their own and others' identities, and their place in the world, with all the challenges this brings in evaluating and adopting social behaviours and understanding social difference and meaning, youth are asked to do so in social spaces that are often defined and shaped for them. Typically, this means the age-graded institution of school or of work – Amit-Talai (1995a: 153) calls this "institutionalized adolescence" (see also Danesi 1994; Eckert and McConnell-Ginet 1995; Eckert 2003, 2004, 2005). Within relevant societies, in many cases late industrial ones, adolescence can thus become regarded as a time of understanding and responding to the constraints and opportunities that are set by others; and a time when young people construct their own social responses, rules and parameters inasmuch as they can within those broader limitations (Amit-Talai 1995a; Miles 2000; Eckert 2003, 2004; Levikova 2004; Wilson 2015; Green 2016). Furthermore, as they respond to these limitations and negotiate the social and identity-related challenges that come their way, and as they develop speech styles in combination with other style elements such as clothing, tattoos, gesture, dance, musical taste and other activities to these ends, the moves they make are often seen as part of the growing-up process, something *not quite adult* and something of a phase on the way to a place that is more responsible, considered, serious and mature. They may thus be seen as "incomplete adults" (Wulff 1995a: 11; see also Miles 2000; Eckert 2004, 2005). The question of whether youth are acting in this way, not as a reaction to the adult sphere or as part of the broader process of growing up, but more proactively as recognisable and active sociocultural agents in their own right can escape attention (Amit-Talai 1995b; Wulff 1995a).

Where youth language practices are concerned – that is to say, linguistic forms that index youth identity – these can also attract criticism on a number of fronts. Sometimes youth can be accused of using infantile, simplistic, lazy, inept, immature or anti-social language (Eckert 2003, 2004; Thurlow 2003b, 2005, 2006, 2007, 2014; Coleman 2012). Such allegations of communicative ignorance or ineptitude can accompany concerns about their use of communication technologies, such as text messaging, Instant Messaging, chat and others (Thurlow 2003a, 2006, 2007), although the use of such technologies need not always be in evidence, as we will see later in the chapter. On other occasions youth are considered to use language that adults claim to have whimsically used in the past but to have given up long ago: in some cases because this is something in which adults are expected not to engage as a result of social convention (Storch 2011 discusses this question with regard to expectations of adulthood in certain African societies, for example) – although notions of youth, adulthood and adult responsibility can themselves change and be contested (Bennett 2007; Wilson 2015),[9] and it is not excluded that youth language practices will not endure beyond youth as a conceptualised life stage (e.g. Stein-Kanjora 2008; Rampton 2015) (see also **Contemporary Urban Vernaculars** on pages 156–7).

Moreover, on other occasions still the use of youth-associated language practices can see them charged with endangering both their own education and future, and the fabric of the broader society and/or culture. The use of the Indonesian youth language Bahasa Gaul, for instance, has been criticised by some commentators as ruining Indonesian and threatening the integrity of the standard language and young speakers' linguistic creativity (Smith-Hefner 2007). In Germany, use of the multiethnolect Kiezdeutsch has attracted negative social evaluation, including from those who fear for the "deterioration of the German language" (Wiese 2009: 15). In the UK in 2006, the former Chief Inspector of Schools, who enjoyed a high profile in the country, proclaimed that 'slang' "contaminates and subverts" (cited in Green 2014: 69; see also Coleman 2012: 9, 264), a claim that chimes greatly with one Kenyan description of Sheng as a "subversive factor in Kenya's language education efforts", where the sale of Sheng dictionaries was believed to greatly damage and impede the development of standard language (Mazrui 1995: 168; see also Mukhwana 2015: 96–7, 99 for criticism of Sheng and Engsh as the "childish" and "vulgar" languages of "spoilt youths", and for fears over the purity of Swahili, *inter alia*).[10] Nouchi has also been painted as a "standard rule-breaking language" that is "despised in educational settings" (Vakunta online interview with Meme Bamba, undated). Finally, practices associated with Japanese youth have been criticised as undermining sociocultural norms, even though some language behaviours may not be theirs alone. Miller (2004), for example, points out that the lack of use in Kogal speech of the infix '-ra-', which is found in prestige dialects, is encountered in many regional dialects and across age groups; nonetheless, the Japanese media have fixed onto the dropping of the infix as "one of the worst transgressions of youth speech, and this association with youth is widespread" (Miller 2004: 235). In this and other respects, Kogals and other young Japanese therefore stand accused of destroying the national language or of having forgotten how to speak it (see also **Language ideology** on page 127).[11]

Young people can thus become criticised not only in terms of their being perceived as a definable social Other in their own right, but through denigration of their language practices as a means of achieving the same end (e.g. Stein-Kanjora 2008; Thurlow 2014).

Of course, just as not all youth oppose mainstream values (e.g. Miles 2000), not all adults or members of the dominant social mainstream are critical of youth as a life stage or as speakers of an inferior or substandard language variety. In much the same way as youth should not be regarded as a homogeneous social category (e.g. Labov 1992; Thurlow 2003a, 2003b, 2007), so attention should be called to the danger of mischaracterising all those in the adult or mainstream spheres also, or of downplaying the part that some youth may play in keeping the adult sphere distant, including through confirmation of negative stereotypes, as Beazley (2003) reports regarding some Indonesian street youth. Stepping aside from the traditional caricature in many societies of parents who inexpertly use youth language to *speak the same language* as their children, much to the latter's chagrin, there are people in the parental, state or institutional domains who accept youth and their language in a non-critical manner. Some younger Cameroonian teachers are reported to have aligned themselves with their young compatriots in pointing to the benefits of speaking Camfranglais, a perspective shared by the country's national pedagogic adviser for French, who didn't see the variety as a "learning obstacle" as such, but indicated that, should its use cause concern, then it should be incorporated into national language syllabi to make speakers aware of risks relating to its use (Vakunta 2008: 944). Equally, against the backdrop of falling Kenyan school exam marks in Swahili in 2010, where the widespread use of Sheng was claimed to have had a negative impact on scores, one educator questioned not so much the place that Sheng had in society as school pupils' inability to correctly select the contexts in which Swahili and Sheng should be used (Muindi 2010) – it would have been all too easy to cast Sheng in a disapproving light altogether, especially as it is often painted as a threat to standards and/or competence (e.g. Ferrari 2014; Beck 2015; Dorleijn, Mous and Nortier 2015; Kioko 2015). While highlighting the risks of speaker miscalculation, this last qualification rests in fact on the notion that young speakers may use Sheng or other in-group language in appropriate situations and in specific ways, as Doran (2004, 2007) notes regarding suburban French youth language, Wiese (2009) with reference to Kiezdeutch, and Bardsley (2014) concerning New Zealand students.

Indeed, as Stein-Kanjora (2008) also fairly points out with regard to the use of Camfranglais, even if the majority of adults surveyed view the use of a variety negatively, this does not account for *all* opinions. In her study, 64% of adult questionnaire respondents between 25 and 63 years of age held a negative view of Camfranglais – they variously opined that it was a bad influence on kids, that its use meant loss or mixing up of French and English, and that its use signified a terrible situation for the country or caused problems. However, 32%, aged between 25 and 40 years, had a favourable or at least neutral view of the use of Camfranglais in that they considered it part of growing up and/or in that it was amusing or creative (Stein-Kanjora 2008: 124). Stein-Kanjora also found that young adults appeared to stop using Camfranglais between 20 and 24 years old, particularly when they got a job or got married, but that adults between 30 and 40 tended to keep using certain Camfranglais words and expressions with friends of a similar age – they thus carried aspects of youth language with them as they progressed through life and crafted and re-crafted their sense of identity beyond their adolescent years (Stein-Kanjora 2008). The behaviour of this last group is reflected to some extent in a study by Ngefac (2010: 155–6), who observed that 65% of Francophone respondents aged 26–39 years spoke Camfranglais. It would appear that this variety is not alone in being utilised beyond adolescence (see Rampton 2015 and **Contemporary Urban Vernaculars** on pages 156–7).

For sure, not all observations by members of the mainstream about the social roles of young people and youth practice more generally are adversarial or deprecating. While some academics argue that mainstream media portrayals of youth have long tended to be over-generalising, negative and misrepresentative, in many cases feeding public fears of moral degradation and decline (e.g. Thurlow 2005, 2014 and Wyn 2005 vis-à-vis the UK, the US, Australia and New Zealand; Drummond and Schleef 2016 with regard to the UK; and Doran 2007 in relation to marginalised suburban French youth), in some contexts depictions can be favourable. For example, although Indonesian street children are often demonised as social pariahs or deviant criminals by the state or the social majority, they can also be depicted as victims discarded by an uncaring society or in over-romanticised terms by charities and the press (Beazley 2003). Young people can also be seen as victims of modernisation and the section of society most at risk due to rapid social progress or, alternatively, as switched-on heralds of and guides to a better future (Wyn 2005) who may even embody familial hopes for betterment or survival, not to mention society's passion and vitality (Santa Maria 2002 regarding Southeast Asian societies, and Coleman 2012: 71 on English-speaking countries such as the UK, the US and Australia). Of course, in each of these instances care must be taken with generalistic and essentialising qualifications of what is in reality a heterogeneous social group and, at the same time, acknowledge the fact that the evaluations in every case have been produced by adults as the main powerbrokers in society (see also **Identity for the self and others** in this chapter).

Whether the mainstream criticises or supports youth language, its value as a vehicle for engaging young people is often recognised, which can lead to its use by mainstream (and other, non-mainstream) out-groups. Hollington and Nassenstein (2015) indicate, for instance, that in Africa urban youth language is achieving greater presence in public discourse, in the campaign speeches of politicians and in advertising – it is thereby being utilised by previous outsiders in new arenas. Such practices correspondingly invite investigation of resistance and project identities. Sheng, for example, has been used by banks, charities, NGOs, religious bodies, government ministries and businesses, among others (Kioko 2015). It has figured in advertisements about HIV and AIDS to help messages about condom use to become accepted and hit home; and it has also been employed by politicians to appeal to youth, including during election campaigns (Mwihaki 2007; Bosire 2009; Ferrari 2014) – no doubt for much the same reasons as Nouchi was used during the 2010 presidential elections in Côte d'Ivoire (Aboa 2011) and Tsotsitaal during South Africa's transition to democracy (Molamu 1995).[12] Moving beyond the public health and conventional political arenas, Bahasa Gaul has been utilised by Muslim preachers attempting to reach out to young Indonesians (Smith-Hefner 2007) and Russian youth language has been employed to attract young speakers, who may further adapt advertising phrases for their own purposes (Biblieva 2007). Verlan, too, has been used in French advertising and media since the 1980s (Méla 1988) while, more recently, in 2013 the French Caisse d'Epargne bank included youth expressions in advertisements aimed at people between the ages of 18 and 25, who they no doubt hoped would constitute a set of potentially profitable clients (my italics):

> Halluciner *grave* (v): effet produit par notre credit étudiant à 1,90% …
>
> Seeing things big time (v. phr.): effect produced by our student credit at 1.90%. …
>
> *Gratos* (adj.): prix de notre carte bancaire la première année.
>
> Buckshee (adj.): cost of our bank card during the first year (see also page 201).

Of course, the use of youth language in these instances is very tactical and instrumental, and in some cases may serve socially benign causes (e.g. HIV and AIDS prevention) – particularly given that young people comprise large proportions of many populations, as noted in the Introduction. However, depending on the agenda, the use of youth language practices by mainstream out-groups such as political parties may also risk accusations of the disingenuous or cynical employment of such language as a vote-gathering device, and – particularly where commercial bodies are involved – as further evidence of the commoditisation and/or exploitation of youth culture. Where mainstream advertising is concerned, a key question can indeed arise as to whether the use of youth language indicates recognition of diversity or evinces corporate moves to increase consumption (Milani, Jonsson and Mhlambi 2015), although in a broader sense consumption need not always imply the victimisation of youth but may form part of a process of active identity formation by young social actors (Wulff 1995b; Miles 2000; but see also Miles' discussion of mass media control of youth, and Thurlow 2007, 2012 regarding the impact of adult-directed commerce regarding youth, consumption and communication technologies).

Overall, then, an interesting picture develops in which some adults see youth or adolescents as immature; write off young people and their language as something of a fad or, alternatively, culturally threatening; and/or regard speakers in overly simplistic, oppositional, even catastrophising terms (e.g. McKay 2005: 226, citing Kelly 2000; Thurlow 2005).[13] At the same time, however, some adults or members of the dominant mainstream leave themselves open not only to accusations of recognising youth language and identity for reasons of political or other expediency, but also of burdening these *not quite adults* with the sociocultural expectations typical of adulthood in the shape of the future health of the language, not to mention culture and society. In this sense, youth "often becomes the discursive screen onto which a society's fears and hopes are projected" (Smaill 2008: 3). As we saw in the Introduction, this situation can occur perhaps because some of these young people are no longer teenagers or adolescents, but are, in fact, *adults themselves*. A combination of these perspectives, antagonisms and contradictions can be seen in Cameroon, for instance, where speakers of Camfranglais can be painted by the dominant mainstream as delinquents, gangsters, school drop-outs and so on, even though they include university students and well-known – including some rebellious – artists (de Féral 2004; Kießling 2004; Ngo Ngok-Graux 2007; Fonkoua 2015).

Yet, as this Camfranglais example implies, these sceptical views of youth and youth language fail to account for the fact that, in some word-formation and stylistic respects, speakers of youth language in many communities often demonstrate elements of linguistic improvisation, innovation and virtuosity that can also be used by writers and poets whose works are deemed to be socially acceptable or even celebrated, and viewed as proper vehicles for taking language and culture forward (see pages 311–12 for examples of **Literary devices**). Nor do these views consider the possibility that youth sometimes adopt items from the non-standard usage of those more typically representative of the adult sphere (Green 2016: 69); or that speakers of youth language can help a language to grow: some youth varieties have actually broadened the vocabularies of their host languages as young speakers become adults and take youth language with them (Kerswill 2010). And by no means gilding the lily are three final points: that – as we saw in Chapter Two – the use of such language does not by necessity constitute a speaker's entire linguistic repertoire, i.e. speakers can often adapt their language according to context and circumstances; that young people may be filling a perceived void where they feel that their values, hopes and aspirations are left unstated and unaddressed in much the same way as any other community; and that, in functional terms and in principle, those engaging in youth language practices can be little different from members of the mainstream who use situationally relevant language for their own ends. Quite aside from the fact that some speakers of youth language may also be regarded as adults in view of their age and responsibilities, for instance, Eckert (2002: 7) argues with real merit that adolescent stylistic practice is not qualitatively different from adult practice insofar as:

> [w]e are all tweaking our styles in one way or another as we proceed through life and from situation to situation, and it is precisely the flux of identity, persona, community and the times that keeps stylistic practice – hence the construction of meaning in and for variation – an ongoing process,

while Thurlow (2005: 4–5; his emphasis),[14] in his discussion of youth, also perceptively points to the ongoing negotiation and representation of identity:

> For most social theorists and critical scholars, it is now received wisdom that identity (cultural, social or otherwise) is an intensely dynamic *lifelong* project … the communicative process of identification never ceases; it is certainly not unique to young people, nor is it their sole preoccupation.

Youth language practices: an impenetrable threat?

So, why are youth language practices seen as such a threat? What is it about them that prompts such apprehensive, anxious or even hostile reactions from some quarters? No doubt there are many reasons why people respond to such practices in a negative or defensive manner. These may range from resistance to or concern about linguistic or sociocultural change, including the compromise of language purity or social identity, to fears among parents that their children will bring social disadvantage upon themselves, perhaps through inappropriate or incorrect use (e.g. Thurlow 2003a; Wyn 2005). These concerns appear to coincide with those cited by Cheshire, Nortier and Adger (2015: 17–8) regarding risks to future employment, social prospects and "the good functioning of society" through the use of "urban youth vernaculars" variously in France, England, the Netherlands and Germany.

A particularly engaging study of an adult cohort's attitudes towards youth language practices can be seen in a survey conducted in Cameroon by Stein-Kanjora (2008). In her work, Stein-Kanjora elicited the opinions of 50 adults aged 25–63 years about the use of Camfranglais by many young people in urban centres (see Table 3.2).

Although these data were provided by a range of social actors, some of whom may nominally have yet engaged in youth practices of some kind, they are nonetheless revealing. They suggest concerns about the effect of Camfranglais on the broader culture and community; on children's sociocultural and linguistic resources; on the status of the state's main languages, English and French; on youths' moral or behavioural compass; and reflect views about Camfranglais being tied to childhood or adolescence. Some of these responses align to some extent with the findings of a study of age and language choice in Cameroon

Table 3.2 Stein-Kanjora: adults' views on the use of Camfranglais

It causes problems; speakers will mix up English and French	26%
It has a bad influence on kids; English and French are lost	26%
It's a normal part of youths growing up; it will stop	18%
It's ok; easy, amusing, creative language	14%
It's a terrible situation for our country and our children	12%
No information	4%

(Stein-Kanjora 2008: 124)

by Ngefac (2010) who – examining the questionnaires of 120 respondents – noted that the two reasons among the 68% of respondents who did *not* speak Camfranglais (35% of Francophone speakers between 26–39 years and 100% of Francophone and Anglophone speakers aged 40 and over) were that it was "the language of rascals and irresponsible children" (76%) and was "childish" (24%) (Ngefac 2010: 158).[15] Indeed, in view of the reactions to Bahasa Gaul, Sheng, Kogal and other youth languages cited previously, we can reasonably expect to see some of the apprehensions cited by Stein-Kanjora and Ngefac's respondents voiced by adults and the mainstream in other societies. For instance, youth language in the Netherlands – now commonly known as Straattaal ('street language') – has been stereotypically characterised as reflecting "social and linguistic deviance, deficiency and even delinquency", has attracted criticism from teachers and has figured in television discussions about "the degeneration of Dutch" (Cornips, Jaspers and de Rooij 2015: 48–9). A number of specific antagonisms can therefore surface, and there is merit in considering underlying tensions. For example, are there conceptualisations regarding inter-generational change? In a discussion of youth and the media in the UK, the US, Australia and New Zealand, for instance, Wyn (2005: 25) notes one perception that: "[i]f young people do not grow up to reproduce the patterns of life and the values of the previous generation, then they appear to represent a threat to the traditional order". This could be a causative factor in a number of societies, although note needs to be taken that sociolinguistic and sociocultural contexts can, of course, differ. For example, some societies might have only one dominant state language (e.g. Spain, Russia), while others may have more than one or a number of widely spoken languages (e.g. Kenya, Zimbabwe; see also **Multilingualism** on pages 111–12 and **Language ideology** on page 127).

Another factor that deserves attention in understanding youth language and reactions to it concerns its accessibility: perhaps it is threatening to the uninitiated because they can't understand it? Although some report that young people do not try to encrypt their language or aim to be cryptic (Duc 2003 on French students; Quist 2008 on the use of multiethnolect in Copenhagen, as cited by Nortier and Dorleijn 2013: 16; Jørgensen 2013, citing Briz 2003 on Spanish teenage language), the allegation to the contrary is widespread (see, for example, Chambert-Loir 1984; Ogechi 2005; Manfredi 2008a; Mugaddam 2008). The reasons underpinning this notion are interesting. It can be argued that there is a tacit suggestion that such disquiet may in some part be based on assumptions that particularly adults/ the mainstream are entitled to and/or should know about young people's communications; on the related premise that youth are "apparently obliged to make themselves understandable to adults" (Thurlow 2014: 490–1); and on worries that adults are being deliberately excluded (which they sometimes are). Whether they have a right to such communications is another matter. One way or another, however, we are led to a fundamental question: do youth language practices really constitute secret language?

A useful way to investigate this question is to consider it in five respects and note that (i) many items that adults believe to be unintelligible may also be incomprehensible to other youth (Labov 1992); (ii) even if it is codified in dictionaries and thus given the status of a language, as Thurlow (2006, 2014) notes with regard to computer-mediated discourse, youth language (and that of criminals, for that matter) tends not to represent a different language as such, but rather is created using lexical, semantic, phonological and other mechanisms, many of which can be found in other domains such as literature and in the standard variety more broadly. Indeed, in many cases, only parts of an utterance may be difficult to comprehend at the first attempt; (iii) many varieties popularly thought to be secret often end up revealed and examined in social or academic studies, or used in literature and the media (for example, in advertising, where notions of who is and who is not supposed to use youth language may be exploited – see, for instance, Cheshire, Nortier and Adger 2015); (iv) the degree of exclusivity brought about by in-group communication may be exaggerated as youth become painted in sweeping terms as a socially distant Other. A "clear set of reinscribed assumptions about young people and the nature of youth" thus become consolidated or perpetuated, especially by the media (Thurlow 2014: 490); and (v) there are so many mechanisms used by so many groups, for whom cryptolect may or may not be important, that it is impossible to give an all-embracing, catch-all answer regarding secrecy *as a prime motive*, even within a single larger Community of Practice. In some cases, an individual's or group's practices may enable them to establish a sense of peer group solidarity or to bolster individual status. Correspondingly, a tough-to-crack cryptolect, or any cryptolect at all, might not be required: it's the use of the in-group language, the resultant social sharedness, the desire to convey a message with the appropriate affect and force, the use of appropriate language, and/or the underlining of social status that counts (although this does not necessarily preclude claims of distinctiveness). For example, when asked in 2012 why they used their particular language variety (identified as 'slang'), linguistics students at Victoria University of Wellington, New Zealand cited a number of reasons, none of which referred explicitly to secrecy or exclusivity (esoterogeny). Instead, their responses focused greatly on other motivations, including the ability to achieve communicative aims such as expressing feelings or irony, the value of creativity, social cachet, and the use of contextually appropriate language. The replies, not given in order of prominence, can be seen in Table 3.3.

This compares with a survey carried out by Nad'iarova (2014) of 70 Humanities students at several higher education establishments in Simferopol', Crimea.

Table 3.3 Bardsley: motives of students at Victoria University of Wellington, New Zealand, for using slang

- ease of communication
- to give the speaker street cred
- to be ironic
- to be creative
- to combine words and feelings
- to exaggerate feelings
- it is more appropriate than Standard English in socially relaxed situations

(Bardsley 2014: 102–3)

Table 3.4 Nad'iarova: motives of students in Simferopol', Crimea, for using in-group youth language

- desire not to stand out from others (75%)
- habit (60%)
- desire to be up-to-date (57.5%)
- influence of company and friends (42.5%)
- possession of insufficient standard vocabulary (20%)

(Nad'iarova 2014: 72)

Of the respondents, 30% noted using in-group youth language "quite often", 60% "sometimes" and 10% "never". Again, none specifically highlighted the need for encryption, as Table 3.4 shows.

In other cases, however, groups *will* go to some lengths to ensure that access to their communication remains out-of-reach to out-groups, with this secrecy in turn bringing a sense of security and, sometimes, solidarity:

- Street youth in Indonesia, for example, use in-group language that both protects against unwanted intrusion by out-group members and fosters feelings of autonomy and solidarity (Beazley 2003). Harchaoui (2015) advances a similar proposition regarding solidarity vis-à-vis the use of certain loanwords by adolescents in Eastern Oslo.
- In Zimbabwe, urban youth language can contain elements from a number of languages such as English, Shona, Ndebele and other African languages to ensure secrecy and to exclude elders (Veit-Wild 2009; Hollington and Makwabarara 2015).
- In France and Sudan, speakers of Verlan and Randuk deliberately create new unintelligible vocabulary if they feel that terms have become too widespread or well-known (Méla 1991; Manfredi 2008a).

So, access to a large extent can depend on the lengths to which a group will go when they encrypt.

In many instances, youth language forms can be fairly easily recovered and some understanding of what is being communicated possible (see, for example,

Thurlow 2003a, 2006 on youth use of SMS in English, and Smith-Hefner 2007 on Bahasa Gaul). One thing that may stand in the favour of the out-group is that youth language *tends* to observe the core syntactic and grammatical frameworks of local colloquial forms – so, Russian youth practice, for instance, largely observes standard Russian grammar and is used within the framework of general colloquial syntax (the same happens with many other varieties, such as Sheng and French youth language, for example – see Beyer 2015). What is more, some word-creation methods such as metathesis may have been used by out-group members in years gone by (Davie 1998; Doran 2007), and so they might be able to deduce meaning, especially if change in a word's form through a known mechanism is the only thing that hampers understanding (i.e. there is no semantic change). Or a word might previously have been used by out-group members as an in-group item in their youth: a good example of this is a Russian word for 'cool' ('klëvyi') – popular in the 1980s and 1990s – which was documented as far back as 1786 with broadly the same meaning ('splendid') (Davie 1998: 123. Leaving aside the question of what is considered *old*, see also Stalker 1995; Coleman 2012; Widawski 2012, 2015; Green 2016 on the longevity of 'slang' words in English; Levikova 2004 on Russian; and Deumert (in press) on Tsotsitaal). Alternatively, the form or use of items may be sufficiently clear for out-group members to correctly guess meaning, or some vocabulary may become so widely used that it becomes colloquial: Camfranglais, for example, has spread to other cities in Cameroon and among other social groups, partly due to adolescents using it in the workplace and other social milieux when they leave education (Kießling 2004). This is also the case in Côte d'Ivoire with Nouchi, which has spread sufficiently widely among students and pupils so that it is no longer secret, in part due to its association with the early 1990s *zouglou* musical style and large-scale urbanisation (Aboa 2011). Indeed, such has been its spread that parents might use Nouchi to communicate with their children; all of the Côte d'Ivoire population is reported to have some passive knowledge of it (Aboa 2011).

So, in writing off youth language practices as indexing immaturity and faddishness, in perhaps catastrophising about deviance and the sociocultural consequences of its use, in sometimes seeing it in the most secretive and inaccessible terms, and in not thinking more deeply into why youth may situationally use certain forms of language to express how they view themselves and others, members of the mainstream can leave themselves open to charges of:

- failing to comprehend why such language is used and what this use means for the individual and others in respect of identity;
- not understanding the dynamics of how such language varieties develop to convey and construct what is happening socially *on the ground*;
- underestimating the complexity of social negotiation as seen in youth discourse;
- exaggerating claims of the impenetrability of youth language practices, in some cases to accentuate claims of a definitive break with standard language and thereby cast speakers as Others;

- overstating the impenetrability of youth language practices to underline perceptions of youth as a distinct and profitable market (e.g. Thurlow 2007, 2012, 2014 on digital discourse); and
- selectively criticising users of language varieties of which they don't approve, while praising those who may employ similar or the same linguistic devices for other creative ends (in line with the thoughts of Tajfel and Turner 1986, as outlined in Chapter Two).

Language ideology

Questions of language ideology address beliefs and assumptions about how people communicate and the relative value assigned to linguistic practices and varieties within sociocultural systems. Foci for language ideology questions include, *inter alia*, the socio-political and sociocultural premises that underpin models of standard or appropriate usage and concordant beliefs about the social value of standard varieties relative to dialects or vernaculars; and the use of languages as a sign of national identity in the construction of states. Correspondingly, language ideologies must be "understood and investigated as cultural constructions" (Lytra 2015: 185).

Language ideologies can be both maintained and contested. By exploring the views of young people concerning their own and others' contextually situated practices, we can further interrogate their perspectives on ideology. Cutler and Røyneland (2015: 140), for instance, posit that youth from both immigrant backgrounds and host communities in Norway and the US connect with the oppositional expressivity of hip hop and engage in language practices that "challenge hegemonic language ideologies" through which dominant social establishments propagate bias in favour of an "abstract, idealized homogeneous standard language". Indeed, Cutler and Røyneland propose that while groups (such as immigrants) who lack proficiency in the national language are disadvantaged through such ideologies, multiethnolectal and non-standard practices linked to hip hop can help the youth they discuss to set themselves apart from others, resist and/or transform entrenched traditional notions of ethnicity and social configuration, and positively underscore their identity. See also **Overt and covert prestige** on page 73, **Mainstream perceptions vis-à-vis the standard** (Introduction), **Youth language practices: how they're perceived** and **Youth language practices: an impenetrable threat?** (this chapter, both).

Identity for the self and others

As some commentators suggest (e.g. Thurlow 2003b, 2005; Bucholtz and Skapoulli 2009), in some societies there have been tendencies to regard youth and their identity monolithically, as concepts or phenomena that are somehow fixed. Furthermore, in classifying the semantic fields of interest that are commonly reflected in youth discourse, there has also been a tendency to generalise the preoccupations and concerns of young people as a larger collective (i.e. young people like X). Of course, a certain degree of thematic and linguistic consistency will be found among the language varieties of many different youth collectives, especially as some cultural values and practices gain appeal across societies (see also **The global and the local** and subsequent sections, and Chapter Five's discussion of fertile semantic fields).

However, as a social constituency young people are neither homogeneous nor static (Thurlow 2003a, 2003b, 2007; Levikova 2004). As youth negotiate the surrounding social world, they make sense of their own place, and those of others, within it. They derive meaning from, and create meaning within, different contexts. They explore, shape and express identities for themselves and look to understand the identities and modes of expression associated with others and how they compare with their own – be those others parents, the dominant social mainstream, other social constituencies, or other youth. Furthermore, in a highly mobile world (in social, cultural and physical senses) youth can act as diverse and dynamic sociocultural agents. They might traverse national and/or social borders; and they might express affiliation with larger, boundary-crossing groups and/or with collectives occupying a quite different sociocultural space. Moreover, they might also adapt broader practices, or create novel ones, within varying *local* contexts. Scholars have been interested in how rappers, for example, might talk about their immediate situation or neighbourhoods while identifying with broader hip hop values and/or practices (e.g. Androutsopoulos and Scholz 2002; Stein-Kanjora 2008; Alim 2009; Androutsopoulos 2009; Cutler and Røyneland 2015), and in how young people of North African descent have fused French and Arabic terms in their creation of urban French youth language and identity (e.g. Méla 1988; Pozas 2000).

Insofar as we acknowledge that young people come in a variety of social and cultural shapes and sizes, so it is incumbent that we recognise that the language wells from which they draw also vary (in line with thinking on repertoires; see also **Multilingualism** on pages 111–12). Each individual may have different linguistic resources on which to call: most, if not all, no doubt draw on local vernacular usage which develops around and among family and local sociocultural networks – for some, this vernacular may be a variety of a single language which is dominant in a given society; for others, a second language might be spoken at home and not within the wider community; for others still, access may be to more than one language within broader society (e.g. the use of French and Arabic in parts of Paris, popular Ivorian French and Dioula in parts of Abidjan). Additionally, some young people might call on global cultural markers such as hip hop and the language believed to index hip hop identities and activities as a means of connecting with aspects of other (e.g. US) cultures or subcultures while not living in the originating society.

Indeed, by drawing on potentially differing linguistic resources; by determining which and how language forms will be used; and by deciding how these linguistic choices will sit or fit with other or others' ideologies and identity markers (such as demeanour, musical taste, dance, clothes – locally or globally recognised, or highly individualised), young people often draw on *many* rich and varied resources to help them meet their goals. For example, to show how up-to-date they are; to index coolness and/or establish social currency or attractiveness; to provide means for feeling socially and emotionally secure about themselves; to authenticate a particular identity; to know to what extent one style, stance or idea is close to or distant from another or is shared or not by others; and to make socio-stylistic decisions based on these understandings.

As a matter of fact, youth's appreciation of the significance of the diverse links between language, style, interaction and identity, and how others perceive these interstices, can be important. Such knowledge and sensitivity can be used to advantage to make choices in different social situations: they allow young people to know how to accentuate or downplay identities when they want to project images of coolness and urban awareness, for example; or to know how to cross what might be perceived as ethnic, class, political or other boundaries and operate in, and borrow and adapt from, different spaces (see also **Crossing boundaries**).[16] And they allow youth to gain social and material benefits, as Githinji (2006: 458) intimates regarding the use of Sheng by petty prostitutes:

> They claimed that there is no kind of Sheng that they could not understand. Knowledge of many varieties was what enabled them to interact with different clients,

and by other youth from different groups, or 'bazes':

> By pointing to these lexical differences, Makadara respondents sought to show their baze's Sheng variety as unique and distinct from that of Dandora, Kariobangi and Makongeni. However, in a free conversation recording soon afterwards, one of the respondents, Joe, used both mbevo and chuja unconsciously. In the same conversation Bill called thieves mapunju, while seeking clarification from Joe. Since they had claimed they do not use those words, such mismatches may be attributed to language crossing abilities among speakers from different bazes, *who in the case of their daily transactions, have to modify their linguistic behavior in order to gain admission into various networks.*
> (Githinji 2006: 465; my italics)[17]

What kind of difference? Many actors, many contexts, many Others

So far, we have discussed the ongoing construction (and reconstruction) of identity both by individuals and groups. We have established that young people use youth-associated language forms to create identities and express or recognise distinguishable stances, worldviews, and others' positions in the sociocultural universe. They use and recognise these images, symbols and other resources to establish commonality, belonging and difference when in- and out-groups form, and to navigate social spaces. Insofar as style and symbols have social meaning, the projection of image and worldview or ideology cannot happen within a vacuum; social meaning draws currency from the larger collective's or others' views, activities and dispositions (Irvine 2001).

With this in mind, it's perhaps worth thinking more about difference and differentiation. What are they? We've already considered how some youth groups might use language forms that parents or others don't understand to hide meaning. In some cases, this may be to conceal criminality;[18] however, that certainly need not always be the case – sometimes the main driver may instead be to emphasise who is and is not in the social loop or to index opposition to the mainstream. What is the nature of the difference that the use of youth language serves to underline?

In our discussion of the depiction of youth as a social constituency, we have noted that they are sometimes painted as a monolithic Other by those in the mainstream sphere. However, just as there are dangers in viewing youth in such sweeping terms, so the context for the use of youth language – and, by extension, criminal practices also – varies. Méla (1991: 73) crystallised this perceptively in her seminal work on Verlan when she observed that Verlan is the "language mirror in which the many tensions of society and the diversity of those people and things referenced by Verlan speakers are reflected".[19] As Méla intimated, these tensions can be manifold, with different referents and, ultimately, actors and circumstances reflected (we'll explore the motivations behind Verlan more in Chapter Eight).

Méla (1991: 74) also posited that Verlan "by its nature transmits another reality than the standard language through its speakers".[20] Here the very use of an alternative, non-standard mode of expression is a rejection, supplanting, reshaping or disfiguring of a standard language and the values and social structures with which it is felt to be associated (see also, for example, Halliday 1978; Méla 1997; Mayr 2004; Brook 2010; Vakunta 2011). Although Méla's comments focused on Verlan as it was spoken and the reasons for its use in early 1990s France, Verlan is still widely used (indeed, it can even be a vehicle, if not focus, for irony by some out-groupers), and Méla's observations about it continue to resonate elsewhere. For example, Nouchi and Camfranglais are partly used to protest against French in Côte d'Ivoire and Cameroon where French, a colonial language, is often held to index the identities and values of social and political élites and of those who benefit materially from mastering it (Kießling 2004; Kouassi Ayewa 2005; Vakunta 2008). Its status and form are therefore subverted by Nouchi and Camfranglais speakers for whom the use of French has a different meaning and impact.

Indeed, the range of Others against and from whom youth language practices may be used to convey protest and difference, or establish distance – both on an ongoing, consistent basis and dynamically as stance and identification are negotiated – can be broad. It might encompass older generations: in Germany, for example, speakers utilise Kiezdeutsch as a means of distinguishing themselves from other groups such as parents, teachers and adults more generally, not to mention siblings (Paul, Freywald and Wittenberg 2009), while in Cameroon, speakers of Camfranglais use or replace vocabulary to ensure that understanding remains difficult or impossible for adults (Kießling 2004; Vakunta 2008). Thurlow (2003a: 14), moreover, observes that certain technological affordances such as SMS texting can enable youth to operate "outside the purview of, and beyond the immediate reach of, parents and other authority figures". Indeed, moves by youth to establish distance from adults are no doubt enabled or consolidated in some places where youth repertoires are fed by sociocultural resources and practices to which older speakers have more limited or no access, such as social media, some film and television genres and music, as Nassenstein (2016) suggests with regard to the organisation of speaker repertoires in urban Africa, and Kraidy and Khalil (2008) in respect of Arab youth. However, it is noteworthy that the negotiation of difference, distance and exclusion can apply both ways – viz. the use of "undisclosed codes" in Uganda to exclude young people from discussions involving older speakers (Namyalo 2015: 334). Equally, it is conceivable that the practices of older generations may be prized, as Deumert (in press) notes with regard to the esteem with which old-style Tsotsitaal terms are held by some present-day youth actors both on- and offline.

Furthermore, the Other may include those who maintain a rural or more traditional lifestyle and who may be thought to be remote from or disinterested in modernity, and/or to be lacking the sophistication or cultural currency associated with urban spaces (e.g. Kießling 2004 and Vakunta 2008 on Camfranglais; Ahua 2006 on Nouchi; Githinji 2006 on Sheng; Smith-Hefner 2007 on Bahasa Gaul). There is a strong emphasis in much of the literature on youth and criminal language practices within urban spaces, in no small part because this is where the ramifications of migration and urbanisation can be clearly seen, if not keenly felt: for example, in urban areas of Sudan, Kenya, Indonesia and Northern Europe (see, for instance, Dorleijn and Nortier 2013 on multiethnolects). It is instructive that Hagedorn (2005) indicates that the overwhelming majority of gangs and gang members are from Africa, Asia and Latin America and ties this phenomenon directly to urbanisation, while Green (2016: 36) also sees direct links between generic English 'slang' and the town or city more broadly:

> Still, the city provides slang's consistent home. The history of slang is also the history of the urbanization of modern life as reflected in this influential subset of the language. One may suggest a simple rule: no city, no slang.

Certainly, a number of varieties are linked closely with urban practice: for example, Bahasa Prokem is frequently associated with criminals, street kids and students in Jakarta (e.g. Chambert-Loir 1984); Randuk is reported to index the identity of urban youth in Northern and Central Sudan, having arisen in the 1970s after large-scale urbanisation in Khartoum and having later spread to other urban centres in the 1980s and 1990s (Manfredi 2008a); Sheng is largely – but not exclusively (see Kioko 2015) – associated with marginalised urban Kenyan youth, having originally developed in the poor areas of Nairobi's Eastlands in the 1960s or 1970s (Ferrari 2006; Githinji 2006; Beck 2015); and, going back further in time, Lunfardo is often associated with the Buenos Aires underworld of the nineteenth century (Grayson 1964), to cite but a few examples. With these facts in place, it is little surprise that, in the introduction to her study of teenage language in London and Madrid, Stenström (2014: 8–9) advances the view that "[n]ew tendencies in teenage talk usually make their first appearance in the big cities, often capitals, from which they spread to other regions".

However, as compelling as the links between urban life and youth language practices may be, not to mention how these help to construct ideas of the rural Other, there are three qualifications to this association that merit attention.

First of all is the consideration that a concentration of use in urban spaces does not necessarily mean in and of itself that a variety is used to index a rejection of rural life and/or the practices and principles thought to be associated with it *tout court*. That some urban youth choose to espouse and project identities that promote images of, and practices related to, urbanity is undoubtedly the case: young people in Zimbabwe, for instance, employ youth language for a number of reasons, including to signal difference from those in rural areas (Hollington and Makwabarara 2015), while many of their counterparts in Cameroon may use Camfranglais "in opposition to other groups such as the older generation, the rural population and the elite" (Vakunta 2008: 942). Thus, there appear to be cases where young people resist the traditions held to be valued by those in rural spaces, and – potentially – reject associated traditional outlooks and/or sociocultural practices which they feel are synonymous with rural life (i.e. with tribalism, traditional beliefs, cultural practices and customs, specific social roles and so on).

However, as we will explore in discussion of the implications of globalisation later (**The global and the local** and following sections), many young people in Africa, to continue with examples from that continent, intertwine urban and rural practices within their repertoires and social meaning-making, and in doing so underline the value of both the urban *and* the rural and elements of what each is held to implicate. Samper (2004), for example, posits that while rappers from Nairobi use Sheng because it is the variety with which they and their audience are most familiar, those from rural places may use their mother tongues or Swahili, although this is not a universal practice. In doing so they thus interlink questions of identification and affiliation that span the transnational (for instance, rap, hip hop), the ethnic or tribal and the urban/rural (notably, Ogechi (2005) observes that many African Kenyans, particularly those working or living in towns, may have two homes: the urban place in which they live and a rural home where they were born and grew up, and where family members may still live). At the same time, youth from rural France rank among those living in Parisian suburbs (Doran 2004), leaving open the possibility – at least nominally – of fused practices.

A second consideration concerning immediate associations between youth practices and urbanity questions propositions that it is in urban spaces that hubs of youth-inspired creativity are to be found. Leaving aside the bigger question of what constitutes sophistication or creativity (on which see Carter 2004), it is noteworthy that Stenström, in the introduction referenced in the previous section, postulates that "[n]ew tendencies in teenage talk *usually* make their first appearance in the big cities, often capitals, from which they spread to other regions" (Stenström 2014: 8–9; my italics). In other words, while urban centres are *typically* regarded as the locus of creation and subsequent propagation, this is not *always* the case; they need not be seen as the sole forges of innovation. Naturally, as Kerswill (2010: 13) notes, it may well be the case that "[u]rban settings allow for development of adolescent peer groups" and that conditions of (super)-diversity in urban spaces can provide more ample ingredients and a more fertile setting for new forms of language practice to unfold. However, as Nassenstein (2016) postulates with regard to Africa at least, knowledge about youth practices in rural areas can be patchy at best or lacking. Therefore, a question arises about the extent and nature of, and dynamics behind, creativity, innovation and expression among rural youth. Indeed, Nassenstein (2015c) points to village youth inventing "new rural registers that express regional identity, agency and subversive style".

This is not to say that the rural has been completely ignored: Nassenstein (2015c) cites the existence of 'Luo slang' in Alendu, Kenya; and Karanja (2010) talks of the use of Sheng by rural as well as urban youth, an observation supported by Kioko (2015), who states that rural Sheng has a number of registers where different mother tongues provide the base language. Nevertheless, Nassenstein (2015c, 2016) is correct in claiming that, with a few exceptions, youth language practices in Africa – to continue with that continent – have mostly been considered within urban settings (see, for example, numerous chapters in Nassenstein and Hollington 2015), despite ongoing movement and increasing connectivity between urban and rural spaces through social media and mobile telephony, all of which facilitate the creation of cryptolect in the towns where urban youths adopt items from little-known rural practices, and the incorporation online of rural youth into global flows where they can borrow a number of transnational practices, much as we see in conditions of super-diversity (Nassenstein 2015c). In other words, conditions can also exist for the agency of rural speakers – who may elect to create their own rural varieties – to be realised in very dynamic ways that need not by necessity involve identity creation and the negotiation of social meaning using symbols of urbanity. Notably, this tendency towards the urban is not just present in African studies: if we look at recent discussions of youth practice in Europe and elsewhere (Stenström, Andersen and Hasund 2002; Garza 2008; Dorleijn and Nortier 2013; Stenström 2014; various chapters in Nortier and Svendsen 2015), we see that these too tend towards the urban.

A third point concerns the perceived homogeneity of the rural Other, that is to say, there is merit in challenging notions that youth practice in rural areas is homogeneous or seen by all as such (a point that also holds for practices and perceptions in urban localities – see, for instance, Aarsæther, Marzo, Nistov and Ceuleers 2015 on youth linking language practices with different spaces such as cities and neighbourhoods in Genk and Oslo, and Kioko 2015 on the use of Sheng in different districts of Nairobi). Indeed, great value might potentially be derived from comparison and contrast between rural varieties, and perceptions of linguistic/semiotic commonality and difference within discrete rural locales. Such work depends, of course, on greater research coverage of rural language practice in the first place. However, analysis of rural youth language practices vis-à-vis a number of factors, considered either singly or in combination – for example, comparative rural linkage to online communities, distances from urban, peri-urban or other locations, influence of local dominant languages/dialects, demographic dimensions, etc. – alongside urban–rural comparisons may provide no less interesting insights than comparison between urban varieties, including inner–outer city practices (as in, for instance, Kioko 2015). And such analyses might ultimately help to better understand the practices and identities which Nassenstein (2015c) has in mind when he states that, whether carried out in the town or village, youth language practices should be regarded as "global repertoires" where the polar understandings of urban and rural are challenged (see also Hurst 2017 on African rural and urban linguistic resources not being "mutually exclusive as markers of identity").

Returning to the Other more generally, one final point is that not only can it take a number of forms (older generations, rural inhabitants, other youth groups, etc.), but that it is also likely that youth actors will stand against a number of Others at the same time. Urban youth in Yaoundé and Douala, for example, can use Camfranglais to exclude outsiders such as the older generation, *and/or* rural populations *and/or* a corrupt élite who sign up to the norms that come with *francophonie* and who block access to many aspects of the modern world and the benefits that might accrue (Kießling 2004). Put simply, there may be many and varied causes and stances which these and other urban youth might oppose. Multiple drivers have also been postulated for other youth varieties, such as the French suburban youth practices documented by Doran (2004, 2007), where marginalised minority youth rejected official language practices and ideologies associated with a dominant bourgeois who, they believed, both held a different set of values and enjoyed a different socio-economic/class status (see also **Language ideology** on page 127). Furthermore, it is also noteworthy that ranging against Others need not be the only undertaking by speakers as they communicate: as they position themselves against one or more Others, they may also simultaneously stand alongside other in-group members as a mark of solidarity (e.g. Kießling 2004 on Camfranglais; Cornips and de Rooij 2013 on minority youth usage in Rotterdam).

Youth language practices: not just about men and boys

The question of gender and youth practices has a number of dimensions to it, with girls and young women often implied or explicitly considered to constitute the Other among subjects in a number of studies. Manfredi (2008b), for instance, indicates that Randuk must not be used in linguistic interaction between boys and girls, while Stein-Kanjora (2008) records how some Camfranglais speakers may alter words so that female listeners cannot understand males. In both cases, a perspective is taken by the subject that views the male social actor in a primary or central position and as enjoying certain social privileges. This centrality of young males as social actors is not limited to Randuk and Camfranglais: Méla (1997: 31) described the use of Verlan in the mid- to late 1990s as a "slang for guys, made for guys to speak with guys",[21] although clearly girls and young women have also used it in interaction (Méla 1991), while Grachëv (2007, cited in Gromov 2009: 3) considered it "curious" that young women were actively involved in creating Russian youth language terminology.

Although in some societies young males in particular can be liable to be regarded as communicatively inept (Thurlow 2003b), the depiction of females as the Other often reflects ideologies where masculinity is especially esteemed and where, to extend the scope of Miller's observation regarding female engagement in some Japanese popular cultural initiatives, "girls and 'girl culture' are marginal to primary (male) culture" (Miller 2011: 1). Correspondingly, where such privilege is in evidence, and males may be accorded greater latitude and scope as social agents, the researcher may well be providing an accurate or reasonable description of a general gender bias and/or understandings and discourses about communication (e.g. Thurlow 2003b) in the broader sociolinguistic environment. In her work on tsotsitaals in South Africa, for example, Hurst (2007, 2015) observes that they constitute varieties that are *mainly* spoken by urban males or associated with masculinity and street smarts. Although there are versions spoken by (some) women, girls and non-criminals that have developed into a broader vernacular in some locations, Tsotsitaal was originally born in part out of a masculinity that celebrated violence and crime (Hurst 2007; Milani, Jonsson and Mhlambi 2015), and its use by women can still carry some stigma (Hurst 2017). However, while there is no question of the male agency that has underpinned the initial creation and propagation of Tsotsitaal, the picture around who uses Tsotsitaal is more nuanced than one that can be accounted for through identifying general gender biases. An important factor here may revolve around what kind of Tsotsitaal we have in mind – there may be more than one version with different degrees of access, images of prototypicality and attendant perceptions surrounding use. Hurst (2013), for example, refers to males being more likely to be involved in the generation and use of new Tsotsitaal lexis where a deep, less accessible variety is used, while women, very young children and the older generations have at their disposal versions that can be characterised as "milder" and "more accessible" (Hurst 2013). Furthermore, although Tsotsitaal can index roughness and street culture, this does not exclude the possibility of women using Tsotsitaal words and expressions consciously to convey a specific social persona (Deumert, in press). Its performative use and its value in the construction of identity also require more nuanced consideration.

The conceptualisation of male language practices has also been articulated in view of a greater association with social resistance, conflict and the breaking of social convention (Bucholtz 2002; Kiessling and Mous 2004; de Klerk 2005), as well as with in-group youth language and swearing (Danesi 1994; Beazley 2003; de Klerk and Antrobus 2004; de Klerk 2005; Stenström 2014). In a thought-provoking study, Stenström, Andersen and Hasund (2002), for instance, analysed teenage language practices in the London area using a quantitative approach and used the resultant statistics to draw conclusions about different behaviours relating to class, age and gender. Their study, they noted, "showed, not unexpectedly, that the boys (especially the 10–13 year-olds) used more slang and dirty language than the girls", and that this usage extended to swearing (Stenström, Andersen and Hasund 2002: 212). This qualification is instructive: although they included male subjects together with teenage girls in the research and produced statistically informed insights about gendered language practices, the authors were not surprised to see a link emerge between certain youth language practices and young males. Indeed, it could be argued that a correlation of some description involving agentive male behaviour was to be anticipated, not least when we consider that a similar connection ties in-group hierarchies and verbal competitiveness to male peer collectives (e.g. Stenström, Andersen and Hasund 2002; de Klerk 2005; but see Eckert 2005 and also **Verbal contests and ritual insults** later in the chapter) and in view of a potentially gendered understanding that may arise from the historical ties some youth varieties and emerging vernaculars are believed to have with criminality and images of violence or danger (e.g. Hurst 2007, 2015 and Deumert (in press) on Tsotsitaal; Mensah 2016 on gangs in Africa more broadly).

While the direction of research and concomitant analytical paradigms relating to youth cultural practices have been influenced by underlying popular associations involving masculinity and sociocultural agency (Bucholtz 2002), and while within youth literature young women have correspondingly tended to be less commonly studied as full-status social agents in their own right, it is noteworthy that this phenomenon is neither new nor limited to the study of language practices. Wulff (1995a, 1995b), for example, relates that most major studies of youth culture until the mid-1990s focused on urban, Western male youth in sociological and anthropological research, while in his engaging sociological analysis Miles (2000: 147–8) notes Jeffs and Smith's (1998) proposition that the idea of youth was mostly understood in masculine terms.

This is not to say that girls and young women have not figured as research subjects in investigations of youth language practices in any way, shape or form. Méla (1991), for example, noted how in 1990s France many 'beur' girls (i.e. girls of North African background) used Verlan to rebel against the expected image of young women; Veit-Wild (2009: 687, citing Chuma) has documented how in Zimbabwe some young women distinguish themselves not only through wearing hipsters, skin-tight blouses and high-heeled shoes, but also by speaking in a particular accent to mould and project identity; and Miller (2004) has reported how in Japan, where the standard language has masculine and feminine forms, and where young women are traditionally expected to comply with conservative social expectations, girls have developed their own lexis at least since the Meiji era spanning 1868–1912. Finally, in their study of Eastern Cape Province youth practices, including deprecating and pejorative usage, de Klerk and Antrobus (2004: 279) also underline moves by young women to use such language to "assert a new image of women which runs contrary to stereotyped images of being pure, sensitive and caring".

Nor is this to say that to improve the overall analytical picture, young women need to be studied as agents relative only to the practices of young males. As intimated previously, it is certainly the case that in some societies, settings and situations young women have been relegated to the role of bit-part players or auxiliaries in a male-centred and/or -dominated social universe (for more see Beazley 2002), cast as second-order *bricoleuses* and as passive reactors to male-driven cultural moves, and thus variants on a male theme. Some female rappers in the early 1990s, for example, felt compelled to assume a "male aesthetic" to develop an audience for their art (Keyes 1993). At the same time, street girls in Indonesia have not only enhanced their chances of survival but have also gained confidence and street status and resisted traditional notions of femininity by adopting male practices and approaches to street life, such as smoking cigarettes, scarification, getting tattoos, wearing men's shirts and cutting their hair short (Beazley 2002). However, examination of the practices of young women beyond traditional male–female associations is also important. In her discussion of the language of Japanese women, for instance, Okamoto (1995: 310) observes that they are "socially and ideologically diverse and constantly changing". As social agents, they may use informal speech styles incorporating faddish expression, quick conversational tempos and contracted sentence-final forms ahead of more formal ones to project an image of playfulness and youthfulness. In doing so, they not only take a lead in establishing solidarity and in constructing and expressing their own sense of identity and relationships, but socially and linguistically differentiate younger women from older counterparts (Okamoto 1995).[22] This does not deny space for analysing male social practitioners and practices among and across genders *tout court* (see, for instance, Williams' 2016 interesting discussion of verbal duels, including opponent feminisation, in Cape Town hip hop ciphas as an example). However, de Klerk (2005) rightly questions whether the activity of young women should be treated as mimicry or rather as substantive attempts to create new representations of femininity that counter conventional stereotypes. Furthermore, in cases where such practice does apply, there is also the question about what forms(s) of masculinity they are trying to engage.

One way or another, although in his discussion of African youth languages Mensah (2016: 7) suggests that "[m]odern social realities triggered by the spread and development of these languages seem to deemphasize gender differentiation and other forms of bias in the use of youth languages", it is clear that more work needs to be done to correct a relative dearth of research into girl culture and the practices of and identity construction among young women (Hurst 2007, 2015; Hollington 2015; Hollington and Makwabarara 2015). This includes not just in terms of gender as a single criterion but also across other sociological factors such as class and race: Krohn and Suazo (1995) note, for instance, that black women are possibly doubly disadvantaged in respect of their gender and their race. At the same time, how young women are conceptualised as agents who actively negotiate social meaning through language should also figure centrally in deliberations. The last 20 years or so have witnessed the recognition of certain girls and young women as agents of linguistic innovation (Stenström,

Andersen and Hasund 2002; Miller 2003, 2004; Quenqua 2012; but note also Demisse and Bender's 1983 study of the language of unattached girls in Addis Ababa, for example); as active seekers and creators of distinct resistance identities (Beazley 2002; Miller 2004); as more disposed to self-disclosure in discussing personal experiences with friends (Stenström 2014); as social actors who use discrete methods of verbal duelling for particular social and communicative outcomes (Keyes 1993); as speakers employing in-group terms and/or expletives to negotiate or defy conventional concepts of femininity (Miller 2003, 2004; de Klerk 2005); as members of all-female gangs (Hagedorn 2005); as speakers utilising the same linguistic manipulations as boys but for different ends (Mugaddam 2012); as agents whose lexical borrowing trends may set them apart from young males in the same area (Harchaoui 2015: 229–30, citing Opsahl, Røyneland and Svendsen 2008); as speakers addressing discourse topics in different ways, compared both with other female groups and males (Stenström, Andersen and Hasund 2002; Stenström 2014; Hollington and Makwabarara 2015); and as actors who – in the case of teenage girls – "come to understand, value, and pursue communication differently" from teenage boys (Thurlow 2003b: 55; see also Labov 1992 for youth terms recognised and used across genders in the US), to name but a few instances. Promising ground therefore exists for more exploration of what separates the practices of some young women as social agents from those of others (see, for example, Bucholtz 2004), including young men.

Youth language practices and class: not just the lower rungs

The practice of associating specific linguistic behaviours with social classes is long-established in sociolinguistics. In some cases, commentators relate to this phenomenon in terms of social dialects or sociolects (see also **Social dialects, speech communities and Communities of Practice** on pages 84–5), which can be defined as "differences in speech associated with various social groups or classes" (Wardhaugh 1998: 45–6). The linking of certain criminal, youth or vernacular language practices with social classes is also well-established. In his discussion of English 'slang', Green (2016: 71) states that "[t]he working class, criminal or not, have always been and remain slang's leading creators and speakers" (see also Coleman 2012 on 'slang' and social class in the UK). This general connection has been reflected in individual studies. Mallik (1972), for example, noted class-related trends in his particular study in West Bengal where he indicated that it was only rarely that criminals and their associates came from the middle and upper classes in West Bengal in the 1960s; instead, they typically emerged from the lower social strata (here Mallik specified the children of criminals, prostitutes, labourers and peasants). Indeed, "[a]bout one-half of the underworld persons interviewed hail[ed] from the low income agricultural and industrial working class families having no criminal antecedents" (Mallik 1972: 3).

Where youth language practices are concerned, Beyer (2015: 33) intimates connections with class-related cohorts in a number of countries:

the beginnings of specific youth ways of speaking are usually traced back to marginalized groups, often situated in juvenile male-dominated low income and low-education class milieus where specific ways of speaking become a marker of 'resistance identities'.

A connection between resistance and social class is also identified by Bucholtz (2006), who observes that, in certain societies, many young people may construct identities in a social landscape where ideas of resistance may be especially associated with cultural styles linked to particular social classes – although this is not to say that youth identities will forever stay tied to those class-based styles.

Although class is one of a range of variables to have featured in both sociological and sociolinguistic discussion over several decades (e.g. Lodge 1993; Miles 2000; Stenström, Andersen and Hasund 2002; Verma and Saraswathi 2002; Stenström 2014; Widawski 2015), when trying to understand links between class and youth or criminal language practices, and also how these intersect with speaker motivations and identity, a number of considerations are noteworthy.

The first is that binary connections between criminal or youth language practices and stigmatised or lower-status social classes do not always reflect the greater sociolinguistic or stylistic complexity that is evident in much usage. For instance, within the context of British 'slang', Coleman (2012: 303) points to repeated adoption by the socially "privileged" of terms created by the "dispossessed" at least since the nineteenth century. In a discussion of the use of Luyaaye by youth in Kampala, Uganda, Namyalo (2015: 319) documents its use by "many youths, irrespective of social class, gender, educational background or ethnic composition". In his analysis of verbal duelling among Toronto youth, Danesi (1994) refers to the language practices of a group whose members (aged 14–16) came from middle-to-upper-middle class homes. And, in her examination of Bahasa Gaul in Indonesia, Smith-Hefner (2007) points to its use by middle-class youth who adopt language practices believed to be characteristic of those in marginal social positions such as criminals and street children, as well as loanwords. In doing so, they highlight their opposition to mainstream social conventions and traditional expectations. However, while middle-class youth may adopt items linked with disaffected counterparts at the social margins for this and other purposes (including demonstrating links to *cool* or *authentic* youth cultural practices or outlooks), such adoption need not mean that they will distance themselves altogether from that class and its attendant benefits. Instead, such speakers may maintain their middle-class associations and aspects of identity and gain the benefits that accrue, while others do not have the same options. As Eckert (2005: 105) notes with reference to Brazilian youth as profiled by Roth-Gordon: "The use of slang by the white middle class, thus, is very much part of the construction of privilege whereas its use by the kids in the favela is very much part of the construction of disenfranchisement".

A second consideration concerns the potential heterogeneity that may escape reflection in some broad-brush definitions of class. While the definition of class can be problematic and ambiguous (Miles 2000), even among social cohorts with apparently similar class or other socio-economic profiles, and both within and across societies, there can be distinctions that call for more refined analysis and interpretation and thus question the value of class as a broad variable. Indeed, more discrete social/socio-economic gradations or distinctions may be in evidence (Montgomery 2008). Nairobi provides an illuminating backdrop in this regard insofar as two varieties, both linked with the "lower class", have been associated with different subgroups. Mutonya (2007: 170) reports, for instance, that

> while Sheng is widely perceived to index urban sophistication and an association with the lower class, Kinoki indexes street sophistication and membership of a different group of the lower class: those with a shared knowledge of the experiences and harsh realities of homelessness.

Indeed, the association of broad categories such as class with varieties such as Sheng can be further challenged by dint of their becoming sufficiently widespread so as to become effectively vernacularised. As we noted already, Sheng, for example, has been chiefly associated with marginalised Kenyan youth in urban spaces, principally from the lower class and the slums. However, its emergence has been so marked that it has become the first language of many young people born in the shanty towns *and beyond*. Indeed, by 2004, it was spoken in practical terms by all young people from poor areas *as well as from the middle class* – all in, by more than 80% of the youth of Nairobi (Ferrari 2006). This too would suggest that correlations involving broad-brush class definition can bring limitations to analysis of distinct practices.

Of course, even where researchers are content with the definitions they have reached, class may not be the only sociological variable that they explore. Multilayered approaches folding in other factors can paint a richer picture than investigation of class alone. In 2005, Thurlow pointed to a requirement to understand young social actors beyond their youth, observing that identity may also be interleaved with nationality, ethnicity, gender and class, etc. Such cross-currents are certainly evident in many analyses of vernacular and/or youth social practices (not least in Beyer's observation earlier in this section). Widawski (2015: 14), for example, indicates that both the extent of use and competence in 'slang' among African Americans are linked to factors such as age, habitat and socio-economic status: "younger, inner-city working-class African Americans are naturally more prone to use slang than their older, upper-class counterparts from wealthy suburbia". Further, Stenström, Andersen and Hasund's (2002) small-scale study of ritual conflict among London-area teenagers points to contrasting language practices among black working-class girls and white and middle-class subjects (see also **Verbal contests and ritual insults**). And, in her discussion of the language practices of teenagers in London and Madrid, Stenström (2014: 94) notes that the quotative markers 'like' and 'en plan' ('like') were most typically used not only by upper/middle-class girls, but by those between 14 and 16 years of age (see also **Youth, age and language practices**).

Stenström, Andersen and Hasund's and Stenström's studies are certainly very insightful and thought-provoking in terms of drawing a picture of usage by specific cohorts: they identify sociolinguistic patterns and – in Stenström's (2014) case – also explore some of the discourse strategies and markers that speakers use. However, as our discussion of the practices of middle-class youth suggests, to reach a deeper understanding of the social meaning being explored in interaction moment-by-moment, other approaches such as those that focus on usage as stylistic practice also hold value. To this end, Eckert (2008) suggested that a new outlook is needed to support more situationally focused understandings that extend beyond those yielded by quantitative survey-based approaches, especially on a large scale. So, while there may be certain social collectives that are prototypically linked with certain language practices, further insight is needed into *specific contexts of use* to understand how class fits into the social meaning, including questions of identity, that is being situationally negotiated. As we noted previously (page 129), youth actors may select aspects of identity, including those relating to class, as they operate in different social situations. They may choose to emphasise or downplay certain facets and ascertain when and how to cross what might be perceived as class, political, ethnic and other boundaries as they operate in, and borrow and adapt from, different social spaces. In this sense, then, attention needs to be paid to social meaning as it is being negotiated in the moment, and how understandings of class fit into this dynamic, including within in-groups. The language practices of some middle-class youth who situationally index stances of social marginality are a good example of this general principle (for more, see **Style (stylistic practice) as an explanation of linguistic variation** in Chapter Two).

Youth, age and language practices: one age group or many?

In the Introduction, we acknowledged that there are a number of questions that specifically tie matters of age to youth language practices. The first of these concerns the definition of youth. We saw that, although it recognises fluidity in defining youth, an acceptable parameter for the UN is to consider age range, especially when education and employment are also assessed. To support statistical consistency across societies, the UN categorises as youth those between 15 and 24, although it also acknowledges that definitions in different parts of the world may vary. For example, the African Youth Charter views as youth everyone between 15 and 35 years of age (UNESCO 2016).

We also noted that many researchers examining youth language practices provide age ranges for subjects who we may infer to be prototypical social actors. Kießling (2004), for instance, considered Camfranglais to be used by speakers aged 10–30 years old, while Miller (2004) specified a 14–22 years age range in her discussion of the language practices of Kogals. Such ranges are not unusual and, in some cases, may be the results of data collection processes where the researcher has access to cohorts with a similar profile (e.g. school pupils).

While it is helpful to identify such age ranges for discrete subject groups, they are not absolutes: they may not necessarily capture the full range of actors or language practices beyond immediately studied cohorts. In other words, while some subject groups can be defined in age and other macrosociological terms, they might not represent the broader user communities with and from whom any given practices are shared or imported (see also **Community of Practice** on pages 84–5). At the same time, even if we accept the age ranges suggested by the UN and researchers, there is a question as to how to account for continued language practices that extend beyond youth as a perceived life stage, as Rampton (2015) notes. Again, this is not to say that establishing age ranges in studies of language practices has no value. Apart from providing tightly defined sociological data for exploration by the researcher, the question of how groups actively define themselves as in-groups, including as older or younger youth (Wilson 2015) or as distinct from other generations, remains important in terms of investigating social meaning.

A further consideration concerns the ways in which linguistic behaviours may be linked to specific age-graded youth subgroups. Such distinctions have been captured in statistical analyses (although these are less common than other types of investigation). For example, in her corpus-based study of the language practices of teenagers in London and Madrid, Stenström (2014: 94) suggests that the quotative markers 'like' and 'en plan' ('like') were most typically used by upper/middle-class girls aged between 14 and 16. This approach complements a previous study in which Stenström, Andersen and Hasund (2002) examined teenage talk in London. Here again certain trends were noticeable. For instance, the use of certain tags (items such as 'yeah' and 'innit') fell sharply after late adolescence (17–19 years) or young adulthood (20–29 years). Overall, such tags could be regarded as very characteristic of teenage talk (Stenström, Andersen and Hasund 2002: 185, 191). Equally, the same study indicated that subjects aged between 17 and 19 were the most prolific users of 'slang' (Stenström, Andersen and Hasund 2002: 105; for a definition of types of usage studied, see especially their discussion at pages 63–76).

These statistical insights are also accompanied by those of Labov (1992), who studied US high school youth language practices. Her analysis indicated, *inter alia*, that fourth-year students were more likely to recognise certain 'slang' lexis than first-year counterparts. Items included 'rents' ('parents'), 'za' ('pizza'), 'wasted', 'trashed', 'pot heads' and 'chill out'. At the same time, the item 'generic' was recognised more by those in the first year, possibly suggesting that this was a newer term (Labov 1992: 355–6).

These studies are not only instructive from a quantitative analysis point of view, but also call to attention questions about identity work. If some statistics suggest that certain items are more likely to be used by members of specific youth sub-cohorts in peer-group interaction then, given principles of in-groupness (see page 90 for a definition of **in-groups**), questions arise as to whether such items are consciously or unconsciously selected by group members with particular age profiles to index particular in-group identities, social qualities or stances. At the same time, questions also arise about whether such items are used when a speaker is in contact with other (especially socially desirable) groups with a different age or other profile. While quantitative approaches such as those cited previously cannot in and of themselves deeply explore speaker motivations, the trends they bring to light may provide a platform for investigating in more granular fashion not only which practices might be more age-graded among any given population and which less so, but also which social meanings are being negotiated relative to that grading. At the same time, and no less importantly, they serve to further underline the point that youth is not a homogeneous social group, as many commentators point out (e.g. Thurlow 2003a, 2003b, 2007; Levikova 2004; Wilson 2015).

Difference within groups

While depictions of Others are important to studies of youth and criminal practice, differentiation *within* youth groups or movements should also be considered. Just as there are problems in defining youth (or criminals, for that matter) as a fixed homogeneous social configuration, so it is possible that groups may also have different sub-elements which might share sufficient commonality to establish a measure of common identity, but which have divergent views about particular aspects of the group vision. Or who compete to gain prestige or status within the ensemble, thereby setting distinctiveness and differentiation in train.

In her engaging analysis of Camfranglais, Stein-Kanjora (2008) explored both the linguistic aspects of usage and why it was used. As part of that work, 324 youths aged 12–24 were asked why they learned Camfranglais. The main reasons can be seen in Table 3.5.

Stein-Kanjora's data make for very interesting reading, not least when we compare them with the ranking of social and cryptolectal motivations found in Mallik's data (page 113), and with some of the aims cited by Bardsley's linguistics

Table 3.5 Stein-Kanjora: youth explanations for learning Camfranglais

To code certain messages/ keep secrets from parents	14.4%
To be like the others/ because everybody speaks it	13.5%
To be integrated/accepted by friends	10.3%
For better/faster/easier communication between friends	9.7%
Because it was modern/to be 'in'	8.5%
Because it belongs to us/it's the language of youths	7.2%
Because I liked it/I found it amusing	6.0%
Not consciously/for no special reason	5.6%
I didn't want to/I was obliged to learn it	5.3%
I don't speak it	5.0%

(Stein-Kanjora 2008: 120)*

*Stein-Kanjora's data appear to chime somewhat with the findings of Ngefac (2010), who studied 120 questionnaires on age and language choice in Cameroon. Of the 32% of respondents who said they spoke Camfranglais, 79% claimed that they spoke it because it was the language for people of their age group (it was spoken by all those between 15 and 25 years, and by 65% of those between 26 and 39), while 21% explained that it was the fashionable language of the day. Ngefac also suggested that Camfranglais was preferred by Francophone youths to express their involvement in fashion and to mark off their world from that of the older generation.

students (particularly those relating to solidarity). Her respondents have an understanding of what Camfranglais is and why they and others use it. However, while the notion of Camfranglais as reflected in Table 3.5 at least nominally suggests a similarly – but not necessarily identically – understood set of language practices among respondents, the range of motivations for using it reminds us that there can be different types of Camfranglais speaker. They may share many commonalities with other group members, say in socio-economic or worldview terms. However, Stein-Kanjora's data hint that some group members were more active than others in adopting, generating, developing and using the language variety, and by extension espousing certain values associated with it, than others (e.g. "I didn't want to, I was obliged to learn it"). Levels of investment may thus differ.

That different levels of engagement are evident within a group is not entirely surprising. Indeed, Stein-Kanjora also alludes to differing degrees of perceived reward through usage when she correlates skills in using, interpreting and re-crafting youth language practices either with time spent in the peer group and/ or with status, an observation broadly in keeping with Scholten (1988), who found "a correlation between the frequency of non-standard features and popularity in the peer group" (cited by Androutsopoulos 2005: 1500). More specifically, Stein-Kanjora (2008: 121, 127) notes that:

> Being able to converse skilfully in this variety, producing new words and phrases and thus making the listener laugh inevitably accords a high in-group status to the speaker ... Verbal skills are extremely important if a speaker wants to impress his audience, and the admiration and laughter of the spectators are a precious reward for him. There is an obvious connection here to Hip-Hop culture.

Other commentators also point out that innovation and play not only consolidate solidarity among the in-group but also give speakers a means of demonstrating their creativity and individual distinction and distinctiveness to underscore or improve in-group status (Danesi 1994; Gil 2002; Androutsopoulos 2005, citing Deppermann and Schmidt 2001; Harchaoui 2015). Of course, where social esteem is influenced by innovation the converse is also true: an individual's status may suffer if their language play or neologism is seen to fail.

Indeed, establishing and maintaining status within the group through language would appear to be a consistent concern. Higgs (2014: 8), for instance, reports that "[m]astery of prison argot indicates the criminal's status in prison and his commitment to the convict identity" (see also Coleman 2012: 58). Nad'iarova (2014) suggests that some Russian youth may use items borrowed from criminal usage to appear tougher than and superior to others. In her study of Californian youth culture, Bucholtz (2006) notes that displaying knowledge of the rapidly changing lexicon of youth language allows teenagers to bolster their credentials as individuals who are on top of current trends. Similarly, Doran (2004) alludes to a number of French studies (e.g. Bachmann and Basier 1984; Lefkowitz 1989) indicating that the use of youth language practices can point to a speaker's social status; while de Klerk (2005) notes that youth language can be used coercively within a group as a way of controlling in-group values and behaviour, an observation that implies status and power. Some group members may actively vie for status through verbal contests or improvisation: for example, the invention of original, authentic and creative language forms as well as other style markers can also underline kudos in a competitive sense in the hip hop world (Alim 2009; Androutsopoulos 2009) (see also the next section, **Verbal contests and ritual insults**). Those prestigious leaders whose pioneering and innovative language practices are adopted by others have been described as *saccadic leaders* (Labov 2001), a term applied in African contexts by Nassenstein in his studies of Imvugo y'Umuhanda in Rwanda (Nassenstein 2015a) and Langila in the Democratic Republic of Congo (Nassenstein 2015b); by Vierke (2015) in her discussion of Kenyan rappers; and by Hollington and Makwabarara (2015) in their overview of youth language practices in Zimbabwe.

Finally, and no less worthy of note, are the notions that prestige can mean different things to different groups (de Klerk 2005), and that it need not be sought within youth groups alone. One language game originating in Mecca and used in the mid-twentieth century allowed speakers in the local community not only to mask conversation from visiting pilgrims and to establish social solidarity but also to gain social distinction (Walter 2002).

Whether the distinction is between or within groups, the importance of youth language practices for signalling and maintaining both difference and distance from others should therefore not be underestimated. It is arguably because of the importance of wanting to be and remain different and differentiated from others, and perhaps in some cases to be up-to-date, *au fait*, sophisticated or enjoy particular prestige, that youth language has such a productive turnover of terms (of course, ephemeral practices, consumer included (Miles 2000; Coleman 2012: 201–2), and the desire for and dynamics of language play are no less important in this respect – on the latter see, for example, Cheeseman's 1998: 213 observation regarding "a delight in linguistic play which characterizes the best contemporary German rap"). In Verlan, words created through inversion that have become known to and used by out-group members, especially the mainstream, may be reordered yet again to enable clear social water to be re-established between groups and thus reinforce ideas of social distinctiveness. In this way, as we will see in Chapter Eight, the Verlan term 'beur', an inverted form of 'arabe' ('arab') which has been found in standard French dictionaries for several years, was modified again to become 'reubeu'. When the Randuk term 'rendók' ('the beautiful language') started to be commonly used in Khartoum, it was changed to become 'dernók', which in turn became 'gernót' (Manfredi 2008a: 118–9). And when the Sheng word 'mozo' – used by youths to hide references to smoking from their parents – lost its secrecy (and no doubt social distinctiveness), an amended form of the English 'fag' ('fegi') was adopted, until this too was replaced in time by 'fwaka' (Ogechi 2005: 346). As the adoption and eventual replacement of 'fegi' indicate, users of a language variety may switch between different means to create a new item and maintain distance. Furthermore, as subsequent chapters will show, speakers may deliberately combine word-formation mechanisms, such as Verlan and suffixation, not only to make meaning more opaque but also to underscore their linguistic dexterity and social currency – whether as a group or as individuals – and/or foreground ideas of social difference.[23]

Verbal contests and ritual insults

A number of studies (e.g. Labov 1972; Danesi 1994; Stenström, Andersen and Hasund 2002; Beazley 2003) point to the importance of ritualised verbal contests and particularly to a connection between duelling and young men. These behaviours have been especially linked with young African American males in practices known as *sounding, signifying* or *playing the dozens* (e.g. Labov 1972). In this duelling, extravagant insults and quick retorts that build on preceding utterances, sometimes in rhyming couplets and involving swearing, are exchanged in front of an audience of peers. These insults often refer to an opponent's family members (mostly their mother), appearance, sexuality and/or personal circumstances (e.g. 'Your mother raised you on ugly milk'). Opponents understand that they are not to be taken personally or as presentations of fact. Prestige is gained by surpassing opponents through linguistic dexterity and deftness of wit: the winner provides the most entertaining and/or pointed (as well as varied) repertoire and delivery. Through such duels speakers often assert dominance and gain in-group capital; those with higher status or central roles within a group often have greater duelling ability (Labov 1972; Danesi 1994; James 1995).

Although some commentators suggest that these terms are synonymous (Montgomery 2008; Labov 1972 points, *inter alia*, to certain similarities in activity and potential synonymy but also notes terms being favoured in different geographical areas in the US), there may exist differences between them. In her discussion of female rappers, for example, Keyes (1993) indicates that *sounding* differs from *the dozens* insofar as it does not entail deleterious comments about the addressee's forebears, but directly targets the addressee instead. These comments may touch on the recipient's physicality or sexual or other prowess, often as markers of masculinity. *The dozens*, correspondingly, involve direct statements about relatives (especially the addressee's mother) through rhymed couplets. *Signifying*, on the other hand, which Samper (2004) suggests has its roots in Africa, involves talking down another person ('dissin') indirectly, where a certain degree of ambiguity or allusion is brought into play.

An instructive examination of verbal duelling is given by Danesi (1994), who studied a male adolescent cohort aged 14–16 years over two months in Toronto. The group had ten members from different racial and ethnic backgrounds; all came from middle- to upper middle-class homes. Danesi noted that verbal skill and dexterity arguably helped to achieve power and that the following were especially prized:

- swearing and abusive language;
- the ability to provide a *mot juste* and sarcastic retorts;
- novel insults in reply to verbal challenges;

- keeping cool in the face of mocking;
- the ability to entertain through humour;
- *besting* – providing the most entertaining example of a shared experience, such as recounting a funny film.

(Danesi 1994: 117, 121–2)

Verbal duels occur in a wide variety of contexts across the globe. Many do not involve insults or are the preserve of young people or males: *the dozens*, for example, were also performed by women; 1960s Black Nationalist H. Hubert 'Rap' Brown, for instance, noted the prowess of some female players (Keyes 1993; see also Pagliai 2009). Keyes (1993) also points to greater female use of *signifying* in rap duels in the early 1990s, with the more direct *sounding* more highly esteemed by males. Moreover, duels between the sexes were also in evidence, with male rappers directly insulting women in often highly sexist and misogynistic terms and with female rappers dissing after their own fashion – although female appropriation of male behaviours implies that not all females were indirect (Keyes 1993; see also Stenström, Andersen and Hasund 2002 for more on female duelling). In some senses, this may have been seen as women wishing to underline their linguistic virtuosity; however, the case has also been made that women rappers, in their use of more aggressive, challenging and pointed rapping, including duelling, were seeking to establish their status as peers in a male-dominated domain (Keyes 1993). One way or another, these activities appear to have been evident in rap and hip hop over the last 30–40 years in particular as cultural forms where competitiveness, improvisation, inventiveness and originality remain highly valued (Alim 2009; see also Williams' 2016 study of verbal duels in freestyle rap battles in Cape Town, South Africa).

This exploration of verbal duelling reflects perspectives in a youth literature set that focuses on English, although such contests are also found in other languages and varieties (see Doran 2004 for examples of ritual insults in suburban France, Ferrari 2014 for discussion of 'Mchongoano' duelling in Sheng, and Sherzer 2002 for an overview spanning a number of societies). Furthermore, discussion about duelling can also address social dimensions other than gender alone. For example, although in their small-scale study of ritual conflict among London-area teenagers, Stenström, Andersen and Hasund (2002: 213–4) state that "[r]itual insult is primarily a male activity" – a perspective often alluded to or explored in the literature (e.g. Danesi 1994; Sherzer 2002; Coleman 2014) – they also draw attention to combined factors including race and class, where they observe that in one comparison of girls' discourse, ritual conflict only figured in the recorded speech of black working-class girls as opposed to that of white and middle-class subjects.

Furthermore, insofar as she views such duels as "a genre of argumentative language that entails exchanges between two persons, parties, or characters that challenge each other to a performative display of verbal skilfulness in front of an audience", Pagliai (2009: 63) posits that another aspect of duelling also deserves attention – the heightening of language's "poetic dimension" (see also Sherzer 2002 for discussion of duels as verbal art). And no less important is the point that duelling in a broader sense need not be a verbal process, nor occur solely among friends; graffiti tagging, for example, can constitute "a collective conversation among writers, a process of symbolic interaction by which writers challenge, cajole, and surprise one another" (Ferrell 1995: 37). Moreover, Androutsopoulos (2007) cites examples of challenges and dissing in German online hip hop practice, while some fashion-driven Skhothane groups in South Africa regularly compete with and denigrate one another not only through creative language practices, but also through clothing and innovative dance (Bristowe, Oostendorp and Anthonissen 2014). Duelling can therefore extend beyond the verbal.

The global and the local: youth language practice in a connected world

So far, we have discussed why young people might use in-group language and other resources to create, project and negotiate identity, belonging, affiliation, distance and status. We have taken stock of approaches that seek to define youth and their culture in (sometimes abstract) macro terms and suggested that local and micro-practice are important to understanding the diversity of identities that make up this social cohort. We have noted that the linguistic resources on which youth might call may be influenced by a number of cultural, social and other background factors, such as the variety of contact languages and cultures; mobility; and access to other sociocultural spaces and practices. The creation of Multicultural London English (MLE) – the speech of young Londoners, often from or associated with black communities that grew after immigration to London around the 1950s (see, for example, Green 2006, 2014 and initial data provided by Thorne 2006) – and the ongoing re-creation of French youth language arising from multilingual contact in the housing estates of Paris and other cities (e.g. Méla 1997; Tetreault 2000; Doran 2004, 2007) are evidence of the rich use of different resources.

We have also considered that identity isn't something that is static or fixed: youth may work and rework their identity and/or may choose to belong to a number of groups or networks at the same time, dynamically importing and exporting values and practices between communities. They may thus identify with many groups and display a number of different identities within their social universe.

As Chapter Four will reflect, those using youth and criminal language have consistently benefited from varied social or cultural contacts to shape and update their linguistic repertoire. The language of nineteenth-century Russian criminals and traders, for instance, included lexical items associated with geographically diverse and distant groups, most probably as a result of the circulation of Ofeni hawkers as they plied their trades throughout central Russia (Davie 1998). Staying with Russian, many young people in the Soviet Union during the twentieth century learned about domestic and foreign events, trends and values through acquiring black market Western records and publications, or through listening to Western radio and, later, watching MTV. Access to these views and commodities posed a threat to the Soviet state, which wanted to control identities within the Soviet social and political structure. However, such access enabled Soviet youth to tap into other resources to construct alternative identities, inform their view of the world and to acquire new linguistic resources as they managed their social lives within the Soviet system (Soviet hippies are perhaps a good example of this in their espousal of imagery, values and language consistent with those found in the West; see, for example, Davie 1998). Moving beyond Russia, in Sophiatown, Johannesburg, in the 1940s young male criminals ('Tsotsis'), who fought over territory and trade, modelled themselves on the stylish gangsters they saw in American movies, adopting terms used by those on screen (Hurst 2007; Deumert in press), while more recently, in Côte d'Ivoire, Ahua (2006) implies contact between criminal and youth groups in the use of Nouchi in the ghetto. Here the speech variety has two "levels of style": a more opaque, ambiguous and secret variety spoken by criminals and those in the margins of Abidjan's shanty towns; and another, reportedly associated with youths in urban surroundings, which relates more to everyday life and enables speakers to show awareness of or index a Western-facing urban world or to appear up-to-date in fashion terms (Ahua 2006: 143–4. For accounts of Russian youth language and Tsotsitaal also having two distinct elements – general and subcultural – see Gromov 2009 and Hurst 2013). Whatever form it takes, contact between groups increases the number of linguistic, sociocultural or other wells from which individuals or groups can draw as they seek to cast or recast identity and how this is expressed.

When we consider the various possibilities that now exist for sharing and circulating cultural and social values, information and practices, then the Soviet scenario seems older than the *mere* 20–30 years that have passed since the collapse of the USSR in 1991. The possibilities that come with learning about, adopting and adapting others' values and practices through the Internet and mobile communications easily surpass the then-innovative satellite TV that was becoming the next big social and cultural gateway at the turn of the 1990s. But this leaves us with questions: what are the implications of global social and cultural access and of practice at the local level (however local is defined)? And what effect does globalisation writ large have on youth culture and attendant means of expression? These, of course, are complex and far-reaching questions. However, perhaps the most productive approach for our immediate purposes is to consider how youth use local, extra-local or global accesses to shape more immediate youth cultural practice and how this is expressed.

Moving beyond fixed positions

Numerous scholars have considered the question of the local and the global and what impact there might be on local youth practices (e.g. Wulff 1995b; Miles 2000; Samper 2004; Cutler and Røyneland 2015). Bucholtz and Skapoulli (2009: 4) describe the global and local dynamic particularly well when they state that:

> youth have access to identities that are both global, with respect to transnational, nonterritorial youth culture, and local, by virtue of the particular

meanings which the insertion of such forms takes on in local youth-centred linguistic and cultural practices.

This is not an abstract or theoretical qualification; rather, it accords with many descriptions of how local and global resources have been identified and utilised, with differing balances and emphases, by many youth groups (e.g. Gidley 2007; Alim 2009; Androutsopoulos 2009). A typical example cited in studies of the global and the local is the spread of hip hop.

Hip hop grew as an inner-city street counterculture represented by dress, dance and musical styles such as rap. Created by marginalised African American youth in the US in the 1970s, it fuses local sociocultural and linguistic expression with a socio-political current (Krohn and Suazo 1995; Cheeseman 1998; Widawski 2015). For some, its expression, particularly through rap, can be viewed as "innovative oral poetry with ancient roots in African story-telling" (Stavsky, Mozeson and Mozeson 1995: vii; see also Keyes 1993; Krohn and Suazo 1995; Cheeseman 1998). Its robust messages, representation of social experience, socio-political critique, and accentuation of identity, status, resistance and verbal creativity have seen its popularity spread hugely beyond the US to the point that a hip hop nation has become more widely recognised and identified worldwide (see, for example, Androutsopoulos and Scholz 2002; Roth-Gordon 2007; Alim 2009).

Since its rise in popularity in the 1980s and 1990s, many young people in a number of countries have drawn on hip hop to demonstrate belonging to what is effectively a transnational youth movement. They have noted many of the social tensions and stances articulated in US versions (for example, racism, socio-economic marginalisation, police violence), identified how these apply to their own lives, and have adapted them to represent and articulate local values, issues and priorities, while at the same time remaining part of a global hip hop community (Samper 2004; Alim 2009; Androutsopoulos 2009; Williams 2016). Some German youth, for example, have used the US representation of hip hop as a scaffold or frame for local versions, evoking elements of the global hip hop phenomenon (such as phrases in English) and mixing them with locally valued elements (Androutsopoulos 2009). In this sense, "'local' hip-hop does not completely separate from, but emerges in a constant dialogue with its 'mother culture'" (Androutsopoulos 2007: 281). Other hip hop practitioners have used US hip hop practice and ethos as the basis of a "more complex resistance identity ... modeled after African American rebellion to White authority" (Hagedorn 2005: 159, citing Short 1996). In other cases still, such as in some parts of Africa, identification with foreign linguistic practices, including those associated with hip hop, has facilitated "modes of representation for people's identification with their African-American 'brothers' and the latters' culture" (Beck 2010: 25). Whatever the case, affiliation with hip hop need not necessarily mean that a singular US hip hop model has been exported widely abroad without regard to the local (indeed, there are various regional flavours of hip hop in the US); that transnational forms have automatically replaced local ones – although some accounts point to African youths initially trying to imitate American rappers (Ferrari 2007) or "embracing globalization and rejecting tradition" as part of a preoccupation with international, principally North American, culture (Hurst 2007: 9; see also Kiessling and Mous 2004); or that only one local interpretation of hip hop has occurred within any given local context (Cheeseman 1998; Ferrari 2007; Androutsopoulos 2009).

Indeed, hip hop is a particularly interesting practice because their engagement in it points to how, in a great many cases, youth have sought to see themselves as members of a culture or spaces that are variously both *global and local*. This can be seen in some African and South American contexts where engagement in global hip hop culture has been viewed as a means of demonstrating first-world connections but may be merged with local practices to create something specific to and distinct for the local area (or parts of that area), *and* to ensure that older cultural practices are not abandoned but are instead adapted. The use of Camfranglais, for example, indexes a Cameroonian urban youth identity that is, among other things, modern, up-to-date and streetwise. In embracing hip hop, speakers may associate with young Americans in borrowing relevant terms and in their dress, music, etc. However, they do not all rush to import hip hop practices and what they represent wholesale or blindly; rather, some youth are keen to demonstrate their African background (Stein-Kanjora 2008).[24]

Correspondingly, there are numerous instances where youth remain connected to their local community and/or familial linguistic and cultural background and draw on hip hop strands while reflecting the problems and circumstances they face more immediately. Many young people in Kenya may be drawn to rap or hip hop because practice can be local and global at the same time, with a new local form arising through the use of Sheng and/or local languages (as opposed to English). The use of these languages adds more immediate social meaning and emotional connection and enables young people not only to craft and re-craft identity and practice (Samper 2004) but also to emerge as innovative producers rather than mere consumers of a global commodity (Karanja 2010; Vierke 2015). Furthermore, some young Kenyans see hip hop's root source as African: when tapping into global hip hop practices, they are reconnecting with cultural practice that originated on and has returned to their continent (Karanja 2010) or has always been African (Samper 2004). At the same time, some Brazilian youth intermesh and modify broader understandings of hip hop with ideas of racial and national status, rights and belonging relevant to their own situation (Roth-Gordon 2009), while in Europe, rap lyrics have been found neither to fully imitate US models nor to remain totally free from US influence – they thereby represent a form of sociocultural fusion (see, for instance, Cheeseman 1998; Androutsopoulos and Scholz 2002).[25] These examples show not only the relevance of movements such as hip hop in local and transnational senses, but also underline the importance of those who play an active role in merging and reshaping the global and the local. Hip hop actors in particular can span a cosmopolitan, global identity and a traditional, local one, and thus can play a key role in interweaving strands of local ethnicity, identity and/or tradition through more globally spread ideologies and practices to create meaningful new values and identities that go beyond imitation of African American sociocultural practice (e.g. Samper 2004; see also Bucholtz 2002).

Indeed, by interpreting something that originates beyond the local space; by assessing its suitability and compatibility with the practices, views and interests of local actors (mindful of the potential heterogeneity of practices in any one locale); by merging it with local, more traditional resources; and by shaping local practice in a new direction, youth cultural actors are able to demonstrate cultural currency and dexterity in understanding the values and direction of global movements and how these sit with the local – even protecting local culture and values from outside (Western) harm, where necessary (Samper 2004). These activities underline their role as interpreters for those who don't have the same insights, as facilitators for those in local spaces who might not have the same transnational access, and as agents tapped into a global scene. Further, such actors underscore their linguistic tradecraft and adroitness by creating new terms that express new notions or practices, fused or otherwise. In these senses, the mobilising and meshing of the global and the local, and how this fusion is conveyed linguistically, can be carefully considered by young people serving as active social and cultural agents as part of a linguistic, social and stylistic avant-garde.

In situating themselves within global and local cultural practices, such young people are, it could be argued, positioning themselves as they have in the past, but perhaps nowadays with more and more variables and vectors at play. For instance, access to more global cultural practices and forms of expression through TV, mobile communications and the Internet further enables youth to remain up-to-date with trends taking shape and events unfolding elsewhere in the world. It enables them to continue to create or find new forms of cultural portrayal that can be merged with local resources, but also to determine just how much value the global or local can bring to the table and to have an impact on distant practice. And, equally, it helps them to compare long-standing or emergent representations not just of the global and the local, but of tradition and modernity, of the old and the new, of what is indexical of generations, and also to determine their relevance to identity construction and how this is effected linguistically (e.g. Githinji 2006 on Kenya; Smith-Hefner 2007 on Indonesia; Hollington and Makwabarara 2015 on Zimbabwe).

In this sense, it can be said that such youth cultural actors operate as cultural brokers in a liminal *Third Space* (Samper 2004, citing Bhabha 1994). Acting as *bricoleurs*, they "negotiate between various styles, between binary opposites such as local/global, urban/rural, and traditional/modern" (Samper 2004: 38) in a way that brings these opposite poles together to invent new styles, forms and meanings – although in many respects these divisions actually may be more "blurry and ambiguous" (Bucholtz 2002: 531) than dichotomised or mutually exclusive. Samper sees such Third Space brokering in the activities of Kenyan rappers who occupy a position between a cosmopolitan, global identity and a traditional, local one, and who feed aspects of the traditional and the ethnic (including local language) into the construction of a modern Kenyan identity – for them "an authentic Kenyan identity must also include elements from traditional culture" (Samper 2004: 43). A Third Space perspective is also proposed by Karanja (2010), who views urban youth in Kenya as having charted their way to a position between the global and the local, thereby pointing to the fuzzy boundaries between the two spaces. She notes that Sheng embodies the aspiration of urban youth to move beyond fixed (and therefore essentialised) ethnic and localised identities into a "third hybridized space that is fluid and shifting" (Karanja 2010: 1), one that has "enabled them to go beyond the binaries of the traditional and the urbanized" and that fosters new forms of creativity (Karanja 2010: 6, 8). This means not only occupying a different, in-between position but also challenging constraining or restrictive definitions of culture and identity and resisting "the established and rigid norms that provide limiting views of the *other*" (Karanja 2010: 3; Karanja's emphasis). Doran (2004, 2007) similarly argues that certain suburban youth in France use particular language practices (*linguistic bricolage*) to negotiate on their own terms a Third Space where their multidimensional, hybrid identities – multilingual, multicultural, working class – can be presented and interpreted in a manner that is not catered for by mainstream society. Such moves towards liminality are not restricted to early twenty-first–century Kenya or France: Liechty (1995: 191) documents how, for young people in Kathmandu, Nepal:

> life in the present is the experience of modernity. It is a life in the 'in-between' space: between expectations and reality; between past and future; between village and an external, modern metropole; between child- and adulthood; between high and low class; between education and meaningful employment.

The active merging of the local and the global, the traditional and the modern and/or the old and the new, whatever forms they might take, thus helps to avoid a binary, fixed or polarised understanding of youth as either one thing or the other, as many elements – language included – are dynamically utilised for identity construction and comprehension in newly defined spaces. As forms of communication and cultural access enjoy ever greater reach, as young social actors' language practices remain "locally bound, but at the same time globally contingent in multi-layered and comprehensive ways" (Svendsen 2015: 4), the context exists for youth actors to interpret the global, assess the local, identify their respective meaning and complementarity, and consider liminal sociocultural spaces with a larger and more varied linguistic and sociocultural palette.

Crossing boundaries: youth language, race and ethnicity

In the preceding section, we saw how some youth actors may occupy liminal spaces in the ongoing construction and negotiation of identity and social practice. Samper (2004), for example, identifies Kenyan rappers who, as part of their identity formation, occupy a Third Space position. Here the global and the cosmopolitan are intermeshed with the local and the traditional, while the rappers also interweave elements of the ethnic into the definition of a modern Kenyan identity. In this section, we explore a little more how race and ethnicity have been investigated in studies of youth language practices and how these might also relate to questions of identity.

In Chapter Two we noted that traditional sociolinguistic approaches have examined correlations between linguistic variables and certain social categories, such as age and race. These factors have continued to be researched over the years, sometimes in combination. For example, Stenström, Andersen and Hasund's (2002) small-scale analysis of ritual conflict among teenagers in the London area pointed to contrasting language practices among black working-class girls and white and middle-class subjects (see also **Verbal contests and ritual insults**).

Social associations linking questions of language practice to race and ethnicity – as well as perceptions of such – are not uncommon in the youth literature. Roth-Gordon (2009), for instance, points to an association among certain middle-class residents of Rio de Janeiro between the slang of favela (shanty town) inhabitants and ideas of danger, marginality and race (here: blackness) (see also **Enregisterment** on page 280). Roth-Gordon (2016) has also explored how, through *racial malleability*, male Brazilian youth look to situationally influence others' perceptions of them in racial terms (blackness, whiteness) through combining sociocultural and linguistic practices with the physical features with which they were born: how they sound to others contributes to their racial image and the racial interpretation of interlocutors, including the police and politically conscious youth. As Roth-Gordon (2016: 61) points out: "one's racial appearance and one's stance toward (or against) whiteness are constantly negotiated through daily practices that include language".

Indeed, there are several indications of links between language, race and ethnicity being used by some speakers to demonstrate affiliation and to foster social solidarity across races or ethnic groups. With the rise of hip hop, for instance, elements of AAVE have been adopted by speakers of different races and with different ethnic profiles worldwide who wish to affiliate with African American youth culture and a hip hop identity. At the same time, in the Netherlands a Moroccan accent and lexis are highly valued by speakers of other languages who want to identify with people with Moroccan backgrounds. It is believed that Moroccans and their language have "very strong covert prestige" (Dorleijn, Mous and Nortier 2015: 275; for more on **Overt and covert prestige**, see page 73).

Questions concerning language and ethnicity have become particularly prominent due to the emergence of multiethnolects – globally found, mainly urban youth peer-group language varieties, principally of speakers from multiple ethnic backgrounds, in many cases including the host community, that incorporate elements from migrant languages to index social identity (Dorleijn and Nortier 2013). These have developed in many urban areas that have become increasingly diverse in ethnic and linguistic respects as a result of immigration. As loci of language contact involving majority languages and minority ones, multilingual areas have become home to "new linguistic variation and the emergence of new linguistic patterns" (Freywald, Cornips, Ganuza et al. 2015: 73).

The rise of such phenomena as multiethnolects as part of youth sociocultural practice is certainly very important: in their discussion of Kiezdeutsch, Paul, Freywald and Wittenberg (2009: 92), for example, suggest that using a multiethnolect "constitutes an important factor in the construction of young people's identities. It serves as a means to express their hybrid self-perception between the culture they live in and the culture of their ethnic background". In this sense, we see social agents using varied linguistic means from within and beyond their own languages (though see the discussion of competence and repertoires in Chapter Two) as they seek to define themselves in their own terms.

An important concept in the study of cross-linguistic usage, ethnicity and identity among youth actors is that of *language crossing* (Rampton 2010 [1995]). This is where speakers use language that is believed to be "beyond their normal range" (Rampton 2015: 25): in traversing borders in linguistic terms, speakers adopt or engage with elements of the identity of those speakers to whom that language is believed to belong.

The research most associated with this concept is that of Rampton, who in the 1980s and 1990s analysed how white and Asian adolescents used Caribbean Creole, black and white adolescents used Punjabi, and all three used Indian English as a way of recasting their ethnic identities and affiliations (Rampton 2010). Since the 1970s, styles or language linked to specific ethnic minority groups had sometimes become dominant in the local vernacular usage of people with different backgrounds in areas in the UK and Europe (Rampton 2015). Rampton posited that, in their crossing, the speakers he observed had "developed a set of conventionalised interactional procedures that enabled them to reconcile and rework their ethnic differences within broadly shared experience of a working class position in British society" (Rampton 2010: 134). As a result, speakers were able to create a sense of solidarity through the cross-ethnic use of elements of migrant speech.

Rampton's research subjects were youth in the UK. However, other studies also point to this idea of language crossing being in evidence in other youth language practice. Doran (2004) suggests that the minority youth she studied in suburban France demonstrated a form of crossing when they underscored their linguistic and cultural hybridity through borrowing terms from different minority languages such as Arabic, Romani and Berber, that is to say, from languages they did not inherit from their own families. This practice helped them to affirm their joint membership of a multiethnic collective. Androutsopoulos (2009: 58–9) also proposes that the "short, formulaic switches into English" that he has observed in German hip hop discourse, such as 'word' and 'how you like me now' also constitute language crossing insofar as they entail the use of linguistic elements that do not belong to the speaker, but instead to another ethnic or social group. In this way he suggests that the use of English enables questions of identity to be addressed by German speakers. Among other things, the use of English underlines cultural engagement and appeals to shared values important to hip hop practice (Androutsopoulos 2009).

That said, the idea of crossing as outlined in Rampton's work is not embraced in all discussion where youth language practices in some way transcend or cut across ethnic boundaries. One of the functions of Sheng, for instance, is to help speakers to transcend ethnic differences and thus create and project what is for many a "general, supra-ethnic, urban identity" (Dorleijn, Mous and Nortier 2015: 287). For Dorleijn, Mous and Nortier, however, the crossing witnessed in London is not, strictly speaking, seen in Nairobi, where the closest model involves the use of items taken from other varieties of Sheng which are determined by neighbourhood and class as opposed to ethnicity.

Finally, as we considered in Chapter Two, there is merit in exploring language, ethnicity and race as part of an expressly dynamic, ongoing negotiation of identity. Bucholtz (2009: 146) observes, for example that:

> [t]he social meaning of linguistic forms is most fundamentally a matter not of social categories such as gender, ethnicity, age, or region but rather of subtler and more fleeting interactional moves through which speakers take stances, create alignments, and construct personas.

In this connection, there is value in examining the *multiplicity and dynamicity* of identity, particularly insofar as speakers may create, recast, emphasise or de-emphasise aspects of identity in the moment, including as they move between different Communities of Practice. This means not only acknowledging the multi-layered, dynamic nature of identity and how it is defined and expressed but – where ethnicity is concerned – understanding that it need not be conceptualised in static terms but viewed instead as negotiable (Cutler and Røyneland 2015). Indeed, social actors may identify with more than one ethnicity, irrespective of their origins, or seek to oppose traditional categorisations of speakers by ethnicity, not to mention racialisation (Cutler and Røyneland 2015).

Whatever the perspective, questions of race and ethnicity remain key factors in the exploration of identity and youth language practices.

Contemporary Urban Vernaculars

The Contemporary Urban Vernacular is a concept used by Rampton (2015 [2010]) that describes a "set of linguistic forms and enregistering practices (including crossing and stylization) that

- has emerged, is sustained and is felt to be distinctive in ethnically mixed urban neighbourhoods shaped by immigration and class stratification,
- ... is seen as connected-but-distinct from the locality's migrant languages, its traditional non-standard dialect, its national standard and its adult second language speaker styles, as well as from the prestigious counter-standard styles (such as American Vernacular Black English) circulating in global popular culture,
- ... is often widely noted and enregistered beyond its localities of origin, represented in media and popular culture as well as in the informal speech of people outside".

(Rampton 2015: 39)

As we can appreciate, the Contemporary Urban Vernacular develops in urban locations with marked levels of linguistic and ethnic diversity and consists of relatively stable language features that are used in daily exchanges and are not limited to individual ethnicities or to young people. It can also influence the language practices of groups beyond a given locale.

The Contemporary Urban Vernacular has been used by some scholars as an analytical anchor in their investigation of youth urban language practices in multilingual settings. It is cited, for instance, by Aarsæther, Marzo, Nistov and Ceuleers (2015) in their analysis of youth language practices in Genk and Oslo, where young people saw their practices as indexing one or more locality. Ekberg, Opsahl and Wiese (2015: 93) also posit that multilingual urban spaces in Europe have provided a "rich sources of language contact involving the majority languages and a range of typologically diverse minority languages" and have led to the emergence of Contemporary Urban Vernaculars.

One of the reasons for Rampton proposing the Contemporary Urban Vernacular lies in the maintenance by speakers of language practices beyond their youth. In charting the continuities into middle age in the repertoire of a 40-year-old British-born man with a Pakistani background, Rampton challenges the suitability of designations such as *youth language*. Indeed, he proposes that as a term this "risks the 'juvenilization' of a style that we can now see lasting well into adulthood" (Rampton 2015: 43). Among other things, the Contemporary Urban Vernacular is not age-graded but accommodates enduring practices.

The diffusion of youth and criminal language into broader usage

As we have seen, the use and/or circulation within broader society of items associated with youth or criminal language and the identities and values they are held to typify has prompted criticism and concerns about lower educational standards, compromised cultural levels and an undermined status of language and society (e.g. Miller 2004; Stein-Kanjora 2008; Wiese 2009; Mukhwana 2015). When viewed from another perspective, however, it can be argued that language has always developed and, in some cases, assimilated youth and criminal vocabulary – newer forms and frequencies of contact simply provide more cogs and wheels to enable the dynamic of linguistic creativity and diffusion to run.

Language change as a result of social contact is mostly to be expected. And where there are larger gatherings of young social groups – for instance, due to immigration into an area by ethnically diverse populations speaking different languages – there may be faster or more pronounced language change (for discussion see, for instance, Ekberg, Opsahl and Wiese 2015). This certainly seems to be the case in parts of Africa, for example, where peer groups have met particularly in contexts of rapid urbanisation, and where this contact has spawned new youth language varieties that have been used, among other things, to span ethnic boundaries (e.g. Kouadio N'guessan 2006 and Aboa 2011 on Nouchi; Manfredi 2008a and Mugaddam 2015 on Randuk; Karanja 2010 and Mukhwana 2015 on Sheng). What is more, as the scope and use of a new youth language variety grows, and as more people in more towns, cities and areas adopt it, the greater the chance that it may become vernacularised – everyday informal usage – and that some aspects may even proceed along the path to becoming viewed as standard.

Naturally, in painting the process of language change in such broad-brush strokes, there is a risk of oversimplifying the picture. However, while we are not proposing that vernacular or standard language varieties are shaped or develop in a universal manner, nonetheless the principle of some youth or criminal terms eventually working their way into broader usage does hold across many communities and societies. In French, some terms created through Largonji and Largonji des Louchébems, which rely heavily on metathesis and suffixation, have passed into common parlance among the public, and have even been found in standard dictionaries –, for example, 'louf' and 'loufoque' ('nuts', 'crazy') from 'fou' ('mad') (Robert L'Argenton 1991). And in Russian, the noun 'tusovka', probably originally borrowed by youth from criminal vocabulary with the meaning 'mob', 'gang' or 'fight', was used by politicians in the 1990s, after the fall of the USSR, in non-youth-related contexts (e.g. 'politicheskaia tusovka' – 'political gathering', 'élite') and has gone on now to become universally used to refer to events, get-togethers or meetings. These are but two of a host of examples that could be cited across a number of languages.

The role of youth as agents in this diffusion from non-standard to standard cannot be underestimated; indeed, a number of linguists testify to their central role. In her 2006 analysis, Ferrari noted that Sheng was spoken practically by all young people from poor areas and the middle class, a cohort amounting to more than 80% of the youth population of Nairobi. Indeed, its rise and spread had been such that Sheng had become the first language of the latest generation of young people born in the shanty towns, and the most used informal language variety in everyday life (Ferrari 2006; see also Kioko 2015 and Vierke 2015 on its considerable expansion). Similarly, Beck (2010: 32) notes that African urban language varieties such as Sheng, Tsotsitaal, Nouchi and Camfranglais "can be viewed as generalizations of youth languages, which themselves are evidence of the tremendous social and cultural importance of this age group as observable in the sediment of speech". What is more, going considerably beyond Ferrari's cohort, in 2010 Beck crucially pointed to the fact that roughly 60% of those inhabiting African cities were under 25 – i.e. 60% fell within the group held to be most linguistically innovative and associated with youth language (Beck 2010: 12). The picture Beck paints has become more concentrated since then: in 2015, some 60%

of the *continent's* population was under 25 years of age (UN 2015b: 7), while the percentage of those aged between 15 and 34 and living in urban locations in Africa rose between 2010 and 2015 by 18%. Some 74% of Africa's total urban population of approximately 472 million people was aged below 35 in 2015 (Mo Ibrahim Foundation 2015: 6, 14).

When we marry these figures with Cooper's (1989) view of the role of youth in the diffusion of criminal language forms (mentioned with regard to Russian but applying more generally), we see that significant numbers of the African youth described by Ferrari and Beck play and will no doubt continue to play an important role in the spread of language forms:

> it is through the young that cant words can gain wider currency in general slang before possibly being raised to the level of acceptable colloquialisms and finally, perhaps, literary usage.
>
> (Cooper 1989: 61)

While they point to smaller cohorts in percentage terms, statistics produced in 2015 also suggest the importance of youth as a diffusing social cohort in that one out of every six people worldwide was aged between 15 and 24 (UN 2015a: 1). While these figures do not account for adults beyond 24 who still remain as agents within youth sub- and countercultures and exponents of language varieties associated with them, they point to a potential for significant parts of the population to act as linguistic innovators and conduits for linguistic forms to be circulated more widely.

Of course, the role of young people and/or those occupying the social margins as contributors to language change is nothing new. And, of course, it is possible that non-standard forms used by a wider local community will also be adopted by more discretely bounded youth groups, such as those speaking certain multiethnolects (Cheshire, Nortier and Adger 2015). One way or another, social movement and the realities that go with it have occurred and recurred throughout time, bringing new circumstances within which the marginalised have had to assess and shape or reshape their social and cultural space. Cockney rhyming slang, which may have been used in part as a cryptolect to operate beyond the knowledge of the London police in the early nineteenth century (see, for instance, Adams 2009), may owe its spread not only to the transportation of criminals, Cockneys included, to Australia from the late eighteenth century until the mid-nineteenth, hence its presence in Australian English, but also to the mixing of UK servicemen during World Wars One and Two, not to mention nineteenth- and twentieth-century British media and entertainment (Green 2003; see also Maurer 1981). Similarly, the forced disbanding and movement of French criminal communities and the mixing of social classes during and after World War One brought conditions where new forms of contact were made possible, and where diffusion of previously group-specific varieties and colloquial forms was facilitated (e.g. Lodge 1993; Ellis 2002). It was no doubt with this principle in mind that, in his 1920 publication *Le Langage Populaire*, Bauche commented of

French that "[t]he argot of criminals, the argot of prisons, plays a large part in the formation of popular language" (Bauche 1920, cited in Cooper 1989: 61);[26] while in 1931, Straten – commentating chiefly on a time of great social upheaval in Russia – observed:

> Criminal or thieves cant is the latest form of the special, secret jargons or argots. Different nations have secret languages, and their inception dates back to ancient times ... These were real jargons, that is, secret languages accessible only to professionals, members of closed guilds ... It must be added to this that these professional (and not class-based) languages, gradually fading away with the growth of factory-based industry (and not only with the rise of new methods of communication), did not die out completely, but left behind successors – the jargons of town low-lifes, the criminal world, various argots still used until this very day both in France, and in other countries, and primarily in big cities.
>
> (Straten, cited in Davie 1997/98: 44, endnote 38)

In fact, a scenario depicting the diffusion of in-group terms among wider populations emerges in a number of languages. Criminal forms such as 'gabbā' ('room', from 'ḍabbā' meaning 'tin box') and 'māchi' ('policeman', from the word for 'fly', in that it irritates and gets everywhere, even the dirtiest places) were circulated by the media in West Bengal (Mallik 1972: 43–4). GDR youth language penetrated into 'Spoken Standard' usage in the old East Germany (i.e. until 1990) (Salmons 1991: 7); while Verlan vocabulary associated with marginalised, mainly urban French youths in the 1980s and 1990s made its way into standard French dictionaries by the mid-1990s, and French adults adopted, among other things, informal suffixes once typical of criminal and youth speak such as '-oche' in 'cinoche' ('cinema', 'flicks') (Červenková 2001: 81). Finally, Randuk terms have found their way into widely circulated newspapers as part of its "steady penetration ... into the media domain" (Mugaddam 2015: 117), while items initially used by youth have progressed into colloquial and *prostorechie* lexicons in Russian (Biblieva 2007; Gromov 2009).

Although we can see diffusion from in-group lexicons to those of broader collectives in a number of societies, we cannot say, however, that youth-, criminal- or other in-group–associated forms will be viewed universally in the same stylistic and indexical light as they become used more widely. Furthermore, even allowing for traditional stylistic demarcation (though see **Stylistic headaches, stereotypes and indexicality** in the Introduction), there is no universal graduated stylistic path down which words and phrases proceed to wider use, or even a guarantee of ongoing use with the same meaning or in the same way (e.g. Coleman 2012: 76). We can see this if we look at the stylistic categorisation of French terms such as 'fric' ('dosh', 'dough', which has been used with this meaning at least since the early twentieth century) and 'flic' ('pig', 'cop', probably from the German 'Fliege' ('fly' → 'cop'); compare West Bengal criminal 'māchi', seen previously).

Item	1905	1938	1957	1993	1994
Fric	Argot	Argot	Argot	Argot	Familiar
Flic	Argot	Popular	Familiar	Popular	Familiar

(Adapted from Červenková 2001: 79–80)*

*Although she fails to specify the dialect, Wise (1997: 208) suggests that the 'familier' 'flic' is derived from a dialectal word for 'fly'. This does not exclude the possibility of ultimate provenance from German, of course.

Another term used in the late-nineteenth and early twentieth century to refer pejoratively to policemen (and guards) was 'vache'. It is possible that the term is a nativised French version of the German 'Wache' ('guard'). It can be seen in a line from an early twentieth-century anarchist song *Cayenne*: 'Mort aux vaches! Mort aux condés!' ('Death to the pigs! Death to the cops!') – both 'vache' and 'condé' were used to refer to the police. The author of the song is unknown, although it is commonly associated with Aristide Bruant. The slogan has since become popular among punks and an example can be seen on the *eResource*. Further discussion of the phrase can be found in scribium.com/jessie-chevin/a/cayenne-la-chanson-du-bagnard-injustement-condamne/.

The media: enabling diffusion, and movement on the stylistic radar

The relationship between youth/criminal culture and the media is generally thought to be a close one. Where young people are concerned, for example, there is a widely held belief that "it is impossible to undertake an effective examination of youth cultures without exploring young people's relationship with the media" (Kraidy and Khalil 2008: 336, citing the United Nations 2005; see also Miles 2000: 70–86 for an instructive discussion of youth and the mass media, principally in a Western context).

Where youth language practices are concerned, these can be closely intertwined with the media, both in terms of youth access to channels of popular or mainstream discourse, and in respect of those channels' use as platforms or vehicles for sociocultural practice. Post-Soviet Russia in the early to mid-1990s, for example, witnessed an explosion of homemade fanzines and more corporate glossy magazines aimed at youth, as well as an increase in the use of youth language on television and in the mainstream press (Beregovskaia 1996; Davie 1998; Garza 2008). These gave young Russians new, previously denied and less regulated arenas for discussing youth culture and subcultures; the chance to express and experiment on a larger social and cultural scale; the chance to advance positive images of youth practice and identity; and the opportunity to set news trends and create and take new cues (Davie 1998). The relative liberalisation of the media vis-à-vis youth cultural practice, and the new role played by youth in the creation, depiction and ongoing generation of social values and meaning through those media have not, however, been limited to Russia and its youth. In Indonesia, greater media liberalisation and expansion – including publishing houses producing youth publications – and a publishing boom were central to the spread and popularity of Bahasa Gaul after the fall of Suharto in 1998 (Smith-Hefner 2007). In parts of Africa, the media have been important in helping terms circulate with great effect. Camfranglais, for example, has a rather prominent place in the Cameroonian media, particularly where adolescents may serve as the target audience, while terms associated with youth practice are also found in youth journals, song lyrics, commercials, daily newspapers and in chat rooms or online fora (Stein-Kanjora 2008). In Sudan, significant numbers of items from the vocabularies of Randuk speakers can be found in daily newspapers (Mugaddam 2015), while in Kenya, the use of Sheng has grown to the point where it appears in such spheres of mass communication as radio, advertising, public information on issues of particular relevance to young people, youth columns in newspapers and in music. Indeed, hip hop has played a considerable part in the diffusion of Sheng as a vehicle for social and political expression (Ferrari 2006; Mwihaki 2007; Kioko 2015).

What is noteworthy about all these instances is that marginalised, subordinated and/or previously controlled or regulated groups found a new voice and were able to express their thoughts more freely across a range of media. In Russia, magazines, homemade fanzines, radio, MTV and then the Internet were all instrumental in facilitating youth expression and in the circulation of items popularly associated with the youth scene and criminal (under)world, not to mention in supporting a popular discussion, if not re-evaluation, at the time of what was stylistically and socially acceptable language (Davie 1998; see also Garza 2008). In fact, MTV and radio and television more broadly remained a powerful vector for youth-associated language practices into the twenty-first century (Biblieva 2007). A range of media has also enabled the circulation of other language varieties such as Camfranglais, for instance, where in the past at least young people relied not only on television or the Internet, both of which could be costly to acquire and use, but on other forms that were (or may still be) more accessible: Stein-Kanjora (2008: 134) reported in 2008 that, of 263 respondents asked about the media form most likely to spread Camfranglais, 42.5% pointed to music they listened to on tape or compact disc; 17.5% indicated the radio; and 15.6% suggested magazines and newspapers. Indeed, with reference to hip hop, Alim (2009: 105) also alludes to the multiplicity of means that can serve as conduits for expression when noting that:

> globalization has created multiple new opportunities for youth in particular to rework, reinvent, and recreate identities through the remixing of styles which are now, as a result of a multitude of technological innovations, more globally available than ever before.

However, as significant as the role of the media is in circulating language that is typically associated with youth and the criminal world, it is not always the case that they will instantaneously or compliantly reflect usage at street level. Ferrari (2006), for instance, notes that although it was often used in music shows and youth programmes (especially those featuring rap and reggae), Sheng only really figured in Kenyan television and radio after the late 1990s, i.e. quite some time after its initial use and subsequent growth.

Over and above their role in helping items to circulate and cross what are perceived to be stylistic boundaries, the media's embrace of youth-associated varieties is significant for other reasons. For example, analysing mass media attitudes to youth language in particular can help commentators to identify movement from the social and stylistic periphery to the corresponding centre, where youth language is no longer necessarily perceived as indexing opposition to the mainstream from the social margins but becomes associated more with the social centre (i.e. resistance versus project identities). Of course, this does not herald widespread acceptance by the wider society of previously socially marginal language and of what its use means in social terms – but it may create the backdrop for greater integration both socially and stylistically through time and create a new context where new identities and forms of representation can be crafted, initially employed and eventually used more widely. Then there is a question over the degree to which the mass media in particular control youth practices, and why: is their agreement to accommodate previously decried youth practices a sign of a new-found wholesale alignment, or is it contingent on institutional interests, principles and constraints? In other words, while the media are often used by youth actors to construct and make sense of their lifestyles (Miles 2000), youth language practices as promulgated through and in the mass media can raise questions regarding youth agency and the presentation if not perpetuation of certain images of youth: to what extent are youth language practices, as part of a broader semiotic process, unconstrained, or are they in any way legitimised and/or marketised by mass media proprietors and institutions?

Unsurprisingly, more consideration is currently being paid to the role of the Internet and the impact this has and will have on youth and/or criminal practices and colloquial forms (e.g. Cutler and Røyneland 2015; Hollington and Nassenstein 2015; Nassenstein 2015b, 2016). In view of its wide and expanding reach, the Internet not only increases the range of influences and platforms from which youth can draw linguistic and other resources in the shaping and expression of stance and identity, but also potentially accelerates the diffusion of colloquial, youth and criminal forms in vehicular terms, as Vertovec (2007) and Blommaert and Bacchus (2011) intimate in their discussion of super-diversity (for more detail, see **Repertoires** in Chapter Two). And by doing so, it has an impact on the broader social, cultural and linguistic environment. In some respects, of course, the Internet is but a recently appeared vector for the reflection of social contact in and through language. And insofar as it can serve as an accelerant for the use and circulation of language forms that draw disapproval from some quarters (e.g. certain educators) as they wind their way more broadly through sociocultural fabrics, the Internet too will be drawn into age-old debates about the appropriateness of language, about modes and contexts for expression and about perceived language progression or regression (see, for example, Thurlow 2006, 2014; Drummond 2016).

What does the Internet mean for youth and colloquial language?

The arrival of newer means of communication over the last 20 years or so has led to a number of studies which have explored how modern-day youth language is developing or circulating in light of the latest technological innovations (e.g. Thurlow 2003a; McKay, Thurlow and Toomey Zimmerman 2005; Tagliamonte and Denis 2008 on English; Dunn 2006; Biblieva 2007; Berdicevskis 2011 on Russian; Hollington and Nassenstein 2015 on a number of African varieties). In their study of Sheng and Dutch Urban Youth Speech Styles (UYSS), Dorleijn, Mous and Nortier (2015: 277, footnote 7) point to the importance of youth language practices online where they state: "The Internet is a rich source of UYSS, specifically in comments on *YouTube* videos... Computer-mediated communication is increasingly important among adolescents". This is not to say that the literature on the online language practices of youth and criminal groups is routinely comprehensive – Hollington and Nassenstein (2015: 352) conclude that "[y]outh language practices in digital spaces are still largely unstudied and thus comprise a huge new field that offers a broad range of possible research projects". Nonetheless, it is possible to draw out some key themes relating to how youth language can be used on the Internet in particular and what reactions this stimulates. To do this, we will look at the case of Russian.

Russian use of the Internet has been an attractive topic for those who follow the language's development. In statistical terms, for example, in 2015, 73.4 % of the country's population used the Internet. This was an increase of some 30% from 2010, when around 43% went online (some 60 million users), an increase from 24.6 % in 2007 and from a mere 4.1% in 2002 – therefore, approximately an 18-fold increase in 14 years (World Bank).[27] If we step back from this overall trend and look at the use of one blogging platform, LiveJournal (LJ), we also see significant adoption: even as far back as 2004, Russian was the second-most highly used language on LJ among the 30 or so languages into which LJ was translated, coming second to the international *lingua franca* of the Internet, English. Moreover, the Russian LJ (RLJ) user community was the largest virtual Russian-speaking community online with 40,000 users (Gorny 2004: 1).

These figures should certainly catch the eye of anyone interested in how language is used as Russian society encounters and/or embraces new sociocultural enablers. They suggest a strong uptake within and by a large speech community. When we combine the desire of many young Russian Internet users to project identity online, and to index stance, then it appears indeed that the Internet is providing another outlet both for the use of colloquial usage and youth language, and for the broader language to change, both stylistically and sociolinguistically. Where a new context for youth language is concerned, the Russian Internet, or Runet, has been described by some as a place where non-mainstream language stands in contrast to that preferred by more conventional and controlled media (Schmidt and Teubener 2006). Among other things, it has become home to a mainly youth-associated variety known as Olbanskii iazyk (a play on 'albanskii iazyk' – 'Albanian language'), Afftarskii iazyk (Afftar Language, from 'afftar' – an amended written form of the standard 'avtor' ('author')), or 'Iazyk padonkoff' ('Dregs' Language'), a language variety that emerged most likely in the mid- to late 1990s to challenge social and linguistic convention, and perhaps to avoid language filters, and gained popularity with the emergence of RLJ in late 2003 (Dunn 2006). As yet uncontrolled by the state to the same extent as most of the traditional media (although this situation may change), the Internet provides a platform both for youth language practice itself and for the sub- or countercultural perspectives and distinctions it is thought to index. In her article on Russian Internet news and usage, for example, Lapina-Kratasiuk (2009: 13) observes: "Since counter-cultural modes of expression and behaviour in everyday life still provoke suspicion and hostility, Runet helps members of different communities, societies, professional associations and fan-clubs unite and express themselves". And it does so as a still relatively new and far-reaching vehicle for expression.

In terms of the language changing in a more general sense, linguists are aware of developments here too – although naturally, more time is needed to draw any firm conclusions on middle- to long-term change. As Crystal (2005) intimates, some aspects of the written language have changed with the advent of the Internet (and texting, for that matter). Chat, for example, allows real-time, instantaneous interaction with a number of interlocutors at the same time; interactants may also be communicating with others through additional online media. Furthermore, it bears many of the hallmarks of spoken language, although it is not completely like face-to-face spoken language in that, for example, it lacks the kinds of non-verbal cues that go with conversation – although emoticons partly make up for the lack of certain paralinguistic signals (Crystal 2005: 4–6; Androutsopoulos 2007, 2011; see also Dorleijn, Mous and Nortier 2015: 277, footnote 7).[28]

While Crystal mainly focuses his observations on English, they are also relevant to Russian (and other languages), where the Internet also provides a context for sociolinguistic and stylistic change. The use of informal Russian modes of address and other forms that are often suggestive of closer social proximity, such as the use of youth language and colloquial vocabulary, for instance, can be found where social commonality and group affiliation are understood, but true identities remain unknown among interlocutors – in the outside, *physical* world, formal modes of address and more careful language would normally be expected between strangers, although there are some exceptions, such as in advertising, where prospective customers are directly addressed in a more personal and informal way. Equally, new social and stylistic norms and features are taking shape and becoming more commonplace in computer-mediated exchanges as Russians increasingly communicate online. The Russian used in chat sessions, for instance, involves fewer sentences, end marks (such as full stops) and capital letters, most likely because of the speed of interaction and because clarity of message can still be maintained even if they are omitted. Furthermore, comparative stylistic weighting also appears to be accorded insofar as chat is viewed as less formal than email, and so the breaking of certain norms, such as spelling or punctuation, is more acceptable in that medium (see, for example, Berdicevskis 2011: 90; Androutsopoulos 2011 similarly discusses orthographic strategies varying according to online application more broadly). Of course, these examples of chat session Russian do not constitute youth language practices writ large;

rather, they are typical of a specific form of written language on a particular platform where features of colloquial speech are strongly represented. But these forms are taking hold as acceptable, or even appropriate, for certain means of interaction online.

As some of these chat examples suggest, temporal and technical factors associated with online interaction, such as the need to reply quickly to others' posts or to work within character limits, appear to be leading to certain social–stylistic practices with the result that some of the traditional hallmarks of colloquial Russian or the less approved *prostorechie* are encountered online. To that end, some commentators consider certain forms of online Russian to be part of a hybrid sometimes referred to as 'ustnaia pis′mennaia rech′' ('spoken written speech') (Lysenko 2008: 69) or 'pis′mennaia razgovornaia rech′' ('written conversational speech'). Examples include:

- the use of colloquial items such as 'marshrutka' (a contracted form of 'marshrutnoe taksi' – 'taxi', with a suffix added), and 'slykhat' (for standard 'slyshat' – 'to hear');
- greater entrenchment of elements of casual, colloquial language in the written mode, such as the use of particles ('nu …' – 'well …') and unexpected or variant word order, which is possible in spontaneous spoken Russian;
- the discarding of standard rules of spelling and punctuation ('budm' for 'budem' – 'we will', 'raskazali' for 'rasskazali' – 'told'), often through lack of editing time;
- greater use of abbreviations and/or acronyms, including 'kmk' for 'kak mne kazhetsia' ('it seems to me'), to save time, and some Cyrillic–Roman keyboard switching taking root – 'lytdybr' for 'дневник' ('diary' – 'dnevnik').[29]

Internet Russian: is it contagious?

As a medium mainly, but not exclusively, used by educated Russians aged 18–30 (Miodushevskaia 2009) – i.e. youth as the cohort most popularly thought to push social and stylistic boundaries in the West, at least (Miles 2000; Eckert 2005: 94, citing Chambers 1995; de Klerk 2005: 117; Stenström 2014) – the Internet provides a new stage for sociocultural expression; for experimenting with stylistic norms and parameters; and for mixing and matching language resources to enable social practices and values to be created, contested or maintained. The question is: will its main features be seen in other situations of language use?

The answer to this question would so far seem to be a qualified yes. By a *qualified yes*, what is meant is that certain parts of the Internet serve as platforms for elements of Russian youth language practices or colloquial Russian that pre-existed it, such as ellipsis and shorter sentence length, as also found in SMS text messages (e.g. Dunn 2006; Androutsopoulos 2011). So, youth-associated or colloquial vocabulary is simply used by speakers in another, new communication environment from and through which it might proliferate. In this respect, there is no wholesale spill-over of Internet 'slang' to the outside world as such, but a process where many elements of what are perceived to be colloquial language or youth language practice become popular online.

Another argument underlining this *qualified yes* concerns the Internet-specificity of some language forms from varieties such as the Iazyk padonkoff, in that it is possible that certain items could be generated as part of Iazyk padonkoff and spread from the Runet into other domains. Berdicevskis (2012), for example, points to the use of the noun ending '-o', which is normally found in neuter nouns, in Iazyk padonkoff instead of the unstressed standard feminine ending '-a'. Nouns like 'devushka' ('girl') and 'nauka' ('science') therefore become 'devushko' and 'nauko'. In changing the ending in this way, which is one of the Padonkis' favoured twists, intelligent users are variously playing with the written representation of spoken language, innovating, making their text less serious and more informal, creating ironic forms of in-group expression, and subverting the generally accepted rules. However, despite occasional reports of its spread from the Internet page to the spoken word, in reality most Padonki items retain their Internet–Padonki indexicality to the extent that the Runet remains their primary, or in some cases sole, context for use (indeed, Androutsopoulos 2011 notes that the influence of computer-mediated language on speech in English and other languages is typically limited).

However, a *qualified yes* suggests less than total certainty, and it can't be excluded that the Internet will give rise to new group-associated items that will then be used in the outside world, sometimes even on an enduring basis, even if the extent of this diffusion cannot be truly quantified. In fact, such diffusion is arguably inevitable, although the degree to which it unfolds remains to be seen, and analysis of Internet use in other languages suggests that its impact can be exaggerated (see Thurlow 2014: 486). If we consider that youth-associated lexis in the non-virtual, physical world can endure in non-standard lexicons, and that some semantic fields have large numbers of competing (near-)synonyms – for example, the police, drugs, alcohol, women – it is not unreasonable to expect that some youth-associated or colloquial terms will emerge from Internet usage and embed themselves in the wider language. Nominally, one might imagine that the use of Padonki terms by radio stations, on t-shirts, in graffiti and advertisements, and even in political protest in the outside world could perhaps be a precursor to further, stronger waves that could well hit parts of Russia's linguistic shoreline (Dunn 2006). Be that as it may, Zvereva (undated), in her study of Internet news, observes that between 2004 and 2007 some Padonki terms and phrases such as 'afftar zhzhot!' ('the author rules!') were borrowed and used more widely but then went out of fashion.

The relatively brief shelf-life and Internet-specificity of certain youth language items do not, however, seem to soothe the anxieties of some. As with Russian youth and criminal language practices more broadly (e.g. Grachëv 1992; Likhovit′ko and Ivantsova 2015), concerns have been expressed that the rise of Internet varieties such as Iazyk padonkoff will pollute standard Russian or national cultural levels – even though there are many areas of the Internet where formal or stylistically neutral language is used. Unsurprisingly for Russian-watchers, and in an echo of our previous discussion of Sheng and the classroom (see page 118), these concerns are in part based on errors reported in school work: in 2009 the Russian Ministry of Education ascribed mistakes in the written work of schoolchildren directly to Olbanskii iazyk, where spelling rules are deliberately manipulated to convey pronunciation in colloquial speech. So, 'preved' ('hi'), 'grit' ('says') and 'toka' ('only') were preferred to standard 'privet', 'govorit' and 'tol'ko' (*Novosti* 2009).[30]

Of course, those worried about the spread of Iazyk padonkoff or other nonstandard varieties are right to look for signs that youngsters might use it/them in ways that compromise their ability to use language both correctly and appropriately in broader life, especially in institutionalised writing. The range of forms that are misspelt in Iazyk padonkoff extend beyond those highlighted, e.g. 'mine', 'ispatstula', 'smeiatso', 'ni skem' and 'kakdila?' are used instead of 'mne' ('to me'), 'iz-pod stula' ('ROTFL/ROFL' – 'rolling on the floor laughing'), 'smeiat'sia' ('to laugh'), 'ni s kem' ('not with anyone') and 'kak dela?' ('how are things?'). And concerns centre not only on unconscious errors; standard terms may be disfigured deliberately as a sign of identity construction and projection, subcultural cachet and/or as a challenge to those who seek to ensure adherence to established mainstream linguistic rules where subverting the standard rules of spelling may index the snubbing of mainstream rule-makers and what they stand for (hence a social and cultural challenge to and for educators). Furthermore, when we look at the rapidity with which new, more colloquial or stylistically expressive forms might *potentially* take hold on the Internet, and then *potentially* spread into the non-virtual world, and the view of some commentators that the Internet may "privilege nonstandard forms" (Crystal 2006: 9) or that we are witnessing the "rapid 'internetization' of society" (Lebedeva and Astakhova 2016: 125), we gain even further insight into educators' concerns about ubiquitous, uncontrolled *linguistic corruption*. The data cited previously on the increased numbers of Internet users in Russia over 2002–2015 – although in truth hiding a variety of different sociolinguistic uses – no doubt bring home the perceived power of the Internet to take root in parts of society, to foster freer, unchecked (in both senses) usage and to act as a context for new forms of expression to be learned and to spread: when it was first used, for example, Olbanskii iazyk changed *in a matter of weeks* from being a fairly marginal countercultural language variety into a "mainstream Internet movement" where the subculture had "lost its ideological edge, but its slang gained enormous popularity" (Hristova 2008). Seen from educators' and mainstream perspectives, where knowledge of the standard can be tied to concepts of citizenship (Doran 2004; Blommaert 2013) and where the educators in question undoubtedly have vested professional interests tied to the fate and status of language and an authority that becomes challenged (Thurlow 2006, 2014), these factors must surely frighten those who feel that they are acting benignly as the moral guardians of Russian language, education, culture and society, not to mention a sometimes protective and ideologically managed or driven media (Thurlow 2006; Androutsopoulos 2011).

However, educators and the media cannot blame the Internet for the phenomenon and consequences of language diversity, desired or not. In Russian, there were many examples of non-standard forms, language play and incorrect usage in the years before the explosion of the World Wide Web (e.g. Beregovskaia 1996), and the problem of language variation and how to cater for this in language learning and society more generally is not at all new to Russian educators (see, for instance, Ryazanova-Clarke and Wade 1999). The use of forms such as 'toka' and 'grit', which are orthographic representations of colloquial speech found online, is little different from Russia's pre-Internet days, where the same pronunciation and orthographic representation were witnessed. Moreover, such concerns about youth language online are seen in the physical world and point to tensions concerning the use of youth language more broadly. In her discussion of youth language, for example, Nad'iarova (2014: 64) identifies some of the merits of 'slang', but at the same time replays some of the anxieties articulated about youth language online where she states that 'slang' "impoverishes speech, thereby impeding an individual's intellectual and creative development".

In addition, as Dunn (2006) points out, the Iazyk padonkoff is probably part of the stëb tradition ('mocking') which emphasised the undermining of sociocultural and political hierarchies and which emerged in the 1970s but gained prominence after the collapse of the USSR in 1991, i.e. before the rise of the Internet as a popular medium in Russia. Indeed, although the Internet may pose particular problems for educators in terms of usage reinforcement due to its popularity, economy, range of content and scale, by and large they have successfully managed the use of youth and criminal sub- and countercultural terms, the consequences of colloquial usage and stëb in the past. They still retain workable functional stylistic frameworks for using the language in a variety of contexts, so much so that a prominent user cohort of the Internet in Russia nowadays – members of the vanguard of language use in this newer medium – is young, urban and educated to graduate level, as Miodushevskaia suggests.

Given that the importance of the Internet as a means of communication between young Russians is unlikely to decrease in coming years (even if users become more careful about what they communicate due to state restrictions on expression), those who fear for the future of Russian may well face more challenges in balancing the concepts of the Internet as a sociocultural, societal and educational enabler with encouraging or teaching the use of Russian in a situationally and socially appropriate and adaptive manner. Whatever path they choose, considered thinking will perhaps be required to avoid the reflexes seen in media treatments of in-group usage in a number of languages and societies:

- to avoid demonising the Internet as a/the sole cause of linguistic or educational decline;
- to recognise that many errors found in Internet usage may well have predated online and SMS communication (see Thurlow 2003a for similar observations regarding spelling in youth SMS messages in English);

- to consider that other sociolinguistic factors may also be prompting some language seen in homework and assessments, such as linguistic interference (e.g. Busch 2012);
- to acknowledge the sociostylistic adroitness and sociocultural importance to be found in diversity, experimentation and language play in appropriate contexts – for example, use of the Russian ending '-o' instead of unstressed '-a' has been seen in literature as a literary device (Berdicesvskis 2012);
- to keep in mind the fact that different online spaces still require different styles, such as those required in news-writing (Androutsopoulos 2007);
- to consider that some online usage may in fact be more conservative than fears suggest, as Tagliamonte and Denis (2008) indicate regarding teenage use of Instant Messaging in English;
- to reflect that new linguistic practices rarely develop in a vacuum: developments in language used online may potentially reflect changes in the broader language (Tagliamonte and Denis 2008); similarly, they do not neatly replace or utterly break with longer-term patterns of usage (Thurlow 2006);
- to remember that the Internet can serve as a vector through which social meaning and identity might be negotiated and explored, and through which youth might learn about the rest of the world (Karanja 2010);
- to register that time spent together by youth online and in SMS exchanges can complement offline contact and ameliorate social interaction (Thurlow 2003a; McKay, Thurlow, Toomey Zimmerman 2005; Coleman 2012) or communication (Thurlow 2006);
- to consider that conscious variation in youth language practice may point to "fluid mastery of the sociolinguistic resources in their speech community" (Tagliamonte and Denis 2008: 27) as opposed to language deficit; and
- to note that youth are not the only social actors who use new digital communication media and linguistic forms associated with them: people in the mainstream adult sphere also employ them (Thurlow 2014).

This thinking will not, it seems, be required exclusively for Russian. Of course, it would be unwise to simplistically transpose the factors that influence and characterise Russian online usage and how that is perceived among Russian speakers onto other languages, cultures and societies. Stein-Kanjora's information on the relatively minor role that the Internet played in the spread of Camfranglais in the pre-2008 climate, mainly because few young people could afford regular online access, is a salutary reminder of sociocultural and socio-economic relevance, for one thing. However, tensions between online (and, indeed, SMS) usage and perceived language standards and literacy are found beyond Russia's borders, as Thurlow (2003a, 2006, 2014) and others point out. In 2010, Canadian academics bemoaned poor spelling and grammar, punctuation errors, the use of emoticons, and inappropriate abbreviations and reduced words ('cuz' for 'because') by candidate university students. In some instances, the cause was seen as a lack of grammar teaching at primary and secondary level; however, texting and social networking were also advanced as causative factors (Kelley 2010). In 2010, one-third of young Thais were reportedly unconcerned about the kinds of misspellings, abbreviations and grammatical mistakes common in texting and social media exchanges (Suchaovanich 2010). And in 2012, a survey conducted by the *China Youth Daily*, for instance, suggested that 67% of participants felt that "the popularity of Web language had weakened standard Chinese usage" (Mo Ting 2012). These reports would appear to coincide to a considerable extent with Thurlow's observation about the extent to which the broader English-language media claim that Instant Messaging, emailing and, particularly, SMS variously not only corrupt, destroy, ruin and erode Standard English, but compromise literacy standards with regard especially to grammar, spelling, punctuation, capitalisation and sentence structure (Thurlow 2014: 487).

Naturally, there can be many reasons why such fears are articulated, even if the complaints are similar. Busch (2012: 1) helpfully sheds light on the tensions that can arise in the educational domain in particular when she notes how schools have historically been viewed as "a key institution to implement language policies aiming at the enforcement of a unitary (state) language and at the homogenization of linguistically diverse populations" – which in turn often brings pressure to prioritise and support standard varieties (of course, how this qualification applies across societies will differ, but the core pressure to encourage homogeneity is evident in many countries). The potential for vernacular practices to gain in status could thus be viewed as a threat to such homogeneity:

> digital media enable an expansion of vernacular writing into new domains of practice, and therefore a diversification of writing styles and pluralisation of written language norms. The expansion of digital literacy practices affords vernacular written usage more space, visibility and status than ever before, and vernacular usage itself is diversified in what we might call 'old vernaculars', representing locally bound ways of speaking that traditionally didn't find their way into (public) writing, and 'new vernaculars' – new patterns of differentiation from written standards, indexing practices and networks of digital culture.
>
> (Androutsopoulos 2011: 2)

Furthermore, and as we saw already, it is also noteworthy that such concerns may be shared by those outside the education sector, particularly the media: the common accusation that youth are "reinventing or destroying not only the (English) language but also *the entire social order*" is listed by Thurlow (2007: 216; my italics) among adult concerns vis-à-vis young people's use of mobile telephony and texting. At the same time, as it has attracted criticism through its use more broadly, the Straattaal of the Netherlands, for instance, has been described as reflecting "social and linguistic deviance, deficiency and even delinquency" (Cornips, Jaspers and de Rooij 2015: 48–9).

In point of fact, over and above the criticism aimed at Chinese, Canadian, Thai and other youth, experiences registered by commentators in other countries do suggest that concerns are widely articulated,[31] but can be exaggerated or misinformed. In an excellent review of language change and online use covering a wide range of issues, Androutsopoulos (2011) points to other languages with non-Roman scripts, such as Greek and Arabic, continuing to see variation in the use of Roman letters (for example, between phonetic transcription and transliteration), while the three main components of innovation in online language across a range of languages also coincide with trends referenced concerning the use of Russian online:

- orality: where elements of casual speech appear in written text;
- compensation: keyboard-based moves to mitigate the absence of intonation or facial expression (e.g. emoticons, abbreviations);
- economy: moves to shorten the form that text takes, including through the need to communicate rapidly, but also moves to frame exchanges in an informal light.

(Androutsopoulos 2011: 5)

However, Androutsopoulos notes a "widely publicised linguistic myth" that school pupils might use netspeak or texting styles in their school work that is not supported by the evidence, as well as claims that online usage increases tolerance of typographic errors (Androutsopoulos 2011: 4, 7; see also Thurlow 2006, 2007).

How these trends are analysed within and across languages requires, of course, detailed attention, as well as time to establish their longevity and impact. However, if anything is to be taken away from the frequently voiced criticisms of youth language practices offline, perhaps it is that care should be taken not to assume that, in online usage, young people are necessarily being lazy, inept or sloppy. Inasmuch as Internet access will vary among social groups across the globe, the Internet will surely continue to serve as a platform for young people to take important steps in comprehending, negotiating and shaping linguistic and social landscapes, including in contextually appropriate ways (see, for example, Doran 2004 on context-specific usage by suburban French youth offline); to move and operate across social, national and/or other boundaries; to assess and reassess their background and traditions; to scope out, craft, distinguish and share identity; to explore the expression and understanding of social meaning more broadly; and to advance alternative worldviews or protest in many of the same respects as in the past. And to undertake all this through the medium of language. Against the ongoing need for expression for social purposes, and the backdrop of antagonisms between standard language and what it is held to stand for and other linguistic–sociocultural alternatives, the Internet should provide fertile ground for youth to construct positions and express sociocultural viewpoints in novel and inventive usage, including for positive social gain, for quite some time yet (see also **Language ideologies** on page 127).

Youth Internet use: statistics and significance

The use of the Internet and associated technological affordances can vary per country. In one 2015 study, 92% of US teenagers aged 13–17 stated that they went online daily, with 24% going online "almost constantly" (Lenhart 2015). Some 56% of this cohort went online several times a day. The most utilised social media site was Facebook (71%), with just over half using Instagram (52%) and 41% using Snapchat. Of the teenagers studied, 71% made use of more than one application (Lenhart 2015). This picture compares with less than 55% Internet access among the Millennials generation in some large emerging economies such as India, Nigeria and South Africa, although statistics suggest that access among that age range is currently approaching 100% in many of the world's largest economies (Poushter 2016).

Use can vary across age groups. One study has found that, across 40 countries surveyed in 2015, people between 18 and 34 were more likely to report using the Internet or owning a smartphone than those aged 35 and over. The size of the gap varied from country to country, but the pattern was reported to be "universal" (Poushter 2016). The largest age gaps in Internet access were found in emerging economies such as Vietnam (a 56% gap between those aged 18–34 and those 35+), Ukraine (+49), China (+44), Poland (+42), Malaysia (+41) and Turkey (+40) (Poushter 2016).

The importance of online access has been noted for a number of youth language varieties. Nassenstein (2015b: 86), for example, indicates that Facebook, Twitter and YouTube are important to the circulation of Langila vocabulary (from a variety in the Democratic Republic of Congo) and the manipulations that ensure that the youth language remains "in a steady state of flux". At the same time, in Northern Europe and the US, YouTube and other social media sites have been reported to greatly increase the potential for practices such as hip hop to shape "the narrative about ethnic differences and belonging in both national and regional contexts" (Cutler and Røyneland 2015: 163).

Taking other options

In much the same way as we noted that youth do not constitute a homogeneous social group, and that youth often look to distance themselves from other youth groups, it is also important to register that some youth actors may not use what is understood to be youth language. In some cases, they might not be aware that such a variety exists (e.g. Paul, Freywald and Wittenberg 2009), an observation that reaches into questions of metalinguistic awareness that may be far from uniform across youth cohorts. Alternatively, speakers may reject the language practices in which either the broader peer group, or *cool* or anti-social elements of it, may be engaging. Instead, they may construct their own alternative styles, of which some may be more palatable to the social mainstream, or choose a palette that has no forms typically associated with youth language practices.

The rejection of such practices may occur for a number of reasons. In a study of Laotian American youth, Bucholtz (2004) compared two girls who selected stylistic practices against a backdrop of broad racial and ethnic stereotypes of Southeast Asian Americans as either minority nerds or gangsters. Nikki used elements of African American phonology, grammar and youth language that indicated affiliation with African American youth culture. Ada, on the other hand, was part of a circle of friends that valued nerdiness in contradistinction to the images of coolness and trendiness that were valued and promoted by others at their school. This circle invested more in intelligence and wit, conveying their rejection of the cooler Others in a number of ways, including by dressing differently and by choosing not to indulge in 'slang', colloquial and non-standard English (Bucholtz 2004: 137–8). Although it is possible that Ada elected not to employ the youth language practices used by others not so much through a strategy of avoidance as a lack of access to the necessary linguistic resources (as a non-native speaker of English and an out-grouper), Bucholtz (2004: 139) suggests that "in not pursuing slang as a desirable stylistic commodity as cool teenagers did, Ada signaled her nonparticipation in trendy youth culture. In this way she clearly distinguished herself from cool teenagers like Nikki".

Bucholtz acknowledges that this is but one example of diversity among what is a broad and varied Asian American community, and that working-class immigrant Asian American youth are not limited to the two stereotypes she cites in her study. By implication, the identity choices available to youth actors need not be reduced to a simple dichotomy where they embrace one or another option – instead, other alternatives or conclusions in an understudied community may emerge, including the possibility that social agents may be less disposed to subscribing to one identity than avoiding another (here Ada with regard to the nerd identity ahead of that of a gangster group). One way or another, Bucholtz's study is highly instructive insofar as, whatever Ada's motivations, the group with which she was aligned clearly elected not to share the youth language practices of the cool Others.

A further example of groups rejecting certain youth cultural practices and, in doing so, creating alternative and more socially valued styles can be seen with Langila. Langila is a variety spoken by at least 20,000 young people in Kinshasa, Democratic Republic of Congo, since 2003–2004. It is mostly associated with a creative set – young musicians, dancers, choreographers and painters – and has emerged within the shadow of a dominant youth culture created by speakers of Yanké – a more established variety traditionally associated with street children, gangsters (who are sometimes known as Bayanké), criminality, lack of education and rebellion (Nassenstein 2015b). Insofar as it indexes notions such as education and sophistication, Langila fills a void left by the active exclusion of Others such as artists by the street-focused, socially marginalised Yanké speakers who had hitherto monopolised youth culture and language (Nassenstein 2015b: 82).

Langila speakers aim to distance themselves from the streets and from non-Langila speakers and will tolerate its use by anyone except the crime-fuelled, anti-social Bayanké. In view of their variety's association with education, creativity and the arts, speakers of Langila enjoy positive social prestige, in contrast with the covert prestige that comes with the use of Yanké (Nassenstein 2015b. For a description of **Overt and covert prestige**, see page 73). Given that low-status varieties such as Yanké are often characterised as antilanguages, and that the use of Langila supports a more sophisticated and socially valued identity than that enjoyed by the lowly Yanké speakers (even though Yanké appears to be on the verge of losing its resistance identity and gaining popularity among young people who had previously not used it as an in-group variety), Nassenstein (2015b) posits that Langila may thus be classed as an *anti-antilanguage* – one that occupies an oppositional position to Yanké, while not representing linguistic and ideological resistance to the social mainstream but still serving to differentiate its speakers from peers. A similar claim could also be made, he suggests, for Engsh – a variety spoken in the more affluent Westlands area of Nairobi which, in contrast to Sheng, appears to be based on English grammatical–syntactic structure and to have a greater share of English lexis (Nassenstein 2015b). Indeed, a similar conclusion regarding Engsh had also been reached by Kiessling and Mous in 2004 (for more details of Engsh, see Ogechi 2005; Kioko 2015; Mukhwana 2015).

Summary

In this chapter, we have examined the motivations thought to underpin the expression of stances, values and identities through youth and criminal language practices. We have seen that, in discourse about linguistic forms and practices associated with criminal groups and other social marginals, they are often seen merely as ways of masking malign purpose. However, we have equally established that there can be social identity dimensions to the use of such in-group language practices, such as prisoner socialisation, and that criminals and the déclassé are not the only people who conceal what they mean: speakers may, for example, wish to underscore group identity (Manfredi 2008a, 2008b), control access to shrines (Storch 2011) or observe rules of politeness and hospitality (Wolfer 2011). Cryptolect is thus not all about the criminal.

We have also examined the use of youth language practices and acknowledged the way in which criticism of language practices associated with youth can stand for criticism of the group or individual (e.g. Stein-Kanjora 2008). We have noted that youth language can be regarded as something of a phase to a more meaningful adult place, and its use viewed as inept, rebellious, sloppy or faddish (Wulff 1995a; Miles 2000; Thurlow 2003b, 2007, 2014; Eckert 2004, 2005; Jørgensen 2013), but that care needs to be taken when generalising about youth language in that:

- The use of youth language practices is closely connected to questions of identification, identity, and the interpretation of social meaning. In this sense, it is used to underscore social distance, affiliation, and so on within a social universe (e.g. Eckert 2005, 2012).
- Many people engage in language practices that index youth and elements of youth identity as it is typically understood. Such social actors can include adults who may, for example, situationally choose to use certain items that they have retained since adolescence when communicating with adult friends or peers (e.g. Stein-Kanjora 2008; Rampton 2015).
- The core stylistic, sociolinguistic and socio-psychological considerations that sit around youth language practices are in some ways no different to the situation-dependent use of language by speakers in the mainstream space (e.g. Eckert 2002).
- Youth often make sense of and operate within a universe whose rules are set by the dominant mainstream adult population (e.g. Amit-Talai 1995a; Ferrell 1995; Miles 2000; Eckert 2005), who may create and maintain highly oppositional, hostile and even pathologising stereotypes of youth through media control (e.g. Thurlow 2005, 2007; Wyn 2005; Doran 2007) but may also praise (e.g. Wyn 2005). Either way, such adults are able to maintain the social order (Thurlow 2007, 2014) and propagate corresponding narratives.
- Where the life stage is salient, the creation of space for and by youth, where they can have greater freedom of action and expression and define themselves in their own terms, can be important as they negotiate social meaning (e.g. Amit-Talai 1995a; James 1995; Miles 2000; Eckert 2003, 2004, 2005).
- As a variety associated with a considerable part of some populations, urban youth language in particular can be an important driver behind language change in the broader sociolinguistic environment (e.g. Ferrari 2006; Beck 2010; Kioko 2015, all discussing Sheng).

Another important feature of this chapter has been the discussion of the Other. We have noted that youth or criminal speakers may, through certain language practices, identify certain out-groupers as an Other, just as they too can be cast in this role by members of the (adult) mainstream. For youth, the Other can take a number of forms, including representatives of rural life (e.g. Githinji 2006; Smith-Hefner 2007; Hollington and Makwabarara 2015), the opposite sex (e.g. Manfredi 2008a), older generations (e.g. Paul, Freywald and Wittenberg 2009) or the authorities (e.g. Beregovskaia 1996; Vakunta 2008), to name but a few. It is noteworthy, however, that in drawing social distinctions, speakers may identify a range of Others from whom they distance themselves simultaneously (e.g. Doran 2004, 2007; Kießling 2004).

At the same time, we discussed how – through practices such as hip hop – youth can draw from global and local *(glocal)* resources. There are a number of reasons why this might occur: for example, to demonstrate sociocultural agency in global and local contexts or to create new modern identities (e.g. Samper 2004). Whatever the motivation, in a variety of settings transnational practices such as hip hop are frequently modified to meet immediate local needs by social actors conversant in global and local cultural flows. Furthermore, insofar as such actors are *bricoleurs* who negotiate complex, fused and/or hybrid practices and identities, they occupy a liminal Third Space (e.g. Samper 2004; Karanja 2010). In this respect, then, we can see that fixed, binary understandings of the motivations behind youth and criminal language practices, and of identity, can be limiting. As more young people gain access to global communications and sociocultural activity, so their practices and identities should continue to remain "locally bound, but at the same time globally contingent in multi-layered and comprehensive ways" (Svendsen 2015: 4).

We have also discussed the potentially important role that the Internet has to play as a relatively new platform for youth-associated and colloquial forms to be used, and for their diffusion. A number of educators and social commentators have expressed concern about the potential for Internet 'slang' to undermine young speakers' ability to use their language appropriately and have feared negative consequences for the standard language. In many cases, such fears draw attention to errors made in school work and point to the Internet as a causative factor. However, many of these concerns are not supported by evidence (Androutsopoulos 2011; see also Thurlow 2006, 2007). Indeed, some language practices of concern predate the advent of the Internet. That being said, the Internet does offer a fertile context for novel expression and new trends, and the potential exists for further diffusion into the offline world. Thurlow (2012: 186) captures its creative potential and sociocultural significance well when he opines:

> The language play and verbal art of new media communicators is certainly no less creative, no less imaginative, no less reflexive than, say, concrete poetry or other verbal art. Nor is new media language any less significant for language and culture.

Youth and criminal language practices are thus strongly functional, enabling speakers to meet various communicative and social goals. Their functions are many. For example, through youth language practices, in-groups and individuals can lay out their social and linguistic ground and select and apply their own social rules in an adult-dominated world. They can help speakers to overcome and avoid ethnic difference, as we see in Africa through the use of Sheng. They can enable speakers to co-construct social meaning on an ongoing basis, and to affiliate or (dis)affiliate themselves with/from others. They can help social actors to negotiate questions of globalisation and to explore new fused practices and redefined identities. And they can enable speakers to push stylistic and sociolinguistic boundaries and potentially shape the greater sociolinguistic environment in particular ways (viz. emerging vernaculars such as Nouchi). In these respects and others, their value should not be underestimated.

Finally, we have seen that some young people choose *not* to use youth or criminal language. There are several reasons why this might be the case. However, in doing so they are undertaking their own identity work and adopting particular

178 *Youth and criminal language practices*

stances in light of the prevalence and social importance of what are conceptualised as youth language practices (e.g. Bucholtz 2004; Nassenstein 2015b).

Notes

1 Green (2008) also notes that the Coquillards mainly consisted of ex-soldiers from the 100 Years' War (1337–1453) and that the Chauffeurs were so called due to their heating the feet of their victims (from the French 'chauffer' – 'to heat').
2 It is not known definitively when the mechanisms involved in the creation of Largonji were first employed in France. However, Robert L'Argenton (1991) notes an observation that they were in use in the country during the times of the criminalist Vidocq (1775–1857). Additionally, Bullock (1996: 190, endnote 10) cites a claim that the first attestation of Largonji – 'lombem' from 'bon' ('good') – was in a document regarding the 'slang' of the Brest prison dated 1821, while Wise (1997: 212) notes that Largonji was "first brought to light in an account of nineteenth-century criminal slang" and, like Loucherbem/ Louchébem, "involve[d] the same kinds of phonological manipulation of words, in order to disguise them".
  Finally, while suggesting that Largonji probably came from former French Indochina, Strutz (2009) also observes that Louchébem is a variation of Largonji created by Lyon and Paris butchers.
3 Nedelec (1986) cites the first appearance of 'argot' referring to the group-specific language of street sellers, peddlers, cut purses, beggars, haberdashers and tricksters in 1628. Lodge (2004) indicates that the term 'jargon' ('incomprehensible babbling') was used in the twelfth century and continued to be used to refer to criminal language until the seventeenth century, when it began to be replaced by the term 'argot'. Lodge notes that this latter designation seems to be Parisian pronunciation of 'ergot', which was derived from the verb 'ergoter' ('to haggle', 'to hassle clients') and which was used to designate the city's thieves and beggars as a collective.
4 "Mais l'argot moderne n'est plus vraiment un langage secret, il est plutôt un des éléments dans la palette de choix dont dispose le locuteur… Certains emploient, pour suivre la mode, des mots argotiques qu'ils découvrent grâce aux médias. D'autres, qui ont créé ces mots vont en créer d'autres pour maintenir la distance entre leur groupe et ses imitateurs" (my translation).
5 Interestingly, Green (1999, online version) observes that Roma were first to be found in England circa 1500 and were almost invariably "seen (then as now) as 'bad'". Indeed, he notes the description of itinerant criminal beggars by the magistrate, Thomas Harman, circa 1560, as largely associated with Roma, insofar as Harman referred to "the wretched, wily, wandering vagabonds calling and naming themselves Egyptians, deeply dissembling and long hiding and covering their deep, deceitful practices… in short, all thieves and whores".
6 The use of in-group language and reasons for its use are echoed elsewhere. In a groundbreaking study of "Hungarian prison slang", Szabó (2006: 221, 223, 226) also notes: "Slang is a medium which helps its users to survive a difficult period of their lives"; that "prison slang is not only an interesting set of words and expressions, but a very lively internal language operated by informal groupings that make up a language variety to be used as a substantial tool for everyday social contacts"; and that "prisoners go through a resocialization process in prison which is revealed by the individual appearance of prison slang, too". Szabó collated prison language data over 1996–2005, using questionnaires and interviews. The questionnaires were distributed among prisoners in 18 larger corrective institutions across Hungary, with most interviews conducted in groups and with individuals at the Penitentiary and Prison of Sopronkőhida.
7 Sourdot (1991) also indicates that cryptic use is not the only reason for using what he terms 'argot': the reinforcement of social identity and pleasure through language

play are also reasons for developing and maintaining a variety. However, he suggests that they are not as pertinent as the cryptic functions when the variety emerges in the first place. Furthermore, he indicates that there are also different degrees of secrecy required by different groups; and that for criminals the ludic element is of secondary importance. That said, even prison language can have a ludic quality to help prisoners deal with circumstances as they await release.

8 Roth-Gordon (2009) similarly points to an association among Rio de Janeiro middle-class residents between users of what she terms 'slang' and the 'favela' (shantytown) and states: "For the elite and middle class, Brazilian Portuguese gíria [slang] has long symbolised disorder, where the unauthorized breaking of linguistic convention indexes the breaking of laws" (Roth-Gordon 2009: 64). She further documents an association made by wealthy residents of the city between the favela and ideas of poverty, danger, marginality, dirt and race (blackness), and that youth are highly aware that this language practice marks them as residents of the favela and thus can associate them with crime and danger (Roth-Gordon 2009).

9 Bennett (2007: 35) points to changing perceptions of adulthood and adult responsibility and states that, since the 1950s, "successive generations have come of age during particular youth cultural eras, this experience remaining with them as they have aged and giving rise to a new construction of youth as an attitudinal sensibility rather than necessarily connected with age". Much of Bennett's engaging discussion centres on youth in UK and Western contexts. However, shifts in notions of adulthood may be possible elsewhere.

10 Another African example can be found in Cameroon, where Camfranglais has been described as threatening the moral health of younger Cameroonians and the French language; as undermining knowledge of and ability in French and English; as responsible for lower academic achievements; and as leading young people astray. For those reasons it is forbidden in classrooms and in many homes. In this sense, public disapproval is not necessarily being directed against Camfranglais as a language variety alone, but against the youth themselves and the values they hold. Stein-Kanjora cites Bell when she says that, as often happens with such language varieties, the "social evaluation of the group is transferred to the linguistic features associated with the group" (Stein-Kanjora 2008: 123, footnote 15).

11 Interestingly, with regard to Japanese, Okamoto (1995) notes that prominent female politicians are regularly reported as contravening traditional speech conventions and employing less formal and more direct speech styles. In this way, they too appear to protest against conservative social expectations.

12 The use of language to reach out to young voters need not contain items typically associated with youth – indeed, where it is tactically deployed by the dominant mainstream its use may come across as fake, contrived or insincere.

13 In a very interesting analysis of *risky* behaviour in adolescence, McKay (2005: 226) notes that Kelly sees "a danger in the microanalysis of adolescent behaviors and young people's activities, especially those categorized as risky, because they problematize, even catastrophize, adolescent behaviors and dispositions".

14 In his discussion Thurlow was working on the basis of adolescence covering 11–21/22 years.

15 Ngefac (2010: 155–6) noted that Camfranglais was mostly spoken by Francophone speakers between 15 and 25 years (indeed, all Francophone respondents of this age group spoke it), and also by 65% of Francophone speakers aged 26–39 years. It was not spoken by Francophone or Anglophone speakers over 40 years old. In all, 32% of his 120 respondents spoke Camfranglais.

Elisabeth Ngo Ngok-Graux (2007) also produced an engaging study of Camfranglais which was based on answers provided by 150 people who belonged to five groups (two young and three adult) located in Douala and Yaoundé. The respondents were categorised into three age groups: 6–20, 25–40 and those over 45. The field work spanned late 2003 to early 2004. In brief terms, this study shows that the vast majority of those questioned considered Camfranglais to be a language variety of young people, mainly pupils, students, young traders and street hawkers; and that the primary user group was aged between 12 and 35. Furthermore, Camfranglais was viewed as used mainly in informal situations (for example, in the street, bars, markets, games halls, among neighbours, with family), although it was also clearly used in the school playground. Camfranglais was learned in school, but also through family and in the street and workplace, and mainly by word of mouth (Ngo Ngok-Graux 2007).

16 For example, Boellstorff (2004) observes with regard to Bahasa Gay that when heterosexual Indonesians use Bahasa Gay forms, such usage does not mark them as gay but as in tune with popular culture.

17 A parallel of this principle of actors moving across networks and adjusting usage accordingly can be seen in one study of UK student language practices. In a study focusing on students at the University of Leicester, Coleman (2014: 61) notes that there is no single UK student variety used by all students in the UK and only them; that use of relevant lexis will depend on the preferences of individual networks; and that "students may modify their own speech as they move between social networks".

18 The question of criminality is a nuanced one. Eckert and McConnell-Ginet (1995) indicate, for example, that drug use is a potent marker for rejecting adult authority and asserting autonomy. The use of drugs by young people in the light of this assertion need not centre on a desire for criminal involvement in its procurement and sale, for instance, but could be based on a motivation centring more on rejecting mainstream ideologies or showing solidarity with peers.

19 "… c'est la langue miroir dans laquelle se reflètent les multiples tensions de la société, la diversité des références des verlanisants" (my translation).

20 "Le verlan, de par sa nature, transmet à travers ses locuteurs une autre réalité que la langue standard" (my translation).

21 "C'est un argot de mecs, fait pour parler entre mecs" (my translation).

22 Okamoto (1995: 298, 310–3, 317) observes that "Japanese norms of behaviour have traditionally been highly gendered" and that the language is also held to have distinct female and male speech registers.Interestingly, Adams (2009) points to reflections of how girls and young women used a 'slang' in nineteenth-century American literature, citing Louisa May Alcott's *Little Women* as an example. He notes: "In other words, *Little Women* should lead us to a set of conclusions: in nineteenth-century New England, slang was framed as masculine; girls spoke it unconsciously but heard it consciously and socialized one another out of its use by the time they became adults; women well past adolescence, like Alcott when she wrote *Little Women*, used slang anyway" (Adams 2009: 78–80).

23 Storch (2011: 45, citing Koji 2006) also comments that Yarada K'wank'wa items used by Ethiopian urban youth are replaced once they become known to members of the out-group. Yarada K'wank'wa is based on Amharic and is spoken in Addis Ababa and beyond. Storch (2011: 73) underlines the importance of secrecy for some speakers when she notes: "Speakers may use one manipulation strategy first then switch to another one. This mixing of secret codes is claimed to increase the difficulty adult listeners experience in deciphering what has been said". Her account of speaker ability to move between strategies would appear to echo the thoughts of Bachmann and Basier (1984: 175) who, writing about the use of Verlan, note: "First of all, an expert in using Verlan is rarely limited to his mastery of Verlan alone. He knows other secret languages at the same time" ("Tout d'abord, un expert en verlanisation s'en tient rarement à la maîtrise du seul verlan. Il connaît simultanément d'autres langues cryptiques").

24 Gidley (2007: 149) provides a particularly adroit qualification regarding globalisation and urban culture: "A simplistic view of the corporate globalisation of 'urban culture' sees 'cultural imperialism': a US-centric aesthetic replicated wholesale, overriding the particularity of 'local' or 'native' cultures outside the United States. This critique –

politically radical but culturally conservative – misses the way that the products of the global cultural industries are never consumed in a purely passive way. They are always adapted to local needs and desires".

25 An engaging analysis of this question within a London context is provided by Gidley (2007). Referring to one record – *This Is How We Talk Down South* – he notes that the 'we' talks in a South London accent that is "the sole possession of neither black nor white", and that "the 'we' is not contrasted against white Londoners but against African-Americans. Responding to debates within the U.K. hip hop scene of the time, the record was asserting the possibility of taking up the American idiom of rap and rendering it in a profoundly British – and specifically local – voice in order to express the experiences of life as lived in south London" (Gidley 2007: 150).

26 My translation: "l'argot des malfaiteurs, l'argot des prisons, entre pour une part importante dans la formation du langage populaire".

The importance of social networks for the circulation of items is also demonstrated well by Boellstorff (2004). In his work on Bahasa Gay, for example, Boellstorff notes that all of the derivational models used to create its lexis had originated in one region of Indonesia but had circulated nationally through gay social networks. Boellstorff himself had sought out regional or local distinctions of Bahasa Gay but was only able to find what he described as "minor and temporary variations" (Boellstorff 2004: 249).

27 Alternatively, Internet World Stats (www.internetworldstats.com/euro/ru.htm) suggests the following population percentages for Internet use in Russia: 2.1% in 2000, 20.8% in 2007, 27% in 2008, 32.3% in 2009 and 42.8% in 2010. Zvereva (2012) cites ComScore statistics that indicate that, in 2012, there were some 50.8 million Internet users in Russia (unique visitors aged 15 or above) – about one-third of the Russian population (Zvereva 2012).

28 Crystal (2006: 8) also states: "The Internet is altering our conception of what the written language is for. The vast majority of traditional writing has represented the language of public record and debate ... It is formal in style, for the most part constructed with care, and expressed in the standard language".

29 Gorny (2004) suggests that 'lytdybr' was coined by Roman Leibov, whom he describes as the father of Russian LiveJournal and one of the pioneers of the Russian Internet.

30 It was further suggested that some 14–15% of all Russian Internet queries in 2008 were reportedly written incorrectly ("s iskazheniiami"). These data on incorrect queries were provided by Marina Purim, Manager for Social Engagement at Yandex (*Argumenty i fakty*, 2008). The most common errors were technical, where the user didn't change the keyboard from Roman to Cyrillic. Second place was occupied by spelling errors.

31 For instance, a 2008 study of US middle- and high-school students shed light on the accidental use of instant messaging–style vocabulary and emoticons in assignments (Amari 2010: 7).

References

Aarsæther, F., Marzo, S., Nistov, I. and Ceuleers, E. (2015) 'Indexing locality: contemporary urban vernaculars in Belgium and Norway', in J. Nortier and B.A. Svendsen (eds.) *Language, Youth and Identity in the 21st Century*, Cambridge: Cambridge University Press. 249–70.

Aboa, A.L.A. (2011) 'Le Nouchi – a-t-il un avenir?', *Revue Electronique Internationale de Sciences du Langage*, 16(Décembre), 44–54.

Adams, M. (2009) *Slang: The People's Poetry*, Oxford: Oxford University Press.

Ahua, B.M. (2006) 'La Motivation dans les créations lexicales en Nouchi', *Le Français en Afrique*, 21, 143–57.

182 Youth and criminal language practices

Alim, H.S. (2009) 'Translocal style communities: hip hop youth as cultural theorists of style, language and globalization', *Pragmatics*, *19*(1), 103–27.

Amari, J. (2010) 'Slang lexicography and the problem of defining slang', *The Fifth International Conference on Historical Lexicography and Lexicology*, Oxford.

Amit-Talai, V. (1995a) 'The waltz of sociability: intimacy, dislocation and friendship in a Quebec high school', in V. Amit-Talai and H. Wulff (eds.) *Youth Cultures: A Cross-Cultural Perspective*, London: Routledge. 144–65.

Amit-Talai, V. (1995b) 'The "multi" cultural of youth', in V. Amit-Talai and H. Wulff (eds.) *Youth Cultures: A Cross-Cultural Perspective*, London: Routledge. 223–33.

Androutsopoulos, J. (2005) 'Research on youth language', in U. Ammon, D. Norbert, K.J. Mattheier and P. Trudgill (eds.) *Sociolinguistics/Soziolinguistik: An International Handbook of the Science of Language and Society (Ein internationales Handbuch zur Wissenschaft von Sprache und Gesellschaft), Vol. 2*, Berlin: de Gruyter. 1496–1505.

Androutsopoulos, J. (2007) 'Style online: doing hip-hop on the German-speaking web', in P. Auer (ed.) *Style and Social Identities: Alternative Approaches to Linguistic Heterogeneity*, Berlin/New York: de Gruyter. 279–317.

Androutsopoulos, J. (2009) 'Language and the three spheres of hip-hop', in A. Ibrahim, H.S. Alim and A. Pennycook (eds.) *Global Linguistic Flows: Hip Hop Cultures, Identities, and the Politics of Language*, Mahwah, NJ: Lawrence Erlbaum. 43–62.

Androutsopoulos, A. (2011) 'Language change and digital media: a review of conceptions and evidence', in T. Kristiansen and N. Coupland (eds.) *Standard Languages and Language Standards in a Changing Europe*, Oslo: Novus. 145–61.

Androutsopoulos, J. and Scholz, A. (2002) 'On the recontextualization of hip-hop in European communities: a contrastive analysis of rap lyrics'. www.fu_berlin.de/phon/phin19/p19t1.htm, accessed April 2012.

Argumenty i fakty (2008), 29 October.

Bachmann, C. and Basier, L. (1984) 'Le verlan: argot d'école ou langue des Keums?', *Mots*, *8*, 169–87.

Bardsley, D. (2014) 'Slang in Godzone (Aotearoa – New Zealand)', in J. Coleman (ed.), *Global English Slang*, London: Routledge. 96–106.

Beazley, H. (2002) '"Vagrants wearing make-up": negotiating spaces on the streets of Yogyakarta, Indonesia', *Urban Studies*, *39*(9), 1665–83.

Beazley, H. (2003) 'The construction and protection of individual and collective Identities by street children and youth in Indonesia', *Children, Youth and Environments*, *13*(1). www.colorado.edu/journals/cye/13_1/Vol13_1Articles/CYE_CurrentIssue_Article_ChildrenYouthIndonesia_Beazley.htm, accessed July 2015.

Beck, R.M. (2010) 'Urban languages in Africa', *Africa Spectrum*, *45*(3), 11–41.

Beck, R.M. (2015) 'Sheng: an urban variety of Swahili in Kenya', in N. Nassenstein and A. Hollington (eds.) *Youth Language Practices in Africa and Beyond*, Berlin/Boston: Walter de Gruyter, Inc. 51–79.

Beier, L. (1995) 'Anti-language or jargon? Canting in the English underworld in the 16th and 17th centuries', in P. Burke and R. Porter (eds.) *Languages and Jargons: Contributions to a Social History of Language*, Cambridge: Polity Press. 64–101.

Bennett, A. (2007) 'As young as you feel: youth as a discursive construct', in P. Hodkinson and W. Deicke (eds.) *Youth Cultures: Scenes, Subcultures and Tribes*, New York: Routledge. 23–36.

Berdicevskis, A. (2011) 'Elektronnaia pochta vs. Chat: vliianie kanala kommunikatsii na iazyk', in *Computational Linguistics and Intellectual Technologies. Papers from the Annual International Conference "Dialogue"*, Moscow: RGGU. 84–93.

Berdicevskis, A. (Berdichevskiy, A.) (2012) '"Orfograficheskii" srednii rod: grammaticheskaia innovatsiia v iazyke russkogo interneta', in L.L. Fedorova (ed.) *Variativnost' v iazyke i kommunikatsii*, Moscow: RGGU. www.uib.no/filearchive/berdichevskij_neuter.pdf, accessed June 2014.
Beregovskaia, E.M. (1996) 'Molodëzhnyi sleng: formirovanie i funktsionirovanie', *Voprosy iazykoznaniia*, 3, 32–41.
Beyer, K. (2015) 'Youth language practices in Africa: achievements and challenges', in N. Nassenstein and A. Hollington (eds.) *Youth Language Practices in Africa and Beyond*, Berlin/Boston: Walter de Gruyter, Inc. 23–50.
Biblieva, O.V. (2007) 'Molodëzhnyi sleng kak forma reprezentatsii molodëzhnoi kul'tury v sredstvakh massovoi informatsii', *Vestnik Tomskogo Gosudarstvennogo Universiteta*, 304(Noiabr'), 62–5.
Blommaert, J. (2013) 'Language and the study of diversity', in *Working Papers in Urban Language and Literacies*, 113.
Blommaert, J. and Backus, A. (2011) 'Repertoires revisited: "knowing language" in superdiversity', in *Working Papers in Urban Language and Literacies*, 67.
Boellstorff, T. (2004) '*Gay* language and Indonesia: registering belonging', *Journal of Linguistic Anthropology*, 14(2), 248–68.
Bosire, M. (2009) 'What makes a Sheng word unique? Lexical manipulation in mixed languages', in A. Ojo and L. Moshi (eds.) *Selected Proceedings of the 39th Annual Conference on African Linguistics*, Somerville, MA. 77–85.
Bristowe, A., Oostendorp, M. and Anthonissen, C. (2014) 'Language and youth identity in a multilingual setting: a multimodal repertoire approach', *South African Linguistics and Applied Language Studies*, 37(2), 229–45.
Brook, K. (2010) 'Interactions of South African Languages: case study of Tsotsitaal', paper presented at the *GlobalWordnet Conference*, Mumbai, India. www.cfilt.iitb.ac.in/gwc2010/pdfs/13_challenges_Tsotsitaal_wordnet__Brook.pdf, accessed 20 May 2016.
Bucholtz, M. (2002) 'Youth and cultural practice', *Annual Review of Anthropology*, 31, 525–52.
Bucholtz, M. (2004) 'Styles and stereotypes: the linguistic negotiation of identity among Laotian American youth', *Pragmatics*, 14(2/3), 127–47.
Bucholtz, M. (2006) 'Word up: social meanings of slang in Californian youth culture', in J. Goodman and L. Monaghan (eds.) *A Cultural Approach to Interpersonal Communication: Essential Readings*, Malden, MA: Blackwell. cloudfront.escholarship.org/dist/prd/content/qt0c7141bs/qt0c7141bs.pdf;v=lg, accessed November 2016.
Bucholtz, M. and Skapoulli, E. (2009) 'Youth language at the intersection: from migration to globalization', youthful concerns: movement, belonging and modernity, *Pragmatics*, 19(1), 1–16.
Bullock, B. (1996) 'Popular derivation and linguistic inquiry: Les Javanais', *The French Review*, 70(2), 180–91.
Burke, P. (1995) 'Introduction', in P. Burke and R. Porter (eds.) *Languages and Jargons: Contributions to a Social History of Language*, Cambridge: Polity Press. 1–21.
Busch, B. (2012) 'The linguistic repertoire revisited', *Applied Linguistics*, 33(5), 503–23.
Buzek, I. (2012) 'Presence of gypsy origin vocabulary in Latin American Spanish varieties: the case of Mexican Spanish and its *Caló*', paper presented at the *Tenth International Conference on Romani Linguistics, Barcelona*, 5–7 September.
Caputo, V. (1995) 'Anthropology's silent 'others': a consideration of some conceptual and methodological issues for the study of youth and children's cultures', in V. Amit-Talai

and H. Wulff (eds.) *Youth Cultures: A Cross-Cultural Perspective*, London: Routledge. 19–42.
Carter, R.A. (2004) *Language and Creativity*, London: Routledge.
Červenková, M. (2001) 'L'influence de l'argot sur la langue commune et les procédés de sa formation en français contemporain', *Studia Minora Facultatis Philosophicae Universitatis Brunensis*, L.(22), 77–86.
Chambert-Loir, H. (1984) 'Those who speak Prokem', *Indonesia*, 37, 105–17.
Cheeseman, T. (1998) 'Hip hop in Germany', *Debatte*, 6(2), 191–214.
Cheshire, J., Nortier, J. and Adger, D. (2015) 'Emerging multiethnolects in Europe', in *Queen Mary's Occasional Papers Advancing Linguistics*, 33.
Coleman, J. (2012) *The Life of Slang*, Oxford: Oxford University Press.
Coleman, J. (2014) 'Slang used by students at the University of Leicester', in J. Coleman (ed.) *Global English Slang*, London: Routledge. 49–61.
Cooper, B. (1989) 'Russian underworld slang and its diffusion into the standard language', *Australian Slavonic and East European Journal*, 3(2), 61–89.
Cornips, L. and de Rooij, V.A. (2013) 'Selfing and othering through categories of race, place, and language among minority youths in Rotterdam, The Netherlands', in P. Siemund, I. Gogolin, M.E. Schulz and J. Davydova (eds.) *Multilingualism and Language Diversity in Urban Areas: Acquisition, Identities, Space, Education*, John Benjamins Publishing Company. 129–64.
Cornips, L., Jaspers, J. and de Rooij, V. (2015) 'The politics of labelling youth vernaculars in the Netherlands and Belgium', in J. Nortier and B.A. Svendsen (eds.) *Language, Youth and Identity in the 21st Century*, Cambridge: Cambridge University Press. 45–69.
Council of Europe (2012) *Council of Europe Descriptive Glossary of Terms Relating to Roma Issues*, 18 May.
Crystal, D. (2005) 'Johnson and the internet', Hilda Hulme Lecture.
Crystal, D. (2006) 'Diversity? We ain't seen nothing yet!', Plenary paper to the Fédération International des Professeurs de Langues Vivantes, Diversity in Language Learning and Teaching Conference, Göteborg, 16 June.
Cutler, C. and Røyneland, U. (2015) 'Where the fuck am I from? Hip-hop youth and the (re)negotiation of language and identity in Norway and the US', in J. Nortier and B.A. Svendsen (eds.) *Language, Youth and Identity in the 21st Century*, Cambridge: Cambridge University Press. 139–63.
Danesi, M. (1994) *Cool: The Signs and Meanings of Adolescence*, Toronto: University of Toronto Press.
Davie, J.D. (1997/98) 'Missing presumed dead? The *baikovyi iazyk* of the St. Petersburg *mazuriki* and other pre-Soviet argots', *Slavonica*, 4(1), 28–45.
Davie, J.D. (1998) *Making sense of the nonstandard: a study of borrowing and word-formation in 1990s Russian youth slang, with particular reference to the language of the fanzine* (Doctoral thesis, 2 volumes). University of Portsmouth.
De Féral, C. (2004) 'Français et langues en contact chez les jeunes en milieu urbain: vers de nouvelles identités' in *Penser la francophonie: concepts, actions et outils linguistiques, Actes des premières Journées scientifiques communes des réseaux de chercheurs concernant la langue*, Ouagadougou (Burkina Faso), 31 mai–1er juin.
de Klerk, V. (2005) 'Slang and swearing as markers of inclusion and exclusion in adolescence', in A. Williams and C. Thurlow (eds.) *Talking Adolescence: Perspectives on Communication in the Teenage Years*, New York: Peter Lang Publishing, Inc. 111–27.
de Klerk, V. and Antrobus, R. (2004) 'Swamp-donkeys and rippers: the use of slang and pejorative terms to name "the other"', *Alternation*, 11(2), 264–82.

Demisse, T. and Bender, L.M. (1983) 'An argot of Addis Ababa unattached girls', *Language in Society*, *12*(3), 339–47.
Deumert, A. (in press) 'Tsotsitaal online – the creativity of tradition', in C. Cutler and U. Røyneland (eds.) *Analyzing Multilingual Youth Practices in Computer Mediated Communication (CMC)*, Cambridge: Cambridge University Press.
Doran, M. (2004) 'Negotiating between bourge and racaille: Verlan as youth identity practice in suburban Paris', in A. Pavlenko and A. Blackledge (eds.) *Identities in Multilingual Contexts*, Clevedon, UK: Multilingual Matters Ltd. 93–124.
Doran, M. (2007) 'Alternative French, alternative identities: situating language in la banlieue', *Contemporary French and Francophone Studies*, *11*(4), 497–508.
Dorleijn, M., Mous, M. and Nortier, J. (2015) 'Urban youth speech styles in Kenya and the Netherlands', in J. Nortier and B.A. Svendsen (eds.) *Language, Youth and Identity in the 21st Century*, Cambridge: Cambridge University Press. 271–89.
Dorleijn, M. and Nortier, J. (2013) 'Multi-ethnolects: Kebabnorsk, Perkerdansk, Verlan, Kanakensprache, Straattaal, etc.', in P. Bakker and Y. Matras (eds.) *Contact Languages: A Comprehensive Guide*, Berlin: de Gruyter. 229–72.
Drummond, R. (2016) 'Slang shouldn't be banned… it should be celebrated, innit', *The Conversation*, 3 May, theconversation.com/slang-shouldnt-be-banned-it-should-be-celebrated-innit-58672, accessed October 2016.
Drummond, R. and Schleef, E. (2016) 'Identity in variationist sociolinguistics', in S. Preece (ed.) *The Routledge Handbook of Language and Identity*, London: Routledge. 50–65.
Duc, C. (2003) 'Confidences des jeunes sur leur langage', *Résonances*, 10(Juin), 13.
Dunn, J.A. (2006) 'It's Russian – but not as we know it', *Rusistika*, *31*, 3–6.
Eckert, P. (2002) 'Constructing meaning in sociolinguistic variation', paper presented at the Annual Meeting of the American Anthropological Association, New Orleans, November.
Eckert, P. (2003) 'Language and adolescent peer groups', *Journal of Language and Social Psychology*, *22*(1), 112–18.
Eckert, P. (2004) 'Adolescent language', in E. Finegan and J. Rickford (eds.) *Language in the USA*, Cambridge and New York: Cambridge University Press. Pre-publication copy. web.stanford.edu/~eckert/PDF/adolescentlanguage.pdf, accessed February 2013.
Eckert, P. (2005) 'Stylistic practice and the adolescent social order', in A. Williams and C. Thurlow (eds.) *Talking Adolescence: Perspectives on Communication in the Teenage Years*, New York: Peter Lang Publishing, Inc. 93–110.
Eckert, P. (2008) 'Variation and the indexical field', *Journal of Sociolinguistics*, *12*(4), 453–76.
Eckert, P. (2012) 'Three waves of variation study: the emergence of meaning in the study of sociolinguistic variation', *Annual Review of Anthropology*, *41*, 87–100.
Eckert, P. and McConnell-Ginet, S. (1995) 'Constructing meaning, constructing selves: Snapshots of language, gender and class from Belten High', in K. Hall and M. Buchholtz (eds.) *Gender Articulated: Arrangements of Language and the Socially Constructed Self*, London and New York: Routledge. 469–507.
Einat, T. and Einat, H. (2000) 'Inmate argot as an expression of prison subculture: the Israeli case', *The Prison Journal*, *80*(3), 309–25.
Einat T. and Livnat, Z. (2012) 'Words, values and identities: the Israeli argot (jargon) of prisoners', *International Journal of Political Science, Law and International Relations*, *2*(2), 97–118.
Einat, T. and Wall, A. (2006) 'Language, culture, and behavior in prison: the Israeli case', *Asian Criminology*, *1*, 173–89.

Ekberg, L. Opsahl, T. and Wiese, H. (2015) 'Functional gains: a cross-linguistic case study of three particles in Swedish, Norwegian and German', in J. Nortier and B.A. Svendsen (eds.) *Language, Youth and Identity in the 21st Century*, Cambridge: Cambridge University Press. 93–115.

Ellis, Y. (2002) 'Argot and Verlan', *Contemporary France Online*. www.well.ac.uk/cfol/argot.asp, accessed May 2011.

Ferrari, A. (2006) 'Vecteurs de la propagation du lexique sheng et invention perpétuelle de mots', *Le Français en Afrique*, *21*, 227–37.

Ferrari, A. (2007) 'Hip-hop in Nairobi: recognition of an international movement and the main means of expression for the urban youth in poor residential areas', in K. Njogu and H. Maupeu (eds.) *Songs and Politics in Eastern Africa*, Dar es Salaam/Nairobi: IFRA and Mkuki na Nyoka Publishers. 107–28.

Ferrari, A. (2014) 'Evolution of Sheng during the last decade', *Les Cahiers de l'Afrique de l'Est*, *47*, 29–54. rekebisho.wixsite.com/aureliaferrari/publications, accessed March 2015.

Ferrell, J. (1995) 'Urban graffiti: crime, control, and resistance', *Youth and Society*, *27*, 73–92.

Fonkoua, H.K. (2015) *A Dictionary of Camfranglais*, Frankfurt am Main: Peter Lang AG, Volume 107.

Fortier, J. (2002) 'The arts of deception: verbal performances by the Rāute of Nepal', *The Journal of the Royal Anthropological Institute*, *8*(2), 233–57.

Freywald, U., Cornips, L., Ganuza, N., Nistov, I. and Opsahl, T. (2015) 'Beyond verb second – a matter of novel information-structural effects? Evidence from Norwegian, Swedish, German and Dutch', in J. Nortier and B.A. Svendsen (eds.) *Language, Youth and Identity in the 21st Century*, Cambridge: Cambridge University Press. 73–92.

García, M. (2005) 'Influences of gypsy *Caló* on contemporary Spanish slang', *Hispania*, *88*(4), 800–12.

Garza, T.J. (2008) '"Ne trozh′ molodëzh′!" A portrait of urban youthspeak and the Russian language in the 21st century', *Russian Language Journal*, *58*. www.academia.edu/1974996/Не_трожь_молодёжь_A_Portrait_of_Urban_Youthspeak_and_the_Russian_Language_in_the_21st_Century, accessed December 2016.

Geipel, J. (1995) 'Caló: the "secret" language of the gypsies of Spain', in P. Burke and R. Porter (eds.) *Languages and Jargons: Contributions to a Social History of Language*, Cambridge: Polity Press. 102–32.

Gidley, B. (2007) 'Youth culture and ethnicity: emerging youth interculture in South London', in P. Hodkinson and W. Deicke (eds.) *Youth Cultures: Scenes, Subcultures and Tribes*, New York: Routledge. 145–60.

Gil, D. (2002) 'Ludlings in Malayic languages: an introduction', *PELBBA 15, Pertemuan Linguistik (Pusat Kajian) Bahasa dan Budaya Atma Jaya: Kelima Belas Pusat Kajian Bahasa dan Badaya*, Jakarta: Unika Atma Jaya. Pre-publication copy.

Githinji, P. (2006) 'Bazes and their shibboleths: lexical variation and Sheng speakers' identity in Nairobi', *Nordic Journal of African Studies*, *15*(4), 443–72.

Gorny, E. (2004) 'Russian LiveJournal: national specifics in the development of a virtual community', Version 1.0, 13 May. www.ruhr-uni-bochum.de/russ-cyb/library/texts/en/gorny_rlj.pdf, accessed June 2012.

Grachëv, M.A. (1992) 'Tret′ia volna', *Russkaia rech′*, *4*, 61–4.

Grachëv, M.A. (2007) *Slovar′ sovremennogo molodëzhnogo zhargona*, Moscow: Eksmo.

Grayson, J. (1964) 'Lunfardo, Argentina's unknown tongue', *Hispania*, *47*(1), 66–8.

Green, J. (1999) 'Romany rise', *Critical Quarterly*, *41*(3), 118–22. jonathongreen.co.uk/wp-content/uploads/2010/09/12_RomanyRise.pdf, accessed March 2014.
Green, J. (2003) 'Rhyming slang', *Critical Quarterly*, *45*(1–2), 220–6. jonathongreen.co.uk/wp-content/uploads/2010/09/7_RhymingSlang.pdf, accessed March 2014.
Green, J. (2006) 'Diction addiction', *Critical Quarterly*, *48*(3), 99–104. jonathongreen.co.uk/wp-content/uploads/2010/09/1_DictionAddiction.pdf, accessed March 2014.
Green, J. (2008) 'Argot: the flesh made word', *Critical Quarterly*, 50(1–2), 258–64. jonathongreen.co.uk/wp-content/uploads/2010/09/10_Argot.pdf, accessed March 2014.
Green, J. (2014) 'Multicultural London English: the new "youthspeak"', in J. Coleman (ed.) *Global English Slang*, London: Routledge. 62–71.
Green, J. (2016) *Slang: A Very Short Introduction*, Oxford: Oxford University Press.
Gromov, D.V. (2009), 'Sleng molodëzhnykh subkul′tur: leksicheskaia struktura i osobennosti formirovaniia', extended version of article in *Russkii iazyk v nauchnom osveshchenii*, *1*(17), 228–40.
Hagedorn, J.M. (2005) 'The global impact of gangs', *Journal of Contemporary Criminal Justice*, *21*(2), 153–69.
Halliday, M.A.K. (1978) *Language as Social Semiotic*, London: Edward Arnold.
Harchaoui, S. (2015) 'Lexical innovations in the speech of adolescents in Oslo, Norway', *Proceedings of ConSOLE XXIII*. 220–47.
Heller-Roazen, D. (2013) *Dark Tongues*, New York: Zone Books.
Hensley, C., Wright, J., Tewksbury, R. and Castle, T. (2003) 'The evolving nature of prison argot and sexual hierarchies', *The Prison Journal*, *83*, 289–300.
Higgs, E. (2014) 'Inmate subcultures', in J.S. Albanese (ed.) *The Encyclopedia of Criminology and Criminal Justice*, Chichester: John Wiley and Sons, Ltd. shareslide.org/inmate-subcultures-higgs, accessed June 2015.
Hollington, A. (2015) 'Yarada K'wank'wa and urban youth identity in Addis Ababa', in N. Nassenstein and A. Hollington (eds.) *Youth Language Practices in Africa and Beyond*, Berlin/Boston: Walter de Gruyter, Inc. 149–68.
Hollington, A. and Makwabarara, T. (2015) 'Youth language practices in Zimbabwe', in N. Nassenstein and A. Hollington (eds.) *Youth Language Practices in Africa and Beyond*, Berlin/Boston: Walter de Gruyter, Inc. 257–70.
Hollington, A. and Nassenstein, N. (2015) 'Conclusion and outlook: taking new directions in the study of youth language practices', in N. Nassenstein and A. Hollington (eds.) *Youth Language Practices in Africa and Beyond*, Berlin/Boston: Walter de Gruyter, Inc. 345–56.
Hristova, D.S. (2008) 'Velikiy i moguchiy "olbanskii yazyk": the Russian internet and the Russian language'. aatseel.org/100111/pdf/program/2008/29d7_2hristova_daniela.pdf, accessed July 2012.
Hurst, E. (2007) 'Urban discourses and identity in a South African township: an analysis of youth culture in Cape Town', paper presented at the African Studies Association 50th Annual Meeting, New York, 18–21 October.
Hurst, E. (2013) 'Youth shape the way we communicate', *Mail & Guardian*, 2 July mg.co.za/article/2013-07-02-youth-shape-the-way-we-communicate, accessed October 2017.
Hurst, E. (2015) 'Overview of the tsotsitaals of South Africa; their different base languages and common core lexical items', in N. Nassenstein and A. Hollington (eds.) *Youth Language Practices in Africa and Beyond*, Berlin/Boston: Walter de Gruyter, Inc. 169–84.
Hurst, E. (2017) 'African (urban) youth languages', *Oxford Research Encyclopedia of Linguistics*. linguistics.oxfordre.com/view/10.1093/acrefore/9780199384655.001.0001/acrefore-9780199384655-e-157, accessed October 2017.
Internet World Stats, www.internetworldstats.com/euro/ru.htm, accessed July 2012.

Irvine, J.T. (2001) '"Style" as distinctiveness: the culture and ideology of linguistic differentiation', in P. Eckert and J.R. Rickford (eds.) *Style and Sociolinguistic Variation*, Cambridge: Cambridge University Press. 21–43.

James, A. (1995) 'Talking of children and youth: language, socialization and culture', in V. Amit-Talai and H. Wulff (eds.) *Youth Cultures: A Cross-Cultural Perspective*, London: Routledge. 43–62.

Jeffs, T. and Smith, M.K. (1998) 'The problem of "youth" for youth work', *Youth and Policy*, *62*, 45–66.

Jørgensen, A.M. (2013) 'Spanish teenage language and the COLAm-corpus', *Bergen Language and Linguistic Studies*, 3(1), 151–66 (shared through https://creativecommons.org/licenses/by/3.0/legalcode).

Karanja, L. (2010) '"Homeless" at home: linguistic, cultural and identity hybridity and third space positioning of Kenyan urban youth', *Education canadienne et internationale*, *39*(2), 1–11.

Kawase, I. (2005) 'Musical performance and self-designation of Ethiopian minstrels: Azmari', *African Study Monographs*, Suppl. *29*, 137–42.

Kelley, S. (2010) 'Texting, Twitter contributing to students' poor grammar skills, prof says', *The Globe and Mail*, 1 February.

Kerswill, P. (2010) 'Youth languages in Africa and Europe: linguistic subversion or emerging vernaculars?', *Language in Africa: An Inter-University Research Seminar Exploring Language Usage and Values in a Range of Contexts*, Edge Hill University, 24 November.

Keyes, C.L. (1993) '"We're more than a novelty, boys": strategies of female rappers in the rap music tradition' in J. Radner (ed.) *Feminist Messages: Coding in Women's Folk Culture*, Urbana: University of Illinois Press. 203–20.

Kießling, R. (2004) 'bàk mwà mè dó – Camfranglais in Cameroon', *Lingua Posnaniensis*, *47*. www.aai.uni-hamburg.de/afrika/personen/kiessling/medien/kiessling-2004-camfranglais.pdf, accessed September 2012.

Kiessling, R. and Mous, M. (2004) 'Urban youth languages in Africa', *Anthropological Linguistics*, *46*(3), 1–39.

Kioko, E.M. (2015) 'Regional varieties and "ethnic" registers of Sheng', in N. Nassenstein and A. Hollington (eds.) *Youth Language Practices in Africa and Beyond*, Berlin/Boston: Walter de Gruyter, Inc. 119–47.

Kouadio N'guessan, J. (2006) 'Le Nouchi et les rapports Dioula-Français', *Le Français en Afrique*, *21*, 177–91.

Kouassi Ayewa, N. (2005) 'Mots et contexts en FPI et en Nouchi', *JS LTT/AUF, AUF*, Bruxelles. 1–11.

Kraidy, M.M. and Khalil, J.F. (2008) 'Youth, media and culture in the Arab world', in K. Drotner and S. Livingstone (eds.) *International Handbook of Children, Media and Culture*, London: Sage. 330–44.

Krohn, F.B. and Suazo, F.L. (1995) 'Contemporary urban music: controversial messages in hip-hop and rap lyrics', *Et cetera: A Review of General Semantics*, *52*(2), 139–54.

Labov, T. (1992) 'Social and language boundaries among adolescents', *American Speech*, *67*(4), 339–66.

Labov, W. (2001) *Principles of Linguistic Change: Social Factors*, Vol. 2 (Language in Society), Oxford: Blackwell.

Lapina-Kratasiuk, E. (2009) 'News in the Russian internet: the growing indifference of a closing society', *Russian Analytical Digest*, *69*(9), 12–4.

Lebedeva, S.V. and Astakhova, N.V. (2016) 'Main features of youth jargon: synchronic analysis', *Russian Linguistic Bulletin*, *3*(7), 125–6.
Lefkowitz, N.J. (1989) 'Verlan: talking backwards in French', *The French Review*, *63*(2), 312–22.
Levikova, S.I. (2004) 'Molodëzhnyi sleng kak svoeobraznyi sposob verbalizatsii bytiya', *Bytie i iazyk*, 167–73.
Liechty, M. (1995) 'Media, markets and modernization: youth identities and the experience of modernity in Kathmandu, Nepal', in V. Amit-Talai and H. Wulff (eds.) *Youth Cultures: A Cross-Cultural Perspective*, London: Routledge. 166–201.
Likhovit'ko, E.S. and Ivantsova, N.A. (2015) 'Argotizmy i zhargonizmy v molodëzhnoi srede v Rossii', *Molodëzhnyi vestnik IrGTU*, dek, 1–2.
Lodge, R.A. (1993) *French: From Dialect to Standard*, London: Routledge.
Lodge, R.A. (2004) *A Sociolinguistic History of Parisian French*, Cambridge: Cambridge University Press.
Lysenko, S.A. (2008) 'Oralizatsiia kak tendentsiia razvitiia Internet-kommunikatsii', *Vestnik VGU, Seriia: Filologiia. Zhurnalistika*, *2*, 69–71.
Lytra, V. (2015) 'Language and language ideologies among Turkish-speaking young people in Athens and London', in J. Nortier and B.A. Svendsen (eds.) *Language, Youth and Identity in the 21st Century*, Cambridge: Cambridge University Press. 183–204.
Mallik, B. (1972) *Language of the Underworld of West Bengal*, Calcutta: Sanskrit College Research Series No. LXXVII.
Manfredi, S. (2008a) 'Rendók: a youth secret language in Sudan', *Estudios de dialectología norteafricana y andalusí*, *12*, 113–29.
Manfredi, S. (2008b) 'Le Rendok: un parler jeune Soudanais. Analyse linguistique et sociolinguistique en comparaison avec le Verlan', Centre Culturel Français de Khartoum, 7 April.
Maurer, D.W. (1981) *Language of the Underworld* (collected and edited by Allan W. Futrell and Charles B. Wordell), Lexington: University Press of Kentucky.
Mayr, A. (2004) *Prison Discourse: Language as a Means of Control and Resistance*, Basingstoke: Palgrave MacMillan.
Mazrui, A.M. (1995) 'Slang and code-switching: the case of Sheng in Kenya', *Afrikanistische Arbietspapier*, *42*, 168–79.
McKay, S. (2005) 'Communication and "risky" behaviour in adolescence', in A. Williams and C. Thurlow (eds.) *Talking Adolescence: Perspectives on Communication in the Teenage Years*, New York: Peter Lang Publishing, Inc. 265–81.
McKay, S., Thurlow, C. and Toomey Zimmerman, H. (2005) 'Wired whizzes or technoslaves? Young people and their emergent communication technologies', in A. Williams and c. Thurlow (eds.) *Talking Adolescence: Perspectives on Communication in the Teenage Years*, New York: Peter Lang Publishing, Inc. 185–203.
Méla, V. (1988) 'Parler verlan: règles et usages', *Langage et société*, *45*, 47–72.
Méla, V. (1991) 'Le verlan ou le langage du miroir', *Langages*, 101, 73–94.
Méla, V. (1997) 'Verlan 2000', *Langue française*, *114*, 16–34.
Mensah, E. (2016) 'The dynamics of youth language in Africa: an introduction', *Sociolinguistic Studies*, *10*(1–2), 1–14.
Milani, T.M., Jonsson, R. and Mhlambi, I.J. (2015) 'Shooting the subversive: when non-normative linguistic practices go mainstream in the media', in J. Nortier and B.A. Svendsen (eds.) *Language, Youth and Identity in the 21st Century*, Cambridge: Cambridge University Press. 119–38.
Miles, S. (2000) *Youth Lifestyles in a Changing World*, Buckingham: Open University Press.

Miller, L. (2003) 'Graffiti photos: expressive art in Japanese girls' culture', *Harvard Asia Quarterly*, 7(3), 31–42.
Miller, L. (2004) 'Those naughty teenage girls: Japanese Kogals, slang, and media assessments', *Journal of Linguistic Anthropology*, 14(2), 225–47.
Miller, L. (2011) 'Taking girls seriously in "cool Japan" ideology', *Japan Studies Review*, 15, 97–106.
Miodushevskaia, T. (2009) '15-letie Runeta: "olbanskii" iazyk stanovitsia dlia molodëzhi osnovnym?', *Argumenty i fakty*, 7 April.
Mo Ibrahim Foundation (2015) *African Urban Dynamics: Facts and Figures*. static. moibrahimfoundation.org/u/2015/11/19115202/2015-Facts-Figures-African-Urban-Dynamics.pdf, accessed October 2016.
Molamu, L. (1995) 'Wietie: the emergence and development of Tsotsitaal in South Africa', *Alternation*, 2(2), 139–58.
Montgomery, M. (2008) *An Introduction to Language and Society* (3rd ed.), London: Routledge.
Mo Ting (2012) 'New survey reveals deterioration of national Chinese language skills', *People's Daily Online*, 11 January. en.people.cn/90882/7701810.html, accessed June 2012.
Mugaddam, A.H. (2012) 'Identity construction and linguistic manipulation in Randuk', paper presented at the *Youth Languages and Urban Languages in Africa Workshop*, Institut für Afrikanistik, Cologne University, Germany.
Mugaddam, A.H. (2015) 'Identity construction and linguistic manipulation in Randuk', in N. Nassenstein and A. Hollington (eds.) *Youth Language Practices in Africa and Beyond*, Berlin/Boston: Walter de Gruyter, Inc. 99–118.
Mugaddam, A.R. (2008) 'Youth language in Khartoum', paper presented at the University of Cologne Institute for African Studies, 28 May.
Muindi, B. (2010) 'Kenya: Sheng blamed as candidates post poor results', *Daily Nation*, 29 December.
Mukhwana, A. (2015) 'Sheng and Engsh: what they are and what they are not', *International Journal of Scientific Research and Innovative Technology*, 2(1), 94–102.
Mutonya, M. (2007) 'Redefining Nairobi's streets: a study of slang, marginalization, and identity', *Journal of Global Initiatives*, 2(2), 169–85.
Mwihaki, A. (2007) 'Viewing Sheng as a social dialect: a linguistic approach', *ChemChemi*, Kenyatta University, 4(2), 57–75.
Nad′iarova, E.Sh. (2014) 'Rasprostianenie slengovykh vyrazhenii v molodëzhnoi polil-ingvokul′turnoi srede', *Uchënye zapiski Tavricheskogo natsional′nogo universiteta im. V.I. Vernadskogo. Seriia "Filologiia. Sotsial'nye kommunikatsii"*, 27(66), No. 2, 64–74.
Namyalo, S. (2015) 'Linguistic strategies in Luyaaye: word play and conscious language manipulation', in N. Nassenstein and A. Hollington (eds.) *Youth Language Practices in Africa and Beyond*, Berlin/Boston: Walter de Gruyter, Inc. 313–44.
Nassenstein, N. (2015a) 'Imvugo y'Umuhanda: youth language practices in Kigali (Rwanda)', in N. Nassenstein and A. Hollington (eds.) *Youth Language Practices in Africa and Beyond*, Berlin/Boston: Walter de Gruyter, Inc. 185–204.
Nassenstein, N. (2015b) 'The emergence of Langila in Kinshasa (DR Congo)', in N. Nassenstein and A. Hollington (eds.) *Youth Language Practices in Africa and Beyond*, Berlin/Boston: Walter de Gruyter, Inc. 81–98.
Nassenstein, N. (2015c) 'Rural youth language practices, social media and globalization in Africa: New sociolinguistic arenas', presentation given at the Institut für Ethnologie & Afrikastudien, Universität Mainz, 23 November.

Nassenstein, N. (2016) 'The new urban youth language Yabacrâne in Goma (DR Congo)', *Sociolinguistic Studies*, *10*(1–2), 235–59.
Nassenstein N. and Hollington, A. (eds.) (2015) *Youth Language Practices in Africa and Beyond*, Berlin/Boston: Walter de Gruyter, Inc.
Nedelec, C. (1986) 'L'argot des gueux aux XVIe et XVIIe siècles', *Dix-Septième Siècle*, Jan–Mar., 147–54.
Ngefac, A. (2010) 'Linguistic choices in postcolonial multilingual Cameroon', *Nordic Journal of African Studies*, *19*(3), 149–64.
Ngo Ngok-Graux, E.N. (2007) 'Les Représentations du Camfranglais chez les Locuteurs de Douala et Yaoundé', *Le Français en Afrique*, *21*, 219–25.
Nortier, J. and Svendsen, B.A. (eds.) (2015) *Language, Youth and Identity in the 21st Century*, Cambridge: Cambridge University Press.
Novosti E.1.Ru (2009) '*Deputaty Gosdumy vnov' khotiat borot'sia s "olbanskim" iazykom*', 30 April.
Ogechi, N.O. (2005) 'On lexicalization in Sheng', *Nordic Journal of African Studies*, *14*(3), 334–55.
Okamoto, S. (1995) '"Tasteless" Japanese: less "feminine" speech among young Japanese women', in K. Hall and M. Bucholtz (eds.) *Gender Articulated: Language and the Socially Constructed Self*, New York: Routledge. 297–325.
Opsahl, T., Røyneland, U. and Svendsen, B.A. (2008) '"Syns du jallanorsk er lættis, eller?" – om taggen [lang=x] i NoTa-Oslo-korpuset', in J.B. Johannessen and K. Hagen (eds.) *Språk i Oslo. Ny forskning omkring talespråk*. Oslo: Novus forlag. 29–42
Pagliai, V. (2009) 'The art of dueling with words: toward a new understanding of verbal duels across the world', *Oral Tradition*, *24*(1), 61–88.
Paul, K., Freywald, U. and Wittenberg, E. (2009) '"*Kiezdeutsch* goes school" – a multi-ethnic variety of German from an educational perspective', *JoLIE*, *2*(1), 91–113.
Pozas, M. (2000) '"De Remps, de Reufs et de Reus: Approximation au lexique de la famille dans le "langage" jeune', *La Philologie Française à la croisée de l'an 2000*, 95–103.
Quenqua, D. (2012) 'They're, like, way ahead of the linguistic currrrve', *The New York Times*, 27 February.
Rampton, B. (2010) 'Crossing into class: language, ethnicities and class sensibility in England', in C. Llamas and D. Watt (eds.) *Language and Identities*, Edinburgh: Edinburgh University Press. 134–43.
Rampton, B. (2015) 'Contemporary urban vernaculars', in J. Nortier and B.A. Svendsen (eds.) *Language, Youth and Identity in the 21st Century*, Cambridge: Cambridge University Press. 24–44.
Robert L'Argenton, F. (1991) 'Larlépeem largomuche du louchébem. Parler l'argot du boucher', *Langue française*, 90, 113–25.
Roffé, A. (1993) 'Dénominations des argot en France', *Revista de Filología Francesa*, *4*, 215–29.
Roffé Gómez, A. (1994) 'Propriétés essentielles des langues spéciales: coïncidences et différences par rapport aux argots', *Revista de Filología Francesa*, *5*, 283–93.
Roth-Gordon, J. (2007) 'Racing and erasing the playboy: slang, transnational youth subculture, and racial Discourse in Brazil', *Journal of Linguistic Anthropology*, *17*(2), 246–65.
Roth-Gordon, J. (2009) 'The language that came down the hill', *American Anthropologist*, *111*(1), 57–68.
Roth-Gordon, J. (2016) 'From upstanding citizen to North American rapper and back again: the racial malleability of poor male Brazilian youth', in H.S. Alim, J.R. Rickford and A.F. Ball (eds.) *Raciolinguistics*, New York: Oxford University Press. 51–64.

Ryazanova-Clarke L. and Wade, T. (1999) *The Russian Language Today*, London: Routledge.

Salmons, J. (1991) 'Youth language in the German Democratic Republic: its diversity and distinctiveness', *American Journal of German Linguistics and Literature*, *3*, 1–30.

Samper, D.A. (2004) '"Africa is still our mama": Kenyan rappers, youth identity, and the revitalization of traditional values', *African Identities*, *2*(1), 37–51.

Santa Maria, M. (2002) 'Youth in Southeast Asia: living within the continuity of tradition and the turbulence of change', in B.B. Brown, R.W. Larson and T.S. Saraswathi (eds.) *The World's Youth*, Cambridge: Cambridge University Press. 171–206.

Schmidt, H. and Teubener, K. (2006) '"Our Runet"? Cultural identity and media usage', in H. Schmidt, K. Teubener and N. Konradova (eds.) *Control + Shift. Public and Private Usages of the Russian Internet*, Norderstedt, Germany: Books on Demand. 14–20.

Scholten, B. (1988) *Standard und städtischer Substandard bei Heranwachsenden im Ruhrgebiet*, Tübingen.

Sherzer, J. (2002) *Speech Play and Verbal Art*, Austin: University of Texas Press.

Slone, T.H. (2003) *Prokem. An Analysis of a Jakartan Slang*, Oakland: Masalai Press.

Smaill, B. (2008) 'Asia Pacific modernities: youth and media locations', in U.M. Rodrigues and B. Smaill (eds.) *Youth, Media and Culture in the Asia Pacific Region*, Newcastle: Cambridge Scholars Press. 1–15.

Smith-Hefner, N.J. (2007) 'Youth language, *Gaul* sociability, and the new Indonesian middle class', *Journal of Linguistic Anthropology*, *17*(2), 184–203.

Sourdot, M. (1991) 'Argot, jargon, jargot', *Langue française*, *90*, 13–27.

Stalker, J.C. (1995) 'Slang is not novel', *Annual Meeting of the American Association for Applied Linguistics*, Long Beach, California, March 25–8.

Stavsky, L., Mozeson, I.E. and Mozeson, D.R. (1995) *A2Z: The Book of Rap and Hip-Hop Slang*, New York: Boulevard.

Stein-Kanjora, G. (2008) '"Parler comme ça, c'est vachement cool!"', *Sociologus*, *58*(2), 117–41.

Stenström, A. (2014) *Teenage Talk: From General Characteristics to the Use of Pragmatic Markers in a Contrastive Perspective*, Basingstoke: Palgrave MacMillan.

Stenström, A., Andersen, G. and Hasund, I.K. (2002) *Trends in Teenage Talk: Corpus Compilation, Analysis and Findings*, Amsterdam/Philadelphia: John Benjamins Publishing Company.

Storch, A. (2011) *Secret Manipulations*, New York, Oxford University Press.

Strutz, H. (2009) *Dictionary of French Slang and Colloquial Expressions*, New York: Barron's.

Suchaovanich, K. (2010) 'Facebook and Twitter blamed for decline in language skills', *The Winnipeg Free Press*. www.winnipegfreepress.com/breakingnews/facebook-and-twitter-lingo-blamed-for-decline-in-language-skills-among-thailands-youths-99086794.html, accessed March 2012.

Svendsen, B.A. (2015) 'Language, youth and identity in the 21st century: content and continuations', in J. Nortier and B.A. Svendsen (eds.) *Language, Youth and Identity in the 21st Century*, Cambridge: Cambridge University Press. 3–23.

Szabó, E. (2006) 'Hungarian prison slang today', *Revue d'Études Françaises*, *11*, 219–29.

Tagliamonte, S.A. and Denis, D. (2008) 'Linguistic ruin? Lol! Instant messaging and teen language', *American Speech*, *83*(1, Spring), 3–34.

Tajfel, H. and Turner, J.C. (1986) 'The social identity theory of intergroup behavior', in S. Worchel and L.W. Austin (eds.) *Psychology of Intergroup Relations*, Chicago: Nelson-Hall. 7–24.

Tetreault, C. (2000) 'Adolescents' multilingual punning and identity play', paper presented at the American Anthropological Association, San Francisco.
Thorne, T. (2006) 'Slanguistics or just lemon meringue?', *Proceedings from the Crossing Frontiers: Languages and the International Dimension Conference*, Cardiff University, 6–7 July. www.llas.ac.uk/cardiff2006, accessed June 2012.
Thurlow, C. (2003a) 'Generation txt? The sociolinguistics of young people's text-messaging', *Discourse Analysis Online*, *1*(1), 1–27. www.researchgate.net/publication/259258527_Generation_Txt_The_sociolinguistics_of_young_people%27s_text-messaging, accessed August 2016.
Thurlow, C. (2003b) 'Teenagers *in* communication, teenagers *on* communication', *Journal of Language and Social Psychology*, *22*(1), 50–7.
Thurlow, C. (2005) 'Deconstructing adolescent communication', in A. Williams and C. Thurlow (eds.) *Talking Adolescence: Perspectives on Communication in the Teenage Years*, New York: Peter Lang Publishing, Inc. 1–20.
Thurlow, C. (2006) 'From statistical panic to moral panic: the metadiscursive construction and popular exaggeration of new media language in the print media', *Journal of Computer-Mediated Communication*, *11*, 667–701.
Thurlow, C. (2007) 'Fabricating youth: new-media discourse and the technologization of young people', in S. Johnson and A. Ensslin (eds.) *Language in the Media: Representations, Identities, Ideologies*, London: Continuum. 213–33.
Thurlow, C. (2012) 'Determined creativity: language play in new media discourse', in R. Jones (ed.) *Discourse and Creativity*, London: Pearson. 169–90.
Thurlow, C. (2014) 'Disciplining youth: language ideologies and new technologies', in A. Jaworski and N. Coupland (eds.) *The Discourse Reader* (3rd ed.), London: Routledge. 481–96.
Tonkov, V. (1930) *Opyt issledovaniia vorovskogo iazyka*, Kazan': TATPOLIGRAF.
UNESCO (2016) *Learning to Live Together*. www.unesco.org/new/en/social-and-human-sciences/themes/youth/youth-definition/, accessed July 2016.
United Nations (2015a) *Population Facts*, New York: United Nations Department of Economic and Social Affairs, May. www.un.org/en/development/desa/population/publications/pdf/popfacts/PopFacts_2015-1.pdf, accessed July 2016.
United Nations (2015b) *World Population Prospects. The 2015 Revision*, New York: United Nations. esa.un.org/unpd/wpp/publications/files/key_findings_wpp_2015.pdf, accessed July 2016.
Vakunta, P. (undated) 'Nouchi – the making of a new Ivorian language: an interview with Mema Bamba', blog entry. vakunta.blogspot.co.uk/p/interviews_02.html, accessed July 2016.
Vakunta, P.W. (2008) 'On translating Camfranglais and other Camerounismes', *Meta Translators' Journal*, *53*(4), 942–7.
Vakunta, P.W. (2011) 'Ivorian Nouchi, cousin to Cameroonian Camfranglais'. www.postnewslive.com/2011, accessed September 2012.
Veit-Wild, F. (2009) '"Zimbolicious" – the creative potential of linguistic innovation: the case of Shona-English in Zimbabwe', *Journal of Southern African Studies*, *35*(3), 683–97.
Verma, S. and Saraswathi, T.S. (2002) 'Adolescence in India: street urchins or Silicon Valley millionaires?', in B.B. Brown, R.W. Larson and T.S. Saraswathi (eds.) *The World's Youth*, Cambridge: Cambridge University Press. 105–40.
Vertovec, S. (2007) *New Complexities of Cohesion in Britain: Super-Diversity, Transnationalism and Civil-Integration*, UK Commission on Integration and Cohesion.

Vierke, C. (2015) 'Some remarks on poetic aspects of Sheng', in N. Nassenstein and A. Hollington (eds.) *Youth Language Practices in Africa and Beyond*, Berlin/Boston: Walter de Gruyter, Inc. 227–56.

Walter, M. (2002) 'Kalaam, Kalaarbaam: an Arabic speech disguise in Hadramaut', *Texas Linguistic Forum 45, Proceedings of the Tenth Annual Symposium about Language and Society*, Austin, April, 177–86.

Wardhaugh, R. (1998) *An Introduction to Sociolinguistics* (3rd ed.), Malden, MA: Blackwell.

Widawski, M. (2012) 'Twentieth century American slang and its sociocultural context: part one', *Kwartalnik Neofilologiczny, LIX*(3), 381–91.

Widawski, M. (2015) *African American Slang*, Cambridge: Cambridge University Press.

Wiese, H. (2009) 'Grammatical innovation in multi-ethnic urban Europe: New linguistic practices among adolescents', *Lingua, 119*, 782–806.

Williams, Q. (2016) 'Ethnicity and extreme locality in South Africa's multilingual hip hop Ciphas', in H.S. Alim, J.R. Rickford and A.F. Ball (eds.) *Raciolinguistics*, New York: Oxford University Press. 113–33.

Wilson, C. (2015) 'Kindoubil: urban youth languages in Kisangani', in N. Nassenstein and A. Hollington (eds.) *Youth Language Practices in Africa and Beyond*, Berlin/Boston: Walter de Gruyter, Inc. 293–311.

Wise, H. (1997) *The Vocabulary of Modern French*, London: Routledge.

Wolfer, C. (2011) 'Arabic secret languages', *Folia Orientalia, 47*, Part II.

World Bank, data.worldbank.org/indicator/IT.NET.USER.P2/countries/RU?display=graph, accessed July 2012.

Wulff, H. (1995a) 'Introducing youth culture in its own right: the state of the art and new possibilities', in V. Amit-Talai and H. Wulff (eds.) *Youth Cultures: A Cross-Cultural Perspective*, London: Routledge. 1–18.

Wulff, H. (1995b) 'Inter-racial friendship: consuming youth styles, ethnicity and teenage femininity in South London', in V. Amit-Talai and H. Wulff (eds.) *Youth Cultures: A Cross-Cultural Perspective*, London: Routledge. 63–80.

Wyn, J. (2005) 'Youth in the media: adult stereotypes of young people', in A. Williams and C. Thurlow (eds.) *Talking Adolescence: Perspectives on Communication in the Teenage Years*, New York: Peter Lang Publishing, Inc. 23–34.

Zarzycki, Ł. (2015) 'Socio-lingual phenomenon of the anti-language of Polish and American prison inmates', *Crossroads. A Journal of English Studies*, Wydział Filologiczny Uniwersytetu w Białymstoku, *8*, 11–23.

Zhirmunskii, V. (1936) *Natsional'nyi iazyk i sotsial'nye dialekty*, Leningrad: Khudozhestvennaia literatura.

Zvereva, V. (undated), 'Comments on Ru.net news: speech formulas and cultural meanings'. www.uib.no/filearchive/zvereva2.pdf, accessed July 2012.

Zvereva, V. (2012) 'On new media: memory and identity in Russia', blog entry, 13 February. cambridgeculturalmemory.blogspot.co.uk/2012/02/on-new-media-memory-and-identity-in.html, accessed January 2015.

A new saint, Florence, 2012

'All cops are bastards', Bordeaux, 2015

'Blank walls = silent people', Paris, 2013

'ILY' ('JtM'), near Rambouillet, 2013

'Illuminati' or '*Kill*uminati'?, Florence, 2012

Rabzette and friends, Strasbourg, 2013

Electricity 'for nowt', Saintes, 2015

'New Year shindig …', Almaty, 2016

'Treize (13) NRV': 'Très énervé' ('very irritated') or 'Trop déter(miné') ('Too determined')?, Paris, 2013

'Keuj', Metz, 2011

'À ma mifa' ('To my family'), Geneva, 2013

'The Little Diner', Strasbourg, 2013

'Shut Your Trap!' ('Ta gueule'), Rouen, 2013

Part II

4 Invention and borrowing

Introduction

As we will discover in this and later chapters, there are many ways in which new items can be created to supplement a lexicon. One such way is through lexical borrowing. Interaction between communities often brings with it an exchange or flow of terms from one language to another; colloquial, youth and criminal language practices are no different. Indeed, it is often the case that such varieties develop a well-established history of borrowing vocabulary from other languages. In his study of the English criminal cant of the sixteenth and seventeenth centuries, for example, Beier (1995) cites the use of items such as 'shappeau' (from the French 'chapeau') for 'hat', while in his analysis of Spanish prison and criminal language, Salillas (1896) points to 'sacocha' ('small purse', 'handbag', 'pocket') being borrowed from Italian 'saccoccia' ('pocket') and to 'dupa' ('one easily duped') being based on the French 'dupe' ('dupe', which was also used by the Coquillards). Equally, Tikhanov (1895), discussing the language variety reportedly used by beggars in Briansk, Russia, in the late nineteenth century, observed that it included vocabulary from, among others, Greek, German and Romani, an example of the latter being 'raklo' ('thief'), a term designating a non-Roma boy in Romani and surviving as an albeit uncommon item with the meaning of 'petty thief'.[1]

In this chapter, our primary focus is on lexical borrowing and what happens when items move from one language or lexicon to another. We'll explore three particular manifestations:

- lexical borrowing from one language to another – in addition to the aforementioned examples, criminals in 1960s West Bengal borrowed from Arabic, English and Persian, for example (Mallik 1972); speakers of French youth and colloquial language have borrowed words from African languages, Arabic and English, among others (e.g. Goudailler 2002; Kortas 2003; Doran 2004; Strutz 2009); Russian criminals and traders historically borrowed from Greek and German, *inter alia* (e.g. Davie 1997/98); while Lunfardo, originally the language variety associated with the Buenos Aires underworld and lower classes, included lexis from Italian, French and English (e.g. Grayson 1964; Vázquez Ríos 2009; Blake 2010);

- transfer between lexicons associated with certain groups, such as between criminal and youth language; and
- calques, or loan translations, where the sense of a word is borrowed across languages, e.g. the Russian and Spanish drugs terms 'trav(k)a' and 'hierba', respectively, are translations of the English 'grass'.

Before we investigate these areas, we briefly discuss the concept of coining – the invention of new lexis.

Coining and currency

On some occasions, speakers may create completely new words as they interact. These words may be invented because the desired word doesn't come to mind, or to get a point or attitude across in a novel and unexpected way, and don't last any length of time in the language. Words created on the spur of the moment and to keep the conversation flowing are known as *nonce words* or *nonce-formations*. In using them, speakers creatively bend the shape of the language as we commonly know it.

When speakers create new words or phrases, they *coin* them. Also employed in literature, coining is an interesting example of a speaker mobilising their linguistic abilities in a creative way. The aims behind inventing new terms are manifold, ranging from maintaining secrecy to in-group competition and social association/dissociation (see Chapters Two and Three). Many language varieties have coinages in their lexicons – Nouchi, for example, generally sources its vocabulary from three categories of word: items of European origin; words of Ivorian origin; and those either of unknown provenance or coined locally (Ahua 2008).

It can sometimes be difficult for researchers to find and record new items, in particular those that are invented locally. In some instances, coinages may be created, used by large cohorts and then become available for subsequent analysis. However, in others, an item may be created, used within a very small group and then quickly pass out of use. Or indeed, it may remain used by only one or two people and no more. Unless there is broader dissemination of the word or phrase, it is unlikely that it will be picked up by other users and circulated more broadly, or noticed by researchers, although fieldwork can help in this regard.[2]

When an item is found, it is *generally* likely that its creation will adhere in large part to the word-formation practices that account for the creation of other non-standard forms. This does not mean, however, that the construction of a coined item will be routinely transparent: in his study of criminal language practices in 1960s West Bengal, Mallik (1972) cited 'bigi' ('metals') and 'binu' ('radio') as coinages of unknown provenance. Furthermore, the invented element need not be an entire word: nonsense suffixes might also be created, for example '–le/–les' in Pachuco Caló 'Mexicles' – 'Mexico', from 'México' (García 2005).

Although finding invented items and explaining their linguistic and social provenance can be difficult (see also **Difficulties in defining word origin**), there are nonetheless terms that do acquire longevity or gain broader currency after initially being used as part of colloquial, youth and criminal varieties. Sheng, for example, has a number of items that have been created and survived long enough to be documented: 'stra' ('words'), 'mrenga' ('car'), 'weng' ('tyre') and 'kiwii' ('buttocks') are but a few examples (Mazrui 1995; Githinji 2006). And, even when an item is found, it is possible that it might have more than one meaning: Sheng again provides an interesting example in the use of the coined adjective 'noma', where 'mtu noma' can mean either a 'good person' or a 'nuisance' (person), while 'kipindi noma' refers to an interesting TV or radio programme (Ogechi 2005; Kioko 2015).[3]

Of course, if an invented word is to continue being used it must gain traction, either within the immediate user group or more widely. Either way, initial group use is key. Furthermore, it should be remembered that not all words are created with the intention of ongoing use – some may be invented on the spur of the moment and/or for the sake of fun within an immediate conversation or exchange.

Lexical borrowing across languages: why?

Lexical borrowing is typically where items of vocabulary are imported by speakers of one language from the lexical stock of another. We say *typically*, because other forms of lexical borrowing are possible and are sometimes overlooked – for example, in the case of youth and criminal language, borrowing between subgroups sharing the same language. Moreover, there may be words which are borrowed by speakers of another language, used only for a brief time or in very specific circumstances, but are not retained or used sufficiently widely on an ongoing basis – such items are sometimes known as *ephemeralisms*. Lexical borrowing is distinct from code-switching, where speakers move between languages or dialects as they interact.

On a broader level, borrowing might not only involve the transfer of individual words and phrases between languages, but also the borrowing of phonological or syntactic elements.

A number of reasons may explain why lexical borrowing occurs between languages. These include:

- the inadequacy of the receiving language where new phenomena and terms arise in other societies/cultures and the terms are borrowed to fill the lexical gap;
- language economy, where a borrowed term might be less clumsy or more convenient than an equivalent in the borrowing language;
- semantic specificity to add greater accuracy: a loanword may offer more granularity in detail;
- specific social or cultural reference, where an item describes a phenomenon particularly associated with the society or culture of the donor language;
- the expression of sociocultural closeness, distance, commonality, cultural cachet, or language play to gain prestige. The use of foreign loanwords in Bahasa Gaul, for example, enables speakers to identify with *cool* Western

youth culture (Smith Hefner 2007) – although in some cases, the borrowing of items from prestige groups can show an ability to use vocabulary from a donor language without having a mastery of it;
- to affirm links to different minority cultural and linguistic backgrounds, including in cases where there may be broader homogenising cultural discourse (Doran 2007);
- expressive force: a foreign item might have greater perceived directness, emphasis or impact, while items in the borrowing language might be seen to have less effect;
- euphemism: where a foreign word is deemed less shocking than equivalents in the receiving language – it can be easier to talk about embarrassing or even taboo subjects if borrowed items are used that don't have the same emotive effect or perceived sociocultural *baggage*;
- hiding meaning from others: this factor might be particularly important where knowledge of foreign languages and/or cultures may be limited (see, for example, Méla 1991; Harchaoui 2015).[4]

Lexical borrowing by speakers of colloquial and in-group language varieties has formed the focus of a number of studies, both academic and popular. Sornig (1981: 4) has noted that "[w]hen one tries to observe some of the characteristic features of slang usage the very first thing that strikes the eye is the great amount of seemingly foreign lexical material that makes up slang vocabularies". This is certainly the case for a number of youth and criminal varieties such as French youth and criminal language, Lunfardo, African youth languages and West Bengal criminal language, to name but a few, all of which point to the flow of items between foreign lexicons. Such a flow can be seen, for example, in vocabulary that has moved between Lunfardo, which is used by Spanish speakers in Argentina, and Gíria, a non-standard Brazilian variety used by speakers of Brazilian Portuguese (Chamberlain 1981), while a similar dynamic has developed where words from German criminal lexicons are used by Hungarian prison inmates (Szabó 2006). In the same vein, youth speakers of Yabacrâne in Goma, Democratic Republic of Congo, may use the term 'demu', a loanword from Sheng, to refer to a girl (Nassenstein 2016: 247). In light of the conditions of linguistic super-diversity explored in Chapter Two, where access to foreign media and diaspora may enable contact across geographical spaces, and where migration and major sociopolitical events also lead to dynamic language contact, lexical borrowing is likely to continue to remain a prominent subject in the literature.

Where youth and criminal language practices are concerned, there can be a number of reasons why foreign lexical items are borrowed. With criminal language, there can be a desire to use foreign words where it is thought that the local population will not know the originating language. Sourdot (1991) points out, for example, that it would be difficult to fully appreciate the cryptic capability of French argot if we didn't consider borrowing from Arabic and Romani. Moreover, Harchaoui (2015) raises the use of Arabic loanwords by youth in Eastern Oslo to encrypt their utterances when discussing questions of legal or moral sensitivity, thereby underlining the cryptic potential for certain youth actors in certain social situations.

However, as we saw in Chapter Three, while obfuscation can be a motivation for borrowing in youth language practices, there can be other drivers. In her study of the language practices of young people in Eastern Oslo, for example, Harchaoui (2015) indicates that adolescent speakers there define their identity in terms of their local area and its multiethnic composition to set themselves against allegedly superficial adolescents in Western parts of the city – significantly greater borrowing from languages such as Berber, Arabic and Indo-European languages beyond English and Norwegian is one way of achieving this aim (Harchaoui 2015: 229–30, citing Opsahl, Røyneland and Svendsen 2008). At the same time, they are aware of the contexts within which certain loanwords are used (Harchaoui 2015). Social differentiation is thus supported and communicated through language choices.

The aspiration to generate social currency through borrowing is often regarded as important: knowledge of a foreign language can enable identification with foreign prestige groups or practices, and the ability to adopt and adapt select foreign vocabulary can enhance status within a group. In her examination of several hundred Gaul items used by university students, Smith-Hefner (2007: 193) found that over 30% of these were from English – the most productive source of borrowed items. For speakers of Gaul, borrowing items from English points to

> the speaker's identification with a fashionably cosmopolitan youth style widely identified with Western and East Asian print media, films, radio and television. Western, even global, youth culture emphasizes the positive value of cool nonchalance and casual informality.
>
> (Smith-Hefner 2007: 195)

Examples of the importance of borrowing from foreign sources can also be seen in Camfranglais and German youth language. In his analysis of 462 Camfranglais items, Kouega (2003: 524) found that roughly 60% resulted from borrowing,[5] while Androutsopoulos (2003: 2) noted in one study that vernacular English represented an important resource for projecting identity among German youth. Of course, masking and prestige are but two motivations for lexical borrowing in language practices; the reasons can be many, particularly as borrowing occurs through contact between varied groups in different circumstances (see also Chapters Two and Three, and **Multilingualism** on pages 111–12).

While the given examples of why lexical borrowing occurs cover a lot of ground, they don't tell the whole story. It is also worth noting that other, perhaps less obvious, considerations also emerge when an item is being borrowed. These include:

- It is easier to borrow from other sources, create new meanings for existing words, or even invent new lexis than to create new grammatical rules. Criminal and youth language practices tend to unfold within the syntactic

214   *Invention and borrowing*

and grammatical systems of their base languages. Camfranglais, for example, integrates vocabulary originating from English, German and Cameroonian languages into a French structure. Similarly, Bahasa Gaul adapts both dialectal and foreign loanwords while observing the patterns practiced in informal spoken Indonesian. It is thought that elements that can be easily taken from the originating language and which do not affect the structure of the borrowing language are those which are most commonly and readily borrowed (Aitchison 1991: 114).

- Some collectives such as youth groups may be keen to express affinity with foreign trends in particular, and thus will actively look to identify markers of foreign cultures, ranging from the use of in-group lexis to the use of untransliterated items. Good examples of this can be seen in the borrowing of English forms such as vernacular and hip hop terms by German youth through access to song lyrics, magazines, video clips and so on (e.g. Androutsopoulos 2003).

As these considerations suggest, analysis of borrowing can require some deep digging to understand not only why such borrowing occurs, but also how a word may or may not be modified for use as it enters the receiving lexicon. For example, whether a word will be changed in terms of its grammatical number, gender or word class; whether its meaning will change when borrowed; whether it will keep a foreign alphabet through non-transliteration and why (or why not); whether it will be combined with a word or suffix from another language to make a new item, and so on. These are areas that all require some consideration when thinking about the use of borrowed items, especially in cases where the item in question appears to have been modified in some way when imported into a new lexicon.

Semantic change in the borrowing process

Although there are some varieties that are reported not to rely on borrowing from other languages to any great extent (e.g. US college student language as outlined by Eble 1996;[6] Finnish 'slang' as referenced by Nahkola and Saanilahti 1999; Imvugo y'Umuhanda in Kigali, Rwanda, as noted by Nassenstein 2015; African American 'slang' as described by Widawski 2015), lexical borrowing tends to constitute an important process for supplementing youth and criminal lexicons. Indeed, a great deal of attention has been paid in various studies of youth, criminal and colloquial usage to items that derive from other languages. For example, Mallik's (1972) study of the language practices of criminals in 1960s West Bengal documented items such as:

nagdi	'money', from the Arabic for 'cash';
cillar	'small coins', compare Hindi 'cilar' ('small coins');

Invention and borrowing 215

while Chambert-Loir's (1984) study of 1980s Jakartan youth language recorded:

fly	'in a high' (from marijuana), from English 'fly';*
fotocopy	'to go back and forth', 'to hang around', from English 'photocopy';

*In addition to 'fly', 'flai' is also given in Indonesian dictionaries.

Colloquial French from 2002 to 2009 had:

casba(h), kasba(h)	'house', 'pad', 'joint', 'brothel', from the Arabic 'kasba' ('citadel');

and Einat and Livnat's (2012) study of Israeli inmate language identified:

madroob	'violent prisoner', from the Arabic 'slang' for 'crazy';
cowboy	'uncontrollably violent prisoner', from the English.

As some of these examples show, borrowing an item from another language is not always a simple case of transferring the item and accommodating it in the receiving language with the same grammatical, semantic or other properties. There are several changes that *can* occur during the borrowing process that mean that the word might be altered in some way by the receiving group. For example, a change in meaning might occur:

1960s West Bengal criminals:

ṭiṅ	'pocket'. Mallik (1972: 30) compares with English 'tin' ('tin can') and notes that the term was used by pickpockets;
katil	'stay of execution in death penalty', from Arabic 'qātil' ('murderer');

1990s Israeli prisoners:

wiseh	'informer', from the Arabic for 'dirty';

2006 Russian colloquial usage and youth language:

katso (*coll., neg.*)	'Georgian', from the Georgian for 'friend';*
ask (*yth.*)	'cadging', 'begging', from English 'ask';

*Writing about Russian youth, criminal and colloquial language as well as vulgarisms in the 1980s, von Timroth (1986: 110, 124) noted the use of 'katso' to mean 'Georgian', suggested provenance from the Georgian 'kazo!' meaning 'Good God!', 'what on earth?', and indicated that Georgians used this item to address one another.

2012 Randuk:

sakandhand	'wife who has married before', from English 'second hand';
chooma	'food', from English 'chewing'.

On some occasions, the nature of the semantic change might mean that the borrowed item is given a different meaning through *semantic narrowing*: an example of this can be seen in the Israeli military's late-1960s use of the English word 'job' – not to refer to any task or professional activity, but specifically to mean a 'soft, non-combatant job'. Similarly, as noted by Ogechi (2005), Sheng has incorporated 'ngiri' ('one thousand shillings', 'one thousand shilling note') from the less specific Kikuyu 'ngiri' ('one thousand'). Additionally, a number of varieties have borrowed the English 'business' and narrowed its application to something criminal or *dodgy*: early 1960s criminals in West Bengal used it to refer to criminal activity, as did speakers of colloquial Russian in the early to mid-1990s, while speakers of colloquial Spanish in 2008 also used the term 'bisnes' to refer to 'shady business'.

Borrowed forms can also be subject to the reverse process, *semantic broadening*. This is when a word is borrowed with a fairly specific meaning, but that meaning is expanded. Again, 1960s colloquial Hebrew provides a good example: the item 'pantsher', from English 'puncture', was used by speakers not only to mean a (tyre) puncture, but any unforeseen mishap or unfavourable occurrence. To further underline the potential variation that can come into play when vocabulary is borrowed, the term 'puntcher' was also noted in a study of prison inmate language practices in Israel four decades later to mean 'a stabbing' (Einat and Einat 2000).

Functional shift

We have seen from the previous examples that some borrowed lexis might be subject to meaning transfer. However, this is not the only change that a borrowed item might undergo, and it is possible that a word will be altered in some other manner. One such possibility is a change in grammatical category or word class, which is known as *functional shift* or *conversion*. Youth in the former East Germany (GDR), for example, used the English 'rock and roll' not as a noun but as a verb; in Camfranglais, the English noun 'thief' has become a verb 'tiff' ('to steal'), while the adverb 'back' has become a verb 'to give back', as in the sentence 'bàk mwà mè dó' ('Back moi mes do!' – 'Give me back my money!') (Kießling 2004: 1). In a similar vein, the Caló of Spanish Roma ultimately provided colloquial Spanish with the noun 'andoba' or 'ondoba' ('bloke', 'guy') on the basis of the Caló pronoun for 'that one', while changes in word class can also be seen in Russian youth language in:

forin	'foreigner' (noun), from the English adjective 'foreign';
frei	'free spirit' (noun), from the German adjective 'frei'.

While a number of examples highlight such functional shift occurring as words are borrowed from another language, Mallik's (1972) study of the language practices of criminals in West Bengal also shows that a change of word class is also possible *within* a language – hence the noun 'uṭhāo' ('thrower of fake gold bar'), which had meant '(you) pick up', which in turn developed from the infinitive 'to pick up'. Similarly, Sourdot's (1997) study of Parisian student usage in 1987 and 1994 points to a change of category from adjective to adverb in 'grave' (lit. 'serious' → 'big time', 'really'; we saw an example of this in the 'Halluciner grave' advertisement in Chapter Three); and from verb to noun in 'discute' (lit. 'discusses' → 'discussion'), while Eble (1996) cites the following changes in her study of US college usage:

Item	Meaning	Old Word Class	New Word Class
harsh	to criticise	adjective	verb
later	to end a relationship	adjective/adverb	verb
bad	fault	adjective	noun

Adapting borrowed words to a new system

In addition to questions of semantic change and functional shift, it is possible that the shape of a word in one language may suggest particular grammatical characteristics, such as number, to speakers of another. For example, when borrowed into Russian the English 'punk' and 'drug dealer' become 'pank' and 'drag-diler' ('панк' and 'драг-дилер' in Cyrillic). Insofar as these words are seen to end in a consonant, they will *generally* be viewed as masculine singular nouns in keeping with Standard Russian practice (compare standard 'mal'chik' – 'boy', 'stol' – 'table'). Examples of similar loanwords include 'reiv' ('rave'), 'smart-drag' ('smart drug') and 'trip' (*dr.* 'trip').

In these examples, singular nouns in English ('punk', etc.) have retained the same grammatical number when borrowed into Russian. However, in some instances it is possible that a borrowed item's grammatical number might change. For example, the colloquial Russian 'shuz' ('shoes'), which phonetically transcribes the plural ending '-s' in the originating English item (becoming 'шуз' in Cyrillic), is singular. There are, notionally at least, a number of reasons for such a change during the borrowing process: sometimes amendments might be made to deform a word, subvert rules or common practice and/or to indicate some form of in-group appropriation (for more on **Appropriation**, see pages 243–4). Equally, however, 'shuz' may be singular in Russian due to its being seen to end in a consonant and thus having the hallmark of a masculine singular noun. Alternatively, some speakers may choose to add the regular nominative case plural noun ending '-ы' ('-y')[7] because an analogous Standard Russian equivalent ('tufli') is plural, as are the referents themselves. The resulting form – 'шузы' ('shuzy') – thus possibly gives speakers more certainty in usage.

What amounts effectively to the use of more than one plurality marker can also be seen in some African varieties such as Sheng, where the English plural marker '-s' and a Swahili plural marker 'ma-' can co-exist in the same item (for example, 'maspots' for 'spots', 'mabits' for 'bits' and 'marhymes' for 'rhymes'), and in

Town Nyanja (known in some places as 'Nyanja Slang'), where items such as 'guys' and 'rules' become 'magaiz' and 'marulz'.[8]

The above outline suggests that there is no guarantee that a borrowed item's grammatical status will be clear to all users when an item is borrowed. We have looked at changes in grammatical number; however, there are other possible changes a term can undergo, for example, in *grammatical gender*.

When a word is borrowed into a language that assigns grammatical gender, it is possible that there may be some uncertainty about which gender should be applied. Our Russian 'shuz' example primed us to the possibility that in some languages the shape of a word may be important when determining both the number *and* gender of a noun: 'shuz' is singular in number and masculine in gender. With youth and criminal language practices (and, indeed, in Standard Russian), we can never be certain that items will retain the gender they had in the donor language, assuming that it recognises gender in the first place. Two examples illustrate what can happen to a borrowed item when considerations regarding its gender are made.[9]

On the one hand, it is possible that the speaker of the borrowing language may be guided by analogy. Are there synonyms in the receiving language that might help (especially if the item does not fit easily within the receiving language's structures)? If so, these may prove helpful. In his excellent overview of Camfranglais, for example, Kießling (2004) observes that Camfranglais classifies nouns as either masculine or feminine in keeping with French rules of morphology and syntax and suggests that the gender of non-French nouns is mostly determined by those of French equivalents. So, the Duala 'jobajo' ('beer') is seen as a *feminine* noun on the basis of the French feminine noun 'bière'. The gender of a synonym can also be important in Russian. For example, the loanword 'gerlfrend' (from English 'girlfriend') is often – although not always – treated as a grammatically feminine noun in Russian youth language by analogy with Standard Russian feminine 'devushka' ('girl', 'girlfriend'), even though – as we saw with 'shuz' – its ending bears the hallmark of masculine singular nouns.

However, as suggested previously, for Russian at least, the gender of a synonym might not always settle the matter. The attribution of grammatical gender can, in some instances, vary and be tied to the expression of attitude/intentional differentiation from existing variants or speaker uncertainty, as we can see in the Russian term 'monstra', meaning 'ugly person', 'monster' (sometimes also used as a collective noun; most likely from the English 'monster', where there is no gender). This noun can be found with masculine or feminine grammatical gender. In both instances they contrast with the Standard Russian noun 'chudovishche', which is neuter, and – in the latter – with the masculine figurative 'monstr', which can sometimes be seen as bookish. We can also see differentiation if we compare the masculine youth item 'flet' (from English 'flat', 'apartment') with Standard Russian 'kvartira', which is feminine.

We can see therefore that the borrowing process can give rise to changes in grammatical characteristics. Other examples may include changes in declension. For example, should a Russian say 'khipp*i* net' (undeclined), 'khipp*ei* net' or 'khipp<u>ov</u> net' (all meaning 'there are no hippies')? Technically, the item 'khippi' ('hippy') should not decline, and thus should remain 'khipp<u>i</u>' when used with 'net' ('there are no'). However, examples from 1990s youth fanzines show that endings such as '-ei' and '-ov' might nonetheless be found as speakers play with the standard language for particular effect (Davie 1998).

Mimicry, and altering how a borrowed word sounds

As we saw in Chapter Three, some youth, criminal and colloquial items are created through a desire to engage in language play. This is an interesting motivation which can be seen across a whole range of languages, and the expressivity that comes with it can point to a desire to demonstrate social cachet, wit, irony or other stances and attitudes. One mechanism used for language play centres on sound similarity or mimicry (for more on mimicry, see Chapter Eight).

Mimicry can be achieved by altering the sounds of words within a language to create similarity with another word or phrase, for example, the phrase 'New World Mordor' satirised George Bush Senior's 'New World Order' (Breva Claramonte and García Alonso 1993: 24). However, mimicry can also involve items which are borrowed from other languages: even a slight measure of similarity in sound between items across languages, as well as their foreign status, may mean that one is used to replace another, often for jocular or parodic effect. We can see this in the 1980s–1990s US college term 'gorbachev', where the borrowed German 'Gesundheit' ('bless you', said when someone sneezes) was replaced with the name of the former Soviet leader. Alternatively, the similarity in sound between a foreign word and one in the receiving language may also prompt the latter's use in a new way. The Russian Internet term 'khomiak' (Russian for 'hamster'), for example, refers to a 'home page' on the basis of the similarity of 'khom' to English 'home'. Similarity of items across English and Russian has additionally led to humorous new terms, such as 'korol' drov' – 'king of firewood', which may replace the name of the *Coral Draw* graphic programme.

As these examples suggest, speakers can set great store by their ability to create new items, or at least new versions of established words and phrases.[10] For some speakers, improvisation and creativity are highly prized, and it is therefore no surprise that many youth and colloquial varieties contain innovations based on borrowed, or indeed indigenous, words that are either given new meanings or new forms (or sometimes both). Hence in Sheng, the English 'dead' and 'Hilton' ('Hilton hotel') become 'dedi' ('finish') and 'muhilton' ('tall person'), while Swahili 'duka' ('shop', 'corner store') becomes 'odukoo'.

However, language play, the desire to be creative, and showing off might not be the only reasons why borrowed items are amended. In fact, borrowed items may be altered as much to match the typical phonological behaviour of borrowing users, as for any other reason. The principle of words being adapted in this way to fit in with the structures of the receiving language is long-standing and not limited to youth, criminal or colloquial language. However, where these varieties are

220 *Invention and borrowing*

concerned, it is widespread practice. For example, items borrowed into Sheng can undergo phonological change so that, for example, English 'game' and 'come' become 'gemu' and 'kamu', while Harare 'Shona Slang' has items such as 'taimi' and 'pini' from English 'time' and 'pin'.[11]

It is also possible that a desire to contort a donor language's vocabulary as a means of protest, to hide meaning or to stretch stylistic boundaries may lie at the heart of amendments made. As Mallik (1972) demonstrates, criminal language in 1960s West Bengal included items that had been modified by borrowing users either to match their speech habits *or* to deliberately distort. In many cases, items were also subject to semantic change:

ṭæciṅ	'bomb', from English 'touching';
bisuni	'thief', from English 'business'.

More recent cases where items have been distorted can be seen in Nouchi, where some speakers seek to deform French lexis both to undermine the status of French and to create new forms with hidden meaning – hence 'caire' for 'coeur' ('heart') and 'oridjidji' for 'original' ('original').

A final example shows how certain borrowed items may be adapted to reflect the pronunciation of those borrowing. For instance, Smith-Hefner (2007) notes how English items in Bahasa Gaul are adapted to reflect Indonesian pronunciation, so 'married' is written 'marit' or 'merit', whereas others remain spelled as in English.

Hybrids and mixed text

Hybrids, words consisting of elements from different sources to make one item, can be created for many reasons. At a time when we are interested in the merging of the global and the local (as discussed in Chapter Three), the creation of hybrid forms has real resonance among many communities. It allows speakers to demonstrate sociocultural cachet, to engage in language play and improvise, to experiment stylistically, and to test and challenge the compatibility of different concepts and values in and through new linguistic forms.

In view of the many linguistic components that can be brought to bear across languages, hybrids can naturally have multiple guises. One frequently cited example of hybridisation involves the addition of affixes (i.e. suffixes and prefixes) found in the/a language typically used by the borrowing speaker to foreign loanwords. In some language varieties, such as Camfranglais, the addition of a prefix to a French or other foreign word can give a Bantu feel and can also serve to deform the original item as a mark of protest.

Indeed, combining affixes and borrowed lexis in this way is a common occurrence within some language varieties and can form part of the adaptation of a loanword when it is imported into the receiving lexicon, as these Russian and French examples demonstrate:

Colloquial French (early 1990s):

hard<u>eux</u>	'hard style', from the English 'hard' and the adjectival suffix '-eux';

Russian (2006):

am<u>urchik</u> (*crim.*)	'protector of a gang of women thieves'; 'p(a)edo', from the French 'amour' ('love') and the masculine nominal suffix '-chik';
allor<u>ets</u> (*yth.*)	'Itye', from the Italian 'allora' ('then'), with the masculine nominal suffix '-ets'.

For their part, borrowed items can serve as productive catalysts for the creation of new vocabulary, and speakers of the borrowing language may add a variety of affixes to foreign bases to create new words. In early 1990s French drugs usage, the verb 'se shooter' was created on the basis of the English 'shoot' from 'to shoot up'. As we can see, this was formed by combining the English 'shoot' with the infinitive ending '-er' (and the reflexive 'se'). However, the borrowed form has also acted as a productive base leading to related terms such as 'shooteuse' ('syringe'), 'shooterie' ('place where people shoot up') and 'shooté' ('stoned'). The same pattern can be seen with 'snif' ('cocaine', 'nose candy'), 'sniffer' ('to snort cocaine'), 'sniffeur' and 'sniffeuse' ('cocaine snorter', 'glue sniffer').[12]

'Se shooter' has the status of a non-standard term largely through its connection with the anti-social and illegal act of drug-taking, not to mention the drugs milieu, and has a sense of expressiveness and informality attached. The word is therefore not seen as stylistically neutral. The suffixes found in 'shooteuse', 'shooterie', 'shooté' are not non-standard *per se* and are commonly found in Standard French. That said, in some cases a stylistically marked or non-standard suffix can be combined with a loanword to create a new item – the French '-os', for example, which is thought to derive ultimately from older criminal language, was added to the English youth term 'cool' in the 1980s–1990s to produce 'coolos' ('cool').

These examples show that there is real potential for speakers to be innovative through combining foreign items with suffixes from a borrowing language. However, this need not be the only recipe to create new hybrids; elements such as affixes can themselves be borrowed and combined either with other borrowed lexis, or with items in the borrowing language to create new vocabulary.[13] Speakers of Nouchi, for example, mainly borrow suffixes from French, English and Dioula when creating new terms such as 'gbasseur' ('drug addict') from Mande 'bàási' ('medicine') and the French '-eur', 'percing' ('success') from 'percer' ('to succeed', from French) and English '-ing', and 'daïko' ('drunk'), from English 'die' and Dioula '-ko'; while in Camfranglais the French suffix '-iste' is added to 'mbengue' ('European country', 'abroad') to describe someone who often travels abroad in 'mbenguiste'. Hebrew and US college language have also borrowed suffixes for expressive effect: '-chik', the Russian diminutive nominal suffix, was

222   Invention and borrowing

added to 'katan' ('small', 'little') to produce 'katanchik' ('very small', 'infant') in 1960s colloquial Hebrew;[14] and '-ment', the French adverbial suffix, was added in 1970s–1990s US college language to make items more emphatic, hence 'solid' became 'solidment'. This type of hybridisation need not only affect nouns, adjectives and adverbs, of course; verb forms might also be created through, for example, combining loanwords with verb endings from another language, as in the Camfranglais 'nous go-ons' ('we are going'), from English 'go' and the regular French ending '-ons', and 'je knowais' ('I knew'), from the English 'know' and the French imperfect ending '-ais'. However, although these make for interesting examples, it is not always the case that verb forms will be changed, as we can see in 'Tu l'as deja meet?' ('Have you ever met him?') (Kouega 2003: 512).[15]

Communication Accommodation Theory (CAT)

Drawing in part on Social Identity Theory, CAT is a theoretical framework that explains how interlocutors consciously and unconsciously adjust the ways in which they communicate as they interact with others, both as individuals and as group members, and how others perceive and react to these changes (Gallois, Ogay and Giles 2006; Dragojevic, Gasiorek and Giles 2015).

There are thought to be two main motives for amending our communication by accommodation: to regulate social distance and identity and to heighten communicative effectiveness (Dragojevic, Gasiorek and Giles 2015). Through **convergence** with the various (non-)linguistic behaviours of others, such as choice of vocabulary, information density, utterance length, accent, speech rate, posture, gaze and so on, speakers may aim to appear more socially similar or appealing (Gallois, Ogay and Giles 2006; Dragojevic, Gasiorek and Giles 2015). Alternatively, through **divergence** they may wish to emphasise social distance and dissimilarity; while through **maintenance**, where there is no adjustment in behaviours, they may signal a desire for the social *status quo* (Gallois, Ogay and Giles 2006). Where there is **full convergence** there can be a danger that this may come across as patronising – depending on how the accommodation is expressed. For example, addressees may feel that they can be easily mimicked.

Accommodation can be **symmetrical**, where change is reciprocated by an interlocutor, or **asymmetrical**, where there is no such reciprocity. Furthermore, it can be **unimodal,** where adjustment is made in one respect (for example, topic initiation), or **multimodal**, where shifts occur in a number of respects at the same time (e.g. speech rate and posture).

An important consideration within CAT is the degree to which interlocutors converge or diverge in view of perceptions that one may hold of the other, as opposed to particular characteristics and personality (Gallois, Ogay and Giles 2006; Dragojevic, Gasiorek and Giles 2015). In this way, interactants' views of others as stereotypes may play an important role in how they act. No less important are addressee perceptions of adjustments. A speaker may **overaccommodate** if they exceed an interlocutor's desired degree of adjustment – for example, talking to an elderly person as if they were a child, or parents using youth language to figuratively *speak the same language* as their children. The opposite of this is **underaccommodation**, where insufficient adjustment is made relative to the listener's needs or preferences (Dragojevic, Gasiorek and Giles 2015).

Indeed, context and addressee expectation can be important factors in the success of accommodative moves. Interactants often have expectations about the types and levels of accommodation that are acceptable or to be expected within certain contexts which may be shaped by their own history of personal or group-based interaction (Gallois, Ogay and Giles 2006; Dragojevic, Gasiorek and Giles 2015). Personal preferences may thus play a real part in the perception of accommodative moves and may account for different interpretations by different recipients of the same behaviour (Dragojevic, Gasiorek and Giles 2015).

Generally speaking, CAT is not utilised greatly as a theoretical model in studies of youth language practices, although the principle of accommodation may be referenced. For example, in their study of London teenage talk, Stenström, Andersen and Hasund (2002: 212) discuss how recorded mixed-age conversations "demonstrate how teenagers talk differently in various social settings, accommodating their language as they tell a joke to a friend, answer the teacher's question in class or discuss homework with their parents".

It is also possible that hybridisation might involve the concatenation of words and phrases from different languages. Eble (1996) documents the conjoining by US college students of standard words from Spanish and English to create a phrase whose meaning derives from the Spanish 'hasta la vista' in 'hasta la bye bye'; in his overview of Estonian 'slang', in which he includes expletives, Tender (1996) notes a combination of English and Russian in 'getnaahui' ('Fuck off!', 'Get to fuck!') – here English provides 'get' and Russian 'na khui' ('to fuck').[16] Other examples of compounding across languages include:

Hindi and Persian:

khopiākhānā	'empty room used by a whore in the evening', formed by joining the Hindi 'khuphiyā' ('secret') and Persian 'khānā' ('dwelling house');

Bengali and English:

cākār-line	'railroad', formed by combining Bengali 'cākā' ('wheel') and the English 'line';

Sheng and English:

zeiks-man	'father', from Sheng 'zeiks' ('old man') and English 'man';

Nouchi and English:

gbassman	'drug addict', from Mande 'bàási' ('medicine') and English 'man', a variant of 'gbasseur';

Spanish and Caló:

gilipollas *(coll.)*	'bloody fool', 'jerk', formed through joining Caló 'jilí' ('mad') and the Spanish 'polla(s)' ('prick').

Alternatively, some hybrid forms may be created through blending, where an element of one word is merged with part of another. So, in Bahasa Gaul, 'jaga imej' ('to protect one's image'), containing an adapted form of the English 'image', becomes 'jaim' (for more on blends see also Chapter Seven).

It is also possible that some hybrid combinations may involve items from languages with different orthographic systems. One study of Russian youth language practices in the 1990s, for instance, showed that some youth combined English and Russian words and phrases in Roman and Cyrillic script as part of their stylistic repertoire: hence 'техно-dance party' ('techno dance party'), 'funky-версия' ('funky version') and 'хиппи-girl' ('hippy girl') (Davie 1998). These demonstrate the respective users' awareness of a prestige foreign language/vocabulary and of items and practices important to the subculture. However, they also emphasise this awareness through what could reasonably be viewed as the *unexpected* appearance of Roman letters, pointing all the while to shared interests across the local Russian and foreign cultural domains. Another example of the fusion of alphabets at that time can be seen in a discussion of the band BRICKS ARE HEAVY in the Russian magazine *Rock Fuzz* in 1995, where the Russian nominative case plural ending '-ы' ('-y') was added to provide 'BRICKSы' (*Rock Fuzz* 1995, 26: 6). Again, it seems that the author wanted the reader to appreciate the foreignness of the BRICKS; however, as with 'shuzy', there may also have been a need to clarify the BRICKS' plurality and/or to innovate for appreciative readers (of course, such non-transliteration is neither new nor the preserve of Russian youth – we need only look at Russian advertisements in newspapers, magazines or online to see examples that incorporate lexis from different alphabets).

Invention and borrowing 225

Hybridisation can also be seen in other domains. Japanese hip hop lyrics, for instance, can place English phrasing in Roman script together with Japanese lyrics written in kanji (Chinese characters), katakana (used for transcribing non-Japanese words) and hiragana (used for Japanese inflectional endings and grammatical items):

Yo Bringing That, Yo Bring Your Style,
人類最後のフリーキーサイド
Yo Bringing That, Yo Bring Your Style,
The last freaky side of the human race.
(Alim 2009: 117, citing Pennycook 2003)[17]

Russian youth language also provides interesting examples of the insertion of untransliterated and untranslated foreign phrases. This can result in a sense of surprise, lend expressive emphasis and/or enable the author to express more complex ideas (not to mention avoid the pains of translation):

Я - Uzi-minded-human-being!
I am an Uzi-minded human being!
(DVR II 1990: 69)

while shock can be effected through borrowing an expletive phrase carrying expressive force:

В который уже раз мы говорили: FUCK YOU MILICIA!
How many times have we already told you: FUCK YOU POLICE!
(Russkii fan vestnik 1993: 31)[18]

So far, we have focused largely on Japanese and Russian, in great part due to questions around the integration and stylisation that occur when incorporating items represented in one orthographic system into a text dominated by another. However, the desire to achieve a particular effect can also be seen where the orthographic system is largely the same: it is the change in language that lends the desired force and enables aims to be met. As Androutsopoulos (2003) demonstrates with regard to German youth fanzines, English items may routinely be used in specific contexts such as greetings, as slogans, as discourse markers or due to expressive directness, to cite a few manifestations and reasons. Indeed, a parallel can be seen between the preceding Russian example and the following German illustration he cites:

Ich möchte mich noch beim Bremer Kultursenator bedanken, das er uns ohne einen Ersatz zu stellen aus unserem Bunker geworfen hat. FUCK OFF YOU BASTARD!
I'd also like to thank Bremen's Minister of Culture, who threw us out of our depot without providing any substitute. FUCK OFF YOU BASTARD!
(Androutsopoulos 2003: 5)

As with Russian, the use of English forms in German fanzines provides us with opportunities to see whether and how such foreign items are integrated into the receiving structure. In Androutsopoulos' data, for instance, and as he himself indicates (2003: 4), the phrase 'die exhausting Kickdrum' sees the use of the English 'exhausting' without a German inflection. However, Androutsopoulos raises another interesting question where he points out that the extensive use of English in German fanzines, including routines such as opening or closing or other phrases, may not only involve borrowing as it is commonly understood, but may also constitute a form of code-switching (Androutsopoulos 2003: 6–7. Paul, Freywald and Wittenberg 2009: 98 also point to consistent use in Kiezdeutsch of borrowings from migrant languages as introductory and closing remarks, while Doran 2004 notes the use of borrowings by suburban Parisian youth as conversational discourse markers).

Calques and literal translation

Calques are sometimes known as loan translations and refer to processes where the constituents of a word in one language are replaced by the corresponding elements in another. Items created through calquing can be found in the lexicons of standard and non-standard varieties. Examples of the latter include, for example, Italian 'merda' and French 'merde', which are most likely loan translations of the English 'shit' (as a synonym for 'drugs'), while Prokem 'rumput' and Spanish 'hierba' are probably calques for 'grass'. The same principle applies to the Russian words for 'acid' ('kislota'), 'grass' ('trava') and 'track' ('doroga'), which are most likely based on the English 'acid', 'grass' and 'track mark'. The drugs scene is one of many fields where calquing is in evidence; it has also been seen in other domains, as exemplified by Russian 'tantseval'naia muzyka' (compare English 'dance music') and 'novaia volna' ('new wave'); Spanish and German 'está en la casa' and 'ist im Saal', from English dance music 'is in the house'; and Sheng 'poa' (lit. 'chill') to mean 'cool' and 'tarehe' (lit. 'time period') to mean 'date' in a romantic sense, both also from English.

An additional means of translation between languages involves literal translation. Through literally translating phrases into another language, speakers can create jocular and sometimes absurd combinations. Two interesting examples can be seen in Bahasa Gaul, where the Indonesian phrases 'tidak apa-apa' ('don't worry about it') and 'terima kasih' ('thank you') become 'no what-what' and 'receive love' in English. A similar phenomenon can also be seen in the colloquial English use of 'grand fromage' to mean 'boss' or 'big shot', where speakers have playfully translated the colloquial term 'big cheese' into French.

Borrowing within a language

A regular feature in the creation of new terms in colloquial, youth and criminal language centres on the borrowing not of geographical dialectal terms (which is possible, as Tender 1996 notes concerning Estonian 'slang', Smith-Hefner 2007 with regard to Bahasa Gaul and Green 2016 in respect of English 'slang'; de Klerk 2005: 113 also observes that youth practice can be "regionalized", as do Labov 1992 and Pozas 2000[19]), but on the movement of words and phrases between social sub- or countercultural groups. This process relies on a measure of contact, for example, virtually on the Internet, or physically in places such as prisons and urban centres. Prisons appear to provide the context for a lot of group-to-group borrowing: as we saw in Chapter Three, they and other corrective institutions hold inmates from many walks of life who are faced with the need to socialise and survive. The circumstances are ripe, therefore, for items denoting prison reality and prisoner requirements (such as secrecy from prison guards), denotation of rank within prison society, and so on, to be shared among the diverse prison population and then with interlocutors outside. A good example of inter-group transfer in a prison setting can be found in a fascinating discussion of prison language in El Jadida, Morocco, where Berjaoui (1997) notes that it could only be learned during incarceration and that it contained words from the "secret languages" of drug addicts, alcoholics, poets, thieves and sellers of livestock.

Similarly, young people also come into contact with a range of groups as part of their social and professional lives. They may pick up and recirculate military lexis if they undertake military service; they may adopt elements of student usage if they go to university or college; and they may pick up criminal terms if in direct or indirect contact with criminal elements or related groups (such as drugs users).

For many languages, this principle of inter-group borrowing is not new. Indeed, in the case of Russian Elistratov (1991: 84) has observed that: "[i]t is already very difficult in this regard to determine precisely to which jargon a word belongs. There are words that belong to several jargons at the same time" (i.e. that index different kinds of identity or activity). A good illustration of different groups using the same items to mean the same thing, and thus benefiting from inter-group borrowing, is provided in one study of nineteenth-century Russian criminal and military language practices (see Table 4.1).

As our discussion of diffusion in Chapter Three established, ultimately it is likely that many terms will progress from tighter, more limited usage to the language of larger social collectives, and that this may be the result of greater, sometimes forced, social movement and mobility. Nineteenth-century Paris, for instance, saw the breaking-up of criminal and marginal social groupings as the police were re-organised to become more effective and the districts where the underclasses predominated demolished. As these criminal and marginal

Table 4.1 Examples of inter-group borrowing among Russian criminals and sailors

Criminal lexicon	Sailors' lexicon	Meaning
smola	smola	sailors
krupa	krupa	soldiers
amba	amba	death
ksiva	ksiva	document

(Amended from Davie 1997/98: 34)

communities became dispersed throughout urban centres, some of the poor and working class of Paris reportedly became (more) exposed to the language of the criminal (Ellis 2002). This is, of course, but one cause. It is also likely that the diffusion of criminal terminology occurred as a result of a combination of factors. For instance, nineteenth-century Paris underwent "unprecedented demographic and social changes which were transforming western Europe at the time of industrialisation" (Lodge 2004: 207, 244).

Given the number of possible routes by which in-group items can make their way into broader circulation, and the myriad social network touchpoints provided by global telecommunications (Eble 2014), the borrowing paths taken by such terms as they make their way into society at large can be difficult to trace: some terms may be borrowed between a number of subgroups before being drawn into broader colloquial usage, while others find a more direct route (Coleman 2012). However, we can be confident that inter-group borrowing and diffusion take place and can see evidence of their occurrence in certain languages:

- *1990s colloquial Spanish* had items that ultimately emerged from Romani, either directly or via criminal language, such as 'estaribel' ('stir', 'prison'), 'bastes' ('fingers'), 'diñar' ('to give') and 'chaval' or 'chabal' ('lad'). Additionally, Pachuco Caló had the imported criminal word 'taris' ('jail'), for example, which, as García (2005: 809) indicates, can be traced back to Spanish Caló, where it appeared as 'estari', 'estarú', 'estaribel' and 'estaribó'. Similarly, items described as Lunfardo by Grayson (1964) can also be traced back to Caló through criminal language: 'guita' ('money'), from the Caló 'gui' ('wheat'), was recorded in 1896 by Salillas as meaning 'money' in Spanish criminal usage;[20] there is also 'chorro' ('thief') – Salillas (1896) notes 'choro' with the same meaning from the Caló 'choro' ('theft', 'robbery').
- *2008 colloquial Argentine Spanish* had 'bagayo', meaning 'ugly person', and the alternative 'bagarto', which can also mean 'burden'. 'Bagayo' was documented by Grayson in 1964 as a Lunfardo item meaning 'loot' and retained the meanings of 'loot' and 'bundle' in 2008.[21]
- *Colloquial French and French criminal language* have retained items associated with older criminal varieties, such as 'taule' ('jail', 'the nick'), 'naze' ('knackered'; 'mad') and 'baston' ('fighting').[22]

Notably, however, even where there is contact between youth, criminal and/or other communities, different groups may attribute different meanings or connotations to the same lexical items at the same time. Good illustrations of these differences can be seen in criminal and student usage in West Bengal in the 1960s:

Item	Criminal	Student
āoāj	knife	to tease, exaggerate
kānki	eyes	to draw a girl's attention by winking
pāgli	prison warning bell	entertaining girl

This can also be seen in Israeli inmate language as described by Einat and Livnat (2012). Here, the derogatory 'manyak' – or the plural 'manayek' – is applied to a number of referents by different groups to refer to those who are of questionable social value or who trespass a moral code of some kind. In broader Israeli colloquial usage, it refers to a malicious or immoral person; prisoners may use 'manayek' to variously describe a lowlife, informer, prison officers or the police more widely, while in military usage it refers to the military police.

Great diversity could also be found in the 1960s West Bengal underworld and related collectives with regard to the meaning of 'saodā' ('merchandise'): procurers and frequenters of brothels ascribed the meaning 'young girl'; luggage lifters used it to mean 'a suitcase' or 'goods bundle'; pickpockets – 'a note' (money); and prostitutes – 'a customer'.

It is also possible that a word will be adopted from one group by another, with its pre-borrowing meaning lost at a later point. One example of this is 'bola', which was originally a Germanía word meaning 'fayre', 'festival', and which came to mean 'freedom' when incorporated into broader criminal usage by the late-nineteenth century. The item still means 'prisoner release' in contemporary Spanish criminal language.

Youth language and links to criminal communities

A number of youth varieties are believed to have had bridges to the language of criminal communities:

- Many African varieties are thought to have had early links with the criminal underworld: Kießling (2004) noted the apparent criminal origins of Sheng in Nairobi (Kenya), Iscamtho in Johannesburg (South Africa), Indoubil and Lingala ya Bayankee in Kinshasa and Brazzaville (Congo), Nouchi in Abidjan (Côte d'Ivoire) and Camfranglais in Yaoundé and Douala (Cameroon). Similarly, Yarada K'wank'wa in Ethiopia possibly had its origins in the language practices of prostitutes and criminals (Demisse and Bender 1983; Hollington 2015).
- Indonesia's Bahasa Prokem appears to have had similar origins in Medan and Jakarta. Boellstorff (2004) pointed to the spread of terms from the criminal world to that of street youth and university students when he describes Prokem as apparently having originated in the criminal underworld of Jakarta and Medan in the early 1960s, having spread to street youth by the end of that decade, and then being used by university-educated youth by the mid-1970s.
- In his study of the underworld of 1960s West Bengal, Mallik (1972) observed that anti-social elements might transmit criminal lexis to

230 *Invention and borrowing*

> students; concluded that the underworld and general population met at certain points; and posited that criminals, near-criminals and students might use common vocabulary with identical meanings.
>
> As we discuss in Chapter Three, there are many youth language practices where the social agents need not have links to the criminal milieu or to criminal behaviour as we typically envisage it – although legal definitions of criminality can, naturally, differ across states or regions.

Difficulties in defining word origin

Some borrowed terms exist as representations of in-group and wider colloquial usage for some considerable time. For example, a number of items of Caló origin have been in use in Spanish for at least two hundred years, partly through the language of prisons and the underworld, and partly through language mixing, popular literature and flamenco. Indeed, much as with English words such as 'cosh(er)', 'cushti' and 'chav(vy)', many Caló items have become so deeply rooted in colloquial Spanish that their Romani provenance may go unnoticed. Examples include:

chinel	'screw', 'prison officer', 'constable', 'guard';*
chucho	'dog', 'mutt';
lacha	'shame';
parné	'money'.[†]

*Salillas recorded the use of 'chinel' in 1896. He also noted the use of 'chino' to mean 'constable', 'guard' from 'chinar' ('to cut') (Salillas 1896: 319).

[†]Of these examples cited by Geipel (1995), only 'parné' was attested in Mahler's 2008 *Dictionary of Spanish Slang and Colloquial Expressions*. Interestingly, some items of Romani provenance may mean different things in different languages. Geipel (1995: 131, endnote 35) points to the French colloquial item 'costaud', meaning 'heavy', 'strong', and suggests that this derives from the Romani 'kushto' ('good'), whence the term 'cooshti' in colloquial English, and the Spanish drugs term 'costo' ('drugs', 'dope').

Given that out of all the European vernaculars Castilian reportedly retains the largest number of terms of "Romani inspiration", Geipel (1995: 128) posits that "indeed, it may be predicted that colloquial Spanish – the language of the streets – will, within the next generation or so, come to represent the final repository of the largest number of Romani survivals in Europe". That said, considerable influence by Romani on another in-group language variety may also be seen in Hungarian prison usage, where Romani reportedly provides more loanwords than other languages (Szabó 2006: 224).

While there are clear advantages to tracing the provenance of such items, it is not always possible to definitively determine their origins. This is not unusual for youth, criminal and colloquial language (or, indeed, for many items within standard vocabularies), with provenance often remaining opaque and, occasionally, folk etymologies taking hold (for more on which, see Coleman 2012: 40–1).

Sornig's (1981: 11) observation that "[t]he bulk of slangisms in any language remains etymologically obscure", Widawski's (2015: 13) caveat that "[e]stablishing a definitive origin of slang expressions is not always feasible due to the largely oral and often mutable nature of slang", and Sourdot's (1997) tentative conclusion in his analysis of Parisian student usage:

> In this 1994 list some forms *still pose a problem as to their origin and formation*. If there are no other explanations, *we might therefore suppose* a regional or dialectal origin for items such as 'jarter' ('to leave'), 'ratrusher' ('to wipe') and 'piouquer' ('to smell bad')
>
> (Sourdot 1997: 70; my italics)[23]

are regularly echoed by other scholars. In his study of Bahasa Prokem, for instance, Chambert-Loir (1984: 110) indicates that Prokem words consist of three groups, of which one comprises "new words, the origins of which cannot be determined". Kortas (2003) similarly refers to some lexis in colloquial French having obscure origins; while Mallik (1972: 55) observes, for instance, that some 1960s West Bengal criminal terms such as 'igāni' ('cattle thief'), 'gosti' ('stolen property'), 'ghaskantu' ('to run away') come from an unknown source. Equally, Mallik (1972: 38) cites lexis where the provenance of only one part is known, for instance, 'jārkāno' ('to come'), where 'āno' (from 'ānā') means 'to bring', 'to come', but the meaning of 'jār' is unknown; and points to items with more than one meaning, such as 'kāṭi', for which he considers a number of origins possible:

Meaning	Possible Provenance
false key	'cābikāṭi' ('key');
match stick	'deślāikāṭi' ('match stick')
cartridge	abbreviation of 'cartridge'
knife	'kāṭā' ('to cut')
arrest	from English 'cut off'
fountain pen	'kaṭhi' ('stick')

(Mallik 1972: 39)

At the same time, where explanations have been advanced, these may not be universally embraced. Russian commentators, for example, have forwarded different explanations of the provenance of youth words such as 'chmo' ('idiot', 'useless person'): Beregovskaia (1996: 35) suggests that it is an acronym based on '<u>ch</u>elovek <u>m</u>oral'no <u>o</u>pushchennyi' ('morally lacking person'), while Nikol'ski (1993: 156) posits that it is borrowed from Yiddish. Analysis of another Russian youth item – 'gliuk' ('hallucinations', 'seeing things') – offers no more unanimity: Rozhanskii (1992: 19) suggests that this is probably an abbreviated form of 'galliutsinatsiia' ('hallucination'; 'galiuki' or 'galiuniki' ('seeing things') also exist), whereas Corten (1992: 51) indicates that it is derived from the German 'Glück' ('happiness').

Summary

In Chapters Two and Three, we considered the many reasons why in-groups may create and develop their own lexicons. These included the need for cryptolect, the demonstration and negotiation of identity and the need for prestige or cachet, to name but a few. We also recognised that a merging of the local and the global is often seen where youth cultural actors in various societies may choose to adopt common strands of hip hop, for example, and mould them with traditional or local practices to reflect something that is more immediate and relevant to their environments.

With these thoughts in mind, it is no real surprise to see that borrowing has figured strongly in youth and criminal language practices. In this chapter, we have seen that the reasons for borrowing between languages and group-specific lexicons can correspondingly be manifold, but that they support some of the themes from Chapters Two and Three: to facilitate cryptolect, especially where knowledge of a given foreign language is weak (although this is arguably becoming more difficult where there is access to the media and the Internet); to enable speakers to demonstrate affiliation and alignment with high-value groups, identities and practices; to push stylistic limits in a language; and to enhance speaker status, should they wish to do so. The use of English by youth the world over during the past 60 years or so is a very good demonstration of borrowing and the reasons for its occurrence (for an interesting discussion of the use of English by young speakers of a foreign language – in this case, Norwegian teenagers – see Hasund and Drange 2014).

We also noted the possibility that borrowed items may change in some respect when imported from one language into another (e.g. grammatical number). This change may be for reasons of inventiveness or improvisation – some users may change a word's properties for highly expressive or specific ends. However, it may also be to fit the new word more clearly into the structure of the receiving language. In this latter respect, they may not be alone: users of what are regarded as less expressive (or even antagonistic) forms of standard language may consider the same or similar changes as they adopt and adapt items of foreign provenance for their own purposes, i.e. they may alter an item to match local phonological practices or to fit in with standard analogues (for example, English 'shorts' becomes 'un short' in French by analogy with the French singular 'pantalon' ('trousers')).

One way or another, there are different reasons why items may be integrated or not, or why certain modifications may be made. At a time when there is extensive contact between young speakers of different heritage languages, including speakers of local dominant languages, and when young people can tap into the sociocultural practices of social agents in other parts of the globe, knowledge of context, speaker aspiration and attitude are important when it comes to interpreting borrowing and any attendant modifications: who is the speaker, with whom are they communicating, in what circumstances, and what are they trying to achieve? (For very good overviews of developments in lexis, morphosyntax and syntax in multiethnolects across a number of languages, for example, see Dorleijn and Nortier 2013; Cheshire, Nortier and Adger 2015.)

These considerations also bring us back to questions of hybridity. In Chapters Two and Three we examined questions surrounding language contact in conditions of super-diversity, and the merging of the global and the local, where elements of the old and new, modern and traditional and so on might be merged with a particular purpose in mind. As this chapter further indicates, we also see these trends in the use of language, for instance, in the creation of compounds consisting of words from different languages or with different orthographic systems, and in the application of foreign affixes to indigenous vocabulary, to name but a few instances. The use of such linguistic means is certainly very important: as we noted in Chapter Three, in their discussion of Kiezdeutsch, Paul, Freywald and Wittenberg (2009: 92) for example, suggest that using a multiethnolect "constitutes an important factor in the construction of young people's identities. It serves as a means to express their hybrid self-perception between the culture they live in and the culture of their ethnic background" (compare the use of Pachuco Caló by speakers who perceived a lack of identification with either their heritage or adopted cultures (Daniels 1997; De Katzew 2004; García 2005)). We can thus see varied linguistic resources found both within and outside traditionally delineated linguistic boundaries employed by social actors looking to define themselves in their own terms. As we see greater access to the Internet and evolving communications, increases and differences in migration flows, rising awareness of foreign sociocultural (including sub- and countercultural) practices and the crossing of traditional boundaries, the creation and use of hybrid forms will continue to be an especially interesting area to study.

Notes

1 Indeed, the feminine 'racli' is still used in colloquial French to mean 'girl' (from 'rakli' – 'non-Roma girl').
 Compare the contemporary colloquial Spanish use of 'gacho' ('man', 'guy') and the feminine form 'gachí' ('woman', 'girl'), where 'gacho' is derived from the Romani 'gadjo' ('non-Roma man'). The same provenance is also shared with colloquial French 'gadjo', meaning 'average Joe', 'naive, nondescript person', 'guy'. Strutz (2009: 169) additionally gives 'gadji' as a variant of this, while Bachmann and Basier (1984: 181, 187) suggest in their study of French youth language that 'gadjo' referred to a non-Roma man and 'gadji' to a non-Roma woman.Bachmann and Basier (1984: 181) provide more fascinating insights when they note that French youth language in 1984 included the Romani items 'câlo', meaning 'arab male', and 'câli' as its feminine equivalent.
2 Notably, in her study of US college student words and expressions in use between 1972–1993, Eble (1996: 6, 14) pointed to a rapid change in vocabulary – roughly speaking, under 10% of the number of items in her corpus lasted over a 15-year period – and noted that many items may be introduced and tried out but that very few become adopted by large numbers of users. Interestingly, this incidence of turnover in Eble's analysis contrasts with a discussion of the lexis used by Russian criminals and traders over the period 1850s–1927. Davie (1997/98) shows that 112 of the 139 entries cited in a glossary of 1850s St. Petersburg thieves' language were to be found in a 1927 dictionary of criminal usage. Most items coincided fully in semantic reference.

234   Invention and borrowing

3   Ogechi (2005: 352) refers to 'noma' as "a coined and the most variantly used adjective".
4   When discussing borrowing, Sornig (1981: 4) suggests: "The utilization of foreign or strange lexical material is an old practice and might at some time or other have served the purpose of camouflage and/or secrecy". A recent example is cited by Bardsley (2014: 104) in her description of New Zealand 'slang', where Maori terms such as 'kupenga' ('net') or 'hinaki' ('eel trap') may be used by prisoners as code to refer to punishment cells. Both borrowing and semantic change are utilised here.
5   Notably, in a study of the "secret language" of Anglophone students in the state universities of Cameroon, Kouega (2009: 97–8, 102) documented that some 96 of 222 items in the students' lexicon were borrowed. They came from four main sources: Camfranglais (59.3%), Pidgin English (22.9%), French (12.5%) and Nigerian English (5.2%). Cameroon Pidgin English is a *lingua franca* spoken by almost all Anglophone Cameroonians. Borrowing was the most productive process of all those used to extend the lexicon.
6   More specifically, in her study of US college usage from 1972–1993, Eble (1996: 39) indicates that borrowing from foreign languages was not a feature of 'slang' in general or of college student usage, although she does record some foreign words and expressions as being found in her corpus.
7   Or its softer equivalent '-и' ('-i'), where required.
8   Mutunda (2007: page unknown), however, points out that some English loans do not retain the '-s' in Town Nyanja, e.g. 'matrabo' ('troubles'), while Vierke (2015: 252) cites 'mapiercing' ('piercings') and 'matatoo' ('tattoos') in Sheng.
9   In some cases, a lack of Cyrillic form can also add to uncertainty in the attribution of gender. In material analysed in the mid- to late 1990s, the word 'boogie', for example, was regarded as either masculine, presumably by analogy with standard 'tanets' ('dance'), or neuter, in keeping with the shape of the word had it been transliterated, giving 'буги' ('bugi') – many loanwords ending in '-i' are neuter, such as 'taksi' ('taxi') (Davie 1998: 221–2).

Note also untransliterated items such as 'настоящий "industrial"' ('real industrial music'), 'хипповый look' ('hippy look') and 'британский underground' ('British underground'), where 'industrial', 'look' and 'underground' are modified by adjectives with masculine singular endings.
10 The recasting of well-known expressions, phrases and proverbs for expressive effect using loanwords can also be seen in a Japanese practice known as 'Lu-go' (lit. 'Lou language', after Lou Oshiba, a comedian and actor). Here English loanwords are used to replace key Japanese equivalents while maintaining Japanese grammar and word order. For example, the Japanese 'uso kara deta makoto' ('a truth which has emerged from a lie', i.e. 'many a true word is spoken in jest') becomes the humorous 'uso kara deta turū', where the modified English loanword 'turū' ('true') replaces 'makoto' ('true') (Stanlaw 2014: 165–7).
11 Mawadza (2000: 96–7) notes, however, that "some slang words do not conform to Shona syllable structure constraints. Such words end in a consonant for example, finaz 'funeral'". Other examples cited by Mawadza include 'chilaz' ('chill'), 'coldaz' ('cold') and 'monaz' ('morning').
12 In a paper on street French ('français branché'), which included analysis of verbs, Verdelhan-Bourgade (1991: 75) noted that there were no infinitives derived from borrowed lexis ending in '-ir', '-oir' or '-re', and that the new verbs cited in the paper aligned themselves "sans risque" ("without risk") per the first conjugation model.

Entries in more recent studies of colloquial French (2009) also show the addition of a French suffix to an English base in items such as 'lapeuse' ('lap dancer'), formed from the English 'lap' and the French suffix '-euse' (Strutz 2009: 214).
13 The idea of borrowing affixes or what are believed to exist as such across languages to create youth, criminal or colloquial items is not a new phenomenon: Leroy's

A *Dictionary of French Slang* (1935: 136) included the item 'infectados', meaning 'cheap cigar', 'cabbage leaf', 'stinkador', where Leroy suggested that this was formed through adding a "jocular Spanish ending" to 'infect'.
14 Other Roman character representations of 'katan' include 'qtn', 'qaton' and 'kaataan'.
15 Kouega's example did not have the accents customarily found in Standard French 'déjà'.
16 Tender also notes that Estonian 'slang' contains examples of suffixes being borrowed from other languages, although this process is not thought to be productive.
17 Alim is citing Pennycook's analysis of the Rip Slyme lyrics in the song "Bring Your Style". The transliteration of the line is: "Yo Bringing that, Yo Bring your style Jinrui saigo no furikiisaido". I have added the comma in the example to differentiate the example from the translation.
18 This example is all the more interesting in that in 'MILICIA' we see the romanisation of the Russian 'militsiia' ('police').
19 In French, criminal items such as 'pieu' ('bed') and 'cambrioleur' ('burglar') are held to derive from the regional Picard words 'piau' ('skin') and 'cambriole' ('small room') – this is probably evidence of criminals borrowing lexis from regional dialect. Leroy (1935: 52, 177) notes the use of 'pieu' to mean 'bed' and 'cambriole' to mean 'room', 'burglar's trade' and the "Act of *cambrioler* (breaking into a room)".

Similar borrowing can be seen in Russian *prostorechie* in the use of archaic dialectal items such as 'chislennik' for 'kalendar'' ('calendar').
20 Interestingly, French 'blé' ('wheat') is also used to refer to money ('dough', 'bread'). An intriguing parallel is provided for 'guita' by Guella (2010: 488–9), who notes the use in Algeria of 'ḥabbāt' ('grains', 'seeds') to refer to money (it can also be used to refer to testicles). Similarly, Nassenstein (2016: 249) notes the use of 'bunga' ('money'), from the Swahili for 'flour', by youth speakers of Yabacrâne in Goma, Democratic Republic of Congo, while Burke (1995: 5) points to the use of the US term 'bread' being reminiscent of the sixteenth-century Italian slang term 'grano' (lit. 'grain', 'wheat') for a ducat.
21 An interesting comparison can be found in 1960s West Bengal criminal language 'pur' ('fold', 'bundle') which was subject to meaning transfer to mean 'currency notes'. The term 'saodā' ('merchandise') was also used by pickpockets to refer to a note (money) while luggage-lifters used it to refer to a bundle of goods or suitcase (Mallik 1972: 32–3).
22 Notably, Wise (1997: 207) suggests that 'taule' is an example of a "Northern variety" providing a term that has spread among broader informal French.
23 My translation. Sourdot stated: "Dans ce relevé de 1994, quelques formes posent encore un problème quant à leur origine et à leur formation. On supposera donc, à defaut d'autres explications, une origine régionale ou dialectale, à des unités comme jarter 'partir', ratrusher 'essuyer', piouquer 'sentir mauvais'." Sourdot's qualification is also reflected to some degree by Lodge (1993: 148), who describes the survival of items recorded as low-status in the seventeenth century thus: "Some of the low-status forms gradually diffused upwards and became accepted into the standard language ... Others appear never to have done so and to have survived only in regional *patois*... Yet others continued a subterranean existence in colloquial usage only to resurface in the twentieth century as non-standard French and labelled 'slang' or 'français populaire'. It is indeed currently a matter of some debate to know which vernacular forms in lower-class usage in our own day represent recent innovations and which represent long-standing features which a powerful normative tradition has kept hidden from published view".

References

Ahua, B.M. (2008) 'Mots, phrases et syntaxe du Nouchi', *Le Français en Afrique*, 23, 135–50.
Aitchison, J. (1991) *Language Change: Progress or Decay?* (2nd ed.), Cambridge: Cambridge University Press.

Alim, H.S. (2009) 'Translocal style communities: hip hop youth as cultural theorists of style, language and globalization', *Pragmatics*, *19*(1), 103–27.
Androutsopoulos, J. (2003) 'Non-native English and sub-cultural identities in media discourse', in S. Helge (ed.) *Den fleirspråklege utfordringa/The Multilingual Challenge*, Oslo: Novus. Pre-publication copy. file.setav.org/Files/Pdf/non-native-english-and-sub-cultural-identities-in-media-discourse.pdf, accessed May 2015.
Bachmann, C. and Basier, L. (1984) 'Le verlan: argot d'école ou langue des Keums?', *Mots*, *8*, 169–87.
Bardsley, D. (2014) 'Slang in Godzone (Aotearoa – New Zealand)', in J. Coleman (ed.), *Global English Slang*, London: Routledge. 96–106.
Beier, L. (1995) 'Anti-language or jargon? Canting in the English underworld in the 16th and 17th centuries', in P. Burke and R. Porter (eds.) *Languages and Jargons: Contributions to a Social History of Language*, Cambridge: Polity Press. 64–101.
Beregovskaia, E.M. (1996) 'Molodëzhnyi sleng: formirovanie i funktsionirovanie', *Voprosy iazykoznaniia*, *3*, 32–41.
Berjaoui, N. (1997) 'Parlers secrets d'El-Jadida: notes préliminaires', *Estudios de dialectología norteafricana y andalusí*, *2*, 147–58.
Blake, B. (2010) *Secret Language*, Oxford: Oxford University Press.
Boellstorff, T. (2004) '*Gay* language and Indonesia: registering belonging', *Journal of Linguistic Anthropology*, *14*(2), 248–68.
Breva Claramonte, M. and García Alonso, J.I. (1993) 'Categories, morphological features, and slang in the graffiti of a United States Western university', *Revista Alicantina de Estudios Ingleses*, *6*, 19–31.
Burke, P. (1995) 'Introduction', in P. Burke and R. Porter (eds.) *Languages and Jargons: Contributions to a Social History of Language*, Cambridge: Polity Press. 1–21.
Chamberlain, B.J. (1981) 'Lexical similarities of Lunfardo and Gíria', *Hispania*, *64*(3), 417–25.
Chambert-Loir, H. (1984) 'Those who speak Prokem', *Indonesia*, *37*, 105–17.
Cheshire, J., Nortier, J. and Adger, D. (2015) 'Emerging multiethnolects in Europe', in *Queen Mary's Occasional Papers Advancing Linguistics*, *33*.
Coleman, J. (2012) *The Life of Slang*, Oxford: Oxford University Press.
Corten, I.H. (1992) *Vocabulary of Soviet Society and Culture*, London: Adamantine Press.
Daniels, D.H. (1997) 'Los Angeles zoot: race "riot", the Pachuco, and black music culture', *The Journal of Negro History*, *82*(2), 201–20.
Davie, J.D. (1997/98) 'Missing presumed dead? The *baikovyi iazyk* of the St. Petersburg *mazuriki* and other pre-Soviet argots', *Slavonica*, *4*(1), 28–45.
Davie, J.D. (1998) *Making sense of the nonstandard: a study of borrowing and word-formation in 1990s Russian youth slang, with particular reference to the language of the fanzine* (Doctoral dissertation, 2 volumes). University of Portsmouth.
Demisse, T. and Bender, L.M. (1983) 'An argot of Addis Ababa unattached girls', *Language in Society*, *12*(3), 339–47.
De Katzew, L. (2004) 'Interlingualism: the language of Chicanos/as', in A. Muñoz (ed.) *Chican@ Critical Perspectives and Praxis at the Turn of the 21st Century*, National Association for Chicana and Chicano Studies. 61–76.
de Klerk, V. (2005) 'Slang and swearing as markers of inclusion and exclusion in adolescence', in A. Williams and C. Thurlow (eds.) *Talking Adolescence: Perspectives on Communication in the Teenage Years*, New York: Peter Lang Publishing, Inc. 111–27.

Doran, M. (2004) 'Negotiating between bourge and racaille: Verlan as youth identity practice in suburban Paris', in A. Pavlenko and A. Blackledge (eds.) *Identities in Multilingual Contexts*, Clevedon, UK: Multilingual Matters Ltd. 93–124.
Doran, M. (2007) 'Alternative French, alternative identities: situating language in la banlieue', *Contemporary French and Francophone Studies*, *11*(4), 497–508.
Dorleijn, M. and Nortier, J. (2013) 'Multi-ethnolects: Kebabnorsk, Perkerdansk, Verlan, Kanakensprache, Straattaal, etc.', in P. Bakker and Y. Matras (eds.) *Contact Languages: A Comprehensive Guide*, Berlin: de Gruyter. 229–72.
Dragojevic, M., Gasiorek, J. and Giles, H. (2015) 'Communication Accommodation Theory', in C.R. Berger and M.L. Roloff (eds.) *International Encyclopedia of Interpersonal Communication*, New York: Blackwell/Wiley. Pre-publication copy.
DVR II (1990).
Eble, C. (1996) *Slang and Sociability*, Chapel Hill, NC: University of North Carolina Press.
Eble, C. (2014) 'American college student slang: University of North Carolina (2005–12)', in J. Coleman (ed.) *Global English Slang*, London: Routledge. 36–48.
Einat, T. and Einat, H. (2000) 'Inmate argot as an expression of prison subculture: the Israeli case', *The Prison Journal*, *80*(3), 309–25.
Einat T. and Livnat, Z. (2012) 'Words, values and Identities: the Israeli argot (jargon) of prisoners', *International Journal of Political Science, Law and International Relations*, *2*(2), 97–118.
Elistratov, V.S. (1991) 'Russkoe argo v iazyke, obshchestve i kul'ture', *Russkii iazyk za rubezhom*, *1*, 82–9.
Ellis, Y. (2002) 'Argot and Verlan', *Contemporary France Online*. www.well.ac.uk/cfol/argot.asp, accessed May 2011.
Gallois, C., Ogay, T. and Giles, H. (2006) 'Communication Accommodation Theory: a look back and a look ahead', in W.B. Gudykunst (ed.) *Theorizing About Communication and Culture*, Thousand Oaks, CA: Sage. 121–48. Pre-publication copy.
García, M. (2005) 'Influences of gypsy *Caló* on contemporary Spanish slang', *Hispania*, *88*(4), 800–12.
Geipel, J. (1995) 'Caló: the "secret" language of the gypsies of Spain', in P. Burke and R. Porter (eds.) *Languages and Jargons: Contributions to a Social History of Language*, Cambridge: Polity Press. 102–32.
Githinji, P. (2006) 'Bazes and their shibboleths: lexical variation and Sheng speakers' identity in Nairobi', *Nordic Journal of African Studies*, *15*(4), 443–72.
Goudaillier, J-P. (2002) 'De l'argot traditionnel au français contemporain des cités', *La Linguistique*, *1*(38), 5–24.
Grayson, J. (1964) 'Lunfardo, Argentina's unknown tongue', *Hispania*, *47*(1), 66–8.
Green, J. (2016) *Slang: A Very Short Introduction*, Oxford: Oxford University Press.
Guella, N. (2010) 'La suppléance linguistique en arabe dialectal: reflet d'une dynamique conversationnelle', *Arabica*, *57*, 477–90.
Harchaoui, S. (2015) 'Lexical innovations in the speech of adolescents in Oslo, Norway', *Proceedings of ConSOLE*, *XXIII*, 220–47.
Hasund, I.K. and Drange, E. (2014) 'English influence on Norwegian teenage slang', in J. Coleman (ed.) *Global English Slang*, London: Routledge. 139–49.
Hollington, A. (2015) 'Yarada K'wank'wa and urban youth identity in Addis Ababa', in N. Nassenstein and A. Hollington (eds.) *Youth Language Practices in Africa and Beyond*, Berlin/Boston: Walter de Gruyter, Inc. 149–68.

Kießling, R. (2004) 'bàk mwà mè dó – Camfranglais in Cameroon', *Lingua Posnaniensis, 47*. www.aai.uni-hamburg.de/afrika/personen/kiessling/medien/kiessling-2004-camfranglais. pdf, accessed September 2012.

Kioko, E.M. (2015) 'Regional varieties and "ethnic" registers of Sheng', in N. Nassenstein and A. Hollington (eds.) *Youth Language Practices in Africa and Beyond*, Berlin/Boston: Walter de Gruyter, Inc. 119–47.

Kortas, J. (2003) 'Expressivité Dérivationnelle en Français Contemporain: Noms d'Action', *Studia Romanica Posnaniensia*, Poznań, Adam Mickiewicz University Press, Vol. XXIX, 155–70.

Kouega, J.-P. (2003) 'Word formative processes in Camfranglais', *World Englishes, 22*(4), 511–38.

Kouega, J.-P. (2009) 'The slang of Anglophone Cameroonian university adolescents: a glossary', *Syllabus Review, 1*, 88–116.

Labov, T. (1992) 'Social and language boundaries among adolescents', *American Speech, 67*(4), 339–66.

Leroy, O. (1935) *A Dictionary of French Slang*, London: George G. Harrap and Co. Ltd.

Lodge, R.A. (1993) *French: From Dialect to Standard*, London: Routledge.

Lodge, R.A. (2004) *A Sociolinguistic History of Parisian French*, Cambridge: Cambridge University Press.

Mahler, M. (2008) *Dictionary of Spanish Slang and Colloquial Expressions*, New York: Barron's.

Mallik, B. (1972) *Language of the Underworld of West Bengal*, Calcutta: Sanskrit College Research Series No. LXXVII.

Mawadza, A. (2000) 'Harare Shona Slang: a linguistic study', *Zambezia, XXVII*(i), 93–101.

Mazrui, A.M. (1995) 'Slang and code-switching: the case of Sheng in Kenya', *Afrikanistische Arbietspapier, 42*, 168–79.

Méla, V. (1991) 'Le verlan ou le langage du miroir', *Langages, 101*, 73–94.

Mutunda, S. (2007) 'Language behavior in Lusaka: the use of Nyanja slang', *The International Journal of Language, Society and Culture, 21*. www.edu.utas.au/users/tle/JOURNAL/, accessed May 2012.

Nahkola, K. and Saanilahti, M. (1999) 'Finnish slang as a linguistic and social phenomenon', in A. Fenyvesi, T. Kis and J.S. Várnai (eds.) *Tanulmányok a szleng fogalmáról*, Debrecen; Kossuth Egyetemi Kiadó, *76*.

Nassenstein, N. (2015) 'Imvugo y'Umuhanda: youth language practices in Kigali (Rwanda)', in N. Nassenstein and A. Hollington (eds.) *Youth Language Practices in Africa and Beyond*, Berlin/Boston: Walter de Gruyter, Inc. 185–204.

Nassenstein, N. (2016) 'The new urban youth language Yabacrâne in Goma (DR Congo)', *Sociolinguistic Studies, 10*(1–2), 235–59.

Nikol'ski, V. (1993) *Dictionary of Contemporary Russian Slang*, Moscow: Panorama.

Ogechi, N.O. (2005) 'On lexicalization in Sheng', *Nordic Journal of African Studies, 14*(3), 334–55.

Paul, K., Freywald, U. and Wittenberg, E. (2009) '"*Kiezdeutsch* goes school" – a multi-ethnic variety of German from an educational perspective', *JoLIE, 2*(1), 91–113.

Pozas, M. (2000) 'De Remps, de Reufs et de Reus: Approximation au lexique de la famille dans le "langage" jeune', *La Philologie Française à la croisée de l'an 2000*, 95–103.

Rock Fuzz (1995) No. 26 (October).

Rozhanskii, F.I. (1992) *Sleng khippi*, Paris: Izdatel'stvo Evropeiskogo Doma.

Russkii fan vestnik (1993), No. 8 (February).

Salillas, R. (1896) *El Delincuente español – El Lenguaje (studio filológico, psicológico y sociológico) con dos vocabularios jergales*, Read Books. 2011 reprint.
Smith-Hefner, N.J. (2007) 'Youth language, *Gaul* sociability, and the new Indonesian middle class', *Journal of Linguistic Anthropology*, *17*(2), 184–203.
Sornig, K. (1981) *Lexical Innovation: A Study of Slang, Colloquialisms and Casual Speech*, Amsterdam: John Benjamins.
Sourdot, M. (1991) 'Argot, jargon, jargot', *Langue française*, *90*, 13–27.
Sourdot, M. (1997) 'La dynamique du français des jeunes: sept ans de mouvement à travers deux enquêtes (1987–1994)', *Langue française*, *114*, 56–81.
Stanlaw, J. (2014) 'Some trends in Japanese slang', in J. Coleman (ed.) *Global English Slang*, London: Routledge. 160–70.
Stenström, A., Andersen, G. and Hasund, I.K. (2002) *Trends in Teenage Talk: Corpus Compilation, Analysis and Findings*, Amsterdam/Philadelphia: John Benjamins Publishing Company.
Strutz, H. (2009) *Dictionary of French Slang and Colloquial Expressions*, New York: Barron's.
Szabó, E. (2006) 'Hungarian prison slang today', *Revue d'Études Françaises*, *11*, 219–29.
Tender, T. (1996) 'Some fragments about the Estonian slang: its essence and research', in M. Kõiva (ed.) *Contemporary Folklore: Changing World View and Tradition*, Tartu: Institute of Estonian Language and Estonian Museum of Literature. www.folklore.ee/rl/pubte/ee/cf/cf/25.html, accessed July 2015.
Tikhanov, P.N. (1895) *Brianskie startsy: tainyi iazyk nishchikh. Etnologicheskii ocherk*, Briansk.
Vázquez Ríos, J. (2009) 'Linguistique et sociolinguistique du verlan à travers le monde', *AnMal Electronica*, *26*, 197–214.
Verdelhan-Bourgade, M. (1991) 'Procédés sémantiques et lexicaux en francais branché', *Langue française*, *90*(1), 65–79.
Vierke, C. (2015) 'Some remarks on poetic aspects of Sheng', in N. Nassenstein and A. Hollington (eds.) *Youth Language Practices in Africa and Beyond*, Berlin/Boston: Walter de Gruyter, Inc. 227–56.
von Timroth, W. (1986) *Russian and Soviet Sociolinguistics and Taboo Varieties of the Russian Language*, Munich: Verlag Otto Sagner.
Widawski, M. (2015) *African American Slang*, Cambridge: Cambridge University Press.
Wise, H. (1997) *The Vocabulary of Modern French*, London: Routledge.

5 Semantic change

Introduction

Another major means of creating youth, criminal and colloquial vocabulary involves semantic transfer. This is where new meaning is given to existing words or phrases, stylistically neutral or otherwise. Where youth and criminal varieties are concerned, when a word is given a new meaning, this new sense remains the preserve of the in-group until such times as it gains broader use. For the new item to be understood, it is important that users know what it means and how it is used.

Semantic transfer can be a particularly important way of supplementing a lexicon and has been employed as a means of creating in-group terms for centuries. Wolfer (2011: 25) notes that "semantic changes are predominant in almost all Arabic argots. Metaphors, metonyms, euphemisms, proper names and onomatopœa have been used since the tenth century in the old argot of the Banu Sāsān" (a variety spoken by crooks and beggars). Heller-Roazen (2013) also points to the creation of new senses for often well-known words by the Coquillards in fifteenth-century France.[1]

Semantic transfer has been productive in many youth and criminal varieties in recent history also. Slone (2003: 29) indicates in his study of Prokem that some 44% of the prostitution-related words he collated were formed through meaning transfer, as were 52% of other criminal words. Hollington and Makwabarara (2015) indicate that semantic manipulations appeared to be the most prominent of all strategies among speakers of the youth language they studied in Zimbabwe, a trend also seen in the language of Luyaaye speakers in Uganda (Namyalo 2015). More broadly, Mugaddam (2008: 9) has suggested that "[s]emantic processes like metaphor, metonymy, synecdoche, hyperbole, and euphemism are used frequently in youth languages", a position shared in part by Vierke (2015: 242), who considers metaphor to be "the key means of creating new terms" in youth language. Addressing certain semantic modifications of items borrowed from English in Yarada K'wank'wa, a youth variety spoken in Ethiopia, Hollington (2015: 154) underlines the agency manifested in manipulations where she notes that such "deliberate changes reflect the role of agency and consciousness with regard to the youths' linguistic practices". In view of the innovation demonstrated through the many varied examples in this chapter, a similar claim could be advanced regarding many of the items that have been semantically altered in other varieties.

The mechanisms most often cited to create new meaning are metaphor and metonymy.[2] Metaphor involves the creation of new meaning for an existing item based on comparison. Sornig (1981: 36–7) posits that metaphor "tries to span a semiotic distance, i.e. to establish equivalence between concepts originally not equivalent", and that any metaphorical expression constitutes "a kind of (implicit) comparison, a prerequisite of any comparison being that the two concepts should be comparable, i.e. that they should have something in common, e.g. certain semantic features".

Metonymy, by contrast, rests on a *contiguity relation* where an association between objects or concepts is the key factor (Sornig 1981: 37–8). This means that an item is referenced by its features or attributes, or by something linked with it – for instance, the use of the term 'the press' to refer to journalists due to the machinery once used to produce newspapers. With metonymy the connection may not be entirely clear to those not in the know, but an association exists, nonetheless. A third mechanism, which is less cited in studies and is conceptually close to metonymy, is synecdoche, where a part of something comes to represent the whole (e.g. 'the Crown' representing 'the monarchy' or 'the state') or the whole represents a part (e.g. 'Britain won two gold medals' where 'Britain' stands for the 'British athletics team'). The former type of synecdochic representation is the most commonly cited in studies of in-group and colloquial language and is sometimes referred to as a *pars pro toto* or *part for the whole* relationship, whereas the latter is sometimes known as *totum pro parte* or *whole for the part*.

Semantic transfer is used in cryptic and expressive language because it has great potential to hide in-group meaning and/or to facilitate language play, exclusivity and expressiveness. Mugaddam (2008: 9) notes the way in which such communicative aims are realised when he observes that "[e]xtension or change of the meaning of words with the purpose of insulting, ridicule, secrecy, exaggeration or fun is a characterizing feature of youth languages". Hyperbole, for example, allows speakers to be emphatic through exaggeration, and in some cases may help the speaker to be funny, in others ironic or sarcastic. In East Germany, for instance, youth used words involving the item 'Schleuder' ('catapult') to talk about transport that emphasised speed. In some cases, this feature was the main object of focus, so 'Schleuder' could refer to a car or train. However, in compound forms, more pointed, dysphemistic expression was possible, hence a 'Mumienschleuder' or 'mummy catapult', referred to a train that took old East Germans for trips to West Germany, and a 'Bullenschleuder' was a police car, created through use of the pejorative 'Bullen' (lit. 'bulls', for 'cops', 'pigs' (police)).

As we can see in these colourful examples, the use of hyperbole enables the speaker to create a new meaning with certain connotations or attitudes attached – old people are irreverently called 'mummies'. With semantic transfer there are many ways of conveying such attitude. Dysphemism, where a neutral idea is made negative through focus on an unfavourable element of the person or thing referred to, is produced to real effect in the Camfranglais item 'cou-plié', which refers to a rich old person by pointing to their wrinkled neck (lit. French 'cou plié'). Similarly, *onomastic synecdoche*, where the name of a place, object or person is used by dint of its/their properties or associations, or represents generic terms, gives us the sardonic use of 'Beirut' in English to mean a dangerous place, while 'Kosovo' and 'Bakassi' (a peninsular area subject to dispute between Cameroon and Nigeria) are used in the same vein in Sheng and Camfranglais, respectively.

Of course, items created through semantic transfer need not always emphasise the negative or critical. While in the previous examples dysphemism, onomastic synecdoche and hyperbole have all been used to create new words with disparaging or sardonic connotations, semantic transfer can be used for other purposes. Changing the meaning of a word can enable a speaker to talk about a sensitive or taboo subject in a less direct or embarrassing way, hence euphemisms in colloquial English for genitalia (e.g. 'family jewels', 'privates', 'private parts', 'wedding tackle' – Thorne 2005: 157, 346, 470). These terms are used widely within at least British English-speaking communities and are predicated on the perceived desirability of not referring explicitly to subjects deemed to be in some way sensitive or uncomfortable to discuss (see also **Euphemism and dysphemism**).

No matter the mechanism, an essential component of successful semantic transfer is context. This can be vital to understanding new meaning in terms of comprehending the comparisons and associations that make the transfer possible (at least initially), knowing what a new item means, and understanding how it is being used – especially as more than one meaning may be possible. The standard Russian word 'veteran' ('veteran'), for example, refers to a veteran in the commonly understood sense, e.g. a veteran of a war or other experience. However, in Russian hippy circles, 'veteran' can refer to an experienced hippy, someone who has been on the hippy scene for some time. Were two hippies to meet and talk about veterans, then the subject, the surrounding text (cotext) and context of their discussion, not to mention their shared hippy affiliations, could be important for a third party to determine whether they were discussing experienced hippies or former soldiers who have served in military campaigns (or other types of veteran). Those in on the newer meaning as well as the context are therefore better able to cut through any ambiguity and know what is being discussed, whereas those who are not in the know may be left trying to join the dots. In his discussion of semantic variation and Sheng, Githinji (2006: 462) captures the importance of context particularly well by showing how meanings given to the same word can be shared or differ across different Sheng 'bazes' (groups hanging out in Nairobi city estates such as Kibera, etc.):

Item	Kibera	Sinai	Kariobangi	Shaurimoyo
manga	steal	eat, have sex	–	–
kizee	father	boyfriend	boyfriend	father

and in his qualification that "[o]nly the members of a baze who share the norms of interpretation … are able to disambiguate problematic words in such changing contexts" (Githinji 2006: 464; for further information on usage across 'bazes', see also Kioko 2015).[3]

As this suggests, colloquial, youth and criminal vocabularies tend to have a number of words and phrases created through semantic transfer and other means that can be called on by speakers for use in a given situation. Indeed, many semantic mechanisms are widely used across such varieties to create new forms. It is perhaps unsurprising therefore that García's qualification that Pachuco Caló

> shares many characteristics with other in-group argots around the world, such as word creation, taboo words, semantic extension, and metaphor, to name a few. Such speech characteristics might be considered universals for this type of speech variety, which would include English cockney, Argentinian Lunfardo, and the Gypsy *germanía*,
>
> García (2005: 805)

chimes with the words of Partridge concerning prison language:

> The principle of "one word equals one meaning" is not relevant in the case of argot: there is a constant desire on the part of its speakers to introduce dramatic changes. Metaphors and creative elements are adopted for their entertainment and illustrative value, for their power to attract the attention of listeners, as well as to soften the harsh realities of prison life and to ensure secrecy and group cohesiveness.
>
> (Cited in Einat and Einat 2000: 319)

Appropriation

There are many respects in which questions of appropriation and re-appropriation are addressed in studies of youth and criminal practices. In our discussion of youth language practices and class in Chapter Three, for example, we noted how some middle-class youth in Indonesia appropriate aspects of the speech styles of social marginals such as criminals and street kids, as well as using dialectal forms and foreign loans, to distance themselves from traditional social expectations and conventions (Smith-Hefner 2007).

The appropriation of linguistic features by youth actors is commonplace. Large numbers of white youth in the UK, the US and beyond, for example, have adopted linguistic features from AAVE as part of their stylistic performance and identity work (e.g. Eckert 2012; Widawski 2015, both on the US). In this case, they appropriate to index elements of African American and hip hop identity that they particularly value. We also see appropriation by youth actors in France to emphasise multiethnic peer-group bonding, racial and ethnic diversity and shared identity at a time when traditional French mainstream discourse has avoided specific questions of race and ethnicity because they are seen as divisive (Doran 2004, 2007). To this end, they have replaced or reconfigured Standard French terms relating to race and ethnicity and used the resulting lexis in playful new ways, including through mock teasing or ritual insults (e.g. 'reub' for 'Arabe' ('Arab'), 'black' for 'noir' ('black person'), 'clandax' for 'clandestin' ('illegal alien')). The youth have thus created circumstances within which questions of race, ethnicity, immigration status and diversity can be discussed and negotiated positively in their own terms, using items that "[lack] the kinds of racist and stigmatizing connotations that they might have in the dominant language" (Doran 2007: 503). Indeed, not only have some youth appropriated and modified terms to these ends, they have also arguably appropriated the discussion itself of race, ethnicity, diversity and status as part of regular in-group discourse and a more open negotiation of identity while such questions have not been addressed or have even been erased within broader social discourse (Doran 2007).

Finally, youth actors may appropriate in other ways. Beazley (2003), for instance, describes how, in response to their marginalisation and subordination in Yogyakarta, Central Java, street children have occupied certain spaces within the city to earn money, feel secure, experience enjoyment and build identities. In this regard, the physical notion of space and how and why it is appropriated may have parallels in the discursive practices of some youth groups. See also **Crossing boundaries** in Chapter Three.

Popular thematic areas and richness of options

A number of thematic domains are prominently represented in colloquial, youth and criminal language practice, including where words and phrases have been created through meaning transfer. In his study of the colloquial forms of a number of languages, Sornig (1981: 49) identified a number of "fertile semantic areas". He pointed out that there are specific conceptual areas which are "extremely productive as to the paraphrastic proliferation of expressive lexical material" and that "the semantic areas of special lexical productivity (because of their special interest), are also areas of specific emotive charging" (Sornig 1981: 50). The areas he identified were:

- part of the human body, including the use of names of inanimate objects or personal names for body parts;
- bodily functions, sexual and otherwise;

- eating and drinking, alcohol, cigarettes, etc.;
- mental and physical deficiencies, diseases and death;
- money, payment and insolvency;
- other areas, such as work, the police, vehicles and fast movement, dress, God and the Devil.

(Sornig 1981: 50–3)

These underlying and mostly closely related topics are to some extent also in evidence in the subject areas covered by González and Stenström (2011) in their interesting study of London and Madrid youth language:

- sex and physical attraction;
- drugs (especially drinking and smoking);
- music;
- pastimes;
- school;
- fashion and physical culture;
- leisure activities;

(González and Stenström 2011: 252, 254)

and by Davie (1998) in his study of 1990s Russian youth language:

- the human body and the sexual act;
- emotional states (highs and lows) and feelings of enjoyment, appreciation, disappointment;
- members of traditional sub- or countercultural youth groups (including adherents of musical styles);
- non-members of the same groups (including representatives of the authorities and their supporters; foreigners);
- institutions within which young Russians play a prominent part (school, college, armed forces, etc.);
- money;
- consumer items connected to the youth milieu (e.g. clothing);
- alcohol and its consumption;
- drugs (their distribution and use);
- music and the music scene;
- recreational events or activities (e.g. gigs);
- places;
- comprehension or lack of understanding;

(Davie 1998: 248–301, 422–3)[4]

while Einat and Einat (2000) identified the following six main categories in their study of Israeli prisoner language:

- prisoner status (informers, inmate ranks);
- drugs;

246 *Semantic change*

- sexual relations in the prison;
- violence;
- nicknames for police officers and prison staff;
- other.

(Einat and Einat 2000: 313)

Sornig's, González and Stenström's, Davie's and Einat and Einat's thoughts on fertile semantic areas are very much evidenced by many of the in-group varieties that we consider in this book. If we look at the use of animal metaphors describing criminals and the police (and, by extension, the authorities), for example, we see that there are a number of terms in various languages that refer to different criminal occupations, prisoner status and their traditional foes (in respect of Sornig's "other areas", including the police):

1960s West Bengal criminals:	billi	'cat' → 'prostitute';
	khæk seāl	'fox' → 'police';
1990s Israeli inmates:	klavim	'dogs' → 'inmates who obey the boss';
Russian (1990s–2006, *crim., coll.*):	pës	'dog' → 'prison warden';
	nochnaia babochka	'moth' → 'hooker', 'prostitute';*
2008 colloquial Spanish:	gato	'cat' → 'pickpocket', 'petty thief';
2009 colloquial French:	fourmi	'ant' → 'small-time drug dealer';
	grue	'crane' → 'hooker', 'prostitute';
2012 Randuk:	dubbaana	'fly' → 'intruder', 'unwanted official'.[†]

*Notably, Zarzycki (2015: 20) also records the use of 'ćma' (literally 'moth') in Polish prison language to refer to a prostitute.

There is surely a parallel at least between 'ćma', the Russian 'nochnaia babochka', a term used by eighteenth-century German students – 'Buttervögel' (lit. 'butter bird'), which is used in some German dialects to mean 'butterfly' and was used in the eighteenth century to refer to a prostitute (Zhirmunskii 1936) – and the Hungarian 'pillangó', which literally means 'butterfly' but is found in 'éjszakai pillangó' to mean 'hooker' and 'bat' ('éjszakai' meaning 'all-night'). Further, and no less interestingly, Nassenstein (2016: 250) records the use of 'popo' (Swahili for 'bat') to refer to a prostitute in Yabacrâne youth language in Goma, Democratic Republic of Congo, on account of nocturnal working.

[†]Compare West Bengal criminal 'māchi' ('policeman', from the word for 'fly', in that it irritates and gets everywhere, even the dirtiest places – Mallik 1972: 44), and French 'flic' ('pig', 'cop'; its origin is undetermined but it is probably from the German 'Fliege' ('fly')). In her description of language practices in New Zealand, Bardsley (2014) cites 2001 doctoral work by Looser covering prison language known as Boobslang in 18 New Zealand prisons from 1996 until 2000. Among the data cited by Looser were the following dysphemistic terms for a 'pimp': 'fly', 'gannet', 'hyena', 'leech', 'magpie', 'seagull', 'piranha' and 'vulture' – some of these are scavenging or parasitic creatures. Bardsley additionally noted that terms involving words for animals were also found outside prison as terms of reference for angry, foolish or unreliable people or situations.

Of course, as we saw in the discussion of antilanguage and overlexicalisation in Chapter Two, we might reasonably expect criminal language to contain many terms referring to criminal acts, those who commit crime, and those who seek to stop it or who work in corrective institutions: in one study, Einat and Wall (2006: 182) pointed to at least 20 different terms used to describe informers and 15 expressions for prisoners who observed the inmate code and would not betray their colleagues. They also observed that over 29% of the 503 terms they examined related to drugs, 14% to violence and 14% to loyalty (Einat and Wall 2006: 185).

If we look at other language varieties, we see that many areas can be rich in lexical options. In Nouchi, for example, a number of terms exist relating to girls and young women, with 'djague', 'go', 'gnan', 'produit', 'stéki' and 'daye' all referring to a girl or girlfriend (Kouadio N'guessan 2006: 187), while Sheng – on a completely different topic – was described in 2006 as having six words for 'ten' (Ferrari 2006). English has a number of synonyms and near-synonyms for consuming alcohol, with varying degrees of expressive strength: to be 'bladdered', 'hammered', 'out of it', 'pissed', 'plastered', 'sloshed', 'smashed', 'steaming', 'wasted', 'wrecked' (Coleman 2014b: 56–7); or for relaying a positive evaluation: 'banging', 'boss', 'cool', 'mega', 'sick', 'sound', 'wicked', to quote items used in British English alone over the last few decades (Coleman 2014b: 57). On another tack, colloquial French has at least eight synonyms for the verb 's'en aller' ('to go away') and at least the same again for money (Červenková 2001: 83), while colloquial Russian and Russian youth language have at least fifty words for 'face' and over fifty for 'alcoholic' (Nikitina 2009: 1027, 1060). And so the list goes on.

Indeed, the creation of several synonyms or near-synonyms across subject areas of particular interest to an in-group is regarded by some as a defining feature of youth and criminal language (Halliday 1978; Eble 1996; Mayr 2004; Einat and Wall 2006; Mugaddam 2015; see also **Antilanguage** in Chapter Two) and can be one of the main impediments to understanding by out-groupers.[5] There are many reasons both why they might exist and why their use might be seen as characteristic of youth or criminal language: in some cases, a number of items may exist because different (sub)groups use different terms, as with Githinji's 'bazes'; alternatively, in situations of language contact it is possible that groups from different ethnic and linguistic backgrounds might bring alternative items to group usage that compete with other (near-)synonyms, especially as some words become more current or *en vogue*; in other circumstances, some already used or established terms may be considered to have lost their expressive effect or potency, and so replacements are needed – again, different groups may use certain items longer than other groups; equally, some varieties can have a high turnover of items to ensure secrecy, with older words and phrases even being restored to use when it is thought they might ensure the required level of obfuscation; and, finally, perhaps one of the most significant drivers in youth language practice is the constant aspiration to remain current, creative, sophisticated and socially and linguistically dextrous. González and Stenström (2011: 236) capture the significance of synonyms and near-synonyms in youth language practice well when they state:

> the language of youth groups becomes highly connotative, full of synonyms for concepts that are very dear to them and related to a few semantic fields, such as love, drugs and student life. What matters is not the denotative meaning of the words, but their associations and their connotations.

As the Nouchi examples demonstrate, not all of the items used by its speakers need to be created through semantic transfer alone: 'produit', to take but one, has been taken from French (lit. 'product') and then subjected to meaning change. Similarly, Randuk can trace productivity in certain semantic fields not only to the use of semantic transfer to create new items but also to borrowings from African and European languages that cover the same phenomena (Manfredi 2008). As a result, speakers can often have a number of options available to them when they wish to achieve their communicative goals, including, of course, stylistically neutral items and youth or criminal in-group terms for which no stylistically neutral equivalent exists.

Metaphor: comparison to create new meaning

As with the creation of new items in language more generally, metaphor is, without doubt, one of the predominant mechanisms that enable semantic change in colloquial language and in youth and criminal language varieties. Carter (2004: 109), for example, notes that metaphor is one of the methods of linguistic creativity most frequently found in a spoken English-language corpus he studied, while – in Africa – Shona 'slang' "characteristically employs metaphor to describe many different kinds of events" (Mawadza 2000: 98, citing Mashuta 1997).

In colloquial, youth and criminal varieties, it is reasonable to assume that many speakers may use an item as the most relevant word to meet their purposes without knowing the specifics of the semantic change involved. For them, the non-inventors, the most important thing is using the new item to meet a particular aim. However, for the metaphor to work in the first place, speaker–inventors must have an appreciation of the underlying comparison. In many cases, this comparison will be readily understood: for instance, the use by Israeli prison inmates of 'bakbak' ('bed bugs') to refer to tea leaves can be understood on account of their small, black appearance. However, even when a comparison is made, there is no guarantee that the rationale for that comparison will be understood by interlocutors in the same way, particularly where different cultures are involved – viz. the varied use of animal metaphors, where anthropomorphic qualities may vary from one culture or group to the next. Many British and North American English speakers, for instance, may be surprised by the positive Sheng use of 'kenge' ('monitor lizard', probably from Swahili) to refer to a girlfriend – when the comparison was made both were regarded as having special qualities that speakers wanted to emphasise (Ogechi 2005: 347).[6]

Even if cultural differences make it difficult to fully understand the comparison that makes a metaphor appreciable by others, it is nonetheless possible to identify a number of comparative mechanisms that facilitate metaphorisation. One such comparison involves *physical properties* such as composition, texture or sensation. An example of this is the traditional French criminal item 'poudre' – its meaning has been changed from the literal 'powder' to 'heroin', 'cocaine' on account of its physical form. Compare Russian 'belaia pudra' ('white powder') for 'cocaine' and 'pyl'' ('dust') to refer to drugs in powder form, cocaine.

These examples illustrate that an item's physical properties can serve as a vehicle for comparison to enable new meanings to be created. In the same vein, comparison based on physical *shape* is also possible. In the following table we can see examples from a range of colloquial, youth and criminal lexicons where shape serves as the principal conceptual criterion. Notably, in both West Bengal criminal language and colloquial Spanish we see a comparison between a broom and a thin woman, which is also echoed in colloquial French 'manche à balai' ('broomstick' → 'skinny person'):

1960s Lunfardo:	coco	'coconut' → 'head';
	bagayo	'bundle' → 'loot';*
1960s West Bengal criminals:	jhāṭā kāṭi	'broomstick' ('jhāṭā kāṭhi') → 'tall thin girl';
1990s Israeli inmates:	galgalim	'wheels' → 'ball-shaped hashish';
2006 Russian criminals:	maslina	'olive' → 'bullet';
2008 Spanish:	bellota (*crim.*)	'acorn' → 'bullet';
	calabaza (*coll.*)	'pumpkin' → 'head';†
	escoba	'broom' → 'thin woman';
2012 Randuk:	bagara	'cow' → 'fat woman'.

*The use of terms denoting a 'bundle' for 'loot' is not limited to Lunfardo: in his 1935 description of old-timers or professionals who had given up their criminal careers ('good people'), Maurer (1981: 72; my italics) gives the following definitions for 'bundle': "1. A woman. (Obs.) 2. A package sent from home to a prisoner. 3. *The loot from a burglary*. 4. *Any stolen property*.".

†Sornig (1981: 39) similarly cites the German use of 'Kürbis' ('pumpkin') for 'head', 'skull', while colloquial Russian also uses 'tykva' ('pumpkin') and 'repa' ('turnip'), both also meaning 'noggin' ('head'). Colloquial Russian also has 'orekh' ('nut') for 'head', as does English (Thorne 2005: 314), while 2009 colloquial French had 'praline' ('praline', 'sugared almond'). Words for 'head' seem to be plentiful in colloquial varieties. 'Praline' aside, colloquial French lists a number of items where shape can be viewed as a motivating factor, for example, 'caillou' ('pebble'), 'citron' ('lemon'), 'patate' ('potato') and 'melon' ('melon'). Moreover, French colloquial use of 'théière' (lit. 'teapot') for the same referent also has an echo in colloquial Russian 'chainik' (lit. 'teapot'), which can mean a 'noggin', 'head', 'dummy' or 'idiot'.

The use of foodstuffs such as fruit and vegetables more generally is also reflected in the West Bengal criminal item 'ālu' ('potato'), which was cited by Mallik (1972: 35) as used to mean 'bomb'.

Other metaphors may be based on *sound*. Colloquial Spanish (2008) draws a comparison between a 'tartamuda' ('stutterer') and a machine gun, in much the same way presumably that German troops did in the trenches of World War One when they called the machine gun a 'Stottertante', or 'Stuttering Aunty' (Zhirmunskii 1936: 117). The 1990s Israeli inmate term 'krav hatoolim' is also based on sound comparison, where its literal meaning of 'cat fight' comes to refer to a fight with much noise but no violence. Finally, mechanics speaking Randuk may refer to someone laughing by using the term 'yagasim' – Arabic for the sound of a well-functioning engine.

Another prominent comparison concerns *function* – creating new meaning tied to the utility and purpose of an object, and so on. In the following examples, we can see a cross-section of items indicating parts of the body, feeding, communication and drugs:

250 *Semantic change*

1990s Israeli inmates:	antenna	'antenna' → 'stool pigeon';*
	ekdah	'pistol' → 'injector' (for shooting);
Russian (1990s–2009, *coll.*):	lokator/y	'radar/s' → 'ear/s';
2008 Spanish:	buzón (*coll.*)	'mailbox' → 'big mouth';
	caldo (*coll.*)	'broth' → 'petrol', 'gasoline';†
	camisa (*dr.*)	'shirt' → 'heroin hit wrapping'.

*Presumably someone who picks up and/or transmits information. Compare colloquial Spanish 'antenas' ('antennae') for 'ears'.

†The feeding-fuelling theme in 'caldo' is seen in reverse in colloquial French 'carburant' – 'liquor' (lit. 'fuel') and colloquial Russian 'goriuchee' – 'booze', 'alcohol' (lit. 'fuel'). Shona 'slang' also has the items 'mafuta endege' ('aeroplane fuel') and 'mafuta etractor' ('tractor fuel') to mean 'clear beer' and 'cloudy beer', respectively. Interestingly, in terms of fuel and narcotics, Israeli prisoner language has 'metudlak' (lit. 'fuelled') for 'stoned'.

Dimmendaal (2009: 8) cites the use in Randuk of 'baboor', which literally means 'machine', but is used to mean 'hash'. Dimmendaal explains that hash is viewed as just as important to the brain to be able to function as a machine (presumably *engine*) is to a car. Mugaddam (2012: 8), on the other hand, notes its use by 'Shamasha' street boys to refer to a fat woman, and points to different varieties of Randuk being used by different groups. Additionally, Mugaddam (2015: 110) notes the Randuk phrase 'mashi bi jaazelmasaafi' (Arabic for 'the last little fuel left in the tank') to mean 'one who is almost dead/becoming penniless'). The phrase was associated with mechanics.

In our discussion so far, we have seen that when the meaning of a word is changed, this is often done deliberately with a particular purpose in mind. In some instances, this may be to hide meaning: we can all understand why Spanish-speaking drug dealers or purchasers might want to talk about a 'camisa' rather than something more understandable to out-group members. However, alternative purposes are possible: a speaker may want to use 'camisa' to underline group belonging, or to signal that they have a certain knowledge about drugs. In other cases, it is possible that the speaker may wish to express particular attitudes towards drugs or those in the drugs milieu (such as irony, sarcasm, *black humour*). Comparison of function certainly prompts us to think about speaker circumstance and attitude regarding handcuffs: Russian criminal language (1990s–2006) referred to 'braslety' ('bracelets'), while 1960s West Bengal criminals spoke of 'bālā' and 'kākan' ('bangles'). Similarly, with regard to corrective institutions, 2014 New Zealand prisoners might talk of 'Bahamas', 'Barbados', 'Club Med' or 'Siberia' (among many other options) to describe a solitary confinement cell (Bardsley 2014: 104); Spanish counterparts might use the word 'hotel' (lit. 'hotel') for 'jail'; while 1990s Israeli prisoners might refer to 'malon' ('hotel') and 'Hilton' – in the case of 'Hilton', with regard to a particular prison wing. Alternatively, Russian criminals might call prison an 'akademiia' ('academy'), while speakers of Luyaaye in Kampala, Uganda, might use the phrase 'okugenda ku yunivasite' ('to go to the university') to refer to being sentenced to prison (Namyalo 2015: 333). The comparison of prison with a place of learning is not particularly new or surprising: speakers of Nouchi in the early 1990s referred to Yopougon prison as the 'lycée de Yop', or 'Yop high school'; while in 1990s El Jadida, Morocco, prisoners referred to the 'ḥəbs' ('prison') as the 'məd̪rasa' ('school') (Berjaoui 1997: 157). Further back in time, Maurer (1981: 61) documented the use of 'college' to mean a 'penitentiary' in the in-group language of 1920s–1930s US safe-crackers, while speakers of English cant in the seventeenth and eighteenth centuries used the term 'academy' to refer to a brothel, and 'boarding schools' for London bridewells (Beier 1995: 78, 84). As we consider why such terms have been created, it is reasonable to assume that criminals may want to ironise about prisons and the rigours of life inside by referring to them in opposing and less oppressive terms, notwithstanding the learning of criminal tradecraft in jail (for more details, see Einat and Wall 2006; Szabó 2006; Einat and Livnat 2012).

A further link between education and corrective establishments or experiences is also reflected from the other perspective in the ironic 1990s–2006 Russian youth term 'katorga' ('hard labour') to refer to 'school', while in the 1970s–1990s US college students spoke of 'doing time in jail' to mean 'required time in a study hall'.

Given the importance to young people (and criminals) of locating themselves within a social context (e.g. Eckert 2003, 2005), it is perhaps consistent that another common subject for metaphorisation concerns *status, experience and roles*. Status can be an important field for speakers of youth and criminal language: youth can use linguistic virtuosity as a means of demonstrating their skill and intelligence and of underlining and enhancing their group standing (e.g. Danesi 1994; Stein-Kanjora 2008; Pagliai 2009), while – as we saw previously – Einat and Einat's study identified that prisoner status, designation and rank was one of six main subjects to emerge in their Israeli prison language sample. In the following examples, we can see a need to identify the standing of people within criminal environments, i.e. in places where individuals have a formal position as prisoners, but where informal or non-formal ranking can also be important:

1990s Israeli inmates:	hayalim	'soldiers' → 'inmates who obey the boss';
	poel	'worker' → 'drug dealer';
	melech hata	'king of the castle' → 'prison leader'.

This kind of comparison need not be limited, however, to the underworld: colloquial Russian items such as 'vratar'' (lit. 'goalkeeper' → 'bouncer') and 'gonets' ('herald' → 'someone sent for booze') enable speakers more generally to create jocular forms relating to the roles people play.

Of particular note in status terms are those that involve *familial role*. In the Spanish military, the word 'bisabuelo' ('great-grandfather') is used to refer to a soldier with less than three months of service to see out. This word carries a clear (albeit non-formal) connotation of seniority, and in this sense is very similar to Russian military usage where 'ded', a contracted form of 'dedushka' ('grandfather'), is used to refer to a barrack-room senior in the last year or 100 days of their military service, as well as to someone who may be involved in 'dedovshchina' ('hazing', 'barrack-room brutality'). Other forms of seniority, role or status can be seen in the Russian use of 'papa' ('dad') to mean 'commander' in the military and 'gang, prison or cellblock boss' in criminal circles; and in 1960s criminal usage in West Bengal, where 'kākā' (lit. 'uncle') meant 'accomplice', while 'bābā' (lit. 'father') referred to a gang leader or known policeman.

As we have seen, speakers of many varieties make extensive use of *animal metaphors*. These are predicated on comparison of an animal's physical or other perceived characteristics and can be found in many languages: in Shona, for example, animal metaphors have been described as "the most obvious set of metaphoric words" (Mawadza 2000: 97). In many cases, the sense can be negative, demonstrating the low status that certain animals have in specific cultures when compared with man. So, in the criminal language of 1960s West Bengal 'kuttā' ('dog') related to a 'contemptible person', while 1990s Israeli inmates referred to prisoners who obeyed the boss as 'klavim' ('dogs'). In Shona 'slang' (2000), 'imbwa' ('dog') was used to refer to a debased person; this insult is also used by Yabacrâne speakers in Goma, Democratic Republic of Congo (Nassenstein 2016: 251), while Town Nyanja has reportedly had a similar equivalent in 'galu' ('dog').[7] Prisoner language in New Zealand also includes the dysphemistic use of animal terms – a pimp or parasite, for example, may be known as a 'fly', 'gannet', 'hyena', 'leech' or 'vulture', to list but a few descriptions (Bardsley 2014: 104, citing Looser 2001), while colloquial Russian (1990s–2006) has seen the disparaging use of 'baran' (lit. 'ram') to mean 'thicko'. For all the evidence outlined, however, animal metaphors need not always be negative, as 'orel' and 'farasa' demonstrate, or refer to animate objects, as we see with 'sargeel':

1980s Bahasa Prokem:	kijang	'antelope' → 'stubborn';
GDR youth:	Krabbe	'crab', 'shrimp' → 'girl', 'young woman';
	Käfer	'bug' → 'girl', 'young woman';
1990s Israeli inmates:	shafan	'rabbit' → 'coward';
	dag shamen	'fat fish' → 'person robbed easily';
Russian (1990s–2006):	orël *(mil.)*	'eagle' → 'paratrooper, with open parachute';
	tëlka *(coll.)*	'heifer' → 'chick', 'piece of skirt';
2008 colloquial Spanish:	besugo	'red snapper' → 'idiot';
2012 Randuk:	farasa	'female horse' → 'beautiful girl';
	sagur	'eagle' → 'ugly boy';
	sargeel	'long worm'→ 'train'.

Over and above the use of animal metaphors is the replacement of *parts of the human body by those of animals*. This can often be used to refer to others in an informal, blunt or even disrespectful manner (much as we might say 'paws off!' in English). The following examples all focus on hands, feet/legs and the face:

1960s Lunfardo:	pata	'paw' → 'leg';*
Russian (1990s–2009, *coll.*):	lasty	'flippers' → 'paws': 'lasty uberi!' ('paws off!');
	morda	'snout' → 'face', 'ugly mug';
	lapa	'paw' → 'hand';

2008 colloquial Spanish:	pezuña	'hoof' → 'foot';
2009 colloquial French:	patte	'paw', 'animal leg' → 'leg';
	museau	'muzzle', 'snout' → 'face';
	gueule	'maw', 'mouth' → 'trap': 'ta gueule!' ('shut your trap!').

*'Pata' is additionally found in the colloquial Spanish phrase 'a pata' – 'on foot', while colloquial French has 'aller à pattes' ('to go on foot'). Sornig (1981: 38) also cites examples such as German 'Flossen' ('fins') for 'hands' and 'feet'.

An interesting extension of animal comparison concerns references to *mythological creatures*. In these cases, a characteristic of a mythological being is transposed to an individual. Thus the criminal language of West Bengal in the 1960s saw the use of 'monsā' ('snake goddess') to mean 'spiteful woman' (see also page 265), while Russian has seen the term 'oboroten'' ('werewolf') mean 'dirty cop' (presumably a good cop turned bad), 'course manager' or 'orderly' (military usage); and 'vamp' (from 'vampir' – 'vampire'), which can refer to a 'pervert' or 'rapist' (compare Sheng 'mavampires' for 'police').

One final instance that demonstrates the popularity of metaphor for creating new terms focuses on the comparison of *drug use and travel*. As the following examples show, words and phrases normally associated with travel can be used either to describe forms of drug taking or a state of mind after the narcotic has taken effect. Indeed, the metaphorical link between the effect of being carried off somewhere, the way a drug seems to work, and the manner in which the drugs are taken appears to be fairly transparent (although it is possible that some terms are actually calques). A 'paravoz' ('steam train'), for example, involves one person drawing on a joint and then blowing the smoke into another's mouth, while 'Haifa/Tel-Aviv/Haifa' refers to snorting lines of cocaine through a rolled-up paper one way and then the other. Another Israeli prison term, 'shvilim' (lit. 'paths'), is also used to refer to drugs arranged in rows. Both 'shvilim' and 'Haifa/Tel-Aviv/Haifa' have a parallel in the 1990s US hip hop item 'line', which refers to a gram measure of cocaine based on how it is usually prepared for snorting (Stavsky, Mozeson and Mozeson 1995: 63). As for the trip itself, Eble (1996: 71) cites the use by US college students of the expression 'to ride the E Train' to mean 'to feel the effects of (the drug) Ecstasy'. The travel theme also extends to destinations, which were implied in 1990s Russian in the names of drugs, including 'Oblako deviat'' ('Cloud Nine') and 'Nirvana' (compare the more recent 'rai' ('heaven') to refer to cocaine):

1990s French drug users:	voyager, faire un voyage	'to trip', 'to get high';
1990s Israeli inmates:	Haifa/Tel-Aviv/Haifa	way of doing lines;
1990s–2014 Russian drug users:	parovoz	'steam train' → 'blow-back';
	dvigat'sia	'to move' → 'to shoot up', 'to get a hit';
	kolësa	'wheels' → 'tabs';
	prikhod	'arrival' → 'trip';
	ekskursiia	'excursion' → 'search for drugs'.

254   Semantic change

While these examples all point to an appreciable travel–drugs theme, not all travel or movement metaphors describe drug-taking, drug-induced intoxication or what it feels like. The use of Russian 'gruzilo', a military term literally meaning a 'sinker' or 'lead weight', shows a form of gallows humour in its secondary meaning of 'submarine' or 'sailor'. Similarly, Russian youth may refer to 'going in' ('v''ezzhat'') to articulate that they have understood or know about something, while a speaker of colloquial Russian may refer to someone running them down ('naezzhat'') if they want to intimate that they are being given a hard time.

As we can see from the previous examples, the potential for metaphors to be created by users who value hidden meaning and/or linguistic novelty or virtuosity, or who want to convey how they feel about something, is great.[8]

Metonymy: associations and connections

Whereas metaphor rests on comparison, metonymy relies on association (Sornig 1981: 37–8). Unsurprisingly, given that associations between items or concepts are not always easily appreciable, the use of metonymy can make a new term arguably more difficult for the uninitiated to understand. Furthermore, metonyms need not be linguistic: Androutsopoulos (2007), for example, points to the use of visual metonyms in German hip hop discourse where images of turntables, microphones or spray cans might represent dj-ing, rapping and graffiti.

Just as with metaphor, a wide range of connections may be utilised to create new meaning. One involves the *representation of cause by effect*. In this case, there is no comparison as with metaphor, but a representation of one thing by another associated phenomenon. For example, in Israeli prisoner language the term 'shofech shinaim' (lit. 'spilling teeth') is used to refer to hitting someone; among Russian drug users, 'rai' ('heaven') may be used to refer to cocaine; and in colloquial English we might ask about the 'damage' when wanting to know how much something costs (Thorne 1994: 122; still in use). A similar question might also be heard in colloquial French, were someone to ask about the 'douloureuse' ('the painful one') when talking about a hotel or restaurant bill, a quite different association from the Randuk 'dahaakaat' ('money', from an item meaning 'causing laughter/happiness').

Interesting cases of cause being represented through effect can be seen with regard to HIV and AIDS in some informal African varieties. In Nyanja (Zambia), HIV may be called 'ka-onde-onde', or 'the thing that makes you thinner and thinner'; while in Zimbabwe, the Shona expression 'ari pachirongwa' means that someone is on a treatment programme, and so by implication has HIV/AIDS (*IRIN/Plus News* 2008). Other examples of effect representing cause include:

1960s Lunfardo:	corte	'cut', 'cutting', 'notch' for 'chisel';
1960s West Bengal criminals:	kāpā	'shiver', 'shake' for 'fever';
Russian (1990s–2006):	beda (*crim.*)	'trouble' for 'drugs', 'gear';
	dur' (*yth., dr.*)	'foolishness', 'nonsense' for 'drugs', 'gear'.

The reverse principle, where the *cause is used to describe the effect*, is also fairly commonplace. In 1960s West Bengal criminal language the word 'pālok' (lit. 'feather') might be used to describe its effect ('titillation'), while 2009 colloquial French saw the use of 'gerbe' (lit. 'bouquet') to refer to vomit.

Four other metonymic connections can be considered to be act-associated: where an *act describes a place, adornment or person*; where a *location represents an act, event, facility or occupant*; where a *service represents a location*; and where the *tool represents the actor* (which is often known as *objectification* where a negative attitude is imparted). With the first of these, colloquial French uses words such as 'fouille' (lit. 'search(ing)', 'excavation(s)') to refer to a pocket, and 'frappe' (lit. 'punch', 'kick') to refer to a hoodlum, lout or yob – an interesting contrast with Sheng 'teke', which literally means 'kick' but is used to refer to a beautiful woman.[9] Moreover, in the Randuk of 'Shamasha' street boys, the term 'shaloot' ('kick') comes to mean 'shoes'. Remaining in Sudan, Randuk speakers may also use 'intarnet' ('Internet') to denote a place where they can go online. Indeed, where a place is used to represent an act, event, facility or occupants, we can see a number of examples in different languages:

1960s West Bengal criminals:	pāṭsālā	'village primary school' → 'training';
2000 Shona slang:	madziro	'wall' → 'ATM cash machine';
2009 colloquial French:	galerie	'gallery' → 'crowd'.*

*An example in colloquial French, for example, is 'amuser la galerie' – 'to be the life of the party'. Compare English 'to play to the gallery'.

With regard to a tool representing the actor, criminals in 1960s West Bengal used 'lāṭhi' ('stick', 'cudgel') to refer to the police, and 'kãici' ('scissors') to refer to a pickpocket or gardener; Soviet soldiers referred to a driver (lit. 'shofër') as the 'steering wheel' ('rul''); while in Sheng speakers may refer to a policeman as a 'karau', which is a shield used by riot police.

A very common association found in criminal, youth and colloquial language concerns the use of *personal, place, brand or organisational names*, or *nationalities* (onomastic synecdoche; the term *eponym* is also used, mostly to refer to specific people or characters such as 'Picasso' in the bulleted list below). Although these are widely found, and the fact of their use is therefore not particularly surprising, these can still be difficult for out-group members to decode unless they have at least some idea about the relevance and the association. Some particularly good illustrations of this process can be found in 1980s Bahasa Prokem, where 'nisan' was used to refer to marijuana on account of the Nissan jeeps reportedly used by police to pursue marijuana users; and in colloquial French, where personal names may be used: 'Jacques' (lit. 'James') in 'faire le Jacques' ('to act the clown', 'to play the fool'); 'Julie' (lit. 'Julie') meaning 'girl', 'wife' or 'steady girlfriend'; and 'Julie du Brésil' (lit. 'Julie from Brazil') as a term of reference for cocaine. Other examples include:

1990s Israeli inmates:	Glickstein	name of the tennis player ('the white sport') → 'heroin' (due to its white colour);
	Picasso	'face wound' (after the painter Picasso, who produced many abstract works with unconventionally aligned faces);
	Colombia	'Colombia' → 'prison full of drugs';
Russian (1990s–2006):	arnol'd (*yth.*)	'bodybuilder' (from Arnold Schwarzenegger);
	adidas (*yth.*)	'cool', from the name of the German sports company, Adidas, whose goods were viewed as high-quality;
	kamchatka (*sch.*)	'last row of desks', from the name of the area in the Russian Far East;
Sheng (2015):	honda	'motorcycle', from the name of the motorcycle manufacturer;
	ndai	'car', from the name of the Hyundai car.

Even if the new meaning brought about through the transfer is disclosed, there is no guarantee that the original association will be either objectively correct or totally transparent. In 2008 Argentine Spanish colloquial usage, the word 'Turco' (lit. 'Turk', 'Turkish') referred to an Arab, *perhaps* due to peoples' presumed descent.

Naturally, there are cases where associations may be quite clear, as happens when a nationality is widely known by a product or cultural practice. In this sense, the disparaging reference to Italians as 'macaroni' in French, 'macarronista' in Spanish and 'makaronnik' in Russian arguably seems to underscore the power of both association and stereotypes.

A final example of metonymy in colloquial, youth and criminal language concerns *colour*. Colour associations can be more or less difficult to appreciate, depending on factors such as, for instance:

- (shared) sociocultural knowledge: is a newbie green or blue? English uses green to refer to inexperience, whereas French has 'bleu' (lit. 'blue') to refer to a novice, rookie or raw recruit. At the same time, in English we talk about turning the air blue with bad language, whereas in French 'langue verte' ('green language') refers to what many call 'slang' and the adjective 'vert' ('green') can be used to describe a 'smutty or spicy story';
- awareness of a referenced item's attributes: it is not too difficult to understand the use in 1960s West Bengal criminal language of 'holud-āḍḍā' (lit. 'yellow den') to mean 'jeweller's shop', where 'holdi', 'holde' ('yellow') referred to gold.

The use of colour to refer either informally or surreptitiously to something is not new: Beier (1995: 87) documents the use of 'yellow' for a piece of gold in the criminal language of sixteenth- and seventeenth-century England, while Sornig (1981: 39) has pointed to colour association in the Austrian 'Jeans' to refer to '1000 shillings', on account of the colour the trousers and bank note had in common. The colour of jeans also figured in the synecdochic use of 'blue jeans' to refer to the police in 1990s US hip hop usage; the same community additionally used the items 'green' and 'red' to mean 'money' and 'high on marijuana', respectively (Stavsky, Mozeson and Mozeson 1995: 9, 44, 84). Remaining on the drugs theme, in 1936 Maurer (1981: 87, 96) documented the use of 'black stuff' for 'opium' and 'white stuff' to mean 'morphine' among "underworld narcotic addicts". Forty-five years later, Sornig (1981: 38) additionally cited the use of 'naftalina' ('naphthalene', 'mothballs') in Italian to mean 'cocaine' due to its colour, while in the 1990s French saw the use of 'naph', 'naphte' ('naphtha') and 'naphtaline' to mean 'cocaine' or 'heroin', 'blanc' to mean 'cocaine', 'heroin', and 'noir' for 'opium', 'black stuff'. More recently Mattiello (2014: 153) has documented the Italian use of 'neve' ('snow') and 'bianca' ('white'), again for 'cocaine'.[10] Other examples of the use of colour terms include:

1960s West Bengal criminals:	kālo	'black' → 'opium', 'cocaine';
	sādā	'white' → 'cigarette', 'silver';
1990s Israeli inmates:	cachol meza'azea	'shocking blue' → 'patrol car';
Russian (1990s–2014):	zelënye (coll.)	'green ones' → 'money';
	chërnye (yth., dr.)	'blacks' → 'drugs';
	cherniashka (yth., dr.)	'black' → 'raw opium';
	belye (yth., dr.)	'whites' → 'drugs', 'tab(let)s';
	beliashka (yth., dr.)	'white' → 'cocaine';
	fioletovo (coll.)	'lilac' → 'all the same';
	kapusta (coll.)	'cabbage' → 'money' (banknote colour).*

*Mahler (2008: 307) also points to the use of 'lechuga' (lit. 'lettuce') to mean 'dollar bill' or 'green back' in Spanish, while Green (2017: 297) notes that the use of 'cabbage' in English for 'dollars' or 'pounds' (old pound notes) goes back to 1903. Although colour is the most likely association, a potential alternative explanation relates to the sound of new notes being flicked.

Synecdoche

This method rests on representation on a *part for the whole* or *whole for the part* basis. Like metonymy and metaphor, it is commonly found in standard usage, such as 'London' meaning 'the United Kingdom'. In general terms, it has a number of functions: for example, it enables more concise description; it can make usage more vivid; it can help conceal meaning; and, where required, it can also attract the attention of listeners where a speaker uses terms that may not be expected.

Examples from colloquial Spanish, colloquial Côte d'Ivoire French, colloquial Russian and West Bengal criminal usage point to a number of items created through synecdoche to designate various kinds of people:

258   Semantic change

1960s West Bengal criminals:	beni	'woman's braided hair' → 'woman';
	cok	'eye' → 'police';
	hāt	'hand' → 'pickpocket';
1990s Côte d'Ivoire:	deux doigts	'two fingers' → 'pickpocket';*
Colloquial Russian (1990s–2006):	boroda	'beard' → 'bearded man';
Colloquial Spanish (2008):	barbas	'beards' → 'bearded man';
	bigotes	'mustaches' → 'mustachioed person'.

*Compare (old) English thieves' use of 'fork' to refer to pickpocketing, alluding to use of the fore and middle finger for stealing (Green 2017: 150).

Synecdoche is also in evidence where *form is represented by substance*. Sornig (1981: 53), for example, notes the use of 'papel' and 'kağit', both meaning 'paper', to refer to money in 1980s Turkish usage. Similarly, 1990s US hip hop artists also referred to 'papes' and 'papers' for 'paper money' (Stavsky, Mozeson and Mozeson 1995: 76); and speakers of 2014 Multicultural London English might talk about 'papers' with the same referent in mind (Green 2014: 70).[11] Moreover, many people in the UK and US will be familiar with paying for something with 'plastic' ('credit card') – much the same, in fact, as people in Spain who pay with 'plástico'. Other examples include:

Russian (1990s–2006):	tsink (*mil.*)	'zinc' → 'coffin' (extending to 'casualty');
	plastmassa	'plastic' → 'record' (by extension, 'CD');
	zhelezo (*crim.*)	'iron' → 'gun', 'weapon';
Spanish (2008):	piel (*coll.*)	'skin' → 'wallet';
	hierro (*crim.*)	'iron' → 'pistol', 'sawn-off shotgun'.

Over- and understatement

A range of studies of colloquial, youth and criminal language underline the use of over- and understatement not just to hide meaning, but to variously express social solidarity, antagonism or for other effects, such as humour and attracting attention (e.g. Einat and Einat 2000; Miller 2003, 2004; Stein Kanjora 2008; González and Stenström 2011; Dorleijn, Mous and Nortier 2015; Hollington and Makwabarara 2015). Indeed, Jørgensen (2013) and Stenström (2014) identify intensification and having one's voice heard as especially important in youth discourse.

The emphasis and intensification that can be carried in expressive language can be clearly seen when we look at hyperbole, where items gain a secondary meaning through exaggeration, such as the use of lexis referring to illness, damage, injury and harm:

1970s–1990s US college students:	obliterated	'drunk';
	wiped out	'drunk';
Colloquial Russian (1990s–2009):	trup (*joc., neg.*)	'corpse' → 'drunk person';*
2008 Spanish:	colgar (*yth.*)	'to hang' → 'to fail a student';
	quemado (*coll.*)	'burned' → 'emotionally exhausted';
	infanticida (*coll.*)	'infanticide' → 'cradle robber'.

*Sornig (1981: 39) also points to the Austrian German use of 'ein Patient' ('a patient') to refer to someone who is bad at playing cards.

Interestingly, the reference by young Germans to those who were particularly loyal to the authorities in the GDR as 'the inoculated' ('die Geimpften') also highlights the use of medically related terminology for expressive effect.

The use of items referring to deleterious conditions as vehicles for (negative) expression can also be seen in 1960s West Bengal criminal language: 'mæleriā' ('malaria') → 'policeman'; in 1990s Israeli inmate language: 'wisach' ('contaminated', from Arabic) → 'prison staff'; in 1990s Russian criminal usage 'likhoradka' ('fever') → 'trial', 'court process', colloquial 'marazm' ('senility') for 'garbage', 'crap', and youth 'bred' ('delirium') → 'crap', 'rubbish'; and in the language of Indonesian street children in the 1990s who referred to the police as 'penyakit' ('the disease').

Indeed, heightened expressive force and a number of aims, including irony, may be achieved through overstatement and (over-)accentuation:

1970s–1990s US college students:	to bomb	'to fail';
	to blitz	'to perform well';
Russian (1990s–2009):	predki (*yth.*)	'ancestors' → 'parents';
	pushka (*crim.*)	'cannon' → 'piece', 'revolver';
Colloquial French (2009):	(les) vieux	'old people' → 'parents';
	incendier	'to set fire to' → 'to reprimand';
	plongeur	'diver' → 'dishwasher'.

For overstatement to work successfully, relative or excessive emphasis is placed on a feature or element of the activity or referent: parents have their age emphasised ('les vieux', 'predki'; notably, the term 'fossiler' (lit. 'fossils') is also used by Norwegian teenagers to refer to parents, as documented by Harchaoui 2015: 225), as is a train or car's fast movement in the previously cited 'Schleuder'. Indeed, selective accentuation can be important in creating ironic items, as the following 1990s Russian youth terms suggest, where an accepted or understood feature of a referent is focused on and used to describe something that is markedly dissimilar or antithetical:

basketbolist	'basketball player' to mean 'short person';
Rembo	'Rambo' to mean 'weakling', 'skinny person'.

The opposite process to hyperbole is understatement, sometimes referred to as *litotes* or *meiosis*. This allows a speaker to make an item or concept seem less serious, emphatic or important than it is, and involves the use of words that nominally have less semantic force or perceived import than the word that is replaced. Its use can facilitate irony, such as the Israeli criminal phrases 'shalach lo zer' (lit. 'sent him a bouquet/wreath') meaning 'liquidated' and 'yatsa letayel' (lit. 'went for a walk') to mean 'was kidnapped'. Additionally, the use of understatement can help to hide meaning or to talk about a sensitive or threatening subject euphemistically. Examples of understatement include:

260 *Semantic change*

1960s West Bengal criminals:	cij, ciz	'thing' → 'hemp';
1960s Lunfardo:	enfriar	'to cool' → 'to kill';
Russian (1990s–2006):	kusok	'piece' → 'grand', '1000 roubles';*
	bessrochnyi dembel'	'indefinite discharge' → 'death';
2008 Spanish criminals:	abrazado	'embraced' → 'detained (police)';†
	colocar	'to place' → 'to detain', 'to arrest';
Colloquial French (2009–2010):	larguer	'to release' → 'to dump'.

*Colloquial Russian also has 'shtuka' ('item', 'piece') used to mean 'grand' in the same way. Notably, Sappan (1969: 75–80) documented the use in late 1960s colloquial Hebrew of the word 'khatikha' (lit. 'piece') to mean 'pretty girl'; Manfredi (2008: 126) recorded the Randuk inversion of 'ḥādʒa' ('thing', 'stuff') to become 'dʒāḥa' ('girl'); and Nassenstein (2016: 250) reported the use of 'matière' (from the French for 'material') for 'girl' among Yabacrâne speakers in Goma, Democratic Republic of Congo.

†Salillas (1896: 265) documented the use of this item to mean 'prisoner', 'someone caught, arrested'.

Euphemism and dysphemism

As can be seen with 'larguer', 'abrazado' and 'bessrochnyi dembel'', understatement can enable a speaker to avoid direct reference to something negative or unpleasant through employing attenuated, gentler or more carefully couched terms. However, while on some occasions understatement may be appropriate for euphemistic purposes, it is also possible that understatement can serve to convey informality, levity, rhetoric or irony.

As we noted previously, euphemism is often associated with discussing sensitive, unpleasant, taboo or embarrassing subjects in a less offensive, easier or milder way. For example, contracting or having HIV/AIDS may be referred to indirectly in a number of informal varieties of African languages, especially while some communities struggle to discuss the problem formally or openly:

Language	Country	Term	Meaning	Refers to
Swahili	Tanzania	amesimamia msumri	standing on a nail*	AIDS
Kikuyu	Kenya	kagunyo	the worm	HIV
English	Uganda	slim	slim	HIV/AIDS

(IRIN/Plus News 2008)

*Interestingly, Coleman (2012: 228) points to the wide use in the Caribbean of the phrase "pick up a nail" to mean "to catch venereal disease", attested during 1938–1994.

However, it is also worth noting that euphemism may also be used for other purposes. In some contexts, it may be employed to avoid thoughts of danger (e.g. in wartime); in others, a speaker's aims might range from minimising negative impressions to creating positive ones (for more information and examples see, for instance, Cooper 1993; Blake 2010; Namyalo 2015; Nassenstein 2015).

Some examples of euphemism can be seen in 1960s West Bengal criminal usage in 'saṛak-soāri' (Hindi for 'street passenger') to mean 'beggar', and in the use by Bengali prostitutes of 'bādhā-paṛā' (lit. 'to be hindered', 'hindrance') to refer to a menstrual period – compare the use of English 'injury' for 'menstruation' in Kampala, Uganda (Namyalo 2015: 334). Over and above the select use of softer or attenuated terms, euphemistic items may also have some degree of similarity in sound to the words they replace, as the following French and English examples indicate:

Item	Literal meaning	Euphemistic meaning	Replaced item	Replaced meaning
Flute!	Flute	Gosh! Drat!	Foutre!	Fuck! Fuck it!
Miel!	Honey	Sugar!	Merde!	Shit! Bloody hell!
Punaise!	Bug	Damn it!	Putain!	Bloody hell!
Flip!	Flip	Damn (it)!	Fuck!	Fuck!
Sugar!	Sugar	Damn (it)!	Shit!	Shit!

Where euphemism sees speakers couch their utterances in softer, more sensitive or palatable terms, dysphemism involves the substitution of a neutral or agreeable description by one that is unpleasant, disparaging or offensive. Given the pervasiveness of semantic change in youth and criminal language, and the desire of speakers to meet expressive and/or verdictive communicative aims (as we saw previously with the German examples 'Mumienschleuder' and 'Bullenschleuder'), it is perhaps not surprising that examples of dysphemism can be found frequently in youth and criminal discourse. Dysphemistic labels and expressions to insult, such as Randuk 'kilabelamn' ('security dogs') and 'kilablahab' ('wild dogs') for security officials are reported as being used by university students in Sudan (Mugaddam 2015: 113), while youth in Zimbabwe may refer to the police as 'orovai' (Shona for 'beaters'). These examples echo dysphemistic designations across a number of languages, as we have seen in the examples provided for members of the criminal world or authorities ('klavim', 'pës', 'fourmi') and in other animal metaphors ('imbwa', 'galu', 'besugo', 'baran').

Expansion and contraction of meaning

In our discussion of lexical borrowing in Chapter Four, we saw that speakers of colloquial, youth and criminal language can create new items through the expansion and contraction of meaning ('pantscher', 'bisnes'). This can also apply to lexis that is not borrowed. With the former, meaning is extended to encompass broader concepts. Examples of this process can be seen in the creation of words referring to money: in 1960s West Bengal usage, for instance, speakers would use 'phuṭi' to refer to 'small coins'. This word came from 'phuṭo' ('hole') and from the fact that the coin with the lowest denomination was hollow. This association expanded to refer to small coins more broadly. Similarly, colloquial French has

262 Semantic change

'thune'. This originally referred to a five-franc coin; however, it was subsequently used to refer firstly to any coin, then to money in general.

A similar process can be seen with some terms relating to narcotics, prisons and clothing. One word used in Russian circles to refer to drugs in general is 'igla', which literally means 'needle', while in Sheng 'tembe' literally means 'tablet' but is used to refer to drugs more broadly. In Camfranglais, the term 'kondengui' originally referred to the main prison in southern Cameroon, but later came to refer to any prison, while 'kenzo' relates to any pricey footwear or clothing, having originally been a brand name for expensive shoes.

Semantic contraction, by contrast, involves a more specific or narrower sense, such as the use of the 1990s French drug users' item 'marchandise' ('merchandise') specifically to mean 'drugs' or the 2006 Israeli prisoner item 'poel', the meaning of which was narrowed from 'worker' to 'drug dealer'.

Polysemy

Polysemy is where a lexical item has a number of different meanings. As a linguistic phenomenon, it is not limited to colloquial, youth or criminal varieties. However, its appearance in these varieties provides some striking examples of variation in meaning, domains of particular significance or salience, and the importance of context and cotext to determining what speakers might be communicating. Some good illustrations of polysemy can be seen in the different meanings for 'saodā' that we saw in Chapter Four (page 229) and in Austrian German, where Sornig (1981) noted a number of meanings for 'Blitzen', 'Fleck' and 'Häfn':

Item	Literal meaning	Meaning 1	Meaning 2	Meaning 3
Blitzen	to flash, to sparkle	to drink	to drive fast	to cohabit
Fleck	patch	shot	money	bad mark at school
Häfn	pot	prison	motorbike	motor car

(Sornig 1981: 49)

In some instances, the same words or phrases can refer to opposite meanings or concepts. Colloquial French has, for example, 'c'est trop', which literally means 'that's too much'; the phrase can be used in either a positive or negative sense. In the same way, 1970s–1990s US college students used the word 'trip' to mean something positive or negative (e.g. 'it's a trip'), depending on the speaker's position and aims at the time. In such cases, voice qualifiers such as sounding ironic may play a role in enabling the speaker to impart their particular attitude.

Quite apart from the potential for words and phrases to designate either of two extremes, it is also possible that a word may have both a narrow and a broader meaning. Eble (1996) provides the following examples from US 1970s–1990s college student practice:

Item	Narrow meaning	Broader meaning
ace	to get an A for a test	to perform any action well
jones	craving for drugs	craving for anything

(Eble 1996: 57–8)

Antiphrasis

As we saw with polysemy, certain items (e.g. 'c'est trop') can refer to either of two poles. However, there is another area where opposites seem to meet – antiphrasis, where opposite sense is given to the normal meaning of a word – and it is fairly common in informal usage. A classic example in 1990s US youth culture was the ameliorative 'bad' to mean 'good', 'cool', 'great' (Dalzell 2014: 18; British youth culture popularly used 'wicked' in the same way. 'Sick' is a more recent favourite meaning 'excellent' – Coleman 2014b: 51, 57). There are different reasons why antiphrasis appears in informal usage: in some cases, the speaker may wish to use a mirror version of the generally accepted meaning to express their antipathy to or disagreement with society and/or convention – Slone (2003: 42), for example, observes that mirroring can be a "symptomatic reaction of an oppressed minority within a society" (see also **Antilanguage** and **Resistance and resistance identities** in Chapter Two).[12] In other instances, it may serve as a form of linguistic experimentation (perhaps for language play) or as an in-group code. The frequency of negative terms used to convey positive meaning in youth language practices in Holland has led Dorleijn, Mous and Nortier (2015: 277) to observe that such antiphrasis is commonplace among youth in the country.

We have already encountered an example of antiphrasis in Chapter Four, in the West Bengal item 'uṭhāo'. This normally means 'to pick up'; however, in 1960s criminal usage it referred instead to someone who would throw false gold to induce a prospective victim. Similarly, Sheng has 'm-see/mzee' and 'imbaya'/'vi-baya sana', meaning 'youth' and 'very well' instead of the literal 'old man' and 'bad'/'very badly'; and speakers of Luyaaye in Uganda might use the antonymic 'okwesala obuwero' (literally 'to be dressed in torn old clothes') to refer to being dressed smartly and expensively (Namyalo 2015: 333). Returning to areas outside Africa, Dutch youth have used 'gruwelijk' (lit. 'horrible') to mean 'fantastic' or 'great' (Dorleijn, Mous and Nortier 2015: 271), while teenagers in Norway might also sardonically refer to a foolish person as 'einstein' ('Einstein') (Harchaoui 2015: 225) in much the same way as speakers of British or American English.

Finally, the idea of turning accepted and expected meanings on their head also partly accounts for friends jokingly calling each other otherwise insulting names, of which some may be expletives, in banter (e.g. Stenström, Andersen and Hasund 2002). Such examples include 'motherfucker', as noted by Widawski (2015: 79) in his study of African American usage, and 'You stupid bastard!'.

Counterlanguage

In his discussion of English 'slang', Green (2016: 27) notes that its "unifying essence" – if it has one – is opposition. Insofar as it enables subversion of Standard English, which Green sees as its primary function, and helps speakers to define themselves as outsiders beyond the "standard world", it represents a *counterlanguage*.

In using this term, Green emphasises the contrastive, oppositional functions which some non-standard language practices can serve (see also **Antilanguage** and **Resistance and resistance identities** in Chapter Two). That said, he does not employ it within a new theoretical construct (which is not his aim). There is, however, another interpretation of the term that seeks to conceptualise specific language practices within particular sociocultural spaces and language ideological contexts. This is the notion of counterlanguage proposed by Morgan in her work on African American discourse.

Morgan states that, from the days of slavery until particularly the 1960s in southern states of the USA, African Americans lived in a hostile environment where the rules of communication were determined by dominant whites. Those rules were built on a presumption that the latter were superior and their communication and interactional control could go unchecked and unpunished (Morgan 2002). When communicating with whites, for example, African Americans were expected to talk only when allowed; to avoid direct eye contact with white interlocutors; to never ask about the intentions of a white person; and to never contradict. Failure to observe these rules could lead to severe sanctions (Morgan 2002).

In the face of this oppression and attendant ideologies, African Americans correspondingly developed a counterlanguage. This counterlanguage, which made great use of indirectness in communication, enabled them to resist, contest and undermine the values and attitudes of restrictive white society. Based on practices from African discourse, indirectness enabled African American speakers to positively maintain their sense of agency and self in a generally oppressive environment where a black audience could tell a speaker's real intention. The use of ambiguous words or phrases with many different meanings, including contradictory, beyond those traditionally attested in English, facilitated satirical, ironic and critical expression, among other things, about which the uninitiated (whites) would be unaware (Morgan 2002, 2009). In this way speakers represented an alternative African American reality through ambiguity and indirectness and, indeed, set in train practices that survive in hip hop, rap and African American English discourse (Morgan 2002, 2004, 2009).

Context and culture

Context and cotext are important for a new item to be successfully used and understood. Polysemy provides a good example of this importance: the colloquial Russian adjective 'sinii' (blue), for example, means 'a thief' or 'convict' (due to the colour of tattoos thieves or prisoners might have). However, it is also commonly used to refer to an alcoholic. Similarly, the noun 'avtomat' can mean a 'machine gun' or 'automatic machine' in Standard Russian, whereas in certain contexts some youth may use it to mean an 'automatic pass' or 'exemption from final exams'.

The internal social, cultural or other ties and values important to a small ensemble or subgroup can be significant; however, appreciation of broader shared values, knowledge, assumptions, markers and practices can also be influential as the group draws on sociocultural resources that surround it to create new items and achieve expressive effect (see also **Repertoires** in Chapter Two). Speakers of colloquial Russian, for example, may well have drawn on Russian social and cultural history (cultural allusion) in producing items such as 'T'mutarakan'' to mean 'middle of nowhere', although nowadays many may be unaware of why this term is used. This item derives from the name of the ancient city near the Black Sea, and knowledge of its faraway location can be important to understanding what it means and why a speaker may choose to use it to emphasise physical distance as they qualify a position in conversation (compare the distance implied in the colloquial English use of 'Timbuktu', which was first documented in 1863 – Green 2017: 80). And in Goma, Democratic Republic of Congo, speakers of Yabacrâne youth language, if using the term 'muganda' (Swahili for 'Ugandan') to refer to a very dark-skinned person, are relating to a stereotype that is often linked to certain Ugandans and to invasion by Ugandan troops (Nassenstein 2016: 250). Social and cultural knowledge is indeed "needed for the impact of wordplay and humour to be at its most effective", as Carter (2004: 21) intimates – although many speakers will no doubt accept some phrases as a matter of convention without questioning their provenance or sociocultural merit.

Shared knowledge of mythology can also be used to create new items that enable a speaker to meet expressive aims: 1960s West Bengal criminal usage saw the interesting use of 'Behulā' for 'bride' (or 'new bride' in the eunuch community). This originally referred to a woman who became a widow when, as a result of a curse from Manasā the snake-goddess, her husband was bitten by a snake. According to the story, Behulā made extensive efforts to get her husband back through devotion, and thereby became the symbol of a dedicated wife or bride. For her part, Manasā was recalled in the use of 'monsā' to mean an 'ill-tempered or spiteful woman' (Mallik 1972: 42–3, 102).

History and mythology aside, other *everyday* social and cultural associations can also be important, whether it is in vernacular or narrower, in-group usage, advertising, the media or literature. In Sheng, the word 'makabelo' is used to refer to teeth – this word was based on the name of a radio broadcaster who had 'funny teeth' (Githinji 2006: 45); while, also in Kenya, 'mteja' can be used to mean 'missing' on the basis of the Swahili voicemail message for 'customer unavailable' (Bosire 2009: 80). Similarly, Mallik's (1972) study of West Bengal criminal language cited items such as 'kānpuri' ('knife', because Kanpur is famous for its cutlery); 'nācgoli' ('Calcutta police intelligence branch office', after the old name of the place where the branch was situated as of 1972); and 'haringhāṭā' ('young woman', named after the location of the West Bengal Government dairy) (Mallik 1972: 40–1). These items all point to the advantage of sociocultural knowledge to define and derive meaning, although an item's origins might not always be clear-cut, hence the possible provenance of 'gāchi' ('amorous relationship with a public woman') – Mallik indicates *possible* derivation from 'Sonāgāchi', a notorious brothel area of Calcutta (Mallik 1972: 40).

Naturally, the propensity for sociocultural institutions, mythological and historic figures, trends and events to inspire or appear in colloquial, youth or criminal varieties is not unique to areas beyond Europe as we traditionally understand it. European rappers commonly employ cultural referencing such as citing the names of celebrities, consumer products, companies and the like in their narratives. For example, one line by the German rap group Rödelheim Hartreim Projekt reads: "du bist weich wie ein Kissen, ich bin hart wie Thyssen Stahl" ("You are soft like a cushion/I'm coming hard like Thyssen steel") (cited in Androutsopoulos 2009: 49). In English, an improbable story may be described as 'like tea from China', that is to say, 'far-fetched'; while colloquial French has items such as 'amazone' (lit. 'amazon'), 'coup de Trafalgar' (lit. 'Trafalgar blow' – after the location of a French naval defeat in 1805) and 'gnaf' (from 'Gnafron', a character in traditional Lyon puppet theatre) meaning 'car-based prostitute', 'violent situation or behaviour' and 'shoemaker', respectively (Strutz 2009: 11, 107, 175).

As we might appreciate, for those who do not share the same sociocultural background, the task of understanding others' cultural allusions and what their use means can be considerable. What is more, it can be complicated by the fact that speakers might adopt points of cultural reference and adapt them to their own particular groups or circumstances. Russian again provides a number of examples where common cultural phenomena such as song or film titles are subject to meaning change to refer to something specific to a certain group. According to Shlyakhov and Adler (2006), some military, for example, have changed the original reference of book or film titles to describe phenomena more relevant to their everyday lives:

teni ischezaiut v polden'	literally 'the shadows disappear at midday', the title of a popular TV series – this is said of privates heading for absence without leave;
khozhdenie po mukam	often translated as *The Ordeal*, this title of the novel by Aleksei Tol'stoi comes to refer ironically to a drill.

(Shlyakhov and Adler 2006: 267, 297)

Summary

In this chapter, we have identified the main semantic processes through which youth, criminal and colloquial words and phrases are created. As in many standard language varieties, these primarily involve metaphor and metonymy. Both mechanisms are very widely used, and the multitude of examples for both is testament to their productivity in a number of varieties across a range of languages.

We have acknowledged the importance of context and of sociocultural and other insights to the successful creation, use, understanding and (where possible) unmasking of words created through semantic transfer. And we have discussed the significance and utility of onomastic synecdoche, euphemism, dysphemism, understatement and overstatement in enabling a speaker to express attitude and evaluation, to innovate and improvise, and even to escape the repetition, rigours and monotony of everyday life and language. In this regard we have covered most of the comparisons and associations that arise in usage of interest to us, but not all. For example, we might also have mentioned expressive practice through simile, such as in colloquial English 'drunk as a skunk' or one of its Russian translations 'p'ianyi, kak svin'ia' (lit. 'drunk as a pig'). One way or another, we have seen that, through use of semantic transfer, speakers are able to create a number of synonyms or near-synonyms, a phenomenon held to characterise youth language practice in particular, and one which can aid in the masking of meaning.

The use of semantic transfer by in-groups helps them to reach the quasi-professional and/or socially driven destinations outlined in Chapters Two and Three: to describe who they are and who they aren't; to create and consolidate social bonds through shared language; to keep others at a desired distance; to modify and negotiate expressive force within ongoing discourse; to communicate beyond the knowledge of others and exclusively among themselves; and to challenge, if not subvert, the mainstream and its standard language and ideology by changing conventional meaning for their own, sometimes radically different ends. These are but a few of the purposes served by the creation of new items through conscious meaning transfer. However, ultimately, no matter the aim, while others continue to use the original sense of any given word more conventionally, in-groups not only create a new meaning, but also make it their own.

Notes

1 Heller-Roazen (2013: 23) writes of the Coquillar[d]s: "The words contained in the legal documents would have been known in large part to the inhabitants of Burgundy, but not in the meanings lent to them by the Companions of the Shell [the Coquillards]. The rogues, in other words, had selected certain words and phrases, withdrawn their usual sense from them, and conferred upon them a new and impenetrable significance".

2 A number of studies of colloquial, youth and criminal language focus on metaphor and metonymy. Their importance was described by Sourdot (1997: 72) in one study of French youth language, for instance, when he said: "Sans entrer dans le détail des opérations sémantiques qui les sous-tendent, on peut être d'accord avec D. François et dire que les glissements de sens s'effectuent essentiellement à travers la métaphore et la métonymie" ("Without getting into the detail of the semantic operations which

underpin them, one can agree with D. François and say that meaning change is carried out essentially via metaphor and metonymy" (my translation)).

3 The Sinai group's definition of 'manga' is noteworthy in that parallels between consuming, food and sexual activity can be found in other languages. For example, Danesi (1994: 106) points to the use by teenage girls in Toronto of 'He's a stud muffin', 'He's a burger' and 'He's got great buns' with regard to male teens whom they might want to *eat sexually*. Equally, Nassenstein (2015: 197) points to the use of 'kurya' ('to have sex', from standard Kinyarwandan 'to eat') in Imvugo y'Umuhanda, a youth variety spoken in Kigali.

4 Compare also Kouega's (2003) description of the most frequent topics discussed by users of Camfranglais, which include: food and drink, money and ways of getting it, sex and relationships with women, the physical appearance and feelings of people, ways of addressing people and referring to them.

5 Androutsopoulos (2000: 8, footnote 11) points to Kotsinas (1997) having collected 425 synonyms for 'stupid', for instance. With regard to colloquial and in-group French, Červenková (2001: 83) notes: "The richness of argot in synonyms is explained by the essentially emotive nature of this language" ("La richesse synonymique de l'argot s'explique par le caractère essentiellement émotif de ce langage" (my translation)).

6 Ogechi (2005: 347) describes it as "a rare creature that lives in hot climates and even here, it does not expose itself carelessly. In the same way, a dear girlfriend is not considered an ordinary human being but a special creature".

Another example of cultural specificity in Sheng is cited by Kiessling and Mous (2004: 10), where they point to the use of 'kiboko' ('hippopotamus') to refer to a beautiful girl.

7 Note also the use of the dysphemistic 'wambwa' (literally 'he/she is like a dog') to refer to a poor, not presentable, low-class person or nobody in the Luyaaye youth language in Kampala, Uganda (Namyalo 2015: 335).

Sornig (1981: 39, 40–1) points to a number of animal and plant metaphors to represent humans and suggests: "Persons are likened to an animal or plant because of some vague similarity in their psychological behaviour or physical appearance". As a result, verbs may be derived to denote human activities, e.g. Austrian German 'Tigern' – 'to work hard', from German 'Tiger'. Animal–human meaning transfer is also seen, according to Sornig, in the Austrian use of 'Taubn' ('dove') to refer to a female, and German 'Biene' ('bee') and Austrian 'Käfer' ('beetle') for 'girl'. Salmons (1991: 19) also points to the use of terms denoting fruit in this way in his article on GDR youth language, viz. 'Kirsche' ('cherry') for 'girl', 'young woman' and 'Kirschkern' ('cherry pit') for 'boy', 'young man', not to mention 'Krabbe' ('crab', 'shrimp') and 'Käfer' ('bug') also for 'girl'.

8 In addition, examples of position comparison include colloquial Spanish 'tejado' ('roof') for 'head' and the older English 'slang' 'attic' for the same purpose (Green 2017: 138), as well as colloquial Russian 'bagazhnik' ('car trunk') for 'backside'.

Examples involving similarity in acts include colloquial French 'emballer' ('to wrap up') for 'to arrest'; Spanish 'cantar' ('to sing') to mean 'to confess' (compare the Israeli prison verb forms 'sharim' and 'lezamer' (lit. 'sing') for informing, as well as the loanword 'musician'; and the English 'sing'); and Russian 'gruzit'' ('to load') to mean 'to bore rigid'. Comparisons involving quantity or numerical value include colloquial Russian 'tonna' ('tonne') for 'grand', 'thousand roubles', and colloquial French 'carat' ('carat') for 'year', 'age'.

9 According to Ogechi (2005: 344), the use of the noun 'teke' to refer to a beautiful woman may be associated with the attractiveness of a woman's leg as a sign of beauty. The significance of the leg, which is obviously used to kick, may well relate to the use of 'teke' in the Swahili saying 'asante ya punda ni mateke' – 'a donkey's thank-you is a kick'. This interpretation as a probable explanation is supported by Mwihaki (2007). Associations based on body contact also include the 1960s West Bengal item 'kobji' ('wrist') for 'wrist-watch'.

Semantic change 269

10 Interestingly, Coleman (2012: 198) notes the use of 'snow' by African American writers to mean 'cocaine' from 1913. Compare also the 2009 use of 'white T-shirt', 'brown T-shirt' and 'green trainers' for 'cocaine', 'heroin' and 'cannabis', respectively, by prisoners in Rochdale, UK, as cited by Thorne (2014: 77).

An interesting additional example of identification of police officers by the colour of their uniform is provided by Mugaddam (2015: 113), who notes the Randuk use of 'loohtalij' (from Arabic for 'bar of ice') for traffic police on account of their white uniform and the colour of ice.

11 Green (2014: 70) suggests that MLE use of 'papers' may come from "white London slang or cockney". Interestingly, the same author suggests the use in English of 'paper' for 'money' as far back as 1786 (Green 2017: 297).

12 Slone (2003: 42) comments thus: "Negation of the original meaning of a word is a common process in slang ... The process of negation is a symptomatic reaction of an oppressed minority within a society, e.g. African-Americans have used a process that Sims Holt (1972) calls 'inversion': the exaggeration of labels for insult (e.g. calling a white army corporal a 'captain') or for solidarity (e.g. African-American use of 'nigger' in some circumstances)".

References

Androutsopoulos, J.K. (2000) 'Extending the concept of the (socio)linguistic variable to slang', in T. Kis (ed.) *Mia szleng*, Debrecen: Kossuth Lajos University Press. 1–21. jannisandroutsopoulos.files.wordpress.com/2009/09/slangvar.pdf, accessed April 2014.

Androutsopoulos, J. (2007) 'Style online: doing hip-hop on the German-speaking web', in P. Auer (ed.) *Style and Social Identities: Alternative Approaches to Linguistic Heterogeneity*, Berlin/New York: de Gruyter. 279–317.

Androutsopoulos, J. (2009) 'Language and the three spheres of hip-hop', in A. Ibrahim, H.S. Alim and A. Pennycook (eds.) *Global Linguistic Flows: Hip Hop Cultures, Identities, and the Politics of Language*, New Jersey: Lawrence Erlbaum. 43–62.

Bardsley, D. (2014) 'Slang in Godzone (Aotearoa – New Zealand)', in J. Coleman (ed.) *Global English Slang*, London: Routledge. 96–106.

Beazley, H. (2003) 'The construction and protection of individual and collective identities by street children and youth in Indonesia', *Children, Youth and Environments*, *13*(1), online version.

Beier, L. (1995) 'Anti-language or jargon? Canting in the English underworld in the 16th and 17th centuries', in P. Burke and R. Porter (eds.) *Languages and Jargons: Contributions to a Social History of Language*, Cambridge: Polity Press. 64–101.

Berjaoui, N. (1997) 'Parlers secrets d'El-Jadida: notes préliminaires', *Estudios de dialectología norteafricana y andalusí*, 2, 147–58.

Blake, B. (2010) *Secret Language*, Oxford: Oxford University Press.

Bosire, M. (2009) 'What makes a Sheng word unique? Lexical manipulation in mixed languages', in A. Ojo and L. Moshi (eds.) *Selected Proceedings of the 39th Annual Conference on African Linguistics*, Somerville, MA. 77–85.

Carter, R.A. (2004) *Language and Creativity*, London: Routledge.

Červenková, M. (2001) 'L'influence de l'argot sur la langue commune et les procédés de sa formation en français contemporain', *Studia Minora Facultatis Philosophicae Universitatis Brunensis*, L.(22), 77–86.

Coleman, J. (2012) *The Life of Slang*, Oxford: Oxford University Press.

Cooper, B. (1993) 'Euphemism and taboo of language (with particular reference to Russian)', *Australian Slavonic and East European Studies*, 7(2), 61–84.

270   Semantic change

Dalzell, T. (2014) 'Hip-hop slang', in J. Coleman (ed.) *Global English Slang*, London: Routledge. 15–24.
Danesi, M. (1994) *Cool: The Signs and Meanings of Adolescence*, Toronto: University of Toronto Press.
Davie, J.D. (1998) *Making sense of the* nonstandard: *a study of borrowing and word-formation in 1990s Russian youth slang, with particular reference to the language of the fanzine* (Doctoral dissertation, 2 volumes). University of Portsmouth.
Dimmendaal, G.J. (2009) 'Randuk: Arabisch in Khartoum/Sudan', 2 November.
Doran, M. (2004) 'Negotiating between bourge and racaille: Verlan as youth identity practice in suburban Paris', in A. Pavlenko and A. Blackledge (eds.) *Identities in Multilingual Contexts*, Clevedon, UK: Multilingual Matters Ltd. 93–124.
Doran, M. (2007) 'Alternative French, alternative identities: situating language in la banlieue', *Contemporary French and Francophone Studies*, *11*(4), 497–508.
Dorleijn, M., Mous, M. and Nortier, J. (2015) 'Urban youth speech styles in Kenya and the Netherlands', in J. Nortier and B.A. Svendsen (eds.) *Language, Youth and Identity in the 21st Century*, Cambridge: Cambridge University Press. 271–89.
Eble, C. (1996) *Slang and Sociability*, Chapel Hill, NC: University of North Carolina Press.
Eckert, P. (2003) 'The meaning of style', *Texas Linguistic Forum 47, Proceedings of the Eleventh Annual Symposium about Language and Society*, Austin, April, 41–53.
Eckert, P. (2005) 'Stylistic practice and the adolescent social order', in A. Williams and C. Thurlow (eds.) *Talking Adolescence: Perspectives on Communication in the Teenage Years*, New York: Peter Lang Publishing, Inc. 93–110.
Eckert, P. (2012) 'Three waves of variation study: the emergence of meaning in the study of sociolinguistic variation', *Annual Review of Anthropology*, *41*, 87–100.
Einat, T. and Einat, H. (2000) 'Inmate argot as an expression of prison subculture: the Israeli case', *The Prison Journal*, *80*(3), 309–25.
Einat T. and Livnat, Z. (2012) 'Words, values and identities: the Israeli argot (jargon) of prisoners', *International Journal of Political Science, Law and International Relations*, *2*(2), 97–118.
Einat, T. and Wall, A. (2006) 'Language, culture, and behavior in prison: the Israeli case', *Asian Criminology*, *1*, 173–89.
Ferrari, A. (2006) 'Vecteurs de la propagation du lexique sheng et invention perpétuelle de mots', *Le Français en Afrique*, *21*, 227–37.
García, M. (2005) 'Influences of gypsy *Caló* on contemporary Spanish slang', *Hispania*, *88*(4), 800–12.
Githinji, P. (2006) 'Bazes and their shibboleths: lexical variation and Sheng speakers' identity in Nairobi', *Nordic Journal of African Studies*, *15*(4), 443–72.
González, F.R. and Stenström, A. (2011) 'Expressive devices in the language of English- and Spanish-speaking youth', *Revista Alicantina de Estudios Ingleses*, *24*, 235–56.
Green, J. (2014) 'Multicultural London English: the new "youthspeak"', in J. Coleman (ed.) *Global English Slang*, London: Routledge. 62–71.
Green, J. (2016) *Slang: A Very Short Introduction*, Oxford: Oxford University Press.
Green, J. (2017) *The Stories of Slang*, London: Robinson.
Halliday, M.A.K. (1978) *Language as Social Semiotic*, London: Edward Arnold.
Harchaoui, S. (2015) 'Lexical innovations in the speech of adolescents in Oslo, Norway', *Proceedings of ConSOLE, XXIII*, 220–47.
Heller-Roazen, D. (2013) *Dark Tongues*, New York: Zone Books.
Hollington, A. (2015) 'Yarada K'wank'wa and urban youth identity in Addis Ababa', in N. Nassenstein and A. Hollington (eds.) *Youth Language Practices in Africa and Beyond*, Berlin/Boston: Walter de Gruyter, Inc. 149–68.

Hollington, A. and Makwabarara, T. (2015) 'Youth language practices in Zimbabwe', in N. Nassenstein and A. Hollington (eds.) *Youth Language Practices in Africa and Beyond*, Berlin/Boston: Walter de Gruyter, Inc. 257–70.
IRIN/Plus News (2008) '*AFRICA: mind your language – a short guide to HIV/AIDS slang*', *IRIN*, 18 June. www.irinnews.org/news/2008/06/18/mind-your-language-short-guide-hivaids-slang, accessed June 2014.
Jørgensen, A.M. (2013) 'Spanish teenage language and the COLAm-corpus', *Bergen Language and Linguistic Studies*, 3(1), 151–66 (shared through https://creativecommons. org/licenses/by/3.0/legalcode).
Kiessling, R. and Mous, M. (2004) 'Urban youth languages in Africa', *Anthropological Linguistics*, 46(3), 1–39.
Kioko, E.M. (2015) 'Regional varieties and "ethnic" registers of Sheng', in N. Nassenstein and A. Hollington (eds.) *Youth Language Practices in Africa and Beyond*, Berlin/ Boston: Walter de Gruyter, Inc. 119–47.
Kotsinas, U.-B. (1997) 'Young people's language: norm, variation and language change', in *Stockholm Studies in Modern Philology New Series 11*, Stockholm: Almqvist and Wiksell. 109–32.
Kouadio N'guessan, J. (2006) 'Le Nouchi et les rapports Dioula-Français', *Le Français en Afrique*, 21, 177–91.
Kouega, J.-P. (2003) 'Word formative processes in Camfranglais', *World Englishes*, 22(4), 511–38.
Mahler, M. (2008) *Dictionary of Spanish Slang and Colloquial Expressions*, New York: Barron's.
Mallik, B. (1972) *Language of the Underworld of West Bengal*, Calcutta: Sanskrit College Research Series No. LXXVII.
Manfredi, S. (2008) 'Rendók: a youth secret language in Sudan', *Estudios de dialectología norteafricana y andalusí*, 12, 113–29.
Mattiello, E. (2014) 'The influence of English slang on Italian', in J. Coleman (ed.) *Global English Slang*, London: Routledge. 150–9.
Maurer, D.W. (1981) *Language of the Underworld* (collected and edited by Allan W. Futrell and Charles B. Wordell), Lexington, KY: University Press of Kentucky.
Mawadza, A. (2000) 'Harare Shona slang: a linguistic study', *Zambezia*, XXVII(i), 93–101.
Mayr, A. (2004) *Prison Discourse: Language as a Means of Control and Resistance*, Basingstoke, UK: Palgrave MacMillan.
Miller, L. (2003) 'Graffiti photos: expressive art in Japanese girls' culture', *Harvard Asia Quarterly*, 7(3), 31–42.
Miller, L. (2004) 'Those naughty teenage girls: Japanese Kogals, slang, and media assessments', *Journal of Linguistic Anthropology*, 14(2), 225–47.
Morgan, M. (2002) *Language, Discourse and Power in African American Culture*, Cambridge: Cambridge University Press.
Morgan, M. (2004) 'Speech community', in A. Duranti (ed.) *A Companion to Linguistic Anthropology*, Oxford: Blackwell. 3–22.
Morgan, M. (2009) 'The African-American speech community: reality and sociolinguists', in A. Duranti (ed.) *Linguistic Anthropology*, second edition, Oxford: Blackwell. 74–92.
Mugaddam, A.H. (2012) 'Identity construction and linguistic manipulation in Randuk', paper presented at the *Youth Languages and Urban Languages in Africa Workshop*, Institut für Afrikanistik, Cologne University, Germany, 31 May–1 June.
Mugaddam, A.H. (2015) 'Identity construction and linguistic manipulation in Randuk', in N. Nassenstein and A. Hollington (eds.) *Youth Language Practices in Africa and Beyond*, Berlin/Boston: Walter de Gruyter, Inc. 99–118.

Mugaddam, A.R. (2008) 'Youth language in Khartoum', paper presented at the University of Cologne Institute for African Studies, 28 May.
Mwihaki, A. (2007) 'Viewing Sheng as a social dialect: a linguistic approach', *ChemChemi*, Kenyatta University, *4*(2), 57–75.
Namyalo, S. (2015) 'Linguistic strategies in Luyaaye: word play and conscious language manipulation', in N. Nassenstein and A. Hollington (eds.) *Youth Language Practices in Africa and Beyond*, Berlin/Boston: Walter de Gruyter, Inc. 313–44.
Nassenstein, N. (2015) 'Imvugo y'Umuhanda: youth language practices in Kigali (Rwanda)', in N. Nassenstein and A. Hollington (eds.) *Youth Language Practices in Africa and Beyond*, Berlin/Boston: Walter de Gruyter, Inc. 185–204.
Nassenstein, N. (2016) 'The new urban youth language Yabacrâne in Goma (DR Congo)', *Sociolinguistic Studies*, *10*(1–2), 235–59.
Nikitina, T.G. (2009) *Molodëzhnyi sleng: tolkovyi slovar'*, Moscow: AST: Astrel'.
Ogechi, N.O. (2005) 'On lexicalization in Sheng', *Nordic Journal of African Studies*, *14*(3), 334–55.
Pagliai, V. (2009) 'The art of dueling with words: toward a new understanding of verbal duels across the world', *Oral Tradition*, *24*(1), 61–88.
Salillas, R. (1896) *El Delincuente español – El Lenguaje (studio filológico, psicológico y sociológico) con dos vocabularios jergales*, Read Books. 2011 reprint.
Salmons, J. (1991) 'Youth language in the German Democratic Republic: its diversity and distinctiveness', *American Journal of German Linguistics and Literature*, *3*, 1–30.
Sappan, R. (1969) 'Hebrew slang and foreign loan words', *Ariel*, *25*, 75–80.
Shlyakhov V. and Adler, E. (2006) *Dictionary of Russian Slang and Colloquial Expressions*, New York: Barron's.
Sims Holt, G. (1972) 'Stylin outta the black pulpit', in T. Kochman (ed.) *Rappin and Stylin Out*, Urbana: University of Illinois Press. 189–204.
Slone, T.H. (2003) *Prokem. An Analysis of a Jakartan Slang*, Oakland: Masalai Press.
Smith-Hefner, N.J. (2007) 'Youth language, *Gaul* sociability, and the new Indonesian middle class', *Journal of Linguistic Anthropology*, *17*(2), 184–203.
Sornig, K. (1981) *Lexical Innovation: A Study of Slang, Colloquialisms and Casual Speech*, Amsterdam: John Benjamins.
Sourdot, M. (1997) 'La dynamique du français des jeunes: sept ans de mouvement à travers deux enquêtes (1987–1994)', *Langue française*, *114*, 56–81.
Stavsky, L., Mozeson, I.E. and Mozeson, D.R. (1995) *A2Z: The Book of Rap and Hip-Hop Slang*, New York: Boulevard.
Stein-Kanjora, G. (2008) '"Parler comme ça, c'est vachement cool!"', *Sociologus*, *58*(2), 117–41.
Stenström, A. (2014) *Teenage Talk: From General Characteristics to the Use of Pragmatic Markers in a Contrastive Perspective*, Basingstoke, UK: Palgrave MacMillan.
Stenström, A., Andersen, G. and Hasund, I.K. (2002) *Trends in Teenage Talk: Corpus Compilation, Analysis and Findings*, Amsterdam/Philadelphia: John Benjamins Publishing Company.
Strutz, H. (2009) *Dictionary of French Slang and Colloquial Expressions*, New York: Barron's.
Szabó, E. (2006) 'Hungarian prison slang today', *Revue d'Études Françaises*, *11*, 219–29.
Thorne, T. (1994) *Dictionary of Contemporary Slang* (1st ed.), London: Bloomsbury.
Thorne, T. (2005) *Dictionary of Contemporary Slang* (3rd ed.), London: A & C Black.
Thorne, T. (2014) 'The new canting crew', in J. Coleman (ed.), *Global English Slang*, London: Routledge. 72–82.

Vierke, C. (2015) 'Some remarks on poetic aspects of Sheng', in N. Nassenstein and A. Hollington (eds.) *Youth Language Practices in Africa and Beyond*, Berlin/Boston: Walter de Gruyter, Inc. 227–56.

Widawski, M. (2015) *African American Slang*, Cambridge: Cambridge University Press.

Wolfer, C. (2011) 'Arabic secret languages', *Folia Orientalia*, *47*, Part II.

Zarzycki, Ł. (2015) 'Socio-lingual phenomenon of the anti-language of Polish and American prison inmates', *Crossroads. A Journal of English Studies*, Wydział Filologiczny Uniwersytetu w Białymstoku, *8*, 11–23.

Zhirmunskii, V. (1936) *Natsional'nyi iazyk i sotsial'nye dialekty*, Leningrad: Khudozhestvennaia literatura.

6 The role of affixation

Introduction: a focus on suffixes

In this chapter, we turn our attention to affixation, that is, to prefixes, infixes, circumfixes and suffixes. Discussion of affixation in youth, criminal and colloquial language practices is one of the most recurrent in studies of the varieties (e.g. Gooch 1970; Mallik 1972; Khomiakov 1992; Sherzer 2002; Kießling 2004; Bosire 2009). As we saw in our exploration of affixation and borrowing in Chapter Four, affixes can be used to create new words that meet speakers' expressive and evaluative aims (e.g. 'coolos').

Within the literature, suffixation attracts great attention in particular (e.g. Mandelbaum-Reiner 1991; Červenková 2001; Ahua 2006; Doyle 2007; Doludenko 2012). In US college student usage, for example, the standard English suffix '-er', which is often used to create nouns designating the agent of an action, can be added to colloquial words such as 'bum' to create 'bummer'. Alternatively, adding '-y', which is used to create adjectives, to the nouns 'dork' or 'geek' provides 'dorky' and 'geeky' (Eble 1996: 33). In colloquial Spanish, the noun 'chorizo' ('thief') consists of the Romani word 'choro' ('thief') and the standard Spanish suffix '-izo' (Geipel 1995: 123).[1] Similarly, 1990s Russian youth language had items where the standard suffix '-ost′', which is used to create abstract nouns, was added to youth variety adjectives in 'vlomnost' ('can't be bothered feeling', from 'vlomnyi' – 'tough going'; both also seen in 2009) and 'klëvost′' ('coolness', from 'klëvyi' – 'cool') (Davie 1998: 355).

In the above examples, new words are created through adding a standard suffix to what might be described as a non-standard base, and it is the base that marks the item as indicative of youth, criminal or colloquial language and not stylistically neutral. However, in some languages it is also possible to create an item not through using a youth, criminal or colloquial word base, but by selectively using a *stylistically marked* suffix that conveys a particular connotation or connotations, not to mention social value. Good examples of the use of suffixes in this way can be seen in languages such as French, Spanish and Russian, where a word (or base) can be taken from the standard lexicon and combined with a stylistically marked suffix to produce an item which possesses a stylistic or evaluative hue not present in the original, stylistically neutral word; in some cases, this might mean replacing the word's original suffix. The result is a colloquial, criminal or youth term that can be used for jocular, deprecative and other expressive effect, with context and cotext important factors in successful use and interpretation. Examples from Russian provide a good illustration of this process, where a base ('alk') is derived from the standard noun 'alkogol''/'alkogolik' ('alcohol'/'alcoholic') and combined with various suffixes:

alkofan	produces an often jocular youth term for a heavy drinker;
alkarik	results in an often jocular term for a drunkard;
alkash	gives an often deprecative term for a heavy drinker (see also Introduction);
alkashnia	produces an often uncomplimentary collective noun for a group of drunks;*
alkushnik	results in an often derogatory term for a drunkard.

*The suffix '-nia' is often viewed as colloquial or pejorative when referring to human collectives but can also be found in stylistically neutral lexis such as 'pashnia' ('arable land').
 More broadly, the productivity of what is known as *expressive affixation* as a word-formation process in Russian is underlined by Doludenko (2012). In her study of 135 words not found in dictionaries at all or with the same sense but used on the Russian *Vkontakte* social networking site, Doludenko noted that 65 were created through affixation – 39 of these were examples of *expressive affixation*. Doludenko further observed that "[b]oth inflectional and derivational processes are used to make the language more expressive and to emphasize certain ideas that the users share in the network", and distinguished augmentative, affectionate, diminutive and pejorative meanings in suffixes (Doludenko 2012: 17–9, 22).

The use of marked suffixes to create youth, criminal and colloquial terms is fairly widespread. In Finnish, 'slang' words are often created through employing a "special 'slangy' suffix" (Nahkola and Saanilahti 1999: 76), while speakers of Bahasa Gay can also rely on unique suffixes to create new items (Boelstorff 2004: 248). Social actors engaged in rap and hip hop have also used suffixes such as the now waning and much-parodied '-izzle' for jocular and cryptic purposes (e.g. 'shizzle' for 'shit', 'sure') (Widawski 2015: 35). And those engaged in German youth language practices might employ "colloquially marked suffixes" (Androutsopoulos 2000: 11) to produce equivalents to standard words: for instance, the use of '-i' in 'Studi' for 'Student' ('student'). Finnish 'slang', English-language hip hop, Bahasa Gay and German youth language practices are not alone in this respect: García (2005: 809), for example, cites the use of *nonsense suffixes* such as '-les' in Pachuco Caló 'Mexicles' (for 'México' – 'Mexico') to enable speakers to playfully confuse and ironise.

In the two preceding examples (e.g. 'Studi', 'Mexicles'), when we compare the standard words with the alternative (non-standard) versions, we can see that there is no change in the referent: the student remains the student and Mexico is still Mexico. However, one significant difference emerges: the speaker has moved from referring to the student and Mexico in a denotative way to using a new word with a new suffix which helps connote some form of attitude and evaluation. Indeed, such suffixes, which can help to express various and often subtle degrees of emotiveness and evaluation, are often linked to youth, criminal or colloquial language, where they can enable speakers to meet their communicative goals and/or mark social affiliation, where such a link is thought to exist between suffixes/words and user groups (e.g. Chambert-Loir 1984; Mandelbaum-Reiner 1991; Grachëv 1994; Kortas 2003; Widawski 2015) (see also **Enregisterment** on page 280).[2] Using a suffix thus enables a particular attitude and social message to be imparted, and the choice of suffix becomes an important factor when a user wants to meet a particular communicative goal within a particular context (habitual and unconscious expression notwithstanding).

With varied communicative possibilities in mind, it is perhaps no surprise that languages which rely on suffixation in this way may have a number of suffixes to meet varying expressive needs. Russian is one such language, one which – in the words of Friedrich (1997, cited by Wierzbicka 1999: 218–9) – has "an enormous number of simple and complex affixes" with an "affective suffixal system" that is "more richly evolved ... than in any other Slavic language or, apparently, any language in the world" and with a system of expressive suffixation that is "imagination boggling". The use of various suffixes with 'alk' gives us a good initial taste of this system.

Some other languages also have a range of suffixes, many of which are marked as typical of demotic, youth or criminal language, on which speakers can call. As noted previously, one such language is French, which has a number of suffixes that are added to bases, including standard words, to create colloquial, criminal and youth items, including derogatory or deprecative terms.[3] Many of these are often called *pejorative* or *evaluative suffixes*.[4] Although some can also be used to create stylistically neutral words in Standard French (such as '-aille' in the collective 'volaille' – 'poultry'), several are used to create words that could be viewed as indicative of youth, criminal or colloquial language, and stylistically marked nonetheless:[5]

Standard item	Standard meaning	Suffix	Item created	New meaning
vin	wine	-asse	vinasse	cheap wine, plonk
pourri	rotten	-av(e)	pourrave	lousy, rotten
Américain	American	-loc(k)/-que	amerloc(k)/~que	Yank
matériel	equipment	-os	matos	gear, kit
crasseux	dirty, filthy	-pec	craspec	filthy; crummy*
partie	part, party	-ouse	partouse	orgy, party
bague	ring	-ouze	bagouze	ring
Arménien	Armenian	-ouche	arménouche	Armenian (*neg.*)
Américain	American	-(l)uche	amerluche	Yank
cinéma	cinema	-oche	cinoche	flicks, cinema

*Writing in the late 1990s, Sourdot (1997: 66) also notes the use of 'crade' to mean 'dirty'.

Again, it can be seen in these examples that the semantic and stylistic properties of the suffix play an important role both in marking the word as informal and/or non-standard, and in helping the speaker to signal a particular message or evaluation. These considerations help to determine how and where the suffix and word should be used: it is easy to appreciate the difference between cheap plonk and wine, and a Yank and an American. 'Wine' and 'American' are straightforward designations, whereas 'cheap plonk' points verdictively to a wine's poor quality, and 'Yank' is often disparaging.

Equally, in French expressive or evaluative suffixes can be applied to bases that are themselves associated with colloquial, youth or criminal language practices. Items such as the (youth) term 'bombax' (here – 'hottie', 'hot girl') are created by adding a suffix to a word that is already marked as indexing youth language ('bombe', also meaning 'hot girl') when used in the appropriate context. In this case, 'bombe' has been created through semantic transfer (from standard 'bombe' – 'bomb'). Other examples involving youth, criminal or colloquial bases in French include:

Base Word	Base Meaning	Suffix	Item Created	New Meaning
flic*	cop, copper	-aille	flicaille	the cops, the fuzz
défoncé†	spaced out; pie-eyed	-arès	défonçarès	spaced out; pie-eyed
mec	guy, bloke; pimp	-ton	me(c)queton, mecton	pimp, petty criminal
poulet	cop, copper	-aga	poulaga	cop, copper
trouille	fright, fear	-ard	trouillard	yellow, chicken

*'Flic' and 'mec' are widely used colloquial terms for 'copper' and 'guy', respectively.
†'Défoncé' also means 'smashed'.

As we can see, adding a marked suffix to a youth or criminal language base produces forms that are quite different from the motivating word. However, the question arises as to why such items might be created. After all, to refer to a 'cop' the speaker can notionally select 'flic' or 'poulet', as the context and the speaker's positionality dictate.

There are a few possible reasons why a marked suffix might be added to a word that is already understood to be indexical of colloquial, youth or criminal language practices. The speaker may want to more explicitly mark a given word as youth, etc.; they may want to add further emphasis to their expression through use of a suffix known to carry a particular sense or attitude (e.g. pejoration) or even add a new sense as they create a new word; or they may wish to create a word that, although substantially similar in form (e.g. to an item such as 'bombe'), feels more up-to-date, fresher, or resonant with a particular group. Whatever the motivation, the application of a marked suffix can form part of a highly creative, innovative and experimental process, as demonstrated in the following examples, where a suffix has been added to a base formed through Verlan:[6]

Original item	Verlan	Verlan + Suffix	Meaning
(les) arabes	rabza	rabzouille	Arabs*
pétasse	taspé	taspèche	fear; a mess, fix; tart; bint; queer

*Note also 'rabzette' ('girl', 'woman of North African descent'; also a nickname) consisting of 'rabza' and standard '-ette' (see illustration on page 200).

278   The role of affixation

So far, we have focused mainly on suffixation in Russian and French, with brief nods in the direction of Caló, Finnish and German. However, the principle of using suffixes to create colloquial, criminal or youth items can also be seen elsewhere. Khomiakov (1992: 97) pointed to suffixation in 1980s–1990s colloquial English when he referred to a stool pigeon being known also as a 'stoolo', 'stooly', 'stoolie' or 'stoolola'; in Sheng, *dummy affixes* such as '-o' or '-sh' may be added for stylistic or dialectal reasons: so 'chokora' ('street children'), 'darasa' ('classroom') and 'uhuru' (the name 'Uhuru') become 'chokosh', 'daroo' and 'uhush' (see also **Dummy affixes** later in the chapter); while colloquial peninsular Spanish also has a number of evaluative suffixes:

Base word	Base meaning	Suffix	Item created	New meaning
tinto	wine	-orro	tintorro	plonk, cheap wine
jefe	manager	-azo	jefazo	big shot; big boss
libro	book	-aco	libraco	trashy book; boring read
papel	paper	-eo	papeleo	red tape; bumph
abogado	lawyer	-esco	abogadesco	legal-eagle (ironic)

In contrast, some varieties, such as Randuk, may not have the same range of pejorative or expressive ('slangy') suffixes as, say, Spanish, French or Russian. Manfredi (2008), for example, was only able to identify two suffixes in his 2008 study.[7]

As we might imagine, a considerable degree of sensitivity to the language and contextual culture and social setting is required to understand the often subtle connotations that come with words created using in-group or colloquially marked suffixes, or even a standard suffix in an unexpected or pointed way (for example, the sometimes ironic use of French '-esse' in 'cheffesse' ('female boss')): if a suffix conveys criticism, is it mild or scathing?; does the suffix and its context for use suggest more than one connotation or sense?;[8] is the suffix indexical of any particular collectives? – in the case of youth language practices, with youth in general, or smaller, discrete groups?; how will its use be received by an interlocutor, and will different interlocutors understand the word differently, perhaps depending on context and different personal social history? (see also **Enregisterment** on page 280). These are important considerations, because some suffixes can help to impart quite different connotations. Gooch (1970: 20) underscores the expressive potential of diminutive, augmentative and pejorative suffixes, as well as the importance of context, in Spanish:

> Precisely because of the popular and intimate nature of the diminutive, augmentative and pejorative suffixes, words can be created which, perhaps more than any others, have to be used by the right person, in the right place, at the right time.

An example of how a word created using an *expressive suffix* might be understood differently can be seen if we return to one of the Russian items we looked at earlier, 'alkash'. As we noted in the Introduction, whereas Shlyakhov and Adler (2006: 3) document it as being "rude", Ozhegov and Shvedova (1995: 20) describe it as *prostorechie* (stigmatised colloquial Russian) and disapproving, the online *Collins Russian Dictionary* (undated) qualifies it as "pejorative", Marder (1994) sees it as "colloquial" and Nikitina (2009: 20) suggests that the item she cites is "jocular–ironic".[9] In reality, each of these meanings and senses is possible, depending on factors such as word and utterance context, newly attributed definitions at any given time, relationships between interlocutors, speaker attitude and delivery (e.g. tone, facial expression).

A further complication is that not only do some suffixes convey more than one meaning (such as '-aille'), but some can be used interchangeably. Colloquial and youth language in French have 'crado' and 'cradingue' ('filthy'), 'amerlo' and 'amerluche' ('Yank'), while Russian youth and criminal language have 'dinamshchik' and 'dinamist' ('let-down', 'unreliable person') and 'mesilovo', 'mesilovka' ('scrap', 'fight'). Additionally, the use of a suffix might result in the production of a homonym: in the 1990s French students used the term 'péteuse' ('moped'), which involved adding the suffix '-euse' to a truncated form of 'pétrolette' (also 'moped'). However, this item was also a homonym of the word 'péteuse', meaning 'pretentious person', 'coward' or 'cowardly'.

These considerations combine to make the use of many suffixes associated with youth, criminal and colloquial language a subtle affair. As they engage in the ebb and flow of everyday communication and interact with others either spontaneously or in considered fashion (see also **Conscious choice in language practice** on pages 297–8), speakers rely on a number of social, cultural and linguistic associations and cues to be able to use words and phrases both appropriately and creatively. And these associations can be deep-rooted: for example, besides referring to something that can be physically small or smaller, diminutive suffixes can also be used to express endearment, whereas augmentatives may enable more critical, negative or even pejorative hues. Moreover, Sherzer (2002: 16) notes that in languages such as Spanish words created using these suffixes are imbued with sound symbolism, where certain sounds are associated with particular notions. So, there are Spanish diminutives with *i* ('-ito', '-illo', as in 'hermanito' – 'little brother'), and augmentatives with *a* or *o* ('-aco', '-ón', as in 'hombrón' – 'big tough guy').[10] Further examples of the use of Spanish suffixes to create negative terms also include '-acho' as in 'ricacho' – 'arrogant rich guy', and '-ucha', as in 'casucha' ('hovel', from 'casa' – 'house') and the Pachuco Caló 'capirucha' ('decrepit capital city', from 'capital').

A final consideration concerning suffixes relates to their role in the creation of cryptolect. As important as the use of marked suffixes can be to the creation of youth and criminal items and the communication of stance, it is also possible that some suffixes might be used to disguise a word and hide meaning. In Randuk, for instance, the suffix '-īs', only found in Kadugli (at least in 2008), serves to change a word's form; it has no semantic value of its own. So, 'baggār' ('cattleman') becomes 'baggār-īs'.[11] A similar phenomenon has been seen in French, where suffixes with no semantic properties are added in Largonji des Louchébems to serve as a further barrier to guessing a word's meaning (for more on Largonji des Louchébems, see Chapter Eight) (see also **Dummy affixes**).

> ### Enregisterment
>
> Proposed by Agha (2003), this is the process through which a linguistic repertoire or features become(s) indexical of particular social practices and the people who undertake them. Particular sets of linguistic forms become differentiable, (widely) socially recognised and associated with places, identities, personas and their attributes within a given population. Smith-Hefner (2007) suggests, for instance, that through enregisterment, Bahasa Gaul has become broadly associated with contemporary middle-class youth culture, while Roth-Gordon (2009) discusses how 'slang' in Rio de Janeiro is enregistered where both it and its speakers are associated with blackness and social marginality.

Prefixing

The importance and role of prefixation in youth and criminal language practices vary across languages. In some languages, there are relatively few prefixes that are thought to be characteristic of or unique to youth, criminal or colloquial varieties. For example, they tend not to be productive in Bahasa Prokem, where only a small number of words have been reportedly created using a combination of 'kos-' and truncated lexis, including 'kospul' (from 'pulang' ('return home')) and 'kosmob' (from 'mobil' ('car')), and 'cong-': 'congtipu' ('trick', 'fraud') from ('tipu' – 'deceit', 'fraud'). When they are used, however, prefixes can enable emphatic expression, as can be seen in the ubiquitous English colloquial use of 'mega-' (e.g. 'megastar', 'megabucks'), or the more recent use in the UK of German 'über' (e.g. 'uber-cool', 'uber-trendy').

Given youth language's highly inventive and expressive nature, some youth make great use of prefixes as intensifiers. For example, the prefixes 'mega-' and 'súper-' are held to typify youth language practices in Spanish (Jørgensen 2013). In Japan, Kogals have been reported to frequently employ emphatic prefixes such as 'chô-', meaning 'super-' or 'ultra-', and to combine them with abbreviations: so 'chôSW' stands for a 'super bad personality', where the Roman letters 'SW' represent 'seikaku' ('personality') and 'warui' ('bad') – a phenomenon known as 'KY-go' ('KY Language') (Stanlaw 2014: 163). Indeed, Miller noted in 2004 that 'chô-' was the intensifier of choice among Kogals, although the English loan 'sûpâ-' ('super-') and Japanese 'meccha' ('awesomely') were also commonly used (Miller 2004: 232).

As well as lending expressive emphasis, the use of prefixes such as 'chô-' with abbreviations also makes new items less comprehensible to older Japanese. As we saw with suffixation, some speakers may change the form of a word by adding an affix to disguise what they are communicating (see also **Dummy affixes**). We can see this in Randuk, where prefixes can also be used for encryption. In this connection, Mugaddam (2015: 105) describes prefixation as "a very important morphological process in Randuk" that functions to hinder comprehension by out-groupers.

There is a final category of prefix that deserves recognition in discussion of youth, criminal and colloquial language – those which identify what something is not. One prefix that fulfils this role is Russian 'ne-' ('non-', 'not'), which can be seen in standard vocabulary: for example, Russian 'neurozhai' for 'poor harvest' (lit. 'non-harvest'). 'Ne-' still very much retains this negating function when combined with colloquial or youth forms, where it can help speakers to indicate their cultural and linguistic non-conformism or social opposition, describe people not in the in-group, or point to actions and concepts that are incompatible or inconsistent with in-group values or beliefs. In the following examples, we see use of the negating or absence function in youth and colloquial vocabulary:

nevrubon *(coll.)*	not getting, not twigging;
neprokhodniak *(coll.)*	something that has no chance of success;
nekaify *(yth.)*	'hassles' (from the first criminal and then youth 'kaif' – 'high', a word originally from Arabic);
neprukha *(coll.)*	'bad luck' (*neg.*, from criminal 'prukha' – 'luck', 'success');
nerusskii *(coll.)*	'bad', 'strange' (lit. 'non-Russian'). Compare the ironic 'nerus'' – 'foreigner', 'foreign language lecturer'.

Indeed, in the above examples we can see that 'ne-' can be used not just to produce a sense of negation or opposite condition, but in 'nerusskii' to quite substantively change meaning: 'nerusskii', means 'bad' or 'strange', and thus departs somewhat from its literal meaning of 'non-Russian'.

Of course, not all languages rely on prefixes to convey negation. Sherzer (2002: 89–90), for example, points to the use of a negative suffix '-suli' by the Kuna of Panama as part of their humour and language play, where 'pippisuli' ('small-negative') means 'enormous'.

Infixing

Infixing occurs when new words are created through the insertion of an affix, or sometimes even another word. In youth, criminal and colloquial varieties, infixing is often used for the purpose of language play; however, it can also serve other ends such as, for example, to disguise speech, enable a speaker to stand out from others, to lend emphatic effect, or to underscore group affiliation.

The intercalation of elements into words to create new youth or criminal language items has been evident in some languages for some considerable time. German speakers between 1583 and 1663, for instance, are believed to have created new words such as 'dipir' for 'dir' ('(to) you') (Zhirmunskii 1936: 154–5). Somewhat closer to the present day, in his study of criminal language practices in West Bengal, Mallik (1972: 82) noted words such as 'bituri' ('old woman') from 'buri' and 'kimire' ('what') from 'kire', while, more recently still, US hip hop has provided the now dated '-iz-' and '-izz-'. These infixes are mostly jocular in nature but can also be employed to mask meaning and for emphatic and euphemistic purposes (Widawski 2015: 34–5, 63; examples he cites include 'shizzit' for 'shit' and 'hizzouse' for 'house').

Indeed, a number of language varieties employ some form of infixing or interpolation to create new words. For example, Indonesian youth language, including the in-group language of school children, employs infixes such as '-arg-/-ark-' and '-ok-' (which is strongly associated with Prokem) to create their own new items where the original meaning is retained but the form is different:[12]

Base item	Base item meaning	Infix	New item	New item meaning
anjing	dog, despicable guy	-arg-	anjargin	dog
dingin	cold	-ark-	dingarkin	cold
berat	heavy, weight	-ok-	berokat	heavy, weight

As the association between '-ok-' and Prokem suggests, in some cases the insertion of a constituent may not only bring change in the form of an item but may also mark it as typical of a particular language variety (and thus social constituency). Prokem is not alone in this respect; Caló has also provided examples where insertion was used to *gitanise* Spanish verbs, as the following criminal language examples provided by Salillas (1896) indicate:

Spanish verb	Spanish meaning	Caló verb	Caló meaning
andar	to go, to walk	andivelar	to go, to walk
comprar	to buy	comprinchar	to buy
engañar	to cheat	engañisar	to cheat
ayunar	to fast	ayunisarar	to fast

Perhaps one of the most intriguing examples of infixing is to be found in French in the form of Javanais (sometimes known as *Infixing Javanais*). This was recorded in 1857 and often involved the insertion of '-av-' within syllables;[13] in this way, a word such as 'jardin' ('garden') became 'javardavin', with no change in meaning:

Base Item	Javanais Form	Meaning
poulet	pavoulavet	cop, copper*
jeudi	javeudavi	Thursday
gros, grosse	gravos, gravosse	fat

*Bullock (1996: 189) indicates that the popular usage of 'poulet' to mean 'copper' is derivable from its meaning of 'horse', not 'chicken'. The reason for this is expanded by Wise (1997: 216, endnote 5, citing Guiraud 1985), who notes that the term 'poulet' was probably influenced by Italian 'slang' 'pula' for 'polizia', and that the term's use to mean 'horse' provides the basis for a whole series of items referring to the police.

Although descriptions of Javanais as a process often cite the intercalation of '-av-', some accounts (e.g. Bullock 1996: 186, citing Queneau 1947) propose that in Javanais the inserted element might alternatively replicate the vowel found in the base. A noun such as 'midi' ('noon') would thus become 'mividin' rather than 'mavidavi'.

The height of Javanais' popularity as a means of facilitating secret communication is thought to have been the late nineteenth century; however, some people still used the mechanism in the late twentieth.[14] In some cases, Infixing Javanais could be combined with other forms of word masking, such as Largonji des Louchébems, to make recognition even more difficult. As we saw in Chapter Three, Largonji des Louchébems mostly involved substituting a word's first letter by *l* and adding the original first letter and a suffix to the end of the new base – the addition of the suffix was a further step to disguise the word's meaning. However, this model also had an amendment where a word such as 'trou' ('hole') would become 'loutré'. When this new item was then subject to Javanais, it would undergo even more change to become 'lavoutravé'.

The example of 'lavoutravé' points to a phenomenon that we have encountered in previous chapters, albeit with regard to different means of creating and extending youth and criminal lexicons: the use of more than one method to create a new item (we might also recall 'coolos' from Chapter Four). Combining mechanisms is a widespread practice among in-groups looking to develop group-specific vocabulary. In varieties such as 1980s Bahasa Prokem, for example, some words were created through inserting the infix '-ok-' and dropping the final part of the original word. So, 'rumah' ('house') would become 'rokum' while 'preman' ('street kid') became 'prokem'. Chambert-Loir (1984) also highlights the existence of a Javanese mechanism where the final part of a word was removed and 'so-' added to the beginning. Thus 'aku harep lungo' ('I want to go') would become 'soak sohar solung'.[15] Alternatively, combinations found in other language varieties such as Sheng might involve a word being borrowed, rearranged through metathesis, clipped and a suffix added, as in 'nosh' ('porn'): 'porno' (English) → 'nopo' → 'no' → 'nosh'.

A final example of infixing concerns what is sometimes termed *expletive infixation*. This is where an expletive word or euphemism is positioned within a word, for example 'absobloodylutely!' instead of 'absolutely!' in English. Unsurprisingly, the use of such infixation can bring strong and emphatic effect: there's quite a difference in emphatic force between, for example, 'hallelujah!' and 'hallebloodylujah!' or 'Armageddon' and 'Armafuckingeddon'.

Circumfixes: before and after

In some languages, affixes may be added to both edges of a word to create a new item. As we might imagine, this kind of mechanism might well result in a new word that looks substantially different from the original. In Chapter Four, for instance, we discussed the importance that some groups place on inventiveness and noted that speakers of Sheng might alter the Swahili word 'duka' ('corner store', 'shop') to become 'odukoo'. This is an example of circumfixation, where dummy affixes are added to both edges of the word: here 'o-' is added to the beginning, while 'a' is removed and replaced with '-o' (lengthened and represented orthographically as '-oo'). Apart from the clear difference in the form of the word, what is interesting about these affixes is that, much like some of the suffixes and prefixes we have already encountered, they carry no semantic value of their own; instead, their function is to change the shape of the word and make it sound different, to make it sound like Sheng (see also the next section, **Dummy affixes**).

Not all cases of circumfixation, however, involve affixes with no meaning value. In 1990s Russian youth language, for example, standard prefixes and suffixes were added to verbs such as the youth item 'torchat′' ('to get high', 'to hang about') and colloquial 'drinchat′' ('to booze') to provide 'storchat′sia' ('to die through drug use'; 'to get high together') and 'sdrinchat′sia' ('to drink oneself to death'; 'to get sloshed together'). Similarly, the noun 'liuber' ('yob') became 'sliubernut′sia' ('to join the yobs'). In these cases, the prefix 's-' was used together with the reflexive suffix '-sia' to indicate excessive or joint action (Russian largely relies on prefixes in particular to create new verbs, e.g. 'priekhat′' ('to arrive'), 'uekhat′' ('to go away')) and applies '-sia' to create reflexive verbs). A similar process to 'storchat′sia' and 'sdrinchat′sia' could also be seen in 'udolbat′sia' ('to get really high') and 'utorchat′sia' ('to get really high'), where the combined use of the prefix 'u-' and '-sia' suggests extensive state or action.[16]

Dummy affixes

In our discussion of circumfixation, we noted that speakers of Sheng might amend Swahili items such as 'duka' ('corner store', 'shop') to become 'odukoo' through the use of certain affixes. In this instance affixes were added to both edges of the base to create a word whose form differed significantly from the original. The affixes had no semantic value in their own right, but served to alter the shape and sound of the original item and to make it appear as Sheng. In this sense, the affixes helped articulate social positioning, among other things.

Such affixes, which may sometimes be described as "semantically empty" (Namyalo 2015: 336), are commonly known as *dummy affixes*. They can be found in a range of youth and criminal usage. Recorded examples include their use by speakers of Kindoubil, an urban youth language spoken in Kisangani, Democratic Republic of Congo (Wilson 2015); by those speaking Luyaaye, a youth language in Kampala, Uganda, who most commonly utilise dummy suffixes (Namyalo 2015); and by speakers of Camfranglais, who may employ the suffixes '-sh' and '-o' with truncation to provide 'takesh' ('cab') and 'loco' ('home') from the French 'taxi' ('taxi') and 'location' ('rental'). The same two dummy suffixes have also been documented as used by speakers of Sheng, resulting in items such as 'safoo' and 'chokosh' from 'safari' ('safari', 'safari rally') and 'chokora' ('street children'). The use of dummy affixes is not an entirely new phenomenon: Vierke (2015), for instance, observes that dummy affixation was found in nineteenth-century classical Swahili poetry. Nor are they limited to languages spoken in Africa: Nahkola (1999) points to the existence of a "special slang suffix" with no semantic content which can be added to create a word with the same meaning as the corresponding standard item in Finnish.

Another term that may be employed to describe affixes with no overt semantic meaning is *parasitic*. Androutsopoulos (2000: 11) points to the use of parasitic suffixes in German youth language, where '-o' can be found in adjectives such as 'tollo' ('mad', 'awesome') and 'geilo' (cool), from 'toll' and 'geil'. Sourdot (1991: 18) similarly documents the uncommon French parasitic prefixes 'bé-' and 'te-' which served to make lexis more opaque – thus 'cave' ('cellar') and 'pris' ('taken') become 'bécave' and 'tepris'.

Back formation

This is where a new word is created from an existing item which is assumed to derive from it. In colloquial English, for example, this means removing what is mistakenly considered to be an affix from 'janitor', 'burglary', flaky' and 'sleazy' to provide 'janit', 'burgle', 'flake' ('oddball') and 'sleaze'.

Other examples of back formation can be found in colloquial French where, for example, a number of nouns have been created from verbs: 'bouffe' ('grub') and 'merdouille' ('crap', 'a crock of shit') from 'bouffer' ('to eat', onomatopoeic) and 'merdouiller' ('to screw up'); while Nouchi provides the splendid 'braillé' ('smart', 'elegant') from 'débraillé' ('untidy', 'dishevelled').[17]

Summary

In this chapter, we have particularly underlined the considerable role that affixation can play in the creation of youth, criminal and colloquial items in some languages. Naturally, languages can have very different structures, and will rely on affixation to varying degrees (if at all). However, in the examples we have discussed, we can see that the use of affixes can be very important in helping a speaker to hide meaning, or to create *attitudinally loaded* items to attain communicative goals.

One important consideration that we see with items such as 'bombax' and 'lavoutravé' is that affixation can often be used in tandem with other means of word-creation. This echoes our discussion in Chapter Four, where suffixes were added to loanwords to form hybrids, and underlines both a consistent preparedness to use varied resources to create new items, and/or the intention to develop something that is clearly different from what already exists. In utilising the various resources available to them to create new words and phrases, some of which will be covered in subsequent chapters, speakers kindle the fires of linguistic creativity and novelty on the one hand, and social and interpersonal expressiveness and positioning on the other.

However, these speaker aspirations come with a caveat for the linguist researcher – to know what is thought to be typical of standard usage, and what is not. In the introduction to this chapter, we saw the use of two standard English suffixes '-er' and '-y' to create US college student terms. By definition, these suffixes are not unique to colloquial or youth language. However, as Mattiello (undated) notes, there are some that are either novel or used differently from Standard English, such as '-o' and '-ers', as in 'thicko', 'dumbo', 'saddo', 'sicko', 'preggers' and 'bonkers'.[18] And as we saw in French, there are some suffixes that are indicative of colloquial, criminal or youth varieties, such as '-os' and '-asse', and some that are also found in certain instances in Standard French, such as '-aille'. So, it is important to know which mechanisms and markers (in this case, affixes) are found solely in the colloquial, youth or criminal variety, which are most productive within those varieties, which are used more widely to create stylistically neutral (standard) items, and what conclusions can be drawn from their use in context.

Notes

1 Veraldi-Pasquale (2011: 78) lists 'choro' as meaning 'robbery', 'theft', 'damage', 'harm', 'injury'.
2 Mandelbaum-Reiner (1991: 112) notes with regard to French in-group suffixes that this kind of suffix signals the use of a variety in text, and is used as an identification call between speakers so that they can better recognise one another ("Ce type de suffixe prend valeur de signal d'argot, dans le texte, et sert à se faire "coucou" entre argotisants pour mieux se reconnaître" (my translation)).

The association between suffixes and users would also appear to be reflected to some extent in Bahasa Prokem. In his article describing Indonesian youth language practices and the criminal Bahasa Prokem, Chambert-Loir (1984: 110) suggests that "transvestites are generally known to use words with the suffix ong". To that end, he cites items such as 'polesong' (from 'polis' ('police')) and 'kemenong' (from 'ke mana' ('where to?')). Whether the transvestite community, or also the homosexual community (with whom he also links words with this suffix), was or is alone in using this suffix is implied but unclear.

With regard to the use of suffixes to express attitude in Spanish, Gooch (1970: 1) captures this well: "It can certainly be said that in Spanish the diminutive, augmentative and pejorative suffixes represent a deeply rewarding study, for they not only give contact with a very wide range of many of the most fundamental words in the language, but, in addition, they reveal speakers' and writers' attitudes, in varying circumstances, to the concepts expressed by those words." Somewhat similarly, Ahua (2006: 151) suggests that the use of Dioula suffixes such as '-ya', '-ko' and '-li' allows Nouchi speakers to express a quality or feeling or a way of being, and that their use brings "a certain impressive force".
3 The principle of substituting word endings is not new in French, for example. Roffé (1993: 223–4) points to a method in nineteenth-century French known as Le Zéral, where words ending in '-aux', '-eaux', '-ots', or '-os' would have their ending replaced with '-al'. So, 'drapeaux' ('flags') and 'boyaux' ('guts') would become 'drapal' and 'boyal'. Roffé notes that it was recorded in 1894 as being used by students, where 'zéral' meant 'zéro' ('zero').
4 Pilard (1998: 413) discusses the use of suffixes such as '-asse', '-ard', '-oche', '-os', '-ouille', '-ouiller', '-ouse' and '-muche' and states: "It must be noted that almost all

slang suffixes have a *pejorative* value in French" ("Il faut remarquer que presque tous les suffixes argotiques ont une valeur *péjorative* en français" (my translation and italics)). In her treatment of *evaluative* suffixes, Corbin (1999) includes '-asse', '-ard', '-oche', '-ot', '-ille', '-aille', '-et(te)' and '-eau/el'. Importantly, she notes that the semantic value of evaluative suffixes allows speakers to bring a quantitative judgement in terms of diminution and augmentation, or a qualitative one, which could involve a negative or positive judgement, or allows a speaker to situate himself or herself in relation to the interlocutor to indicate association, distance, and so on.

5 Over and above underlining differing interpretations of which French suffixes are pejorative, Doyle (2007: 51, 66) gives an interesting perspective where she suggests: "Pejorative suffixes in particular often fall prey to folkloric definitions, assertions that they are simply pejorative without consideration for a broader meaning or even an alternative one", and that "Slang is looked down upon if only for the fact that it has as one of its purposes to the exclusion of one or more groups of people, to create inclusion among the users of a particular slang and exclusion for those who do not use it. It is often this negative stigma which carries over onto certain suffixes, creating the negative value often attributed to them. However, this negative value is not necessarily inherently pejorative and is rather merely indicative of the suffix's label as slang, which causes it to be looked down upon".

6 Notably, inversion can also be used to create bases in Lunfardo, for example, 'batidor' ('beater', 'informer') is inverted to become 'ortiba', from which the verb 'ortibar' ('to rat', 'to inform') is created.

7 Manfredi (2008: 121) notes that he found two suffixes while discussing "ungrammatical suffixation".

8 Gronemeyer (1994: 25) observes, for example, that the Russian secondary suffix '-en′k-' has compassionate, attenuating, pejorative and ironic senses in addition to its regular profile as diminutive and affectionate, while '-enn-' and '-ushch-' can convey either positive or negative emotion. Similarly, Gooch (1970: 5) notes that in Spanish the suffix '-ito', regarded as a diminutive suffix, often expresses affection but sometimes "carries augmentative force", and can be used ironically with strong pejorative implications.

9 We can see a parallel of sorts in French. In her study of French pejorative suffixes and discussion of whether they are all pejorative, Doyle (2007: 99) notes: "There were many additional aspects of this study which surprised me. The sheer fact that there was not more agreement among authors as to the use and morphology of pejorative suffixes was one, but the most surprising was the general lack of agreement as to which suffixes were pejorative at all. Many authors disagreed as to the nature of most of the suffixes such as *-aille* and even *-asse*, ranging their descriptions from 'slang' and 'pejorative' to simply 'evaluative'."

10 The examples are mine. Jurafsky (1996: 535–6) notes that diminutives can have a number of senses, including imitation, approximation, intensity/exactness and children/offspring. He indicates that they are associated with pragmatic senses, including marking affection, contempt and playfulness in a number of languages.

A number of suffixes, including '-aco', '-aca', '-acho', '-acha', '-ucho' and '-ucha' are regarded as pejorative in Spanish and can suggest some form of undesirability or contempt. Argentinian Spanish, for instance, has the item 'escracho', meaning 'something or someone ugly or dirty', or 'something that or someone who should not be seen'.

Geipel (1995: 123) also points to the addition of popular "quasi-Caló" suffixes such as '-saro' and '-zuno' to create forms such as 'unosaro' ('one' – 'uno' + 'saro') and 'calzonzuno' ('pants' – 'calzón' + 'zuno') in Spanish Caló.

11 Not all affixes cited by Manfredi (2008: 121–2) served to hide meaning alone. He also cites the use of the suffix '-ōk' to convey positive attitude.

12 Chambert-Loir (1984: 109, 111–2) also notes that the infixes '-in-', '-arg-'/'-ark-' have been noted in Javanese. See also Slone (2003: 64–5) and Boellstorff (2004: 257).
13 Most commentators reviewed cite '-av-' and '-va-' as elements inserted as part of Javanais. Strutz (2009: v), however, also points to the use of '-ag-' in the vulgarism 'chagatte' ('pussy'), from 'chatte' ('she-cat').
14 It is possible that Javanais was used by a number of different in-groups. However, Heller-Roazen (2013: 40) indicates that Javanais was "the cryptic special tongue of nineteenth-century French prostitutes, invented, if one believes the historians, for protection from male clients".

Plénat (1991: 5–6) points out that the term 'Javanais' was used in the nineteenth century to refer to secret languages utilising affixation or substitution and displacement (such as Louchébem), although he acknowledged that it tended to be used mostly with regard to the insertion of '-av-' in syllables, or to infixing-based language varieties. He suggests, however, using the term to apply to a variety of language games or *secret languages* across languages; the term is thus sometimes used to refer to a number of *secret languages* or ludlings in the literature.
15 Notably, citing Chambert-Loir, Slone (2003: 4, 68–9) suggests that many users of Prokem items are not aware of how the words have been transformed for ludic purposes, and that Prokem "is learned organically, not formally".
16 Doludenko (2012: 24) also identifies this phenomenon in her analysis of the language of users of the Russian social networking platform *Vkontakte*, citing 'obamerikanit' sia' ('to acquire American traits') from 'Amerika' ('America').
17 An example of the removal of a supposed affix in a standard language can be seen in the etymology of the Russian 'zontik' ('umbrella'). This item was originally an eighteenth-century loanword from the Dutch 'zonnedek' ('awning', 'canopy'). When borrowed, it initially had the Russian form 'zondek', meaning 'sun canopy stretched across a deck' but was later seen as 'zontik' ('parasol', 'umbrella'), with what was believed to be a diminutive '-ik' suffix. As a result, the form 'zont', meaning 'umbrella' or 'awning', evolved in the nineteenth century without the supposed suffix (Wade 1996: 67).
18 Mattiello (undated) sees both '-o' and '-ers' as novel suffixes.

References

Agha, A. (2003) 'The social life of cultural value', *Language and Communication*, 23, 231–73.
Ahua, B.M. (2006) 'La Motivation dans les créations lexicales en Nouchi', *Le Français en Afrique*, 21, 143–57.
Androutsopoulos, J.K. (2000) 'Extending the concept of the (socio)linguistic variable to slang', in T. Kis (ed.) *Mia szleng*, Debrecen: Kossuth Lajos University Press. 1–21. jannisandroutsopoulos.files.wordpress.com/2009/09/slangvar.pdf, accessed April 2014.
Boellstorff, T. (2004) '*Gay* language and Indonesia: registering belonging', *Journal of Linguistic Anthropology*, 14(2), 248–68.
Bosire, M. (2009) 'What makes a Sheng word unique? Lexical manipulation in mixed languages', in A. Ojo and L. Moshi (eds.) *Selected Proceedings of the 39th Annual Conference on African Linguistics*, Somerville, MA. 77–85.
Bullock, B. (1996) 'Popular derivation and linguistic inquiry: Les Javanais', *The French Review*, 70(2), 180–91.
Červenková, M. (2001) 'L'influence de l'argot sur la langue commune et les procédés de sa formation en français contemporain', *Studia Minora Facultatis Philosophicae Universitatis Brunensis*, L.(22), 77–86.
Chambert-Loir, H. (1984) 'Those who speak Prokem', *Indonesia*, 37, 105–17.

Collins Russian–English Dictionary, online version, via dictionary.reverso.net/english-russian/, accessed July 2016.
Corbin, D. (1999) 'Pour une théorie sémantique de la catégorisation affixale', *Faits de langues*, 14(Octobre), 65–77.
Davie, J.D. (1998) Making sense of the nonstandard: a study of borrowing and word-formation in 1990s Russian youth slang, with particular reference to the language of the fanzine (Doctoral dissertation, 2 volumes). University of Portsmouth.
Doludenko, E. (2012) 'Morphological analysis of the lexicon used in the Russian social network "Vkontakte"', *Studies in the Linguistic Sciences: Illinois Working Papers*, 17–31.
Doyle, E. (2007) French pejorative suffixes: meaning and morphology (Master's thesis). Indiana State University.
Eble, C. (1996) *Slang and Sociability*, Chapel Hill, NC: University of North Carolina Press.
Friedrich, P. (1997) 'Dialogue in lyric narrative', in. M. Macovski (ed.) *Dialogue and Critical Discourse: Language, Culture, Critical Theory*, New York: Oxford University Press. 79–98.
García, M. (2005) 'Influences of gypsy *Caló* on contemporary Spanish slang', *Hispania*, *88*(4), 800–12.
Geipel, J. (1995) 'Caló: the "secret" language of the gypsies of Spain', in P. Burke and R. Porter (eds.) *Languages and Jargons: Contributions to a Social History of Language*, Cambridge: Polity Press. 102–32.
Gooch, A. (1970) *Diminutive, Augmentative and Pejorative Suffixes in Modern Spanish* (2nd ed.), Oxford: Pergamon Press, Ltd.
Grachëv, M.A. (1994) 'Ob etimologii v russkom argo', *Russkaia rech'*, *4*, 67–70.
Gronemeyer, C. (1994) 'Productivity in derivational morphology – a case study of Russian secondary suffixes', *Lund University Department of Linguistics Working Papers*, *42*, 15–33.
Heller-Roazen, D. (2013) *Dark Tongues*, New York: Zone Books.
Jørgensen, A.M. (2013) 'Spanish teenage language and the COLAm-corpus', *Bergen Language and Linguistic Studies*, *3*(1), 151–166 (shared through https://creative commons.org/licenses/by/3.0/legalcode).
Jurafsky, D. (1996) 'Universal tendencies in the semantics of the diminutive', *Language*, *72*(3), 533–78.
Khomiakov, V.A. (1992) 'Nekotorye tipologicheskie osobennosti nestandartnoi leksiki angliiskogo, frantsuzskogo i russkogo iazykov', *Voprosy iazykoznaniia*, *3*, 94–105.
Kießling, R. (2004) 'bàk mwà mè dó – Camfranglais in Cameroon', *Lingua Posnaniensis*, *47*. www.aai.uni-hamburg.de/afrika/personen/kiessling/medien/kiessling-2004-camfranglais. pdf, accessed September 2012.
Kortas, J. (2003) 'Expressivité Dérivationnelle en Français Contemporain: Noms d'Action', *Studia Romanica Posnaniensia*, Poznań, Adam Mickiewicz University Press, Vol. XXIX, 155–70.
Mallik, B. (1972) *Language of the Underworld of West Bengal*, Calcutta: Sanskrit College Research Series No. LXXVII.
Mandelbaum-Reiner, F. (1991) 'Suffixation gratuite et signalétique textuelle d'argot', *Langue Française*, *90*, 106–12.
Manfredi, S. (2008) 'Rendók: a youth secret language in Sudan', *Estudios de dialectología norteafricana y andalusí*, *12*, 113–29.
Marder, S. (1994) *A Supplementary Russian–English Dictionary*, Columbus, OH: Slavica Publishers, Inc.

Mattiello, E. (undated) 'The pervasiveness of slang in Standard and non-Standard English'. www.ledonline.it/mpw/allegati/mpw0506mattiello.pdf, accessed December 2012.

Miller, L. (2004) 'Those naughty teenage girls: Japanese Kogals, slang, and media assessments', *Journal of Linguistic Anthropology*, 14(2), 225–47.

Mugaddam, A.H. (2015) 'Identity construction and linguistic manipulation in Randuk', in N. Nassenstein and A. Hollington (eds.) *Youth Language Practices in Africa and Beyond*, Berlin/Boston: Walter de Gruyter, Inc. 99–118.

Nahkola, K. (1999) 'Aspects of word formation in Finnish slang', online abstract, *Virittäjä Magazine*, 2(103). www.kotikielenseura.fi/virittaja/hakemistot/jutut/vir99nahkola.html, accessed July 2013.

Nahkola, K. and Saanilahti, M. (1999) 'Finnish slang as a linguistic and social phenomenon', in A. Fenyvesi, T. Kis and J.S. Várnai (eds.) *Tanulmányok a szleng fogalmáról*, Debrecen; Kossuth Egyetemi Kiadó, 76.

Namyalo, S. (2015) 'Linguistic strategies in Luyaaye: word play and conscious language manipulation', in N. Nassenstein and A. Hollington (eds.) *Youth Language Practices in Africa and Beyond*, Berlin/Boston: Walter de Gruyter, Inc. 313–44.

Nikitina, T.G. (2009) *Molodëzhnyi sleng: tolkovyi slovar'*, Moscow: AST: Astrel'.

Ozhegov, S.I. and Shvedova, N.Iu. (1995) *Tolkovyi slovar' russkogo iazyka*, Moscow: Az''.

Pilard, G. (1998) 'Argot, slang et lexicographie bilingue', *Eurelex '98 Proceedings*, 411–20. www.euralex.org.

Plénat, M. (1991) 'Présentation des javanais', *Langages*, 101, 5–10.

Roffé, A. (1993) 'Dénominations des argot en France', *Revista de Filología Francesa*, 4, 215–29.

Roth-Gordon, J. (2009) 'The language that came down the hill', *American Anthropologist*, 111(1), 57–68.

Salillas, R. (1896) *El Delincuente español – El Lenguaje (studio filológico, psicológico y sociológico) con dos vocabularios jergales*, Read Books. 2011 reprint.

Sherzer, J. (2002) *Speech Play and Verbal Art*, Austin, TX: University of Texas Press.

Shlyakhov V. and Adler, E. (2006) *Dictionary of Russian Slang and Colloquial Expressions*, New York: Barron's.

Slone, T.H. (2003) *Prokem. An Analysis of a Jakartan Slang*, Oakland: Masalai Press.

Smith-Hefner, N.J. (2007) 'Youth language, *Gaul* sociability, and the new Indonesian middle class', *Journal of Linguistic Anthropology*, 17(2), 184–203.

Sourdot, M. (1991) 'Argot, jargon, jargot', *Langue française*, 90, 13–27.

Sourdot, M. (1997) 'La dynamique du français des jeunes: sept ans de mouvement à travers deux enquêtes (1987–1994)', *Langue française*, 114, 56–81.

Stanlaw, J. (2014) 'Some trends in Japanese slang', in J. Coleman (ed.) *Global English Slang*, London: Routledge. 160–70.

Strutz, H. (2009) *Dictionary of French Slang and Colloquial Expressions*, New York: Barron's.

Veraldi-Pasquale, G. (2011) *Vocabulario de caló-español*, Bubok Publishing S.L.

Vierke, C. (2015) 'Some remarks on poetic aspects of Sheng', in N. Nassenstein and A. Hollington (eds.) *Youth Language Practices in Africa and Beyond*, Berlin/Boston: Walter de Gruyter, Inc. 227–256.

Wade, T. (1996) *Russian Etymological Dictionary*, London: Bristol Classical Press.

Widawski, M. (2015) *African American Slang*, Cambridge: Cambridge University Press.

Wierzbicka, A. (1999) *Emotions Across Languages and Cultures*, Cambridge: Cambridge University Press.

Wilson, C. (2015) 'Kindoubil: urban youth languages in Kisangani', in N. Nassenstein and A. Hollington (eds.) *Youth Language Practices in Africa and Beyond*, Berlin/Boston: Walter de Gruyter, Inc. 293–311.
Wise, H. (1997) *The Vocabulary of Modern French*, London: Routledge.
Zhirmunskii, V. (1936) *Natsional'nyi iazyk i sotsial'nye dialekty*, Leningrad: Khudozhestvennaia literatura.

7 Compounding and reduplication

Introduction

In basic terms, compounding involves joining together separate words to create a new item of vocabulary. This method of word-formation is frequently encountered in some standard language varieties. English makes extensive use of compounding, for example – 'boyfriend' ('boy' + 'friend'), 'headache' ('head' + 'ache') and 'blackbird' ('black' + 'bird'); while French has 'lave-vaisselle' ('dishwasher') and 'pare-brise' ('windscreen'); and Russian – 'student-inostranets' ('foreign student'). A variety of word classes such as nouns, adjectives and adverbs can form part of compounds, as can – much less commonly in English, at least – letters, as Widawski (2015: 22) documents in his study of African American 'slang' (e.g. 'A-Town' for 'Atlanta, Georgia').

In youth, criminal and colloquial language, compounding variously allows a speaker to be specific, creative and expressive. In varieties such as 1990s US college language and present-day colloquial English (UK and US), it has proved to be a popular method for creating lexis that can refer to someone in an informal, ironic, humorous, irreverent or even rude way. A variety of items with the word 'head', for example, refer to a person, often negatively:

pothead	marijuana smoker	petrolhead	car enthusiast
crackhead	user of crack	thickhead	dunce, dimwit
pisshead	habitual drunk	airhead	fool, empty-headed person
metalhead	fan of heavy metal	dunderhead	dimwit, oaf*

*Breva Claramonte and García Alonso (1993: 25, endnote 8) point out that 'head' "increased in productivity as the main element of compounds in the 1960s and 1970s in connection with the drug culture. It meant a hippy or a person who drops out of society because of drug use". They also observe that 'deadhead' had existed in Britain since 1841. Vulgar terms with 'head' include 'dickhead' and 'shithead'.

In her engaging analysis of 1970s–1990s US college student usage, Eble (1996) noted that compounding was a major source of new vocabulary. She found that compounds were often easy to understand when used in a context, breathed new life into old or more routine information, and often relied on metaphor, metonymy, or linguistic–cultural knowledge to be used successfully – for instance, 'sofa spud' for 'couch potato', 'lunch box' for 'out to lunch' (i.e. someone out of touch with reality)

(Eble 1996: 31). In terms of their composition, she cited combinations of lexis from two word classes that might create an item belonging to a third, for example an adjective and a noun to create an adverb in 'big time'; and observed that some compounds can be grammatically ambiguous: 'face rape' could be Noun + Noun (for 'passionate kissing') or Noun + Verb ('kiss passionately') (Eble 1996: 31).

It is undoubtedly the case that compounding has been used to great effect in English (other examples include the disparaging 'ratbag', 'dirtbag', 'scumbag', 'shitbag' and so on). However, the mechanism has been used to create eye-catching and clever terms in other languages also. Examination of the language practices of criminals in 1960s West Bengal, for instance, shows that compounding was a particularly productive form of lexical creation among them. For example:

ābchā-megh	'dark night', from 'ābchā' ('fleeting shadow') and 'megh' ('cloud');
nalgiṭṭi	'bullet', from 'nal' ('gun') and 'giṭṭi' ('broken stone or brick pieces'), a Bengali–Hindi compound.

Indeed, compounding is not a recent phenomenon, and has been used to create youth and criminal items in some languages for quite some time. In his nineteenth-century study of Spanish criminal language practices, for example, Salillas (1896) pointed to compounds such as 'guardacoimas' ('brothel keeper's servant'), which was derived from standard 'guardar' ('to keep') and the criminal 'coimas' ('hookers').

Composition, and extending expressive and descriptive boundaries

Given that words from a number of different classes can be used to create compounds, many kinds of word combination are possible, for instance, Noun + Noun, Noun + Adjective, Verb + Verb, and so on. The following sample provides a few examples where words are brought together to create a noun, adjective or verb. The first involves Noun + Noun combinations. These have been held to be particularly prolific in colloquial French (Verdelhan-Bourgade 1991: 71) and by some margin the most common in African American 'slang' (Widawski 2015: 20), while Eble (1996: 31) stated that they were the most frequently found in her study.

Noun + Noun (to create a noun):	
1960s West Bengal criminals:	
kāli-billi	'taxi cab', especially used by burglars as they steal; from 'kali' ('dark colour of cab') and 'billi' ('cat', due to its motion);
2006 Russian criminals:	
blatkhata	'den', 'place of illegal or seedy activities' (such as gambling, prostitution or drinking); from the colloquial 'blat' ('pull', 'connections') and the mainly dialectal 'khata' ('house', ultimately from Ukrainian or Belarussian);*

Noun + Adjective (to create a noun or adjective):

1960s West Bengal criminals:

kāli-pharsā 'dark, rainy night'; from 'kāli' ('ink', here used to refer to rain) and 'pharsā' ('fair');

1990s Russian youth:

tomveitsopodobnyi 'Tom Waits-like'; from 'Tom Waits' and 'podobnyi' ('similar');

2003 Camfranglais:

cou-plié 'stout rich man'; from French 'cou' ('neck') and 'plié' ('folded');

Verb + Verb (to create a noun):

1960s West Bengal criminals:

calā-khāoā 'member of kidnapping gang who does the scouting before the act'; from 'calā' ('to move') and 'khāoā' ('to eat');

Numeral + Noun (to create a noun):

1990s Côte d'Ivoire:

deux doigts 'pickpocket', from 'two fingers';

Noun + Numeral (to create a verb):

2003 Camfranglais:

Renault-deux 'to tramp', from 'Renault' (car make) and French 'deux' ('two'), representing a pedestrian's feet.

---

*'Blat' was originally associated with criminals and criminality. Grachëv (2003: 80–2) also notes other compound forms which include 'blat': 'blat-zadachnik' ('argot/criminal dictionary' – lit. 'criminal problem book'), 'blatkvartira' ('den' – lit. 'criminal quarters'), 'blatkomitet' ('criminal meeting' – lit. 'criminal committee'), 'blatpedali' ('computer keys' – lit. 'criminal pedals') and 'blat-khaza' ('den' – lit. 'criminal house').

As Eble (1996: 31) intimates, some compounds may rely on meaning change (metaphor, metonymy) or cultural appreciation for the new item to work, hence 'dead soldier' is a metaphor for an empty beer container (notably, empty beer glasses in the UK are often called 'dead'), while a 'wounded soldier' is a partially empty one. An awareness of words from different stylistic categories can also be important, as 'guardacoimas' and the 2009 Russian 'biznesment' show. An item that sounds like the standard 'biznesmen' ('businessman'), 'biznesment' is used to refer to a corrupt policeman and involves the joining of standard 'biznes' ('business', which can also refer to shady dealings) and criminal 'ment' ('pig', 'cop').

Compounds need not be limited, of course, to two elements. Arguably some of the most expressive, if not impressive, examples of compounding in colloquial Russian and Russian youth language practices over the last 25 years or so have involved the use of three or more elements to add a sense of specificity and/or jocularity:

1990s:	'stëb-rok-bard' ('satirical rock-bard');
2006:	'tele-moto-baba-liubitel'' ('skirt-chaser', 'playboy').

Indeed, the concatenation of several items to create highly descriptive, expressive and sophisticated forms is demonstrated in the following 1991 example from the Russian magazine *Mitsar*:

Rezul'tat ili Providenie, s techeniem obstoiatel'stv vstrechaetsia kuchka nenormal'nykh panko-khipo-roko-psikhodelo-teatralo-foto-kino-radio-avto-moto-seksualov.

Result or Providence, but with the flow of events you meet a small group of wacky punk-hip-rock-psychedelic-theatrical-photographic-cinematic-radio-auto-motor-sexuals.

(Mitsar 1991: 51)

The creation of compounds can often have a phonological dimension to it also, with some forms based on rhyming or similar-sounding elements. Eble's 1996 study of US college student language, for instance, cited items such as 'sight delight' ('good-looking guy') and 'frat rat' ('member of a fraternity'), while examples from other languages also show either full or partial reduplication. Colloquial French, for example, has 'copain-copain' ('buddy-buddy', from standard 'copain' – 'friend') and 'fric-frac' ('burglary'), while Russian *prostorechie* has the dismissive 'tary-bary' ('blah-blah-blah', 'tittle-tattle', 'empty talk', sometimes seen as 'tary-bary-rastabary'; see also Chapter Eight and **Reduplication** later in this chapter).

Blends

Also known sometimes as *portmanteau words*, blends are typically formed by combining elements of two words, as we see in English 'smog' from 'smoke' and 'fog'. In the example of 'smog', the first and last parts of the words in question are brought together, as are aspects of their meaning. This method enables users to create inventive and clever forms, ranging from the light-hearted to the dismissive or off-hand, which push the stylistic boundaries of the language. A number of particularly inventive items can be seen across youth, criminal and colloquial varieties:

1960s West Bengal criminals:	ghapā	'den', from 'ghar' ('room') and 'gopā' (c.f. 'gopan' – 'concealment');
	bharoti	'late midnight', from 'bhor' ('dawn') and 'rāti' ('night');
1970s–1990s US college students:	droned	'out of it (from drink and drugs)', from 'drunk' and 'stoned';
2009 French:	alicament	'therapeutic food', from 'aliment' ('food') and 'medicament' ('medicine').

Additionally, some blends are based on how alike certain words, or parts of words, might sound. In these cases, the speaker plays on similarity to create a new item the use of which may have some form of evaluation, attitude or connotation attached. This process can be seen in the French 'beurgeois' ('highly assimilated person of North African descent'), which acts on 'beur' and 'bourgeois'; in Spanish 'burrócrata' ('stupid bureaucrat'), which plays on 'burro' ('ass', 'dimwit') and 'burócrata' ('bureaucrat'); and in the Russian 'kabakterii' ('restaurant'): Shlyakhov and Adler (2006: 113) and Nikitina (2009: 300) note that this is a jocular play on 'kabak' ('bad restaurant', 'dive') and 'kafeterii' ('cafeteria'). However, the presence of the bulk of the word 'bakteriia' ('bacteria') is surely no accident.

Satire about officialdom: stump compounds

Stump compounds are created through joining a number of truncated forms to produce a new item. In some languages, this type of compounding, along with the abundant creation and use of acronyms, can be associated with bureaucratic language and military jargon – Slone (2003) associates the proliferation of acronyms in Indonesia with the Sukarno era (1945–67), for example. In view of this link to bureaucracy and the military, stump compounds were also unsurprisingly popular in Soviet-era Russian, for example, where combinations of initial elements provided 'komandarm' from 'komanduiushchii armiei' ('army commander'); 'disbat' from 'distsiplinarnyi batal'on' ('disciplinary battalion'); and 'sukhpai' from 'sukhoi paëk' ('dry ration'). A more recent Russian military example takes the shape of 'morpekh' ('marine'), from 'morskaia' ('marine') and 'pekhota' ('infantry') (see also **Acronyms** in Chapter Nine).

Hybrid forms

This category of compound incorporates items from different languages or language varieties. In some cases, the use of hybrid forms as a means of creating new lexis is not new: in his 1896 analysis of Spanish criminal language, for example, Salillas recorded the use of 'gurapandó' ('sun') from Germanía 'gura' ('justice') and Caló 'pandar' ('to tie up', 'to roll up', 'to squeeze'), reportedly due to the sun being a finder of criminals. Several decades later, and in quite another part of the world, Mallik (1972: 47) recorded 'cākār-line' ('railroad'), from Bengali 'cākā' ('wheel') and English 'line', while Kouega (2003: 523) documented the Camfranglais compound 'big rémé' ('grandmother'), from English 'big' and 'rémé', an inverted form of French 'mère' ('mother').

Additionally, as we saw in Chapter Four, some compounds may consist of words in different alphabets:

техно-dance party	'techno dance party', from the Russian loanword 'техно' ('techno') and the English 'dance party', used in 1990s Russian youth language.

In some languages or varieties, the use of words of foreign origin in compounds is not unusual. For instance, magazines and fanzines written by and for youth in 1990s Russia contained many examples of loanwords combined with Russian lexis:

pank-boginia	'punk goddess', from English 'punk' and Russian 'boginia' ('goddess');
tresh-korol'	'thrash king', from English 'thrash' and Russian 'korol'' ('king').

This trend would appear to have continued in the language with items such as 'putiniugend' ('pro-Putin youth'), which incorporates the name of the Russian president and the German 'Jugend' ('youth'). A pointed allusion to the Hitler Youth ('Hitlerjugend') almost certainly figures in such usage, which was recorded in 2009.

Conscious choice in language practice

Language can be deliberately used by social actors to achieve particular goals. Cryptolect, for example, is mostly created with a specific aim in mind: so that others can't understand what is being communicated. Equally, in verbal duelling phrases are deliberately used to gain social capital; while speakers of Nouchi and Camfranglais (and others) have been documented as intentionally distorting the language of the establishment/élite as a sign of protest (e.g. Kießling 2004; Vakunta 2011). With euphemisms, a conscious move is also made to mitigate offence or observe social or interpersonal sensitivities.

Many examples of items created through conscious use are cited in this book. These range from those invented through inversion and the transposition of syllables in Sheng and Randuk, or non-transliteration and non-translation in Japanese or Russian youth text, to the use of more than one mechanism to create new lexis – for example, hybrid compounds in criminal language practices in West Bengal, or Verlan and suffixation. In many cases, speakers aim to achieve an appreciable effect, which suggests some thought may be given as to whether the linguistic means is likely to meet a social end. However, this does not account for all usage. One speaker may use a given term, aware of the underlying mechanisms (perhaps as its creator); however, others may later use it as an established lexicalised in-group item, unaware of derivational intricacies, as a matter of routine or even unconsciously (see, for example, Mallik and Stein-Kanjora's drivers behind usage in Chapter Three and **Communication Accommodation Theory (CAT)**).

Particular attention should be given to what is considered to constitute vernacular usage, or whether some varieties enjoy the status of vernaculars. We have noted that Nouchi, Sheng and Camfranglais have become sufficiently widespread as to be considered vernaculars. Vernaculars can be seen as a "'basic', unmarked, unreflecting, unmonitored variety" (Cheshire, Nortier and Adger 2015: 3, noting Labov's view of the vernacular). Sheng and others may well fit this description, although the sociolinguistic picture across geographical spaces can vary (e.g. Kioko 2015). At the same time, Cheshire, Nortier and Adger (2015: 3) also note that multiethnolects, for example, cannot be universally regarded as vernaculars because their use is sometimes documented as "deliberate and marked". Indeed, Dorleijn and Nortier (2013: 8) report that "metalinguistic awareness among speakers of multi-ethnolects is high … the use of multi-ethnolects is a deliberate choice". Questions of the definition of **vernacular** usage and of intentional selection, particularly where speakers are seen as social actors consciously engaging in stylistic practices, are thus important to how we understand the social significance attached to a speaker's language practices.

Reduplication

Reduplication is where a new item is created through the repetition of all or part of a base word. In English, for instance, we can see examples of *exact* or *full reduplication* where people talk about a 'no-no', *rhyming reduplication* in 'super-duper', or *ablaut reduplication*, where the vowel is replaced, in the dismissive 'riff raff'. Reduplication can be used in a number of ways and for a number of purposes across many languages. For example, in some languages full reduplication can be used to create plural nouns. It is not surprising, therefore, that Sornig (1981: 26) describes reduplication as something that "has always been a familiar and common device in grammar and word-formation".

Reduplication is fairly commonplace in youth, criminal and colloquial varieties, not only in English, but also in French, Russian and other languages. Furthermore, it is not a recent invention: the French 'frou-frou' ('burglar's or thief's master key'), for instance, is believed to come from old French criminal language, having been documented at least in the late-nineteenth century (Boutler 2012); while colloquial English 'hurly-burly' dates back to 1530 (*Slang Phonology* 2014).[1]

There are many reasons why reduplication might be employed in youth, criminal and colloquial language. In his very engaging discussion of the subject Sherzer (2002: 17), for example, points out that it can be particularly typical of "baby/caretaker talk, the language of respect as well as insult, and emotive language", that it is used to mark out augmentation, diminution, endearment and contempt, and that it is "often felt to be playful, even humorous and/or aesthetically pleasing" (see also Sherzer 2002: 18–25 for further discussion). It can thus help speakers to meet the (evaluative) communicative goals they want to reach: for instance, disparaging others through descriptors such as 'namby pamby', 'wishy-washy' or 'hoity-toity' in English. Equally, it may be used to foreground close social relationships through the informal, if not sometimes endearing, 'night-night' or 'bye-bye'. Examples of *full reduplication*, where there is complete repetition of the word, include:

1990s US rap and hip hop:	boo-boo	'girlfriend' (Stavsky, Mozeson, Mozeson 1995: 10);
2006 colloquial Russian:	vas'-vas'	'on first name terms', from a form of the name 'Vasia'.

As we saw with 'super-duper' and 'riff raff', there are items where the second element largely, but not wholly, replicates the first. Terms created through rhyming reduplication often (but not always) involve change in the initial consonant. Together with ablaut reduplication, this mechanism has also been found in criminal language practices in West Bengal, in Russian *prostorechie* and in colloquial French:

1960s West Bengal criminals:	gāḍḍā guḍḍā	'danger', from the Hindi for 'ditch';
2006 Russian *prostorechie*:	tyr-pyr	'any which way', 'pointlessly', 'no way out';*
2009 colloquial French:	ric-rac	'strict', 'touch-and-go'.

*For example, 'Otvechaiu na ekzamene, tyr-pyr, vizhu, govoriu ne to' ('I was just answering at random on the exam; I could see that what I was saying wasn't right') (Shlyakhov and Adler 2006: 278).

In some instances, the forms that are reproduced may be clipped, for example through *apocope*, where part of the end of a word is dropped, or through *aphaeresis*, where an element from the beginning is discarded. In her study of French 'argot', for example, Červenková (2001: 82) cites items consisting of clipped constituents ('gogo' for 'gobeur' – 'easily taken in'), some of which may be used for and with children ('mémé' for 'grand-mère' – 'grandmother'). Other examples of reduplicated clipped forms in colloquial French include:

cracra	'filthy', presumably from standard 'crasseux' ('dirty');
gengen	'money', from phonetic rendering of 'gent' in 'argent' ('money');
zonzon	'prison', from phonetic rendering of 'son' in 'prison' ('prison').

Summary

In keeping with examples cited in other chapters, items formed through compounding, blending and reduplication remind us of the varied means by which speakers can seek to achieve particular goals. We have seen that a variety of word classes can be represented in compound forms, ranging from Noun + Noun to Verb + Verb. We have also seen that, in some cases, compounds may have a hybrid character, for example, where different orthographic systems or words from different languages are in evidence. One way or another, in items such as 'burrócrata', 'blockhead' and 'tyr-pyr', we can see the speaker's desire to create evaluative, expressive terms which point to how they feel about what they are referencing – such as in a critical, dismissive and/or ironic way – or to create semantically opaque lexis to hide meaning (viz. 'calā-khāoā'). At the same time, it is evident that in items such as 'blatkhata', a real sense of specificity can be discerned – the 'blatkhata' is no everyday or ordinary house, or 'khata'; it is a place where under-the-counter, illegal and socially questionable acts occur. So, a new word emerges with a new meaning.

As with other coined items (for more see Chapter Four), sometimes compound forms come to light spontaneously and are sufficiently funny, catchy and so on to become part or typical of an individual's or group's repertoire. In other cases, they can be consciously created and tested: a speaker thinks up a new combination and introduces it into a conversation in the hope that the desired communicative goal is reached. Others hearing the new item may react with a smile or with surprise because the combination is unexpected and/or because it facilitates what they as speakers might also want to achieve. They may then start using it themselves. Alternatively, they may opt to use it temporarily or not at all, thereby shortening the item's life cycle. When such items are adopted, it can be argued that this acceptance testifies both to the inventiveness that underpins their creation and the social interaction insights with which they have been shaped. Such acceptance points to the inventor's awareness of and sensitivity to meaning, sound, expectation, and a whole range of contextual considerations and processes that wrap around what is written or said. When seen in this light, the fact that successful compounding or reduplication might involve other mechanisms such as borrowing or truncation ('gengen', 'zonzon') speaks even more to the intelligence behind the creation of some youth, criminal and colloquial items.

Note

1 The *Slang Phonology* web site contains an interesting overview of sound repetition/reduplication in English.

It is also worth noting that reduplication need not consist of one instance of repetition. Khomiakov (1992: 98) notes the use of the French 'bla-bla-bla' ('waffle', 'chatter'), for instance; this, of course, is mirrored in the English 'blah-blah-blah'.

References

Boutler, C. (2012) *Argoji*. www.russki-mat.net/page.php?l=FrFr&a=Frou-Frou, accessed December 2017.

Breva Claramonte, M. and García Alonso, J.I. (1993) 'Categories, morphological features, and slang in the graffiti of a United States Western university', *Revista Alicantina de Estudios Ingleses*, 6, 19–31.

Červenková, M. (2001) 'L'influence de l'argot sur la langue commune et les procédés de sa formation en français contemporain', *Studia Minora Facultatis Philosophicae Universitatis Brunensis*, L.(22), 77–86.

Cheshire, J., Nortier, J. and Adger, D. (2015) 'Emerging multiethnolects in Europe', in *Queen Mary's Occasional Papers Advancing Linguistics*, 33.

Dorleijn, M. and Nortier, J. (2013) 'Multi-ethnolects: Kebabnorsk, Perkerdansk, Verlan, Kanakensprache, Straattaal, etc.', in P. Bakker and Y. Matras (eds.) *Contact Languages: A Comprehensive Guide*, Berlin: De Gruyter. 229–72.

Eble, C. (1996) *Slang and Sociability*, Chapel Hill, NC: University of North Carolina Press.

Grachëv, M.A. (2003) *Slovar' tysiacheletnego russkogo argo*, Moscow: RIPOL KLASIK.

Khomiakov, V.A. (1992) 'Nekotorye tipologicheskie osobennosti nestandartnoi leksiki angliiskogo, frantsuzskogo i russkogo iazykov', *Voprosy iazykoznaniia*, *3*, 94–105.

Kießling, R. (2004) 'bàk mwà mè dó – Camfranglais in Cameroon', *Lingua Posnaniensis*, *47*. www.aai.uni-hamburg.de/afrika/personen/kiessling/medien/kiessling-2004-camfranglais. pdf, accessed September 2012.

Kioko, E.M. (2015) 'Regional varieties and "ethnic" registers of Sheng', in N. Nassenstein and A. Hollington (eds.) *Youth Language Practices in Africa and Beyond*, Berlin/ Boston: Walter de Gruyter, Inc. 119–47.

Kouega, J.-P. (2003) 'Word formative processes in Camfranglais', *World Englishes*, *22*(4), 511–38.

Mitsar (1991), 3.

Mallik, B. (1972) *Language of the Underworld of West Bengal*, Calcutta: Sanskrit College Research Series No. LXXVII.

Nikitina, T.G. (2009) *Molodëzhnyi sleng: tolkovyi slovar'*, Moscow: AST: Astrel'.

Salillas, R. (1896) *El Delincuente español – El Lenguaje (studio filológico, psicológico y sociológico) con dos vocabularios jergales*, Read Books. 2011 reprint.

Sherzer, J. (2002) *Speech Play and Verbal Art*, Austin, TX: University of Texas Press.

Shlyakhov V. and Adler, E. (2006) *Dictionary of Russian Slang and Colloquial Expressions*, New York: Barron's.

Slang Phonology (2014). duermueller.tripod.com/slangphon.html, posted 28 April, accessed June 2015.

Slone, T.H. (2003) *Prokem. An Analysis of a Jakartan Slang*, Oakland: Masalai Press.

Sornig, K. (1981) *Lexical Innovation: A Study of Slang, Colloquialisms and Casual Speech*, Amsterdam: John Benjamins.

Stavsky, L., Mozeson, I.E. and Mozeson, D.R. (1995) *A2Z: The Book of Rap and Hip-Hop Slang*, New York: Boulevard.

Vakunta, P.W. (2011) 'Ivorian Nouchi, cousin to Cameroonian Camfranglais'. www. postnewslive.com/2011, accessed September 2012.

Verdelhan-Bourgade, M. (1991) 'Procédés sémantiques et lexicaux en francais branché', *Langue française*, *90*(1), 65–79.

Widawski, M. (2015) *African American Slang*, Cambridge: Cambridge University Press.

8 Phonetics and phonology

Introduction

There is a well-established history of phonetic and phonological manipulations being used to create new words and phrases in in-group and colloquial language. Walter (2002) suggests that language games and speech disguise typically involve the subtraction, addition, replacement or transposition of sounds, and that such alterations have been observed among many of the world's languages, from Hebrew to Cantonese.[1] In his discussion of language associated with adolescents, Androutsopoulos (2005: 1499) observes that a high incidence of "colloquial phonological processes" is sometimes considered to typify adolescent speech. Boellstorff (2004), in his analysis of Bahasa Gay, points to the popularity of substitution, where Bahasa Gay words might replace Standard Indonesian items if they share a syllable, so that 'jelek' ('bad') and 'semak' ('to like') are replaced by 'jelita' (original Indonesian meaning: 'lovely') and 'semangka' (originally: 'watermelon'). And, going further back in time, Khomiakov (1992), Blake (2010) and Coleman (2012) point to the reordering of lexis in nineteenth-century English in-group usage. For example, among traders: 'bad' and 'sweet' provided the now unused 'dab' and 'eetswe', while 'yob', which is still in use meaning 'thug', 'hoodlum', was derived from 'boy'.

The reasons for the use and productivity of phonological and phonetic methods of word-creation are many and can vary from group to group. They include: criminals changing the way a word sounds to hide intentions – in many cases, the meaning won't change as it's enough to change a word's form; street kids disguising their vocabulary for survival; speakers wishing to change their intonation to make it closer to that of foreign prestige groups; and youth engaging in language play and/or showing off or subverting others through mimicry.

As for the mechanisms themselves, these can be found in a number of languages and variously include:

- the use of accent, such as the Moroccan accent in the Netherlands, where speakers of other languages seek to align themselves with people with a Moroccan background (Dorleijn, Mous and Nortier 2015);
- a shift in stress – for example, in French, where a shift to the first syllable became more frequent in 1990s urban language; this does not accord with general

French phonological practice. We also see variant stress in colloquial Russian, for instance, 'ud<u>a</u>los'' ('succeeded') for 'udal<u>o</u>s'', including through error;[2]
- rhyming, such as Cockney rhyming slang 'dog and bone' for 'phone';
- word reordering, such as French 'kecla' for 'claque' ('smack', 'slap'), 'kecra' for 'crack' ('crack', *dr.*), 'mifa' for 'famille' ('family' – see page 205) and 'keuj' for 'Jacques' ('James'; see also page 204; 1980s Bahasa Prokem 'jaker' for 'kerja' ('work'); and Argentine 'slang' 'javie' ('old') for 'vieja' ('old', 'old woman'; 'mother'). A language game popular among some English-speaking children is Pig Latin, where consonants positioned before a word's first vowel are placed at the end of the word and are followed by '-ay'. So, 'sheet' would become 'eetshay'.

Furthermore, in some languages we can see that certain sounds can be particularly representative of colloquial, youth or other-in-group varieties. In colloquial English, for instance, "/z/ has taken on a special marked status as particularly representative of slang, since its frequency in slang is out of all proportion to its frequency in formal speech" (e.g. 'snazzy', 'fuzz', 'whiz', 'jazz') (*Slang Phonology* 2014).

What is especially interesting about some of the processes identified is that they can show a sensitivity to sound and meaning and can be used in colloquial and in-group language by a number of different groups. Some children, for example, might use rhyming words and phrases as a means of teasing (for example, 'Elvis the pelvis', 'Anna banana'), while adults might employ them for jocular, sarcastic or ironic reasons as well as different discourse functions:

1970s–1990s US college students:	'Come in, Berlin!': a call for someone to pay attention;
1990s colloquial French:	'À la tienne, Étienne!': 'Cheers!', 'Good health!' (lit. 'To yours, Étienne!');
2006 colloquial Russian:	'Genii sredi udobrenii': A phrase used to undermine someone's pretensions to cleverness (lit. 'A genius in a dung heap').

Together with the mechanisms cited later in the chapter, these examples of rhyming phrases can point to a desire to consciously play with language; to make it more colourful by replacing safer, stylistically neutral options; to give a new spin to a phrase, perhaps as a means of fun, teasing or mocking; to make an exchange more informal; and even to step back and take time out from the rigours or monotony of everyday life (for more on language play see, for instance, Sornig 1981; Crystal 1998; Sherzer 2002; Blake 2010).

Changing how a word sounds (or looks)

By replacing sounds in a word, it is possible to create entirely new lexis. This can be a fairly important mechanism in word-creation – indeed, playing with or altering expected sound is important to the cut and thrust of everyday interaction, ranging from the desire to underscore difference and/or in-group competition to engaging in banter.

Sound substitution can happen for several reasons. In addition to the motivations outlined earlier, speakers may change how a word sounds so that out-groupers cannot grasp what is being communicated. Equally, change may occur due to a desire to give a variety a particular, 'special' sound. Such an aspiration is ascribed to speakers of Sango Godobé, for example, a variety associated with street children in Bangui in the Central African Republic. Landi and Pasch (2015: 216–7) have observed that in disyllabic nouns speakers replace the vowel sequences *a – a* or *e – e* with *ú – è*: this latter sequence is regarded as uncommon in Sango, one of the country's two official languages, together with French. Nouns such as 'tèré' ('body') and 'gàrá' ('market (place)') may thus become 'túrè' and 'gúrè' and then potentially subject to syllable inversion (resulting in 'rètú' and 'règú', which have a new tonal sequence).

Alternatively, speakers may wish to signal a particular attitude (e.g. irony, sarcasm) or impart levity as part of language play. For example, in the 1990s one Russian youth magazine replaced the *zh* in the title of the Russian journal *Nauka i zhizn* (*Science and Life*) by *sh* to give the ironic *Science and Lunacy* ('shiz-' is the root for many Russian *prostorechie* items meaning 'loony' or 'nutty') (Davie 1998: 383). Similarly, deliberate change to words such as 'bumazhka' ('document') and 'detektiv' ('detective') gave rise to the ironic 'bamazhka' and 'diudiuktiv',[3] while the use by Russian goths in 2015 of 'mogil'nik' (lit. 'burial ground') to mean 'mobile (phone)' surely involved conscious consonant replacement from the regular 'mobil'nik'. Goths referring to a burial ground in this way no doubt reproduced symbolism associated with their group's stylistic practices.

Examples of sound substitution can also be found in other languages. Pilard (1998: 413), for instance, notes how in French consonant replacement brought a humorous change from the 'storming of the Bastille' ('la prise de la Bastille') to 'the storming of the arse' ('la prise de la pastille'). Other examples of sound substitution include:

1960s West Bengal criminals:	konā	'gold', from 'sonā';
1980s Indonesian Prokem:	gorang	'thief', from the criminal 'garong' ('brigand');
1997 French youth:	panoque	'panic', from 'panique' ('panic').

Changing distinct sounds in a word can also help to create euphemisms as a way of avoiding less socially acceptable, vulgar or taboo items. English, for instance, has 'beggar' for 'bugger' and 'muck about' for 'fuck about'. Some particularly interesting examples of change to avoid taboo terms can be seen in Caló, where speakers amended the Common Romani word for 'devil' ('beng') to 'mengue' (also to mean 'devil'), as found in the Spanish phrase 'Malos mengues te lleven' ('Go to hell!'), to avoid use of the word (Geipel 1995: 122). Taboo is also thought to account for other Caló distortions such as 'orú', 'orióz' and 'ollarub' to avoid pronouncing 'aruje' ('wolf') (Geipel 1995: 122) (see also **Euphemism and dysphemism** in Chapter Five).[4]

In some cases, we can see that replacement need not always occur on a like-for-like basis. As Grachëv (1994) has noted, Russian criminal language has had items such as 'vlika' ('piece of evidence') as a replacement for the standard 'ulika' – in this case, a vowel has been replaced by a consonant. Moreover, the substitution of syllables might also be seen, such as in Prokem 'murse' ('cheap') for 'murah' ('cheap'), and even in nineteenth-century Russian trader language, where words such as 'tovar' ('a good') and 'povozka' ('cart') became 'shivar' and 'shivozka' without any change in meaning. In words such as the English 'opporchancity', from 'opportunity', we see replacement arguably taken to a different level, where replacement with 'chance' (a synonym of 'opportunity') creates an item that conveys a sense of levity which 'opportunity' and 'chance' ordinarily lack (see also **Infixing** in Chapter Six).

Other ways of changing the shape and sound of a word are also possible. One such manipulation is to add letters or sounds. Again, this can help speakers to create new terms insofar as the known and expected form of the word is altered and, in some cases, a new meaning attributed (which can make the new word even more unintelligible to the uninitiated). The 'Illuminati' scrawled on a wall in Florence acquired a different sense when a *k* was added to the beginning by another individual, most likely in a pointed expression, as seen in 2012 (see also page 199). A sense of playfulness is also evidenced by the jocular Russian 'vechedrinka'. This is a version of 'vecherinka' ('party') that incorporates the English loan 'drink' through the addition of *d* to underscore the consumption of alcohol. Similarly, the addition of *m* turns Russian 'uchitel'' ('teacher') into a tormentor, in that 'muchitel'' means 'torturer'. In another context altogether, word-internal consonant doubling has also been documented, for example, by criminals in 1960s West Bengal in the item 'thābbā'.

1960s West Bengal criminals:	ārelā	'hubbub', from 'relā' ('abundance');
	thābbā	'large amount of uncounted money', from 'thābā' ('handful');
Russian criminals:	freiger	'crime victim', from criminal 'freier' ('crime victim', 'mug', 'non-crim').

The opposite mechanism to addition is vowel or consonant dropping. This can sometimes occur through relaxed pronunciation or the desire to create a new word for humorous purposes. Additionally, where youth and criminal language practices are concerned, it can also be employed to create an item that is unrecognisable to the uninitiated. Again, in some instances the meaning of the word will not need to change:

1960s West Bengal criminals:	āli	'ink', from 'kāli';
	thuri	'old woman', from 'thubri';
	gun	'danger', from 'āgun' ('fire');*
2007 Bahasa Gaul:	emang	'right', 'indeed', from 'memang';
	udah	'already', from 'sudah'.

*According to Mallik (1972: 73–4), the dropping of the initial vowel, as in 'gun', occurs where there is emphasis on the following syllable.

Furthermore, it is possible to lengthen sound for emphasis. For example, 'That is soooo not gonna happen!', 'Niiice!', 'Noo waaay!' and 'Waay!'? may be found in English. Although with sound we mainly think of the spoken mode, such emphasis can also be imparted in written language, where underlining, capitalisation, vowel repetition and punctuation help to express author attitude: 'He is totally barking!!', 'That's SO unreal!'. Two consecutive posts on one French graffiti forum provide particularly good illustrations (over and above non-standard orthography, the long-since borrowed 'cool' and Verlan 'keurma' for 'marqueur'):

> cooooooooooool ...sa fait a peu prés 10ans que tout le monde s'en sert 😊
> cooooooooooool... that means it's about 10 years that everyone's been using it ... 😊
>
> et si si sa marche TRES bien comme keurma
> and if that works VERY well as a marker

(Bombing Art, April 2006)[5]

Substitution strategies: some examples

As our nineteenth-century English and Russian criminal and trader language examples ('yob', 'shivar') suggest, changing the form of a word to hide meaning is not new to the human experience. Man has been creating substitution codes for thousands of years: both Julius Caesar and Augustus substituted letters of the alphabet to conceal messages from prying eyes, while a system known as Atbash, which saw the last letter of the Hebrew alphabet replace the first, with the penultimate replacing the second and so on, was noted in the Book of Jeremiah (Heller-Roazen 2013). With these historical precedents in mind, it is arguably not surprising to see substitution protocols practised by groups such as criminal gangs or young people in more modern times, as a few examples from Russia, Indonesia and Japan show.

In 1902, a form of word-masking was documented as being used by Russian school children to disguise commonplace words. It consisted of arranging the first ten consonants of the Cyrillic alphabet in order and lining up the last ten against them in reverse order (there was no change in vowels). This gave two rows, reproduced here in Roman letter form:

b	v	g	d	zh	z	k	l	m	n
shch	sh	ch	ts	kh	f	t	s	r	p

Swapping corresponding consonants meant that everyday words such as 'вокруг' ('vokrug' in Roman script, meaning 'around'), 'что' ('chto' – 'what') and 'друг' ('drug' – 'friend') became the very different and otherwise incomprehensible 'шотмуч' ('shotmuch'), 'гко' ('gko') and 'цмуч' ('tsmuch') (Smirnov 1902). Somewhat similarly to this, in 1952 police in the city of Sverdlovsk (now Yekaterinburg) documented the use of a code based on arranging the letters of the Cyrillic alphabet (except ё) in two parallel rows: the top consisted of the first 16 letters, *а* to *п* (in Roman *a* to *p*), and the second the letters *р* to *я* (*r* to *ia*). Letters were then swapped between the rows so that words such as 'Иван' ('Ivan') and 'убить' ('ubit′' – 'to kill') would, again, read incomprehensibly as 'штрэ' ('shtre') and 'гсшвм' ('gsshvm') (*Materialy otdela rezhima i operraboty UITLK* 1952).

The systems outlined were based on Russian, but they are conceptually close to Atbash and to a system seen in Javanese, where two columns of syllabary letters are arranged. In this case, the first ten are written from top to bottom and the second ten from the bottom up. Those letters forming pairs are then swapped, so that 'ha' is exchanged with 'nga', for example. As a result, words such as 'sewu' ('1000') and 'lanang' ('male') become 'jedu' and 'patang' (Chambert-Loir 1984).

As we can see from these examples, an element in one line has been substituted by a corresponding element from another to create entirely new vocabulary. However, it is also possible to create new sentences through reassigning the syllables of constituent words across different lines. One extravagant obfuscation mechanism employed in nineteenth-century Russian word-masking saw the phrase 'khosha delo ne veliko' ('although it's not a big deal') become 'khodeneli kovelosha':

kho		de		ne		li	
	sha		lo		ve		ko

Here, the original words are split into syllables, which are then placed alternately across two lines; the word in the second line is read in inverted syllable order (Smirnov 1902: 94).

Closer to the present day, another example of substitution can be seen in a code used by Japan's Kogals. The code, known as Gyaru moji ('Girl characters') and normally employed in text messaging, involves the use of mathematical symbols, numbers, Roman, Greek or Cyrillic letters and parts or combinations of characters to replace Japanese syllabic characters. Loanwords and symbols such as love hearts may also be used, while mathematic symbols and Greek letters might replace single-stroke hiragana characters (e.g. 'ω' for 'ん', or '§' for 'す'), and kanji characters might replace similar-looking katakana ('世' for 'せ'). Furthermore, each syllabic character may have a number of alternatives. This kind of code not only figures in texts, in part to ensure secrecy of message content from prying eyes, but also features in pointedly expressive graffiti photos. The result is an unusual and sometimes unexpected visual mix:

Gyaru moji *form*	Standard equivalent	Transliteration	Translation
⊇ω(こチ(よ	こんにちは	Konnichiwa	Hello
カゝ"ωレよ"Яĕ	がんばれ	Ganbare	Don't give up
内糸者ナニ"Ɔ	内緒だよ	Naisho da yo	It's a secret*

(Examples from *Japan Times* 2005)

*For more, see *Japan Times Kanji Clinic #69* (2005), 'Japanese girls devise their own written language' and Miller (2004: 229–30).

Stanlaw (2014: 162–5) additionally points to the use of different writing systems in Japanese for the purpose of wordplay and describes the use of *KY-go* (lit. 'KY language'), a technique popular among high school girls (among others), where Roman initials are used to refer to Japanese words and phrases. Examples cited by Stanlaw include 'IW' for 'imi wakaranai' ('I don't get it'; 意味 わからない), as well as the allocation of a Roman letter to each syllable within a word: 'kwsk' for 'kuwashiku' (詳しく) – 'in detail' (compare 'SW' in **Prefixing**, Chapter Six).

Substitution strategies also have an echo of sorts in today's Internet, where Russian again provides a particularly interesting example. In some blogging circles the Russian word дневник ('dnevnik' – 'diary') might be referred to as 'lytdybr' after Roman Leibov, one of the first main Russian Internet users and bloggers, switched from a Cyrillic to a Roman keyboard and typed 'lytdybr'. The word has since gained currency among bloggers and Internet users, with other forms such as 'PS' and 'pls' also becoming the otherwise bizarre 'ЗЫ' ('ZY' – see *eResource*) and 'зды' ('zdy'). Another example from the Internet takes the form of the English 'to pwn', meaning 'to dominate'. This is a form of the English verb 'to own' which emerged through a typing error and gained popularity:

'Btw, Celtic *pwned* St Mirren 5–1, awesome! ': 😁 a reference to the Scottish football team Celtic soundly beating an opponent.

(Ichimaru Gin n Tonic 2007; my italics)

'**32 min**: A Lallana volley from the edge of the area whistles past the far post. Leeds are being *pwned* right now': a media update on a 2011 English football match between Southampton and Leeds.

(Gardner 2011; my italics)

Reduction: making it short and sweet

Another way in which the sound of a word might change in colloquial usage in particular is through reduction. Whereas more formal social and professional situations often require speakers to produce more deliberate or careful pronunciation, this is typically not the case in informal settings. Partly for reasons of informality and language economy, speakers may instead alter pronunciation of an item from the full *formal* variant to something that is in some way reduced or shortened – for instance, in English we might say 'wanna' and 'gonna' for 'want to' and 'going to'; the Russian words 'seichas' ('now'), 'tebia' ('you') and 'budesh'' ('you will') can often sound more like 's'chas' or 'shas', 'tya' and 'bush' in colloquial speech; while French 'voilà' ('there'), 'there is'), 'je suis' ('I am') and 'autre' ('other') may sound more like 'v'là', 'chui' and 'aut'.

Not surprisingly, reduction does not only involve change in the pronunciation of standard items. The French criminal and youth term 'jet(t)ard' meaning 'inside' (prison) or 'pigs' (police) may also be written as 'chtar(d)' or 'schtar(d)' to reflect casual pronunciation (when the word is pronounced the *d* is silent):

Les petit frère qui rend fou les chtard.
The little brothers who drive the cops mad.

(*kinkin83*: 2012)[6]

Given that youth, criminal and colloquial usage can rely heavily on the principles of informality and language economy, where the least effort necessary may be expended in communication, and in view of the rise of text- and computer-mediated communication through instant messaging, chat and other platforms, the context certainly exists for elements of informal or non-standard pronunciation to become more widely represented in the written mode – particularly where solidarity is sought. Stylistic boundaries may thus become challenged and stretched. In his study of German fanzines, for example, Androutsopoulos (2000a: 528) notes: "By regularly reproducing colloquial speech, fanzine writers project an intimate relationship with their audience; by exploiting further graphemic resources, they both style relevant others and self-consciously signal their own cultural orientation".

Colloquial speech can also be imitated and reproduced to connect with how people speak in their everyday lives in other spheres such as advertising (such as English 'coz', 'innit?' for 'because' and 'isn't it?' – for more on the use of English 'slang' in advertising, see Coleman 2012). Generally speaking, in everyday interaction the context should help to explain why and when such behaviour might be reproduced. However, even if the evidence suggests otherwise in some regards (Thurlow 2007; Androutsopoulos 2011), it is possible that with some speakers, colloquial forms of pronunciation and resultant spelling may be used in more formal domains where they are not typically expected to appear, hence the concern of educators as we saw in Chapter Three.

Sounds like ...

Playing on similarity in sound can be important for creating new words to produce particular effects. For instance, in his article on the language practices of what he termed "the déclassé" (criminals, tramps, street kids, etc.), Grachëv (1994: 67) noted that similarity to existing words was an "important feature" of their lexis, while Zaikovskaia (1993) has also pointed to the expressive potential in mimicry when writing about Russian youth language.

Indeed, by replacing one word with a homophonous or similar sounding one, speakers can create witty words and phrases for a number of purposes – for instance, to add a sense of levity, or for play or entertainment. One example of mimicry, albeit a far-from-full one, can be seen in the use of the name 'Emilio' to replace the word 'email' in colloquial Spanish.[7] Equally approximative or partial is the colloquial French 'vice-Versailles' for 'vice versa'. As we can see in these examples and in the jocular replacement by US college students of names such as 'Pizza Hut' and 'Student Health Services' with 'Pizza Slut' and 'Stupid Health Services' (Eble 1996: 128), sometimes it is enough to effect a broad or partial similarity for the impact to occur. At the same time, however, more similar sounding words can also convey wit, surprise and/or entertain. A theatre troupe advertising Olivier Maille's comedy in Paris in July 2017 comically played on sound similarity when they noted that were Death to catch you it would *death* you, as opposed to *bite* you – playing on the similarity in sound between the words 'mords' ([I] 'bite') and 'mort' ('death'). And in advertising a New Year's party in 2016, a bar in Almaty, Kazakhstan, where both Russian and Kazakh are commonly spoken, described it as a 'kipish' ('shindig', 'loud party' in Russian) while noting that those looking to attend were already 'boiling up' ('kipish'' – 'you are boiling'; see page 202).

Given the effects of such artifice, it is perhaps not surprising that similarity in sound can also be a core property in games, again where agility, depth of resource and quick wit can be tested competitively. Tetreault (2000), for example, describes the use by Arabic-French youth in France of linguistic resources from French, American and North African culture and language in a game known as 'hachek' (Arabic, approximating to 'I'm sorry'). The game is started by a speaker pronouncing this word; a second player must juxtapose this with an incongruous word that rhymes with it (e.g. 'milkshake', 'biftek' ('steak', 'muscle man')).

As Tetreault intimates, exploiting sound similarity need not be limited to a speaker's native or main language. Veit-Wild (2009) cites a particularly witty example from Zimbabwe youth usage in 'Bhombi stombi', where the English 'bottle store' has been altered by Shona speakers to provide an item that rhymes and jocularly alludes to both being 'bombed' and 'stoned' ('drunk'). The aspiration to be playful can also be seen in the use by 1970s–1990s US college students of 'sarajevo' for the Japanese 'sayonara' to mean 'goodbye', and in the replacement by Indonesian youth of terms such as 'perawan tulen' ('an authentic virgin') and 'Ridwan' (i.e. a man's name) by similar sounding phrases which include English elements, 'pra one two land' and 'read one'. Where a person or place name, or that of a concept, replaces a similar sounding word stem or word, this has been termed *onomastic substitution* (Nassenstein 2015b: 88, 90) – for example, in Langila, a variety spoken in the Democratic Republic of Congo, the item 'miamí' means 'hunger' or 'hungry' by virtue of Yanké 'myá' ('hunger') and the name of the US city, Miami: no semantic connection between the items is required for the mechanism to be used. Equally, youth speakers of Yabacrâne, another youth language in the country, may refer to a house as a 'palestine' by dint of similarity to the Yanké use of the euphemised French 'palais' ('palace') (Nassenstein 2016: 247). In Randuk, the name of a well-known Sudanese singer, Faatna Elhaaj, may be used to refer to breakfast due to a certain similarity with 'fatoor' ('breakfast'); while those in the Russian drugs sphere may talk about 'Fedia' ('Fedia', diminutive male name) when discussing 'efedrin' ('ephedrine'), and have indeed expanded the principle to abbreviations where 'Liusia' ('Liusia', girls' name) is used for 'LSD' (possibly inspired by the English 'Lucy in the sky with diamonds').

Importantly, these examples point not only to a knowledge of words of foreign origin, but also to their similarity to words in a speaker's own language and to a judgement that the resulting item will produce a specific effect in a given situation. In this respect, they differ from the unwitting use of malapropisms, where a word is incorrectly used instead of another due to similarity in sound, albeit often with humorous results.

The use of mimicry to parody another's voice or pronunciation is not a new phenomenon and is also fairly commonplace in language play (for more on mimicry see, for instance, Crystal 1998; Sherzer 2002). It can allow for an aspect of another's personality or identity to be evoked through characterisation, again for a specific effect. The accent of people from Northern Ireland may often be humorously reflected in reference to their being from 'Norn Iron' (Quinn 2017); while Eble (1996: 43, 79) has noted the use of *Cajun talk*, where US students pronounced any word "ending in *-(t)ion* as *shawn* (such as educa*shawn*), in imitation of the way Cajuns speak", and the rendering of 'Spencer Dormitory' (for women) as 'Spinster Dormitory', on the basis that there is no distinction in North Carolina pronunciation in items such as 'pin' and 'pen'. Such play can be used not just for banter, jocular or witty ends but also to criticise or undermine. Equally, however, the imitation of foreign accents can also emphasise a sense of social and/or cultural prestige and association, such as when non-US rappers imitate North American (US) pronunciation.

Devices used to create new words and phrases in literature

Links between literature and invention are commonplace. Some regard literature as "the creative use of language" which may involve deviating from norms (Awa 2015b: 56). Crystal (1998: 137) notes that "a considerable proportion of the language used in literature is indeed ludic", and that "there is no clear boundary between the way in which 'authors' play with language and the way everyone else does"; while Osundare (1982, cited by Awa 2015c: 31) suggests that "the remarkable writer is one who has been able to bend or break the preset rules of language, the linguistic outlaw who has flouted its hallowed thou-shall-nots. Every Language (sic) has within its system a loophole, an elastic edge for the adventurous user to widen and stretch".

Writers use many devices for stylistic effect. These can range from assonance, alliteration, rhyme and onomatopoeia to parallelisms, personification and citing or amending sayings or proverbs. Many devices are used in literature across the globe: for example, colour association with socio-political movements and animal metaphor in Indonesian literature (see, for example, Laksana 2015: xiii), and coining in English. In Africa, various devices are used for creativity where English is chosen as the language for expression but amended to distance the work from Western influence. These devices may lend authenticity, as well as local flavour, salience and perspective, and emphasise the value of local resources for uniqueness and distinctiveness (Awa 2015a: 264, 266).[8] Devices used by African writers include, for example:

- references to females through male terms to protest against patriarchal structures;
- the coining of new terms;
- lexical borrowing and expressions from African languages as discourse markers;
- concatenated English and African items;
- transporting African modes of expression into English (for example, proverbs);
- metaphor;
- hyperbole and antithesis;
- onomatopoeia and alliteration (Awa 2015a, 2015b, 2015c).

What constitutes literature and literariness can be subject to debate, and new and emerging language varieties may contribute to new forms of literature and literary production. Furthermore, there is also music and other forms of artistic expression to consider. Many see links between 'slang', art and literary practice: referring to English 'slang', Amari (2010: 9) writes: "However, slang does share certain characteristics of art, particularly poetry in its manipulation of linguistic codes, conventions and processes, its creative handling of metaphor, allusion, irony, humor, its wit and inventiveness".

A number of criminal and youth language items have figured in poetry written by members of socially marginal in-groups. François Villon wrote poetry in the language of the Coquillards (for more see Heller-Roazen 2013), while others have used Lunfardo as a medium of expression, or to give a more authentic feel to certain characters (see, for instance, Grayson 1964 on the use of Lunfardo in poetry, prose and in lyrics to the tango). In a separate domain García (2005) points to the use of Pachuco Caló terms by the singer Lalo Guerrero in the 1950s, while there are several discussions of the artistic merits of the use of youth items in hip hop (e.g. Journo 2009; Veit-Wild 2009; Vierke 2015).

Insertion

Insertion is a practice that has been in evidence in a number of languages for some considerable time. One example of this practice has already been encountered in Chapter Six in the shape of French's Infixing Javanais, where the same element – typically '-av-' – was inserted to provide words such as 'javardavin' from 'jardin' ('garden').

France is not the only country where intercalation has been evident. In nineteenth-century Russia, some criminals and down-and-outs utilised a system known as the 'Razgovor po kheram' ('Kher talk'), where 'kher' (now mostly translated to mean 'dick', 'cock') was appended to and inserted between syllables. The sentence 'Pokurim trubochki' ('Let's smoke some pipe') would thus become:

Kher<u>po</u>kher<u>ku</u>kher<u>rim</u>kher<u>tru</u>kher<u>boch</u>kher<u>ki</u>kher

(Tikhanov 1895: 5)

A more recent example of insertion has been seen in Jordan in 2008. Abu-Abbas, Al-Kadi and Al-Tamimi (2010: 77–9) noted, for example, that '-irb-' or '-urb-' would be added to the initial syllable in each word, so that Arabic 'salaam' ('peace') and 'suuri' ('Syrian') would become 'sirbalaam' and 'surbuuri', while the syllable 'tin' would be placed within the penultimate syllable in a language game in Cairo in 1970.[9] Additionally, a combination of inserting '-in-' into syllables and subsequent clipping produces new items in Bahasa Gay. To create the in-group term for 'man', 'laki' is lengthened to '<u>linakini</u>' before being shortened to 'linak' – leading to a quite different looking and sounding word.

Not all systems rely on the repetition of a pre-defined element. Some young Indonesian speakers, for example, have been known to add a consonant and vowel to syllables according to a series of letter codes such as *p*, *f*, and *g*. While the consonant to be added is determined by the letter code selected, it is followed by the vowel found in a given syllable. In this way, were the *p* code applied to the Sundanese word 'eta' ('that'), this would result in 'epetapa'.[10] An analogous system can be seen in 1930s Russia, where school children might playfully transform a word such as 'pribezhali' ('ran up' (plural)) into '<u>prikibekezhakaliki</u>' (Zhirmunskii 1936: 155);[11] while nowadays French youth may employ *F language* (known as Langue de Feu or Langue de F) by adding *f* after each syllable and repeating the vowel; so 'salut' ('hi' – the *t* is not pronounced) becomes 'safa lufu'. Alternatively, they may opt for Gueu language (Langue de Gueu), where 'gu' follows each syllable, again with the vowel reproduced – so, 'la' ('the') and 'je' ('I') become 'lagua' and 'jegue'.[12]

Rhyming and alliteration

As we saw with the use of 'Come in, Berlin!', 'À la tienne, Étienne!', and 'Genii sredi udobrenii', it is possible that speakers may wish to produce a rhyming effect. Colloquial English, for example, has items such as 'chick flick' and 'chill pill'; Yiddish-influenced deprecative compounds of the type 'letter-schmetter'; and Cockney rhyming slang, where 'apples and pears' means 'stairs' and 'trouble and strife' means 'wife' (although the rhyming phrases are often shortened, making 'apples' and 'trouble').

The last of these three examples, rhyming slang, is particularly associated with London; however, it can also be found in Australia, Ireland and Scotland.[13] The Scottish term 'Bertie Auld', for instance, means 'cauld' [kɔːld] (dialect for 'cold') – Bertie Auld is a famous former football player who enjoyed great success with

Glasgow Celtic. As in other forms of rhyming slang, the Scottish phrase might simply be shortened, in this case 'It's Bertie!'. Similarly, 'Very Annie' may be used to apologise (i.e. 'sorry') after the name of the traditional Scottish song 'Annie Laurie' (for more on rhyming slang, see Blake 2010; Coleman 2012; Green 2016).

Alliteration, where sounds – usually initial consonants – are repeated, can also be used for expressive effect; it is therefore often found in literary works and in advertising. A number of youth and colloquial varieties provide examples: Widawski (2015: 31), for instance, notes its prominence in African American usage such as 'main man' and 'soul sister', while Eble (1996) points to its use in 1970s–1990s US college language:

'brain burp'	'random thought';
'Woodstock wannabe'	'someone with sensibilities and styles of the 1960s'.

At the same time, alliteration is frequently used in hip hop along with devices such as repetition and rhyming. The use of these devices in Kenyan hip hop, for instance, has been documented by Journo, who accords with Alim's suggestion that the language of the Hip Hop Nation represents a "synergetic combination of speech, music, and literature" (Journo 2009: 10, citing Alim 2006).

Backslang and reordering

Backslang, where items are written or pronounced as if they are spelled backwards, and word reordering, which is achieved mainly through transposing syllables or inverting their order, are well-known mechanisms in criminal and youth language practices, and are used for play and/or disguise in many languages. Writing in 1936 about the historical development of secret language varieties associated with beggars, vagabonds and criminals in Russia, England, Spain, France and Germany, Zhirmunskii (1936: 154–5) intimated that the rearrangement of words to hide meaning was long-standing. German writers from the 1580s, 1620s and 1660s, for example, outlined several Rotwelsch manipulations for distorting words, such as 'Teper' for 'Peter' or 'feiren' for 'reifen' ('to age', 'to mature'), while eighteenth-century criminal language saw the use of 'ückbre' for 'Brücke' ('bridge'). Writing almost 30 years after Zhirmunskii, Grayson (1964) also talked of syllable displacement in his 1964 description of Lunfardo Vesre (from 'revés' – 'other side'; 'al revés' means 'the other way round' in Spanish);[14] while Mallik (1972) documented the use of inversion in his study of the language practices of criminals in West Bengal. Closer to the present day, Manfredi (2008) and Mugaddam (2015) have recorded the extensive use of metathesis, the process of changing the position of elements within a word to create another, in Randuk; Slone (2003) has noted its frequent application in Prokem; Githinji (2006) and Bosire (2009) have pointed to its appearance in Sheng; while Landi and Pasch (2015) have documented the use of syllable inversion in Sango Godobé, the language of street youth in Bangui, Central African Republic.

Not all users and motivations for reordering vocabulary are identical. However, in many cases we can see "astonishing similarities between the argotic creations of different countries" (Vázquez Ríos 2009: 197). Furthermore, although found in many varieties across the globe, backslang and reordering can be absent or unproductive in some languages and varieties. Androutsopoulos (2000b), for example, intimates this with regard to German, Nassenstein (2015b) with reference to Langila in the Democratic Republic of Congo, and Widawski (2015) concerning African American 'slang' (one notable exception being the 1991 N.W.A. album title *Efil4zaggin* ('niggaz 4 life') cited by Krohn and Suazo 1995: 152).

To dig deeper into how and why backslang and reordering are employed to create new forms, it is useful to explore what is probably the most famous of all types of transposition, the Verlan of French youth.

Opposite in name

Apart from Verlan and Vesre, there is evidence of other language games or varieties being named through the use of inversion or a word or phrase pointing to realignment or incomprehensibility. In some cases, the names of extant in-group varieties are reordered to designate distinct new language practices:

- School students in Zimbabwe use metathesis, including inversion, that they variously refer to as 'verers' (from 'reverse'), 'cabdwa' or 'kabwards' (from 'backwards') (Hollington and Makwabarara 2015).
- Slone (2003) notes the use of 'Cakap Balik', literally "reverse words", by children in the Negri Sembilan State of Peninsular Malaysia to keep secrets from adults.
- Nassenstein (2015a) cites the use by children in Kigali, Rwanda, of a metathesis-based language game called 'Igifefeko', which translates as 'speaking backwards'. Use of the ludling does not implicate a particular youth identity.
- A secret variety known as Ṣawġ was noted in El Jadida, Morocco, as being used by adults aged 23–30. It relies greatly on inversion; its name is an amended form of Ġawṣ, a variety spoken by 19–25-year olds in the same town (Berjaoui 1997).
- Where Sheng is spoken in Nairobi's Eastlands, a variety known as Engsh is spoken in the more affluent Westlands area of the city. Engsh appears to be based on English grammatical–syntactic structure, with a higher incidence of English lexis, while Sheng relies more on Swahili (Ogechi 2005).
- Blake (2010) points to a secret Portuguese variety in Rio de Janeiro and São Paulo known as 'Gualin', from 'lingua' ('language').

> Two other examples of note are the 'upside down language' ('maʔlūbe') spoken by men in country areas near Damascus (Wolfer 2011), and 'Rendók', an alternative name for Randuk. 'Rendók' is an amended form of 'ruṭāna', which means 'tribal language' in Sudanese Arabic. Notably, Modern Standard Arabic has 'raṭāna', meaning 'unintelligible language', 'jargon' or 'gibberish' (Manfredi 2008: 114, endnote 2).

The case of Verlan

Much as with Vesre and some other terms designating backslang (see also **Opposite in name**), the word 'Verlan' almost certainly comes from inverting the French '(à) l'envers' ('backwards').[15] It especially rose to prominence as a means of creating new vocabulary in the 1970s–1990s, particularly among young 'beur' males living in city estates and occupying the social margins. However, the concept of rearranging lexis in French extends way beyond that time, albeit in limited instances. In her commentary on Verlan, Lefkowitz (1989: 321, endnote 10) cites Paul's (1985) view that Verlan was first attested in the twelfth century. It has certainly been documented that words such as 'Bourbon' were rearranged into 'Bonbour' in the late sixteenth century, while 'Lontou' was used to refer to the Toulon penal colony in the first half of the nineteenth century (Vázquez Ríos 2009). Furthermore, the word 'brelica' for 'revolver' (from 'calibre' – 'revolver') was attested in the *Dictionnaire de L'Argot Moderne* in the 1950s (Sandry and Carrère 1957). Insofar as they substantially changed the form and sound of words, there is little doubt that the mechanisms for which Verlan is famous were previously used by criminals and social marginals as a form of cryptolect and to consolidate in-group identity and solidarity.

Verlan's use in the present day, as part of a range of linguistic behaviours among youth groups, remains considerable. Doran (2007: 501), for example, suggests that the sound structure of terms such as 'keuf' and 'meuf', together with lax vowel articulation, imbues suburban youth language with "a marked vocalic quality that immediately distinguishes it from the more 'precise' diction of standard French". When considered alongside rapid speaker delivery, uncommon intonation patterns and the influence of Arabic phonology, "these marked sound features can be viewed as a refusal of the measured, careful pronunciation of normative French, the language of a cultural elite by whom minority youths feel negatively judged" (Doran 2007: 501; see also Sourdot 2003).

There are many reasons why Verlan is and has been used to create new lexis, and these can vary from speaker to speaker. They include:

- establishing social acceptance, identification and distance, where speakers engage in the same shared social code or wish to sound different from those using the standard language – potentially employing a metaphor of difference, opposition and rejection by *talking backwards* or *talking differently*;

- to establish social cachet or status, create a positive impression, index a cool identity. For example, social prestige may be acquired by those who can produce such manipulations more speedily than others (Kiessling and Mous 2004, on youth use of metathesis more generally);
- for language play and fun;
- concealing discussion of private matters – even though it is no longer a secret code as such, many terms, including disguised insults, can still be unknown to the uninitiated;
- euphemism, through making crude terms sound less derogatory or seem less taboo;
- its use by some girls to reject traditional notions of female behaviour, especially as youth language practices and Verlan are often associated with young men.

The success of Verlan has been marked, and both the mechanism and resultant vocabulary spread in popularity in the late-twentieth century from the language of marginalised youths in Parisian suburbs to practically all parts of France, including better-off social groups. Its use in youth culture, advertising, song and film played a role in its circulation, so much so that certain Verlan words have become established in Standard French as *bona fide* lexical items or, alternatively, have spread to other language varieties such as Camfranglais and Nouchi, not to mention the French spoken in Switzerland. As we saw in Chapter Three, the very word 'beur' is an inverted form of 'arabe' and is to be found in many mainstream dictionaries.

Although in principle any word can be adapted through Verlan, in reality there are limitations. Generally, nouns, adjectives, adverbs and certain verbs are reordered, whereas functional words such as prepositions and articles aren't. Where verbs are rearranged, they are often – but not always – used in the new infinitive form and left unconjugated, such as 'Je l'ai pécho' ('I picked her up') from the colloquial verb 'choper' ('to pick up'; other uses include 'J'ai pécho mon bus' – 'I got my bus', and 'se faire pécho' from 'se faire choper' – 'to get nabbed, caught'). Words created through Verlan will be used in sentences that largely observe established French morphological and syntactic practice. Interestingly, in terms of word order, the use of Verlan is consistent with sixteenth- and seventeenth-century German criminal and 1980s Indonesian youth language, where standard word order is retained even though – in the German and Indonesian cases – entire sentences can consist of inverted items:

> Verlan: Quand irons-nous à Ripa? ('When are we going to Paris?' – here only the syllables in 'Paris' are inverted; the rest of the sentence is Standard French);
> (Strutz 2009: 309)

> Historical German: chi sum muz schit ('I must go to the table' – with inverted forms of 'ich muss zum Tisch');
> (Zhirmunskii 1936: 155)

> 1980s Indonesian school pupils: Diab deba katang ('I want to go' – where the syllables in each word in the sentence 'Abdi bade angkat' are inverted).
> (Chambert-Loir 1984: 109)

The most commonly cited method of rearrangement in Verlan is syllable inversion. As a word-formation strategy, this method is fairly easy to comprehend, and extends to the alteration of standard and youth, criminal or colloquial lexis. Furthermore, variants can occur in spelling, and the final product can often rest on the pronunciation and not necessarily the spelling of the elements that have been altered – it's often important that the resulting word sounds right. This means that homophonous or near-homophonous constituents may replace one another. For example, when written, in 'pécho' and 'méfu' the 'e acute' ('é') replaces the infinitive ending '-er'.

ripou	'crooked', 'rotten', from standard 'pourri' ('rotten');
tromé	'underground', 'subway', from standard 'métro' ('Métropolitain', 'subway');
féca	'cafe', from standard 'café' ('cafe');
méfu	'to smoke', from standard 'fumer' ('to smoke');
guédro	'junkie', from standard 'drogué' ('drug addict').

Although reordering in Verlan works most readily with bisyllabic items, monosyllabic words can also be rearranged. With some items, individual segments are reordered, so that standard 'fou' ('mad') becomes 'ouf', and 'ça' ('that') becomes 'aç': a popular orthographic representation of 'aç' – 'asse' – is found in expressions such as 'comasse' for 'comme ça' ('like that').[16] With some other words, '-eu' or 'e-muet' may be added to facilitate inversion. In this way 'truc' ('stuff') becomes 'keutru' ('thing', 'stuff'). The creation of a Verlan word may also require truncation after the word is inverted. So, 'flic' ('cop') becomes 'keuf' ('cop', 'copper') and not 'keufli'. Where the last consonant is not pronounced before inversion, this might not be found in the final written Verlan form, so 'chaud' ('hot') becomes 'auch', 'vieux' ('old') is rendered 'ieuv', and 'pas' ('not') – 'ap':

> et ba c'est tres gentil de nous donner ce super conseil pour un systeme D qui march *ap* alor.
>
> and yea, and it's really very kind of you to give us this great advice for smarts that don't work.
>
> (*Bombing Art*, April 2006; my italics)[17]

Polysyllabic words can be *verlanised* in a number of ways. For example, 'cigarette' ('cigarette') might become 'garetsi', where 'ci' (/si/) is moved to the end of the word, while 'brelica' ('revolver') involves inverting the syllables in 'calibre' ('revolver').

Inversion and reordering in other languages

As the introduction to this chapter indicates, inversion and reordering can be found in a variety of languages. Moreover, they can be used for many of the reasons outlined for Verlan. In the nineteenth century, English street sellers and food vendors used backslang (e.g. Blake 2010; Coleman 2012), as did Russian traders (e.g. Davie 1998), and speakers of Kinyume in Zanzibar (Steere 1894).[18] In South

America, speakers of Lunfardo have been known to invert syllables so that words and phrases such as '¿Qué pasa?' ('What's up?'), 'calor' ('heat') and 'mina' ('bird', 'chick', 'girl') become '¿Qué sapa?', 'lorca' and 'nami'. In Sheng, inverting words such as 'keja' ('house') and 'chali' ('boy') produces 'jake' and 'licha'. And in Randuk, words such as 'baḥar' ('river'), 'dāmm' ('blood') and 'waswas' ('whisper') become 'raḥab' and 'sawsaw' through inversion, and 'mādd' through consonant swapping. In this connection, Mugaddam (2012b: 4) suggests that Randuk's "secretive nature" may encourage the use of metathesis.

In terms of individual manipulations, perhaps the simplest is inversion, where the order of the individual letters or sounds of a word is reversed, for instance:

1980s Indonesian pupils:	koseb	'tomorrow', from 'besok';
1990s Russian youth:	nelch	'member', from 'chlen';
2003 Bahasa Prokem:	askis	'torture', from 'siksa';
2012 Randuk:	sagad	'made a mistake', from 'dagas';
2015 Zimbabwe youth:	vig	'give' (from the English);

As we saw with Verlan, the inversion of syllable order is another means by which words can be reordered:

1960s Lunfardo:	dorima	'husband', from 'marido';
1960s West Bengal criminals:	lokā	'black', 'opium', from 'kālo';
2003 Camfranglais:	dybo	'someone', from English '(some)body';
2008 Argentine Spanish:	zabeca	'head', from 'cabeza';*
2009 Sheng:	nopo	'porn', from English 'porno(graphy)'.†

*'Zabeca' was also recorded by Grayson (1964: 68) with the same meaning in his description of Lunfardo.
†Inversion in personal names is also possible, hence Russian 'Rogi' from 'Igor'' and French 'Vida' from 'David'.

Further methods involve the transposition of consonants:

1960s West Bengal criminals:	kodān	'shop', from 'dokān';
	māglā	'metal', from 'gāmlā';
1980s Indonesian pupils:	sebok	'tomorrow', from 'besok';
2008–2015 Randuk:	damrasa	'school', from 'madrasa';
	burta	'package of banknotes', from 'rubta';
	jiraasa	'cigarette', from 'sijaara'*;

*Alternatively still, in language varieties such as Bahasa Prokem, reordering of vowels may occur, hence 'perkaos' from 'perkosa' ('rape').

and consonant substitution, where one consonant replaces another:

2008 Randuk:	ramma	'time', from 'marra'.

Akin to Verlan 'garetsi', in varieties such as Lunfardo some trisyllabic constructions may see the first syllable moved to the end of the word, so 'berretín' ('obsession', 'mania') becomes 'retimbe'. Alternatively, the final syllable may be moved to the beginning of the word, or the final syllables reversed, again with no change in meaning required:

Lunfardo:	jotraba	'work', from 'trabajo';
	ajoba	'downstairs', from 'abajo';
2012 Randuk:	yalogo	'they say', from 'yagolo';

In other trisyllabic items, initial constituents may also be inverted:

2012 Randuk:	bagartu	'his neck', from 'ragabtu'.*

*Many examples cited in studies focus on metathesis in bi- or trisyllabic words. However, longer items such as the Vesre 'yotivenco' ('messy house', from 'conventillo' – 'tenement', 'inner city slum') can also be found.

An extension to these practices is where elements may be swapped between words, as we can see in a Finnish example cited in the 1980s where 'suomen kieli' ('Finnish language') might become 'kiemen suoli'; and in an example of Estonian 'slang' where 'Juta Silk' ('a girl's name') might become 'sitajulk' ('heap of excrement') (Tender 1996: 3).[19]

The constraints that apply to Verlan in terms of which word categories are reordered and which aren't are not necessarily observed by speakers of other languages (given, of course, that languages can be structured differently, for one thing). In Randuk, for example, apart from some functional elements or markers such as 'but' and 'that', in principle everything can be altered (although, in reality Randuk does observe some conventions where, for instance, the definite article 'al-' or gender and number suffixes do not change their position). And in Sheng, prefixes are not subject to metathesis unless the stem is monosyllabic. For that reason, 'hakuna' ('there isn't'), for example, which consists of 'ha-' (negative) and 'kuna' ('there is'), becomes 'hanaku' (for more see Bosire 2009).

In some instances, reordering can bring about a change in meaning or word class. As many of the examples given indicate, often the word will not change its meaning once its form has been amended – it may be enough to alter its guise to make it incomprehensible to out-group members. However, in some language varieties such as Randuk, meaning can sometimes change: 'duxxān' ('smoke') becomes 'xunnād' ('marijuana'), for example, while the Norwegian 'keeg' is not only an inversion of the English loanword 'geek', which is largely negative when used by out-groupers (i.e. 'a nerd', 'unpopular'), but also has a meaning that many would see as antithetical – 'cool', 'popular' (Hasund and Drange 2014: 144). Equally, as Mallik (1972) noted in his study of the language practices of criminals in West Bengal, a change in word class can also result: once reordered the Hindi borrowed adjective 'sākrā' ('narrow') became a noun in 'sarkā' ('den of criminals').

The backslang and word reordering described are not the only instances where rearrangement may occur in language more generally. Spoonerisms also involve reordering constituents within a word or phrase. Although these can occur accidentally to humorous effect, they can also be contrived, as in 'Coloversity of Univrado' for 'University of Colorado' and 'Barber the Conarian' for 'Conan the Barbarian' (Breva Claramonte and García Alonso 1993: 24), and as can be seen in the introduction to one 1990s Russian youth publication:

за возможные очепятки и ашипки – SORRY!
For possible prismints and errarz – SORRY!

(O.R.Z. 1992)

Here the word for 'misprints' ('opechatki' – 'опечатки' in Cyrillic) is deliberately misspelt to read 'ochepiatki' ('очепятки'), while the word for 'errors' ('oshibki' – 'ошибки') is written 'ашипки' in line with pronunciation.

Double metathesis (reverlanisation)

Perhaps one of the most interesting manifestations of reordering is double metathesis or, in the case of Verlan, reverlanisation. Here a word created through Verlan is once again rearranged if it becomes too well known or readily recognisable. Verlan words such as 'beur' and 'meuf' thus become 're(u)beu' and 'feumeu', while for some items a single syllable might only be changed, so 'trakma' from 'matraque' ('cosh', 'truncheon') becomes 'trakam'. A similar step to ensure secrecy has also been seen in Randuk, where the alternative designation 'rendók' was changed to become 'gernót' via 'dernók' when it became commonly used in Khartoum (Manfredi 2008: 118–9).

Largonji and Largonji des Louchébems

A particularly fascinating method for creating new lexis through rearranging existing and adding new elements can be seen in the French Largonji des Louchébems ('butchers' jargon'). As we saw in Chapter Three, this was a secret language variety mainly used in Paris in the nineteenth century. It is thought to be based on the criminal variety Largonji ('argot'), although a possible link is also suggested in terms of mechanisms used in Hanoi butchers' language (Robert L'Argenton 1991). Some words still remain in use today, such as 'loufoque' ('mad', 'bonkers', 'nutter') from 'fou' ('mad', 'fool'). Such is the difference in the form of words created through Largonji des Louchébems, also known as Argomuche, that it has sometimes been mistaken for another language altogether.

In general terms, with Largonji and Largonji des Louchébems the first letter of a word is substituted by *l* and moved to the end of the new base, where a suffix is also added. Suffixes include '-é', '-em', '-i', '-uche' and '-oque'; '-èm' has been described as the most frequently used in one study, followed by '-ès' and '-é' (Mandelbaum-Reiner 1991: 40).[20] Working from this model, the word 'jargon' therefore becomes 'largonji', while 'patron' ('boss') becomes 'latronpem' ('boss', 'chief'), 'fou' ('mad') becomes 'loufoque', and 'beau' ('beautiful') becomes 'l(e)aubé' or 'l(e)aubiche' ('beautiful'). In items such as 'boucher' ('butcher'), the '-er' may be replaced to give 'louchébem' (compare the Verlan 'pécho' and 'méfu'), while with 'chaud' ('hot'), the *ch* is displaced and substituted with *l*, the unpronounced *d* dropped and a suffix is added to provide 'lauchem'. That all of these items were attested in a late 1980s dictionary of colloquial French and in-group French (Pratt 1989) and that some are also to be found in an equivalent dictionary 20 years later (Strutz 2009) suggests that many of these items have probably been used and circulated as lexical items whose ultimate derivation is down to Largonji and/or Largonji des Louchébems.

The partial similarity of Largonji des Louchébems to a mechanism used by certain workers near Kaluga, Russia, in the late nineteenth century (Dobrovol′skii 1899) and to a language game employed in twenty-first–century Morocco is also noteworthy. In the Russian example, the first consonant was placed at the end of the word and replaced by the letter *sh*; if it had one, the word's original second consonant was then displaced to the end of the new base, after which the vowel which originally followed it was repeated and the consonant *ts* added, hence 'shigaknits' for 'kniga' ('book'):

kniga → shnigak → shigakn → shigakni → shigaknits
(Dobrovol′skii 1899: 1387)

The Moroccan variety, spoken by students in Rabat in the early years of the twenty-first century, involved the first sound being substituted by *f* and then positioned at the end of the word (Wolfer 2011: 14).

Onomatopoeia and ideophones

Very often used as a device in literature, and also known as *echoism*, onomatopoeia is the creation of a word where its form is thought to imitate a sound. It is commonly encountered in the colloquial and youth varieties of several languages, although some discussions consider its use to be relatively marginal (e.g. Widawski 2015 on African American 'slang').

While it is frequently found across languages and cultures, the way sounds are perceived and represented may differ. Interesting examples of onomatopoeia include:

2000 Shona slang:	mungonjo	'policeman', the sound of handcuffs being put on;
	vhuzhi	'car', from the sound of a car travelling;
2002 colloquial French:	chialer	'to blubber', 'cry', from the sound of crying;
2006 Nouchi:	zagazaga	'submachine gun', from the sound of gunfire;
	bao	'pistol', 'to shoot', from the sound of gunfire;
2006 colloquial Russian:	bul′-bul′	'drowning', 'pouring', from the sound of bubbles;
2009 Sheng:	jongolo	'money', from the jingling of coins;
	twatwa	'gun', from the sound of gunfire.

As examples such as 'bul'-bul'', 'twatwa' and 'zagazaga' demonstrate, certain items may not only be based on onomatopoeia, but might also be reduplicative. A further, intriguing example of onomatopoeia combining with another lexical or word-formation process can be seen in the Russian youth term 'chik-faer' ('lighter'). Here a russified form of the English 'fire' is conjoined with an item said to represent the sound of lighting a match.

Ideophones are words that represent or evoke an idea. They can be found in varieties such as Nouchi, which often borrows ideophones from Ivorian languages: 'waha' for 'loads of' and 'foum' to suggest removal or distance, as in the expression 'Y'ai pris foum' ('I got out of there') (Ahua 2006: 145–6) (for more on sound symbolism see, for example, Sherzer 2002; Storch 2011).

Summary

In this chapter, we have considered some of the most interesting and intriguing means by which new vocabulary has been or can be created in youth, criminal and colloquial language practices. We have seen that a number of different motivations might lie behind alteration in the sound and/or form of a word, some of which may tie in closely with the motivations and domains discussed in previous chapters. Verlan, for example, can be used to create items consistent with many of the drivers (e.g. distortion of the standard as a form of rejection) and belonging to fertile semantic areas we discussed in Chapters Three and Five. Examples of the latter include entertainment, places, items or activities important to the group, as can be seen in 'tromé' (for 'métro' – 'underground'), 'keurma' (for 'marqueur' – 'marker') and 'bebom' (for 'bombe' – 'can of spray paint') as used by French graffiti enthusiasts:

> Quand tu te balades dans la rue ou dans le tromé pour marquer, faut pas que t'aies le temps de reboucher ton keurma ou ta bebom.
>
> When you're traipsing round the street or in the underground to put something up, you don't need time to put the top on your marker or spray can.
> (*Skame* 2004)

Although we are looking here at language varieties through the prism of word-formation, the inventiveness of many of the items we meet reminds us that, as interesting as the mechanisms are in themselves, they are created and used by people often as agentive social interactants. In many instances phonological means are deliberately combined with others to create new lexis: in Chapter Six we saw how some words such as 'taspèche' ('fear', 'mess', 'fix' and others) were created by mixing Verlan and suffixation. However, in this chapter we could equally point to inversion and truncation in Verlan 'brelic' ('gun', from 'brelica'); or to borrowing and reordering in the Verlan 'kebla' and 'kecra' from the English 'black' and 'crack' (cocaine), in the Camfranglais 'terma' ('mother') from the Latin 'mater', and in the Sheng 'gashu' and 'daso' from the English 'sugar' and 'soda'. Indeed, combined manipulations are commonplace. In one French example – 'cimer à+ ☺' (i.e. 'merci, à plus [tard] ☺' – 'thanx, laters ☺', from *Bombing Art* May 2005) – we see quite different mechanisms used to create an entire sentence, including a disposition marker in the form of an emoticon.

A key point that therefore emerges is that phonological and other processes can be used sensitively, cleverly and creatively to produce an effect. A case in point is the jocular Russian 'Agdam Sukhein'. This item refers to wine associated with the Azerbaijani town of Agdam, the name of which shares the 'dam' in 'Saddam'. The name of the town is coupled with a reordering of Hussein, where the first syllable is inverted to make 'sukh', which is the root for 'dry' in Russian. The resultant similarity to the name of the former Iraqi dictator Saddam Hussein makes for an especially playful item.

As will be evident, backslang, mimicry and sound symbolism have variously attracted much academic and popular attention over the last few decades, at least (e.g. Sornig 1981; Méla 1988, 1991, 1997; Crystal 1998; Vázquez Ríos 2009; Blake 2010; Mugaddam 2012a, 2012b, 2015), and there is much new ground for readers to cover should they wish to learn more. This includes more detail on Verlan (e.g. Méla 1988, 1991, 1997), Prokem (e.g. Slone 2003), Randuk (e.g. Manfredi 2008) and Sheng (e.g. Bosire 2009); the development of vocabulary through Largonji and Largonji des Louchébems (e.g. Robert L'Argenton 1991; Mandelbaum-Reiner 1991); and the structures of language games more broadly (e.g. Gil 2002; Sherzer 2002; Cahill 2008; Vázquez Ríos 2009). For instance, an interesting mechanism can be seen in an example from the language practices of nineteenth-century Russian beggars, where the phrase 'pokurim trubochki' we met earlier might also be rendered 'shibochkitrutsy rimpokutatsy'. This phrase would be created by first inverting the word order and then moving syllables within the words. Parasitic elements such as *shi*, *ta* and *tsy* would then be added to the end and/or beginning of the new items to create a seemingly impenetrable phrase:

pokurim trubochki → trubochki pokurim → bochkitru rimpoku → shibochkitrutsy rimpokutatsy

(Tikhanov 1895: 5)

A Swiss variety known as Mattenenglisch, which is reported to have almost passed out of common parlance, has also made use of elaborate means (Vázquez Ríos 2009). Named after the Matte, a district of Bern, it was used as a cryptolect by workers and simple everyday inhabitants and was based on the Bern dialect of German. A word in the Bern dialect or a corresponding Matte form was cut after the first vowel and the resulting constituents inverted. An *i* was then added to the beginning of the new word and the final letter/vowel replaced by *e*:

Matte → Mättu (dialect) → Ttumä → Ittumä → Ittume

(Vázquez Ríos 2009: 210–11)

As with many of the examples we have considered in this chapter, in these phrases we see new forms that are very different from the originals, items created by speakers with a particular objective or aims in mind. A very different kind of Russian or Bern dialect emerges from the ones to which many Russian or Swiss German dialect speakers are used.

Notes

1 In her study of Arabic manipulations, Wolfer (2011: 14) reported that no fewer than "[t]en Arabic ludlings are based on the substitution of letters or sounds of the original words by ludling material. This kind of ludlings [sic] is spoken in Morocco, Egypt, Syria and Yemen by children, students, groups of men, craftsmen or entertainers".

   The range of languages in which phonological manipulations have been noted is also mentioned by Zhirmunskii (1936: 133). In his discussion of the historical development of the secret languages of beggars, vagabonds and criminals, he noted that methods of restricting access to words such as the transposition or insertion of syllables was widespread in Russia, England, Spain, France and Germany.

2 Ryazanova-Clarke and Wade (1999: 314) observe with regard to Russian: "Use of non-standard stress is endemic in the speech of many speakers, with a general but by no means universal tendency to move stress closer to the beginning of the word". Apart from 'udalos'', they also cite examples such as 'sredstva' ('means') for 'sredstva'.

3 'Shiz' is derived from the item 'shizofreniia' ('schizophrenia'). Note also the youth language verb 'shizovat'' ('to freak out', 'to go round the bend'). 'Bamazhka' and 'diudiuktiv' are cited by Cobb (2002: 23), who suggests that the effects of deliberate morphological and phonetic change "can be multifold: the connotations vary from the highest degree of informality to expressing strong derogatory or sarcastic attitudes".

4 Veraldi-Pasquale (2011: 40) notes the following Caló lexis: 'bengorré', 'bengorró', 'bengui' and 'benguí', meaning 'devil', and 'benguistano', meaning 'hell'. Cooper (1993: 62) also points to the "supernatural sanctions" that may be invoked when taboo words are pronounced, which leads to common words such as the names of dangerous animals being replaced by euphemisms. Two examples he cites are the replacement in Slavonic languages of the Indo-European word for 'bear' by the euphemism 'honey eater', and the replacement of the word for 'snake' in Common Slavonic by a term from the same root as 'zemlia' ('earth').

   References to religious and mythological beings are found across youth, criminal and colloquial varieties. Indeed, in identifying the fertile semantic areas within metaphorical 'slang' usage, for instance, Sornig (1981) includes items referring to God and the Devil.

5 It is noteworthy that the French has incorrect renderings of 'ça' (in 'sa fait', 'sa marche'), 'à' (in 'a peu prés') and 'près' ('prés').

6 In line with the rules of Standard French, this sentence should have plural endings for 'petit frère' and 'chtard' (i.e. 'petits frères', 'chtards') and a third person plural verb ending where 'rendent' replaces 'rend'.

7 Russian also has the jocular 'mylo' ('email'), which relies on similarities in 'mylo' ('soap') and 'meil' (c.f. English 'mail').

8 While some African writers elect to write in African languages, Awa (2015c: 31) observes that others choose to "capture their cultural, social and linguistic background" and thus reflect African experience through a "new English" that has been amended to suit African circumstances.

9 They quote Burling (1970) regarding the Cairene game.

10 Chambert-Loir (1984: 109) notes that the p code was found in Indonesian and Sundanese; the code for f was found in Sundanese, Javanese and Minangkabau; the code for s in Javanese; and the code for g in Minangkabau.

   The degree to which Indonesian or, more specifically, Javanese insertion-based systems served as the origins of the French Javanais is unclear, although Plénat (1991)

326   *Phonetics and phonology*

points to similarities between the reduplicative Javanais found in French and a secret language code used in Java (among other places).

11   Zhirmunskii additionally indicates that German school children at the time had an insertion-style game known as 'Bi-Sprache' ('Bi-Language').

12   Other examples of insertion are pointed out by Bullock (1996: 189, endnote 2), who notes the insertion of the syllable '-chi-' in the Jeringosa of Puerto Rican Spanish, so that 'dedo' ('finger') becomes 'chidechido'. Separately, Sherzer (2002: 28) states that insertion can involve the addition of one or two consonants after each syllable, followed by a vowel which echoes or copies the vowel of that syllable, in languages such as Balinese, Spanish and Kuna. For example, F Language in Spanish renders 'la casa grande' as 'lafa cafasafa grafandefe'. Finally, Storch (2011: 72–4) considers the insertion of syllables in a language variety known as Ganoore, where Fulfulde words might be changed through the insertion of, for instance, 'r' plus a vowel, or '-si-', so that 'baaba' ('father') might become 'baarabara', while 'ndillen' ('let's go') might become 'ndisillen'.

13   Interestingly, Maurer (1981) recorded its use by American criminals in a study published in 1944. Although often called 'Aussi lingo' by the criminals, of 349 rhyming slang terms collected by Maurer from American criminals, only 3% came from Australia, while 48% came from the United Kingdom and 49% were of American provenance (Maurer 1981: 141, 148–9).

14   Grayson writes of 'Verse', but 'Vesre' is also an accepted term.

15   'L'envers' is most likely the form that was reordered to provide the term 'Verlan'. Lefkowitz (1989: 312), however, points out another (less likely) possibility in the inversion of 'langue verte', a term describing 'slang' or crude language.

16   Verlan does not typically involve rearrangement of word order, although Verlan forms such as 'asmeuk' for 'comme ça' ('like this') are attested in reference works such as Strutz (2009: 21). 'Sakom' is also possible.

17   This example contains a number of misspelt items found on message boards such as 'alor' for 'alors' and 'systeme' for 'système'. www.bombingart.com/forum/billet_36669_colle_marker.html, accessed April 2013. The example dates back to April 2006.

18   Steere (1894) discusses the use of Kinyume in his description of the Swahili spoken in Zanzibar in the latter part of the nineteenth century. He notes that Kinyume involved "going back, shifting, alteration, an enigmatic way of speaking in which the last syllable is put first". Examples he cited from the Merima dialect showed Swahili words and phrases such as 'macho' ('eyes'), 'mutu' ('man'), 'uzingizi' ('sleep') and 'njara inaniuma' ('I ache with hunger') becoming 'choma', 'tumu', 'ziuzingi' and 'ranja mainaniu'. Steere (1894: 310, 425–6).

Storch (2011) suggests that Kinyume was used among Swahili-speaking youth until the early twentieth century. She also points to the use of inversion in initiation language in Africa. In one instance, she cites the views of the Basari in Senegal, who opine that during initiation they speak in a "crazy, opposite way" (Storch 2011: 78, citing Ferry 1981). Storch (2011: 78) further observes: "Inversion can be interpreted as a representation of the initiation candidates' inverted existence during phases of liminality".

19   Tender (1996: no page indicated, online version) also noted that metathesis was popular in Estonian 'slang' and was "used for euphemistic reasons or simply for humour". Estonian and Finnish are both members of the Finnic branch of the Uralic language family.

20   Strutz (2009: v, 220) notes that the most common suffix in Louchébem is '-em' and that, for Largonji, "often fanciful" suffixes such as '-é', '-ès', '-em', '-ic', '-iche', '-oque' and '-uche' are used.

References

Abu-Abbas, Kh.H, Al-Kadi, T.T. and Al-Tamimi, F.Y. (2010) 'On three –rb- language games in Arabic', *Argumentum*, 6, 76–90.
Ahua, B.M. (2006) 'La Motivation dans les créations lexicales en Nouchi', *Le Français en Afrique*, 21, 143–57.
Amari, J. (2010) 'Slang lexicography and the problem of defining slang', *The Fifth International Conference on Historical Lexicography and Lexicology*, Oxford, 16–18 June.
Androutsopoulos, J. (2000a) 'Non-standard spellings in media texts: the case of German fanzines', *Journal of Sociolinguistics*, 4(4), 514–33.
Androutsopoulos, J.K. (2000b) 'Extending the concept of the (socio)linguistic variable to slang', in T. Kis (ed.) *Mia szleng*, Debrecen: Kossuth Lajos University Press. 1–21. jannisandroutsopoulos.files.wordpress.com/2009/09/slangvar.pdf, accessed April 2014.
Androutsopoulos, J. (2005) 'Research on youth language', in U. Ammon, D. Norbert, K.J. Mattheier and P. Trudgill (eds.) *Sociolinguistics/Soziolinguistik: An International Handbook of the Science of Language and Society (Ein internationales Handbuch zur Wissenschaft von Sprache und Gesellschaft), Vol. 2*, Berlin: de Gruyter. 1496–1505.
Androutsopoulos, A. (2011) 'Language change and digital media: A review of conceptions and evidence', in T. Kristiansen and N. Coupland (eds.) *Standard Languages and Language Standards in a Changing Europe*, Oslo: Novus. 145–61.
Awa, J.O. (2015a) 'Language and creativity in African literature: a stylistic examination of Akachi Adimora-Ezeigbo's *The Last of the Strong Ones*', *International Journal of Humanities and Social Science*, 5(1), 260–7.
Awa, J.O. (2015b) 'African literature a celebration of artistic freedom: an examination of Chimamanda Adichie's *Purple Hibiscus*', *Global Journal of Arts, Humanities and Social Sciences*, 3(5), 53–65.
Awa, J.O. (2015c) 'Creativity in the African novel: a Stylistic exploration of Helon Habila's *Measuring Time*', *International Journal of Research in Arts and Social Sciences*, 8(1), 30–9.
Berjaoui, N. (1997) 'Parlers secrets d'El-Jadida: notes préliminaires', *Estudios de dialectología norteafricana y andalusí*, 2, 147–58.
Blake, B. (2010) *Secret Language*, Oxford: Oxford University Press.
Boellstorff, T. (2004) '*Gay* language and Indonesia: registering belonging', *Journal of Linguistic Anthropology*, 14(2), 248–68.
BombingArt.com. www.bombingart.com/forum, accessed April 2013.
Bosire, M. (2009) 'What makes a Sheng word unique? Lexical manipulation in mixed languages', in A. Ojo and L. Moshi (eds.) *Selected Proceedings of the 39th Annual Conference on African Linguistics*, Somerville, MA. 77–85.
Bullock, B. (1996) 'Popular derivation and linguistic inquiry: Les Javanais', *The French Review*, 70(2), 180–91.
Cahill, M. (2008) 'Word games as experimental linguistics', *SIL Forum for Language Fieldwork* (September).
Chambert-Loir, H. (1984) 'Those who speak Prokem', *Indonesia*, 37(April), 105–17.
Breva Claramonte, M. and García Alonso, J.I. (1993) 'Categories, morphological features, and slang in the graffiti of a United States Western university', *Revista Alicantina de Estudios Ingleses*, 6, 19–31.
Burling, R. (1970) *Man's Many Voices: Language in Its Cultural Context*, New York and Chicago: Holt, Rinehart and Winston.

Cobb, M. (2002) 'Changes in the Russian language in the post-Soviet period', *Dialog on Language Instruction*, *15*(1&2), 19–25.
Coleman, J. (2012) *The Life of Slang*, Oxford: Oxford University Press.
Cooper, B. (1993) 'Euphemism and taboo of language (with particular reference to Russian)', *Australian Slavonic and East European Studies*, *7*(2), 61–84.
Crystal, D. (1998) *Language Play*, London: Penguin Books.
Dobrovol′skii, V.N. (1899) 'Nekotorye dannye uslovnogo iazyka Kaluzhskikh rabochikh', *Izvestiia Otdeleniia Russkogo Iazyka i Slovesnosti Imperatorskoi Akademii Nauk*, *IV*, 1386–1410.
Davie, J.D. (1998) Making sense of the nonstandard: a study of borrowing and word-formation in 1990s Russian youth slang, with particular reference to the language of the fanzine (Doctoral dissertation, 2 volumes). University of Portsmouth.
Doran, M. (2007) 'Alternative French, alternative identities: situating language in la banlieue', *Contemporary French and Francophone Studies*, *11*(4), 497–508.
Dorleijn, M., Mous, M. and Nortier, J. (2015) 'Urban youth speech styles in Kenya and the Netherlands', in J. Nortier and B.A. Svendsen (eds.) *Language, Youth and Identity in the 21st Century*, Cambridge: Cambridge University Press. 271–89.
Eble, C. (1996) *Slang and Sociability*, Chapel Hill: University of North Carolina Press.
García, M. (2005) 'Influences of gypsy *Caló* on contemporary Spanish Slang', *Hispania*, *88*(4), 800–12.
Gardner, A. (2011) 'Southampton v Leeds United – as it happened', *The Guardian*, 6 August. www.theguardian.com/football/2011/aug/06/championship-southampton-leeds-united-live, accessed October 2015.
Geipel, J. (1995) 'Caló: the "secret" language of the gypsies of Spain', in P. Burke and R. Porter (eds.) *Languages and Jargons: Contributions to a Social History of Language*, Cambridge: Polity Press. 102–32.
Gil, D. (2002) 'Ludlings in Malayic languages: an introduction', *PELBBA 15, Pertemuan Linguistik (Pusat Kajian) Bahasa dan Budaya Atma Jaya: Kelima Belas Pusat Kajian Bahasa dan Badaya*, Jakarta: Unika Atma Jaya. Pre-publication copy.
Githinji, P. (2006) 'Bazes and their shibboleths: lexical variation and Sheng speakers' identity in Nairobi', *Nordic Journal of African Studies*, *15*(4), 443–72.
Grachëv, M.A. (1994) 'Ob etimologii v russkom argo', *Russkaia rech'*, *4*, 67–70.
Grayson, J. (1964) 'Lunfardo, Argentina's unknown tongue', *Hispania*, *47*(1, March), 66–8.
Green, J. (2016) *Slang: A Very Short Introduction*, Oxford: Oxford University Press.
Hasund, I.K. and Drange, E. (2014) 'English influence on Norwegian teenage slang', in J. Coleman (ed.) *Global English Slang*, London: Routledge. 139–49.
Heller-Roazen, D. (2013) *Dark Tongues*, New York: Zone Books.
Hollington, A. and Makwabarara, T. (2015) 'Youth language practices in Zimbabwe', in N. Nassenstein and A. Hollington (eds.) *Youth Language Practices in Africa and Beyond*, Berlin/Boston: Walter de Gruyter, Inc. 257–70.
Ichimaru Gin n Tonic (2007) *Mangahelpers*, blog post, 22 January. mangahelpers.com/forum/threads/the-football-soccer-thread.25415/page-5, accessed March 2016.
Japan Times (2005) 'Japanese girls devise their own written language', *Kanji Clinic*, #69, 14 April. www.kanjiclinic.com/kc69final.htm, accessed December 2015.
Journo, A. (2009) 'Jambazi Fulani: hip hop literature and the redefining of literary spaces in Kenya', *Postcolonial Text*, *5*(3), 1–22.
Khomiakov, V.A. (1992) 'Nekotorye tipologicheskie osobennosti nestandartnoi leksiki angliiskogo, frantsuzskogo i russkogo iazykov', *Voprosy iazykoznaniia*, *3*, 94–105.

Kiessling, R. and Mous, M. (2004) 'Urban youth languages in Africa', *Anthropological Linguistics*, *46*(3), 1–39.
Kinkin83 (2012), blog post, 29 May. kinkin83.skyrock.com/3093114341-les-petit-frere-qui-rend-fou-les-chtard, accessed December 2017.
Krohn, F.B. and Suazo, F.L. (1995) 'Contemporary urban music: controversial messages in hip-hop and rap lyrics', *Et cetera: A Review of General Semantics*, *52*(2, Summer), 139–54.
Laksana, A.S. (2015) *How to Find True Love and Other Stories*, Jakarta: The Lontar Foundation (BTW).
Landi, G. and Pasch, H. (2015) 'Sango Godobé: the urban youth language of Bangui (CAR)', in N. Nassenstein and A. Hollington (eds.) *Youth Language Practices in Africa and Beyond*, Berlin/Boston: Walter de Gruyter, Inc. 205–26.
Lefkowitz, N.J. (1989) 'Verlan: talking backwards in French', *The French Review*, *63*(2), 312–22.
Mallik, B. (1972) *Language of the Underworld of West Bengal*, Calcutta: Sanskrit College Research Series No. LXXVII.
Mandelbaum-Reiner, F. (1991) 'Secrets de bouchers et Largonji actuel des Louchébèm', *Langage et société*, *56*, 21–49.
Manfredi, S. (2008) 'Rendók: a youth secret language in Sudan', *Estudios de dialectología norteafricana y andalusí*, *12*, 113–29.
Materialy otdela rezhima i operraboty UITLK (1952) Sverdlovsk.
Maurer, D.W. (1981) *Language of the Underworld* (collected and edited by Allan W. Futrell and Charles B. Wordell), Lexington: University Press of Kentucky.
Méla, V. (1988) 'Parler verlan: règles et usages', *Langage et société*, *45*, 47–72.
Méla, V. (1991) 'Le verlan ou le langage du miroir', *Langages*, *101*, 73–94.
Méla, V. (1997) 'Verlan 2000', *Langue française*, *114*, 16–34.
Miller, L. (2004) 'Those naughty teenage girls: Japanese Kogals, slang, and media assessments', *Journal of Linguistic Anthropology*, *14*(2), 225–47.
Mugaddam, A.H. (2012b) 'Identity construction and linguistic manipulation in Randuk', paper presented at the *Youth Languages and Urban Languages in Africa Workshop*, Institut für Afrikanistik, Cologne University, Germany.
Mugaddam, A.H. (2015) 'Identity construction and linguistic manipulation in Randuk', in N. Nassenstein and A. Hollington (eds.) *Youth Language Practices in Africa and Beyond*, Berlin/Boston: Walter de Gruyter, Inc. 99–118.
Mugaddam, A.R.H. (2012a) 'Aspects of youth language in Khartoum', in M. Brenzinger and A-M. Fehn (eds.) *Proceedings of 6th World Congress of African Linguistics*, Cologne: Rüdiger Köppe Verlag. 87–98.
Nassenstein, N. (2015a) 'Imvugo y'Umuhanda: youth language practices in Kigali (Rwanda)', in N. Nassenstein and A. Hollington (eds.) *Youth Language Practices in Africa and Beyond*, Berlin/Boston: Walter de Gruyter, Inc. 185–204.
Nassenstein, N. (2015b) 'The emergence of Langila in Kinshasa (DR Congo)', in N. Nassenstein and A. Hollington (eds.) *Youth Language Practices in Africa and Beyond*, Berlin/Boston: Walter de Gruyter, Inc. 81–98.
Nassenstein, N. (2016) 'The new urban youth language Yabacrâne in Goma (DR Congo)', *Sociolinguistic Studies*, *10*(1–2), 235–59.
O.R.Z. (1992) *1*(96).
Ogechi, N.O. (2005) 'On lexicalization in Sheng', *Nordic Journal of African Studies*, *14*(3): 334–55.

Osundare, N. (1982) *Cautious Paths Through the Bramble: A Critical Classification of Style Theories and Concepts.* Unpublished paper. Department of English, University of Ibadan.

Pilard, G. (1998) 'Argot, slang et lexicographie bilingue', *Eurelex '98 Proceedings*, 411–20. www.euralex.org, accessed December 2014.

Plénat, M. (1991) 'Présentation des javanais', *Langages*, 101, 5–10.

Pratt, J. (ed.) (1984) *Harrap's Slang Dictionary French–English, English–French*, Bromley: Harrap.

Quinn, A. (2017), 'How to speak "Norn Iron" – an A–Z guide', *NewsLetter*, 10 March.

Robert L'Argenton, F. (1991) 'Larlépeem largomuche du louchébem. Parler l'argot du boucher', *Langue française*, 90, 113–25.

Ryazanova-Clarke L. and Wade, T. (1999) *The Russian Language Today*, London: Routledge.

Sandry, G. and Carrère, M. (1957) *Dictionnaire de L'Argot Moderne* (11th ed.), Paris: Librairie Mireille Ceni.

Sherzer, J. (2002) *Speech Play and Verbal Art*, Austin: University of Texas Press.

Skame (2004). jojo882.free.fr/?t=skame, accessed April 2017.

Slang Phonology (2014), posted 28 April. duermueller.tripod.com/slangphon.html, accessed June 2015.

Slone, T.H. (2003) *Prokem. An Analysis of a Jakartan Slang*, Oakland: Masalai Press.

Smirnov, I.T. (1902) 'Melkie torgovtsy g. Kashina Tverskoi gub. i ikh uslovnyi iazyk', *Izvestiia otdeleniia ruskogo iazyka i slovesnosti*, *III*(VII), 89–114.

Sornig, K. (1981) *Lexical Innovation: A Study of Slang, Colloquialisms and Casual Speech*, Amsterdam: John Benjamins.

Sourdot, M. (2003) 'La dynamique du langage des jeunes', *Résonances*, 10(Juin), 4–5.

Stanlaw, J. (2014) 'Some trends in Japanese slang', in J. Coleman (ed.) *Global English Slang*, London: Routledge. 160–70.

Steere, E. (1894) *A Handbook of the Swahili Language, as Spoken at Zanzibar* (4th ed.), London: Society for Promoting Christian Knowledge.

Storch, A. (2011) *Secret Manipulations*, New York: Oxford University Press.

Strutz, H. (2009) *Dictionary of French Slang and Colloquial Expressions*, New York: Barron's.

Tender, T. (1996) 'Some fragments about the Estonian slang: its essence and research', in M. Kõiva (ed.) *Contemporary Folklore: Changing World View and Tradition*, Tartu: Institute of Estonian Language and Estonian Museum of Literature. www.folklore.ee/rl/pubte/ee/cf/cf/25.html, accessed July 2015.

Tetreault, C. (2000) 'Adolescents' multilingual punning and identity play', paper presented at the American Anthropological Association, San Francisco.

Thurlow, C. (2007) 'Fabricating youth: new-media discourse and the technologization of young people', in S. Johnson and A. Ensslin (eds.) *Language in the Media: Representations, Identities, Ideologies*, London: Continuum. 213–33.

Tikhanov, P.N. (1895) *Brianskie startsy: tainyi iazyk nishchikh. Etnologicheskii ocherk*, Briansk.

Vázquez Ríos, J. (2009) 'Linguistique et sociolinguistique du verlan à travers le monde', *AnMal Electronica*, 26, 197–214.

Veit-Wild, F. (2009) '"Zimbolicious" – the creative potential of linguistic innovation: the case of Shona-English in Zimbabwe', *Journal of Southern African Studies*, 35(3), 683–97.

Veraldi-Pasquale, G. (2011) *Vocabulario de caló-español*, Bubok Publishing S.L.

Vierke, C. (2015) 'Some remarks on poetic aspects of Sheng', in N. Nassenstein and A. Hollington (eds.) *Youth Language Practices in Africa and Beyond*, Berlin/Boston: Walter de Gruyter, Inc. 227–56.

Walter, M. (2002) 'Kalaam, Kalaarbaam: an Arabic speech disguise in Hadramaut', *Texas Linguistic Forum 45, Proceedings of the Tenth Annual Symposium about Language and Society*, Austin, April, 177–86.

Widawski, M. (2015) *African American Slang*, Cambridge: Cambridge University Press.

Wolfer, C. (2011) 'Arabic secret languages', *Folia Orientalia, 47*, Part II.

Zaikovskaia, T.V. (1993) 'Mozhno mozzhechoknut'sia? Sabo samoi!', *Russkaia rech', 6*, 40–3.

Zhirmunskii, V. (1936) *Natsional'nyi iazyk i sotsial'nye dialekty*, Leningrad: Khudozhestvennaia literatura.

9 Clipping and the use of acronyms and other abbreviations

Introduction

The clipping of words and phrases to make smaller items is found in many languages. It is regarded as one of the most common markers of colloquial French, and is frequently seen in varieties ranging from Camfranglais, Sheng and Bahasa Gaul to the language of Japanese and Norwegian youth (Kießling 2004; Miller 2004; Smith-Hefner 2007; Bosire 2009; Stanlaw 2014; Harchaoui 2015). Along with borrowing, clipping and other forms of abbreviation are the most productive mechanisms for creating new words in Bahasa Gaul (Smith-Hefner 2007: 192). Its use in some languages also goes back some time: Coleman (2012: 152–3) demonstrates the use of clipping in English at the turn of the eighteenth century; Salillas (1896) points to the use of 'perdi' ('Civil Guard') as a shortened form of the Caló word 'perdinel' ('soldier', 'guard') in his study of eighteenth- and nineteenth-century Spanish criminal language; while Wise (1997) states that clipping began to appear heavily in French student language from the late-nineteenth century. A few decades on from then, Leroy (1935: 34, 145, 186) noted the use of 'mac' for 'maquereau' ('pimp'), 'bis' for 'bistro' ('public house', 'bar', 'inn keeper', 'landlord') and 'Le Popu' for the publication *Le Populaire* variously in 1930s colloquial and criminal French.

In terms of its mechanics, clipping – also known as *truncation* – generally takes two forms: *apocope*, where part of the end of the word is removed; and *aphaeresis*, where an element is removed from the beginning. As many of the examples in this chapter will suggest, in many languages clipping can often involve either creating or amending nouns, such as French 'anarcho' from 'anarchiste', meaning 'anarchist'. However, words from other classes can also be found – such as adjectives, as in the French 'le der des ders' ('the lowest of the low'; 'the war to end all wars'; 'last drink before leaving', 'one for the road'), where 'der' is derived from 'dernier' ('last'). Phrases can also be contracted, as will be shown later.

There can be many reasons why a speaker might use clipping. One commonly cited motivation is language economy (e.g. Červenková 2001 and Kortas 2003 on colloquial French; Sourdot 2003 on French youth language; Stanlaw 2014 on general Japanese 'slang'; Mukhwana 2015 on Sheng and Engsh; Widawski 2015 on 'slang' in general), where shorter forms of words can be easier to use, especially in the ebb and flow of conversation and in SMS and computer-based exchanges, where there may be character and time limitations. However, economy doesn't tell the whole story. As with other markers of youth, criminal or colloquial language, truncation can move a discussion into a more informal place and can signal to interlocutors a more relaxed stance (as well as power or empowerment) on the part of the speaker. It may also facilitate cryptolect (e.g. Sourdot 2003), where the shorter form of a word might be sufficiently different from the full form so as not to be recognised. Where French is concerned, it may even serve a mirror function and thus index social opposition: Goudaillier (2002) suggests aphaeresis emerged in suburban estates because it represented a departure from the general practice where truncation was commonly performed through apocope. Finally, it may also be employed for euphemism, as in the Italian 'bici' ('bicicletta' – 'bike') for 'prostitute' (Cooper 1993: 70).

Truncation is not the only way of shortening words and phrases; abbreviations (initialisms) and acronyms are other examples of smaller or more succinct items representing longer forms. These will be considered in the second half of this chapter.

Apocope

This type of clipping is found in many languages. In many cases, lexis created through apocope is mono- or bisyllabic, for instance, the English 'dis' for 'disrespect' (Coleman 2012: 37) or 'bro' for 'brother' (Eble 2014: 43). In France and Belgium, people might put signs on their doors saying 'Pas de pub' for 'Pas de publicité' ('No advertisements'), study menus outlining options for 'petit déj' ('breakfast', for 'petit déjeuner'), or read Safia Amor's book *'Au secours, j'ai un ado à la maison!'* ('Help! I have a teen at home!'), where 'ado' stands for 'adolescent'. Other examples of apocope, where there is no change in meaning after clipping, include:

Language variety	Original item	Truncated item	Meaning
2003 Camfranglais	Cameroun	Camer	Cameroon
	dangereux	dang	dangerous
2004 Kogals	hazukashii	hazui	embarrassing
	mendokusai	mendoi	pain in the ass
2007 Bahasa Gaul	restoran	resto	restaurant
	minimal	minim	minimal
2006–2014 Russian	komp'iuter	komp (*coll.*)	computer
	Zaporozhets	zapor (*coll.*)	Zaporozhets (car)*
	narkoman	nark (*dr., yth.*)	drug user
Colloquial French	graffito, graffiti	graf	graffiti
	après-midi	aprèm	afternoon[†]

*'Zapor' also means 'constipation', and is no doubt used jocularly with this in mind.
[†]'Aprèm' is derived from an item where the *s* is not pronounced.

In some instances, items may be contracted to a (near-)minimal usable point. In the criminal language of 1960s West Bengal, for instance, the nouns 'dālāl' ('broker') and 'coṭ' ('cheat') were truncated to 'ḍi' ('pimp') and 'ca' ('deception'), while in Spanish youth language 'casa' ('home') may be truncated to 'ca' with the same meaning. Similarly, Nouchi has registered 'pa', 'bou' and 'tri' from French 'parking' ('car park'), 'boutique' ('shop') and 'tricot' ('sweater') (Kiessling and Mous 2004: 22). As we might imagine, context, cotext and precedence can be particularly important when using such heavily contracted words: for example, is the item part of established usage within a given group? If not, will interlocutors know what a speaker means when the new term is used, given that a large part of the original word is absent? Does the new item have a number of meanings?

New lexis created through truncation needn't rely on the clipping of standard items alone. It can also be formed through clipping words associated with youth, criminal or colloquial usage. In the case of French, this can be seen in the truncation of items created through Verlan, such as 'brelic' from 'brelica' (from 'calibre' – 'gun') and 'dèk' from 'dékis' ('plainclothes policeman', an inverted form of the Verlan 'kisdé' from déguisé'). 'Dégueu' ('filthy', 'repulsive') from 'dégueulasse', which has the same meaning, shows that French youth or colloquial items can be shortened without the filter of Verlan. Separately, Russian also includes words most likely derived through clipping youth lexis: the term 'tusovka' ('hangout', 'crew', 'get-together') can be shortened by youth to 'tus' with the same meaning, while the English 'mother', although still vulgar, can partially attenuate the expressive force and taboo of the highly pejorative 'motherfucker' (Widawski 2015: 46–7).

Evaluation and stance

Some scholars see the expression of attitude and stance as pervasive in interaction. Halliday (1978: 203) posits, for example, that "[i]t is impossible to talk about things without conveying attitudes and interpersonal judgements", while Kiesling (2009: 179) states that "stancetaking is always a speaker's primary concern in conversation; even in speech events in which we might think stance is peripheral, it is in fact of central importance".

Insofar as evaluations indicate a person's position vis-à-vis other people, things or concepts, we can say that they are part of the communication and negotiation of stance.

In studies of English-speaking groups, scholars underline the prevalence of evaluation in youth varieties:

- Eble (1996: 52; my italics) notes the role of judgement in her study of 1972–1993 US college language: "Most [meanings] pertain to types of people and to relationships between and among people.

Standards of behavior that one does or does not live up to are implied, as more than one-third of the slang items can be classified as *judgments* of acceptance or rejection. In meaning, then, college slang reflects the users' preoccupation with sociability". This theme continued in the analysis of her 2005–2012 data: "Judgments of approval *(swag)* or disapproval *(whack)*, acceptance *(word)* or rejection *(fail)* are implicit or explicit in most of the vocabulary and aid students in responding to behavior and maintaining group solidarity" (Eble 2014: 38).

- Moore (2014: 7, 17) intimates that "slang is prototypically expressive of attitude" and that it has "a connection to affect or attitude that is called up automatically".
- Eckert (2005: 97) states: "Engaged in a fierce negotiation of social values and differences, adolescents are continually making new distinctions and evaluations of behavior, in the course of which they coin new terms for social evaluation and social types".
- In her discussion of 'global English slang', Coleman (2014: 4, citing Adams 2014) indicates that "[s]lang is often verdictive ... in the sense that it pronounces a judgement not only on the language, but also on the listener and the referent".

In the present book, we can see several cases where a speaker "pronounces a judgement". In some instances, these judgements can reveal what is particularly important, relevant or problematic to the individual or group, and deemed worthy of evaluation, at the time:

- GDR youth use of 'Mumienschleuder' ('mummy catapult') to refer to a train that took old East Germans for trips to West Germany;
- 1990s Israeli inmates: 'klavim' (lit. 'dogs', for 'inmates who obey the boss');
- 2004 Kogals' use of 'chôSW' ('super bad personality') and 'mendoi' ('pain in the ass');
- Indonesian youth: 'rustam lubis' ('really ugly face');
- Russian youth term 'monstra', meaning 'ugly person', 'monster';
- Sheng speakers: 'kenge' ('monitor lizard') to refer endearingly to a girlfriend;
- Colloquial Spanish 'gilipollas' ('bloody fool', 'prat'), 'buzón' ('big mouth'), 'jefazo' ('big shot') and 'burrócrata' ('stupid bureaucrat');
- Colloquial French has seen the use of 'amerlocque' ('Yank'), 'vinasse' ('cheap wine', 'cheap plonk') and 'TBM' ('very good-looking guy').

Aphaeresis

This form of clipping is perhaps less commonly seen in studies of youth, criminal and colloquial language but is found in several varieties nonetheless. As a means of creating youth and criminal items in some languages, it is not new: Salillas (1896) notes 'cal' as a shortened form of 'fiscal' ('public prosecutor') in his record of Spanish criminal language; and Maurer (1981: 101) documents the use of 'cotics' to refer to any kind of narcotics in his study of the language practices of the 1930s US underworld drug user. Particularly good examples of aphaeresis can be seen in the following items, where there is no change in meaning:

Language variety	Original item	Truncated item	Meaning
1970s–1990s US college students	parents	rents	parents
	relatives	tives	relatives
1998 Nouchi	confiance	fiance	trust
2003 Camfranglais	business	ness	business
	bagnole	gnole	car
2004 Kogals	sarariiman	riiman	salaryman
	Shibuya (an area in Tokyo)	Bûya	Shibuya
2007 Bahasa Gaul	begini	gini	like this
	percaya	caya	to believe

As these examples indicate, in some instances the initial word may be standard ('parents'). However, this need not always be the case, as we can see in the colloquial French 'bagnole' ('motor', 'car'; other examples such as 'touse' from 'partouse' ('orgy') could be cited).

Truncation in phrases, change in meaning, and shortening names

In keeping with principles of informality, expressiveness and language economy, in some languages utterances may contain shortened forms of phrases. In Town Nyanja, for example, questions such as 'Ali kuti?' ('Where is (s)he?') and 'Uli bwanji?' ('How are you?') might be rendered 'Ali ku?' and 'Uli bwa?', while in English (mainly US) 'Sup?' may replace 'What's up?' (Coleman 2012: 37). Additionally, in Japanese the phrase 'yoroshiku onegaishimasu' ('Please give my best to ...') may be shortened to 'yoroshiku' or 'yoro' (Stanlaw 2014: 163), while in Russian 'bu sdelano' ('no problem') may be uttered instead of 'budet sdelano' ('it will be done') to mean 'will do'. A less common variant, 'bu ... sde ...', has also been attested (Shlyakhov and Adler 2006: 29). Some truncation can also serve attenuating purposes, as can be seen in 'mo-fo' for the English expletive 'mother fucker' (Widawski 2015: 47).

Truncation can equally be encountered in some languages through the clipping of phrasal verbs – for example, English 'to chill' for 'to chill out'. Alternatively, compounds or noun phrases might also be shortened to create new nouns:

Language variety	Original item, meaning	Truncated item	New meaning
West Bengal criminals	rātkānā ('night blindness')	rāt	blind man, people
Colloquial French	beau-frère ('brother-in-law')	beauf	brother-in-law
Colloquial Russian	federal'nye voiska ('federal troops')	federaly	servicemen

The example of 'rātkānā' suggests that, in some cases, clipping can lead to a change in meaning; consideration may thus be required to correctly interpret clipped forms. Cotext can also be important when trying to determine the word class of the colloquial French 'parano', which can mean 'paranoia' ('paranoïa'), 'paranoiac' ('paranoïaque') or 'paranoid' ('paranoïaque'), for instance.

Ellipsis in names is common in informal British and US English. A sense of levity and playfulness can be created by omitting the surname of a personality or character to refer to an object or state with which that surname is homophonous or near-homophonous. For example, 'Basil' for 'forty pounds' after the TV comedy character 'Basil Fawlty'; 'melanied' ('drunk') after the singer Melanie Blatt and the colloquial 'blatted' ('drunk'); 'Robert Dinero' or 'Robert' ('money') after the actor Robert De Niro, whose surname sounds somewhat similar to the Spanish word for 'money' ('dinero') (Lillo 2007: 435, 437–8). Equally, ellipsis can figure in utterances that are altogether less playful, such as where the verb is dropped in the French 'Ta gueule!' ('Shut it!') from 'Ferme ta gueule' ('Shut your trap!') – see page 206).

Truncation and affixation

In several language varieties, such as German youth language, colloquial English and French, Sheng and Camfranglais, some new items are created through a combination of truncation and suffixation. For example, in German youth language, where clipping is very common (Androutsopoulos 2000: 10), a noun such as 'Asozialer' ('asocial person') can become 'Asi' or 'Asinger';[1] while in colloquial French, where this combination is particularly productive (Kortas 2003), words such as 'alco(o)lo' ('alcoholic') and 'morcif' ('piece') are truncated and resuffixed forms of 'alcoolique' and 'morceau'. In Sheng, truncation can combine with affixation in words such as 'daroo' ('classroom', from Swahili 'darasa') and 'mresh' ('beautiful person', from 'mrembo'); while items such as 'merco' ('Merc') and 'loco' ('home') from 'Mercedes' ('Mercedes car') and French 'location' ('location') can be found in Camfranglais.

As we can see, the youth, criminal and colloquial words differ in form from the originals, and the addition of a suffix is certainly important both to enhancing the 'slang' look and feel of the word and to changing its shape. The new word should both look and feel sufficiently different from synonyms or equivalents in standard usage for the speaker's communicative goals to be achieved. Such changes in form can be seen, for example, in some nouns found in Spanish youth language:

anarco	'anarchist', from 'anarquista' ('anarchist');
manifa	'demonstration', from 'manifestación' ('demonstration');

as well as in colloquial English:

addy	'address', from 'address';
moby	'mobile', from 'mobile (phone)'.

Abbreviations

Another means of representing a word or phrase in a shorter form is to create abbreviations, which are also known as *initialisms* where letters are spelled out individually. This is a process that has been evident in the youth, criminal and colloquial varieties of some languages for some time, and one that allows for language economy (as in text messaging), language play and/or the facilitation of individual or group expression. Abbreviations can also often be found in advertising or in public signs, such as the French 'CB HS' ('carte bancaire hors service' – 'bank card machine out of order'). Examples of abbreviations in youth and colloquial varieties include:

1970s–1990s US college students:	OTL	'Out to lunch' (i.e. out of one's senses);
	MLA	'Massive lip action' (i.e. passionate kissing);
2009 French:	PV *(coll.)*	'traffic ticket', 'fine', from 'procès verbal';
	H *(dr.)*	'hash', 'drugs', from 'hachisch' ('hashish');*
	GDB *(coll.)*	'hangover', from 'gueule de bois' ('hangover');
2009 colloquial French texting:	CPG	'It's not serious' (from 'c'est pas grave');
	MDR	'Rolling on the floor laughing, from 'mort de rire' ('dead from laughing');†
2016 colloquial Russian:	IaTL	'ILY', from 'Ia tebia liubliu' ('I love you')

*The use of abbreviations to refer to drugs is quite commonplace, e.g. 'E' for 'ecstasy'. Maurer (1981: 66) documented the use of abbreviations to refer to drugs in the US in the 1930s. For example, 'O' for 'opium', 'C' for 'cocaine'.

†The use of abbreviations is not a new phenomenon in French: 1980s colloquial French saw the use of 'PPH' for 'old man', from 'passera pas l'hiver' ('won't get through the winter') (Pratt 1984: 346), while the *Dictionnaire de L'Argot Moderne*, published in 1957, attested 'G.D.B.' as meaning 'hangover' (Sandry and Carrère 1957: 121).

In some cases, an abbreviation may extend to an almost absurd length for expressive effect, as in the French jocular 'NDPAMMQJSDLPEMCPDUB' cited by Verdelhan-Bourgade (1991: 74), meaning: 'Ne dites pas à ma mère que je suis dans la publicité, elle me croit pianiste dans un bordel' ('Don't tell my mother that I am in advertising; she thinks I'm a piano player in a brothel'). Despite their impressive artistry, however, extensive examples such as this appear to be less commonplace than shorter constructions.

Abbreviations may also be found in phrases and expressions, such as the French 'Système D' ('resourcefulness', 'smarts', 'thinking on your feet' – also the title of a French home improvement magazine), where 'D' represents 'débrouille' or 'démerde'; and 'avoir les jambes en x' ('to be knock-kneed'; lit. 'to have legs in an X'). They can also be seen in African American 'slang' in the form of 'A-Town' for 'Atlanta, Georgia', 'O-Town' for 'Oakland, California', and 'D Town' for 'Detroit, Michigan' (Widawski 2015: 48, 132).

It is also possible for initialisms to be given new expansions, often as a means of improvisation and for ironic, parodic or humorous effect. Thus, the US college language practices examined by Eble (1996) included a new meaning for the 'ABC Store', from 'Alcohol Beverage Control Store' to 'Aunt Betsy's Cookie Store'. In the same manner, street children in Indonesia may refer to having an 'SH' or 'difficult life', where the regular expansion 'Sarjana Hukum' ('law degree') is replaced by 'Susah Hidup'; or – for those working on Malioboro, the main street in Yogyakarta – to attending 'UGM', which comes to mean 'Universitas Gelandangan Malioboro' ('University of Malioboro's Vagrants') as opposed to the establishment's standard name 'Universitas Gajah Mada'. Other examples include:

1990s Russian criminals:
VLKSM   'Take a spade and dig yourself a grave', from 'Voz′mi lopatu i kopai sebe mogilu'. In the Soviet era, the 'VLKSM' ('Vsesoiuznyi leninskii kommunisticheskii soiuz molodëzhi' – 'All-Union Lenin Communist Youth League') was a state-run political youth body also known as the 'Komsomol'.
2009 French:
BCBG   'part of the smart set', 'Sloane Ranger', from 'bon chic, bon genre'; or 'a pretty face and a good body', from 'beau cul, belle gueule';
TBM   'very good-looking guy', from 'très beau mec'; or 'very well hung', from 'très bien monté'.

Alternatively, although less common, abbreviations might not always be formed by using the first letter of a word. In New York inner-city usage (2005–2008), for example, some abbreviations were created either by using the first two letters of a word, such as 'J.O.' for the standard 'job' – a truncated form that comes to be treated as an abbreviation; or by selecting the first letter of each syllable – 'PJs' ('projects', i.e. housing developments; compare also the commonly used 'PJs' for 'pyjamas') (Kripke 2014: 34).

Acronyms

Acronyms are created through combining the initial letter or letters of a series of words. They have been used in some varieties for a considerable time: 1970s–1990s US college student usage included 'fubar' ('fucked up beyond all recognition', said of students suffering the ill effects of alcohol or drugs; the acronym was also used in World War Two); and 'nail' ('nice ass in Levi's', to refer to a well-built guy). A more recent example is the 2005–2012 US student use of 'yolo' – 'you only live once'.

The use of acronyms to impart speaker evaluation can also be seen in Indonesian youth language where – among other purposes – items might be created for jocular or critical ends:

kuper	'socially awkward', from 'kurang pergaulan';
telmi	'dull', 'slow-thinking', from 'telat mikir';
rustam lubis	'really ugly face', from 'rusak tampang luar biasa';
muklasbakam	'classical face right from the kampong', from 'muka klasik bahan kampung'.*

*The kampong, also seen as 'kampung', is a village, settlement, or residential part of a town or city for lower class inhabitants.

Indeed, Indonesian youth can show considerable deftness where they create new items based on elements of existing words or phrases. In some cases, they might elect to bring together only the final constituents: for instance, the 1980s Indonesian youth item 'tongpes' from 'kantong kempes' ('broke', 'penniless'). In others, the initial element of one word may be concatenated with a medial element from another as part of a play on words, hence 'ANGGUN', a Prokem play on 'anggun' ('well dressed') but redefined to mean 'ugly person', from 'angota ragunan' (lit. 'member of the Ragunan zoo').

As we might appreciate, acronyms in youth and colloquial language can be created at the expense of what is perceived to be the stuffy or self-important language of officialdom and formal structures. Some examples of Indonesian youth language, for instance, show a reinterpretation of official acronyms to provide a satirical, irreverent and ironic meaning:

Puskesmas	where the acronym representing 'Pusat Kesehatan Masyarakat' ('public health centre') is reinterpreted ironically to mean 'pusing keseleo masuk angin' ('nauseous', 'feverish');
APIK	where 'Akademi Pendidikan Ilmu Keguruan' ('Training Academy of Science Teachers') is redefined as 'agak pikun' ('rather senile').

Indeed, as we can see, much as with abbreviations, acronyms can also be assigned alternative expansions (so-called *backcronyms*). A particularly instructive example can be seen in the English 'phat'. This is a word that goes back to the US of the 1960s as a version of 'fat'. Its original meaning was 'physically attractive', however other expansions have emerged from this original acronym, including: 'Pretty, Hot, and Tempting', 'Pretty Hot and Tasty' and 'Perfect Hips and Thighs' (González and Stenström 2011: 239).

The attribution of different expansions to acronyms can also be seen in languages such as Russian. In the 1990s, for example, Russian criminals used the item 'TUZ'. This had a number of potential expansions: 'already know about jail', from 'tiur'ma uzhe znakoma'; 'prison teaches the law', from 'tiur'ma uchit zakonu'; or 'prison captive', from 'tiuremnyi uznik'.[2]

Abbreviations and vocalisation

Some abbreviations may be pronounced as initialisms with the result that new vocabulary emerges. A good example of this can be found in the French 'hachès' or 'hachesse' ('exhausted') from the vocalisation of 'HS' – 'out of order', from 'hors service':

> J'arrête pour aujourd'hui; je suis hachès.
> I'm calling it a day; I'm knocked out.
>
> (Strutz 2009: 189)

Other examples of this process include the French 'tège', a truncated vocalisation of 'T.G.V.', which expands to 'train à grande vitesse' ('high speed train'). Remaining on the rail theme, the 1960s West Bengal criminal 'ṭusi' was derived from 'T.C.' – 'ticket collector'.

In some other cases, a vocalised abbreviation may enable speakers to avoid uttering a vulgar or otherwise sensitive word in its entirety. A good example of this can be found in the Russian item 'zhe', where vocalisation of the first letter ж (zh) replaces 'zhopa' ('arse'). Other examples from Russian include:

be   'whore', from 'bliad'': 'Ia etu be znat' ne khochu' ('I don't want to have anything to do with that whore');
ge   'shit', from 'govno': 'Nu i ge eta kolbasa!' ('This sausage is crap!').
(Shlyakhov and Adler 2006: 31, 64)[3]

An interesting alternative to vocalising the first letter only for euphemistic purposes can be seen in the English attenuating phrase 'C U next Tuesday'/'See you next Tuesday' for the expletive 'cunt'. Here the first two letters are spelled out on the basis that they sound like the words 'see' [siː] and 'you' [juː]. The full spelling of the taboo word is avoided by the replacement of n and t with words starting with the relevant consonants – in this case, 'next' and 'Tuesday'. A plausible variant sentence thus emerges.

At the same time, vocalised letter combinations can sometimes replace whole phrases – for instance the French 'TOQP' might sound like 'T'es occupé?' ('Are you busy?') when letters are pronounced individually. French provides another interesting example in 'L.H.O.O.Q.', which sounds like the sentence 'Elle a chaud au cul' (lit. 'Her ass is hot', but more likely to mean 'She is horny'). As Strutz (2009: 217) indicates, this was the title of a painting of a mustachioed Mona Lisa by Marcel Duchamp.

A final dimension to vocalisation involves the pronunciation of symbols. The colloquial English 'hashtag', for example, can be used as a spoken version of the Twitter hashtag symbol ('#') which is often used to tie an utterance to a topic and/or to convey a particular attitude or message. Its online function can be replicated in colloquial speech for parodic, ironic, sardonic or jocular purposes, and can involve a multitude of constructions, for example: 'hashtag are you kidding me?' (Mack 2012), 'hashtag yolo' (McHugh 2013) and 'hashtag cool' (Hahn, undated).

The Rebus Principle, and abbreviation in text- and computer-speak

Given the popularity of shorthand in text and some computer-mediated communication, it is not uncommon to see some words shortened. For example, in English 'tomorrow', 'holidays' and 'about' may be rendered 'tmrw', 'hols' and 'abt'.

One form of abbreviation is known as the Rebus Principle. Here an author uses a symbol or pictogram to stand for a similar or identically sounding word or element – so in English 'gr8' for 'great' and 'b4' for 'before'. This method is commonplace in texting and in some computer-mediated communication as it provides social actors with a means of expressive language and/or enables language economy.

Indeed, the substitution of words and phrases by shorter forms consisting of or incorporating numerals, symbols and letters is likely to remain productive for some time to come. Examples in English and French include:

English:	4	'for';
	2	'to';
French:	@+	'à plus [tard]' ('see you later');
	TOQP	't'es occupé?' ('are you busy?');
	entouK	'en tous cas' ('in any case');
	je t'M	'je t'aime' ('I love you'; see also page 198);
	Ir'n	'Irène' ('Irene').

With phrases such as 'TOQP', 'entouK' and 'je t'M', the letters in capitals sound like the words or constituents they replace, as does the *n* in 'Ir'n'. A similar case can also be seen in the title of a 1994 song by MC Solaar 'L'NMIACCd'HTCK72KPDP' ('l'ennemi a cessé d'acheter ses cassettes de cape et d'épée' – 'the enemy has stopped buying his cloak and dagger films'). However, while skilfully created, such elaborate examples as MC Solaar's are relatively uncommon.

Borrowed and named abbreviations

In keeping with trends to demonstrate cultural cachet and/or the influence of foreign culture and practice, or through language economy, some groups may choose to borrow abbreviations or abbreviated forms across languages, or items from other languages from which abbreviations can be created:

2001 French	NP	'No problem', from the English;
(texting):	Bcoz	'Because', from the English (cited in *Résonances* 2003: 18);
2009 French:	OD	'To OD', 'to overdose', from the English 'OD';
	X (*dr.*)	'Ecstasy' – this may be pronounced either per French [iks] or English pronunciation [ɛks];
	ACAB	'All cops are bastards', from the English (see page 196);
2007 Bahasa Gaul:	MBA	'Married because [of] accident', from English;
	ML	'Making love';

A final mechanism seen with single letters concerns assigning referents alternative descriptions, in some cases based on letter shape. For instance, Eble (1996) points to the use of words such as 'hook' and 'flag' to describe the grades 'C' and 'F' in her mid-1990s study of US college student usage: 'hook' due to the shape of *c* and 'flag' due both to its form and the letter *F*.[4]

Summary

In this chapter, we have seen how commonplace clipping, abbreviations and acronyms can be as means of creating youth, criminal or colloquial items. Two key themes concern how these mechanisms are used for particular purposes and their use in combination with other manipulations. In many instances, truncating a word lends a sense of informality or levity. However, this needn't always be the case: a speaker may have other purposes in mind, such as protest, irreverence, showing off, or avoiding taboo or vulgar terms. As we saw with stump compounding in Chapter Seven, creating new variants of official or generally accepted terminology can be a sign of opposition and subversion, for example.

We also saw how truncation can be used in tandem with other mechanisms to create new words. We noted, for instance, that truncation might be combined with suffixation. However, we could equally have highlighted the clipping of borrowed lexis in language varieties such as Town Nyanja, which has 'chez' from English 'matches'; Bahasa Gaul, where the English 'sensitive' and 'temperamental' become 'sensi' and 'tempra'; and Sheng, where a word may be borrowed, *bantuized* and then clipped. In this way the English 'practice' becomes 'praktizi', then 'tizi' to refer to practice in the sense of sports exercise.[5]

The use of clipping together with other mechanisms to invent new items underlines another key point: that many new words found in youth, criminal or colloquial usage are created deliberately, and can be novel and clever modifications of pre-existing linguistic resources. The US student 'rotic', the Randuk 'toló' and the (rare) Camfranglais 'den' have been based on a conscious choice to retain and remove constituents and create very different variants: in the case of 'rotic', this involves dropping the 'man' from 'romantic', while 'toló' and 'den' find their origins in what were 'bantalōn' ('trousers') and 'identit[é]' ('identity'), examples of *mixed clipping* where apocope and aphaeresis are both applied.

Notes

1 Androutsopoulos (2000: 10) cites the use of clipping in terms of simple clipping, for example 'Touri' ('tourist') from 'Tourist', and clipping and suffixation/suffix alteration ('Asi', 'Asinger').
2 The Russian 'TUZ' is a homonym insofar as the noun 'tuz' literally means 'ace' (in playing cards). It is also an established youth item meaning 'the man', as in 'Ty prosto tuz!' ('You are the man!').
3 A similar mechanism will be found in euphemistic Russian phrases where only the initial letter is given: for instance, 'slovo na bukvu "b"' – 'a word starting with the letter *b*' (for 'bliad'' – 'whore'). In the same vein, 2006 colloquial Spanish also had 'eme' for 'mierda' ('shit'), and English has 'That c' (for 'cunt') and 'Eff off!', 'Get him to eff' (for 'fuck') as methods for attenuating expressive force.
4 A broadly analogous process can be found in Russian student usage, where the word 'palka' ('stick') is used to represent a low 'Grade 1' marking, while a '2' might be known as a 'gus'' ('goose'); and in 1960s West Bengal gamblers' language, where 'chik-cāki' or 'sik-cāki' meant 'one rupee' due to 'sik' meaning an iron rod, which looked like the numeral one. In these cases, the shape of the orthographic representation plays a role in the creation of the new term.
5 Bantu languages generally have syllables with a Consonant–Vowel structure.

References

Androutsopoulos, J.K. (2000) 'Extending the concept of the (socio)linguistic variable to slang', in T. Kis (ed.) *Mia szleng*, Debrecen: Kossuth Lajos University Press. 1–21. jannisandroutsopoulos.files.wordpress.com/2009/09/slangvar.pdf, accessed April 2014.
Bosire, M. (2009) 'What makes a Sheng word unique? Lexical manipulation in mixed languages', in A. Ojo and L. Moshi (eds.) *Selected Proceedings of the 39th Annual Conference on African Linguistics*, Somerville, MA. 77–85.
Červenková, M. (2001) 'L'influence de l'argot sur la langue commune et les procédés de sa formation en français contemporain', *Studia Minora Facultatis Philosophicae Universitatis Brunensis*, L.(22), 77–86.
Coleman, J. (2012) *The Life of Slang*, Oxford: Oxford University Press.
Coleman, J. (2014) 'Introduction: understanding slang in a global context', in J. Coleman (ed.) *Global English Slang*, London: Routledge. 1–9.
Cooper, B. (1993) 'Euphemism and taboo of language (with particular reference to Russian)', *Australian Slavonic and East European Studies*, 7(2), 61–84.
Eble, C. (1996) *Slang and Sociability*, Chapel Hill: University of North Carolina Press.
Eble, C. (2014) 'American college student slang: University of North Carolina (2005–12)', in J. Coleman (ed.) *Global English Slang*, London: Routledge. 36–48.
Eckert, P. (2005) 'Stylistic practice and the adolescent social order', in A. Williams and C. Thurlow (eds.) *Talking Adolescence: Perspectives on Communication in the Teenage Years*, New York: Peter Lang Publishing, Inc. 93–110.

González, F.R. and Stenström, A. (2011) 'Expressive devices in the language of English- and Spanish-speaking youth', *Revista Alicantina de Estudios Ingleses*, 24, 235–56.

Goudaillier, J-P. (2002) 'De l'argot traditionnel au français contemporain des cités', *La Linguistique*, 1(38), 5–24.

Hahn, H. (undated) 'Abbreviations and slang used while talking on the Internet'. www.harley.com/abbreviations/#A, accessed October 2015.

Halliday, M.A.K. (1978) *Language as Social Semiotic*, London: Edward Arnold.

Harchaoui, S. (2015) 'Lexical innovations in the speech of adolescents in Oslo, Norway', *Proceedings of ConSOLE XXIII*, 220–47.

Kiesling, S.F. (2009) 'Style as stance' in A. Jaffe (ed.) *Stance: Sociolinguistic Perspectives*, Oxford: Oxford University Press. 171–94.

Kießling, R. (2004) 'bàk mwà mè dó – Camfranglais in Cameroon', *Lingua Posnaniensis*, 47. www.aai.uni-hamburg.de/afrika/personen/kiessling/medien/kiessling-2004-camfranglais.pdf, accessed September 2012.

Kiessling, R. and Mous, M. (2004) 'Urban youth languages in Africa', *Anthropological Linguistics*, 46(3), 1–39.

Kortas, J. (2003) 'Expressivité Dérivationnelle en Français Contemporain: Noms d'Action', *Studia Romanica Posnaniensia*, Poznań, Adam Mickiewicz University Press, Vol. XXIX, 155–70.

Kripke, M. (2014) 'Inner-city slang of New York', in J. Coleman (ed.) *Global English Slang*, London: Routledge. 25–35.

Leroy, O. (1935) *A Dictionary of French Slang*, London: George G. Harrap and Co. Ltd.

Lillo, A. (2007) 'Squibs: turning puns into names and vice versa', *SKY Journal of Linguistics*, 20, 429–40.

Mack, E. (2012) 'The spoken hashtag must die – here's how', *CNET*, 2 August. www.cnet.com/uk/news/the-spoken-hashtag-must-die-heres-how/, accessed October 2015.

Maurer, D.W. (1981) *Language of the Underworld* (collected and edited by Allan W. Futrell and Charles B. Wordell), Lexington: University Press of Kentucky.

McHugh, M. (2013) 'WTF, Internet? Keep your hashtags out of my real-life conversation', *Digitaltrends.com*, 6 October. www.digitaltrends.com/social-media/wtf-internet-dont-give-in-to-this-jc-penny-hashtag-nonsense/, accessed October 2015.

Miller, L. (2004) 'Those naughty teenage girls: Japanese Kogals, slang, and media assessments', *Journal of Linguistic Anthropology*, 14(2), 225–47.

Moore, R. (2014) 'Affect-marked lexemes and their relational model correlates', *Faculty Publications*, Rollins College, 107, online version.

Mukhwana, A. (2015) 'Sheng and Engsh: what they are and what they are not', *International Journal of Scientific Research and Innovative Technology*, 2(1), 94–102.

Pratt, J. (ed.) (1984) *Harrap's Slang Dictionary French–English, English–French*, Bromley: Harrap.

Salillas, R. (1896) *El Delincuente español – El Lenguaje (studio filológico, psicológico y sociológico) con dos vocabularios jergales*, Read Books. 2011 reprint.

Sandry, G. and Carrère, M. (1957) *Dictionnaire de L'Argot Moderne* (11th ed.), Paris: Librairie Mireille Ceni.

Shlyakhov V. and Adler, E. (2006) *Dictionary of Russian Slang and Colloquial Expressions*, New York: Barron's.

Smith-Hefner, N.J. (2007) 'Youth language, *Gaul* sociability, and the new Indonesian middle class', *Journal of Linguistic Anthropology*, 17(2), 184–203.

Sourdot, M. (2003) 'La dynamique du langage des jeunes', *Résonances*, 10(Juin), 4–5.

Stanlaw, J. (2014) 'Some trends in Japanese slang', in J. Coleman (ed.) *Global English Slang*, London: Routledge. 160–70.

Strutz, H. (2009) *Dictionary of French Slang and Colloquial Expressions*, New York: Barron's.

Verdelhan-Bourgade, M. (1991) 'Procédés sémantiques et lexicaux en francais branché', *Langue française*, *90*(1), 65–79.

Widawski, M. (2015) *African American Slang*, Cambridge: Cambridge University Press.

Wise, H. (1997) *The Vocabulary of Modern French*, London: Routledge.

10 Final comments

In this introduction to the motivations behind and manipulations used in colloquial language and youth and criminal language practices, we've considered what I believe to be key points. In saying this, I recognise, of course, that researchers can be drawn to areas that they find particularly pertinent or engaging. However, the range of drivers and mechanisms explored in the volume cover what I think many would find as the main analytical ground, leaving room for deeper investigation by readers into individual topics at the same time.

In terms of motivations, for example, we've examined the ways in which youth cultural actors and criminals negotiate social identity and identification through their choice and use of certain language practices; we've considered how notions of the Other/Othering and liminality (including Bhabha's Third Space) are explored by actors in their use of French youth practices and of Sheng; we've identified that cryptolect is not only the preserve of the criminal or used solely to hide malign or nefarious intent; and we've noted how certain mechanisms can be employed to add a sense of levity or informality to what a speaker is saying as they interact either asynchronously or in the moment.

We have also explored some of the theoretical constructs that have been advanced to explain or, at the very least, provide some degree of conceptual anchoring for those seeking to understand criminal and youth practices, in particular. We've noted that emphasis has especially been placed on notions such as resistance (anti-language, resistance identity) and identity formation and negotiation (e.g. in sociolinguistic and social psychological studies). Constructs such as the Community of Practice, for example, allow for social actors to evolve overall identities incorporating different constituent affiliations which are, themselves, dynamically negotiated. Correspondingly, the construct can help us to comprehend how linguistic (and other) practices can be shared across groups as social actors move between them, and how social actors develop individual repertoires. That such multiplicity and dynamicity in the Community of Practice aligns with thinking on the ongoing nature of identity formation and identification (e.g. Wilce 2009; Bucholtz and Hall 2010), as well as its plurality and multifaceted character (e.g. Deaux 2001; Joseph 2004; Feitosa, Salas and Salazar 2012) is perhaps especially noteworthy.

When it comes to manipulations, we've seen how items can be borrowed and then adapted between languages or group lexicons to enable speakers to meet a number of communicative goals; we've noted the ways in which new meaning can be ascribed to create items that convey the values, preoccupations and concerns of a group or individual – for example, English colloquial and criminal 'pig' for 'policeman', Spanish 'camisa' ('shirt') for 'heroin hit wrapping', Randuk 'dubbaana' ('fly') for 'intruder', 1960s West Bengal criminal 'bālā' ('bangles') for 'handcuffs'; we've learned about the ways in which words are reordered in a number of languages, often using the same or similar underlying mechanisms (e.g. Verlan, Vesre); we've observed how similar or the same word-formation methods can be used in criminal, youth and colloquial practices; we've documented how mechanisms can be employed in tandem: borrowing and metathesis, clipping and suffixation, borrowing and semantic change, to name but a few; and we've seen how different methods can be used to create lexis to serve a common purpose. For example, a message of social opposition, dissent or ideological/social distancing can be effected variously through the use of antiphrasis, metathesis and (for example, in French) aphaeresis instead of the more established apocope.

Some general points for reflection

As readers will appreciate, the range of topics that require attention when we try to understand the motivations and manipulations that typically obtain in youth, criminal and colloquial language practices is very broad. However, as I draw the volume to a close, I think it is reasonable to highlight particular points to prompt further reflection.

First of all, it is worth recalling that some of the mechanisms we've seen, such as metaphor and borrowing, are to be found in the engine rooms of many standard language varieties. What we have focused on is how those mechanisms have been used outside what may be described as the standard's fence line. This is an important point to consider, especially because some of the manipulations or features we've encountered might also be used in dominant cultural domains such as mainstream comedy or literature, or indeed in stylistically neutral language. So, what we've done is to prime ourselves to identify the lexis that has become associated with a number of colloquial, youth and criminal varieties and/or identify the attendant manipulations, consider why and how both are used within relevant contexts, but remain conscious of the broader use to which some mechanisms (e.g. borrowing, suffixation and metaphor) can be put. A good example is the use of suffixes such as '-o' and '-ers' in English. As we discussed in Chapter Six, Standard English uses suffixation in its word-formation, but these particular suffixes are used to create colloquial or 'slang' items. Conversely, although a small number of Verlan terms such as 'beur' are to be found in Standard French dictionaries, inversion as a mechanism is not generally used to create new Standard French vocabulary.

Secondly, we should remember that the social, cultural and linguistic backdrops of the usage discussed in this volume are not identical. When comparing mechanisms within the confines of a book, it's easy for the impression to form that we are dealing with wall-to-wall absolutes or universals. However, that would take us to precarious territory. For one thing, languages can be structured very differently, and so certain methods might be (more readily) found in language X as opposed to language Y. Moreover, the sociolinguistic contexts within which youth, criminal or colloquial usage is found can differ in a number of ways: although people from different cultural and linguistic backgrounds can be found in many countries across the globe, there are some states, such as the UK, France and Germany, for example, where a single state language *generally* predominates. That's not to say that in Germany, France and the UK people can't belong to or be influenced by different language communities, ethnicities and cultures, or belong to more than one in-group on a more local level; of course they can – and do. Youth language practices in France provide a good example of diverse source languages serving as wells for urban youth practices, as does the in-group usage of some youth groups in London. However, if we compare the UK, France and Germany overall with countries such as Cameroon, where there are more than 200 languages spoken among a number of different peoples, then it is clear that the background sociocultural and sociolinguistic picture in different societies can differ appreciably. When we think of contexts for usage and communicative goals, we should consider the various influences and dynamics that might be present within individual societies or spaces – for instance, group composition, transnational and local sociocultural influences (however these are defined), sociopolitical and sociocultural history, speaker–interlocutor age, interactant ethnicity, dominant, less dominant and other locally used languages, etc. – and what impact these factors might have at any given time on the negotiation of identity by and other goals of the actors in whom we have an interest.

A third point concerns characterisation and attitudes vis-à-vis the standard. We've seen that youth practices in particular have been described in many contexts as a threat to the status of the standard language, and to culture and society. We've seen disapproval that talks of cultural harm or degradation, and of crude or uneducated usage as a sign of falling standards and a blight on the overall collective and what they are held to stand for. Many of these accusations deserve more careful thought when advanced as platforms for criticism. For example, is it the language variety in question that is the true and ultimate target or cause of the criticism, or is the charge of lowering social, educational and cultural standards that is particularly made against youth language, say, really an articulation of the mainstream's uncertainty and apprehension in a changing world? We have seen that there are many instances where charges of educational, social and sociocultural deficit are made; however, this can be treacherous ground to take. Of course, in the ebb and flow of everyday exchanges there are many occasions when speakers may repeatedly bend and break established language rules, and – yes – some may do so while having a limited formal education. However, care should be taken when sweeping or simplistic statements are made equating youth or criminal language with a lack of culture or education or with social failings. As many scholars (e.g. Sherzer 2002) adeptly point out, speakers may well be engaging in verbal art that evinces sensitivity, dexterity, complexity, artistry and adroitness in linguistic and sociocultural terms. In their 1980s study of Verlan, for example, Bachmann and Basier (1984: 178) observed that the pupils most competent in Verlan were often those who most regularly transgressed school rules. This was taking into account the fact that practically all of the 80 pupils they had interviewed knew some Verlan vocabulary. Of course, the most proficient Verlan speakers in Bachmann and Basier's study could have been, or have been perceived or reported to be, more competent for a number of reasons. One way or another, and although we should be careful about equating inappropriate behaviour in the classroom with linguistic competence (for many reasons), through their use of Verlan and most likely other language manipulations, these *problem pupils* appear to have successfully harnessed intricate linguistic skills.[1]

By reassessing the assumptions and ideology behind such claims, therefore, some critics may realise that the palette we see in youth, criminal and certain colloquial language practice, to continue Červenková's allusion cited in Chapter Three, is not too dissimilar to that employed by artists, literary figures or others celebrated within many social mainstreams as forward-looking, insightful, experimental and brave. The youth, criminal and colloquial palette is more subtle and crafted than may initially appear to be the case.

Indeed, and revisiting Carter's (2004: 215) point that "[c]reative language is not a capacity of special people but a special capacity of all people. It shows speakers as language makers and not simply as language users", the chances are that we all creatively extend linguistic boundaries in language play or experimentation of one sort or another, have almost certainly done so from our early years, and do so beyond our youth, where that life stage is deemed socially salient and however it is determined (see also the next section, **Looking forward**). Many of us may recall the ways in which we, as children, experimented with language, and used it creatively for expressive ends, perhaps using ludlings: in some studies researchers point out, for example, that children may use Pig Latin at about 5 years old, clearly enjoy rhyming at 8, and develop the ability to talk back to front by about 8 or 9 (Crystal 1998: 170–2, citing Cowan 1989). These aren't the earliest ages when verbal play can be detected (Crystal 1998: 165–9), and language play, creativity and experimentation and the social, interactional, identity and other goals being pursued through them are not the preserve of youth, but are in evidence in many life stages and situations. In living our lives and developing our repertoires or engaging in stylistic practice, we all somehow, at some point, bend and break, if not even subvert, the social and linguistic standard.

Fourthly, although this book concentrates on lexical borrowing, semantic transfer and other elements of lexical creation and supplementation, it does not cover the entire waterfront of innovative linguistic and semiotic practices employed by the collectives upon which we focus. There is more ground to cover, for example, in acknowledging the role that cues such as facial expression may play, such as a knowing, playful glance or smile when a pun or otherwise insulting remark is delivered; in thinking about the role of *gestural slang* (for example the English gestured initialisms 'L' for 'loser' or 'W' for 'whatever'; for more on gestural 'slang' in English, for example, see Victor 2014. Mallik 1972 also briefly discusses gesture among criminals in West Bengal); in considering the intonation that may help to convey speaker meaning; and in studying the syntactic hallmarks of colloquial and in-group usage, as we see in the work of Wiese (2009), Dorleijn and Nortier (2013), Cheshire, Nortier and Adger (2015), among others, to name but a few. Analysis of these elements can also help us to understand how speakers consciously and non-consciously apply, bend and shape the rules of a language and/or create new practices for a number of different purposes.

Looking forward

Although it serves as an introductory reference work, it is appropriate that the book also draws attention to some areas that deserve ongoing examination. This is not to say that these topics are more or less deserving than others; but they are pertinent to our evolving understanding and debate.

The first concerns discourse and the value that a discourse-centric analytical approach may bring to the appreciation of the social meaning negotiated by youth actors. In identifying this subject, I draw on the approach that was adopted with no small measure of insight by Mayr (2004), for example, who studied institutional and inmate discourse in Scotland and how this relates to social control in the prison system. Mayr's work analyses interaction in a way that allows us to see both power and ideological alignment as they are expounded institutionally, and positions and antagonisms as they unfold in discourse both over time and in the moment. It brings together questions of power, identity and ideology (including resistance), among other things, and explores how these are articulated in the prison setting. Clearly, there are particular social roles and contextual factors at hand in Mayr's study, and these do not necessarily read across to other groups and circumstances. Nonetheless, from a discourse analysis perspective, Mayr's is a promising study for consideration by those exploring youth or inmate practices and one that may provide additional insights as we seek to understand how actors pursue social, ideological or other goals, including moment-by-moment, through discourse. This is not to say, of course, that discourse has not been examined in analyses of the social interaction of youth actors: Stenström's (2014) investigation of pragmatic markers in Spanish and English teen talk, which utilises corpus-based data from Madrid and London, is one example that offers interesting insights that go beyond word-formation and correlating sociolinguistic observations vis-à-vis class, age and other macrosociological factors (see also, for example, Rampton 2015, Roth-Gordon 2016 and Williams 2016 for analyses that also consider the negotiation of social meaning in particular stretches of discourse). Be that as it may, further insights may well be gained into questions such as the ongoing and emergent negotiation of identity and identification as a dynamic process with greater adoption of discourse techniques.

To be sure, questions of analytical methodology will undoubtedly continue to form a focus of discussion. As Eckert (2012) observes, Labov's ground-breaking quantitative study of linguistic variation in the 1960s also in fact shed light on how linguistic variability forms part of the negotiation of social meaning. This was then initially followed, however, by a predominant focus on correlative analysis linking linguistic variables with macrosociological categories (such as age and gender). Be that as it may, as sociolinguistics has evolved over the decades, so have other analytical approaches been explored. The latest and most recent wave – the third – has seen emphasis placed on the need to understand stylistic practice where, among other things, variation not only reflects but constructs social meaning (Eckert 2012). This approach does not necessarily replace earlier statistical and macrosociologically oriented practices, but complements them. As studies continue to be undertaken using and perhaps integrating and comparing approaches, it will be interesting to see what degree of correspondence and new conclusions emerge.

In parallel to the further incorporation of new or newer analytical principles comes a fundamentally important undertaking: examination of the assumptions that we make, either as researchers or as social actors in our own right, about the types of language and features typically understood to be indicative of youth, criminal and colloquial language practices, and about who those typical speakers are (see also **Enregisterment** on page 208). For example, we have seen an ongoing theme in much youth literature that associates youth language practices chiefly with young males – in part due to the greater agency that males are held to have in some societies (e.g. Bucholtz 2002). Yet at the same time, we have noted that a number of engaging studies have been conducted into various aspects of the language practices of young women in different settings and societies. For all of the latter, there are still perhaps perceptions and predispositions that incline towards the study of male actors, even though there are sufficiently important or numerous bedrock studies or hypotheses pointing to or suggestive of the agency of young women as communicative social actors in particular social, cultural and political contexts. Again, this is not to suggest uniformity in the sociolinguistic geographies or socio-political milieux within which young women operate; rather, it is a call for further research into and awareness of young women as more than *second-order bricoleuses* and as actors worthy of ongoing, detailed study in their own right.

The question of assumptions brings us to one final topic that will no doubt prove to be particularly engaging over the next few years: how we understand youth in relation to adult language practices. We have seen that youth can be depicted as an Other by some adults in the social mainstream and that this can occur for a number of reasons, including the support of adult self-definition (Thurlow 2006, 2007) or protection of standards, values and ideologies by certain adults as *guardians of the mainstream* (e.g. Mazrui 1995; Smith-Hefner 2007; Wiese 2009). At the same time, we have seen in the work of Stein-Kanjora (2008) and Rampton (2015) indications that linguistic forms popularly associated with youth can be employed in life stages that are often considered to lie beyond the youth fence line. Rampton gives as one of his reasons for promoting the concept of the Contemporary Urban Vernacular a speaker's *maintenance* of language practices beyond their youth (although this is not the only criterion or driver for the concept he advances – see also **Contemporary Urban Vernaculars** on pages 156–7). In investigating continuities into middle age in the repertoire of a 40-year-old British-born man with

Pakistani heritage, he calls into question the appropriateness of terms such as *youth language* and suggests that this "risks the 'juvenilization' of a style that we can now see lasting well into adulthood" (Rampton 2015: 43). Rampton raises a fundamental point which, once again, brings into focus some of the *contrastive* assumptions often made in society about youth and the language practices that come to typically index youth actors and their stances, as opposed to those of images of adults. His questioning invites greater understanding of fluid linguistic continuities across perceived life stage boundaries, rather than a focus on certain linguistic practices being boxed within chronological compartments situated either side of a life stage wall. This is an important distinction, given that the social lives of various youth actors, including those who have adult responsibilities, may not (and often do not) adhere to popularly reproduced life stage demarcations (indeed, concepts of adulthood can also change intra-societally). Moreover, this questioning is all the more significant when there is widespread diffusion of language practices and linguistic variables across a number of media and when definitions of youth might centre more on the tastes of social agents as opposed to their age (e.g. Miles 2000).

Indeed, models of discrete, distinct and clearly delimitable life stages have arguably not been reflected in the reality of youth language use if we consider the age ranges reflected in much of the literature. Although tightly drawn or defined youth–adult rubicons may be helpful for certain purposes or domains within certain societies (e.g. in determining thresholds for legal responsibility, lawful ability to engage in sexual relations, marry, consume alcohol, etc.), instead of clear linguistic breaks between life stages, we witness continuities in language and some social practice as speakers advance through life and maintain, craft and/or re-craft their sense of identity beyond their adolescent years. The age ranges of social actors figuring in studies of youth language practices such as those cited in the Introduction, for example, as well as UN or national age-based definitions of youth, indeed raise questions about the assumptions of breaks in linguistic practices that neatly correspond to generally agreed thresholds of adult responsibility – as does the circumstantial onset of familial duties such as adolescent employment across many continents. Many young people simultaneously belong to different Communities of Practice that involve different types of activity and levels of responsibility – some may be leisure-oriented and closer to the prototypical (Western) image of adolescence, while others may entail greater familial responsibility such as wage-earning.

It would seem, therefore, that there is further discussion to be had about where the adult–youth language debate should be socially and behaviourally centred and, indeed, about assumptions that youth language practices do not (regularly) encompass those of many actors who de facto operate in the adult sphere and are expected to do so. Further discussion of continuity in language practices that traverse notional age thresholds, what kind of work these practices are supporting, in which spaces they arise, and whether and in what respects such continuities are commonplace could yield interesting results, particularly if we accept that linguistic practice both reflects and forms part of individuals' multiple social

Thurlow, C. (2006) 'From statistical panic to moral panic: the metadiscursive construction and popular exaggeration of new media language in the print media', *Journal of Computer-Mediated Communication*, *11*, 667–701.

Thurlow, C. (2007) 'Fabricating youth: new-media discourse and the technologization of young people', in S. Johnson and A. Ensslin (eds.) *Language in the Media: Representations, Identities, Ideologies*, London: Continuum. 213–33.

Victor, T. (2014) 'Gestural slang', in J. Coleman (ed.) *Global English Slang*, London: Routledge. 194–204.

Wiese, H. (2009) 'Grammatical innovation in multi-ethnic urban Europe: New linguistic practices among adolescents', *Lingua*, *119*, 782–806.

Wilce, J.M. (2009) *Language and Emotion*, Cambridge: Cambridge University Press.

Williams, Q. (2016) 'Ethnicity and extreme locality in South Africa's multilingual hip hop Ciphas', in H.S. Alim, J.R. Rickford and A.F. Ball (eds.) *Raciolinguistics*, New York: Oxford University Press. 113–33.

Index

abbreviations 338–9; borrowed abbreviations 343; in text- and computer-speak 166, 170–2, 342; named abbreviations 343; in phrases 339; vocalisation 341–2
Abidjanese French *see* Nouchi
acronyms 339–41
adult practices 16, 88, 117, 119, 121–2, 142, 157, 176, 352–3
affixes 274–86; circumfixes 274, 283–4; dummy affixes 278–80, 284–5; emphatic prefixes 51; expletive infixes 283; expressive suffixes 275–6, 278; evaluative suffixes 276–8, 287n9; infixes 281–3; nonsense suffixes 210, 275; parasitic prefixes 285; parasitic suffixes 285; pejorative suffixes 278, 286n4, 287n5, 287n9; prefixes 220, 274, 280–1, 284–5, 308, 320
Afftarskii iazyk 164; *see also* Russian (Internet)
African American Vernacular English (AAVE) 71, 80, 154, 243
African American slang 140, 146, 174, 214, 263–4, 292–3, 314–15, 322, 339
Agha, A. 17, 20–2, 90, 280
AIDS 1–2, 120, 254, 260
alliteration 311–12, 314
Androutsopoulos, J. 15, 23–4, 45, 89, 148, 150, 155, 165, 167, 171–2, 225–6, 254, 268n5, 275, 302, 309, 337, 344n1
antilanguage 8, 68–73, 75–7, 96–8, 175, 246–7, 263–4, 347
antiphrasis 263, 348
antonyms 263
aphaeresis 332, 336
apocope 332–4
appropriation: of debate 244; of language 80, 147, 243–4; of space 244

Arabic, colloquial, criminal, youth practices 4, 53, 316, 325n1: history 60n12; insertion 313; Internet 172; motivations for use 111–12, 115, 128, 212–13; phonology 316; semantic change 240
Argentina 212; Buenos Aires 10, 47, 132, 209
argo (Russian) 49
Argomuche 321
argot: definition of 9, 21, 23
Asian American youth 56–7, 71, 174
Atbash 306–7
Aussi lingo 326n13
Australia 4, 119, 123, 159, 313, 326n13
Azerbaijan: Agdam 324
Azmari 115

backcronyms 340
back formation 285
backslang 314–20
Bahasa Gaul (youth language): abbreviations 343; acronyms 340; affixation 282; blends 224; borrowing across groups 50–1, 214, 227; borrowing from other languages 211, 214–15, 220; clipping 332–3, 336; diffusion 161; enregisterment 280; history 50–1, 229; hybridity 224; language standards 117; letter codes 313, 325n10; literal translation 226; media 119, 161; metathesis 317, 319; motivations for use 50–1, 131, 139; multiple manipulations 283; semantic change 259; use by out-groups 120
Bahasa Gay: affixation 275; diffusion 181n26; motivations for use 50, 72, 115; multiple manipulations 313; sound substitution 302; use by out-groups 180n16

144–6, 153, 155, 158–60, 178n7; multiple manipulations 146, 323–4, 337; onomatopoeia 322; origin of term argot 178n3; phonetic reduction 308–9; prestige of standard French 17–18, 28n3; reduplication 298–9; rhyming 303; semantic change 247, 249, 253, 255–7, 259–62, 266; sound substitution 304; stress change 302–3; use by outgroups 120, 126; use of term argot 44
Fulɓe 115
Fulfulde 326n12
functional shift 216–17

Gacería 110
gangs 8, 44, 50, 75, 77, 131, 136, 138, 306
gangsta (rap) 69
Ganoore 326n12
Gauchos 47
Ġawṣ 15, 315
G code (Sundanese) 313, 325n10
Genoese dialect 59n5
German, colloquial, youth practices: affixation 275, 280–1, 285; borrowing across groups 45, 212; borrowing from other languages 213, 225–6; calquing 226; clipping 337; cultural context 95, 266; diffusion 17, 160; history 58n2, 314, 317; hybridity 225–6; insertion 326n11; language standards 118, 122; metathesis 314–15, 324–5, 325n1; motivations for use 131, 145, 155, 213, 309; multiple manipulations 337; semantic change 241, 249, 253, 259, 262, 268n7, 335
Germanía 9, 29n6, 46, 110, 229, 296
Germany: 7, 28n2, 45, 58n2, 83, 95, 117, 122, 130–1, 314, 325n1, 349; Bavaria 58n2; East Germany (German Democratic Republic, GDR) 45, 216, 259, 335; Hannover 58n2; Saxony 58n2; West Germany 45, 241
gestural slang 1, 350
Gíria 59n5, 179n8, 212
gitanerías 46
gitanos 46, 59n4
G language (Gueu language, Langue de Gueu) 313
globalisation 45, 83, 132, 149–51, 177, 180n24
graffiti 44–5, 48, 53, 56–7, 59n6, 74, 77, 88, 148, 254, 306–7, 323
grammar and syntax: non-standard 26–7
Greek 49, 172, 209, 307

Grypserka 69
Gualin 315
Guerrero, Lalo 312
Gyaru moji 307
Gypsies *see* Roma, Romani language

Hachek 310
Hall, K. 78, 93–4
Halliday, M.A.K. 68–74, 96–7, 334
Harare 55, 60n16, 220
Harrison Act 111
Hebrew 52, 216, 221–2, 260, 302, 306
Hindi 50, 214, 223, 261, 293, 299, 320
Hip hop: African influence 150–1; merging of US and local practices 150, 132, 176–7; mimicry of US practices 150–1; US origins 150
HIV 1–2, 120, 254, 260
homophony, near-homophony 309–10, 318, 337
Hungarian prison slang 178n6, 212, 230, 246
hybridity 53–5, 153, 155, 177, 233, 354; linguistic hybrids 87, 166, 220–6, 285, 296–7, 299
hyperbole *see* semantic transfer (overstatement)

Iazyk padonkoff 164, 167–9; *see also* Russian (Internet)
identity: fixedness in identity 93–4, 96, 128, 148, 153, 177; gender and identity 114, 134–8, 146–7; gay identity 50, 72; hypermasculinity 89; legitimising identity 74; multiplicity of identities 86, 92–4, 96–8, 156, 347, 353–4; personal identity, definition 92; project identity 74–7, 97, 120, 163; resistance identity 68, 97, 120, 138–9, 150, 163, 175, 347; social identity, definition 92
identification: as a constant process 93–4, 96
ideology of the standard 18
ideophones 322–3
Igifefeko 315
Imvugo y' Umuhanda 81, 145, 214, 268n3
indexicality: definition of 20–3; multiple indices 21; multiple indexicality of forms 22–3
India 4, 8, 14, 28n2, 59n4, 97, 173; Bihar 50; Uttar Pradesh 50
Indonesia 50–1; Jakarta 50, 83, 131, 215, 229; Java 51, 59n7, 244; Kediri 59n7; Medan 229; Yogyakarta 51, 94, 239, 244

Indoubil 71, 229
infixes *see* affixes
Infixing Javanais 282–3, 312; *see also* Javanais
in-groups: definition 90
initialisms 338
insertion 312–13
Internet: colloquial language 163–72, 177; youth language 163–72, 177; usage rates 164, 173, 181n27; Afftarskii iazyk 164; *see also* Iazyk padonkoff
inversion 50, 145, 260, 269n13, 287n6, 297, 304, 314–15, 318–21, 326n18, 348
Ireland, Republic of 313
Iscamtho 229
Israel 52
Israeli criminal language: borrowing across groups 229; borrowing from other languages 215–16; motivations for use 52, 89; semantic change 246, 248–54, 256–7, 259, 262, 268n8
Italian 47, 59n5, 209, 221, 226, 235n20, 257, 282, 333
Italian slang 235n20, 282
Italy: Florence 305

Jakartan dialect 50–1
Japan 51, 74, 118, 136
Japanese 118, 135–7, 179n11, 180n22, 225, 280, 297, 307, 310, 332, 336
Javanais 45, 282–3, 288n13, 288n14, 312, 325n10
Javanese 59n7, 283, 288n12, 307, 325n10
Jeringosa 326n12
Jobelin 108–9

Kabwards 315
Kale people 59n3
Kanaksprak 7
Kazakhstan: Almaty 310
Kenya 2, 6, 10, 52, 111, 118, 131–3, 145, 151–3, 162, 265, 314; Nairobi 52–3, 60n11, 83, 85, 132–3, 140, 155, 158, 175, 229, 242, 315
Kher talk 313
Kiezdeutsch 26, 45, 56, 72, 118, 131
Kiezdeutschkorpus (KiDKo) corpus 56, 60n17
Kikuyu language 52, 111, 216, 260
Kinoki/Ki-noki *see* Sheng
Kindoubil 284
Kinyume 318, 326n18
Kogals: abbreviations 280; affixation 280; clipping 333, 336; history 51; hybridity 307; language standards 118; media 118; motivations for use 51; multiple manipulations 51, 280; origin of the term 51; substitution strategies 307
Kuna language 326n12
Ky-go 280

Labov, W. 3, 78, 145–6, 297, 351
Langila 145, 174–5, 310, 315
language crossing 87, 94, 129, 155
language economy 211, 308–9, 332, 336, 338, 342–3
language ideology: definition: 127
Langue de feu *see* F language
Langue de gueu *see* G language
Langue verte 256, 326n15
Largonji: construction 109; history 178n2; speakers 109, 321
Largonji des Louchébems: construction 279, 283, 321–2, 326n20; diffusion 158, 322; history 109, 178n2, 321; and Infixing Javanais 283; motivations for use 109, 114, 283; speakers 109
Latin 323
Leibov, Roman 181n29, 308
liminality 177, 152–3, 326n18, 347
Lingala ya Bayankee 71, 229
literal translation 226
literary devices 311–12
litotes *see* semantic transfer (understatement)
locality: importance of 83, 131–4, 213, 181n25
Lom people 59n3
Lombardo 47
ludic function 10
ludlings 10, 59n7, 115, 288n14, 315, 325n1, 350
Lu-go 234n10
Lunfardo: borrowing across groups 228; borrowing from other languages 47, 59n5, 209, 212; diffusion 47; history 47, 132; metathesis 314, 319–20, 287n6; origin of the term 47, 59n5; in poetry, prose, lyrics 312; semantic change 249, 252, 254, 260; and the tango 47, 312
Luo 52, 111
Luo Slang 133
Luyaaye 81, 139, 240, 250, 263, 268n7, 284
lyrics 151, 162, 214, 225, 312

Magahi 50
malapropisms 310–11

362 Index

Malawi 60n15
Malaysia 4, 14–15, 173; Johor State 59n7; Negri Sembilan State 50, 315
Maori 234n4
Mattenenglisch 324
Maʔlūbe 316
Mboko 54
McConnell-Ginet, S. 180n18
Mchongoano 147 *see also* verbal contests and ritual insults
media: diffusion 161–2; images of youth 119–20; stylistic change 163
meiosis *see* semantic transfer (understatement)
Merima dialect, Zanzibar 326n18
metaphor: animal comparison 246, 252; animal body parts 252–3; definition 241; drug use, travel 253; familial role 251–2; function 249–50; mythological creatures 253; physical properties 248–9; shape 249; sound 249; status, experience and roles 251–2
metathesis 60n13, 69, 158, 283, 314–21, 326n19
metonymy: acts for place, adornment, person 255; cause for effect 255; colour 256–7; effect for cause 254; location for act, event, facility, occupant 255; nationality 256; personal, brand or organisational names 255–6; service for location 255; tool for actor 255
migration 4–5, 82–3, 94, 131, 148, 154, 156, 158, 212, 233, 244; immigrants, immigration 44–5, 54, 87, 91, 94, 112, 127, 148, 154, 156–8, 174, 244
military language practices 216, 227, 229, 251, 253–4, 266, 296
mimicry 137, 219, 302, 309, 311
Morgan, M. 264
Moroccan language 83, 154, 302, 322
Morocco 325n1; El Jadida 15, 227, 250, 315; Rabat 322
Mozambique 55, 60n15
Mtaa *see* Sheng
Multicultural London English (MLE) 95, 148, 258
multiethnolect 5, 26, 45, 82, 87, 117, 123, 129, 154, 159, 233, 298
multilingualism: definition 111
mythology 253, 265–6, 325n4

Nahuatl language 46
Ndebele language 55, 125

Netherlands, the 83, 91, 122–3, 154, 171, 302
New Zealand 1–2, 4, 14, 114, 119, 123, 234n4, 246, 250, 252; Wellington 124–5
Nigeria 115, 173, 242
Nigerian English 234n5
nonce words, -formations 210
non-transliteration 214, 224–5, 297
non-use of youth language 173–5, 177–8
Norway 7, 26, 71–2, 77, 91, 94–5, 98, 127, 232, 263; Oslo 3, 56, 60n17, 83, 111–12, 125, 133, 157, 212
Norwegian 111–12, 213, 259, 320, 333
Nouchi: affixation 221, 286n2; back formation 285; borrowing across groups 149; borrowing from other languages 55, 221, 224, 317; clipping 334, 336; coining 210; diffusion 55, 76, 97, 126, 297; history 54, 229; hybridity 221, 224; ideophones 323; language standards 118; media 55, 126; motivations for use 54, 84, 130–1, 158, 220, 297; multiple manipulations 221, 248; onomatopoeia 322; origin of the term 55, 60n14; semantic change 250; use by out-groups 120
Nsenga language 56, 60n15
Nyanja language 55, 254
Nyanja Slang *see* Town Nyanja

objectification 255
Ochs, E. 21, 26
Ofeni 148
Olbanskii iazyk 164, 168; *see also* Russian (Internet)
onomastic substitution 310
onomastic synecdoche 242, 255, 267
onomatopoeia 240, 285, 311–12, 322–3
Other, the 116, 131, 134–5, 153, 176, 347, 352
out-groups: definition 90
overlexicalisation 69–70, 96, 246
overstatement *see* semantic transfer
overt prestige 73

Pachuco Caló: affixation 210, 275, 279; borrowing across groups 46, 110, 228; borrowing from other languages 46; diffusion 46, 73; history 46; media 46, 312; motivations for use 46, 73, 233; semantic change 243
Padonki *see* Iazyk padonkoff
P code (Sundanese) 313, 325n10
personal names 244, 255, 319, 337

Philippines 4
phonetic reduction 308–9
phonological manipulations 302–26
Piedmontese dialect 59n5
Pig Latin 303, 350
Poland 28n2, 97, 173
polysemy 228, 262, 265
portmanteau words *see* blends
prefixes *see* affixes
prisoners: in Hungary 178n6, 212, 230; in Israel 52, 57, 89, 229, 245–6, 251; in Poland 69, 97, 109; in Scotland 69, 351
Puerto Rico 326n12

race 153–6
Rampton, B. 81–2, 88, 94, 142, 155–7, 352–3
Randuk: affixation 278–9, 281; borrowing from other languages 248; clipping 343; diffusion 53, 60n13, 125, 131, 160, 162; history 53, 131; media 160, 162; metathesis 148, 314, 319–21; motivations for use 84, 115, 158, 281, 297; semantic change 215, 246, 249–52, 254–5, 260–1
rap, rapping 53, 57, 94, 128, 132, 137, 145–7, 150–3, 162, 254, 264, 266, 275, 311; *see also* gangsta (rap)
Rāute 115
re-appropriation *see* appropriation
Rebus Principle 342
reduplication 298–9; ablaut 298–9; full/exact 298–9; rhyming 298–9
regional language varieties 45, 59n8, 85, 110, 118, 133, 150, 181n26, 227, 231, 235n19, 235n23
Rendók *see* Randuk
reordering of words *see* metathesis
repertoires, linguistic 82–8, 90, 98–9, 111, 121, 128, 131–2, 155, 347, 350
resistance: aesthetics and resistance 77; culture and resistance 77; "geographies of resistance" 74; politics and resistance 74, 77
resistance identity *see* identity
reverlanisation *see* double metathesis
rhyming 146, 295, 298, 299, 303, 313, 350; rhyming phrases 303; rhyming slang 313–14, 326n13; *see also* Cockney rhyming slang
ritual insults *see* verbal contests
Roma 59n3; Harman's condemnation in Britain 178n5; history in Spain 110

Romani language 10, 46, 59n4, 109–12, 155, 209, 212, 228, 230, 233n1, 274, 304
Rotwelsch 314, 58n2
Russian, colloquial, criminal, youth practice: abbreviations 310, 338–9, 341; acronyms 340–1; affixation 274–6, 278–9, 281, 284, 287n8; back formation 288n17; blends 295; borrowing across groups 227, 158–9; borrowing from other languages 209, 215–19; calquing 226; clipping 333–4, 336–7; compounding 292–5; cultural context 265–6; diffusion 16, 148, 159; history 16, 49, 148; hybridity 221, 223–6, 296; Internet 164–70, 172, 181n30; language standards 167–9; media 148–9, 161; metathesis 318–19; mimicry 219, 309; motivations for use 10, 144; multiple manipulations 322, 324; online alphabet switching 166, 181n29, 308; onomatopoeia 322–3; phonetic reduction 308; prestige in Standard Russian 17, 28n5; prostorechie 20, 23, 29n9, 49, 160, 166, 235n19, 279, 295, 299, 304; reduplication 298–9; rhyming 303; semantic change 242, 246–60, 262, 268n8; sound substitution 304–5, 321; stress change 303, 325n2; stylistic differentiation 20–3, 29n10, 278–9; substitution strategies 306–8; use by out-groups 120
rural practices 131–4
Russia: Briansk 209; Kaluga 322; Yekaterinburg 306
Rwanda 145; Kigali 81, 214, 268n3, 315

Sango language 304
Sango Godobé 304, 314
Ṣawġ 15, 315
S code (Sundanese) 313, 325n10
semantic fields 70, 96, 128, 167, 244–8, 323
semantic transfer: antiphrasis 263; cultural meaning 265–6; dysphemism 261; euphemism 260–1; metaphor 248–54; metonymy 254–7; semantic broadening 216, 261–2 semantic contraction 216, 261–2; simile 267; synecdoche 257–8; onomastic synecdoche 242, 255, 267; overstatement 240–2, 258–9, 312; polysemy 262–3; understatement 258–9
Senegal 4, 326n18
Seselan 59n7

Index

Shamasha 53, 250, 255
Sheng: affixation 278, 283–4; borrowing from other languages 52, 85, 216–7, 219–20, 234n8; calquing 226; clipping 332; coining 211; compounding 224; cultural context 248, 265, 268n6; diffusion 52, 97, 140, 158, 162, 176, 297–8; history 52, 229; hybridity 224; Kinoki/Ki-noki 53, 59n10; language standards 118; Mchongoano 147; media 53, 162; metathesis 314–15, 319–20; motivations for use 10, 53, 74, 84, 95, 131, 151, 153, 155, 177; Mtaa 52; multiple manipulations 283, 323, 337; onomatopoeia 322; origin of the term 52; rurality and urbanity 131–4; semantic change 242, 248, 253, 255–6, 262–3; use by out-groups 120
Sherzer, J. 279, 281, 298, 326n12
Shona: language 55, 125, 252, 261; slang 55, 220, 234n11, 248, 250, 252, 255, 322
signifying 146–7
Sīm 60n12
Sinti people 59n3
Skhothane groups 148
slang: problems of definition 1–3, 9, 20–3; universality 28n1
social dialects: definition 84–5
Social Identity Theory (SIT) 88–9, 222
sociolects *see* social dialects
sociolinguistics: three waves of 78–82
sounding 3, 146–7
sound symbolism 279, 322–3
sources used in book 43–56, 58
South Africa 1, 4, 14, 16, 26, 74, 87, 120, 135, 147–8, 173; Johannesburg 86, 149, 229
Southeast Asia 4, 174
Soviet Union 111, 169; media 148–9; youth language 158
Spain 9–10, 46–7, 110, 111, 123, 258, 314, 325n1; Madrid 69, 140, 142, 245
Spanish, colloquial, criminal, youth practices: affixation 274, 278–80, 282, 286n2, 287n8, 297n10; blends 295; borrowing across groups 110, 216, 228–30, 233n1; borrowing from other languages 110, 209, 216; calquing 210, 226; clipping 332, 334, 336; colloquial Argentine Spanish 47, 228, 256, 287n10, 303, 319; compounding 224, 293; history 46; hybridity 224, 296; insertion 326n12; metathesis 314, 319; multiple manipulations 337–8; pragmatic markers 353; semantic change 246, 249–53, 256–60, 268n8, 348
speaker motivation: comparison of 9–10
speech community: definition 84–5
Sranan language 83
standard language: association with literary language 17–18; definition 17; as idealised usage 17, 19; ideology of the standard 18; links to privileged dialects 17; preference for written mode 17–18, 28n3, 28n4, 28n5; rise of standard varieties across countries 28n2
stereotypes 21–3, 81, 118, 137, 174, 176, 223, 256
Straattaal 7, 123, 171
stress 28n5, 167, 170, 302–3, 325n2
student language practices: Cameroon 121, 179n15, 234n5, Canada 170; Côte d'Ivoire 55, 126; France 10, 109, 120, 123, 217, 231, 279, 286n3, 332; Germany 45; Indonesia 50–1, 131, 213, 229; Morocco 322; New Zealand 114, 124–5; Russia 124–5; Sudan 53, 72, 261; United Kingdom 71, 96, 180n17; United States 10, 48, 71, 94, 96, 142, 223, 233n2, 234n6, 262–3, 274, 286, 292–3, 295, 309–11, 335, 339–40; West Bengal 228–30; Zimbabwe 315
stump compounds 296
style (stylistic practice) as explanation of variation 78–82
stylistic categorisation: limitations of 20–3
substitution strategies 306–8
Sudan 4, 16, 53, 60n13, 115, 125, 131, 162, 255, 261, 310; Kadugli 53, 279; Khartoum 53, 72, 83, 131, 145, 321; Southern Kordofan State 53
suffixes *see* affixes
Suharto, President 50, 161
Sukarno, President 50, 296
super-diversity: definition 82
Surinamese in the Netherlands 94
Susu language 55
Sverdlovsk *see* Russia (Yekaterinburg)
Swahili 84–5, 111, 118, 132, 217, 219, 235n20, 146, 248, 260, 265–6, 268n9, 283–4, 284–5, 337
swearing *see* expletives
Swedish youth practices 26, 83
Switzerland 317; Bern 324–5; Matte district of Bern 324
synecdoche: definition 241; examples 257–8

synonyms, proliferation of: colloquial English 247; colloquial Russian, Russian youth language 70, 247; Israeli prison language 70, 246–7; Nouchi 247; Sheng 70, 247; Tsotsitaals 70; UK students 70; US college students 70
Syria 325n1; Damascus 115, 316

Taboo 27, 71, 115, 212, 242, 260, 304, 317, 325n4, 334, 341, 343
Tajfel, H. 88–9, 97–8, 127
teasing, mock teasing 224, 303, 124, 131, 138, 140, 171, 177
text speak 342
Thailand 4, 14
Third Space *see* liminality
Thurlow, C. 14, 94, 122
Town Nyanja: borrowing from other languages 56, 218, 234n8; clipping 336, 343; motivations for use 56; multiple manipulations 343; semantic change 252, 254
traders, trade languages 3, 10, 48–9, 109, 110–11, 148–9, 179n15, 209, 233n2, 302, 305–6, 318
transsexuals in Jakarta 50
transvestites in Jakarta 50, 286n2
travellers 59n3, 60n12, 110, 148
truncation *see* clipping
Tsotsitaal(s) 26–7, 70, 74, 81, 87, 120, 126, 131, 135–6, 149, 158
Turkey 28n2, 173
Turkish slang 258
Turner, J.C. 88–9, 97–8, 127

Uganda 15, 131, 240, 260, 263, 265; Kampala 81, 139, 250, 261, 268n7, 284
Ukraine 173
Ulţi, Ulţibãtolã 9, 49, *see also* West Bengal
United Kingdom: London 69, 73, 95, 132, 140, 142, 147–8, 154–5, 159, 181n25, 223, 245, 251, 257–8, 313, 349; Northern Ireland 311; Scotland 313, 351
United States of America: Boulder 48; El Paso 46; North Carolina 48, 311; Philadelphia 56; Southwest 46; college language: abbreviations 338–9; 343; acronyms 339–40; affixation 221–2, 274, 286; alliteration 314; blends 295; borrowing from other languages 214, 221–2, 234n6; clipping 336; compounding 292–3, 295; functional shift 217; hybridity 223; mimicry 219; motivations for use 10, 334; rhyming 303; semantic change 251, 253, 258–9, 262
untranslated phrases 225
UPUS-Oslo corpus 56, 60n17
urbanisation 16, 23, 53, 55, 76, 94, 109, 126, 131, 158
Urban Youth Speech Style (UYSS) 6, 164
Urdu 50
USSR *see* Soviet Union

verbal contests and ritual insults 136, 145–8, 154; dozens, playing the 3, 146–7; Mchongoano 147; signifying 146–7; sounding 3, 146–7
Verers 315
Verse *see* Vesre
Verlan: associated speakers 316; and borrowing 323; construction 317–18; gender of speakers 135–6, 317; history of process 316; items in Standard French 317; motivations for use 130, 316–17; spelling 318; and suffixation 277, 323; word order 317
vernacular 4, 28n3, 71, 76, 97, 122, 127–8, 135–6, 138, 140, 155–8, 171, 213–14, 265, 297; definition of 297–8; multiethnolect as 298; *see also* African American Vernacular English (AAVE), Contemporary Urban Vernaculars
Vertovec, S. 82
Vesre 314–15, 320, 326n14
Vietnam 173
Villon, François 312
vowel dropping 305
vowel replacement 304–5
vulgarisms, vulgar language 27, 215, 288n13, 292, 304, 334, 341, 343; *see also* expletives

West Bengal, criminal language practices: abbreviations 341; affixation 281; blends 295; borrowing across groups 228–9; borrowing from other languages 209, 212, 214–16, 220; clipping 334, 337; coining 210; compounding 223–4, 293–4; cultural context 265–6; diffusion 160, 229–30; functional shift 216–17; gestures 350; history 49–50; hybridity 223–4; media 160; metathesis 314, 319–20; motivations for use 113–14; reduplication 299; semantic change 160, 246, 249–50, 252–61, 263, 348; sound substitution 304
West Germany *see* Germany

word-formation mechanisms: comparison of 19–20
word origins: difficult in defining 230–1
written form: prestige of 17–18, 28n3, 28n4, 28n5

Yabacrâne 212, 246, 252, 260, 265, 310
Yanké 174–5, 310
Yarada K'wank'wa 70, 72, 87, 180n23, 229, 240
Yemen 325n1
Yiddish 49, 231, 313
youth: age ranges, age range comparison 10, 14–15; class 51, 77, 138–40, 153, 155, 158, 179n8, 228; education access 13; employment 10, 13; importance of peer groups 13–14; life stage 10–15; links to criminality 229–30; transition to adulthood 116; UN definition 10; young adults 1, 12, 14, 119, 142
youth language: adult views of 116–27, 172, 175–6; as cryptolect, impenetrable code 122–7, 315; class 51, 77, 138–40, 153, 155, 158, 179n8, 228; practice by age 141–3; ethnicity 153–7; gender 134–8; global and local practices 148–53; how it's perceived 116–27; identity for the self 88, 91, 94–6, 128–9; importance of locality 83, 131–4, 213, 181n25; in-group status 143–8; Internet use 163–73; links to criminal practices 229–30; media 161–3; the Other 129–34; race 153–6; rurality and urbanity 131–4
youth and criminal language commonalities 7–8, 19–20

Zambia 55, 60n15, 254; Lusaka 55–6
Zanzibar 318, 326n18
Zéral, Le: speakers 286n3; construction 286n3
Zhirmunskii, V. 19, 58n2, 314, 317, 325n1, 326n11
Zimbabwe 55, 60n15, 91, 123, 125, 132, 136, 240, 254, 261, 310, 315; Harare 55, 60n16, 220; youth and colloquial language: borrowing from other languages 310; hybridity 55; metathesis 55, 315, 319; motivations for use 55, 72, 91, 125, 132, 136; semantic change 55, 240, 254, 261